Law in Social Work Practice

The Nelson-Hall Series in Social Welfare

Consulting Editor: Charles Zastrow
University of Wisconsin–Whitewater

Law in Social Work Practice

Andrea Saltzman, M.A., J.D.

Kathleen Proch, M.S.W., Ph.D.
University of Denver

Nelson-Hall
Chicago

Project Editor: Dorothy J. Anderson
Text Designer: Claudia von Hendricks
Cover Designers: Claudia von Hendricks and Richard Meade
Compositor: Precision Typographers
Manufacturer: R. R. Donnelley
Cover Art: Fiber Piece, *Thebes For Matios* by Pamela Matiosian

Library of Congress Cataloging-in Publication Data
Saltzman, Andrea.
  Law in social work practice / Andrea Saltzman, Kathleen Proch.
    p.   cm. — (The Nelson-Hall series in social welfare)
  Includes bibliographical references.
  ISBN 0-8304-1161-5
    1. Social workers—Legal status, laws, etc.—United States.
  2. Law—United States.   I. Proch, Kathleen Ohman, 1948–
  II. Title.   III. Series.
  KF390.S6S25   1990
  344.73′017613613—dc20   89-77607
  [347.30417613613]   CIP

Manufactured in the United States of America

10 9 8 7 6 5 4 3 2 1

™ The paper used in this book meets the
minimum requirements of American
National Standard for Information
Sciences—Permanence of Paper for
Printed Library Materials, ANSI
Z39.48-1984.

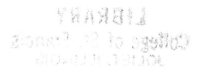

CONTENTS

138,147

v

Refelectcon 28

Due Last Day of class

Nov - 14, Reflect

CHAPTER 16
HEALTH CARE   341

CHAPTER 17
THE RIGHTS OF INSTITUTIONALIZED ADULTS   359

SECTION V ■ LEGAL ASPECTS OF SOCIAL WORK PRACTICE

CHAPTER 18
CREDENTIALING, LICENSING, AND OTHER DIRECT REGULATION OF SOCIAL WORK PRACTICE   379

CHAPTER 19
CONFIDENTIALITY OF COMMUNICATIONS AND RECORDS   391

CHAPTER 20
PROFESSIONAL LIABILITY   411

INTRODUCTION

Since the earliest days of the profession, social workers have been learning about the law and using their knowledge of it to benefit their clients. Since the earliest days of the profession, social workers have found many ways to work within the legal system to further their clients' interests. And the involvement of social workers with the legal system, along with the number and types of roles they play in it, has been steadily growing.

In the course of reading this book, you will learn many roles that social workers have played and can play within the legal system. You will learn that, whatever your speciality as a social worker, you may be able to assist your clients by working in the legal system. You may not be doing all you can for your clients if you do not make use of all available resources—including the legal system. But even if you are never involved with the legal system in your career as a social worker, you still have to learn about the law for several reasons.

The law shapes and regulates all social work practice, whatever form the practice takes. In many States, the law defines who can practice social work and specifies the tasks a social worker can perform. The law may give social workers certain legal rights or may impose certain legal obligations on them. For example, laws in some States give social workers a right to keep client records confidential and laws in every State obligate social workers to report suspected child abuse. The law may also make social workers accountable for certain actions they take on their jobs. For example, clients who believe their social workers injured them through poor practice may be able to sue their social workers for money damages and social workers who fail to report suspected child abuse may be criminally prosecuted.

Just as the social worker's practice may be shaped and regulated by the law, **the lives and actions of social workers' clients may be controlled and restricted by the law.** Social workers have to be aware of the laws which affect their clients in order to assist them effectively. For example, a hospital social worker, in order to arrange for a patient's aftercare, might have to know whether the law allows an adult child to admit a parent to a nursing home against the parent's will or a social worker in a shelter for battered women, in order to help a battered woman make an appropriate decision, might have to know whether the woman risks losing custody of her children if she temporarily leaves them with her husband.

This does not mean that social workers should act as lawyers and dispense legal advice to clients. It means, however, that social workers have to know when the law affects their clients and when it is necessary for their clients to consult lawyers. This brings us to another reason why social workers must know the law: **knowledge of the law enables social workers to recognize certain problems of their clients as legal.** Recognizing a client's problem as legal and making a referral to a lawyer may be the most important service a social worker can perform for a client. As has been stated:

> "Too many clients in the past have endured the painful consequences of festering or unsolved legal problems because neither they nor the social worker recognized the problem as a legal one or knew what to do about it."[1]

People who seek the assistance of social workers or whom social workers seek to assist often have legal problems in addition to their social problems. Their legal and social problems may be intertwined; they may not be able to be resolved independently. For example, a social worker cannot effectively assist a woman with Alzheimer's disease who has come to him for help in facing the disease and ultimately for help in coping with daily living without discussing the need for a legally appointed guardian who can make decisions for the woman when she can no longer make them herself. To give another example, an alcoholic may have several legal problems which will affect his treatment for alcoholism and his well-being. He may be facing a charge of drunk driving and eviction from his home because of his alcoholism. He needs the assistance of both a lawyer and a social worker to resolve these problems.

This interdependence of legal and social problems often requires lawyers and social workers to work together to resolve a client's problems. This is another reason social workers must know the law. **Social workers must be able to communicate with lawyers in order to work successfully with them.** The social worker must speak the lawyer's language. That language is the law.

Social workers also need to know the law because **the law clothes social workers' clients in certain rights.** Social workers must recognize and respect these rights which clients can be forced to shed only in accordance with the law and in conformity with legal procedures. For example, a drug addict has a right to refuse to enter a treatment program; her social worker cannot force her to enter the program against her will—unless certain legal standards are met and certain legal processes are completed. To give another example, an unwed teenage mother has a right to keep her child; her social worker cannot place her child for adoption—again, unless certain legal standards are met and certain legal procedures are followed.

Finally, social workers need to know the law not only because it gives their clients certain legal rights but also because **the law gives others whose lives are affected by social workers' actions certain legal rights.** Social workers cannot ignore these rights. For example, even if an unwed mother client agrees to the adoption of her child, her social worker may not arrange for the adoption without considering the rights of the child's father. If his rights are ignored, any adoption arranged by the social worker may be invalid.

In short, whatever your field of practice as a social worker, you should know the law to help your clients and to do your job effectively and legally. Unfortunately, the law on a given subject is rarely a simple rule which can be easily determined and learned. The law is a complex web of concepts, principles, rules, standards, tests, practices, customs, traditions and modes of thinking and reasoning. It is a vast body of material coming from many sources which must be interpreted be-

---

1. Michael Zander, *Social Workers, Their Clients and the Law,* (Sweet & Maxwell: London 1981), p. vi.

fore it can be applied. It is more process than precept. It is more reasoning than rule.

Even laws that seem to be simple rarely provide simple answers to legal questions. Many seemingly simple laws are difficult to apply to particular fact situations and are not easily used to resolve particular problems. Many seemingly simple laws have hidden qualifications, exceptions and conditions. Think about the commandment: ''Thou shalt not kill,'' which translates into the law: ''Killing another person is a crime.'' This seemingly simple law is not always simple to apply, has many exceptions, and leaves many questions unanswered. For example, is it against the law for a woman to kill a man who raped her? Does an eleven year old boy who kills a friend commit a crime? Can a doctor who heeds a patient's wish to disconnect life support systems be prosecuted for killing the patient? And even those laws that are simple rules which provide unqualified answers to legal questions may be in language completely unfamiliar to you or contain terms that are completely unknown to you.

You, thus, will not know the law essential to your practice if you are simply handed a few laws or are provided with the key to a law library. Learning the law is more difficult than that.

Similarly, learning how the legal system operates and how those who run the legal system—lawyers—think is difficult. The American legal system is complex. It is made up of many different legal systems, each of which is as complex as the law which creates it and governs its operation. The American legal system is often mysterious to those outside of it. It operates in a way that is quite different from other institutions with which social workers are familiar. Lawyers have a unique way of thinking and of approaching their work. Both are very different from the

way social workers are taught to think and to approach their work.

Although learning about the law and the legal system may be difficult, achieving an understanding of them is far from impossible. Many social workers assume that because the law is complex and often written in unfamiliar language, the law is unknowable. Many social workers assume that because the legal system is complex and is run by lawyers, the veils shrouding the legal system are impossible to lift. Neither assumption is true. The law can be found, read and understood by nonlawyers. You, like many social workers in the past and in the present, can lift the veils shrouding the legal system and play important roles in it.

This book is designed to make the law and the operation of the legal system less mysterious to you. It is also designed to improve your legal skills and practices and to enable you to work effectively in the legal system. To these ends, the book begins by providing an overview of American law and the American legal system. In the course of providing this overview, it presents and defines basic legal concepts and terms, decodes the process known as legal reasoning, reveals some aspects of the hearing process and social workers' roles in that process, provides guidance on effective social worker testimony, explains the fundamentals of legal research, sheds some light on constitutional rights and principles, and discusses the criminal law and social workers' roles in the criminal justice process. In other words, in the introductory chapters, the book sets forth the **how**, **what**, **where** and **why** of the law and the legal system in an attempt to give you the grounding necessary to understand specific areas of the law and to operate within specific parts of the legal system.

The book then discusses the specific areas of the law which are most relevant to social work practice: juvenile law; education law; family law; and mental health and health law. It concludes by discussing the laws which directly regulate the practice of social work. In these discussions, general principles, basic concepts, issues, problems and trends are emphasized rather than descriptions of the law. Where the law is presented, to give you practice in understanding the law as you will find it in your work, excerpts from primary sources of the law—mostly court opinions and statutes—are often presented rather than summaries or paraphrases of the law.

The book's approach is designed to enable you to find, figure out and use the law by yourself. Through the book's approach, you should learn how to recognize when a law may be significant to your practice, how to find this significant law, how to understand it when you find it, and, most important, how to use it in your practice. The book's approach is somewhat like giving you a good road map to enable you to get around in unfamiliar territory instead of giving you detailed directions.

This approach is not easy. It can be frustrating. But in the long run it is the best approach to the study of law and the legal system for several reasons.

As we have said, the model of the law as a collection of simple rules which can be committed to memory is far from reality. Further, any rules that do exist may differ from place to place and may change rapidly over time. In addition, there are so many laws which may be relevant to social work practice that it would be impossible for this book to present them all and for you to learn even those relevant to your particular practice. With a basic understanding of the law and of legal principles, however, you should be able to absorb current laws necessary to your practice quickly and easily.

As we have also said, the American legal system is a complex system made up of many different legal systems which take on different forms in different places and which change over time. You will only gain understanding of this complex system and be able to operate effectively within it if you have a basic understanding of the law and of the general principles that control the legal system's functioning—no matter how many specific laws relevant to your work and how much about court procedures you might have learned in your classes related to your field of practice or on the job.

Finally, and perhaps most important, skills acquired in locating, analyzing and interpreting the law remain long after specific laws fade from memory. You can still understand the law after you have forgotten particular laws.

It is necessary to comment, not only on the approach of this book, but also on how you can use the book most profitably.

First, you should use this text in conjunction with the laws from the State in which you practice or intend to practice. As we have said, the laws may differ significantly from place to place. We will provide examples of laws from many States in this book, but the laws of the State in which you practice, not the laws given to you as examples in this book, govern your practice. It is essential that you be familiar with your State's laws.

Second, although learning the law requires you to learn many unfamiliar terms, this book does not provide you with a traditional glossary. A law dictionary would, thus, be a valuable asset. This book does, however, put all unfamiliar legal terms in **bold print** the first time they appear or whenever they are defined for you. All such terms are then included in a special Glossary Index which you can use to locate the definitions and see how the terms are used in context when you next encounter them. Seeing unfamiliar terms used in context may be more useful to you than reading a glossary or law dictionary definition.

Last, while this book includes many excerpts from statutes and court opinions to help you become familiar with legal writing and reasoning, the excerpts are substantially edited and omit many parts of statutes and court opinions you will find in a law library. You may want to read the full statutes and opinions to get a fuller picture. Further, you should understand how we excerpt court opinions so you will not be confused when you read real opinions.

When we excerpt a court opinion for you, and even when we give you relatively short quotations from court opinions, we will delete most citations to authority and most footnotes. These deletions will not be indicated. Other deletions within sentences will be indicated, but deletions of whole sentences, paragraphs or even several pages will not be indicated. What appears as one sentence or paragraph may actually be drawn from two sentences or several paragraphs, but the order of sentences and paragraphs will not be altered. Substitutions of terms and explanatory matter will be placed in brackets. Where there is just a substitution of terms, no deletion will be indicated. Where a sentence begins with a bracketed capital letter (as "[T]he"), there has been a deletion at the beginning of the sentence. Footnotes from the opinion which are retained will be indicated with the symbol *. Long explanatory matter we have written will be included in a footnote instead of in brackets and numbered as other footnotes to the text. Text of particular importance within the excerpts will be emphasized. Any emphasis by the court in the original opinion will be underlined in addition to being emphasized. Internal quotations in the opinions will be indicated with a single quotation mark. The sources of internal quotations will generally not be indicated, but most are from court opinions. Any deletions made by us, not the court, in the quotations in an opinion will be indicated by three asterisks (* * *).

SECTION I

INTRODUCTION TO
THE LAW AND
THE LEGAL SYSTEM

An Overview of the Law and the Legal System

This chapter introduces you to the American legal system and describes the ways laws are produced by this system and the kinds of laws that are produced. It also tells you how you can change the laws that affect your clients.

WHAT IS THE LAW?

"The law" can be defined as those standards, principles, processes and rules, usually written down in some manner, which are adopted, administered and enforced by a governmental authority and which regulate behavior by setting forth what people may and may not do and how they may do what they can do. Put more simply, the law consists of "those guides to social conduct which are created and enforced by public officials."[1]

The keys to these definitions of the law are the phrases "by a governmental authority" and "by public officials." The involvement of government is what makes laws unique among rules of behavior. There are many rules that guide behavior, but only those rules that are adopted and backed by the authority of the government are rules of law. For example, you probably obey the rule that you must wash your hands before you serve dinner, the rule that you should wipe your mouth on your napkin, not your sleeve, while you eat dinner, and the rule that you may not make love with your neighbor's spouse after you finish dinner, but these rules may only be rules of health, of etiquette and of morality, not rules of law prescribed by a government. You may obey these rules, not because of any government sanction, but because of your training, social pressure, habit, your personal morality and beliefs, or a myriad of other reasons. Sometimes rules that you obey for such reasons are also rules of law. For example, a city ordinance may require restaurant employees to wash their hands before serving food, and a statute may make adultery illegal. But these rules do not become rules of law unless and until a governmental authority adopts them and they are backed by the authority of government. They are not considered part of the law until this occurs.

Laws are generally adopted when it is believed that rules of behavior should be backed by governmental authority, because either the rules serve an important societal purpose or are necessary for the safe and healthy functioning of society. Laws should change when beliefs change or society changes. As stated by Justice Oliver Wendell Holmes:

> "It is revolting to have no better reason for a rule of law than that it was laid down in the time of Henry IV. It is still more revolting if the grounds upon which it was laid down have vanished long since, and the rule simply persists from blind imitation of the past."[2]

Laws do not work when the people do not believe in them or they do not fit well with the functioning of society, but sometimes laws should mold, rather than reflect, public opinion or should operate to change the functioning of society. For example, laws forbidding discrimination on the basis of race may be adopted to change beliefs about the races and to end the widespread practice of discrimination.

Laws may be categorized in a variety of ways. First, they may be categorized in terms of how they regulate behavior. When you think about the law, you probably think about those rules

---

1. James L. Houghteling, Jr., *The Dynamics of Law* (Harcourt, Brace & World Inc: New York 1968), p. 5.

2. Oliver Wendell Holmes, "The Path of the Law," *Harvard Law Review*, Vol. 10 (1897) p. 496.

which are enforced by the coercive power of the government. Violators of such rules can be penalized in some way. But many laws merely authorize certain behavior, with no penalties imposed if someone chooses not to engage in the behavior. And some laws may induce certain behavior by rewarding those who choose to engage in the behavior, not by penalizing those who do not. For example, you may be punished if you drive a car without a driver's license, but you would not be punished if you chose not to drive and not to obtain a driver's license. The law permits you to drive if you obtain a driver's license, but it does not require you to obtain a driver's license if you choose not to drive. If you do choose to drive and you drive carelessly, the law may require you to pay damages to anyone you injure. The law attempts to make you drive carefully by imposing such a sanction. It may also induce you to drive carefully by requiring your insurance company to reduce your premium if you have no accidents.

Second, laws may be categorized in terms of whether they impose a **duty**, accord a **right** or grant a **power**. Laws that impose duties may take the form of a command or of a proscription. For example, a law may be phrased either: "You shall drive less than 55 m.p.h. on the highway" or "You are forbidden to drive more than 55 m.p.h. on the highway." Usually if someone has a duty to do something, someone else has a right to insist that the duty be done. The term "right" is also used to refer to privileges or liberties the law accords to all or to certain people. For example, Americans have a right of freedom of speech. Rights are rarely absolute; they also may be withheld from certain people. Thus, for example, the right of free speech does not allow a person to incite violence, to tell lies about someone else, or to utter obscenities. Powers, like privileges, allow someone to do something, but powers differ from privileges in that they create new rights or duties in others. For example, adults have a privilege to

drive; this privilege creates no rights or duties in others. On the other hand, adults have the power to contract for driving lessons; any such contracts create rights and duties in those providing the lessons. Most commonly, powers are accorded to public officials, but private citizens also have certain powers, like the power to sell their homes, which create rights in others, like the right to buy a home put on the market. Powers, like rights, are rarely absolute. The power of one person is often limited by the rights of another. For example, while a woman who is renting her house has the power to refuse to rent it to someone, civil rights laws may prohibit her from refusing to rent her house to a man merely because he is Black.

Third, laws may be categorized as **procedural** or **substantive**. Procedural laws set forth how one must proceed to obtain certain results from the legal system. Substantive laws set forth the possible results and, more important, set forth how one must behave in everyday life. In other words, procedural laws set forth how something is to be done within the legal system while substantive laws set forth what may be done within the law. To illustrate, a law that sets forth how to obtain a driver's license is procedural while a law that requires one obtain a driver's license before driving is substantive.

Finally, laws may be categorized as **criminal** or **civil**. Procedural criminal laws regulate the operation of the criminal justice system. All other procedural laws are civil laws. Substantive criminal laws regulate behavior; they impose duties on people and specify that any violation of these duties may be prosecuted and punished by the government and only by the government. All other substantive laws are civil laws. Substantive civil laws may also regulate behavior and impose duties on people, and the government may also take action against violators of civil laws, but the government may not punish the violators of civil laws and it is mainly private citizens who take action against the violators. Certain acts may be violations of both criminal and civil laws and may have both civil and criminal consequences. For example, a person who drives while intoxicated and injures another person may be criminally prosecuted and punished by the government and civilly sued for damages by the injured person.

WHAT IS THE LEGAL SYSTEM?

The term, the "legal system" encompasses both the governmental systems that produce, administer and enforce the law and the body of law that is produced, administered and enforced. America has a complex legal system made up of many different individual legal systems. There are many laws of many different types produced, administered and enforced by many different branches, levels and types of governments. There are federal laws produced by the federal government, at least fifty different sets of State laws produced by the States[3] and thousands of different sets of local laws produced by the thousands of local

---

3. Lawyers and those discussing the legal system frequently use the word "state" as a synonym for the word "government" or "governmental." When lawyers so use the word "state," it should be uncapitalized. This book will follow that usage. If the word "State" is capitalized in this book, it should be understood as referring to the particular unit of government known as a "State," such as the State of Nebraska. You may sometimes see the uncapitalized word "state" used for this purpose in laws excerpted in this book.

The term "State" should be understood to encompass American territories and special jurisdictions, like Puerto Rico or the District of Columbia, unless the text otherwise indicates. Thus, there may be more than fifty states. The term "State" should also be understood to encompass units of local government within a State. Thus, a statement like "No State may discriminate against Blacks," should be understood as meaning no State or local government may discriminate. Of course, if the uncapitalized word "state" is used as a synonym for "government," it may refer to any type or level of government, whether federal, State or local.

governments, such as counties, cities and towns. There are constitutions, statutes, regulations, ordinances, executive orders and court opinions, all of which are considered law. There are laws produced by constitutional conventions, by the United States Congress and State legislatures, by federal, State and local administrative agencies, by city councils and county boards, by presidents, governors and mayors, and by federal and State courts. All of these laws are administered and enforced by various federal, State, and local governmental entities.

TYPES AND SOURCES OF LAW

Despite the complexity of the American legal system and the vast number of laws coming from so many different sources within the legal system, you should usually be able to determine what the law is on a given subject of interest to you. You may not be able to predict the resolution of a legal problem with absolute certainty, but, frequently, neither can a lawyer. What the lawyer—and the social worker—can do is determine with some degree of certainty what is an acceptable and legal course of conduct and how to achieve a particular goal within the legal system.

Understanding the types and sources of law should help you make such determinations. Therefore, the four main types of law and their sources are reviewed below.

Constitutions

Constitutions are laws that usually are drafted by special conventions and adopted by the people who are to be governed by them. Constitutions are very general documents that provide the framework for all the other laws within their jurisdictions. In other words, constitutions set forth the fundamental principles, procedures and procedural rights which serve as guides for the enactment of other laws and for the making of legal decisions within their jurisdictions. Constitutions generally do not regulate people's conduct directly. Rather, they set up the governmental entities which will regulate it. They set forth what laws can be enacted, by whom and how. They create the legislative bodies which will be primarily responsible for enacting the law. They create the courts which will enforce the laws enacted by legislative bodies and which also may make some law themselves. They grant power to executives to administer the laws enacted by legislative bodies and also to make some law themselves. Constitutions also set the limits of governmental authority and establish the basic rights of those within their jurisdictions which cannot be infringed by government.

There is a constitution for the United States as a whole and all the States have constitutions. Local governments also have constitutions which may be called "charters" or some other term.

The Constitution of the United States, that is, the federal constitution,[4] is the supreme law of the land. This means it prevails over all other kinds of law. A law in conflict with the Constitution—whether it be a State constitutional provision or a State or federal statute or other law—is invalid and without legal force. One may not freely disregard such a law, however, unless and until a court declares it unconstitutional.

State constitutions' relationship to other forms of law in their States is similar to the Constitution's relationship to all other forms of law. In other words, State constitutions are supreme as compared to all other laws in their States.

Legislation

The chief law-making entity of any government in America is its elected and representative legislative body.[5] A law passed by a legislative body, whether Congress, a State legislature or a local legislative body, like a city council or a county board, is called "**legislation**." When you think of legislation, or, indeed, when you think of the law, you probably think of **statutes**, a type of legislation passed by Congress or State legislatures, but statutes are, as we shall see, only one piece in the puzzle of the law and only one type of legislation. **Ordinances**, that is, legislation passed by local legislative bodies, and **resolutions**, that is, legislation of limited authority, are other common forms of legislation. Statutes, also referred to as "**acts**" or "**codes**," are, however, the most important kind of legislation and we will focus on them.

How is a statute enacted? The process for enacting a federal statute is summarized below. Most State legislatures follow a similar process for the enactment of State statutes.

What eventually becomes a statute begins as a **bill** in one of the two branches of Congress, the House of Representatives or the

---

4. For simplicity, this book shall use the capitalized term "the Constitution" standing alone to refer to the United States Constitution. If the word "constitution" is not capitalized, it should be understood as referring to any constitution. If a particular constitution other than than that of the United States is being referred to, the word "Constitution" shall be capitalized and the jurisdiction goverened by the Constitution shall be identified (e.g., the California Constitution).

---

5. The legislative body for the federal government is known as the "United States Congress." The legislatures in the States have a variety of names, but never use the term "Congress." Thus, whenever this book refers to "Congress," it should be understood as referring to the federal legislature.

Senate. Only a member of Congress, that is, a representative or a senator, may introduce a bill.

Let us assume for the purpose of understanding the process, that a representative has introduced a bill in the House. The bill is first read on the floor of the House. It is then assigned to a committee of the House which may hold public hearings or conduct investigations on the wisdom or necessity of the bill. After the committee has considered the bill, it votes on it. If the committee votes unfavorably on the bill, the bill dies. If the committee votes favorably on the bill, the bill may go to another committee for consideration or back to the full body for a vote. There typically will be a debate on the bill on the floor of the House followed by a vote.

If the bill passes in the House, it will go through this whole process in the Senate. (If the bill had started and passed in the Senate, it would have to go through the whole process in the House.) If the bill passes both the House and the Senate, it goes to the President who may sign it or veto it. If the President vetoes the bill, Congress may override the veto with a two-thirds vote. The bill becomes a statute, and thus the law, either when the President signs it or the President's veto is overridden.

The process is not always as simple as it appears above. Amendments may be introduced both in committee and on the floor of the entire body. If a bill is controversial, there may be many amendments, parliamentary maneuvers, and referrals to different committees. Hearings and debates might be extensive. Further, the House and the Senate may pass similar, but not identical bills. In such a case, the differences in the bills must be reconciled before the bill can be sent to the President.

How can a social worker influence legislation? You can intervene at several points in the legislative process. First, you can propose bills to legislators. Second, you can help legislators draft bills. Third, you can submit written statements to committees on bills or seek to orally testify at committee hearings on the bills. Sometimes testimony or statements are solicited by committees, particularly from social workers who work in government agencies. Fourth, you can communicate your views to legislators in person or in writing when floor debates and votes are occurring. No one but a legislator can speak during a floor debate, but anyone can communicate views on a bill to a legislator before a vote is taken. Finally, you can communicate your views to the chief executive officer who must sign or veto a bill that is before him or her.

At times your involvement may seem quite direct. You may be communicating directly with legislators or at least members of their staffs. You may be testifying at hearings. But, you can only influence the process indirectly. Only a legislator can introduce a bill. Only a legislator can participate in a floor debate. Only a legislator can vote on a bill. Your influence, thus, depends on your ability to influence the legislator.

Although it is possible for you to attempt to influence the legislative process as an individual, most social workers rely on the efforts of groups with which they are affiliated. For example, the National Association of Social Workers (NASW) solicits views on needed legislation from its members, develops positions which express the views of the members, and employs lobbyists who communicate these positions to legislators and attempt to convince them to accept NASW's positions. NASW, in turn, works with other groups who have similar interests to it, such as the Children's Defense Fund or the American Association of Retired Persons, to influence legislation.

There are more opportunities for individual involvement in the State legislative process than in the federal process. The State process is closer to home, and State senators and representatives have fewer constituents and experts on whom to rely. Social workers have more opportunity to testify in a hearing before a State legislative committee than to testify before a Congressional committee (though only a few will ever be given the opportunity to testify at any committee hearing.) Thus, at the federal level, social workers rely more on the groups with which they are affiliated to influence legislation than at the State level.

It should be noted that, at both the federal and State level, many bills are introduced at the initiative of public agencies. For example, a State agency with responsibility for mental health services often has its own legislative agenda and works closely with legislators who are interested in the care of the mentally ill. The State agency might suggest bills changing commitment standards or establishing greater local control of services. Or a federal agency that administers a federal welfare program may report to Congress that there is a need for wider coverage and suggest ways to broaden the program. Social workers who have leadership positions in public agencies, therefore, have a powerful opportunity to influence the law.

What can a statute do? A statute can create a social program and tax citizens to raise the money for the program. A statute can create an administrative agency to enforce and produce the law on its own. A statute can establish new rights and obligations of citizens or can outlaw certain conduct and provide sanctions for engaging in it. The only limitation on a statute is that it cannot be inconsistent with the Constitution and, in the case of a State statute, the State constitution.

Statutes, however, are rarely self-enforcing. For example, a legislature can enact a statute authorizing the collection of taxes and the spending of the money raised by the tax for a particular purpose, but it cannot collect the taxes or spend the money itself. Or a legislature can make certain behavior a crime and establish the punishment for it, but it cannot prosecute and punish those who engage in the behavior itself. Administrative agencies, the executive, or the courts usually have to actually enforce statutes in accordance with the will of the legislature as expressed in the statutes.

Statutes also are rarely detailed enough to answer all questions that may arise. Sometimes statutory language is unclear. Sometimes statutes conflict with one another. It is, thus, often necessary for a court to fill in the details of statutes, interpret their terms or choose the controlling statute among several statutes. In other words, a court may have to decide what a statute or several statutes really mean.

A court decision which fills in the details in a statute, determines its scope or interprets its language, merges with the statute. The statute alone is no longer the law. You will not know the law if you know only the statute. You must also know all authoritative judicial interpretations of a statute to know the full law on the subject.

A note on ordinances. Local legislative bodies, like city councils and county boards, also enact laws. These laws, which cover matters of local concern, are generally called "**ordinances.**" The enactment process for ordinances is generally somewhat like that for statutes. That is, there will be a proposal for an ordinance made by a member of the body, a referral of the proposal to a committee, debate and possibly hearings in committee, and then a vote in committee. If the committee passes the proposal, there will be a debate and a vote by the full body. There is usually an opportunity for public input in committee and an opportunity at the time of debate and vote by the full body to lobby but not to have direct input.

Constitutions and State statutes provide the framework for and establish limits on ordinances. No ordinance may conflict with the Constitution or the constitution and statutes of the State in which the local government is located. Further, ordinances may not be allowed on subjects which are fully covered by State statutes, that is, in which State statutes have **occupied the field** or which the State government has **preempted**.

Regulations

Administrative agencies at the federal, State and local levels produce laws which are generally called "**regulations**." Sometimes regulations are referred to as "**delegated legislation**" since a legislative body delegates its power to create law to an agency.

Why are administrative officials, who are not elected, permitted to make law in our democratic system? Why would elected officials delegate their law-making power to the bureaucrats in administrative agencies?

First, legislative bodies do not and cannot fill in all the details in their laws. Congress can, for example, create the Supplemental Security Income (**SSI**) program, which provides cash benefits to those who are poor, disabled, or old and unable to work, but Congress cannot draw fine lines delineating who should be considered poor or disabled and what it means to be unable to work. It has neither the time nor the expertise to do this. Thus, it must authorize some other government entity to draw the lines.

Second, as has been noted, most legislation is not self-enforcing. An administrative agency must, for example, administer the SSI program. It makes sense that this agency should develop its own rules of operation and should work out the details of the broad general legislation enacted by Congress. The agency has the time and expertise that Congress lacks.

Third, legislators are elected to determine policy, not to concern themselves with the day to day functioning of government. The public only expects legislators to enact legislation which sets forth broad policy statements and which leaves the interpretation and effectuation of these policy statements to others. Bureaucrats in administrative agencies cannot be given unbridled discretion to make law, but if legislative bodies clearly define and establish limits on the authority of administrative agencies to adopt (or "**promulgate**," the word often used instead of "adopt" or "enact" for regulations) regulations and if they give agencies authorized to promulgate regulations clear policy guidance on their exercise of discretion, the electorate is satisfied.

Administrative agencies must follow proper procedures in promulgating regulations. Further, they may only promulgate those regulations which are within their statutory or constitutional authority. Moreover, any regulations they promulgate must be within or consistent with **legislative intent** or, in other words, any policy and purposes of the legislature that are revealed in any legislation. If an administrative agency followed proper procedures in promulgating a regulation, if the regulation is within the authority of the agency, if it is consistent with the legislative intent revealed in any authorizing legislation and if it is constitutional, the regulation has the same force and effect as a statute. That is, the regulation is "the law" and, as such, is binding on agency personnel, the courts and the public. It can, however, be overruled or changed by the legislative body which authorized its promulgation at any time. For example, pursuant to a wholly proper regulation, the Social Security Administration used to immediately discontinue Social Security disability benefits when it determined a beneficiary was no longer disabled even if the beneficiary disputed the determination and requested a hearing. When the hardship caused by this practice received a great deal of publicity, Congress, by statute, mandated that, under most circumstances, Social Security disability benefits must be continued if a hearing is requested. Congress, thus, overruled the regulation.

If a regulation is not properly promulgated, is not within the authority of the agency, is inconsistent with legislative intent, or is unconstitutional, a court may declare it invalid. It then is of no force or effect.

As with a statute, a court may interpret a regulation and fill in details left out of a regulation by the administrative agency. The court's decision interpreting or filling in the details of a regulation then merges with the regulation.

As with a court decision which fills in the details, determines the scope of, or interprets a statute, a regulation filling in the details, establishing the scope of, or interpreting a statute merges with the statute; you will not know the full law on the subject if you know only the regulation.

How is a regulation promulgated? Most States and the federal government have statutes which set forth the process by which regulations are to be promulgated. These statutes may be found in something called an "Administrative Procedures Act" (the name used by the federal government and many States) or the like. Usually these statutes provide that after a regulation is drafted by agency personnel (generally with no public input although nothing would prevent such input), it must be published in a designated publication for written public comment. After publication, there may or may not be one or more public hearings required. There may or may not be a requirement that one or more

other government entities, such as a budget agency, a government management office or a legislative committee, review the regulation for cost, necessity, wisdom or consistency with authorizing legislation. After the required procedures are completed, a final version of the regulation is written and the regulation is published in a designated publication.

How can a social worker influence regulations? Some social workers who work in public agencies at the supervisory level may be responsible for drafting regulations, either alone or with agency legal staff. Social workers, thus, can have a direct role in the process of promulgating regulations. But most social workers will not have this direct role. They will only have the indirect role in the process of promulgating regulations that they have in the process of enacting statutes. And very few will have this role.

Despite the usual requirement that proposed regulations be published for public comment, the process of promulgating regulations is much less visible than the legislative process. Most social workers are not aware that a regulation relevant to their practices has been drafted and do not know where to obtain copies of proposed regulations. Few social workers know of or review the publications where proposed regulations are published. Therefore, few social workers impact the process. And yet regulations may be of critical importance to social workers. To give just two examples, most rules for the administration of social welfare programs and most licensing standards, such as those for child care facilities and extended care facilities, are found in regulations. Social workers certainly have a vital interest in such regulations.

Perhaps the best way for you to learn of proposed regulations is to be a member of an interest group that monitors certain public agencies and informs its members of actions proposed or taken by the public agency. Examples are associations of private child care agencies, client advocacy groups and associations of social workers. Such associations will often inform their members of proposed regulations and identify persons to whom comments should be directed. In addition, such associations often will be proactive, proposing regulatory changes to State and federal officials.

Once you know that a regulation has been proposed, you can formally offer your comments in writing or can seek to testify at any hearings on the regulation. Moreover, you can suggest possible regulatory changes either to an agency directly or to the interest groups with which you are affiliated.

What should be promulgated as a regulation? Many agency rules, practices and policies are not formally promulgated as regulations. Agencies have operation guidelines, statements of policies and plans, and internal directives which are never promulgated as regulations and, indeed, may not even be written down. These unpromulgated rules make things difficult for those outside the agency who must deal with the agency. If you have ever been thwarted by a government bureaucrat on the basis of an unknown, unwritten rule, you surely understand the problem.

There have been many law suits in which it has been argued that an agency rule cannot be followed in a given case because it was never formally promulgated as a regulation. If the court in such a suit determines that the rule should have been promulgated as a regulation, the suit will be successful and the unpromulgated rule cannot be applied in the case, for example, to deny benefits or cause sanctions. Thus, if agency personnel wish a rule to be followed, they may have to promulgate it as a regulation. It is, however, difficult to determine what rules must be formally promulgated as regulations. A rule of thumb would be: rules of general applicability which would have a significant impact on members of the general public should be promulgated as regulations. A word of advice for social workers working in public agencies who may be responsible for drafting regulations would be: when in doubt, promulgate.

A note on executive orders Chief executives of governments, like the President, governors and mayors, may also enact law by issuing **executive orders**. Executive orders are somewhat like regulations except that there may be no official promulgation process and there may be no officially designated publication in which they are published.

The executive may be specifically authorized to issue executive orders on a particular subject by a legislative body or may issue executive orders pursuant to the general powers inherent in the office of the executive. Executive orders on non-discrimination in the awarding of government contracts are examples of the latter.

A note on rules of court. Courts may also make laws, called "**rules of court**," which are somewhat like regulations. Rules of court are formal, published rules regulating the operation of certain courts by, for example, prescribing the form of notice to use in a particular kind of law suit or setting forth the amount of a filing fee. Like regulations, rules of court may interpret or fill in the details of legislation.

Court-made law

Courts sometimes make law in the course of resolving disputes. This court-made law is very important in America. We tend to think that judges do not and should not make law and, indeed, that it would be undemocratic for them to do so, but judges do make law. They do it all the time, and they have always done so in our country and in England, the source of our legal system.

Courts make law in two main ways. First, in the course of resolving a dispute, a court may have to determine the meaning and scope of a constitutional provision, statute, regulation or another form of law, may have to resolve a conflict between several laws, or may have to fill in the gaps in existing law. The process of interpreting existing laws in which a court engages is called "**construction**." When construction occurs, the courts make law. As we have said, the courts' construction of the law merges with the existing law, and the existing law alone is no longer the complete law on the subject.

Second, a dispute before a court may involve a novel fact situation or problem not addressed by any existing constitutional provision, legislation, regulation or other law. To resolve the dispute, the court must make law. There are many areas of the law in America which have been totally developed by the courts in this way; there is no legislation on the subject but, over the years, court decisions have created a body of law on the subject. For example, most of the civil law relating to one person's liability for injuring another person, referred to as "**tort**" law, was developed exclusively by the courts.

To understand the two main ways in which courts make law, consider the following example. In every State, doctors are liable for damages if their careless treatment of a patient injures the patient. This type of tort liability, known as "**malpractice**" liability, has been developed solely by the courts although there may be some statutes on the subject. Now assume that a State has a statute which provides that an injured patient cannot sue a doctor for malpractice more than two years "after an injury."[6] Further assume that a patient from the State has been injured by a doc-

tor's careless treatment but that the injury did not become apparent until three years after the treatment. In other words, as is not at all uncommon, the adverse effect of the treatment only appeared after the statute of limitations ostensibly had passed. Finally assume the patient sued the doctor anyway, asserting that the statute of limitations can be read to allow a patient injured by a doctor's careless treatment to sue within two years of the time that the injury first appeared. To decide whether the patient's law suit should be allowed, the court in which the suit was filed must interpret the language of the statute of limitations. In doing so, the court makes law in the first way noted above. Whatever the court decides, its decision may become law.

Now assume that a social worker who works as a family therapist carelessly treated a client, causing the client psychological damage, and that the injured client sued the social worker for malpractice. It is clear in the State where the social worker treated the patient and where she was sued by him that if she were a medical doctor, she could be sued for malpractice, but no one has ever sued a therapist who was not a medical doctor for malpractice before in the State and there is no law on the subject. To decide whether the client's law suit should be allowed, the court in which the suit was filed must make law. In deciding whether clients can sue social workers for malpractice, the court will be making law in the second way noted above.

Law made by courts in the second way, particularly law that was developed by the courts in England and later brought to America and adapted to American needs, is often referred to as the "**common law**." Law made in the first or second way may be called "**case law**" or "**precedent**."

There are limits on courts' ability to make law. First, unlike legislative bodies and administrative agencies which may make law at any time, courts may only make law in the

---

6. This kind of statute is known as a "**statute of limitations**" because it establishes limits on bringing law suits. Statutes of limitations are quite common.

course of resolving disputes that are before them. Second, judges may not make law on the basis of their view of what is right and what is wrong while legislators and administrators can make law on this basis or on the basis of whim, prejudice, public opinion, pressure, political expediency, and so on. Courts may only make law based on a process called "common law reasoning" which will be explained later in this chapter. Third, courts are limited in the kind of law they can make. They cannot appropriate money. They cannot establish social programs. They cannot establish regulatory schemes like social work licensing laws or toxic waste transportation rules. And, they usually cannot mandate how something must be done. They may determine that something was done improperly and what the consequences should be, but they will not specify how it can be done properly.

Despite these limitations on courts' ability to make law, a court can exercise a powerful influence on other law-making entities. For example, although a court cannot appropriate money or create a social program, a court decision that counties are obligated to provide shelter for the homeless may force county boards to appropriate money and establish a shelter program. To give another example, a court cannot establish a regulatory program, but a court decision that social workers may not be sued for malpractice may make a legislature enact a social worker licensing law.

Case law is the law, but a precedent, like a regulation, may be overruled by legislation—except insofar as it interprets a constitution. The courts are the ultimate interpreters of constitutions. For example, assume a State court rules that a battered woman who kills her husband may not use the battered woman syndrome as a defense to a charge of murder. This ruling will be the law in the State. If, however, the State legislature disagrees with this ruling and believes that the battered woman syndrome should be allowed as a defense, it may pass a statute to this effect and thus overrule the court decision. But if the court had ruled that the battered woman syndrome is a constitutionally mandated defense, the legislature could not pass a statute which overruled the court decision by saying the defense could not be allowed.

Before you can fully understand how courts make law and the law they make, it is necessary for you to understand the structure of the court system in America. And before you can fully understand the structure of the court system, you must understand the relation between the federal and State legal systems. Let us, then, turn to those subjects.

THE FEDERAL AND STATE BALANCE

The relationship between the federal and State governments is established by the Constitution. This relationship is often misunderstood. You, like many others, may think that federal government may make law on any subject it chooses and that its law is somehow superior to and governs the law made by State governments. The former is not true, however, and the latter is rarely the case. In fact, all areas of law the fall into one, and only one, of the following categories:

1. Exclusively federal law
2. Federal and State law, federal law superior
3. Federal and State law, neither law superior
4. Exclusively State law

How do you determine in which category an area of the law falls? The easy answer is you look to the Constitution.

Article VI of the Constitution provides: "The Constitution and the Laws of the United States which shall be made in pursuance thereof. . . shall be the Supreme Law of the Land." The 10th Amendment to the Constitution provides: "The powers not delegated to the United States by the Constitution nor prohibited by it to the states are reserved to the states respectively, or to the people." These provisions, coupled with the constitutional principle that the federal government may only act in those areas in which it has been given a power to act by the Constitution, seem to mean: (1) a law will fall into category one if the Constitution gives the federal government the power to make law on the subject and prohibits the States from making law on the subject; (2) because federal law is supreme, a law will fall into category two if the Constitution gives the federal government the power to make law on the subject and does not prohibit the States from also making law on the subject; (3) because federal law must always be supreme, no laws will fall into category three; and, (4) a law will fall into category four if the Constitution neither gives the federal government the power to make law on its subject nor prohibits the States from doing so. Because the Constitution gives the federal government very few specific powers and because it only prohibits the States from acting in a few areas, it would also be expected that most areas of the law would be exclusively State, or in, other words, would fall into category four—with one important qualification. As we have said, the federal Constitution governs all State laws. All State (and federal) laws must be consistent with the Constitution; if they are not consistent with the Constitution, they are invalid.

Unfortunately, the easy answer we just derived from the Constitution is not wholly correct. The powers of the federal government, while not as great as you might have initially imagined, have been greatly expanded over the years and the supremacy of federal law, other than the Constitution, has been greatly limited in areas where both the States and the federal government may enact laws. The result has been that more and more law is falling into category three.

The powers vested in Congress, the chief lawmaking body of the federal government, by Article I, section 8 of the Constitution include the broad, general powers to: "provide for the general welfare of the United States" and "make all laws necessary and proper for carrying into Execution. . . [the] Powers vested by this Constitution in the Government of the United States. . ." They also include the power to "regulate Commerce. . . among the several states," which may seem like a specific power but which has been so broadly interpreted by Congress and the courts that it is really akin to the general powers granted by the "general welfare" and "necessary and proper" clauses. Pursuant to these general powers, in recent years, Congress has enacted numerous laws in areas traditionally considered exclusively State. For example, it has passed laws on child support, on foster care, and on substance abuse treatment.

The courts have usually upheld the federal government's authority to enact laws in these areas against 10th Amendment claims of "States' rights," but the courts have generally been unwilling to make federal law supreme in these areas. The federal government's authority to act in these areas is just too fuzzy. Thus, in all those areas of the law which were traditionally reserved for the States but in which the federal government is now acting pursuant to its general powers, we may have both State and federal laws with neither law supreme, or, in other words, have laws falling into category three.

We also have laws falling into category three if there is no need for consistency between federal and State laws on the subject, and if there is no need for uniformity in laws on the subject among the States. Federal supremacy may yield on these subjects. In many areas, such as criminal law, inconsistent federal and State laws exist side by side, and the laws differ from State to State, but the inconsistency and lack of uniformity cause no problems and, thus, there is no need to assert federal supremacy. In other areas, such as the law related to occupational health and safety, federal law may generally be supreme, that is, the laws on the subject fall into category two, but some inconsistencies and differences between federal and State law may be tolerated because the inconsistencies cause no problems. Again, federal supremacy may yield but for specific laws, not whole areas of the law.

But laws which would seem to fall into category three because the federal government's power to act stemmed from its general powers or because there is no need for uniformity or consistency, may, in fact, fall into category two. If the federal government, pursuant to its general or specific powers, creates a social welfare or other program to be administered by the States with federal financial assistance or if the federal government puts a condition on a State's receipt of federal funds for a specific purpose, federal law will be supreme to the extent that the State is administering the federal program or has accepted funds tied to the condition. For example, the Aid to Families with Dependent Children (**AFDC**) program is a federally created, State administered welfare program providing cash benefits to needy children and their families which States are free to adopt or reject, but because AFDC is partially funded by the federal government, if a State adopts the program, its laws relating to the administration of the program must be consistent with federal law. To give another example, a State which has accepted federal highway funds must set the drinking age in the State at 21 years because this has been made a condition on the receipt of federal highway funds by Congress.

This type of supremacy of federal law is limited, however, to the specific program which is being administered by the State or the specific terms of the condition. And inconsistencies which cause no problems may be tolerated. For example, although a State receiving federal funds for its AFDC program must have AFDC laws which are consistent with federal law, a State can have a program of aid to families with dependent children, even one called AFDC, which is not governed by federal law as long as the program is not funded by the federal government. And even within a federally funded AFDC program, a State can give money to those not eligible under federal law as long as it does not use federal funds in this part of its program or may impose special eligibility requirements in the federally funded part of its program as long as the eligibility requirements serve the federal purpose. The supremacy of federal law related to AFDC merely precludes a State from accepting federal AFDC funds and then denying AFDC to those eligible for it under federal law. To look at the other example, a State can have any drinking age it wants but, if it wants federal highway funds, it must set the drinking age at 21 years. However, just because the federal government has legislated on the drinking age, federal law is not supreme over other State laws related to drinking (e.g., laws establishing when bars close and who can go to bars) or over other State laws related to age (e.g., the age to marry or to quit school).

So where are we in this federal versus State law dilemma? Most laws still fall into category four, that is, they are exclusively, or virtually exclusively, State laws. Although the federal government has been making more law in areas traditionally reserved for the States, its general powers are not seen as unlimited and "States' rights" is a powerful political, if not legal, rallying cry. And most laws enacted by the federal government in areas traditionally reserved for the States only cover a tiny aspect of the law in the area.

When federal law is enacted in areas which were traditionally exclusively State law, this federal law generally does not govern State law. Increasingly, federal supremacy is yielding if federal laws are enacted under the federal government's general powers or there is no need for consistency or uniformity in the law. Thus, more law is falling into category three.

Where federal funds are given to the States, however, laws which would otherwise fall into category three may fall into category two. Federal law will govern State law insofar as the federal funds impose conditions on State law. Laws will also fall into category two in one of those areas where the Constitution gives the federal government a specific power to act and does not prohibit the States from acting, but, even in these areas, the States may sometimes enact laws which are inconsistent with federal law. Only in those few areas where the Constitution gives the federal government a specific power to act and prohibits the States from acting or where it has been determined that the federal government has completely **occupied the field**, or **preempted** State law, is there federal law exclusively, that is, the law falls into category one.

When specific areas of the law are discussed in this text, we will tell you in which category the areas fall. In your practice, you can use the guidelines set forth above to try to determine if federal or State law applies. In doing so, you should remember that there may not be, and, in fact, probably will not be federal law on a subject and that, if there is federal law, it probably will not govern State law unless the federal law is tied to funds given to the States.

THE STRUCTURE OF THE AMERICAN COURT SYSTEM

In America, there is a federal court system and more than 50 State court systems.[7] These systems all have different features, but all of them are basically alike. In all of these systems, there are **trial** courts and **appellate courts** which perform certain distinct functions.

Trial courts

Trial courts resolve disputes. Each separate dispute that a trial court resolves is called a "**case**" or a "**suit**." With very rare exceptions, as between trial and appellate courts, cases begin in trial courts. With no exceptions, trial courts only decide cases that are brought before them by those involved; they do not initiate cases. With no exceptions, trial courts do not decide cases that do not involve an actual dispute between real individuals or entities; they do not issue advisory opinions. With no exceptions, trial courts will not render opinions in cases brought by a person who does not have a real interest in the case. This necessary interest of a party bringing a case is referred to as "**standing**."

Cases must be initiated in a proper court, both in terms of the geographical reach of the court and the ability of the court to rule on the matter in dispute. Both the geographical reach of a court and its authority to rule on the matter in dispute are referred to as the court's "**jurisdiction**." Jurisdiction is a very important concept in law. In order to consider a case, a court must have both **subject matter jurisdiction** over the type of issues involved

---

7. Remember, the term "State" encompasses areas like the District of Columbia and Puerto Rico.

in the dispute and geographical or territorial jurisdiction over the parties to the dispute, that is **personal jurisdiction**, and over any property or objects in dispute.

Federal trial courts have very limited subject matter jurisdiction. They may only resolve disputes in a few kinds of cases, such as some cases in which the parties are from different States (that is, there is ''**diversity of citizenship**''), or, more important, in which the federal government is involved or there is a ''**federal question**,'' that is, a question of federal law. Because, as we saw, federal law is limited, federal question jurisdiction is limited.

State trial courts usually have subject matter jurisdiction over every kind of case, including those that may involve federal law, except for a few types of cases that are exclusively federal, such as bankruptcy cases. Many States, however, have two levels of trial courts. Their lower level trial courts usually have jurisdiction only over less serious criminal cases and over cases involving disputes about money of less than a certain amount while their higher level trial courts usually have jurisdiction over all other cases. Further, some States have one or more specialized trial courts that have jurisdiction only over special kinds of cases while other trial courts have jurisdiction over all but these special kind of cases. For example, some States have special trial courts that only hear cases involving family law; other trial courts in these States have no jurisdiction over such cases. If a State has two levels of trial courts, there may be specialized courts at either or both levels. Some typical specialized courts of importance to social workers are: (1) **family courts**—courts which hear divorces, adoptions and other family matters, and in some States, such as New York, also hear juvenile matters; (2) **probate courts**—courts which deal with estates after death and often with guardianships and in some States,

like Michigan, juvenile matters and commitments of the mentally ill; (3) **chancery courts**, also called **courts of equity**—courts which resolve civil cases involving claims for something other than money damages; (4) **courts of claims**—courts which resolve claims for money against the government; (5) **small claims courts**—low level courts which resolve disputes between individuals involving small amounts of money and which typically have simplified procedures so that lawyers may not be necessary (indeed, in some States, like California, lawyers are not even allowed); and (6) **housing courts**—low level courts which resolve simple landlord-tenant matters.

Sometimes trial courts resolve the cases that are brought before them as a matter of law without having a trial. If they conduct a trial, they resolve a case by deciding the facts and by applying the law to the facts they have decided. They decide facts by listening to testimony, looking at documents and examining objects—in other words, by receiving **evidence**. They decide what evidence to receive and how it must be presented and they decide the facts in accordance with the law.

Appellate courts

A party who believes a trial court made an error in deciding a case generally has a right to have the decision reviewed by an appellate court, or in other words, to ''**appeal**'' the case.

The party who appeals generally cannot question the facts as decided by the trial court. Rather, the party argues that the trial court made an error of law in the way it decided the facts or applied the law. Appellate courts do not receive evidence or decide facts (except for those rare instances when they act like trial courts in cases of great importance.) They look at the record that was made of the proceedings in the trial court and decide questions of law based on this record. An appellate court may decide that a trial court had insufficient evidence to determine a certain fact or that a trial court failed to make a determination on a relevant fact, but, even in these situations, an appellate court will not receive additional evidence or decide the facts itself. Instead, if the trial court's error was significant, the appellate court will overturn the trial court's decision and send the case back to the trial court to decide it again.

In the federal system and most State systems, there are two levels of appellate courts: an intermediate court, usually called a "**court of appeals**;" and a court of last resort, usually called a "**supreme court**." A court of appeals generally must hear all properly appealed cases while a supreme court generally has discretion to refuse cases. A supreme court's decision to accept or refuse a case may have nothing to do with its view of the correctness of the lower court's decision; it may only reflect its view of the importance of the decision. This is because most supreme courts are asked to decide many more cases than they have time to decide.

Generally cases are appealed from a trial court to an intermediate appellate court and from there to the supreme court of a jurisdiction. A few cases may be appealed directly from a trial court to the supreme court. In some States which have two levels of trial courts, cases heard in the lower level trial court may be appealed only to the higher level trial court. When hearing such appeals, the higher level trial court acts as an appellate court.

Court opinions

For the most part, when they decide cases, trial courts do not write opinions setting forth their reasons for deciding as they did. If they do write opinions, generally they will not be published in books available to the general public. (Federal trial courts and higher level trial courts in New York, known as "supreme courts," and in a few other States sometimes write and publish their opinions.) Appellate courts usually do write opinions which are published in books available to the public. Only published opinions create law that affects people in addition to the parties to a case. In other words, only published opinions establish precedent.

The federal and State court systems

The State and federal court systems are parallel systems. Cases do not go back and forth from one system to another. A party may never appeal from a State trial court to a federal appeals court. However, if a party is not happy with a decision of a court of last resort in a State court system and if there is a federal question raised by the case, the party may seek review in the United States Supreme Court.[8]

Most cases are filed and remain in State court systems. As has been noted, federal courts have limited jurisdiction. They may hear far fewer cases than State courts. Further, many disputes which may be heard in federal courts may also be resolved in State courts, at the option of the parties. Moreover, even if the parties chose to go to federal court and even if a federal law may be involved in a case, a federal court may decline jurisdiction if State law is of prime importance in the case. (This is known as "**abstention**.") Finally, even if a federal court has and accepts jurisdiction over a civil case, it may not be able to give the parties complete relief and may not be able to resolve the case fully. Federal courts cannot make many types of orders that

---

8. Hereinafter, the capitalized term "Supreme Court," standing alone, will be used to refer only to the United States Supreme Court.

people regularly seek in civil court actions, like orders for a divorce, an adoption, an appointment of a guardian for a mentally retarded relative, or the like. Usually only State courts may make such orders.

Diagram 1.1 may help you understand the relationship between the State and federal courts in America and how the State and federal courts are structured. Some State court systems have structures different than what is shown on the diagram. For example, they may only have one level of appellate courts or, as has been stated, they may have two levels of trial courts with the higher level functioning as an appellate court for cases from the lower level.

As in the diagram, federal trial courts are called "**United States District Courts.**" There is at least one District Court in every State. There may be several judges and court buildings for each District Court. The bigger States may have several districts and District Courts, each of which may have several judges and several court buildings. For example, the federal trial

court in Charlotte, North Carolina is known as the United States District Court for the Western District of North Carolina. It has two judges and encompasses several cities and areas of North Carolina outside of Charlotte, including Asheville, which, like Charlotte, has a federal courthouse. There are also Eastern and Middle Districts of North Carolina encompassing Raleigh (and other cities) and Durham (and other cities), respectively. By way of contrast, South Carolina has only one district, but it has judges and courts in several cities.

State trial courts have different names in different States. In many States with two levels of trial courts, the lower level courts are called "district courts" and the higher level courts are called "circuit courts." The names of any specialized trial courts also differ from State to State.

As in diagram 1.1, federal intermediate appellate courts are called "**United States Courts of Appeals.**" They are also sometimes referred to as "**Circuit Courts of Appeals**" because there are thirteen divisions, known as "circuits," of

Diagram 1.1

THE AMERICAN COURT STRUCTURE

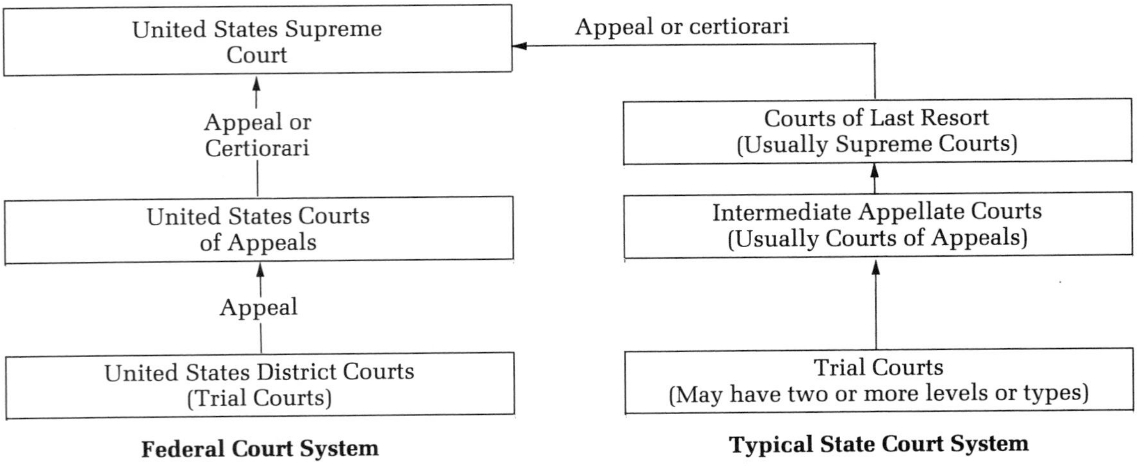

Federal Court System

Typical State Court System

the United States Courts of Appeals. Eleven of the circuits cover particular geographical regions encompassing several States or territories. One circuit covers the District of Columbia. In addition, there is a special Circuit Court of Appeals for special kinds of cases.

There are many appellate judges, usually referred to as "**justices**," in each circuit of the United States Court of Appeals. Usually only three justices in the circuit, selected on a random or rotational basis, hear and decide each appeal. The justices who hear a case are known as the "**panel**." If all the justices hear a case, it is said to have been decided "**en banc**."

State intermediate appellate courts are also usually divided into divisions, districts or circuits. As with United States Courts of Appeals, while there may be many judges in each division, usually only three or some other small number of judges serve as the panel for each appeal.

There is only one United States Supreme Court. It has nine justices. All nine generally hear and decide each case. To have a case heard and decided by the Supreme Court, depending on the nature of the case and the court from which review is sought, one either appeals to the Court or petitions the Court for a **writ of certiorari**. The Supreme Court only takes a tiny percentage of the cases in which certiorari is sought.

COMMON LAW REASONING

The starting point in deciding a case for any court, whether a trial or an appellate court, is to determine if there is any existing law which controls the result. It must look, in order, for an applicable constitutional provision, legislation or regulation. If it finds none, it looks to case law, that is, the law which is found in published court opinions. It examines and applies this law by using the common law reasoning process.

The common law reasoning process is basically a process of reasoning by analogy. That is, when using this process, a court looks for previous published cases with facts analogous to the facts of the case it is deciding. It follows the rulings of law in these analogous cases, known as "**precedent**," in deciding the case before it. Judges are required to follow precedent in deciding the cases before them by the doctrine of "***stare decisis***," a Latin expression meaning "stand by decisions." Under the doctrine of *stare decisis*, if a prior case has significant facts which are analogous to the facts of the case before a court, a court in the same jurisdiction as the court which decided the analogous case and lower in the hierarchy than that court is required to follow the rulings of law in the analogous case and come to the same result. A court in a different jurisdiction or at the same or a higher level in the hierarchy than the court which decided an analogous case is not required to follow the case under the doctrine of *stare decisis* but generally will do so unless substantial considerations dictate a different result. Such a case is considered **persuasive**, not binding.

Stare decisis is not an absolute principle; courts may depart from precedent on occasion. Yet *stare decisis* is the rule in the vast majority of cases for two important reasons. Because of *stare decisis*, like cases are treated alike and people can know in advance the consequences of their actions. To the extent that a court deviates from *stare decisis*, it is not treating like cases alike and it is changing the rules after people have acted. This would be contrary to most people's conception of justice.

The difficulty in using the doctrine of *stare decisis* is determining what facts in a prior case are significant and whether they are analogous to the facts in the case before the court. No two cases are ever exactly alike although they may have similar facts. Only if it is determined that the facts are sufficiently similar in a prior case and the case before the court and only if these similar facts are determined to be significant, should the prior case serve as precedent. But this determination may not be easy. This difficulty, and the entire process of common law reasoning, may best be understood by using one case as an example.

Assume that a woman, Ms. Green, who lives in an apartment building in State X, was injured when she was assaulted in the public hallway of her apartment building. Although no statute, regulation, or ordinance in X provided that a tenant may sue a landlord for such injuries, Green sued her landlord, Mr. Black. She claimed that Black had a duty to make the building safe, that he breached this duty, and that he was, thus, liable to her for her injuries. The trial judge ruled that Black had no duty to keep Green safe from criminals and decided the case in favor of Black. Green appealed the judgment to the X Court of Appeals.[9]

To decide Green's appeal, since no legislation or regulation applies, the justices would look for analogous cases from X. Cases from other States would only be persuasive, not binding. And, since the duty of a landlord to a tenant does not present a federal constitutional or statutory issue, the Court would not look for federal cases, including Supreme Court cases. The Court would probably look

first for opinions of the X Supreme Court and then for cases from its division of the X Court of Appeals. In many States and in the federal system, courts are only bound by *stare decisis* to follow the opinions of the courts of appeals in their own divisions. Each division is treated, in effect, as its own jurisdiction.

Assume that the Court finds only one decision mentioning a landlord's duty to a tenant in the common areas of an apartment building, *Blue v. Brown*. In *Blue*, a tenant sued his landlord when he was injured falling on a broken step leading to the building. The X Supreme Court ruled that a landlord has a duty to keep the common parts of an apartment building in reasonably safe condition and that Brown was, thus, liable for Blue's injuries.

Although the *Blue* facts are somewhat similar to those in *Green*, the court may not be bound by *stare decisis* to follow *Blue*. *Blue* dealt with dangerous physical conditions of a building, not its security. Moreover, in *Green*, there was an intervening criminal act by a third person. The *Green* Court would have to decide if these differences are significant. Whatever it decides, it will make law. Either the *Blue* precedent will be **extended** to the *Green* facts, and landlords in X will have a duty to keep their property safe and secure, or *Blue* will be **distinguished**, and landlords in X will only have a duty to keep their property free from dangerous physical conditions. Either way, *Green* will establish a new precedent which must be followed in later analogous cases.

This new precedent will not have come out of thin air. The new precedent established by *Green* must follow logically from *Blue*. The common law reasoning process and the doctrine of *stare decisis* allow courts to make law but only by building on previous law. There must be a sound and principled reason for the *Green* justices to extend or distinguish *Blue*. Judges should not decide cases based on their

---

9. This example is based on a case called "*Kline v. 1500 Massachusetts Avenue Corporation*," from the District of Columbia. The citation to this case is: 439 F.2d 447 (D.C. Cir 1970). We will explain citation form in Chapter 4. We will also discuss case names in Chapter 4. For now, you should know that a case name often takes the form of the names of the opposing parties separated by a "v.," standing for "versus," and that the name is always underlined or put in italics. Thus, Ms. Green's case would probably be known as "*Green v. Black*."

own notions of right and wrong. They may refer to history, custom, common sense, logic and social policy, but their primary reference should be to prior cases. Even if no prior cases are binding as precedent, prior cases contain general principles which provide guidance to courts. Courts may not depart from the accumulated wisdom found in the common law. The common law should develop slowly, incrementally, and logically, not by great leaps and flights of fancy. Changes in the law should be firmly grounded in existing law.

Nevertheless, a judge's personal belief as to what is right or wrong can influence decision-making. Even if a court finds a precedent which logically points in a particular direction, the court is not likely to extend that precedent to the case before it if the result will produce a decision that is contrary to the justices' view of the "correct" decision. If past precedent is clearly analogous, the judge's determination of law has largely been made for him or her. Thus, if instead of *Blue*, the Green Court found the case of *White v. Tan*, in which the X Court of Appeals ruled that a landlord was liable to a tenant who was attacked in the parking area of his duplex, the Court would have no choice but to follow *White*—even if *White* was decided decades ago and the *Green* justices would not have reached the same result if the case were before them as a matter of first impression. *White* is just not distinguishable from *Green*. But precedent is not always as analogous as *White*, or even *Blue*, is to *Green*. A court may be able to distinguish past cases and need only be bound by their general principles. And these principles may point in different directions, allowing the court to decide as it wishes. For example, if instead of finding *Blue* or *White*, the Green Court found *Orange v. Gray Bank*, in which the X Supreme Court ruled that a bank was liable when a customer was injured during a bank robbery, and *Red*

v. Azure Inn, in which the X Supreme Court ruled that a hotel was not liable when a guest was injured by a drunk driver who drove into the pool area, the *Green* judges could probably decide *Green* as they chose. Both *Orange* and *Red* are distinguishable from *Green*, but could provide guidance to the *Green* justices. The guidance in *Orange*, however, could lead to a very different result in *Green* than the guidance in *Red*.

Moreover, in extraordinary circumstances, a court equal to or above the court which decided a precedent could decide that the precedent was indistinguishable but nevertheless refuse to follow it. The court could **overturn** or **overrule** it as precedent. *Stare decisis* requires adherence to past precedent without regard to a court's view of the precedent's correctness. A court would, however, be justified in overruling a prior case if its rationale is no longer sound because of scientific developments or changes in society or if it is based on assumptions that have been proven inaccurate or on societal beliefs that no longer prevail.

Thus, a court has some freedom in deciding cases, but a judge's ability to make law is restricted by the common law reasoning process and by the doctrine of *stare decisis*. Moreover, a court's creative capacity is limited by the doctrine of *stare decisis* to the particular fact situation before it. If judges reach out and address questions not presented by the cases before them, their answers to the questions will not make law. *Stare decisis* requires adherence only to courts' **holdings**, that is, their rulings as to those matters that had to be settled to decide cases. A holding is limited to the facts before the court. Comments made by court which are not essential to deciding the case before it are called "***dicta***" (or, in the singular, "*dictum*"). *Dicta* are not binding on later courts under the doctrine of *stare decisis*.

To illustrate, *Blue v. Brown*, discussed

above in the *Green* example, dealt with unsafe physical conditions, not security measures. *Blue*'s holding was that a landlord has a duty to repair dangerous physical conditions; *Blue*'s holding says nothing about security measures. Since the issue of security measures was not before the *Blue* Court, any judicial comment about security measures in *Blue* would have been unnecessary to the court's ruling. Even if the *Blue* Court had thought about security measures and commented on them in rendering its decision, the comments would be *dicta* and *stare decisis* would not apply to them. The *Green* justices could ignore these comments.

The common law reasoning process, as described in the *Green* case, was used in the situation where there was no legislation, regulation or constitutional provision available to help decide the case. But, a court may also have to use the common law reasoning process when such law is available. For example, precedent may be used to determine the meaning of a very general constitutional provision, to determine the scope of a statute, or to interpret a regulation.

We will look at the use of precedent in interpreting the Constitution in Chapters 5 and 6. Let us now look to the common law reasoning process when a statute or several statutes appear applicable to a case. The process would be the same for other forms of legislation and for regulations.

If a statute's applicability to a case is obvious, if its language is clear, and if it is sufficiently detailed to resolve the case, the common law reasoning process will not be necessary. But this is not often the situation. Several different and conflicting statutes might all seem to apply to a case. The "plain meaning" of a statutory provision is not always plain; frequently there will be several conflicting interpretations that reasonably can be drawn from statutory language. Few statutes are detailed enough to answer all questions that may arise. Thus, even though a statute or several statutes appear applicable to a case, the court may have to look beyond the statutory language to resolve the case. The first place the court would be required to look is at the purpose of the legislature in enacting the relevant statutes, that is, the **legislative intent**.

To determine the legislative purpose for federal statutes and for statutes of a few States, courts may use the **legislative history** provided by recorded debates and committee reports. In most jurisdictions, however, such recorded history will not be available. Even if it is available, it may not be dispositive. Often legislatures have never considered a situation which has arisen. Courts, thus, must infer the legislative intent. They may infer it from their reading of the statute as a whole, from their understanding of the societal claims and demands that gave rise to the statute, and from their determination of the overall objective of the entire statutory scheme in which the statute is found, if any. But often a court will infer the legislative intent by examining precedent interpreting similar statutes, dealing with analogous situations, or establishing general principles of the law. This is where the common law reasoning process and the doctrine of *stare decisis* come in.

To illustrate, again consider the *Green v. Black* case. Assume that before the case came before the court, the legislature in the State of X had adopted a statute providing that landlords have a duty to keep their buildings "safe." Seemingly, this statute should resolve the *Green* case, but the word "safe" is unclear. The landlord in *Green* argues vigorously that the legislature did not mean "safe" to include "secure." Recorded legislative history is no help to the court in deciding if the landlord is correct. The legislature was not thinking about security measures when it passed the statute and nothing was said about them. The legislature only discussed dangerous physical conditions. Thus, the court must determine what the legislature would have done if it had thought about security measures. It does this by looking at the entire statutory scheme related to landlords, at other statutes talking about duties to keep people safe, and at precedent, specifically at cases with holdings which will enable it to interpret the term "safe" in the statute, and at cases which establish general principles that can guide its determination of the meaning of the word "safe." In other words, the court will use the common law reasoning process to infer the legislative intent and interpret the statute.

The process of common law reasoning and the doctrine of *stare decisis* may seem difficult or confusing to you now, but common law reasoning is really a simple process of reasoning by analogy and *stare decisis* is really a simple rule that a court must follow the law as stated in previous analogous cases in the court's jurisdiction—even when a court is developing new law. The process and the rule will become clearer to you as you read more court opinions.

2

The Hearing Process

Although published appellate opinions are generally the only opinions that make the law, it is crucial that you understand what happens in the trial court. If you do not understand the trial process, you cannot possibly understand an opinion that constitutes an appeal from that process. More important, it is far more likely that you will play a part in a case at the trial level than at the appellate level in the course of your career. Few cases are appealed and the social worker's role in the appeal of a case is virtually nonexistent. On the other hand, many cases go through one or more stages of the trial process, and the social worker can and does perform many roles throughout this process.

THE BASIC NATURE OF THE PROCESS

Three words can be used to describe the nature of the trial process in America: adversarial; accusatorial; and fair. The process, and, indeed, the entire legal system, is shaped by the principles embodied in these three terms. Thus, it is necessary to examine each term in depth.

Adversarial

The American legal system is an **adversarial** system. It is, in other words, a system which arrives at a decision by having each party or side to a dispute present and argue its case and then having a neutral decision-maker decide what is true and who should prevail in light of the opposing presentations and arguments. At the trial level, the parties to a dispute each present their version of the facts to the decision-maker who determines the "true" facts. The parties also present

their views on what law should be used to resolve the dispute to the decision-maker who determines and then applies the "correct" law. At the appellate level, the parties do not present evidence to establish their version of the facts and the decision-makers do not determine the facts, but the parties do argue that certain facts are or are not significant, that certain facts were or were not established by the evidence, and that certain characterizations of the facts are or are not accurate. And, at the appellate level, the parties present their views on what law should have been used at the trial level to decide the case to the neutral decision-makers who determine which side is "right."

Whether at the trial or appellate level, in an adversarial system, the parties in a legal case are advocates for their positions. They are advocates because it is believed that partisan advocacy leads to the best outcome and that people will have the greatest confidence in the decision-making process if they know they may argue for their positions and present their cases as they wish.

In an adversarial system, each side is given the opportunity to present its side of the story, that is, to have its "day in court." The opposing parties frame the issues, advance their interpretation of the law, and, at the trial level, seek out and choose the evidence that they will present. The decision-makers do not develop the case. It is assumed that material presented by the opposing sides will fully develop the relevant facts, accurately present the law and permit the decision-makers to reach an impartial and rational conclusion.

An adversary system operates fairly only if each side has the capacity to present its case fully and if the opposing sides have roughly equal capacities. A primary criticism of the system is that neither this capacity nor this equality always exists, particularly if one party is poor or a government agency opposes a private individual. The government, it is argued, has so many resources that it can overpower a private opponent, particularly a poor one, and that a rich opponent can overpower a poor one.

The American adversary system is also criticized because partisan advocacy is not seen as the best way to arrive at the truth. Some people point out that partisans may suppress evidence that hurts their case or take other actions to prevent a determination of the truth. Some people who are accustomed to the scientific method, cannot accept that the truth will be revealed through the unscientific process of partisan advocacy. Many people see the **rules of evidence**, which restrict what the parties may present as evidence in a trial, as artificial barriers to truth-seeking. The formality and rigidness of the rules of evidence, which also determine how the evidence may be presented, contribute to the perception of a trial as something other than a truth-seeking process; they make a trial seem more like a game than a way to reveal the truth.

The adversary system is further criticized because it is not seen as the best way to achieve a just outcome. It is contended that when emphasis is placed on winning or losing, compromises may be ignored and creative solutions to problems will not be sought. Some say that victory is the goal rather than justice; they see the process as more like a battle than a problem-solving method. And, they say that the winner of the battle may be the party with the best lawyer who best manipulates the rules—not the party with the best case.

While it is true that trials may not lead to the best solutions to problems, most legal disputes are not resolved by trials. The vast majority of cases are settled without trials and many disputes are resolved before they even become "cases." Further, many alternative dispute-resolution methods, like mediation and arbitration, are now being used and more are being tried every year.

The rules of evidence may sometimes seem to restrict the ability of a decision-maker to arrive at the truth, but most of the rules have been designed, not to obscure the truth, but to reveal it. And those that are not so designed have been designed instead to keep trials fair, to prevent the imbalance that results when one party has a greater capacity to present his or her side of the story, or to serve other equally important purposes.

Partisan advocacy may sometimes seem to obstruct the truth-seeking process, but partisan advocacy may be the best way to protect and promote the parties' interests. If the parties had to rely on others to present their stories, their stories might not be told. If the parties had no one to act as their advocates, their desires might be ignored. This would be the case particularly when a private party was involved in a dispute with the government. In an "inquisitorial system," a system without partisan advocacy, the "judge has the responsibility to 'arrive at the truth by his own exertions in conjunction with those of the official prosecutor.' "[1] In such a system, in a case involving the government, the government gets to present, not only its own side of the story, but also its opponent's side, and further gets to act as the judge and jury. This not only seems unfair, but "[e]xperimental studies lend support to the claim that an adversary form of presentation, in contradistinction to an inquisitorial presentation, counteracts bias in decisionmakers."[2]

While the adversarial system is based on partisan advocacy, typically social workers do not perform an advocacy role in the legal system; the role of the social worker in the system is typically different than the role of the lawyer. Lawyers should be concerned with what their clients want. They should ad-

---

1. Ralph Slovenko, *Psychiatry and Law* (Little, Brown & Co.: Boston 1973) p. 19.
2. *Id.*

vocate for their clients' positions even if they do not agree with these positions; they should seek to protect their clients' rights even if they believe their clients or society might be better off if these rights were not protected. On the other hand, social workers typically are concerned with what the parties need. They often try to work out the best solution to a problem even if those involved may not agree it is the best; they work to further their perception of the parties' and society's best interests—even if these interests do not coincide with the parties' desires.

There are some advocacy roles for social workers in the legal system, as, for example, representatives of clients before administrative agencies, but, in the typical legal case involving a social worker, the social worker will be focusing on the parties' best interests while any lawyers will be focusing on their clients' rights. Of course, the best solution to a problem would generally be one which both serves the parties' best interests and protects their rights.

Accusatorial

The American legal system is shaped by an **accusatorial** process of proof as well as an adversarial system of decision-making. The key to an accusatorial process is that one party, usually the party bringing a case, has the **burden of proof**, or in other words, bears the burden of proving that the case has merit.

You can see the accusatorial process in its purest form in the criminal system where the government accuses someone of committing a crime. The government has the burden of proving that the accused is guilty; the accused need not prove his or her innocence but can simply sit back, produce no evidence whatsoever, and be assured of exoneration if the government does not meet its burden of proving guilt.

Although you may not see the accusatorial process in such a pure form in the civil system, the civil system in America is also accusatorial. To get a dispute before a court, one party to the dispute must initiate a law suit. To win the case, the initiating party usually has the burden of proving that his or her claims have merit. The other parties to the dispute need not prove that these claims have no merit or that their claims have merit, but can prevail if the party who initiated the suit does not meet his or her burden of proof.

The accusatorial process sometimes makes legal disputes quite hostile. One party to the dispute is accusing the others of wrong doing in some manner. The parties who are being accused often respond in kind. But the accusatorial process is probably the fairest way to allocate the burden of proof. It is only fair to make the parties who initiate legal actions prove the validity of their claims; the parties being sued, who may be completely free of any wrongdoing, should not be given a burden of proof simply because they were sued. It is not fair to require someone to prove innocence; it is usually extremely difficult to prove a negative. Keeping these reasons for the accusatorial process in mind, might enable you to minimize some of the hostility in cases in which you are involved.

Fair

The adversarial system and the accusatorial process were developed to make our legal system fair. Adjustments are constantly being made to them, and to other aspects of our legal system, to keep it fair. Most rules of procedure and evidence were developed, and are constantly being revised, to insure that our legal system is, and remains, fair to all participants. Thus, for example, because the government in a criminal case has far greater resources than the ordinary defendant, not only is the burden of proof placed on the government, but also the burden of proof is made extremely high.

THE MECHANICS OF THE PROCESS

A discussion of the technical aspects of the hearing process follows. Throughout the discussion, key terms are defined for you. The technical aspects and the terms may differ for different types of cases and in different jurisdictions, but they are generally as described in a civil case. As we shall see in Chapter 6, the process and the terms differ somewhat in a criminal case.

To initiate a civil case in a trial court, one party to a dispute files a document generally called a "**complaint**" or a "**petition**." If it is a complaint, the party filing it is generally called the "**plaintiff**;" if it is a petition, the party filing it is generally called the "**petitioner**." The opponent of a plaintiff is called a "**defendant**" while the opponent of a petitioner is called a "**respondent**." Whether one files a petition or a complaint depends on the type of case and the jurisdiction. Petitions are used more frequently than complaints in most cases involving social workers.[3]

There may be several plaintiffs and defendants on each side in one case. A defendant may file complaints against one or more of the plaintiffs in the case or even against others not originally parties to the case. These complaints of defendants, known as "**cross-complaints**," or "**counterclaims**," become part of the original case.

A single case may involve several related disputes. Each dispute would be set forth separately in the petition as a separate **cause of action, count** or **claim**. As with petitions and complaints, the term used depends on the jurisdiction and the type of case.[4]

Petitioners may have several different reasons, grounds or theories why they are entitled to win a case. These different reasons, grounds or theories would also be included in a single petition but would be set forth in separate causes of action. Causes of action may be cumulative, alternative or even inconsistent. All petitioners may not join in all causes of action; all respondents may not be named in all causes of action.

To illustrate, a single complaint against a marriage counselor who engaged in sex with the wife of a couple he was counseling and who stole money from the couple could have different claims alleging malpractice, undue influence, battery, theft, invasion of privacy, breach of contract, intentional infliction of mental distress, and fraud. The husband could bring some of the claims and the wife others; some could also be against the counselor's supervisor or his agency on the theory that they were responsible for some of the actions.

The petition always asks for something, generally called "**relief**" or the "**remedy**," in something generally called a "**prayer**." A petition may seek several different, alternative, or cumulative kinds of relief.

Often petitions are simple court forms on which the parties have simply filled in the blanks. Sometimes petitions are long, typed documents using highly formal language and containing certain necessary formal allegations. You should ask to see petitions from cases like the ones in which you might be involved before you begin your involvement. Courts will tell you if there is a form petition which can or must be used for a given type of case and, if there is, will provide you with the

---

3.   The two sets of terms will be used interchangeably throughout this book.

4.   These terms will also be used interchangeably in this book.

form. In addition, documents filed with a court in most cases, including the petitions, are generally available to the public;[5] most lawyers have sample or form petitions (and other legal documents) they can show you; there are books of sample forms available in law libraries; and most agencies keep a supply of forms for cases in which they are frequently involved.

Petitions must be filed in courts that have jurisdiction over the case and the parties. If courts do not have this jurisdiction, they usually will dismiss cases rather than transferring them to courts with jurisdiction. If a statute of limitations elapses before the cases can be filed in courts with jurisdiction, the cases may not be allowed to proceed.

Several courts may have geographical and subject matter jurisdiction over a case, but one of these courts may be in the most appropriate location to hear the case. This court is said to have "**venue**" to hear the case. If a case is filed in a court with jurisdiction but not venue, it may be transferred to a court with venue or heard in the court without venue, but generally would not be dismissed.

Usually, plaintiffs must pay fees to file a case. If plaintiffs cannot afford these fees, they may ask courts to permit them to file without paying the fees, that is, to file **in forma pauperis**.

After a petition is filed, it must be served on the respondent. **Service** is the responsibility of the petitioner, not the court. The method of service depends on the nature of the case and the location of the respondent. **Personal service**, that is, actually handing someone the papers, is not always required. Service by mail or even service by publishing a notice in a newspaper may be sufficient. Service may usually be done by any adult who is not a party to a case, although the parties may pre-

fer to have a professional process server or a government agent, such as the sheriff, do the service for them for a fee. When a case has been initiated by a petition rather than a complaint, it may be the petition itself and only the petition which is served on the respondent. When a case has been initiated by a complaint rather than a petition, usually the defendant must be served not only with the complaint but also with something, generally called a "**summons**," which tells the defendant when and how he or she must respond to the complaint.

A defendant must respond to a complaint. If the time to respond to a complaint has passed and the defendant has failed to respond, the plaintiff can enter the defendant's **default**. After the default has been entered, depending on the type of case, the plaintiff may be granted the relief sought in the complaint without further action or there may have to be a hearing to determine the relief. Defendants who have defaulted are not entitled to further notice of the proceedings and cannot appear to argue their positions.

A response may be written or oral or both, depending on the nature of the case. A written response to a petition is generally called a "**response**;" a written response to a complaint is generally called an "**answer**." The petition and the written response together are known as the "**pleadings**." Sometimes the defendant must pay a fee to file a written response to a complaint. If there is a fee, the defendant may request to file in forma pauperis.

In cases where an oral response is required, at the time a petition is filed, the petitioner may set a date and time with the court for the response or even for a hearing at which the response can be given and the hearing proceed. Setting a time and date for an appearance or hearing is called "**calendaring**." Calendaring, whether for initial appearances or trials, is always the responsibility of the petitioners, not the courts.

---

5. The documents filed in some cases, like those involving juveniles, may be confidential.

If the defendant has a legal argument that the case has some legal flaws or should not go forward for some reason, for example, because the court has no personal jurisdiction over her, because the statute of limitations has passed, or because the case was filed in the wrong venue, the defendant would generally make a **motion** raising the argument before or at the time the response is due instead of otherwise responding. The motion would prevent a default from being taken. If a respondent's motion is denied, the respondent would have to respond in a time set by the court or be considered in default. Common motions are **motions to dismiss** (also known as ''**demurrers**''), which argue that even if the petitioner proved everything alleged in the petition, the petitioner would not be entitled to relief under the law, or **motions to quash service**, which argue that there was faulty service or that there is no personal jurisdiction over the defendant. Motions are argued at hearings. The moving party has responsibility for calendaring a hearing on a motion, not the court.

After the pleadings have been filed and all necessary appearances made, there may be **discovery**, a process by which each side determines the facts known to the other side and the facts the other side will seek to prove. A common type of discovery is submission of written questions, known as ''**interrogatories**,'' to the other side. Another type of discovery is taking a **deposition**, that is, questioning a witness in person with an opportunity for both sides to do questioning. A transcript is usually made of a deposition.

There may also be motions filed asking for some legal issues to be resolved prior to trial or that the case as a whole be resolved without a trial. Common motions are motions for a **summary judgment** or for a **judgment on the pleadings** which argue, basically, that there are no disputes as to the facts and applying the law to the undisputed facts, the moving party should win the case.

If the motions made prior to trial do not resolve the case or if the case has not been settled or somehow resolved by the parties, it will go to trial. (Most cases are settled or resolved prior to trial.) The rules of evidence, which will be discussed later in this chapter, and the rules of procedure for a jurisdiction will control the conduct of the trial. Generally the party who initiated the case has the burden of proof and goes first. This party presents his or her case by submitting **evidence**, that is, the testimony of witnesses, documents, actual objects and anything else which may be submitted to a court to establish a fact under the rules of evidence. After this party completes his or her case, the opposing parties may present their evidence or simply argue that the initiating party has not met his or her burden of proof, that is, has not presented enough evidence to win. Usually, if a party without the burden of proof presents evidence, the party with the burden of proof may present further evidence to rebut this evidence.

The trial may or may not be a jury trial. Whether or not there is a jury is determined by the type of the case and the wishes of the parties. In many States, one is not entitled to a jury in the kinds of cases typically involving social workers, like family law or juvenile matters. One is usually entitled to a jury in cases seeking money damages involving personal injuries or contracts. Any party who has a right to a trial by a jury may choose not to have a jury and may ask, instead, to have the case tried before a judge. In other words, the party may **waive** his or her right to a jury. The other party may, however, be able to insist on a trial with a jury. A trial with only a judge is called a ''**bench trial**.''

Juries are supposed to be impartial and representative of the community, but creating such juries may be difficult. Courts have prohibited the systematic exclusion of certain types of prospective jurors from the **jury panel** or **venire**, that is, the group of people from which a trial jury is chosen. Thus, random selection is the basis on which most jury panels are chosen. Making the random selection from lists, such as voter registration lists or lists of utility connections, however, may serve, just as much as systematic exclusion, to exclude large classes of potential jurors, such as the poor.

The judge or the lawyers may question the members of the jury panel before a trial to determine if anything would prevent them from being impartial. This questioning is called ''**voir dire**.'' If jurors would not be impartial, they are **excused for cause**. Usually, both sides may also excuse a certain number of prospective jurors without stating a reason. This is called a ''**peremptory challenge**.''

While juries traditionally have twelve people and while jury decisions, known as ''**verdicts**,'' generally must be unanimous, juries sometimes have less than twelve members, and some cases may be decided by verdicts that are not unanimous.

If there is a jury trial, the jury will decide the facts. If there is a bench trial, the judge will decide the facts. Whether or not there is a jury, only the judge will decide what law to apply to the facts and how to apply it. If there is a jury, the judge will instruct the jury on the applicable law and on how to apply it.

If a case is decided by a judge without a trial or after a bench trial or if a case is decided by a jury verdict, the judge will render or enter a **judgment**. Sometimes, there are jury trials, but the judge will grant a motion to take the case away from the jury and enter a judgment for the moving party. This will be done if the judge determines that, as a matter of law, the moving party must win the case. Sometimes, the judge decides that a jury verdict is erroneous and grants a motion for a **judgment notwithstanding the verdict**.

In suits between private parties, the plaintiffs often seek judgments awarding them **damages**, that is, money compensating them for an injury or wrong. In some such suits and, more commonly, in suits involving the government, plaintiffs may also or alternatively seek **declaratory judgments**, that is, judgments declaring a law invalid or valid, stating the meaning of a document, or setting forth the respective rights and obligations of the parties to the litigation. Plaintiffs may also or alternatively seek judgments granting **injunctions**, that is, orders commanding defendants to do something or, more commonly, to refrain from doing something, like polluting the air or enforcing an invalid law. Sometimes plaintiffs seek, as their judgments or as part of their judgments, special kinds of legal orders called ''**writs**.'' Like injunctions, writs command people to do something or to refrain from something. Sometimes plaintiffs seek special orders or **decrees**, like divorce decrees or orders appointing guardians, as their judgments, as part of their judgments or in addition to their judgments. Decrees, writs, injunctions or other special orders commanding people to do certain things are generally sought in petitions; money damages are generally sought in complaints. Special orders, writs or injunctions may also be sought before judgment, as temporary measures to preserve the *status quo* or to prevent irreparable injury pending final resolution of a case. Orders issued before judgment are often referred to as ''**temporary restraining orders**.'' Injunctions issued before trial are often called ''**preliminary injunctions**.'' Orders or writs may further be sought after judgment, as a means of enforcing a judgment or as a special way to appeal from it. **Writs of execution** are often sought to enforce money judgments while landlords in eviction actions may seek **writs of possession** or **writs of restitution**.

While a party may seek several alternative or cumulative remedies in a complaint, the party will generally not be entitled to receive alternative or cumlative remedies. A party may, however, be awarded more than one nonalternative, noncumulative remedy. For example, a landlord may get a writ of possession commanding a tenant to vacate her apartment, a judgment for past due rent, and a judgment for money damages because of damage to the apartment caused by the tenant.

A judgment is usually the final and complete resolution of a case at the trial level, but some parts of a judgment, like a child custody order, may be modifiable in the future and sometimes matters collateral to the main case, like whether the losing party should pay the winning party's attorney's fees, are resolved after judgment.

The usual method of protesting a judgment is an appeal to an appellate court, but sometimes protests are made in the trial court by motions, like a **motion for a new trial**, and sometimes appellate review is sought through a writ. If an appeal is taken, the party who appeals is called the "**appellant**." The other side is called the "**respondent**" or the "**appellee**." A party seeking review in an appellate court through a writ is usually called the "**petitioner**" and the other side called the "**respondent**." The writ may be called a **writ of certiorari** or a **writ of error**. The effectiveness of a judgment may be **stayed**, that is, delayed, pending appeal or resolution of a writ, by the trial court or the appellate court.

Usually one can only appeal after a final judgment has been entered, but some orders made before judgment, like orders ruling on preliminary injunctions, may be appealed before a final judgment has been entered. An appeal taken before a final judgment is entered is called an "**interlocutory appeal**." Writs are sometimes used to appeal an order from which an interlocutory appeal is not allowed. An appeal from a final judgment does encompass all preliminary orders and actions of a trial court

in the case from which no interlocutory appeal was allowed or taken.

If a trial court has made no significant errors of law in reaching its judgment, the appellate court will **affirm** the judgment. If the trial court has made significant errors of law, the appellate court will **reverse** or **vacate** the judgment. It may also affirm part of a judgment and reverse another part or modify a judgment. Whether the appellate court affirms, reverses or modifies a judgment, the case will probably be **remanded**, that is, sent back to the trial court to take all actions necessary in light of the appellate decision. The trial court, not the appellate court, will make all orders and take all actions necessary to enforce an affirmed judgment.

THE PARTICIPANTS IN THE PROCESS

There are several important participants in the hearing process: the judge; the jury; the parties; the attorneys; the guardian *ad litem*; and the witnesses. All of these will not participate in every hearing and, indeed, you may encounter some of these participants relatively rarely, but you nevertheless should understand each of these participants' role in the hearing process.

The judge

The judge performs three important roles at a hearing. The judge: (1) presides over a hearing; (2) applies the law to the facts presented by the parties; and, (3) either decides the facts if there is no jury or instructs the jury on how to decide the facts. In all three roles, the judge is guided by the law. That is, in the course of presiding over a trial, the judge may have to determine whether certain evidence is admissible or whether a line of questioning is proper under the law. In applying the law to the facts, the judge may have to determine what law to apply and whether a particular legal standard should apply to the facts. In the course of deciding the facts or instructing the jury, the judge may have to decide how to weigh the evidence presented.

To illustrate, in a case seeking to commit a mentally ill man for treatment, the judge may have to decide whether a social worker's evaluation can be used at the hearing, that is, make a legal decision about the admissibility of evidence. The judge will also decide what standard to apply in determining whether the man should be committed, that is, decide the applicable law, and, assuming there is no jury, will decide whether the man meets the standard for commitment, that is, decide the facts in light of the law.

In summary, the judge is the primary legal decision-maker in a hearing and may also be the factual decision-maker.

The jury

If there is a jury, the jury will decide the facts based on the evidence the judge permitted the parties to present and reach a verdict based on these facts in accordance with the judge's instructions on the proper law to apply. The jury will be the primary factual decision-maker at the trial, but it will never decide the law.

The parties

All petitioners and respondents should be named as parties in the pleadings. When petitioners or respondents are government entities, agencies, private associations or corporations, depending on technical rules, the entity or organization may be named as a party or a person in charge of the entity or organization may be so named.

In some cases, known as "**class actions**" or "**representative suits**," one or more named parties act as representatives of unnamed parties who are similarly situated to the named parties. If the named parties in class actions prevail in their suits, the unnamed parties also prevail. If they lose, the unnamed parties also lose and may never be able to bring suit on their own. Thus, for example, if a woman sues an employer in a class action for discriminating against women on her own behalf and on behalf of all other women whom the employer discriminated against and wins her case, the unnamed women who were discriminated against might be entitled to damages or to jobs. If, however, the plaintiff lost her case, the unnamed women might not be able to sue the employer for discrimination themselves.

In some cases, a named party has a smaller stake in a case than a person not named as a party or has no real stake in the case; the party is only named for technical reasons. In such a case, the person who has the bigger or real stake in the case might be named as the "**real party in interest**." For example, a welfare department might bring an action against the father of a child on welfare to obtain support for the child. The welfare department might be named as the plaintiff, but the child would be named as the real party in interest. To give another example, a woman may seek a writ against a court to get it to change a decision to commit her to a mental hospital. The petition for a writ may name the court as respondent, but the person who had petitioned the court to have the woman committed in the first place would be named as the real party in interest.

Sometimes, individuals who have a legitimate and direct interest in a case, for example, a natural father in an adoption action, are not named as parties but may be granted

party status by a statute or a court. Other individuals who are not named as parties or granted party status but who have a stake in the outcome of a case, may ask to be made parties or, in other words, to **intervene** in a case, by filing a **motion for intervention.**

All parties to a case who have not defaulted, including real parties in interest, intervenors who have been made parties, and persons with party status, must be served with all pleadings and other important papers, must be notified of all important motions and hearings, and have a right to be heard at any hearings. Unnamed class members may also be entitled to notice and to be heard.

The attorneys

All parties to a case will not necessarily be represented by an attorney. Whether or not a party has an attorney depends on the party's wishes, the party's ability to afford an attorney, and the type of case. Sometimes parties do not wish to have attorneys because they choose to represent themselves. Sometimes they wish to have attorneys, but cannot afford to hire one. The Constitution specifically grants defendants in criminal cases a right to the assistance of counsel, but a right to the assistance of counsel does not necessarily mean that a lawyer will be appointed to represent a party who cannot afford to pay for one at no cost to the party. The Constitution has been interpreted to provide that a party to litigation is only entitled to the appointment of counsel at no cost in serious criminal cases and in a few civil cases. The States may grant a right to the assistance of counsel and a right to appointment of counsel at no cost in further matters under their constitutions or statutes or as a matter of common law.

The guardian *ad litem*

In certain cases, instead of or in addition to appointing an attorney for a party, judges may be either required or permitted to appoint a **guardian *ad litem***, meaning a guardian at law, for the party. A guardian *ad litem* acts in a given case to protect a party to the case who is assumed to be unable to protect himself or herself because of age or disability. Guardian *ad litems* are typically appointed to represent children who are the subjects of juvenile court actions or custody disputes or adults alleged to be incompetent.

The guardian *ad litem* represents the interests of the party only in the particular case in which he or she was appointed; he or she is not a guardian of the party's interests in any other context or for any other purposes.

A guardian *ad litem* may or may not be an attorney. It is important to note, however, that even if they are attorneys, they do not act like attorneys in the usual sense. As has been stated, the role of the attorney is to represent the client's interests as defined by the client. The guardian *ad litem*, on the other hand, defines the interests of a person thought unable to do so. In other words, unlike attorneys, guardian *ad litems* present to courts what they think best for the party—not what the party wants to present. In a sense, the difference between the roles of the guardian *ad litem* and the attorney in a case is the same as the difference between the usual roles of the social worker and the attorney in the legal system.

The difference between the attorney's and the guardian *ad litem*'s roles can be illustrated by a case of a man whose relatives seek to have him declared incompetent. He may hire an attorney to represent him, and if he wants to object to the allegations of incompetence, the attorney must do so, and should do so vigorously, whatever she thinks about his competence. But if the court appoints a guardian *ad litem* for the man, the guardian *ad litem* may conduct an investigation and may recommend a finding of incompetence because she believes it is in the man's best interests—even if he objects.

The witnesses

Witnesses are called to present evidence to the fact finder, whether it be a judge or a jury. Under oath and under penalty for **perjury**, that is, lying under oath, witnesses typically present information about what they have seen, heard and done through oral testimony. In short, they tell what they know to be the facts. So-called "**expert witnesses**" may also present their opinions. We will discuss expert witnesses in greater depth later in this chapter and in the next chapter.

In some hearings, there may be no witnesses present. Either there may be only a dispute about the law, and thus no testimony is needed, or the facts may be presented through written statements made out of court. Such written statements may be called "**affidavits**" or "**declarations**" if they are made under oath and under penalty of perjury. Transcripts of depositions and responses to interrogatories may also be submitted in some cases. The rules of evidence determine the admissibility of such written evidence. Their admissibility depends on the nature of the hearing and their contents and purpose.

THE RULES OF EVIDENCE

Evidence is everything, exclusive of argument, presented in a hearing to prove the facts. The **rules of evidence** determine what may and may not be presented as evidence

and how evidence must be presented. Legal evidence should be distinguished from social evidence. Evidence of importance to social workers in writing a social history or working with a client may be of no legal significance. Evidence of importance to a lawyer in proving a case may be of no significance to a social worker. For example, evidence that a defendant in a murder case was an alcoholic would probably be of no legal significance but it might be important to the social worker, while evidence that the defendant in a murder case had been threatened by the victim in the past might be legally significant but might not be important to the social worker.

Evidence may be **direct** or **circumstantial**. Direct evidence proves a fact without the need to draw an inference or make an assumption. For example, if John testifies "I saw Jim shoot Jane," this is direct evidence that Jim killed Jane. Circumstantial evidence requires an inference or presumption. For example, if John testifies "I saw Jim standing over Jane's body with a smoking gun in his hand," this is circumstantial evidence that Jim killed Jane. Circumstantial evidence is not "bad" evidence; it's just not direct.

Evidence may be **real** (also called "**demonstrative**"), **documentary** or **testimonial**. Real evidence is a tangible object which is itself the fact to be proven (e.g., the gun, the bruises.) Documentary evidence is, as the name implies, some kind of document that commemorates a fact. It may be, for example, a writing or a photograph. In some instances documents may be real evidence. For example, an x-ray that a doctor in a malpractice case allegedly misread would be real evidence, while an x-ray showing a person's injury would be documentary evidence. Testimonial evidence is oral testimony given in court under oath by a witness.

All documentary and real evidence must be properly identified and authenticated. Certain formalities may be required to authenticate some documentary evidence (e.g., notarizing). Usually a witness must identify and authenticate this evidence through testimony.

All witnesses, whether expert or not, must be found competent to testify. This means the judge must determine, among other things, that the witnesses understand the obligation to tell the truth and either have personal knowledge of the facts about which they are going to testify, in the usual case, or are qualified by virtue of training or experience to give an opinion on a subject beyond the knowledge of the ordinary person, in the case of expert witnesses.

Not all facts in a trial require proof. The parties will **stipulate** to some facts. That is, they will acknowledge their truth. The court will take **judicial notice** of some facts, such as public laws, matters of common knowledge or the laws of nature. That is, the judge will accept some facts, such as that people born in America are United States citizens, Abraham Lincoln was assassinated and it is dark at night, as true without proof or a stipulation.

Not everything the parties seek to introduce as evidence at a trial will be admitted into evidence. To be admitted, first of all, evidence must be **relevant**. Almost any fact may be related to almost any other fact if we pursue a process of reasoning long enough, but courts must save their time for the determination of the case. Thus, only facts determined to be legally relevant or **material** to a particular case will be admitted in the case.

Even if evidence is legally relevant, it may not be admitted for other reasons. For example, logically the character of an individual may be an excellent indication of what a person did or did not do in a given situation. Yet the law usually excludes evidence of character because of the danger of prejudice, because the jury might give such evidence undue weight, and because such evidence will tend to complicate the case with collateral is-

sues and lengthen any trial unduly. **Hearsay** evidence will also be excluded.

Hearsay is a statement made orally or in writing outside of the courtroom which is offered to prove the truth of the matter asserted in the statement. For example, if Jane testifies: "John told me he saw Jim hit his baby in his home," this is hearsay if it is offered to prove that Jim hit his baby. It would not be hearsay if it were offered to prove that John is not always truthful, that John is antagonistic towards Jim, or that John lied when he said he was never in Jim's home.

Hearsay is excluded because the person who made the hearsay statement (the **hearsay declarant**) is not in court and cannot be questioned by the opposing side and the truthfulness of the declarant cannot be assessed by the trier of fact. Rather than letting Jane testify about what John said he saw, John should testify about what he saw so that John can be questioned and so that the trier of fact can determine if John is telling the truth.

Despite these valid reasons for excluding hearsay, there are many exceptions to the hearsay rule. Many oral or written out of court statements may be admitted into evidence to prove the truth of matters asserted in the statements. Most of the exceptions arise because the rule serves no purpose in a particular context or because the rule unduly burdens the truth-seeking process. For example, if John is unavailable to testify about what he saw, the only way to put the crucial evidence of what he saw before the trier of fact may be to allow Jane to testify as to what he said to her. Jane may be allowed to testify, especially if John made his statement to Jane at a time and in such a way as to indicate it was truthful. Thus, dying declarations, admissions, excited utterances and statements of physical sensations may all be admissible if the declarant is unavailable to testify and even in some instances where the declarant is available.

Client files, records or reports, including

those of a social worker, are written statements made out of court. Thus, they would be hearsay if a party seeks to have them admitted into evidence to prove the truth of their contents. Even reports made for a court would be hearsay if a party seeks to admit them to prove the truth of something contained in them. If, however, the reports make recommendations to a court and do not attempt to establish facts, the reports may be considered by a judge. They may be considered even though they are not admitted into evidence; the fact that they would be hearsay if a party sought to admit them into evidence is irrelevant. And many files, records and reports can be admitted into evidence as exceptions to the hearsay rule even if a party seeks to admit them to prove the truth of their contents.

The most commonly encountered exception to the hearsay rule for written out of court statements is that for **business records**. Business records are admissible to prove the truth of facts contained in them if they are made in the ordinary course of business, at or near the time of the event which they record, and in circumstances which indicate their trustworthiness. The "business" maintaining the record need not be a commercial or industrial concern that operates for a profit. Public agencies and non-profit organizations, like hospitals or counseling centers, are considered businesses for the purpose of this exception. If a party seeks to admit business records into evidence, a custodian of the records will usually have to testify about how the records were made and maintained. We will discuss the business record exception for social work records in greater depth in the next chapter.

There is also a **public records exception** to the hearsay rule. Public records are official government documents, like birth certificates or marriage licenses, created and maintained for specific governmental purposes. The records kept by social workers who work for public agencies would ordinarily not qualify as public records but these records may contain public records, like a court order removing a child from her parents or a child's birth certificate.

A record or report which is admissible into evidence as a business record or a public record may contain hearsay or even "double hearsay," like a notation that "Jane said John said he saw Jim hit his baby." Just because the record is admissible into evidence, the hearsay within it would not be admissible. The inadmissible hearsay, and any other inadmissible evidence, will be stricken before the record or report will be admitted into evidence.

In addition to the relevance requirement and the hearsay rule, there are numerous other rules of evidence that operate to exclude evidence which you may consider relevant and important in determining the truth. The rule excluding confidential communications to certain professionals, like psychotherapists, is such a rule yet you would probably agree on the necessity for such a rule. This rule of evidence is of great importance to social workers. Other rules excluding certain evidence are less significant and will not be discussed here. The rule excluding confidential communications will be discussed in Chapter 19.

In addition to operating to exclude certain evidence from a hearing, the rules of evidence establish the form of the questions that may be used to elicit testimony. Questions may not be compound and may not call for a narrative. Most important, questions by the party that called someone as a witness generally may not be leading. A **leading question**, such as, "You left your child alone all day, didn't you?" suggests its answer.

The rules of evidence also establish the order in which parties to a case present evidence, that is, the **burden of going forward**, how much evidence a party must present to win on an issue, that is, the **burden of persua-**

sion, and, most important, how much and how convincing a party's evidence must be to prove a fact or win a case, that is, the **burden of proof**.

If a party with the burden of proof in the case as a whole produces enough evidence to meet the burden, without regard to how convincing the evidence is, the party is said to have established a *"**prima facie** case."* If the party with the burden of proof fails to establish a *prima facie* case, the case will be dismissed—without necessity for the opposing parties to produce any evidence.

While the party with the burden of proof must establish a *prima facie* case in order not to lose the case, this may not be enough to win. In order to win a case, the party with the burden of proof may still have to meet a certain **standard of proof**. The standard of proof, which is encompassed within the burden of proof, depends on the nature of a case, but there are three basic standards.

The normal standard of proof is a **preponderance of the evidence**. Under this standard, the party with the burden of proof merely has to prove that his or her version of the facts is more likely true than not true. If both sides present evidence, the party with the burden of proof needs a mere majority of the evidence to win.

The highest standard of proof, used primarily in criminal cases, is **beyond a reasonable doubt**. Under this standard, the party with the burden of proof only wins if his or her evidence establishes the necessary facts to a very great degree of certainty (in fact, some courts say to a "moral certainty") and the fact finder has no doubts, based on reason, on the facts.

The intermediate standard is called many things but usually is called "**clear and convincing evidence**." This standard is used in cases where there is a great stake in the outcome, like a loss of an important right, but not as great a stake as in a criminal case.

As we shall see, one of the two higher standards of proof may be constitutionally or otherwise required in certain types of cases.

A **presumption** is a rule of law which, after one fact (or several facts) is established, allows one to presume the existence or nonexistence of another fact (or facts) or allows one to draw an inference that another fact (or facts) is true. Presumptions are either **conclusive**, that is, irrebuttable, or rebuttable. Raising a resumption, even if it is rebuttable, may suffice to satisfy a party's burden of proof.

The rules of evidence differ from jurisdiction to jurisdiction although the basic principles are the same throughout America. Where the rules of evidence are found also differs from jurisdiction to jurisdiction. In some jurisdictions, most of the rules of evidence are found in the common law. In other jurisdictions, most of the rules evidence are found in a single code, that is, a group of statutes on a particular topic. Whether or not the basic rules of evidence are in the common law or a single code, most jurisdictions have rules of evidence contained in statutes on other subjects. For example, a statute on child abuse may specify the evidence that may be admitted in a hearing involving an abused child and the burden of proof in such a hearing. As this example demonstrates, the rules of evidence in a particular jurisdiction may differ depending on the type of case. They may also differ depending on the nature of a hearing or the type of a court.

ADMINISTRATIVE HEARINGS

Courts are not the only government entities that resolve disputes through a trial process. Administrative agencies also resolve disputes through an administrative hearing process which may be very much like a trial process.

There are two types of disputes generally resolved by administrative agencies in administrative hearings: (1) disputes which individuals have with the agency; and (2) disputes which are within areas of the law that the agency administers. An example of the first type of administrative dispute resolution is found in the hearings conducted by the Social Security Administration. People who have been denied Social Security benefits by the Social Security Administration may have the denial reviewed by requesting an administrative hearing run by the Social Security Administration. An example of the second type of administrative dispute resolution can be found in the hearings conducted by the National Labor Relations Board. If a union claims an employer engaged in an unlawful labor practice, the union makes its claim against the employer in an administrative hearing run by the National Labor Relations Board.

Administrative hearings are like court trials in that a dispute is resolved by determining the facts and applying the law to the facts. They are unlike court trials in that they may be quite informal, the judge may not be a lawyer, there may be no lawyers involved, there are no juries (although there might be a panel of judges,) the hearing may not be adversarial, and the rules of evidence may not apply.

More social workers may be involved in administrative hearings in more roles than are involved in court trials. In many administrative hearings, unlike court hearings, a party may be represented by a non-lawyer, such as a social worker. Social workers who work for agencies may also represent their agency's position at administrative hearings. Social workers may even act as judges at administrative hearings.

Some administrative agencies have appellate bodies which hear appeals of hearing decisions. Usually parties to administrative hearings may appeal to a court if they are dissatisfied with a hearing decision or any administrative appellate decision. A party who is appealing a federal administrative agency decision to a court would go to a federal court in accordance with the procedures set forth in either the Federal Administrative Procedures Act or in a federal act which applies to the particular kind of hearing involved. A party who is appealing a State administrative decision to a court would appeal to a State court in accordance with a general State administrative procedures act or a particular State act applying to the particular kind of decision involved. You might better understand where one appeals from an administrative hearing decision if, in diagram 1.1, you visualize various federal administrative tribunals below federal trial courts and various State administrative tribunals below State trial courts.

Someone who is seeking court review of an administrative decision, whether in State or federal court, usually goes to a trial court, but the trial court generally operates more like an appellate court than a trial court. That is, the court generally does not receive evidence and decide facts but rather reviews the administrative record and decides if the law was correctly applied.[6]

Often one may not go to court to resolve a dispute with an administrative agency or a dispute in an area of the law usually resolved by an administrative agency without first going to the administrative agency for a decision. In other words, one must go through the administrative hearing process and any administrative appeal process before one may go to court. This is called "**ex-**

---

6. In a few types of cases, a party who appeals from an administrative decision may get a new evidentiary hearing, usually known as a "trial de novo," in the trial court. In a few types of cases of great importance to many people, such as a utility rate case, a party may appeal an administrative decision directly to an appellate court.

hausting administrative remedies.'' When exhaustion is required, one can go to court if, and only if, one has sought all available administrative remedies. For example, because exhaustion is required in this kind of case, a woman who has been denied Social Security benefits cannot go to court directly to protest the denial but must seek an administrative hearing before the Social Security Administration. If she is denied benefits by the administrative law judge after the hearing, she still cannot go to court. She must appeal to the Social Security Administration's appeals board first. If she is still denied benefits by this board, she can go to court in accordance with the procedures set forth in the Social Security Act. Because Social Security is a federal program and the Social Security Administration is a federal agency, she would appeal to a federal trial court, that is a United States District Court.

The proliferation of administrative agencies and the increased demand on administrative agencies to make and enforce the law have meant that administrative agencies are being called on more and more often to resolve disputes. As this has occurred, the doctrine of exhaustion of administrative remedies has become increasingly important. And because many social workers will work for administrative agencies or will work on cases involving administrative agencies, exhaustion is an important concept for them.

The types of cases in which exhaustion is required, which courts hear appeals from which types of administrative decisions, and whether a person who appeals a certain type of administrative decision gets a trial *de novo* or an appellate type of review may be established by a general administrative procedures statute, by statutes covering particular subjects, or by precedent.

3

The Social Worker in the Hearing Process

ROLES PLAYED BY SOCIAL WORKERS IN THE HEARING PROCESS

As we shall see, social workers play many roles in the hearing process. Social workers probably appear most often as witnesses, offering facts or opinion about a given situation, but social workers may also be petitioners, asking the court to take action in a given case. Social workers may occasionally be defendants. And, in some administrative hearings, they may serve as hearing officers or act as advocates.

Perhaps more important than the roles social workers play in hearings are the roles they play related to hearings. Because of their continuing relationship and involvement with their clients, social workers are in a unique position to assist their clients with legal actions, to interpret legal events to them, and to help them live with the outcome of hearings.

The possible roles of social workers in the hearing process and related to a hearing are reviewed below.

Witness

Social workers provide vital information in many hearings. At times the social worker may be avowedly partisan, testifying for a certain position. But, more often, social workers, even though they might desire a certain outcome, are simply providing objective information learned in the course of their work. The social worker's task is not to persuade the court but to inform the court. To give several examples, a social worker, as asked by the attorneys, might provide information from her investigation of alleged child neglect. In a guardianship proceeding, a social worker might provide information obtained while working with the respondent on his adaptive behavior. In a case involving child custody, a social worker might provide information, obtained during evaluative interviews, on the child's relationship with her parents.

Some of the information provided by the social worker in these examples and in other instances is somewhat subjective. But the element of subjectivity does not negate the primary point—the role of the social worker as a witness is that of information provider.

Social workers as witnesses may be asked to make recommendations or state conclusions about the facts. They may be asked, for example, what is the best placement for a child found to be abused, what services should be provided to a person who is involuntarily committed, or whether a child custody plan is workable. The fact that the social worker is asked to make a recommendation or state a conclusion also does not change the social worker's primary role as a witness. The social worker's task is still to inform, not to convince; any recommendation or conclusion must be firmly grounded in facts known to the social worker to be credible and useful.

Sometimes social workers perform a special role as witnesses. Instead of testifying on facts known of their personal knowledge, like any other witness, they may testify on their opinions, not only on the basis of facts with which they are familiar, but also on the basis of their professional expertise. Occasionally, social workers testify on their opinions in cases in which they have no direct or personal knowledge of the facts. In both these instances, social workers testify as expert witnesses. Courts are increasingly recognizing social workers as expert witnesses.

Unlike other witnesses, expert witnesses may testify on or give opinions about matters outside of their personal knowledge. For example, as an expert witness, a social worker might testify on the effects of a proposed separation from a foster parent on a child with whom he is familiar or might testify on the effects of joint custody on a child he has never met. But whether or not social workers know the specific individuals involved, as expert witnesses social workers still provide information—based on their general knowledge and experience, if not their personal knowledge of the facts.

Petitioner

Social workers who work in child welfare agencies are often in the position of asking a court to take action in a case. They may prepare and file the petition themselves or they may ask a government or agency attorney to do it for them. In either case, the social workers are petitioners and perform a different role than that of witness. Social workers as petitioners want to persuade courts that a specific course of action is needed.

Other social workers may also act as petitioners. For example, medical social workers may petition for guardianship or commitment of a patient when family members are unwilling or unable to do so. Social workers who work in community mental health or other mental health facilities may also petition courts for involuntary commitment of clients.

The social worker who is a petitioner may later be called as a witness in the case. As a witness, the social worker's task is, as has been stated, not to persuade but to inform— despite his or her status as the petitioner.

Respondent

Social workers occasionally are respondents in court cases. This occurs most often when the social worker's performance is called into question, for example, in suits for violation of civil rights, for malpractice, or to release records.

Social workers who work for agencies may be also be named as or act as respondents in court or administrative cases when something their agencies have done is called into question or when someone seeks review of agency actions, like denials of Social Security benefits. They may have had no involvement with the action in question but may nevertheless be held responsible because of their supervisory authority or may be asked to represent their agencies.

Judge

Social workers occasionally act as judges. In a few jurisdictions, some court hearings, like those involving juveniles, may be presided over by nonlawyer judges. In appropriate cases, these nonlawyer judges may be social workers. More commonly, non-lawyers may act as judges in administrative hearings. Again, in appropriate cases, these nonlawyer judges may be social workers. For example, in some jurisdictions, social workers serve as administrative hearing officers, reviewing the validity of continuing mental health commitments. Or medical social workers serve as the presiding officers of hospital ethics committee cases, deciding whether life support can be removed from terminally ill patients.

Social workers sometimes work directly for judges. They may be regularly employed as court officers, assisting judges with certain kinds of cases or problems, like adoptions, child custody cases, criminal sentencings or child support determinations. Alternatively, they may work as part-time or occasional consultants to judges, assisting judges when requested to do so. Usually the social worker's role, whether as court officer or consultant, is to make recommendations to the judge in the form of written reports or oral testimony, but sometimes social workers assist judges by performing other roles. For example, they may act as referees in hearings, may mediate contested cases, or may perform what may be described as traditional social work functions, like divorce conciliation or other counseling of those involved in court cases.

Guardian ad litem

In some cases, courts may appoint social workers as guardians *ad litem*. A social worker would be appointed as a guardian *ad litem* most typically in a case where a party is represented by an attorney or where a party might not be able to communicate with an attorney. As a guardian *ad litem*, the social worker may conduct an investigation of the case or may ask others to do the investigation. It is also common for attorneys who act as guardian *ad litems* to employ social workers to conduct assessments and offer recommendations and for social workers appointed as guardian *ad litems* to have attorneys appointed to represent or assist them.

Advisor and advocate

Clients often have legal problems in addition to the social problems that have brought them to a social worker. At times these legal problems are quite independent of the problems the social worker is addressing. At other times the legal problems might be intertwined with the social problems being addressed by the social worker or might even be the reason for or the result of the social worker's involvement. Whatever the source of the legal problems, social workers are in a position to recognize that the problems are legal, even when the client does not recognize them as such. The social worker can then advise clients of the need to obtain legal services and help them do so. In a few situations, the so-

cial worker may even act as an advocate or legal representative for a client in an administrative setting.

The advisory role may be problematic for many social workers, particularly those working for a government agency. The advocacy role may be even more so. But given the nature of the legal system, these roles are not inconsistent with other roles social workers play. For example, if you are working with a parent who is alleged to be neglectful, it is your responsibility to inform the parent that legal action may be taken and strongly suggest that the parent retain an attorney. Doing so will not harm the children who are involved and may even facilitate a more satisfactory outcome. To give a further example, if you are working with a disabled client who has serious financial problems, you should advise the client of his possible eligibility for Social Security disability benefits. If the client is denied these benefits, you might assist him with an appeal, even going so far as acting as his representative in an administrative hearing. Whether it would be appropriate for you to do so and whether you would be the best representative for the client depends on your position and the circumstances of the case.

Interpreter

Legal proceedings are complicated, confusing and frightening to many people. All too often attorneys and social workers assume that the proceeding is understood by the client when in fact it is not. Social workers, because of their relationship with the client, are in a position to explain the proceeding, what is likely to occur, what the possible outcomes are, and what alternatives might exist. This is not to suggest that the social worker should act as an attorney and provide legal advice; to do so would be improper and a disservice to the client. But it is proper for the social worker to provide information in terms understood by the client without trying to advise the client to pursue a certain course of action.

Consider the case of a woman brought to an emergency room during a psychotic episode. Assume the attending psychiatrists believe continued hospitalization is necessary and initiate commitment proceedings. The woman would probably have been informed of her rights at the time of admission, and later she will be informed of the pending hearing and her rights related to the hearing. But can it be assumed she understands what might happen because she has been told once and given some information to read? Obviously not. A knowledgeable social worker can be invaluable in providing her with information in terms she can understand when she is not overly agitated, confused, or medicated. Moreover, a social worker who has continuing contact with the woman can repeat information and answer questions as they arise. To be told once is often not enough.

The social worker can perform the role of interpreter, not only with the client, but also with the client's friends and family members. Friends and family members may be in a position to help the client, but they are often overlooked in the legal process. If they are not informed, they cannot be involved and cannot help the client. Social workers often know who these significant others are and can provide them with information in behalf of the client—as long as the social workers are mindful of the client's right to confidentiality.

As will be discussed in Chapter 19, it may be unethical, or even illegal, for a social worker to release information about clients to third parties without the client's consent. Before social workers discuss a case with a client's family or friends or anyone else—even

when they are trying to assist the client—they should obtain the client's consent. And if the client does not consent, the social worker may not be free to interpret the case or the client's position to anyone.

Keeping the requirements of confidentiality in mind, social workers can provide a further valuable service to clients involved in legal proceedings by speaking to other parties in a case. Attorneys for one party cannot ethically talk to other parties, except through their attorneys, but social workers, who are not partisan advocates, may speak with other parties and perhaps explain the proceedings to them. This is not to say that social workers should take it upon themselves to persuade other parties to go along with their clients' wishes or should interfere with attorneys' handling of cases, but social workers may help facilitate cases in their role as interpreters.

Counselor

What happens after the hearing is over? The judge calls the next case, the attorneys and social workers return to their offices, and the client is left to live with the outcome. In most cases, the attorneys will have little subsequent contact with the client, but the social workers will often continue to be involved. This continuing contact can enable the social worker to help the client accept the outcome and comply with any orders imposed by the court.

This aspect of litigation is often overlooked, but it is an important aspect for several reasons. First, even though a judge has handed down a decision, a dispute is not truly resolved until it is resolved by the parties. Anyone who has been involved in continuing custody battles knows this only too well. Closure must be reached psychologically as well as legally. Second, in many cases one family member has taken action against another, engendering feelings of guilt. For example, a woman who has obtained an order keeping her husband away from their family because he beat her and a man who, at his request, has been named guardian of his elderly mother might be quite ambivalent about their actions. Such people might need help in dealing with their feelings about the actions. Third, in many cases the court imposes orders with which a party must comply. These orders may require substantial changes in a party's life. This is true in most juvenile court cases. Yet a party may not fully understand an order or the duty to comply. A party may further experience difficulties in complying. The social worker can help the parties comply by explaining the orders and working with the clients on compliance.

In sum, the social worker who continues to be involved with the client after a court case is over can help the client reach closure, sort out reactions to what has occurred, and comply with court orders—in other words, to move on with life.

APPEARING IN COURT

As we have said, social workers appear in court in many roles. Many social workers find appearing in court, particularly to testify, frightening and feel unprepared for the experience. While each case in which you might appear is somewhat different, there are some general principles you can learn and some steps you can follow to prepare for a court appearance. These general principles and steps, which are discussed below, can make the process less frightening and your work more effective. In addition, some of what is said on testifying can also enable

you to assist clients who may be called to testify. Appearing in court can be even more frightening for the client than the social worker, particularly if the client is a child. While it is the attorney's role to prepare witnesses for testifying, often attorneys neglect to prepare witnesses psychologically. This is something a social worker can and should do.

Determining whether to initiate a court action

In many situations, social workers' involvement in cases does not begin when they are first called to appear. The social worker may have been actively involved in deciding whether to initiate the court action and may even have been the person who actually initiated the action by filing a petition.

Initiating a court action can be thought of as one type of intervention. It is, however, an intervention that has profound consequences for your clients and that may have a significant impact on your work with your clients. Therefore, it is an action that should never be undertaken lightly. You must determine whether it is the best intervention before attempting to initiate a court action.

There are no hard and fast rules to determine whether court action is desirable, but you can ask yourself certain questions which will help you make such determinations. First, what do you hope to achieve? Second, can the desired result be achieved in any other way? Third, is the desired result likely to be achieved through court action? Fourth, does there appear to be sufficient evidence for the court to act as you hope? Fifth, how have the attorneys and judges who are likely to be involved responded in similar cases?

To illustrate these points, consider the case of a confused, elderly man found wandering outside in freezing temperatures. What you want to do is protect the man; you believe his health is endangered and he is unable to act to protect himself. Appointment of a guardian might thus be indicated. But, can the man be protected without appointment of a guardian? And will the appointment of a guardian assure that he will be protected? Moreover, under the law in your State, does there seem to be evidence sufficient to support a determination that a guardian should be appointed? And are the attorneys and the judge likely to take the action you want to take?

These last two points—your assessment of the sufficiency of the evidence and your evaluation of the willingness of court officials to act as you would like them to act—need further comment.

On the first point, the suggestion that you assess the sufficiency of the evidence is not a suggestion that you should practice law. Generally, the assessment of the evidence is the responsibility of the attorney who will pursue the case either at your request or the request of someone else. However, before going to the attorney, you should consider how strong your case appears to be. Returning to the example of the elderly man, one or two incidents of being found outside, especially in the absence of other information about the man, would probably not be enough to warrant appointment of a guardian. You risk frightening the man and embarrassing yourself by going to an attorney or a court without more evidence.

On the second point, your assessment of the response of court officials should not determine what you do. It simply prepares you for what you might encounter. Again using the example of the elderly man, the fact that judges in a given area are reluctant to appoint guardians should not prevent you from requesting this action if you believe it is truly necessary.

Admissibility, credibility and persuasiveness of evidence

As we have said, the rules of evidence determine what may and may not be presented as evidence in a hearing, that is, what is **admissible**. Admissibility is primarily the concern of the attorneys for the parties. In preparing cases, the attorneys must determine what will be admissible and how they can make evidence admissible. During any hearings, the attorneys must object to evidence offered by the opposing side if they want to keep it out of evidence.

Evidence may be admissible but it may not be given much weight, or may not even be believed, by the trier of fact. That is, admissible evidence may not be persuasive or credible. In contrast to admissibility, persuasiveness and credibility are primarily the concern of the witness. While you, as a social worker, cannot be expected to know exactly whether evidence you might present is admissible, you can be expected to know what evidence is both persuasive and credible and how you can be a witness that is both persuasive and credible.

What is meant by "credible?" Simply put, credible evidence is believable. Evidence is believable if it is consistent with facts that have already been established in a case, consistent with common experience, and consistent with itself. What makes you a credible witness? You are credible as a witness if you appear to be unbiased, are familiar with the facts in a case, demonstrate expertise in the area involved, have done a good job in a case prior to testifying, and have a professional demeanor.

What is meant by "persuasive?" Persuasive evidence or testimony is the kind of evidence or testimony that influences decisions; it is convincing. While we have said that the social worker as a witness is primarily concerned with providing information, you certainly want your testimony to be given due weight by the trier of fact. You do not want to be an advocate, and, indeed, becoming an advocate for a position may weaken the persuasiveness of your testimony, but there is no point to testifying if your testimony has no influence on the decision made by the trier of fact. If your testimony is credible, it may also be persuasive, but sometimes more than mere credibility is necessary. Just because your testimony is believed, it will not necessarily exert an influence on the trier of fact. What makes you a persuasive witness? The conviction with which you testify plays a large part in persuasiveness as does the manner in which you present yourself. A professional demeanor contributes not only to credibility but also to persuasiveness. And, the less you try to persuade and the more natural and knowledgeable you are on the witness stand, the more persuasive you will be.

The desire to be credible and persuasive should influence your work as you prepare to testify and as you testify. It should also influence your work long before that point. Your notes and files, the records you have maintained, and the reports you wrote for your supervisors, yourself, the court, and the parties—indeed, any of your written work which may be admitted into evidence—should be credible and persuasive.

An emphasis on credibility and persuasiveness, as you work on a case, as you prepare to testify, and as you testify, does not mean that you should have no concern about admissibility. You can better investigate and assess a case if you are somewhat aware of what evidence may be admissible and what evidence inadmissible. Moreover, you want what you have to say and what real evidence you want to present to the court to be admissible. After all, credible and persuasive evidence that is not admissible serves no purpose.

Although the lawyers in a case should be primarily concerned with admissibility, you can take two steps which will increase the probability that your evidence and testimony are admissible. First, in your records, reports and testimony, you can and should attempt to communicate what is known directly to you, not secondhand or hearsay information. Second, you should not present conclusions that you cannot support with facts or with your professional expertise. Evidence presented by social workers is probably most often criticized because it is full of hearsay and conclusions, not facts.

As was stated in the discussion of hearsay in Chapter 2, there are many exceptions to the rule excluding hearsay, but hearsay is generally not admissible. And even if it is admissible, it may not be as persuasive or credible as firsthand information. Thus, you want to avoid hearsay whenever possible.

Conclusions can be thought of as judgments you make. Conclusions may not be admissible because they take the responsibility away from the trier of fact to decide the case and place it with the witness. Conclusions may also be mere opinion. With the exception of certain matters which are rationally based on the perception of a witness and which are generally expressed in the form of an opinion, like the speed of an automobile, only the opinions of expert witnesses are admissible into evidence. However, even if you are qualified as an expert witness in a particular case, and thus allowed to give your opinion on a matter, or even if you are permitted to give an opinion on a certain matter as a lay witness, your testimony will be more credible and persuasive, and more likely to be admissable, if you avoid conclusions and testify as to the facts instead.

To illustrate, in most jurisdictions, lay witnesses can give their opinions as to whether someone they observed was drunk; in all jurisdictions, experts on the effects of alcohol use on human behavior would probably be allowed to testify that someone was intoxicated. Thus, you could probably testify in a case, "In my opinion, Mrs. Smith was drunk." But much more persuasive and credible testimony, and testimony that is even more likely to be admissible, would be: "Mrs. Smith's speech was slurred and she bobbed her head and rolled her eyes when she talked. She was unsteady on her feet and her hair and clothes were disheveled. I smelled alcohol on her breath." To further illustrate, instead of testifying, "Mr. Jones seemed nervous," you would be more credible and persuasive, and your testimony would more likely be admissible, if you testified that: "Mr. Jones' hands shook when he spoke to me and he kept avoiding my eyes. I noticed perspiration on his upper lip. His voice wavered and he kept stuttering."

Documentation

If you wait until you are required to appear in court to prepare for court, you have waited too long. The credibility, persuasiveness, and even admissibility, of any evidence you might present can be dependent on the quality of the documentation of your work. This documentation includes your personal case notes, the files and records you have maintained, and, occasionally, audio and video tapes of interviews.

Social workers often believe that a given case will never involve court action. This, combined with a dislike of record-keeping, can result in little or no documentation or vague documentation. If this occurs, important information, such as the dates of contacts, with whom contacts were made, and what was observed and said during contacts, may not be remembered. You cannot always rely on your memory. When memory fails, without documentation, a good case may be

greatly weakened or even destroyed. Moreover, a lack of documentation increases the probability that evidence will be inconsistent and therefore less credible. And even consistent testimony without documentation may be neither credible nor persuasive. Finally, if you do not remember anything about a case or forget aspects of a case, but kept good, contemporaneous records while working on it, your records may be admissible under one of two exceptions to the hearsay rule known as **"past recollection recorded"** and **"present recollection refreshed."**

What should you record? You should record specific information about the dates, places, times, and substance of client contacts or contacts with other persons related in some way to the case. The information should be written in a style that is factual, objective, specific, clear, to the point, and without jargon.

As you record, it is wise to remember that ultimately all your records might be viewed by judges, attorneys and your clients—despite your expectations of confidentiality. As we shall see in Chapter 19, in many States the confidentiality of social workers' and agency records is not protected, and you may be required to allow your client, your client's attorney, and others involved in a case to read your personal notes as well as your agency's records. But even if the confidentiality of your notes and records is protected, it is good practice to be honest, but to record as if anything you write might eventually be read by your client or by your client's attorney.

It is also good practice to record events as soon as possible. The more contemporaneous your records are, the more credible and persuasive they will be. Moreover, records made long after an event may not be considered reliable and thus may not be admissible under an exception to the hearsay rule.

It should be noted that many jurisdictions permit expert witnesses to base their opinions on files, records and reports of others, even if they are inadmissible into evidence or contain inadmissible portions. This is because experts need not rely only on admissible evidence in forming their opinions. Thus, your files, records and reports may not be admissible, but may be examined by an expert and may form the basis of the expert's testimony. This is another reason to take care in preparing your documentation.

Writing court reports

Before social workers ever appear in court, they are likely to have written one or more court reports related to the case. The content and the form of the reports vary according to their purposes and the jurisdiction in which they will be used.

Types of court reports. Social workers who expect to be called to testify might write a report for personal use simply to prepare for a hearing. For example, a child welfare worker who has investigated a complaint of child neglect and who expects to be called to testify might prepare a summary of his personal contacts with the child, the child's parents, and the collateral informants. In preparation for a hearing based on a child's truancy, a school social worker might prepare a list of dates of the child's absences, the dates and times of her contacts with the child's parents, and what occurred during the contacts.

A social worker usually can take this type of report into the hearing and use it to refresh memory during testimony. Such a report would not typically be given in advance to any attorneys who are involved nor would it be admissible into evidence. However, an attorney or the judge can properly ask to inspect the report if it is used during testimony.

You should therefore not include any information in such a report you do not want others to read.

Social workers, particularly those working in child welfare agencies, also might write reports to inform an attorney about a case. For example, in a case of child abuse, a social worker might write a report for the attorney who will file or present the case for the State. Such a report would not only provide information about the child welfare worker's personal observations of the child and the child's parent, it would also identify other individuals who have knowledge of the case— physicians, teachers, day care center staff and others—and briefly summarize what information the social worker expects them to provide. This report helps an attorney decide whether to file a case and forms a basis of the attorney's efforts to build the case.

Even though these reports are written for a specific attorney, they may be given to other attorneys who are involved. This may occur informally or it may occur through discovery. Such reports may be protected from discovery as the so-called **"work product"** of an attorney, but, as with routine case recording, you should work under the assumption that anything you write may be seen by other people.

Social workers also frequently write reports to inform the court. Reports you write to prepare to testify and reports you write to inform an attorney are, in a sense, informal reports. Their content and form are not determined by any particular rules, but by your own preferences and perhaps by local custom. The content and form of many reports whose primary purpose is to inform the court may, however, be determined either explicitly or implicitly by law. Two examples illustrate this point.

First, in many States, the factors a judge should consider in awarding child custody as part of a divorce action are specified in a statute which, typically, also provides that the judge must consider "all relevant factors." Other statutes may allow the judge to ask a social worker to conduct an investigation of the divorcing parents when custody is disputed and to submit a report of the investigation to the judge. Given that certain factors to be considered in decision-making are specifically mentioned in a statute, both the judge and the attorneys will focus on these factors. The social worker's report, to be most useful, should cover these factors but should also cover "all relevant factors." Ignoring something clearly relevant to the court's decision but unmentioned in a statute limits the persuasiveness of a report.

Second, in many States, a statute provides that before committing a mentally ill adult to a hospital, a judge must consider a report on alternatives to hospitalization. The report, which is often done by a social worker employed in a mental health facility, must contain certain information. The required information might be presented to the court in narrative form, but an approved court form, which the person making the report can simply fill in, might also be available. The courts expect and are used to this court form and its use is strongly preferred although perhaps not required.

Principles to follow in writing court reports. No matter what the type of report you are writing, the style of writing should be the same: factual, objective, specific, to the point, and without jargon. Statements such as "they appear to have a close relationship," "he is depressed," "the house was filthy" and "her school attendance was poor" say little that is useful to anyone.

Any report you write must clearly distinguish between what you know from your first hand observation and what you have learned from other sources. When you obtain information from other sources, your report

should, to the extent possible given the law and professional ethics concerning confidentiality, fully identify the sources.

In writing reports where the content is determined or suggested by law, it is important to clearly include the specified content. If the practice or requirement in a given court is to use a certain form, you should use the form. The rule of thumb is to provide information in the format that those who will use it expect to see.

You should carefully proofread any report you write, and any report you submit should be a "clean" report. Misspelled words, typographical errors, poor punctuation and grammar, and excessive erasures not only detract from readability but leave the impression that the writer is careless at best and not intelligent at worst. In short, a poor presentation can mask good information and detract from a report's credibility and persuasiveness.

Admissibility of reports. Depending on the type of case and on the nature and purpose of a report, it may or may not be admissible into evidence. In general, you should keep in mind that a report, even a report prepared at the request of a court, is an out of court statement which constitutes hearsay if it is being admitted to establish the truth of its contents. As such, it would be inadmissible unless an exception to the hearsay rule applies.

As with records, admissible reports may contain hearsay within them. For example, an admissible report might state: "Mr. Smith told me he saw Mrs. Jones hit Jane." The report might be admitted into evidence with the hearsay portions stricken or the whole report may be rendered inadmissible because of the hearsay within it. You make your reports more credible, more persuasive and more likely to be admitted into evidence if you remove hearsay yourself. Of course, you must indicate if information has been obtained from others and is not of your personal knowledge.

Reports contained in your records that are not prepared for courts or for any court case, such as reports for your supervisor, are also written out of court statements which are hearsay if they are being admitted to establish the truth of matters contained in them. Reports in your records might, however, be admissible, with all inadmissible portions stricken, under the business records or another exception to the hearsay rule.

Depositions and interrogatories

As was noted in Chapter 2, in many cases **discovery**, that is, formal and informal investigation of a case by the lawyers for each side, may occur before any hearings. As part of discovery in a case in which you have been involved, you may be asked to respond to interrogatories or may have your deposition taken.

You should always respond to interrogatories with the assistance of a lawyer. In fact, usually your lawyer will actually write the answers after questioning you and you will only approve and sign them. You should make sure the answers are accurate.

If you are only a witness and not a party to a case, you may not have a lawyer available to assist you in a deposition. You should, however, treat a deposition as any other form of testifying and follow the advice given later in this chapter. Despite the informality of some depositions and the fact that no judge is present, you should take depositions seriously. Many cases are settled based on testimony in depositions and, in some cases, deposition transcripts may be admitted into evidence instead of having the **deponent** testify. Further, deposition transcripts or portions of them may be submitted in support of motions.

The mechanics of testifying

If you understand the mechanics of testifying, testifying may be a little less mysterious to you and thus a little less frightening. These mechanics are discussed below. Some of the key terms related to testifying are also defined below. These terms may differ from jurisdiction to jurisdiction, but these are the usual terms.

You will be notified of the hearing in which you will testify in one of several ways. An attorney might call you and ask you to appear on a certain date or you might receive a written request for you to appear, usually called a "**summons**" or a "**subpoena**." Oral requests and some written requests do not require you to appear. A subpoena usually requires you to appear. If you fail to appear as directed by a subpoena or some other written requests to appear, the court may issue a warrant ordering your arrest or may hold you in contempt of court.

Usually a subpoena or summons will tell you to appear at the time a hearing is scheduled to begin, but often several cases will be scheduled for the same date and time as the case in which you are scheduled to appear. And even if your case goes first and you are scheduled to be the first witness in a case, you may not begin to testify until long after the hearing has started. Thus, if you appear at the time set on a subpoena, you may have to wait a considerable time before you are actually called to testify. You should never assume, however, that you will have to wait and therefore appear late. If you are not available when you are called, you risk delaying the proceedings and irritating the judge, at best, and an arrest warrant or contempt citation, at worst.

After a hearing in which you are scheduled to appear begins, you may be asked to remain outside of the courtroom until you are called to testify so that your testimony will not be influenced by the testimony of others or the arguments of the attorneys.

You will be called to testify either by one of the attorneys or by the court clerk or **bailiff**, an officer of the court. When you are called, you will approach the judge's bench and be sworn in by the clerk, bailiff or sometimes by the judge. Whoever swears you in, you will be asked to raise your right hand and then asked whether you swear or affirm to "tell the truth, the whole truth, and nothing but the truth." You simply respond, "I do." You will then be directed to take a seat on the witness stand.

The attorney who requested your appearance will question you first.[1] This questioning is called "**direct examination**." The attorney will usually begin by asking your name and your address or place of work. Typically he or she will also ask some preliminary questions which elicit information about your professional experience and your educational background.

If you are going to be testifying as an expert witness, the questions about your experience and background will be more extensive and probing. After finishing this questioning, the attorney may move to have you qualified as an expert witness. The opposing attorney may question you further on your qualifications before the judge rules on the motion. The judge may also question you on your qualifications before ruling on the motion. This questioning of a potential expert witness by both sides, and possibly the judge, to determine the witness' competence to testify, like the questioning of potential jurors, is known as "**voir dire**." Lay witnesses, particularly child witnesses, may also be voir dired

to determine their competence to testify. Usually child witnesses are questioned to determine if they understand the witness' duty to tell the truth.

After the preliminary background questions and any voir dire, the attorney who called you as a witness will ask you a series of questions designed to elicit information about the case. If you are qualified as an expert witness, you will be asked to provide an opinion on an aspect of the case. Questions on direct examination are supposed to be non-directive or non-leading. Typically they will be questions like: "What happened next?" "What did you see?" and "What is your opinion on the respondent's mental health?" Questions to an expert may be hypothetical, such as: "If this child had been beaten by his mother, in your opinion should he nevertheless remain with his mother?"

After the direct examination is finished, the attorneys for the opposing parties may question you. This questioning is called **cross examination**. During cross examination, the opposing attorney will typically ask questions intended to discredit your testimony during direct examination. Questions on cross examination may also be intended to discredit you. The latter type of questions may go to your credibility, your biases, your motives to testify falsely or, if you are an expert, your qualifications and competence. On cross examination, you may be asked leading questions, such as: "The room was dark when you went in and saw her there, isn't that correct?" "Isn't it true that you were drinking that day?" "Didn't you only interview her for fifteen minutes?" and "You don't have any black friends, do you?"

Following cross examination, there may be **redirect examination**, that is, follow up questions by the attorney who conducted the direct examination. Redirect examination at-

---

1. Throughout this discussion it will be assumed that an attorney will do all the questioning and objecting. Of course, if parties are not represented by attorneys, they may do the questioning and objecting themselves.

tempts to rehabilitate you and your testimony.

During questioning, the attorneys for either side may **object** to a question or to a response. Inadmissible testimony will be admitted and improper questioning allowed unless someone objects to the testimony or questioning or, an infrequent occurrence, the judge rules something inadmissible or improper on his or her own motion. Sometimes, a party whose evidence has been objected to makes an **offer of proof**. This means further evidence will be presented to demonstrate the admissibility of the objectionable evidence.

Disputes about admissibility are sometimes resolved outside of the presence of the jury, and perhaps also outside the presence of the witness. There may be a whispered conference at the bench, the jury or witnesses may be asked to leave the court, or the attorneys and judge may go to the judge's office, usually known as the judge's **chambers**. Sometimes a judge reviews disputed evidence, particularly evidence claimed to be confidential, or questions a witness *in camera*, that is, in chambers. An *in camera* review of evidence or *in camera* testimony is usually not included in the public record.

Following questions by the attorneys, there may be questioning by any guardian *ad litem*. Some judges like to ask questions of witnesses at this point. Judges may ask witnesses questions at any time, but most judges do not do any questioning of witnesses.

When all questioning is finished, the judge will ask you to step down. You may leave unless the judge instructs you differently. In most cases, you will not be recalled for further testimony. However, you are subject to recall at any time until the hearing is concluded. If you are recalled, it simply means an attorney wants to ask you more questions.

Preparing to testify

There are several steps you can follow in preparing to testify that will make the experience less stressful and that are important to your effectiveness in your role as a witness. Some of these steps may, and should, be taken well in advance of the hearing. Others will be taken right before you take the stand in the courtroom.

Steps to follow before the day of the hearing. If you know your presence at a hearing is necessary or expected and if you have not been served with a subpoena, you should ask the attorney with whom you are working most closely to obtain a subpoena. A subpoena can be important to your continuing work with your client. In many cases, you will be providing information that may, from the client's perspective, be damaging to the client. This is clearly the case in juvenile court actions or in hearings involving probation violations or commitments to mental hospitals. And yet you may have to or want to continue to work with the client after the hearing ends. If you testify in response to a subpoena, you can honestly say that you did not choose to testify; you were forced to testify. It lessens the sense that you willingly took sides against the client. A subpoena may also be necessary to show your employer or to obtain compensation for going to court and testifying.

A subpoena may require you to bring certain documents to the court as well as to appear to testify. Subpoenas which require documents are usually called "**subpoenas *duces tecum***." Sometimes you do not have to appear in response to a subpoena *duces tecum*; your obligation may be satisfied if you merely provide the documents. This may not be clear from the subpoena itself. Thus, you should find out your obligation from the attorney who sent you the subpoena.

If you receive a subpoena for documents or for testimony, unless you are very sure of the law concerning confidentiality, it is wise to consult with an attorney before turning over the documents or testifying. If the confidentiality of the information you are asked to provide is protected by law, certain legal actions can be taken to prevent its release.

You need to take several other steps in preparation for the hearing. First, if you have not written a court report, you should prepare notes for use while testifying. Second, you should read and reread the case record, your personal notes, and any reports you have written. Third, you should consult with the attorney who has requested that you appear regarding the questions he or she is likely to ask and the questions you can expect from the other side during cross examination. A role play of your testimony with the attorney would be most helpful. Fourth, you should visit the courtroom where the hearing will be held if you have not appeared there before. Finally, you should verify the date, time and place of the hearing.

It is particularly important to read and reread your material related to the case. While you may believe you have the information firmly in mind, you may have been involved with many other cases and many people. The particular details of this case may easily escape your recall, especially under the stress of actually testifying. You can be sure that the attorneys have carefully read all your documents. As they listen to your testimony, they will compare what you say with what you submitted earlier. They will note discrepancies, and they may use discrepancies to try to discredit you.

If you are testifying as an expert witness, you should prepare a current résumé to show your qualifications to render an expert opinion. You should review your qualifications with the attorney who is calling you. In addition, you should familiarize yourself with the leading treatises and articles on the subject on which you are testifying. You may be questioned on the consistency of your opinion with those of established experts as found in these sources.

As you prepare to testify, it is well to remember that being a witness is simply another role a social worker plays. Like other roles, it is a demanding role, and it requires specific skills. But if you have prepared well, it is no more difficult to perform this role successfully than it is to perform any other role.

Points to remember on the day of the hearing. As in the case of other points made in this chapter, the points that follow may seem simplistic. But they are important and often forgotten and thus need to be made.

First, dress conservatively. A conservative appearance is part of successful role performance. Judges and juries expect professionals to appear and to act professional. If professionals do not meet these expectations, their credibility and persuasiveness is diminished.

Second, be on time. As has been stated, you probably will not be testifying at the time you have been told to appear. While it is irritating to be kept waiting, especially when faced with other work that needs to be done, and tempting to show up late, you should never be late. Sometimes it may be possible to find out from the attorney who subpoenaed you when he or she realistically expects you to testify and to obtain his or her permission to appear at this time rather than at the time stated on the subpoena. Alternatively, if your office is close to the courthouse, it may be possible to arrange to be on call. But unless you make alternative arrangements, you should appear at the time stated in the subpoena.

Third, before going to court you should

check with the attorney who subpoenaed you to make sure that the hearing is going on as scheduled. Hearings are often postponed, that is "**continued**" or "**adjourned**," and cases are often settled after the witnesses have been subpoenaed. Attorneys may forget to notify the witnesses that their appearance is no longer required. There are few things more annoying than preparing for a court appearance and going to court only to be told your appearance is unnecessary. Indeed, it is best to check with the attorney before you start to prepare intensely, and again as soon before the hearing as possible. Postponements and settlements often come at the last minute.

Fourth, review your notes and reports. You do not want to memorize testimony, and you do not want your testimony to sound rehearsed. But you do want to be as prepared and knowledgeable as possible for questioning.

Fifth, while you are in the courthouse waiting to appear, do not discuss the case with anyone and do not show anyone your reports or notes. Act professionally even while you are waiting. There are always many people in the halls of the courthouse. Anyone you see might be a judge, a member of the jury, another witness, a party to a case, or an attorney in the case in which you are appearing. Improper comments or behavior can diminish your credibility and, under some circumstances, provide grounds for dismissal of the case.

Points to remember while testifying

When testifying you are playing a role and you are following certain rules. The role requires you to be serious and dignified and to speak clearly and distinctly, without using jargon.

You should understand that the attorney who asked you to testify is also playing a role. You should answer only the questions this attorney asks. If you volunteer information instead of answering these questions, you infringe on the attorney's right and responsibility to develop the case by asking you questions.

You should remember that the process is adversarial. You should expect the opposing attorney to challenge you and your testimony, and you should not be defensive or hurt when this occurs. The attacks are not personal; this attorney is also simply performing a role and following certain rules.

If an attorney objects to a question another attorney has asked you, do not answer the question immediately. Instead, wait for the judge to rule on the objection. If the objection is **sustained**, you need not answer the question. You only must answer if the objection is **overruled.** If there has been a long argument about the objection, by the time the court has overruled the objection, you may be unsure of the question. You should ask the attorney to repeat the question before you attempt to answer it.

Sometimes you may be troubled by a question, particularly a question on cross examination, to which there is no immediate objection. If you pause before answering or somehow indicate you have a problem with the question, an attorney may object to it. If there is no objection, but you would find it difficult to answer the question, it is better to explain your difficulty than attempt to answer.

A question with several parts is objectionable, but if there is no objection to such a question, you should separate out the parts carefully and answer each part separately.

You are not expected to know and understand everything. If you do not understand a question, say you do not understand it and ask for clarification before you answer. If you do not know the answer to a question, say you do not know. Attempts to guess the meaning of a question or to guess an answer will only cause trouble for you.

If you realize after one question that you have answered a previous question incorrectly, you should correct your error as soon as possible.

Always think before you respond. There is no advantage to rushing out an answer.

Be aware of double negatives, particularly when responding to leading questions on cross examination. If you are asked: "Isn't it true that you didn't see her?" think whether a response of "yes" means you did or did not see her.

Your testimony will be more effective and credible if you answer with facts as much as possible—even if you are testifying as an expert witness. Do not state conclusions. Do not use jargon or buzz words. Use simple English. Say: "Mrs. Brown spoke in a low monotone, gave one word or very brief answers and kept her head lowered when I spoke to her," instead of saying: "Mrs. Brown's affect was depressive when I conducted my examination." Be as exact as possible. Say: "I spoke to her five times," not "several times." Do not offer an opinion unless you are asked to do so.

If appropriate, admit your sympathies and beliefs honestly on direct examination. This will look better than if they are brought out on cross examination. Remember, the goal of the attorney who crossexamines you is to discredit you and your testimony.

Attorneys use a variety of tactics to discredit witnesses and their testimony during cross examination. They use leading questions which require a yes or no answer when no such simple answer is possible or when it would be misleading. They may be condescending, attacking, or overly friendly. They may ask repetitious questions in an at-

tempt to make you answer inconsistently or they may badger you. They may reverse your words. And they may question you about your personal beliefs and your personal life to show possible bias or prejudice or motive to lie. For example, in a child custody case involving a gay father, you may be asked your sexual preference, if you believe in the Bible, or if you know anyone who died of AIDS.

The important point to remember when faced with such tactics is that this is part of the system and not something that is happening to just you. Your best defense is to remain alert and calm. Resist being lulled into a false sense of security when an attorney seems overly friendly and resist becoming defensive or hostile when an attorney seems to be attacking you. Ask the court for permission to explain if a yes or no answer seems incomplete or misleading. Remember that the attorney who asked you to testify should object to inappropriate questioning—if you give him or her an opportunity to do so. But in the absence of a sustained objection to a question, answer as well as you can. Also remember that the attorney who called you to testify can rehabilitate your testimony and give you a chance to explain on redirect examination. This will probably make you feel better and be more relaxed. It should also make you avoid attempts to explain instead of responding to questions during cross examination. Such attempts generally make witnesses look as if they are squirming.

This discussion of cross examination should not make you reluctant to ever be a witness. Rigorous cross examination is rare and cross examination that attacks the witness personally is even rarer. The discussion is included, not because you are likely to encounter such tactics on cross examination, but because you should be prepared if you ever do encounter them.

Learning from experience

Your performance in court can, like all aspects of your professional performance, be improved. You should not just sit back after a hearing is over and heave a sigh of relief—at least if you want to improve your performance the next time you go to court. Instead, you should ask the attorneys who were involved and the judge to critique your petition, your court report, or your testimony. Many attorneys and judges, while not willing to debate the outcome of the case, are quite willing to offer suggestions about how you presented information. In addition, they may be willing to clarify legal points that were made that you might not have understood.

You may also find it useful to read a transcript of your testimony or to listen to a tape recording of it if either is available. In doing so, you will be able to identify patterns of speech and manners of responding to questions of which you were unaware and which you might want to correct.

Confidentiality

Much that has been said in this chapter involves releasing information about clients. Social workers must be sensitive to the consequences to clients of disclosing information about them and must be aware of legal and professional requirements to maintain confidentiality. In working with the courts, social workers must consider how they can fulfill the competing demands to disclose information and to keep information confidential.

Confidentiality will be considered more fully in Chapter 19, but, several points must be made here in relation to appearing in court. First, you must be knowledgeable about the law regarding confidentiality. Second, you should record only information that is essential and factual. Third, you should disclose only information that you are required to disclose. Fourth, you should inform the client that you are recording information and that you may be required to disclose some of it. Fifth, you should consult with your supervisor and, in some cases, with an attorney before you disclose any information.

Locating and Using the Law

Assume you are a social worker in Colorado who has been asked by a judge to conduct a background investigation and write a report in a divorce case where child custody has been contested. You do not want to reveal to the judge that you do not know what is expected of you, but you certainly do not want to risk professional embarrassment by doing something wrong or by failing to do what the judge wants. How can you find out what to do? In other words, how can you determine the law on the subject? This question is answered in this chapter.

This chapter identifies and describes the primary legal references—compilations of statutes, regulations and court opinions—and tells you how to find the law in these references and how to decipher citations to these compilations. It identifies major secondary legal references. It offers suggestions for reading and understanding legal writing. Finally, it presents a procedure to follow when you want to search for answers to legal questions and illustrates the procedure using the above case as an example.

STATUTES

Sources of statutes

In the federal system and in most States, statutes are published in three forms: session laws, codified statutes, and annotated codified statutes. **Session laws** are books of statutes printed exactly as they were enacted and in the order in which they were enacted. **Codified statutes** are books of statutes grouped according to subject matter. **Annotated codified statutes** are codified statutes supplemented with references to court opinions and other legal literature.

Session laws. Rarely do legislatures pass statutes that are single, simple statements of law. Rather, at one time, they pass a group of statutes which constitute a whole legislative scheme. These groups of statutes are often called "**acts**" or "**codes**."[1] All the statutes making up an act will be found in one bill, but each will be individually numbered as separate sections of the bill. Each section may have further subdivisions which will be separately numbered. There may also be groupings of proposed statutes within a bill. These groupings may be designated as "**titles**," "**articles**," or "**chapters**" and numbered individually.

When a bill is introduced in the legislature, it is assigned a number reflecting the chamber in which it has been introduced and when it was introduced. After a bill is passed, it may be assigned another number reflecting when it was passed.[2] Any section, title, chapter, or article numbers used by the legislature in the bill are retained in the new number. For example, after it was enacted, the federal Education for All Handicapped Children Act was assigned the number "P.L. 94-142," meaning it was the 142d public law passed by the 94th Congress, while a Michigan law, requiring the police to report all domestic assaults, after it was enacted was assigned the number "P.A. 1978, No. 319, # 1," meaning it was the first of a group of statutes which were part of the 319th public act passed by the Michigan legislature in 1978.

After being enacted, acts will be placed in the session laws, that is, books containing enacted acts compiled in chronological order. The books of session laws in many States are called "Laws of (Name of State)." The session laws of the federal government are pub-

---

1. This book will use the term "**act**" to refer both to an individual statute and to a group of statutes passed at one time. A "**code**" is always a group of statutes, but it is not necessarily all enacted at one time.

2. Not all jurisdictions go through this process.

lished in the "**United States Statutes at Large,**" abbreviated "Stat."

After being published in books of session laws, acts may be referred to by a number different from their bill number or any public law number. The new number reflects the act's location in the books of sessions laws. For example, the Education for all Handicapped Children Act, P.L. 94-142, is the 773d law in volume 89 of the federal session laws and is referred to as "89 Stat. 773." Again, any section, title, article, chapter or other numbers used by the legislature in its bill will be retained.

All proposed changes to existing acts are also initially introduced as bills. As with other bills, these bills are assigned numbers reflecting the order in which they were introduced. If passed, as with other passed bills, they may be assigned public act numbers reflecting the order in which they were passed. The enacted changes are then compiled in the sessions laws, as are other acts, chronologically rather than with the acts they are changing. Thus, when a Massachusetts act, which forbade discrimination against people using seeing eye dogs, was initially enacted in 1938 it was the 155th act placed in the sessions laws for 1938 and was referred to as "1938 Mass. Acts 155, § 5." When the law was amended in 1978 to include hearing dogs, the amendment was placed as the 458th law in the session laws for 1978, not 1938, and is referred to as "1978 Mass. Acts 458, § 2."

Codified statutes. As you might guess, it would be very difficult to find the current law on a given subject if you could only locate statutes in the session laws. All the statutes on the subject would be scattered depending on when they were passed. Even if you located a statute in the sessions laws, you would not know if changes had been made to it by the legislature at a later date or, indeed,

if it had been repealed. All of the changes to statutes, including their repeals, would also be scattered.

Because of this difficulty with chronological compilations of statutes, most jurisdictions publish their statutes in books organized into subject matter groupings. Each act is placed in an appropriate subject matter grouping as it reads at the time of publication, that is, with additions and deletions. The process of organizing statutes into subject matter groupings is called "**codifying**" and the books are called "**codified statutes**."

In practice you will usually use the codified statutes rather than the session laws. To understand why, think about the request that you conduct a background investigation in a child custody case and your desire to know the relevant law before you begin. You do not need to know that the principal statute in Colorado on such background investigations was passed in 1971 and what the content of this law was. What you need to know is the law as it is now—that is, the 1971 law as it has been amended in 1979 and 1983. You can find the 1971 statute on the conduct of such investigations, and 1979 and 1983 amendments to it, in one place in the codified statutes. The most recent Colorado codified statutes would contain the latest version of the law in the section reserved for law on such background investigations. Moreover, many related laws which could be useful to you would be compiled close by.

When statutes are codified, they are referred to by still another number which reflects their location in their subject matter grouping. The section numbers used by the legislature may not be retained. Section 1 of a bill or an act may be section 23 or even section 2048 of the codified statutes.

The codified United States statutes are published in the "**United States Code,**" abbreviated "U.S.C.". The Code is divided into **titles** which represent groupings of statutes on certain subjects and which are arranged in alphabetical subject order and then numbered to reflect this order. That is, one title is "agriculture;" all statutes dealing with agriculture are placed in this title which is Title 7. This title comes before the title on "education," Title 20, which comes before the title on "public health and welfare," Title 42. A title is not the equivalent of a volume; one title may be in more than one bound volume and several titles may be in one bound volume.

What statutes fall into what titles in the United States Code may not be readily apparent. It may be easy to guess that the Education for All Handicapped Children Act is in Title 20, the title on education, but would you guess that the Civil Rights Act of 1964 and the National Environmental Protection Act are both found in Title 42, the title on public health and welfare? And, knowing that Title 42 is the title on public health and welfare, you might guess that it includes the Social Security Act, but would you guess that the Food Stamps Act is not in Title 42 but in Title 7, the title on agriculture? Fortunately, the Code has a complete topic index. By using the index, you can find the location of specific statutes.

Most State statutes are also codified. The names of the books of codified statutes differ from State to State. Some States call their codified statutes "Revised Statutes of (Name of State)" or simply "Codes of (Name of State)" or "Statutes of (Name of State)." Some States have no official codification, but a private publisher has codified the statutes and the books are referred to by the publisher's name. Thus, in New York, there are codified statutes referred to as "McKinney's."

Subject matter groupings may be called "chapters" rather than "titles." Some States do not number the subject matter groupings, but refer to them by name, such as the Texas Family Code or the California Penal Code.

Some States number subject matter groupings and identify individual statutes within each numbered grouping by using the number followed by a hyphen, colon, or period and the number within the grouping. (E.g., 14-121, 17:05, 17.30)

Like the federal codified statutes, State codified statutes are fully indexed.

Hardbound volumes of federal and State codified statutes cannot be republished each time there is a revision in the law. The revisions are published in supplements to the bound volumes. Often these supplements are inserted in a pocket in the back of a bound volume and are called "**pocket parts**." You should always check the supplements or the pocket parts of codified statutes to assure that you are referring to or relying on current law. Similarly, you should make sure that you are using the most recently published complete set of the statutes. While most libraries will have current materials, it is not unusual to find sets that are several years out of date in an agency's bookshelves.

Annotated codified statutes. As discussed in Chapter 1, the law on a given subject may encompass, not only applicable statutes, but also the statutes as they have been interpreted by the courts and, in some instances, as they have been expanded through regulations. In order to fully understand the law, you must know these decisions and regulations.

References to court decisions interpreting statutes are published with the statutes in **annotated codified statutes**. Annotated codified statutes set forth all the statutes of a given jurisdiction, in the same order as that used by official codifications. Following each statute, they also set forth brief excerpts from or synopses of all authoritative court decisions interpreting the statute. In addition, the annotations may include references to journal articles and other literature on a statute and to regulations interpreting a statute. They may also provide a legislative history.

The two annotated versions of the United States Code are the "**United States Code Annotated,**" abbreviated "U.S.C.A.," and the "**United States Code Service,**" abbreviated "U.S.C.S." They are published by two different private publishing houses. Various private publishing companies publish State annotated codified statutes. Because they are published by commercial publishing houses for private purposes, annotated books of statutes are unofficial. This means that the books are not "the law" but merely republications of the law along with editorial comments and edited bits and pieces of the law.

Like the codified statutes, annotated statutes are fully indexed. Also like the codified statutes, hardbound volumes are not republished each time there is a change in the statutes or a new court opinion interpreting a statute. Instead, as with codified statutes, publishers print pocket parts and supplements. You must check the supplements and pocket parts to assure that you are relying on current law.

Understanding session laws, codified statutes and annotated codified statutes

Appendix 4-1 should help you understand sessions laws, codified statutes and annotated statutes. It is a copy of some pages in the annotated statutes for Colorado as of 1987 related to background investigations in child custody disputes.

Section 14-10-127 of the Colorado Revised Statutes is the Colorado statute dealing with such investigations. It is one section of the Colorado act dealing with divorce, known in Colorado as "dissolution of marriage." This act is called the "Uniform Dissolution of Marriage Act" because it is derived from a model act drafted by legal scholars and proposed for

uniform adoption by the States. It is found in the portion of the codified statutes dealing with "domestic matters." The statutes in this portion of the statutes are all numbered "14-_____," because this is the fourteenth subject matter grouping of the Colorado codified statutes. You can see much of this from Appendix 4-1.

Section 14-10-127 was enacted in its present form in 1971. It can be found in the sessions laws of Colorado for 1971 at p. 530. You can see this from the abbreviations after the word "Source" below the statute on the first page of Appendix 4-1. Section 14-10-127 is similar to a previous law which was codified in the Colorado Revised Statutes for 1963 at section 46-1-27. You can see this from the same place and from the "Annotator's note" further down the page.

In the Colorado annotated statutes, as with most other annotated statutes, any legislative history or comments on a statute are set forth after the statute followed by excerpts from or summaries of cases which have interpreted the statute. You can find such excerpts or summaries for section 14-10-27 at the bottom of the first page of Appendix 4-1 and continuing on the second page.

Appendix 4-1 was copied from pages 394 and 395 of the bound volume of the Colorado annotated statutes containing statutes on domestic matters available in 1987. However, these two pages do not show the 1987 version of section 14-10-127 or the cases interpreting it through 1987. These are found on pages 274 through 276 of the 1987 pocket part to the bound volume. When you look at pages 274 and 275 of the pocket part, duplicated in Appendix 4-2, you can see that section 14-10-127 was amended three times after the publication of the bound volume: in 1976 (the amendment can be found at page 529 of the sessions laws for the 1976 legislative session); in 1979 (page

646 of the 1979 sessions laws); and in 1983 (page 649 of the 1983 sessions laws).[3]

Citations to statutes

Statutes, like all other laws, have **citations**. A citation is the formula for a reference to a law. It is like an address. It tells you in what set of books and where in the set you can find a law. Like an address, citations follow a certain format and use certain abbreviations. For example, a statute, which was first enacted as part of the United States Civil Rights Act of 1871, allows individuals to sue for certain violations of their civil rights. This statute is codified at Title 42 of the United States Code at section 1983. The citation to this statute is: "42 U.S.C. section 1983." Whenever one is referring to this statute in legal writing it should be cited as: "42 U.S.C. section 1983" or "42 U.S.C. § 1983."[4] When the statute was first enacted, it would have been assigned a public law number and would have been compiled in the sessions laws of the 1871 Congress. Sometimes you will see the public law number and a reference to the sessions law in a citation to the statute, most often when the statute's legislative history is being discussed, but in most legal writing, you will only see a citation to the codified statute, that is, 42 U.S.C. § 1983.

Like citations to federal statutes, citations to State statutes follow a certain format and use certain abbreviations. The specific format varies from State to State. For example, the citation to the Colorado statute on background investigations in child custody cases is: "section 14-10-127, C.R.S.;" a similar statute on background investigations in Illinois is cited: "Ill. Rev. Stat. ch. 40, par. 605;" the Wisconsin statute dealing with reports of professionals in child custody matters is cited as: "Wis. Stat. § 767.24;" and an Oklahoma statute on the consideration of a child's preference in custody matters is cited: "Okla. Stat., tit. 12, § 1277.1."

Sometimes the term *"et seq."* is used in a citation to a statute. "Et seq.," meaning "and following," is used to cite a long act with many sections. For example, the Education for the Handicapped Act could be cited: "20 U.S.C. section 1401 *et seq.,*" meaning the act begins at section 1401 and continues in further sections.

Guides to citation form to statutes, as well as other legal material, can be found in *A Uniform System of Citation* published by Harvard Law Review Association. Moreover, many books of statutes have an introductory page giving citation form to the statutes.

REGULATIONS

Federal regulations and regulations in many States are published at least twice during the process of promulgation. They are published first as they are proposed and later as they are adopted.

Both proposed and final federal regulations are published in the "**Federal Register**," abbreviated "Fed. Reg.," in roughly chronological order. The Federal Register is published daily and also contains other matters, such as reports of actions of the executive branch. A citation to a regulation in the Federal Register follows a common format for legal citations. That is, the number of the volume in which the regulation appears is stated first, then "Fed. Reg." and the page in the volume where the regulation begins. The date of publication should be set forth in parentheses at the end of

---

3. Section 14-10-127 was also extensively amended in 1988, L.88, p.639, § 1. Thus, the law shown in Appendices 4-1 and 4-2 is not current, but is used for illustrative purposes only.

4. The symbol "§" means "section."

the citation. For example, a citation to some proposed regulations on substance abuse confidentiality is: "48 Fed. Reg. 38767 (August 25, 1987)."

Federal regulations and regulations in some States are codified after they are adopted. Codified regulations are similar to the codified statutes. That is, the regulations are organized into subject matter groupings, not published chronologically.

Codified federal regulations are published in the "**Code of Federal Regulations**," abbreviated "C.F.R." C.F.R. subject matter groupings, known as "titles," roughly correspond to the titles of the United States Code. A citation to C.F.R. follows the format of a citation to the United States Code. That is, a regulation found at section 200 of Title 38 of the Code of Federal Regulations would be cited as: "38 C.F.R. § 200." The Code of Federal Regulations is republished annually, but, because regulations may change frequently, it is necessary to refer to an index of updates known as "**C.F.R. Sections Affected**." This index refers you to the Federal Register. A citation to the Federal Register must be used until a regulation has appeared in the Code of Federal Regulations.

The Code of Federal Regulations and the codified regulations in the States which have them are fully indexed.

COURT OPINIONS

Court opinions are published in books called "**reporters**." **Official** reporters are published by the courts themselves or by commercial publishing houses under contract to the government. **Unofficial** reporters are published by commercial publishing houses solely for private purposes. The text of an opinion should be the same whether published in an official or an unofficial reporter.

Just as citations identify the location of statutes in books of statutes, citations identify the location of court opinions in reporters. All citations to opinions in reporters, whether federal or State, official or unofficial, follow the same format. The order of the citation is: case name; a comma; the volume number of the reporter in which the case is found; the reporter's abbreviation; the page on which the case begins; and, in parenthesis, the year the case was decided. If the court which decided the case cannot be determined from the name of the reporter, the abbreviated name of the court must be included in the parentheses with the date. If a reference is made to a particular page in an opinion, this page should be noted following a comma and the page at which the opinion begins.[5]

Federal district court opinions are published in two different sets of official reporters, the "**Federal Supplement**," abbreviated "F.Supp." and the "**Federal Rules Decisions**," abbreviated "F.R.D." A federal trial court opinion for a case called "*Jones v. Smith*" could have a citation: "*Jones v. Smith*, 425 F.Supp. 916 (S.D.N.Y. 1978)" or "*Jones v. Smith*, 83 F.R.D. 264 (Wyo. 1980)." The first citation tells you the case is in volume 425 of the Federal Supplement beginning at page 916. It also tells you which district court decided the case (the district court for the Southern District of New York, that is, New York City) and when (1978). The second citation tells you the case is in volume 83 of the Federal Rules Decisions at page 264 and that the case was decided in 1980 by the district court for Wyoming. One must always identify which federal district court issued the opinion in a ci-

---

5. Because of this book's method of quoting from or excerpting opinions (see the discussion of this method in the Introduction), no page numbers for quotations or excerpts will be given in case citations in this book.

tation to F.R.D. or F.Supp. because this cannot be determined from the mere citation to these reporters.

Federal Court of Appeals opinions are published in an official reporter called the "**Federal Reporter**." The Federal Reporter has a first and second series, abbreviated "F." and "F.2d." Later decisions are in the second series. A federal Court of Appeals opinion called "*Jones v. Smith*" could have a citation like: "*Jones v. Smith*, 527 F.2d 92 (2d Cir. 1981)." This citation tells you the opinion can be found in Volume 527 of the Federal Reporter, 2d Series at page 92 and that the case was decided by a panel from the 2d Circuit in 1981. The circuit in Federal Reporter citations must always be identified because the circuit cannot be determined from the mere citation to the Federal Reporter.

United States Supreme Court opinions are found in an official reporter, the "**United States Reports**," abbreviated "U.S.," and two unofficial reporters, "**United States Supreme Court Reports, Lawyer's Edition**," abbreviated "L.Ed." and "L.Ed.2d," and "**Supreme Court Reporter**," abbreviated "S.Ct." Supreme Court opinions are also published weekly in a loose-leaf service called "**United States Law Week**, abbreviated "U.S.L.W." Law Week also contains important recent court decisions by lower courts and recently enacted statutes of importance.

The preferred citation to a Supreme Court decision is to the official reporter. A decision may additionally be cited to one or both of the unofficial reporters. The citation to the official reporter should always be first. Because the official reporter comes out more slowly than the unofficial reporters and because the unofficial reporters come out more slowly than Law Week, it is often necessary to put the official reporter first with blanks for the volume and page number, and then to give the citation to the unofficial reporter or Law Week. Since only decisions of the Supreme Court are pub-

lished in the United States Reports (U.S.), the Lawyer's Edition (L.Ed.), or the Supreme Court Reporter (S.Ct.), there is no need to identify the court. However, the name of the court should be included in a citation to Law Week since decisions of several courts are included in this publication.

A citation to a Supreme Court case may look like this: "*Jones v. Smith*, 325 U.S. 892, 71 S.Ct. 12, 31 L.Ed.2d 643 (1965)." If the decision is recent, the citation may look like this: "*Jones v. Smith*, _____ U.S., _____ 105 S.Ct. 983 (1985)" or like this: "*Jones v. Smith*, 54 U.S.L.W. 3526 (U.S. December 14, 1985)."

State court opinions are generally printed in official reporters. These reporters have different names in different States. There may be one reporter for supreme court cases and another for intermediate appellate court cases. The official reporter for State supreme court cases is typically abbreviated solely by an abbreviation of the State's name (e.g., "Cal.") while intermediate appellate court reporters are typically abbreviated by using the same abbreviation for the State followed by "App." (e.g. "Cal.App."). There may also be one or two unofficial reporters for a State's court opinions.

Most State appellate court opinions are also compiled into an unofficial "**National Reporter System**" published by West Publishing Company. The country has been divided arbitrarily into regions by West; selected published cases of all the States within each region are published in the reporter for that region. In addition, some New York and California cases are separately reported. The regions tend to make more sense historically or impressionistically than geographically. That is, the North Eastern Reporter (N.E.) contains cases from, among others, New York, Massachusetts, Illinois, and Ohio while cases from Pennsylvania, New Jersey, Maine and a number of other States are in the in the Atlantic Reporter (A.). Texas and Tennessee cases are included in the South Western Reporter (S.W.) while Kansas and Oklahoma cases are in the Pacific Reporter (P.).

Some States have no official reporters but designate the West regional reporter as their official reporter.

Citations to State court opinions should be to the official reporter, if any, first and may additionally be to any unofficial reporters. When citing to a case from a State other than where you are located or when citing in something which will be distributed beyond a single State, you should always include the citation to the West regional reporter. This is because most law libraries only contain West regional reporters for out-of-State cases. If the West regional reporter is the official reporter for an opinion, and thus the only reporter to which you cite, you must always identify the court and State in the citation. If you do not indicate the court, the opinion is assumed to come from the State supreme court. Thus, the citation to the case found in Appendix 4-4 is: ''*Pacheco v. Pacheco*, 38 Colo. App. 181, 554 P.2d 97, (1976).'' Since Colorado no longer publishes its own official reporter but designates West's Pacific Reporter as its official reporter, the citation to a case we will discuss in the next chapter is: ''*People v. Beruman*, 638 P.2d 789 (Colo. 1982.)'' *Beruman* was decided by the Colorado Supreme Court.

In a subsequent citation to a case in a document, the term ''**supra**,'' meaning ''above,'' may be used instead of the full citation.

The name of a case found on court documents and at the beginning of a published opinion may be different from the name used in a citation to it. The name used in legal citations is an abbreviated version of the full official name. Use of the full, unabbreviated name in a citation is improper. The name used in a citation is always underlined or put in italics. It is usually two names separated by a ''v.'' standing for ''versus.'' The first name is usually the name of one of the plaintiffs or appel-

lants while the second is the name of one of the defendants or appellees. Usually only one party on each side is included in the name in a citation. If the party is a person, generally only his or her last name will be used. Sometimes pseudonyms or first names will be used to protect confidentiality, particularly of juveniles. An abbreviated name may be used if the party is not a person. Sometimes the name of a case has a slightly different form. You may see a case called ''*In re Smith*,'' ''*Matter of Smith*,'' or ''*State ex rel. Jones v. Smith*.'' There are technical reasons for such names which do not reflect the importance of the case, and may not even reflect the nature of the case.

PARTS OF A PUBLISHED COURT OPINION

When you read a court opinion in a reporter, you will see many things in addition to the text of the opinion. The complete version of an opinion, *Pacheco v. Pacheco, supra*, 38 Colo. App. 181, copied from West's Pacific Reporter, is presented in Appendix 4-4. You should refer to this opinion, which interprets section 14-10-127, C.R.S., as the parts of an opinion are discussed below.

First you will see the full official case name with all the parties and their capacity in the case. As explained above, this full name is not used in citations to or references to the case. The name used in citations is usually found not at the beginning of a case in a reporter but on the top of alternating pages of the opinion in a reporter or in bold face and/or capitalized letters in the name at the beginning of a case.

Below the name, you will see numbers that are the court docket numbers. These numbers, like bill numbers or public act numbers, are chronological numbers used by the courts where the cases have been heard. They are of no importance except if you want to communicate with the court that decided a case to obtain the file.

Next you should see the official name of the court issuing the opinion.

Next you should see some dates. Only the date of the decision is important and generally only the year.

After the dates, you will see a summary of the case. This summary, often called a "**syllabus**," is most helpful, but it is not an official statement of law, even in an official reporter. It may be written by a court official and approved by the court, but even then it is only a summary. It cannot be referred to as the law.

Next, in unofficial reporters printed by West Publishing Company (some West reporters, most notably F.R.D., F.Supp., F., F.2d, and some regional reporters, are official reporters by designation), you will see excerpts from the case headed by a sequential number, a topic, a symbol representing a key, and another number, the key number. These excerpts, known as "**headnotes**" or "**keynotes**," are inserted in the annotated statutes if they relate to a statute. You can see several excerpts from *Pacheco* in the annotations to section 14-10-127, C.R.S., in the pocket part pages reproduced in Appendix 4-1. These excerpts are also entered in books called "**digests**" in alphabetical topical order using the key numbers. As we shall see, digests can be used to find cases discussing a given topic. You might find similar headnotes in reporters printed by other private publishing companies which are used in their books of annotated statutes or digests.

Like the case summary or syllabus, headnotes are not statements of law. They are merely research tools. By skimming the topics and excerpts, you may determine if a case addresses a topic of interest, and you can locate a topic of interest in a lengthy case by finding an excerpt on the topic and looking for the number of the excerpt in brackets in the body of the opinion. You can also find other cases on subjects of interest to you in a case by noting the topic and key number used for the subject and looking in the appropriate digest under the topic and number. Thus, if you want to find cases in addition to *Pacheco* dealing with the exclusion of testimony about disciplining a child (headnote 9), you could look in a West digest under "parent and child," keynote 2(21). Appendix 4-3 shows you this headnote reproduced under the heading "parent and child" at keynote 2(21) in the West digest for the Pacific Reporter. As you can see, there are excerpts from other cases in the Pacific Reporter addressing this topic, including another case from Colorado.

After the headnotes, you find the names of the lawyers for the parties, and for an appellate court with many justices, the names of the justices who heard the particular case, that is, the **panel** members.

The name of the judge who wrote the opinion for the court is then listed and finally one finds that opinion.

Since several appellate justices generally hear and decide each case and since judges may and do disagree, there may be more than one opinion in a case. A **majority opinion** is an opinion written by one justice in which the majority of the justices hearing the case join. A majority opinion decides the case and may make law. Sometimes a majority of the justices do not agree on one opinion. In this situation, there is a **plurality opinion**, the opinion which is joined in by the most justices. The plurality opinion decides the case, but may have little impact on the law. A **dissenting opinion** is an opinion written by a justice who disagrees with the result reached by the majority or plurality. Other justices may join in a dissenting opinion. There may be more than one dissenting opinion in a case if different justices disagree with the majority or plurality for different reasons. A **concurring opinion** is an opinion written by a justice who agrees with the result reached by the majority or plurality but who may not endorse their reasoning or who may want to stress certain points. Other justices may join in a concurring opinion. There may be more than one concurring opinion. Dissenting and concurring opinions neither make law nor have any effect on the result of the case.

To illustrate, the Supreme Court has nine justices. A case could have five justices joining a majority opinion and four joining a dissenting opinion for a total of two opinions. There could also be a case with five justices joining a majority opinion, one writing a concurring opinion, two joining one dissent and one writing her own dissent for a total of four opinions. Or there could be a case with three justices joining a plurality opinion, two concurring with the plurality, one other concurring but for different reasons than the others who concurred and three separate dissenting opinions, for a total of six opinions in one case.

Any concurring opinions would follow the majority or plurality opinion in the reporter and any dissenting opinions would follow any concurring opinions.

Reading a majority or plurality opinion is not easy, but these opinions generally follow a certain pattern and once one understands the pattern, one can read and understand most cases. The essential elements found in most appellate majority or plurality opinions are reviewed below.[6]

---

6. The pattern of opinions and the elements they contain may be more understandable to you if you **brief** each opinion you read. Briefing is the process by which one summarizes or outlines an opinion. (The term ''brief'' may also be used to refer to a written argument presented by an attorney to a court.) Briefing is done differently by different people; there is no single preferred form. You should brief in a way that is comfortable for you. One style of briefing entails setting forth the following information about a case: citation, including name, date, and court; procedural history; facts; issues; holdings; reasoning; decision; and brief summaries of any dissenting or concurring opinions.

Procedural history

The procedural history of a case is a history of the court actions, rulings, and legal maneuvers in the case from the time the case was filed until it reached the court writing the opinion. The procedural history tells you who started the case, where and how it was started, the legal theory of the case or the defense, the relief that was sought, any significant pre-trial motions and the rulings on them, whether there was a trial, whether there was a jury, any significant motions made during the trial and the rulings on them, who won, who appealed, the actions or rulings that are the subject of the appeal, and the decisions of any lower appellate courts that heard the case.

Most procedural history is not important to social workers, but, at a minimum, to really understand a case one should know the nature of the controversy and the relief or remedy sought (e.g., an action for money damages for medical malpractice; a suit challenging a commitment to a mental hospital and seeking an injunction ordering the patient's release).

Facts

As has been noted, appellate courts do not decide facts, but the facts are nevertheless crucial to an appellate court opinion. Appellate courts examine the record and sift through the vast body of facts in the record to determine what facts are significant. The facts that are determined to be significant determine what law will be applied in deciding the case and how it will be applied. The facts that are determined to be significant will also determine the future precedential value of the case.

Issue(s)

An issue is a question of law that the court is deciding. There may be more than one issue in a case. Just as appellate courts sift through the facts to determine which facts are significant, they may sift through all the issues raised by the parties and determine which are worthy of in-depth consideration. Appellate courts may also restate an issue raised by the parties, framing it in broader or narrower terms. The way an issue is stated by a court may be crucial in determining what law to apply, how to apply it, and the future impact of the case.

Holding(s)

As has been stated, a **holding** is a statement of law made by the court which is the basis for the court's decision in a case. It is a statement of the court essential to resolving a case. Put another way, a holding is an answer to the question posed by an issue. It may be as narrow or as broad as an issue. Just as there may be more than one issue, there may be more than one holding. Holdings must be carefully distinguished from *dicta*. As has also been stated, *dicta* are statements made by a court which are not essential to resolving the case or any issues in it.

Decision

The decision is what the court actually does in the case before it. The holding resolves the substantive legal questions while the decision resolves the procedural questions. The decision of an appellate court affirms or reverses a lower court decision.

It should be noted that the word ''decision'' is often used in legal writing to mean ''opinion.'' At times it is said that ''the court decided'' when what is meant is that ''the court held.'' Strictly, however, ''decision'' should be used only to refer to the procedural action taken or directed by the court in the case and ''holding'' to the substantive resolution of issues.

Reasoning

The reasoning is the process by which the court resolves the issues and reaches its holdings and decisions. Understanding a court's reasoning is essential to understanding its opinion.

SECONDARY LEGAL SOURCES

The publications that have been discussed to this point are what are termed ''primary sources,'' that is, they are the sources which present the law as it is written. There are also a number of secondary sources of use to social workers as aids in understanding the law and in locating primary sources. These secondary sources do not present the law. Rather, some present what the authors say about the law. Examples are legal encyclopedias, practice manuals, and articles in law reviews. Such secondary sources may be most helpful but remember, reading about the law is seldom a satisfactory substitute for reading the law itself. Others, termed ''finding aids,'' neither present the law nor what the authors have to say about it but help you to locate it.

Legal encyclopedias

The two legal encyclopedias that are comprehensive and national in scope are *American Jurisprudence* (abbreviated "Am.Jur.") and *Corpus Juris* (abbreviated "C.J."). Both of these publications now have more than one series, so you might see citations such as Am. Jur. 2d and C.J.S. (*Corpus Juris Secundum*). Both encyclopedias provide an overview of the law on given topics, are organized alphabetically by topic, and are fully indexed. They are a useful resource when you are beginning a research project on an unfamiliar subject.

Legal encyclopedias are also published for some States. They tend to be organized as the national encyclopedias.

Similar to legal encyclopedias is the *American Law Reports* (abbreviated "A.L.R."). This publication, now in its fourth series, presents court opinions of note, set forth in full, followed by articles that discuss the law related to the opinions. A.L.R. is not arranged in any particular order so the index is essential. A.L.R. also does not attempt to discuss all topics.

Practice manuals

Practice manuals are books which summarize the law on given topics and provide procedural guidelines to follow in taking cases to court. They are written for attorneys, but they are usually at a fairly simple level and can help you understand legal proceedings in which you might be involved or how to complete legal forms.

Continuing legal education series

Like practice manuals, continuing legal education books are written on various topics primarily for lawyers. They are also generally at a fairly simple level. In States with continuing legal education requirements to retain bar membership or active continuing legal education organizations, there are many such books available.

Law reviews and journals

Law reviews are periodicals published by law schools with editing and article selection done by law students. Almost every law school publishes at least one law review, so there are hundreds of different law reviews. Articles in the reviews are typically written by legal scholars or law students. The articles typically discuss complex legal issues, analyze the law or the legal system, or survey the law on a given subject. The articles usually contain extensive references. Therefore they are a valuable research tool, especially if you are writing a scholarly paper. However, they are often too scholarly, too legalistic, too narrow, too abstract or too detailed to be of use to social workers—or even practicing lawyers.

There are also numerous topical or general interest journals published for lawyers or those interested in the law, just as there are journals, like *Social Work*, *Social Casework* and *Public Welfare*, published for social workers or those interested in social welfare. Many of these legal journals publish articles written by practicing attorneys. Such articles are often practical and timely, and may therefore be more useful to social workers than articles written by legal scholars. Bar journals, published by city, State or national associations of lawyers, often known as **"bar associations,"** may be particularly helpful.

It should be noted that some law school reviews are called "journals," but the use of the term "journal" does not change their essential character. Some topical journals, such as the Journal of Family Law, are put out by law schools and are really law reviews.

Law review and journal articles are indexed by title, author, and subject matter in the *Index to Legal Periodicals*, the *Current Law Index*, and the *Legal Resource Index*. All of these indexes are used just as *Social Work Research and Abstracts*, *Psychological Abstracts*, and the *Social Sciences Index* are used.

Digests

Digests contain brief excerpts of one or two sentences from cases, arranged by topic. There is generally no text at all in a digest, and a topic may be very broad. Therefore one often must wade through hundreds of excerpts to locate useful cases. But digests can help you locate such cases.

Most digests are tied to a particular reporter series. Thus, there are West digests tied to each West Regional Reporter, to West's Supreme Court Reporter, and to it's federal and many of its State reporters. A sample page from the digest for West's Pacific Reporter is duplicated in Appendix 4-3.

Loose-leaf services

There are several loose-leaf services which compile cases, statutes and regulations on particular topics, like programs under the Social Security Act or family law, and which have brief comments on the current law. These loose-leaf services may include court opinions of interest which are not published elsewhere or bills and proposed regulations. Because they publish court opinions, loose-leaf services are sometimes referred to as **"topical reporters."** Sometimes you will see a case citation to a loose-leaf service if an opinion is only published there. For example, "*In re Marriage of Jones*, 12 F.L.R. 97 (Idaho App. 1976)," would be a citation to an Idaho appellate court case in the Family Law Reporter which was not published elsewhere.

Loose-leaf services are kept in binders and are kept current by replacement of superseded pages and additions of new law.

Computerized data bases

Most cases, some regulations and statutes, and a few articles from periodicals are included in computerized data bases for legal research. The two major computerized legal data bases are Westlaw and Lexis. Basically, one finds law in Westlaw and Lexis by using a system of key word searches. Instructions for using the systems are available in libraries which provide access to the systems.

Treatises

There are numerous books and encyclopedias on selected legal topics. Some of these are difficult scholarly tomes not useful to social workers. Others, most notably those referred to as "hornbooks," are simply expositions or summaries of the law on a particular topic. They are designed for practicing attorneys and for students. Hornbooks and other treatises designed for practicing attorneys or students may be quite useful to social workers.

Shephard's Citations

A useful tool for finding cases which interpret a particular statute or rely on a particular precedent or for determining if a case has been overruled or distinguished is *Shephard's Citations*. Different volumes of Shephard's cover specified statutes or case reporters. Each volume sets forth long lists of citations, without case names, courts or dates, to all opinions citing a statute or case. Symbols tell you something about what the opinion did with the cited case (e.g., distinguished, followed, overruled) or what portion of the case it addressed. The lists of citations and symbols with no text can be intimidating, but any law librarian can help you use Shephard's.

LEGAL RESEARCH

This section is written with you as a practitioner in mind. You may be a student at this time, and, if so, you might be required to write a paper that requires you to do legal research. You can follow the steps presented later in this section to complete such a paper. In addition, you will have access to a wide range of legal references and perhaps access to law school libraries with professional law librarians to assist you. When you are in practice, you are unlikely to have these luxuries. Moreover, when you are in practice, the questions you research are likely to be somewhat different than those you research as a student. They will typically arise in the course of your practice and relate to specific aspects of your practice. You will be less concerned with legal principles and issues and more concerned with what the law tells you to do.

When faced with a legal question, how do you proceed? Of course you can always ask an attorney, but we are talking about how you can find and interpret information yourself.

The first step, and one that may seem so simple that it goes without saying, is to determine where physically you are likely to find the legal materials you will need. While this is not problematic if you are a student at a university with a law school and a law library, it is problematic if you are in practice in most places. Where can you find legal materials outside of university law libraries? Many other university and public libraries have state and federal statutes, and if your legal research is not extensive, these sources may be sufficient. Most general university or public libraries do not have the annotated statutes and case reporters, but these materials, at least for your State, should be available in your local courthouse. It should be possible for you to gain access to the collection there, as can any member of the public. You should expect, however, to get little help in using the collection and to do your work during normal business hours. Attorneys have collections related to their own practices, and some might allow you access to their collections.

The second step in finding information is to determine whether the question relates primarily to federal or to State law. Since, as we have said, most laws important to social workers are State laws, it is safe to begin by searching State law. The major exceptions are questions related to federally administered benefit programs, immigration or naturalization, and services to native Americans. Unless you have a question in these areas, begin with the assumption that the relevant law is State law. Move to federal law only if your search of State law is fruitless or takes you to federal law.

The third step is deciding what type of law you should look for first. Usually this will be statutes. Annotations to statutes will lead you to other types of law bearing on your problem. If you can find no relevant statutes, you will have to look for cases, regulations and other types of law.

Assuming you have decided to begin with statutes but have no specific citations, the fourth step is to decide in what books of statutes to look. As has been stated, usually you should look in books of codified statutes, preferably annotated codified statutes.

Next you have to decide what terms to look for in the index to the books of statutes. You can expect the process of using the index to be somewhat frustrating because unfamiliar or legal terms may be used. For example, sections of the statutes referring to children might not be listed under the heading of "children." Instead, they might be listed under "minors" or "infants." Also an outdated term no longer used in common speech or in the law may be used in an index. For example, you may find statutes relating to children whose parents are not married under "children born out of wedlock," "illegitimate children" or even "bastards." It may be easier to look at the table of contents of a title you think may contain the statutes you want.

After you have located the applicable sections of the statutes, remember to look in the pocket parts or supplements for the current law.

If you have looked in the annotated codified statutes, as you should have, you can easily identify relevant court opinions by using the annotations. The annotations might also suggest other helpful sources such as law review and encyclopedia articles.

The annotations often will not identify applicable regulations, so you must decide if there might be applicable regulations and, if so, search for them. For the most part, you can assume that if the statutes give any authority to a public agency, there will be regulations. You will then turn to the administrative code for the state or try to obtain information directly from the agency with authority. As with statutes, if you are faced with a book or set of books containing many regulations, you begin your search with the index or table of contents.

You might also consult a legal encyclopedia and other secondary sources. These sources can provide an overview of a topic and perhaps lead you to additional statutory, regulatory and case references. Indeed, you might go to a secondary source first if you are unfamiliar with a topic or have general rather than specific questions about a broad topic. Secondary sources can also lead you to statutes and cases without using indices, digests, or annotated statutes and can give you an idea about what headings to look for in the indices and digests. For example, you may want to know about fathers' responsibility to support children born out of wedlock. You may not know that actions establishing that a man is the natural father of a child are called "paternity" actions, that the support obligation can only be imposed if paternity is established, and that the obligation is often imposed as part of a paternity action. You cannot find anything in the index to the statutes about fathers' responsibilities for support because the relevant statutes are all under the heading "paternity." A secondary source might use the term "paternity" and lead you to look under this heading in the appropriate index.

At this point you will probably have obtained much of the information you need unless you need to conduct extensive research for some purpose, such as writing a paper for a class or making a presentation at a meeting. If this is the case, you can supplement your review of the statutes, cases and regulations by consulting further secondary sources, like journals.

But assume you have located all the material you believe you need. In fact, your task has just begun. The challenge now is to understand the material you have located, determine what in the material is significant to you as a social worker and identify any additional information you might need.

The statutes must be read carefully. They are written precisely, and there are big differences between a "shall" and a "may" and an "and" and an "or." The rule is to read and then read again, trying to rephrase in common language.

As you read the excerpts of court opinions in the annotations, you need to decide to what extent the cases may apply to your problem as a social worker and therefore whether they are cases you should read carefully. While the holdings in some opinions might enlighten your practice, the holdings in many relate to legal points of no concern to social workers. They address problems for attorneys, not for social workers.

Finally you need to determine if you have all the information you need and if your understanding of what you have is accurate. As questions are answered new questions should arise, and these questions should be pursued until you are sure you have adequate knowledge to guide your behavior. At this point you need to ask if your understanding is consistent with common sense and your experience. This is also the time to consult with colleagues and supervisors, and, if necessary, with attorneys.

To illustrate the process of conducting legal research, again assume you are a social worker in Colorado who has been asked to conduct a background investigation in a divorce case where child custody has been contested and that you wish to determine what is expected of you. What should you do? (You, the reader, should refer to the Appendices to this Chapter, which provide some of the relevant law on the topic, as we explain.)

You correctly recognize that child custody investigations in conjunction with divorce are governed by State law, and probably statutes. Your search for information, thus, leads you to the index of the codified annotated statutes for Colorado. You look under the headings of divorce and child custody and find section 14-10-127, C.R.S., which deals with background investigations. You remember to check the pocket parts. If you did not, you would not discover that the section had been amended since the bound volume was published.

By carefully reading section 14-10-127, you learn you may obtain information from professionals who have served the child in the past without obtaining the consent of the child's parents. You learn you can request the court to order professional assessments. You learn you must mail your report to counsel within 10 days of the hearing on custody. And so on.

By looking at the annotations to the section, you can identify cases interpreting this statute. By reading the annotations, you find some background information related to the section, and you learn that some opinions in Colorado interpret the section. From the annotations, you might decide that the *Pacheco* case is important to you. You would then read *Pacheco* because a mere excerpt is not the law and can be misleading.

But what do section 14-10-127 and *Pacheco* not tell you? They do not tell you what to evaluate. Only by looking further do you find that section 14-10-124, C.R.S., tells you what the court should consider in deciding custody and therefore what you should evaluate. Section 14-10-127 also does not tell you that the court's request to you might have been made under the authority of section 14-10-126, which allows the court to "seek the advice of professional personnel" and which does not give the person giving the advice the specific authority given by section 14-10-127 and which does not impose the same obligations as section 14-10-127. *Pacheco* and the annotations to section 14-10-127 do not tell you, moreover, if there are regulations governing the conduct of investigations by staff of public child welfare agencies, an important point if you are employed by such an agency. Your research may be far from complete at this point.

In summary, legal research demands specialized knowledge and skills. However, it demands knowledge and skills not unique to attorneys. The task of the social worker is to find and use legal information required to practice competently, consulting with attorneys as needed. Legal research, then, is simply one aspect of social work practice.

APPENDIX 4.1

14-10-127. Investigations and reports. (1) In all custody proceedings, the court shall, upon motion of either party or upon the court's own motion, order the court probation department or any county or district welfare department to investigate and file a written report concerning custodial arrangements for the child. Except as otherwise provided in this section, such report shall be considered confidential and shall not be available for public inspection unless by order of court. The cost of each investigation up to a maximum of fifty dollars may be assessed as part of the costs of the action or proceeding, and, upon receipt of such sum by the clerk of court, it shall be transmitted to the department or agency performing the investigation.

(2) In preparing his report concerning a child, the investigator may consult any person who may have information about the child and his potential custodial arrangements. Upon order of the court, the investigator may refer the child to professional personnel for diagnosis. The investigator may consult with and obtain information from medical, psychiatric, or other expert persons who have served the child in the past without obtaining the consent of the parent or the child's custodian; but the child's consent must be obtained if he has reached the age of sixteen unless the court finds that he lacks mental capacity to consent. If the requirements of subsection (3) of this section are fulfilled, the investigator's report may be received in evidence at the hearing.

(3) The court shall mail the investigator's report to counsel and to any party not represented by counsel at least ten days prior to the hearing. The investigator shall make available to counsel and to any party not represented by counsel the investigator's file of underlying data and reports, complete texts of diagnostic reports made to the investigator pursuant to the provisions of subsection (2) of this section, and the names and addresses of all persons whom the investigator has consulted. Any party to the proceeding may call the investigator and any person whom he has consulted for cross-examination. No party may waive his right of cross-examination prior to the hearing.

Source: R & RE, L. 71, p. 530, § 1; C.R.S. 1963, § 46-1-27.

Am. Jur. See 24 Am. Jur.2d. Divorce and Separation, § 793.

C.J.S. See 27B C.J.S., Divorce, § 317(8).

Annotator's note. Since § 14-10-127 is similar to repealed § 46-1-5(7), C.R.S. 1963, relevant cases construing this provision have been included in the annotations to § 14-10-127.

The purpose of the legislation providing for **court assistants in the capacity of investigators of domestic relations cases to assist the court in the transaction of the judicial business of said court** was obviously to assist the court and not to replace it. The general assembly would have no power to substitute an investigator for a judge, and neither would such legislation authorize a trial court to deny to the parties any of the usual attributes of a fair trial in open court upon due notice. Anderson v. Anderson, 167 Colo. 88, 445 P.2d 397 (1968).

The **act of the general assembly (§ 46-1-5(7), C.R.S. 1963), which purported to authorize the trial court to call upon the probation department for a report concerning "the ability of each party to serve the best interest of the child"**, and further directing that "Each report shall be considered by the court" could not be so construed as to deny due process which includes the right to be heard in open court and to have a determination of issues based upon competent evidence offered by persons who submit themselves to cross-examination. Anderson v. Anderson, 167 Colo. 88, 445 P.2d 397 (1968).

A probation officer, or other persons, who have been designated to investigate and report to the court in custody hearings matters involving the ability or fitness of parents to best serve the interests of their children, are subject to examination as witnesses concern-

Reprinted by permission of the State of Colorado, Committee on Legal Service, Office of Revisor of Statutes.

ing matters contained in their reports. Saucerman v. Saucerman, 170 Colo. 318, 461 P.2d 18 (1969).

However, touching upon matters related to them in confidence, the trial court should preliminarily rule in each instance what matters are in fact confidential, and whether the public interest requires the confidence to be preserved, and no examination of the officer should be permitted with respect to such confidential matters. Saucerman v. Saucerman, 170 Colo. 318, 461 P.2d 18 (1969).

But, where the trial court received in evidence the investigative reports of welfare and health department employees in reference to conditions found in the respective homes of the two contestants, and in reference to the psychological effects living with the father or the mother might have on one of the children, and the record indicated that at one hearing after the reports were filed the individuals who made the reports were either in court or could have been made available to the parties for cross-examination, there was no unfairness nor a denial of due process. Aylor v. Aylor, 173 Colo. 294, 478 P.2d 302 (1970).

And in making an order changing the custody of children, the trial court is actually making the decision, though such order is based on the recommendations of a psychiatrist and welfare personnel whose reports constitute nothing more than recommendations. Aylor v. Aylor, 173 Colo. 294, 478 P.2d 302 (1970).

The reports simply furnish specific information of a specialized nature for aid and assistance to the trial court, but in the final analysis the judge makes the decision, and whatever recommendations may be made to the judge, be they by experts or counsel, they are merely recommendations and nothing more. Aylor v. Aylor, 173 Colo. 294, 478 P.2d 302 (1970).

Where objections and exceptions were filed to the report of the probation department, since it was a hearsay document, if the conclusions reached therein were objected to by either party, it would be necessary that competent evidence, upon which the conclusions were based, be presented in open court. Anderson v. Anderson, 167 Colo. 88, 445 P.2d 397 (1968).

And the trial court erred in relying upon the probation report where it afforded no opportunity for the husband to offer evidence in explanation thereof, or to disprove any conclusions based on hearsay that were contained therein. Anderson v. Anderson, 167 Colo. 88, 445 P.2d 397 (1968).

But, it was not prejudicial error for the trial court to have received in evidence the hearsay reports of the case worker of the welfare department in custody proceedings, since the nature of the ''report'' was such that the father could not possibly have been prejudiced by anything contained therein, and furthermore, it affirmatively appeared from the court's decree that it did not in any manner enter into the court's thinking to the prejudice of the father. Suzuki v. Suzuki, 162 Colo. 204, 425 P.2d 44 (1967).

14-10-128. Hearings. (1) Custody proceedings shall receive priority in being set for hearing.

(2) The court may tax as costs the payment of necessary travel and other expenses incurred by any person whose presence at the hearing the court deems necessary to determine the best interests of the child.

(3) The court without a jury shall determine questions of law and fact. If it finds that a public hearing may be detrimental to the child's best interests, the court may exclude the public from a custody hearing but may admit any person who has a direct and legitimate interest in the particular case or a legitimate educational or research interest in the work of the court.

(4) If the court finds it necessary in order to protect the child's welfare that the record of any interview, report, investigation, or testimony in a custody proceeding be kept secret, the court shall make an appropriate order sealing the record.

Source: R & RE, L. 71, p. 531, § 1; C.R.S. 1963, § 46-1-28.

C.J.S. See 27B C.J.S., Divorce, § 317(8).

APPENDIX 4.2

Temporary order is not "in any way res judicata" as to permanent order. In re Lawson, 44 Colo. App. 105, 608 P.2d 378 (1980).

Order granting temporary custody of children is not final for purposes of appeal. In re Henne, 620 P.2d 62 (Colo. App. 1980).

14-10-126. Interviews.

Law reviews. For article, "The Role of Children's Counsel in Contested Child Custody, Visitation and Support Cases", see 15 Colo. Law. 224 (1986).

Section does not mandate interviews. In re Rinow, 624 P.2d 365 (Colo. App. 1981).

Parent may not cross-examine child at interview. The father is not entitled, as a matter of law, to cross-examine the children at the time of the interview. In re Agner, 659 P.2d 53 (Colo. App. 1982).

Making record is for benefit of parties. Though the language of this section is mandatory in form, the obvious purpose of making a record is for the benefit of the parties. In re Armbeck, 33 Colo. App. 260, 518 P.2d 300 (1974).

Requirement for record of interview concerning child's preference not violated. Where the court conducted a 15 minute interview with the two minor children but did not inquire concerning their preference the requirement of this section for a record of an interview concerning the children's preference was not violated. In re Short, 675 P.2d 323 (Colo. App. 1983).

Requirement of making record may be waived. The requirement of making a record, i.e., a verbatim transcript, of the interview between the court and child may be waived either expressly or by implication. In re Armbeck, 33 Colo. App. 260, 518 P.2d 300 (1974).

Waiver of the requirement of making a record by implication held sufficient. See In re Armbeck, 33 Colo. App. 260, 518 P.2d 300 (1974).

As to the standard of the common law with respect to interviews. See Rayer v. Rayer, 32 Colo. App. 400, 512 P.2d 637 (1973).

Applied in In re Schulke, 40 Colo. App. 473, 579 P.2d 90 (1978).

14-10-127. Evaluation and reports. (1) In all custody proceedings, the court shall, upon motion of either party, or may, upon its own motion, order the court probation department, any county or district social services department, or a licensed mental health professional to perform an evaluation and file a written report concerning custodial arrangements for the child, unless such motion by either party is made for the purpose of delaying the proceedings. Except as otherwise provided in this section, such report shall be considered confidential and shall not be available for public inspection unless by order of court. The cost of each probation department or social services department evaluation shall be based on an ability to pay and shall be assessed as part of the costs of the action or proceeding, and, upon receipt of such sum by the clerk of court, it shall be transmitted to the department or agency performing the evaluation. The court shall order an evaluation by an impartial licensed mental health professional selected by the court, upon motion of either party, only if the moving party agrees initially to pay all costs of such evaluation. The moving party shall, at the time of appointment of the evaluator, deposit a reasonable sum with the court to pay the cost of the evaluation. The court may order the reasonable charges of any evaluation and report to be assessed as costs between the parties.

(2) In preparing his report concerning a child, the evaluator may consult any person who may have information about the child and his potential custodial arrangements. Upon order of the court, the evaluator may refer the child to other professional personnel for diagnosis. The evaluator may consult with and obtain information from medical, psychiatric, or other expert persons who have served the child in the past without obtaining the consent of the parent or the child's custodian; but the child's consent must

Reprinted by permission of the State of Colorado, Committee on Legal Service, Office of Revisor of Statutes.

be obtained if he has reached the age of sixteen unless the court finds that he lacks mental capacity to consent. If the requirements of subsection (3) of this section are fulfilled, the evaluator's report may be received in evidence at the hearing.

(3) The evaluator shall mail his report to counsel and to any party not represented by counsel at least ten days prior to the hearing. The evaluator shall make available to counsel and to any party not represented by counsel his file of underlying data and reports, complete texts of diagnostic reports made to the evaluator pursuant to the provisions of subsection (2) of this section, and the names and addresses of all persons whom the evaluator has consulted. Any party to the proceeding may call the evaluator and any person whom he has consulted for cross-examination. No party may waive his right of cross-examination prior to the hearing.

Source: (1) amended, L. 76, p. 529, § 1; (1) amended, L. 79, p. 646, § 1; amended, L. 83, p. 649, § 1.

Law reviews. For article, "Therapist Privilege in Custody Cases", see 15 Colo. Law. 47 (1986).

The purpose of the legislation providing for the preparation and filing of reports in custody proceedings is to make the information contained therein available to assist the court in determining what is in the best interest of the children concerned. Pacheco v. Pacheco, 38 Colo. App. 181, 554 P.2d 720 (1976).

Opportunity to test report's reliability and offer evidence exists. Because any party has the right to call for cross-examination of the investigator and any person he has consulted, and because the investigator's file is available to counsel, ample opportunity exists for a party to test the reliability of the report and to offer evidence in explanation of or to disprove any statements or conclusions based on hearsay. Pacheco v. Pacheco, 38 Colo. App. 181, 554 P.2d 720 (1976).

Compliance with the 10-day provisions of this section is not a condition precedent to the reception of the report. Pacheco v. Pacheco, 38 Colo. App. 181, 554 P.2d 720 (1976).

Effect of noncompliance. Noncompliance with the 10-day rule merely prohibits the court from proceeding with a hearing wherein the report can be considered absent consent of or waiver by the parties. Pacheco v. Pacheco, 38 Colo. App. 181, 554 P.2d 720 (1976).

Waiver of objections to admission of report. Unless a party notifies the court and the opposing party within 10 days after receipt of a copy of the report (or if a copy has not been received at least 10 days prior to the hearing day, then at or prior to the commencement of the hearing at which the report may be used) that he intends to object to the admission of the report on the grounds of noncompliance with the 10-day rule or the hearsay nature of the report, any such objections are waived. Pacheco v. Pacheco, 38 Colo. App. 181, 554 P.2d 720 (1976).

Where a copy of the report was received by counsel a reasonable time prior to the hearing and no objection was made thereto until after the commencement of the hearing, objections as to hearsay and the 10-day rule were waived. Pacheco v. Pacheco, 38 Colo. App. 181, 554 P.2d 720 (1976).

Effect of valid objection. If a valid objection is made within the period specified above, then, on motion of either party or of the court, the court shall grant a reasonable continuance of the custody hearing date in order that the parties may obtain appropriate testimony. Pacheco v. Pacheco, 38 Colo. App. 181, 554 P.2d 720 (1976).

Court did not improperly utilize an investigative report made by an officer of the juvenile probation department in arriving at its decision relative to custody, for while it is true that the investigative report was not formally offered and received in evidence, the report was made a part of the record and had been furnished previously to both parties, and although she did not choose to do so, the wife had the right to call and examine the author of the report. Rayer v. Rayer, 32 Colo. App. 400, 512 P.2d 637 (1973).

Communications disclosed pursuant to this section are not privileged under section 13-90-107 since the information was necessary to make an evaluation for the court, not to treat the person disclosing the information. Anderson v. Glismann, 577 F. Supp. 1506 (D. Colo. 1984).

Actions of a court-appointed expert are made under the authority of the state, but not on behalf of the state, and will not sustain a cause

⟜2(20) PARENT & CHILD

42 P.D.(367 P.2d)—334

For later cases see same Topic and Key Number in Pocket Part

Or.App. 1972. Under circumstances of case, although question of custody was close because of time mother had allowed father to have child, court would not disturb trial judge's order refusing to change custody of child from mother to father.

King v. King, 500 P.2d 267, 10 Or.App. 324.

Wash. 1972. When, on appeal by maternal grandmother and legal guardian of eight-year-old child from order terminating guardianship and restoring custody of child to her natural parents, the Supreme Court was uncertain whether disposition of trial court reflected view that welfare of child was paramount consideration or whether right of parents to custody was given improper weight, case would be remanded to enable trial court to review standards used in deciding case in light of rules enunciated by the Supreme Court.

In re Guardianship of Palmer, 503 P.2d 464, 81 Wash.2d 604.

Wash.App. 1972. Although rarely is an appellate court justified in making new determination of custody of children, since trial judge had disqualified himself from proceedings, many witnesses had testified in the lengthy trial and record clearly substantiated findings, custody of children would be awarded by the Court of Appeals to the mother subject to the six-weeks' visitation time in summer with the father as well as a visitation of every other weekend rather than providing, as trial court had, for the alternating of custody on an annual basis between the father and the mother.

Rickard v. Rickard, 503 P.2d 763, 7 Wash. App. 907.

Wyo. 1968. Supreme Court considered it appropriate in particular case to award mother an attorney's fee of $300 for his representation in the defense of her right to continued custody of children.

Rau v. Rau, 441 P.2d 320.

⟜2(21). —— Scope of review in general; discretion; harmless error.

Ariz. 1970. Granting of visitation rights is a matter in which court enjoys broad discretion, since trial judge is in most favorable position to determine what is best for children, and unless it clearly appears that trial judge has mistaken or ignored the evidence a reviewing court will not disturb his finding.

Armer v. Armer, 463 P.2d 818, 105 Ariz. 284.

Ariz. 1964. Reviewing court should not substitute its opinion as to which parent should have custody.

In re Clay, 393 P.2d 257, 96 Ariz. 160.

Colo. 1969. Denial of father's right to cross-examine probation officer who sub-mitted report of home investigations of both parties in custody proceedings pursuant to stipulation between parties was not prejudicial where father objected only to letter written by medical doctor and such letter was stricken from report and doctor became witness and was examined by both parties. C.R.S. '63, 154–1–7(6).

Saucerman v. Saucerman, 461 P.2d 18, 170 Colo. 318.

Colo.App. 1976. Where objection to challenged testimony of witness as to disciplining of children was sustained, no offer of proof was made following objection and counsel, by other questions, was allowed to go into everything witness had observed concerning mother's treatment of children, no prejudicial error arose because of exclusion of such testimony at custody hearing.

Pacheco v. Pacheco, 554 P.2d 720, 38 Colo.App. 181.

Hawaii 1974. The supreme court will not set aside the findings of fact of the family court unless there is a definite and firm conviction that a mistake has been committed.

Turoff v. Turoff, 527 P.2d 1275, 56 Haw. 51.

Kan. 1978. Judgment of trial court on question of change of custody will not be disturbed on appeal without an affirmative showing of an abuse in exercise of discretion, inasmuch as trial court is in most advantageous position to judge how interests of children may best be served for while an appellate court has only printed page to consider, trial court has advantage of seeing witnesses and parties, observing their demeanor, and assessing character of parties and quality of their affection and feeling for children.

Simmons v. Simmons, 576 P.2d 589, 223 Kan. 639.

Kan. 1973. Paramount consideration in custody disputes between parents is always the welfare and best interests of the children and trial court is in the best position to judge whether those interests are being served; in the absence of an abuse of judicial discretion, its judgment will not be disturbed.

Moudy v. Moudy, 505 P.2d 764, 211 Kan. 213.

Kan. 1968. When issue of child custody is between parents the primary consideration of a court is the best interests and welfare of the children, and in absence of abuse of sound judicial discretion the trial court's judgment determining the issue will not be disturbed on appeal.

Greene v. Greene, 443 P.2d 263, 201 Kan. 701.

Mont. 1977. Where district judge conducting hearing on permanent custody mistakenly assumed that another district judge had

720   Colo.   554 PACIFIC REPORTER, 2d SERIES

Florence M. PACHECO, now known as
Florence M. Sellers, Plaintiff-
Appellee,

v.

Benjamin F. PACHECO, Defendant-
Appellant.

No. 75–799.

Colorado Court of Appeals,
Div. II.

Aug. 12, 1976.

Selected for Official Publication.

Father appealed from orders of the District Court, Jefferson County, George G. Priest, J., denying his motion for permanent change of custody of two children and granting wife's motions for increase in child support and for attorney fees. The Court of Appeals, VanCise, J., held that evidence regarding change of circumstances supported order increasing monthly child support; that trial court's order requiring father to contribute reasonable amount for mother's attorney fees was supported by the evidence; and that where copy of custody investigation report was received by father's counsel a reasonable time prior to custody hearing and no objection was made to report until after commencement of hearing, objections as to hearsay nature of report and the failure to provide father with report at least ten days prior to the hearing were waived.

Affirmed.

1. Parent and Child ⬅3.3(8)

Court has continuing jurisdiction for purpose of later revisions of its orders pertaining to child support as changing circumstances may require. C.R.S. '63, 46–1–5(4).

2. Parent and Child ⬅3.3(8)

If financial ability of father improves and needs of minor children increase, it is proper to make appropriate increases in amount of child support to be paid by father. C.R.S. '63, 46–1–5(4).

3. Parent and Child ⬅3.3(8)

Evidence showing, inter alia, an increase in costs of needs of two children since 1970 support order requiring father to pay $50 per month per child and an increase in father's monthly take-home pay from $376 in 1970 to $516 supported trial court's order increasing child support by $35 per month per child. C.R.S. '63, 46–1–5(4).

4. Parent and Child ⬅3.3(8)

Trial court's finding that mother who brought successful proceeding for increase in child support was entitled to have father contribute reasonable amount for her attorney fees was supported by evidence.

5. Infants ⬅19.3(3)

Compliance with ten-day provision of statute requiring that court mail custody investigation report to counsel at least ten days prior to custody hearing is not a condition precedent to reception of report; noncompliance with ten-day rule merely prohibits court from proceeding with the hearing wherein report can be considered absent consent of or waiver by parties. C.R.S. '73, 14–10–127(2, 3).

6. Infants ⬅19.3(1)

Purpose of legislation providing for preparation and filing of custody investigation report is to make information contained therein available to assist court in determining what is in best interests of children concerned. C.R.S. '73, 14–10–127.

7. Infants ⬅19.3(3)
Trial ⬅76

Unless a party notifies court and opposing party within ten days after receipt of copy of custody investigation report or if a copy has not been received at least ten days prior to custody hearing, at or prior to commencement of hearing at which report may be used that he intends to object to admission of report on grounds of noncompliance with ten-day rule or hearsay nature of report, any such objections are waived; if a valid objection on either of such grounds is made within the period specified, then, on motion of either party or court, court shall grant reasonable continuance of custody hearing date in order that parties may obtain appropriate testimony. C.R.S. '73, 14–10–127(2, 3).

8. Trial ⊜76

Where copy of custody investigation report was received by father's counsel a reasonable time prior to custody hearing and no objection was made to report until after commencement of hearing, objections as to hearsay nature of report and the failure to provide father with report at least ten days prior to the custody hearing were waived and trial court could properly consider the report. C.R.S. '73, 14–10–127(2, 3).

9. Parent and Child ⊜2(21)

Where objection to challenged testimony of witness as to disciplining of children was sustained, no offer of proof was made following objection and counsel, by other questions, was allowed to go into everything witness had observed concerning mother's treatment of children, no prejudicial error arose because of exclusion of such testimony at custody hearing.

10. Parent and Child ⊜2(18)

Evidence, in proceeding by father for change of custody, supported trial court's determination that it was in best interests of children that custody remain with mother.

11. Infants ⊜19.3(2, 7)

Determination of custody is matter left to discretion of trial judge and, absent an abuse of discretion, that determination will not be disturbed on appeal.

———————◆———————

Bettenberg & Stipech, Robert T. Bettenberg, Mark R. Shapiro, Denver, for plaintiff-appellee.

George G. Johnson, Jr., Denver, for defendant-appellant.

VANCISE, Judge.

Defendant, Benjamin F. Pacheco (the father), appeals from the orders denying

his motion for permanent change of custody and granting the motions for increase in child support and for attorney fees of plaintiff, Florence M. Sellers (the mother). We affirm.

In September 1970, custody of the two children of the parties was granted to the mother with prescribed visitation rights to the father, and the father was ordered to maintain medical insurance for the children and to pay $50 per month per child for support. In April 1975, the three motions above referred to were heard. The court denied the motion for change of custody, increased the child support from $50 to $85 per month per child, and ordered the father to pay $300 to the ex-wife's attorney.

I.

The father contends that the court abused its discretion in ordering increased child support payments and in requiring him to pay his ex-wife's attorney fees. No issue is made as to the reasonableness of the amount of the fee; the objection is to his being required to pay any fee.

[1, 2] The court has continuing jurisdiction for the purpose of such later revisions of its order pertaining to child support as changing circumstances may require. C.R.S.1963, 46–1–5(4). And, if the financial ability of the father improves and the needs of the minor children increase, it is proper to make appropriate increases in the amount of child support. *Garrow v. Garrow*, 152 Colo. 480, 382 P.2d 809.

On supporting evidence, the court found that, at the time of the 1970 support order, the father's take-home pay was $376, and that, at the time of the 1975 hearing, his affidavit showed a net monthly take-home pay of $516.30 while an affidavit from his employer, admitted without objection, indicated that his net monthly income was in the $800 to $900 bracket. It further found that, at the time of the hearing, the mother was employed with a net monthly take-home pay of $330, exclusive of child support payments. The evidence was that she was working in 1970, but the amount of her then earnings was not shown. Both parties testified that the costs of the needs of the children had increased since 1970.

[3] The change of circumstances being established, the court could modify support. A monthly increase of $35 per child, under the facts shown, is not unreasonable and is within the sound discretion of the trial court. Thus, its order will not be disturbed on review. *See Franco v. Franco,* 161 Colo. 507, 423 P.2d 327.

[4] Also, the court's finding that the mother was entitled to have the father contribute a reasonable amount for her attorney's fee is supported by the evidence. Hence, there is no abuse of discretion in the order entered.

II.

The father also contends that the court erred in denying his motion for permanent change of custody. He first claims error in the court's considering the custody investigation report prepared by the County Department of Social Services pursuant to court order.

This report is a summary of interviews by a social worker with the parties, their spouses, the two children involved, and with 15 other persons. The report concludes with the social worker's "impressions," but does not contain any specific recommendation or opinion. It is generally favorable to the mother and unfavorable to the father.

The report is dated April 18, 1975, and shows a copy going to each attorney. Counsel for the father received his copy April 23. No objections or exceptions to the report were made prior to or at the commencement of the April 28 hearing.

On cross-examination of the father, he was asked about a statement in the report allegedly made by him. The question was objected to on the ground of hearsay, and the document was objected to on the same ground. The court ruled:

"Well, you can't object to the document because you asked for it, and this is the one you received; but I will sustain the objection."

No further reference was made to the investigation report until the conclusion of the hearing. Its author was not called as a witness. At closing, the mother's attorney moved the admission of the report into evidence. The attorney for the father objected on the ground that the report had not been mailed to counsel "at least 10 days prior to the hearing" as prescribed by § 14–10–127(2) and (3), C.R.S.1973. To this, the court ruled that this objection should have been made at the beginning of the testimony, in which event the hearing would have been set over, and that it was now too late.

[5] Compliance with the 10-day provisions of the statute is not a condition precedent to the reception of the report. Noncompliance with the 10-day rule merely prohibits the court from proceeding with a hearing wherein the report can be considered absent consent of or waiver by the parties.

[6] The purpose of the legislation providing for the preparation and filing of these reports in custody proceedings, § 14–10–127, C.R.S.1973, is to make the information contained therein available to assist the court in determining what is in the best interests of the children concerned. *See Aylor v. Aylor,* 173 Colo. 294, 478 P.2d 302; *Anderson v. Anderson,* 167 Colo. 88, 445 P.2d 397. Because any party has the right to call for cross-examination the investigator and any person he has consulted, and because the investigator's file is available to counsel, ample opportunity exists for a party to test the reliability of the report and to offer evidence in explanation of or to disprove any statements or conclusions based on hearsay. *Cf. Anderson, supra.*

[7] In accordance with the intent and purpose of the statute, we hold that unless a party notifies the court and the opposing

party within 10 days after receipt of a copy of the report [or if a copy has not been received at least 10 days prior to the hearing day, then at or prior to the commencement of the hearing at which the report may be used] that he intends to object to the admission of the report on the grounds of noncompliance with the 10-day rule or the hearsay nature of the report, any such objections are waived. If a valid objection on either of the above grounds is made within the period specified above, then, on motion of either party or of the court, the court shall grant a reasonable continuance of the custody hearing date in order that the parties may obtain appropriate testimony.

[8] Where, as here, a copy of the report was received by counsel a reasonable time prior to the hearing and no objection was made thereto until after the commencement of the hearing, objections as to hearsay and the 10-day rule were waived. *See In re Marriage of Armbeck,* 33 Colo. App. 260, 518 P.2d 300; *Rayer v. Rayer,* 32 Colo.App. 400, 512 P.2d 637. Hence, no reversible error was committed in the court's considering the report.

[9] The father further contends that the court erroneously excluded certain testimony from the mother's present husband as to incidents showing her unfitness to have the children.

The challenged question was:

"[D]id we have a discussion about the disciplining of the children involved, the two Pacheco children?

This was objected to as irrelevant, and the objection was sustained. No offer of proof was made following this objection, and, by other questions, counsel was allowed to go into everything the witness had observed concerning the mother's treatment of the children. There was no prejudicial error here.

[10, 11] The court made a determination that it was in the best interests of the children that the custody remain with the mother. There was sufficient evidence to support that conclusion. Determination of custody being a matter left to the discretion of the trial judge, *Rayer v. Rayer, supra,* and there being no showing of an abuse of that discretion here, we will not disturb that determination.

Orders affirmed.

SILVERSTEIN, C. J., and SMITH, J., concur.

UNIVERSITY HILLS BEAUTY ACADEMY, INC., a Colorado Corporation, Plaintiff-Appellant and Cross-Appellee,

v.

The MOUNTAIN STATES TELEPHONE AND TELEGRAPH COMPANY, a Colorado corporation, Defendant-Appellee and Cross-Appellant.

No. 75–668.

Colorado Court of Appeals, Div. II.

Aug. 19, 1976.

Selected for Official Publication.

Suit was instituted for loss of business profits and expenses in mitigating damages allegedly resulting from negligent omission of a listing in a classified telephone directory. The District Court of the City and County of Denver, Joseph N. Lilly, J., entered judgment in favor of defendant, and plaintiff appealed. The Court of Appeals, VanCise, J., held that enforcement of limitation of liability clause in contract with reference to services to be rendered by telephone utility, with result that utility was not liable to customer for loss of business profits and expenses incurred in mitigating damages allegedly resulting from negligent omission of customer's listing in classified "yellow pages" of directory published by utility, was not so unreasonable as to be unconscionable, where there were other directories and publications in which

5

Basic Constitutional Principles

AN OVERVIEW OF THE CONSTITUTION

As has been stated, the United States Constitution provides the framework for the American legal system. It establishes the federal government and creates the American system of federalism by giving the federal government certain powers and reserving certain powers in the States. It also limits the powers of both the federal government and the States by establishing certain rights in the people which neither the federal government nor the States can infringe. All law, whether federal or State, legislation, regulation or court opinion, must be consistent with the Constitution.

Despite the Constitution's enormous importance, it is relatively short, containing only seven articles and twenty-six amendments. It is far shorter than most State constitutions. You should read the entire Constitution to learn what is and what is not included in it and to become familiar with its key provisions. A brief overview of the Constitution is set forth below to make reading it a little easier for you.

The first three articles of the Constitution establish the three branches of the federal government.

Article I establishes the chief lawmaking branch, the legislative branch. It creates the United States Congress and sets forth the basic rules for the election of its members and for its operation. Section 8 sets forth the powers of Congress and, thus, of the federal government. Sections 9 and 10 limit the powers of the federal and State governments, respectively. Pursuant to these sections, and to the 10th Amendment, the federal government may only exercise those powers granted to it by the Constitution while the States may exercise all powers except those which they

are prohibited from exercising by the Constitution.

Article II establishes the executive branch. It creates the offices of President and Vice-president, sets forth the method of their election, and enumerates the President's powers and duties.

Article III establishes the judicial branch. It creates the United States Supreme Court and authorizes Congress to establish inferior courts (which the first Congress did immediately). It also defines the jurisdiction of the Supreme Court and any other federal courts and establishes some procedural protections in these courts.

The remaining four articles contain several miscellaneous provisions. The most important provisions for social workers are in Article IV, which deals primarily with relations among the States and the relation between the States and the federal government, and Article VI, which contains the so-called "**Supremacy Clause**," making the Constitution and the laws of the federal government "the Supreme Law of the Land."

The first ten amendments to the Constitution are known collectively as "The Bill of Rights." They establish 27 specific rights, like freedom of speech and protection from unreasonable searches, which are protected from government invasion. The Bill of Rights was added to the Constitution immediately after the Constitution was ratified to insure that the newly created federal government would not assume too much power over the States and their residents. Although no language in the Bill of Rights makes this explicit, we know from contemporary accounts of the adoption of the Constitution and the Bill of Rights that the Bill of Rights was designed to limit the power of the federal government, not the power of the States. For over 100 years, the Bill of Rights was so interpreted. In other words, the proscriptions in the Bill of Rights were only seen as proscriptions for the federal government, and the rights guaranteed by the Bill of Rights were only considered to be guaranteed against infringement by the federal government; the States could completely ignore these proscriptions and flagrantly infringe these rights without having their actions declared unconstitutional.

This limitation on the scope of the Bill of Rights changed with the adoption of the 14th Amendment after the Civil War. The 14th Amendment, which is specifically addressed to the States,[1] among other things, provides that "No State shall . . . deprive any person of life, liberty, or property without due process of law." This provision, known as the "**due process clause**," was gradually recognized as requiring the States to comply with the Bill of Rights. In case after case, the Supreme Court ruled that a State's denial of a right guaranteed by the Bill of Rights was not consistent with due process and was, thus, an unconstitutional violation of the 14th Amendment. Put differently, over time the Supreme Court has incorporated most provisions of the Bill of Rights into the due process clause and thus applied them to the States.

The due process clause of the 14th Amendment has not only been interpreted to apply the Bill of Rights guarantees to the States. It, and the equivalent due process clause in the 5th Amendment, has also been interpreted: 1) to require certain procedural protections before a government may deprive a person of certain property interests or certain rights; and 2) to require fundamental fairness and reasonableness in government actions.

In addition to the due process clause, the 14th Amendment contains the **equal protection clause**, which provides that "No State shall . . . deny to any person within its jurisdiction the equal protection of the laws."

This clause basically forbids discriminatory actions by States. There is no equivalent provision anywhere in the Constitution which applies to the federal government. But, just as the courts incorporated most of the specific guarantees in the Bill of Rights into the due process clause of the 14th Amendment, and thus apply them to the States, the courts have incorporated the equal protection guarantee of the 14th Amendment into the due process clause of the 5th Amendment, and thus apply it to the federal government.

THE REQUIREMENT OF STATE ACTION

Whether the Bill of Rights and the equal protection clause apply to the federal government or to the States, it is clear that they, and the other protections of rights found in the Constitution, apply only to governments. This is known as the "**state action**" requirement. Absent state action, which may be loosely defined as governmental involvement or as non-private conduct, there can be no violation of the Constitution, in general, or of the Bill of Rights or the equal protection and due process clauses, in particular, no matter how egregious the conduct, how gross the discrimination or how unfair the procedure. As was stated in the *Civil Rights Cases*, 109 U.S. 3 (1883): "Individual invasion of individual rights is not the subject of the . . . [Constitution]."

To illustrate the state action requirement, suppose you bought a car on the installment plan. Pursuant to the due process clause of the 14th Amendment, you cannot be deprived of property without "due process of law." As we shall see, this language has been interpreted to require, in many circumstances, notice and an opportunity to be heard before your property can be taken

---

1.   The term "State" in the 14th Amendment, as the term "State" in this book, should be understood to include local governments within a State.

away. If you miss several payments on your car, however, the dealer from whom you bought it may go to your house and repossess the car without providing you prior notice and an opportunity to be heard. The dealer's action in so repossessing your car may or may not be legal under State law, but it would most likely be considered constitutional. This is because if the dealer just came and got your car, without any assistance from or involvement of the government, there would have been no state action and if there has been no state action, there can be no violation of the due process guarantee. The due process clause of the 14th Amendment does not require private individuals to give you due process before depriving you of property; it only requires governments to give you due process before taking away your property.

Now suppose that a statute in the State where you bought your car on an installment plan provides that, before repossessing a car, an automobile dealer must go to court and get a court order for repossession and further provides that only the sheriff can actually go out and seize the car pursuant to the repossession order. Given this statute, it would most likely be considered unconstitutional for the dealer to obtain a repossession order for your car or for the sheriff to seize it without giving you prior notice and an opportunity to be heard. The involvement of the court and the sheriff in the repossession means that there is state action and, thus, that there must be due process accorded to you before your car is taken.

It is often not easy to determine if there has been enough governmental involvement in a private action to make the due process clause or other constitutional provisions applicable. For example, if a State statute expressly authorizes automobile dealers to repossess cars themselves without court orders or the assistance of a sheriff, some would argue that the enactment of the statute is sufficient state action to trigger due process guarantees or

that if a dealer repossessed a car on the authority of such a statute, sometimes referred to as acting "**under color of law**," the dealer's action would be state action and the repossession must comply with due process guarantees. Most courts would reject these arguments, however.

In *Burton v. Wilmington Parking Authority*, 365 U.S. 715 (1961), a case addressing the state action requirement in the context of the equal protection guarantee, the Supreme Court stated[2]:

> "private conduct abridging individual rights does no violence to the Equal Protection Clause unless to some significant extent the State in any of its manifestations has been found to have become involved in it. [But] . . . to fashion and apply a precise formula for recognition of state responsibility under the Equal Protection Clause is an 'impossible task' which 'this Court has never attempted.' Only by sifting facts and weighing circumstances can the nonobvious involvement of the State in private conduct be attributed its true significance."

The Court then held that a privately owned and operated restaurant, located in a parking building which was constructed, owned and operated by a city, could not refuse to serve Blacks. The interdependence of the restaurant and the city parking authority

> "together with the obvious fact that the restaurant is operated as an integral part of a public building devoted to a public parking service, indicates that degree of state participation and involvement in discriminatory action which it was the design of the Fourteenth Amendment to condemn. It is irony amounting to grave injustice that in one part

---

2. See the discussion in the Introduction on the method used in this book to excerpt or quote court opinions.

of a single building, erected and maintained with public funds by an agency of the State to serve a public purpose, all persons have equal rights, while in another portion, also serving the public, a Negro is a second-class citizen, offensive because of his race, without rights and unentitled to service . . .''

DUE PROCESS OF THE LAW

As has been stated, the due process clauses of the 5th and 14th Amendments provide that no one may be deprived of ''life, liberty or property'' without ''due process of law,'' but the terms ''due process,'' ''life,'' ''liberty'' and ''property'' are nowhere defined. Thus, the courts have been forced to interpret these terms. Their consistently broad interpretation of these terms has enabled the due process clauses to perform several important functions in our legal system.

First, the due process clauses serve as the source of various protections against government actions and various procedural rights that are not included in the more specific provisions of the Bill of Rights or other portions of the Constitution. Using the due process clauses, a court may fashion standards of fairness not tied to any specific language in the Constitution. The specific protections and procedural guarantees in the Constitution are often restricted by both their language and a narrow historical purpose, but the concept of due process is not so confined. When changes in society have occurred that require changes in the law, when technological advances must be considered, or when problems have arisen that are not addressed by the Constitution, the courts can rely on the due process clauses to provide a solution. For example, when it was questioned whether a State could be required to pay for blood tests

in an action determining the father of a child, the courts analyzed the question in light of due process.

Second, the due process clauses may be relied upon to give recognition to society's continuing development of higher standards of fairness in government actions and higher conceptions of fairness in the legal system. For example, although for many years, children were taken away from allegedly unfit parents with few procedural protections and little concern for the parents, growing recognition that parents also had rights to their children led to a series of due process rulings making the process fairer and the standards employed in determining unfitness clearer.

Further, the due process requirement provides a basis for extending the principles underlying more specific constitutional guarantees to analogous situations. Thus, the 6th Amendment provides for a right to counsel in criminal cases, but makes no mention of a right to counsel in civil cases although some civil cases, like a civil case involuntarily committing someone to a mental hospital or terminating someone's parental rights, may have serious consequences for the individual. The concept of due process has been used to fill this gap.

We shall see the due process clauses used for these and other purposes throughout this book. The clauses have been widely used, but they can only be invoked to protect ''life, liberty or property'' from government actions or laws. In other words, there must be a **protectible interest** under the due process clauses before one can be guranteed due process. As stated, however, the courts have broadly interpreted ''life, liberty or property'' to find protectible interests. For example, in *Meyer v. Nebraska*, 262 U.S. 390 (1923), the Supreme Court decided that a law enacted during World War I which forbade the teaching of German in private or public schools violated due process guarantees in that it unreasonably (i.e., without due process) deprived teachers of liberty (i.e., the freedom to teach whatever they wished). The Court stated:

"While this court has not attempted to define with exactness the [term] liberty . . . [in the due process clause], the term has received much consideration, and some of the included things have been definitely stated. Without doubt, it denotes not merely freedom from bodily restraint, but also the right of the individual to contract, to engage in any of the common occupations of life, to acquire useful knowledge, to marry, to establish a home and bring up children, to worship God according to the dictates of his own conscience, and, generally, to enjoy those privileges long recognized . . . as essential to the orderly pursuit of happiness by free men."

"Property" has come to mean, not only tangible property, like money, bonds, livestock, land or furniture, but also intangible property interests or privileges. For example, in Goss v. Lopez, 419 U.S. 565 (1975), the Court held that an interest in a public education was a property interest so that a temporary suspension from a public high school without a hearing violated due process. The Court stated:

"At the outset appellants contend that because there is no constitutional right to an education at public expense, the Due Process Clause does not protect against expulsions from the public school system. This position misconceives the nature of the issue and is refuted by prior decisions. The Fourteenth Amendment forbids the State to deprive any person of life, liberty, or property without due process of law. Protected interests in property are normally 'not created by the Constitution. Rather, they are created and their dimensions are defined' by an independent source such as state statutes or rules entitling the citizen to certain benefits. Accordingly, a state employee who under state law . . . has a legitimate claim of entitlement to

continued employment absent sufficient cause for discharge may demand the procedural protections of due process. So may welfare recipients who have statutory rights to welfare as long as they maintain the specified qualifications. [T]he limitations of the Due Process Clause [have been applied] to governmental decisions to revoke parole, although a parolee has no constitutional right to that status. In like vein . . . the procedural protections of the Due Process Clause were triggered by official cancellation of a prisoner's good-time credits accumulated under state law, although those benefits were not mandated by the Constitution.

"Here, on the basis of state law, appellees plainly had legitimate claims of entitlement to a public education. Ohio [law] direct[s] local authorities to provide a free education to all residents between five and 21 years of age, and a compulsory-attendance law requires attendance for a school year of not less than 32 weeks. Having chosen to extend the right to an education to [youth] generally, . . . Ohio is constrained to recognize **a student's legitimate entitlement to a public education as a property interest which is protected by the Due Process Clause and which may not be taken away for misconduct without adherence to the minimum procedures required by that Clause.**

In Goss, the Court also recognized that a temporary suspension from school could be a deprivation of liberty.

"The Due Process Clause also forbids arbitrary deprivations of liberty. 'Where a person's good name, reputation, honor, or integrity is at stake because of what the government is doing to him,' the minimal requirements of the Clause must be satisfied. School authorities here suspended appellees from school for periods of up to 10 days based on charges of misconduct. If sustained and recorded, those charges could seriously damage the students' standing with their fellow pupils and their teachers as well as interfere with later opportunities for higher education and employment. It is apparent that the claimed right of the State to determine unilaterally and without process whether that misconduct has occurred . . . collides with the requirements of the Constitution.''

Determining whether one has been deprived of a protectible interest is the first step in determining if one has been denied due process. If it is decided a government law or action has caused or will cause a deprivation of a protectible interest, the second step is to determine whether the deprivation may occur consistently with the Constitution and if it may, how it may so occur. In other words, two inquiries must be made.

First, it must be determined whether there is an adequate reason for the deprivation. That is, the deprivation must be reasonable and fundamentally fair for it to be consistent with the due process clauses. The requirement that all government actions depriving individuals of protectible interests be fundamentally fair is known as the guarantee of **"substantive due process.''**

Second, if there is an adequate reason for the deprivation, it must be determined whether the process by which the deprivation occurs is fundamentally fair. The requirement that governments use fair procedures before permanently depriving individuals of a protectible interest and that all proceedings which may deprive one of a protectible interest be conducted fairly is known as the guarantee of **"procedural due process.''**

Substantive due process

The Supreme Court's early approach to substantive due process is typified by the case of *Lochner v. New York*, 198 U.S. 45 (1905). In *Lochner*, the Court struck down a statute which made it unlawful for an employee to work more than a 60 hour week as an unconstitutional interference with the ''freedom of the master and employee to contract with each other in relation to their employment.''

The *Lochner* approach was repudiated in the 1930's. The Court's new approach was almost the opposite of the old. Under the new approach, no law was to be struck down as a denial of due process unless the law was manifestly arbitrary and capricious. That is, no law could be invalidated on substantive due process grounds if there was any rational basis for its enactment.

This approach to substantive due process was, in turn, partially repudiated in the 1960's when the Court decided that laws which infringed fundamental rights, even those not explicitly guaranteed by the Constitution, should be invalidated as violations of due process unless they served a substantial state interest. *Griswold v. Connecticut*, 381 U.S. 479 (1965), was the forerunner of this new approach to substantive due process. In *Griswold*, a doctor and the head of the Connecticut Planned Parenthood League were arrested because they gave birth control advice to married persons in violation of a Connecticut law which made using, giving information on, or providing contraceptive devices a crime. The Court decided that the Connecticut law intruded unnecessarily upon the right of marital privacy without substantial justification and held that the law, and thus the arrests, were invalid as a violation of due process. The Court stated:

"We do not sit as a super-legislature to determine the wisdom, need, and propriety of laws that touch economic problems, business affairs, or social conditions. This law, however, operates directly on an intimate relation of husband and wife and their physician's role in one aspect of that relation.

"[Our previous] cases suggest that specific guarantees in the Bill of Rights have penumbras, formed by emanations from those guarantees that help give them life and substance. Various guarantees create zones of privacy. The present case . . . concerns a relationship lying within the zone of privacy created by several fundamental constitutional guarantees. And it concerns a law which, in forbidding the use of contraceptives rather than regulating their manufacture or sale, seeks to achieve its goals by means having a maximum destructive impact upon that relationship. Such a law cannot stand . . ."

Moore v. City of East Cleveland, 431 U.S. 494 (1977), typifies the present approach to substantive due process. An East Cleveland housing ordinance limited occupancy of a single dwelling unit to members of a single family. Mrs. Moore, who lived in her East Cleveland home with her son, his son and another grandson who came to live with his grandmother, uncle and cousin after his mother's death, was convicted of violating the ordinance because her family was not a nuclear family within the narrow definition of "family" in the ordinance. In reversing her conviction, the Court stated:

"East Cleveland . . . has chosen to regulate the occupancy of its housing by slicing deeply into the family itself. This is no mere incidental result of the ordinance. On its face it selects certain categories of relatives who may live together and declares that others may not. In particular, it makes a crime of a grandmother's choice to live with her grandson in circumstances like those presented here.

"When a city undertakes such intrusive regulation of the family, . . . the usual judicial deference to the legislature is inappro-

priate.' This Court has long recognized that freedom of personal choice in matters of marriage and family life is one of the liberties protected by the Due Process Clause of the Fourteenth Amendment. A host of cases have consistently acknowledged a 'private realm of family life which the state cannot enter.' Of course, the family is not beyond regulation. But when the government intrudes on choices concerning family living arrangements, this Court must examine carefully the importance of the governmental interests advanced and the extent to which they are served by the challenged regulation.

"[This Court has stated:]

'Due process has not been reduced to any formula; its content cannot be determined by reference to any code. The best that can be said is that through the course of this Court's decisions it has represented the balance which our Nation, built upon postulates of respect for the liberty of the individual, has struck between that liberty and the demands of organized society. * * * No formula could serve as a substitute, in this area, for judgment and restraint.

'. . . [T]he full scope of the liberty guaranteed by the Due Process Clause cannot be found in or limited by the precise terms of the specific guarantees elsewhere provided in the Constitution. This "liberty" is not a series of isolated points pricked out in terms of * * * the freedom of speech, press, and religion; the right to keep and bear arms; * * * and so on. It is a rational continuum which, broadly speaking, includes a freedom from all substantial arbitrary impositions and purposeless restraints, . . . and which also recognizes, what a reasonable and sensitive judgment must, that certain interests require particularly careful scrutiny of the state needs asserted to justify their abridgment.'

"Substantive due process has at times been a treacherous field for this Court. There are risks when the judicial branch gives enhanced protection to certain substantive liberties without the guidance of the more specific provisions of the Bill of Rights. As the history of the era [when this Court freely invalidated laws in the name of substantive due process] demonstrates, there is reason for concern lest the only limits to such judicial intervention become the predilections of those who happen at the time to be Members of this Court. That history counsels caution and restraint. But it does not counsel abandonment, nor does it require what the city urges here: cutting off any protection of family rights at the first convenient, if arbitrary boundary—the boundary of the nuclear family.

"Appropriate limits on substantive due process come not from drawing arbitrary lines but rather from careful 'respect for the teachings of history [and], solid recognition of the basic values that underlie our society.' Our decisions establish that the Constitution protects the sanctity of the family precisely because the institution of the family is deeply rooted in this Nation's history and tradition. It is through the family that we inculcate and pass down many of our most cherished values, moral and cultural.

"Ours is by no means a tradition limited to respect for the bonds uniting the members of the nuclear family. The tradition of uncles, aunts, cousins, and especially grandparents sharing a household along with parents and children has roots equally venerable and equally deserving of constitutional recognition. Over the years millions of our citizens have grown up in just such an environment, and most, surely, have profited from it. Even if conditions of modern society have brought about a decline in extended family households, they have not erased the accumulated wisdom of civilization, gained over the centuries and honored throughout our history, that supports a larger conception of the family. Out of choice, necessity, or a sense of family responsibility, it has been common for close relatives to draw together and participate in the duties and the satisfactions of

a common home. Especially in times of adversity, such as the death of a spouse or economic need, the broader family has tended to come together for mutual sustenance and to maintain or rebuild a secure home life. This is apparently what happened here.

"Whether or not such a household is established because of personal tragedy, the choice of relatives in this degree of kinship to live together may not lightly be denied by the State. [T]he Constitution prevents East Cleveland from standardizing its children—and its adults—by forcing all to live in certain narrowly defined family patterns."

Procedural due process

In order to pass constitutional muster, a government action which may deprive someone of life, liberty or property not only must be fair, it also must be undertaken in a way that is fair. For example, even if the Supreme Court decided in *Moore* that the zoning ordinance was fair in its substance, the Court might not have upheld the ordinance's constitutionality if the ordinance permitted the police to go into peoples' homes and forcibly evict the illegal occupants without any sort of notice or hearing or if the ordinance authorized the jailing of violators without any sort of trial.

As with substantive due process, to determine if a government law or action which is challenged on procedural due process grounds is constitutional, a court must first determine if the government action deprives the challenger of a protectible interest. The due process guarantee will not apply if the action does not cause such a deprivation. If it is determined that the action causes such a deprivation, the court must then determine what procedures should be followed by the government in order to carry out its action. In other words, as was stated by the Supreme Court in *Morrisey v. Brewer*, 408 U.S. 471 (1972): "Once it is determined that due process applies, the question remains what process is due." This question is resolved through a balancing process.

The seriousness of a deprivation is not relevant in determining whether the due process clause applies. As was stated in *Goss v. Lopez, supra*, 419 U.S. 565:

"in determining 'whether due process requirements apply in the first place, we must look not to the "weight" but to the nature of the interest at stake.' The Court's view has been that as long as a property deprivation is not *de minimis* [that is, so minor as to be insignificant], its gravity is irrelevant to the question whether account must be taken of the Due Process Clause."

But the seriousness of a deprivation and the importance of a protectible interest may be crucial in determining what process is due. They are factors to be balanced with the government's interest in an inexpensive and speedy process. As was also stated in *Goss*, which, as you should recall, considered the constitutionality of a 10 day suspension from school without a hearing:

"[T]he length and consequent severity of a deprivation . . . [is a] factor to weigh in determining the appropriate form of hearing, [although it] 'is not decisive of the basic right' to a hearing of some kind.

"[T]he interpretation and application of the Due Process Clause are intensely practical matters and . . . '[t]he very nature of due process negates any concept of inflexible procedures universally applicable to every imaginable situation.' There are certain bench marks to guide us, however. [We have said that] '[m]any controversies have raged about the cryptic and abstract words of the Due Process Clause but there can be no doubt that at a minimum they require that deprivation of life, liberty or property by adjudication be preceded by **notice and opportunity for hearing appropriate to the nature of the case.**' It also appears from our cases that the timing and content of the notice and the nature of the hearing will depend on appropriate accommodation of the competing interests involved.''

In determining what process is due, that is, in balancing the competing interests, it must be determined whether any required procedures must occur before any deprivation or whether it is sufficient if they occur after a temporary deprivation but before a permanent deprivation. *Goldberg v. Kelly*, 397 U.S. 254 (1970), which dealt with the termination of welfare benefits, specifically AFDC and Home Relief, is an important case addressing this question. It also addresses the question of the nature of the hearing to be afforded.

"The extent to which procedural due process must be afforded the recipient [of welfare benefits] is influenced by the extent to which he may be 'condemned to suffer grievous loss,' and depends upon whether the recipient's interest in avoiding that loss outweighs the governmental interest in summary adjudication. Accordingly, as we [have] said . . . 'consideration of what procedures due process may require under any given set of circumstances must begin with a determination of the precise nature of the government function involved as well as of the private interest that has been affected by governmental action.'

"It is true, of course, that some governmental benefits may be administratively terminated without affording the recipient a pretermination evidentiary hearing. But . . . **when welfare is discontinued, only a pretermination evidentiary hearing provides the recipient with procedural due process.**

For qualified recipients, welfare provides the means to obtain essential food, clothing, housing, and medical care. Thus the crucial factor in this context—a factor not present in the case of the blacklisted government contractor, the discharged government employee, the taxpayer denied a tax exemption, or virtually anyone else whose governmental entitlements are ended—is that termination of aid pending resolution of a controversy over eligibility may deprive an eligible recipient of the very means by which to live while he waits. Since he lacks independent resources, his situation becomes immediately desperate. His need to concentrate upon finding the means for daily subsistence, in turn, adversely affects his ability to seek redress from the welfare bureaucracy.

"Moreover, important governmental interests are promoted by affording recipients a pre-termination evidentiary hearing. From its founding the Nation's basic commitment has been to foster the dignity and well-being of all persons within its borders. We have come to recognize that forces not within the control of the poor contribute to their poverty. This perception, against the background of our traditions, has significantly influenced the development of the contemporary public assistance system. Welfare, by meeting the basic demands of subsistence, can help bring within the reach of the poor the same opportunities that are available to others to participate meaningfully in the life of the community. At the same time, welfare guards against the societal malaise that may flow from a widespread sense of unjustified frustration and insecurity. Public assistance, then, is not mere charity, but a means to 'promote the general Welfare, and secure the Blessings of Liberty to ourselves and our Posterity.' The same governmental interests that counsel the provision of welfare, counsel as well its uninterrupted provision to those eligible to receive it; pre-termination evidentiary hearings are indispensable to that end.

"[T]he interest of the eligible recipient in uninterrupted receipt of public assistance, coupled with the State's interest that his payments not be erroneously terminated, clearly outweighs the State's competing concern to prevent any increase in its fiscal and administrative burdens. As [has been said] '[t]he stakes are simply too high for the welfare recipient, and the possibility for honest error or irritable misjudgment too great, to allow termination of aid without giving the recipient a chance, if he so desires, to be fully informed of the case against him so that he may contest its basis and produce evidence in rebuttal.'

"[H]owever, . . . **the pre-termination hearing need not take the form of a judicial or quasi-judicial trial.** [T]he pre-termination hearing has one function only: to produce an initial determination of the validity of the welfare department's grounds for discontinuance of payments in order to protect a recipient against an erroneous termination of his benefits. Thus, a complete record and a comprehensive opinion, which would serve primarily to facilitate judicial review and to guide future decisions, need not be provided at the pre-termination stage. We recognize, too, that both welfare authorities and recipients have an interest in relatively speedy resolution of questions of eligibility, that they are used to dealing with one another informally, and that some welfare departments have very burdensome caseloads. These considerations justify the limitation of the pre-termination hearing to minimum procedural safeguards, adapted to the particular characteristics of welfare recipients, and to the limited nature of the controversies to be resolved.

" 'The fundamental requisite of due process of law is the opportunity to be heard.' The hearing must be 'at a meaningful time and in a meaningful manner.' In the present context these principles require that a recipient have timely and adequate notice detailing the reasons for a proposed termination, and an effective opportunity to defend by** confronting any adverse witnesses and by presenting his own arguments and evidence orally.

"The opportunity to be heard must be tailored to the capacities and circumstances of those who are to be heard. It is not enough that a welfare recipient may present his position to the decision maker in writing or second-hand through his caseworker. Written submissions are an unrealistic option for most recipients, who lack the educational attainment necessary to write effectively and who cannot obtain professional assistance. Moreover, written submissions do not afford the flexibility of oral presentations; they do not permit the recipient to mold his argument to the issues the decision maker appears to regard as important. Particularly where credibility and veracity are at issue, as they must be in many termination proceedings, written submissions are a wholly unsatisfactory basis for decision. Therefore a recipient must be allowed to state his position orally. Informal procedures will suffice; in this context due process does not require a particular order of proof or mode of offering evidence.

"In almost every setting where important decisions turn on questions of fact, due process requires an opportunity to confront and cross-examine adverse witnesses. [As we have said:]

'Certain principles have remained relatively immutable in our jurisprudence. One of these is that where governmental action seriously injures an individual, and the reasonableness of the action depends on fact findings, the evidence used to prove the Government's case must be disclosed to the individual so that he has an opportunity to show that it is untrue. While this is important in the case of documentary evidence, it is even more important where the evidence consists of the testimony of individuals whose memory might be faulty or who, in fact, might be perjurers or persons motivated by malice,

vindictiveness, intolerance, prejudice, or jealousy. * * * '

"Welfare recipients must therefore be given an opportunity to confront and cross-examine the witnesses relied on by the department.

" 'The right to be heard would be, in many cases, of little avail if it did not comprehend the right to be heard by counsel.' We do not say that counsel must be provided at the pre-termination hearing, but only that the recipient must be allowed to retain an attorney if he so desires. Counsel can help delineate the issues, present the factual contentions in an orderly manner, conduct cross-examination, and generally safeguard the interests of the recipient. We do not anticipate that this assistance will unduly prolong or otherwise encumber the hearing.

"Finally, the decision maker's conclusion as to a recipient's eligibility must rest solely on the legal rules and evidence adduced at the hearing. To demonstrate compliance with this elementary requirement, the decision maker should state the reasons for his determination and indicate the evidence he relied on, though his statement need not amount to a full opinion or even formal findings of fact and conclusions of law. And, of course, an impartial decision maker is essential. [P]rior involvement in some aspects of a case will not necessarily bar a welfare official from acting as a decision maker. He should not, however, have participated in making the determination under review."

Because a termination of welfare differs from a short school suspension, both in its seriousness and its nature, far fewer procedural protections must be afforded to students under the due process clauses. In *Goss v. Lopez*, the Court stated:

"At the very minimum, . . . students facing suspension and the consequent interference with a protected property interest must be given some kind of notice and afforded some kind of hearing. We do not believe that school authorities must be totally free from notice and hearing requirements if their schools are to operate with acceptable efficiency. Students facing temporary suspension have interests qualifying for protection of the Due Process Clause, and **due process requires, in connection with a suspension of 10 days or less, that the student be given oral or written notice of the charges against him and, if he denies them, an explanation of the evidence the authorities have and an opportunity to present his side of the story.**

"We stop short of construing the Due Process Clause to require, countrywide, that hearings in connection with short suspensions must afford the student the opportunity to secure counsel, to confront and cross-examine witnesses supporting the charge, or to call his own witnesses to verify his version of the incident. Brief disciplinary suspensions are almost countless. To impose in each such case even truncated trial-type procedures might well overwhelm administrative facilities in many places and, by diverting resources, cost more than it would save in educational effectiveness.

"We should also make it clear that we have addressed ourselves solely to the short suspension, not exceeding 10 days. Longer suspensions or expulsions for the remainder of the school term, or permanently, may require more formal procedures. Nor do we put aside the possibility that in unusual situations, although involving only a short suspension, something more than the rudimentary procedures will be required."

In *Mathews v. Eldridge*, 424 U.S. 319 (1976), the Supreme Court determined that an evidentiary hearing was not required before the termination of Social Security disability payments. The difference between the types of financial assistance programs in-

volved in *Mathews* and *Goldberg v. Kelly* dictated the difference in the due process requirement. The Court stated:

"[I]n *Goldberg* . . . the Court held that due process requires an evidentiary hearing prior to a temporary deprivation. It was emphasized there that welfare assistance is given to persons on the very margin of subsistence . . . Eligibility for disability benefits, in contrast, is not based upon financial need. Indeed, it is wholly unrelated to the worker's income or support from many other sources, such as earnings of other family members, workmen's compensation awards, tort claims awards, savings, private insurance, public or private pensions, veterans' benefits, food stamps, public assistance, or the 'many other important programs, both public and private, which contain provisions for disability payments affecting a substantial portion of the work force . . . .'

"[Typically, it takes more than a year from the time of the cut off of Social Security disability benefits to a decision after an evidentiary hearing.] In view of the torpidity of [the] administrative review process, and the typically modest resources of the family unit of the physically disabled worker, the hardship imposed upon the erroneously terminated disability recipient may be significant. Still, the disabled worker's need is likely to be less than that of a welfare recipient. In addition to the possibility of access to private resources, other forms of government assistance will become available where the termination of disability benefits places a worker or his family below the subsistence level. In view of these potential sources of temporary income, there is less reason here than in *Goldberg* to depart from the ordinary principle, established by our decisions, that something less than an evidentiary hearing is sufficient prior to adverse administrative action."

Many feel that, in *Mathews*, the Court expressed a new attitude towards the imposition of due process safeguards in social welfare programs. Whether or not *Mathews* represents a retreat from the Court's previous support for such safeguards, *Mathews* is of great importance because it enunciated the balancing test to be used by courts in determining what process is due to individuals deprived of life, liberty or property. That test, which we will see used in many due process cases in later chapters, was expressed in the following language in *Mathews*.

''[Our] decisions underscore the truism that ' ''[d]ue process,'' unlike some legal rules, is not a technical conception with a fixed content unrelated to time, place and circumstances.' '[D]ue process is flexible and calls for such procedural protections as the particular situation demands.' Accordingly, resolution of the issue whether . . . procedures . . . are constitutionally sufficient requires analysis of the governmental and private interests that are affected. More precisely, our prior decisions indicate that **identification of the specific dictates of due process generally requires consideration of three distinct factors: First, the private interest that will be affected by the official action; second, the risk of an erroneous deprivation of such interest through the procedures used, and the probable value, if any, of additional or substitute procedural safeguards; and finally, the government's interest, including the function involved and the fiscal and administrative burdens that the additional or substitute procedural requirement would entail.**

''Financial cost alone is not a controlling weight in determining whether due process requires a particular procedural safeguard prior to some administrative decision. But the government's interest, and hence that of the public, in conserving scarce fiscal and administrative resources is a factor that must be weighed. At some point the benefit of an additional safeguard to the individual affected by the administrative action and to society in terms of increased assurance that the action is just, may be outweighed by the cost.

''But more is implicated in [procedural due process] cases than *ad hoc* weighing of fiscal and administrative burdens against the interests of a particular category of claimants. The ultimate balance involves a determination as to when, under our constitutional system, judicial-type procedures must be imposed . . . to assure fairness. The judicial model of an evidentiary hearing is neither a required, nor even the most effective, method of decisionmaking in all circumstances. The essence of due process is the requirement that 'a person in jeopardy of serious loss [be given] notice of the case against him and opportunity to meet it.' All that is necessary is that the procedures be tailored, in light of the decision to be made, to 'the capacities and circumstances of those who are to be heard,' to insure that they are given a meaningful opportunity to present their case.''

THE LEAST RESTRICTIVE ALTERNATIVE

One guiding principle in constitutional interpretation is the notion that whenever the government does something which may impact or restrict the exercise of a constitutional right, it should act in the least intrusive manner possible. This is known as the principle of the ''**least restrictive alternative**.''

No right, even a basic constitutional right like freedom of speech, is absolute. The government may restrict the exercise of a right in certain situations, such as where speech may pose a clear and present danger of violence. But the government should only restrict the exercise of a basic right in the least restrictive manner possible. Put another way, the government should only use the least drastic means to accomplish its purpose. If there are less restrictive alternatives or less drastic means available, government action impacting a basic right or restricting the exercise of a fundamental right must be declared unconstitutional. Thus, in *Shelton v. Tucker*, 364 U.S. 479 (1960), the court held unconstitutional an Arkansas statute requiring teachers to reveal all organizations with which they were or had been affiliated as a means of assessing their fitness and competence to teach. The Court stated:

> "In a series of decisions this Court has held that, even though the governmental purpose be legitimate and substantial, that purpose cannot be pursued by means that broadly stifle fundamental personal liberties when the end can be more narrowly achieved. The breadth of legislative abridgment must be viewed in the light of less drastic means for achieving the same purpose.

> "The unlimited and indiscriminate sweep of the statute now before us brings it within the ban of our prior cases. The statute's comprehensive interference with associational freedom goes far beyond what might be justified in the exercise of the State's legitimate inquiry into the fitness and competence of its teachers."

Closely related to the principle of the least restrictive alternative is the concept of **overbreadth**. Any law restricting the exercise of a basic right must be narrowly drawn to address only a specific problem. "Precision of regulation must be the touchstone in an area . . . closely touching our most precious freedoms." *NAACP v. Button*, 371 U.S. 415 (1963). If a law impacting on fundamental rights sweeps too broadly, it must be declared unconstitutional as overbroad. Thus, in *Dunn v. Blumstein*, 405 U.S. 330 (1972), the Supreme Court invalidated as overbroad a requirement that one must have resided in a State for one year before one could vote, stating:

> "It is not enough for the State to show that du-

rational residence requirements further a very substantial state interest. In pursuing that important interest, the State cannot chose means that unnecessarily burden or restrict constitutionally protected activity. Statutes affecting constitutional rights must be drawn with 'precision,' and must be 'tailored' to serve their legitimate objectives. And if there are other reasonable ways to achieve those goals with a lesser burden on constitutionally protected activity, a State may not choose the way of greater interference. If it acts at all, it must choose 'less drastic means.' "

Also closely related to the principle of the least restrictive alternative is the concept of **vagueness**. When laws impacting on or restricting the exercise of constitutional rights are vague and unclear, there is a real danger that government officials will interpret them in a way that is overbroad and thus violate the principle of the least restrictive alternative. Vague laws are dangerous, moreover, because they permit the unbridled exercise of official discretion.

Vague laws which do not impact on or restrict the exercise of a constitutional right may also be struck down as a violation of due process in that they deprive people of notice of what is expected of them and the ability to conform their conduct to the requirements of the law. Thus, in *People v. Beruman*, 638 P.2d 789 (Colo. 1982), a case involving a child welfare worker who was convicted of the crime of "official misconduct" for failing to respond to a report of suspected child abuse, the Colorado Supreme Court declared a portion of the law establishing the crime of official misconduct unconstitutionally vague. The Court stated:

> "A statute is unconstitutionally vague if persons of common intelligence must guess at its meaning. Penal statutes and regulations must be clearly understandable and reasonably specific so that the defendant may be sufficiently apprised of the crime with which he stands

charged. This affords the defendant due process notice . . . Fundamental fairness requires that no lesser standard be applied.

"The language used to describe the proscribed conduct [in the statute in question here]— 'refrains from performing a duty . . . clearly inherent in the nature of his office'—provides no readily ascertainable standards by which one's conduct may be measured. The legislature has failed to define that phrase, and it is totally without parameters for the determination of guilt or innocence, thus allowing the exercise of unbridled discretion by the police, judge, and jury. The vagueness present in the statutory language impermissibly infringes the constitutional safeguard of fundamental fairness and due process, and creates a danger of arbitrary enforcement."

The principle of the least restrictive alternative and the concepts of overbreadth and vagueness arise most often in the context of 1st Amendment freedoms, but, as we shall see, and as can be seen from *Beruman*, they also arise in many contexts of importance to social workers. For example, removing a child from her home because of parental neglect may violate the principle of the least restrictive alternative, there may be less drastic means than a guardianship to address the problem posed by a frail elderly person, a statute setting forth who may be involuntarily committed for treatment may be overbroad, and a statute defining domestic abuse may be vague.

SOCIAL WELFARE LEGISLATION AND THE CONSTITUTION

Article I, Section 8 of the Constitution gives the federal government the power to "provide for the general welfare." Until well into the twentieth century, however, the courts narrowly construed this power, ruling

repeatedly that the federal government had no power to enact **social welfare legislation**, that is, legislation protecting workers, children or others in need of government protection or creating social welfare programs providing financial assistance or services to the sick, the poor, the disabled, the old or others in need of government help.

There was never any question that the powers reserved to the States by the 10th Amendment to the Constitution included the power to enact social welfare legislation, but most States had little inclination to do so. Moreover, also until well into the twentieth century, the courts' approach to substantive due process led them to declare most social welfare legislation that was enacted by the States unconstitutional on the ground that such legislation impermissibly interfered with basic freedoms, like the freedom to contract.

The massive upheaval caused by the Depression forced a change both in the courts' response towards social welfare legislation and in the conservative attitudes of Congress and the States towards such legislation. State legislatures began enacting laws creating social welfare programs or otherwise fostering social welfare and the courts began accepting the laws as constitutional. In 1935, Congress enacted the Social Security Act, 42 U.S.C. § 301 *et seq.*, which created several financial assistance programs for the elderly, the poor and the unemployed, and in 1937, in *Helvering v. Davis*, 301 U.S. 619 (1937), the Supreme Court ruled that the Act was constitutional and that Congress had the power to enact it. The Social Security Act and *Helvering* signaled a new approach to social welfare legislation.

At the present time, no one would question the power of the federal government and the States to enact social welfare legislation. And, rather than invalidating social welfare programs as unconstitutional denials of due process, as we have seen in *Goldberg v. Kelly*, the courts may act to ensure that the programs operate in such a way as to provide due process. The courts are reluctant to intervene in the administrative process and tell social welfare administrators how they should operate their programs. Where obvious violations of due process occur, however, the courts will act—but only with circumspection. Thus, while the Court mandated evidentiary hearings prior to the termination of certain welfare benefits in *Goldberg*, it gave administrators flexibility, beyond some rudimentary requirements, as to the nature of the hearings. And in *Mathews v. Eldridge, supra*, the Court would not mandate evidentiary hearings prior to the termination of social security disability, noting:

"In assessing what process is due in this case, substantial weight must be given to the good-faith judgments of the individuals charged by Congress with the administration of social welfare programs that the procedures they have provided assure fair consideration of the entitlement claims of individuals."

The courts may also act when social welfare legislation interferes with other constitutional protections, such as the guarantee of equal protection, but, again, the courts will not readily intervene in the administration of social welfare programs and if they must intervene, they will not second-guess administrators or attempt to take over the administration of social welfare programs. As was stated in *Dandridge v. Williams*, 397 U.S. 471 (1970), in which the Court upheld a discriminatory provision in the Maryland AFDC program:

"We do not decide today that the Maryland regulation is wise, that it best fulfills the relevant social and economic objectives that Maryland might ideally espouse, or that a more just and humane system could not be devised. Conflicting claims of morality and intelligence are raised by opponents and proponents of almost every measure, certainly including the one before us. But the intractable economic, social, and even philosophical problems presented by public welfare assistance programs are not the business of this Court. The Constitution may impose certain procedural safeguards upon systems of welfare administration. But the Constitution does not empower this Court to second-guess state officials charged with the difficult responsibility of allocating limited public welfare funds among the myriad of potential recipients."

EQUAL PROTECTION OF THE LAWS

The equal protection clause of the 14th Amendment guarantees all persons equality under the law, but the guarantee is not considered absolute. Despite the clause's unqualified language, the courts have not required the States or the federal government to treat all persons exactly alike. Rather, they have held that governments may recognize and act upon certain differences that exist between classes of individuals without violating the guarantee of equal protection. Legislation which accords some people a benefit or which requires some people to bear a burden while other people, because of some factual difference in their situations, neither receive the benefit nor bear the burden, may be upheld as consistent with the equal protection clause. How can this be?

Legislation generally involves drawing distinctions. Governments continually draw distinctions which discriminate against certain people as part of their normal functioning. If all such distinctions were considered to be unconstitutional violations of the equal protection guarantee, governments would be virtually paralyzed.

The right to legislate implies the right to classify. But classification, by its very nature, gives some classes of people special burdens or benefits not given to other classes. As stated in a classic study of equal protection, Tussman and ten Broek, *The Equal Protection of the Laws*, 37 Cal. L. Rev. 341 (1949):

> "Here, then, is a paradox: The equal protection of the laws is a 'pledge of the protection of equal laws.' But laws may classify. And 'the very idea of classification is that of inequality.' In tackling this paradox the [Supreme] Court has neither abandoned the demand for equality nor denied the legislative right to classify. It has taken a middle course. It has resolved the contradictory demands of legislative specialization and constitutional generality by a doctrine of **reasonable classification**." (emphasis added.)

In accordance with the doctrine of reasonable classification, classifications made by governments are presumed to be constitutional. Even if a distinction drawn by a government causes it to discriminate among classes of people, the distinction will not be considered an unconstitutional denial of equal protection unless the distinction is unreasonable or, to use the courts' terms, is "without any rational basis," or is "wholly arbitrary and capricious." If a government has a reason to discriminate among its people and if those who are discriminated against fall into reasonably drawn categories, based on rational factual circumstances, the government will be permitted to discriminate, as *Dandridge v. Williams, supra*, 397 U.S. 471, illustrates. *Dandridge* involved a challenge to a Maryland law setting a maximum AFDC grant for a family regardless of its size. The

law discriminated against large families, which would receive less AFDC per member than smaller families. The Court stated:

> "In the area of economics and social welfare, a State does not violate the Equal Protection Clause merely because the classifications made by its laws are imperfect. If the classification has some 'reasonable basis,' it does not offend the Constitution simply because the classification 'is not made with mathematical nicety or because in practice it results in some inequality.' 'The problems of government are practical ones and may justify, if they do not require, rough accommodations—illogical, it may be, and unscientific.' 'A statutory discrimination will not be set aside if any state of facts reasonably may be conceived to justify it.'

> "Under [the] long-established meaning of the Equal Protection Clause, it is clear that the Maryland maximum grant regulation is constitutionally valid. [A] solid foundation for the regulation can be found in the State's legitimate interest in encouraging employment and in avoiding discrimination between welfare families and the families of the working poor. By combining a limit on the recipient's grant with permission to retain money earned, without reduction in the amount of the grant, Maryland provides an incentive to seek gainful employment. And by keying the maximum family AFDC grants to the minimum wage a steadily employed head of a household receives, the State maintains some semblance of an equitable balance between families on welfare and those supported by an employed breadwinner. It is true that in some AFDC families there may be no person who is employable. . . . [and that in small AFDC families which receive grants equal to their needs] the employment incentive is absent. But **the Equal Protection Clause does not require that a State must choose between attacking every aspect of a problem or not attacking the problem at all. It is enough that the State's action be rationally based and free from in-**

vidious discrimination. The regulation before us meets that test.''

The doctrine of reasonable classification, enunciated in *Dandridge*, has its limits. All classifications made by governments are not upheld by the courts just because they are reasonable and all distinctions drawn by governments which have a rational basis are not considered consistent with the equal protection clause. Certain classifications are considered **suspect**. These classifications must meet a higher standard than mere reasonableness to pass constitutional muster. And certain distinctions may affect the exercise of **fundamental rights**. The courts will require more than mere reasonableness before these distinctions can be sustained.

For many years, the Supreme Court used a two-tier test when it was determining if a legislative classification violated the equal protection clause. Classifications which were considered inherently suspect or which impinged on the exercise of basic or fundamental rights were subjected to **strict judicial scrutiny**; such classifications could pass constitutional muster only if they served compelling state interests. All other classifications were simply required to be reasonable; they would be sustained if they had any rational basis. In other words, depending on the nature of the classification or on its effect, its constitutionality would be tested using either strict judicial scrutiny or the doctrine of reasonable classification.

San Antonio School District v. Rodriguez, 411 U.S. 1 (1973), illustrates the Court's use of the two-tier test. In *San Antonio*, members of poor families, who lived in school districts with many poor people and thus low property tax bases, challenged Texas' reliance on local property taxes to finance public schools. They claimed that such reliance denied them equal protection in that the public schools in their districts had less money and were thus inferior to public schools in districts with richer residents. The Supreme Court stated, however, that no suspect classification was established and that education was not a fundamental right and, thus, concluded:

"[T]his is not a case in which the challenged state action must be subjected to the searching judicial scrutiny reserved for laws that create suspect classifications or impinge upon constitutionally protected rights. A century of Supreme Court adjudication under the Equal Protection Clause affirmatively supports the application of the traditional standard of review, which requires only that the State's system be shown to bear some rational relationship to legitimate state purposes . . .

Finding that the Texas system of school finance "reflects what many educators for a half century have thought was an enlightened approach to a problem for which there is no perfect solution" and being "unwilling to assume for ourselves a level of wisdom superior to that of legislators, scholars, and educational authorities in 50 States, especially where the alternatives proposed are only recently conceived and nowhere yet tested," the court concluded that the system "rationally furthers a legitimate state purpose or interest," and upheld it as constitutional.

In a concurring opinion, Justice Stewart noted:

"Unlike other provisions of the Constitution, the Equal Protection Clause confers no substantive rights and creates no substantive liberties. The function of the Equal Protection Clause, rather, is simply to measure the validity of classifications created by state laws. There is hardly a law on the books that does not affect some people differently from others. But the basic concern of the Equal Protection Clause is with state legislation whose purpose or effect is to create discrete and objectively identifiable classes. And with respect to such legislation, it has long been settled that the Equal Protection Clause is offended only by laws that are invidiously discriminatory—only by classifications that are wholly arbitrary or capricious. This settled principle of constitutional law was compendiously stated . . . in the following words:

'Although no precise formula has been developed, the Court has held that the Fourteenth Amendment permits the States a wide scope of discretion in enacting laws which affect some groups of citizens differently than others. The constitutional safeguard is offended only if the classification rests on grounds wholly irrelevant to the achievement of the State's objective. State legislatures are presumed to have acted within their constitutional power despite the fact that, in practice, their laws result in some inequality. A statutory discrimination will not be set aside if any state of facts reasonably may be conceived to justify it.'

"This doctrine is no more than a specific application of one of the first principles of constitutional adjudication—the basic presumption of the constitutional validity of a duly enacted state or federal law. Under the Equal Protection Clause, this presumption of constitutional validity disappears when a State has enacted legislation whose purpose or effect is to create classes based upon criteria that, in a constitutional sense, are inherently 'suspect.' Because of the historic purpose of the Fourteenth Amendment, the prime example of such a 'suspect' classification is one that is based upon race. But there are other classifications that, at least in some settings, are also 'suspect'—for example, those based upon national origin, alienage, indigency, or illegitimacy.

"Moreover, quite apart from the Equal Protection Clause, a state law that impinges upon a substantive right or liberty created or conferred by the Constitution is, of course,

presumptively invalid, whether or not the law's purpose or effect is to create any classifications. For example, a law that provided that newspapers could be published only by people who had resided in the State for five years could be superficially viewed as invidiously discriminating against an identifiable class in violation of the Equal Protection Clause. But, more basically, such a law would be invalid simply because it abridged the freedom of the press. Numerous cases in this Court illustrate this principle.

"In refusing to invalidate the Texas system of financing its public schools, the Court today applies with thoughtfulness and understanding the basic principles I have so sketchily summarized."

In a dissenting opinion, Justice Marshall urged the Court to abandon the two-tier test and adopt a balancing test akin to the test used in substantive due process cases. He stated:

". . . I must once more voice my disagreement with the Court's rigidified approach to equal protection analysis. The Court apparently seeks to establish today that equal protection cases fall into one of two neat categories which dictate the appropriate standard of review—strict scrutiny or mere rationality. But this Court's decisions in the field of equal protection defy such easy categorization. [It would be far better to adopt the] . . . sort of reasoned approach to equal protection analysis for which I previously argued—that is, an approach in which 'concentration [is] placed upon the character of the classification in question, the relative importance to individuals in the class discriminated against of the governmental benefits that they do not receive, and the asserted state interests in support of the classification.'

"The majority suggests . . . that a variable standard of review would give this Court the appearance of a 'superlegislature.' I cannot agree. Such an approach seems to me a part of the guarantees of our Constitution and of the historic experiences with oppression of and discrimination against discrete, powerless minorities which underlie that document.''

The Supreme Court has never adopted a balancing test for equal protection cases, as Justice Marshall urged in *San Antonio* and other cases, but, in *Plyler v. Doe*, 457 U.S. 202 (1982), the Court did recognize a new category of classifications, those which were **quasi-suspect**. Such classifications would be subjected to **intermediate scrutiny** and would be sustained only if they served substantial state interests. In addition, in *Plyler*, the court implied that intermediate scrutiny should be used when considering discriminations which impinged important, although not fundamental or constitutional, interests, like education. In effect, *Plyler*, which dealt with the exclusion of illegal alien children from public schools enunciated a three-tier test. The Court stated:

> ''The Equal Protection Clause directs that 'all persons similarly circumstanced shall be treated alike.' But so too, '[t]he Constitution does not require things which are different in fact or opinion to be treated in law as though they were the same.' The initial discretion to determine what is 'different' and what is 'the same' resides in the legislatures of the States. A legislature must have substantial latitude to establish classifications that roughly approximate the nature of the problem perceived, that accommodate competing concerns both public and private, and that account for limitations on the practical ability of the State to remedy every ill. In applying the Equal Protection Clause to most forms of state action, we thus seek only the assurance that the classification at issue bears some fair relationship to a legitimate public purpose.

> ''But we would not be faithful to our obligations under the Fourteenth Amendment if we applied so deferential a standard to every classification. The Equal Protection Clause was intended as a restriction on state legislative action inconsistent with elemental constitutional premises. Thus we have treated as presumptively invidious those classifications that disadvantage a 'suspect class,' or that impinge upon the exercise of a 'fundamental right.' With respect to such classifications, it is appropriate to enforce the mandate of equal protection by requiring the State to demonstrate that its classification has been precisely tailored to serve a compelling governmental interest. In addition, we have recognized that certain forms of legislative classification, while not facially invidious, nonetheless give rise to recurring constitutional difficulties; in these limited circumstances we have sought the assurance that the classification reflects a reasoned judgment consistent with the ideal of equal protection by inquiring whether it may fairly be viewed as furthering a substantial interest of the State.''

It should now be obvious to you that in order to determine whether a law or government action violates the guarantee of equal protection, it is necessary, first, to determine whether the law or action discriminates against an inherently suspect or quasi-suspect class or impinges the exercise of a fundamental or important right. If an inherently suspect class or a fundamental right is involved, the law or action will be subjected to strict scrutiny. If a quasi-suspect or important right is involved, the law or action will be subjected to intermediate scrutiny. If the classification is not suspect and no fundamental or important right is involved, the law or action need only be rationally related to a legitimate government purpose.

Determining the test to be used is a crucial first step in equal protection analysis. In practice, virtually all classifications which have been subjected to strict judicial scrutiny (because they were considered inherently suspect or impinged on a right considered basic) have been declared unconstitutional while virtually all classifications required only to have a rational basis have been declared constitutional. It has been, in other words, all but impossible for a court to find a compelling state interest to justify an inherently suspect classification or a discrimination impinging on a fundamental right and it is highly unlikely a court would be unable to find a rational basis to justify a non-suspect classification or a discrimination which did not affect a basic right.

Because it is crucial that you know which test is to be used in an equal protection analysis, we shall now examine which classifications of importance to social workers have been considered inherently suspect, which quasi-suspect and which neither, and which rights have been considered fundamental or important.

Classifications

A footnote in *Plyler v. Doe, supra,* may help you understand which classifications are considered suspect. In the footnote, the Court stated:

"Several formulations might explain our treatment of certain classifications as 'suspect.' Some classifications are more likely than others to reflect deep-seated prejudice rather than legislative rationality in pursuit of some legitimate objective. Legislation predicated on such prejudice is easily recognized as incompatible with the constitutional understanding that each person is to be judged individually and is entitled to equal justice under the law. Classifications treated as suspect tend to be irrelevant to any proper legislative goal. Finally, certain groups, indeed largely the same groups, have historically been 'relegated to such a position of political powerlessness as to command extraordinary protection from the majoritarian political process.' The experience of our Nation has shown that prejudice may manifest itself in the treatment of some groups. Our response to that experience is reflected in the Equal Protection Clause of the Fourteenth Amendment. Legislation imposing special disabilities upon groups disfavored by virtue of circumstances beyond their control suggests the kind of 'class or caste' treatment that the Fourteenth Amendment was designed to abolish."

Race and national origin. Classifications based on race or national origin are considered inherently suspect and thus subject to strict judicial scrutiny. Such classifications may be upheld only if they are "shown to be necessary to the accomplishment of some permissible state objective, independent of the racial discrimination which it was the object of the Fourteenth Amendment to eliminate." *Loving v. Virginia*, 388 U.S. 1 (1967). The permissible state objective must, moreover, be compelling. This standard of review for classifications based on race or national origin is so stringent that the Supreme Court has only upheld one classification based on race or national origin, the internment of the Japanese during World War II. In a much criticized opinion, *Korematsu v. United States*, 323 U.S. 214 (1944), the Court held the internment was justified for compelling national security reasons.

Just because legislation or another form of state action has a disproportionate impact on certain racial groups, however, it may not be considered a violation of equal protection. Thus, in *Washington v. Davis*, 426 U.S. 229 (1976), the Court made clear that it did "not embrace the proposition that a law or other official act, without regard to whether it reflects a racially discriminatory purpose, is unconstitutional solely because it has a racially disproportionate impact." However, the Court also made clear that:

"This is not to say that the necessary discriminatory racial purpose must be express or appear on the face of the statute, or that a law's disproportionate impact is irrelevant in cases involving Constitution-based claims of racial discrimination. A statute, otherwise neutral on its face, must not be applied so as invidiously to discriminate on the basis of race. It is also clear from the cases dealing with racial discrimination in the selection of juries that the systematic exclusion of Negroes is itself such an 'unequal application of the law . . . as to show intentional discrimination.'

"Necessarily, an invidious discriminatory purpose may often be inferred from the totality of the relevant facts, including the fact, if it is true, that the law bears more heavily on one race than another. It is also not infrequently true that the discriminatory impact . . . may for all practical purposes demonstrate unconstitutionality because . . . the discrimination is very difficult to explain on nonracial grounds. Nevertheless, we have not held that a law, neutral on its face and serving ends otherwise within the power of government to pursue, is invalid under the Equal Protection Clause simply because it may affect a greater proportion of one race than of another. **Disproportionate impact is not irrelevant, but it is not the sole touchstone of an invidious racial discrimination forbidden by the Constitution. Standing alone, it does not trigger the rule that racial classifications are to be subjected to the strictest scrutiny and are justifiable only by the weightiest of considerations.**"

It should be noted that disproportionate impact may be enough to establish a case under **Title VII of the Civil Rights Act of 1964,** 42 U.S.C. § 2000e, which prohibits discrimination in employment by certain employers, and under other statutes prohibiting discrimination. As stated in *Washington v. Davis:*

"Under Title VII, Congress provided that when hiring and promotion practices disqualifying substantially disproportionate numbers of blacks are challenged, discriminatory purpose need not be proved, and that it is an insufficient response to demonstrate some rational basis for the challenged practices. It is necessary, in addition, that they be 'validated' in terms of job performance in any one of several ways, perhaps by ascertaining the minimum skill, ability, or potential necessary for the position at issue and determining whether the qualifying tests are appropriate for the selection of qualified applicants for the job in question. However this process proceeds, it involves a more probing judicial review of, and less deference to, the seemingly reasonable acts of administrators and executives than is appropriate under the Constitution where special racial impact, without discriminatory purpose, is claimed."

The Court has had a difficult time grappling with one problem in the area of discrimination on the basis of race or national origin: the constitutionality of affirmative action plans which discriminate in favor of members of minority groups who have been discriminated against in the past. As has been stated by a commentator:

"In *Regents of the University of California v. Bakke,* 438 U.S. 265 (1978), it took the Court six opinions covering 156 pages to reject the challenged affirmative action program while approving the consideration of race as a factor in medical school admissions. In *Fullilove v. Klutznick,* 448 U.S. 448 (1980), the Court approved a 10 per cent set-aside of federal contract funds for minority businesses, requiring five opinions covering 106 pages to do so. And in *Firefighters v. Stotts,* 467 U.S. 561 (1984), the Court rejected layoff protection for minority firefighters, devoting to the question four opinions covering 61 pages. In [its 1986] Term, the Court decided three major affirmative action cases involving employment issues, twice approving the use of race-conscious remedies. The Court's agonizing continues: the justices wrote 14 opinions covering 179 pages in deciding the three cases.''[3]

In 1987 and in 1988, a badly split Court again approved several different affirmative action plans but in 1989, it disapproved one. It appears that the courts will approve affirmative action plans, particularly in egregious circumstances and where there is evidence of prior discrimination. ''And the more flexible a program is—the more it uses 'goals' rather than 'quotas'—the more likely it is to pass muster. Yet uncertainties still plague the subject.''[4]

Gender. For many years, the Supreme Court refused to consider classifications based on gender suspect, but, in *Frontiero v. Richardson,* 411 U.S.677 (1973), the Court declared that such classifications were, indeed, suspect. *Frontiero* addressed the treatment of women in the military. Servicemen were entitled to claim their spouses as dependents for the purposes of obtaining increased quarters allowances and medical and dental benefits without regard to whether their wives were in fact dependent upon them for any part of their support. Servicewoman, on the other hand, could not claim their spouses as dependents unless their husbands were in fact dependent upon them for over one-half their support. The Court stated:

''There can be no doubt that our Nation has had a long and unfortunate history of sex discrimination. Traditionally, such discrimination was rationalized by an attitude of 'romantic paternalism' which, in practical effect, put women, not on a pedestal, but in a cage. Indeed, this paternalistic attitude became so firmly rooted in our national consciousness that, 100 years ago, a distinguished Member of this Court was able to proclaim:

'Man is, or should be, women's protector and defender. The natural and proper timidity and delicacy which belongs to the female sex evidently unfits it for many of the occupations of civil life. The constitution of the family organization, which is founded in the divine ordinance, as well as in the nature of things, indicates the domestic sphere as that which properly belongs to the domain and functions of womanhood. The harmony, not to say identity, of interests and views which belong, or should belong, to the family institution is repugnant to the idea of a woman adopting a distinct and independent career from that of her husband. . . . The paramount destiny and mission of woman are to fulfill the noble and benign offices of wife and mother. This is the law of the Creator.'

''As a result of notions such as these, our statute books gradually became laden with gross, stereotyped distinctions between the sexes and, indeed, throughout much of the 19th century the position of women in our society was, in many respects, comparable to that of blacks under the pre-Civil War slave codes. Neither slaves nor women could hold office, serve on juries, or bring suit in their own names, and married women traditionally were denied the legal capacity to hold or convey property or to serve as legal guardians of their own children. And although blacks were guaranteed the right to vote in 1870, women were denied even that right—which is itself 'preservative of other basic civil and political rights'—until adop-

---

3.   David O. Stewart, ''Affirmative Action Barely Upheld,'' *ABA Journal,* Dec. 1986, p. 44.
4.   *Id.* at 106.

tion of the Nineteenth Amendment half a century later.

"It is true, of course, that the position of women in America has improved markedly in recent decades. Nevertheless, it can hardly be doubted that, in part because of the high visibility of the sex characteristic, women still face pervasive, although at times more subtle, discrimination in our educational institutions, in the job market and, perhaps most conspicuously, in the political arena.

"Moreover, since sex, like race and national origin, is an immutable characteristic determined solely by the accident of birth, the imposition of special disabilities upon the members of a particular sex because of their sex would seem to violate 'the basic concept of our system that legal burdens should bear some relationship to individual responsibility . . . .' And what differentiates sex from such non-suspect statuses as intelligence or physical disability, and aligns it with the recognized suspect criteria, is that the sex characteristic frequently bears no relation to ability to perform or contribute to society. As a result, statutory distinctions between the sexes often have the effect of invidiously relegating the entire class of females to inferior legal status without regard to the actual capabilities of its individual members."

Later cases seemed to retreat from this position, however. For example, in *Kahn v. Shevin*, 416 U.S. 351 (1974), the Court stated, "Gender has never been rejected as an impermissible classification in all instances," and upheld a property tax exemption plan for widows, but not for widowers. Of course, if gender were a suspect classification, the Court would not have upheld the discriminatory tax. Can you imagine the Court upholding a law which gave all blacks a tax exemption and denied one to all whites? It could well be, however, that the Court's refusal to invalidate the tax exemption for widows in

Kahn was due to its view that, like affirmative action plans designed to remedy the effects of past discrimination on the basis of race, remedial efforts designed to remedy the effects of past discrimination on the basis of gender may be constitutional. In several cases, the Court has specifically held that ameliorative efforts which discriminate against men in order to remedy past discrimination against women are constitutional.

While cases like *Kahn* may have backed down from the Court's prior position that discrimination on the basis of gender is inherently suspect, there can be no question that gender is considered a quasi-suspect basis for a classification.

It has frequently been claimed that discrimination on the basis of pregnancy is sex-based discrimination. In *Geduldig v. Aiello*, 417 U.S. 484 (1974), however, the Court upheld the exclusion of pregnancy from the disabilities covered by California's public disability insurance system, stating: "We cannot agree that the exclusion of this disability from coverage amounts to invidious discrimination under the Equal Protection Clause." The Court reasoned that:

"The California insurance program does not exclude anyone from benefit eligibility because of gender but merely removes one physical condition—pregnancy—from the list of compensable disabilities. **While it is true that only women can become pregnant it does not follow that every legislative classification concerning pregnancy is a sex-based classification** . . . The program divides potential recipients into two groups—pregnant women and nonpregnant persons. While the first group is exclusively female, the second includes members of both sexes."

It appears that Congress did not agree with the Court that discrimination against pregnant people is not discrimination against women or that discrimination on the basis of pregnancy is not sex-based discrimination. Soon after the *Geduldig* opinion was issued, Congress amended Title VII of the Civil Rights Act of 1964, 42 U.S.C. § 2000e, the law forbidding sex-based discrimination in employment, to provide that discrimination on the basis of pregnancy is sex-based discrimination and, thus, prohibited. In *California Savings and Loan Association v. Guerra*, 479 U.S. 272 (1987), the Supreme Court held that this provision in Title VII, while seeming "to mandate treating pregnant employees the same as other employees," does not prohibit discrimination in favor of pregnant women. In other words, pregnant women may be accorded certain privileges not granted to men or to non-pregnant women, like the maternity leave from employment which was upheld in *Guerra*, if the privileges ameliorate discrimination against women. The maternity leave in *Guerra* did not run afoul of Title VII because, unlike "the protective labor legislation prevalent earlier in this century" that had the effect of keeping women out of the workplace, such a privilege "promotes equal employment opportunity" by allowing "women, as well as men, to have families without losing their jobs."

It should be noted that sexual harassment should also be considered a form of sex discrimination under Title VII. In *Meritor Savings Bank v. Vinson*, 477 U.S. 57 (1986), the Supreme Court held that a woman can establish a case of sexual harrassment under Title VII without proving "economic injury" as a result of the harassment and that proving a "hostile environment" is enough.

It should further be noted that no case has ever held that discrimination on the grounds of sexual preference constitutes discrimination on the basis of gender. Whether gays and lesbians constitute a suspect or quasi-suspect class has not been established, but it is unlikely that homosexuality would be considered a suspect or quasi-suspect basis for a classification given that the constitutionality of a law making homosexual relations between consenting adults criminal was upheld in *Bowers v. Hardwick*, 478 U.S. 186 (1986).

Age. In *Massachusetts Bd. of Retirement v. Murgia*, 427 U.S. 307 (1976), the Court held that classifications based on age are neither suspect nor quasi-suspect and thus sustained a law mandating the retirement of all Massachusetts State Police officers at age 50, regardless of their physical or mental health. The Court stated:

"[T]he class of uniformed state police officers over 50 [does not] constitute a suspect class for purposes of equal protection analysis. [We have] observed that a suspect class is one 'saddled with such disabilities, or subjected to such a history of purposeful unequal treatment, or relegated to such a position of political powerlessness as to command extraordinary protection from the majoritarian political process.' While the treatment of the aged in this Nation has not been wholly free of discrimination, such persons, unlike, say, those who have been discriminated against on the basis of race or national origin, have not experienced a 'history of purposeful unequal treatment' or been subjected to unique disabilities on the basis of stereotyped characteristics not truly indicative of their abilities.

"[The compulsory retirement law] cannot be said to discriminate only against the elderly. Rather, it draws the line at a certain age in middle life. But even old age does not define a 'discrete and insular' group in need of 'extraordinary protection from the majoritarian political process.' Instead, it marks a stage that each of us will reach if we live out our normal span.

"We do not make light of the substantial economic and psychological effects premature and compulsory retirement can have on an individual; nor do we denigrate the ability of elderly citizens to continue to contribute to society. The problems of retirement have been well documented and are beyond serious dispute. But '[w]e do not decide today that the [Massachusetts statute] is wise, that it best fulfills the relevant social and economic objectives that [Massachusetts] might ideally espouse, or that a more just and humane system could not be devised.' We decide only that the system enacted by the Massachusetts Legislature does not deny [healthy police officers over age 50] equal protection of the laws.''

It should be noted, as we shall see in the next section of this chapter, that Congress has acted to prohibit certain discrimination on the basis of age.

Legitimacy. For a time it appeared that classifications based on illegitimacy were inherently suspect. In several opinions, however, the Court retreated from this position. For example, in *Mathews v. Lucas*, 427 U.S. 495 (1976), dealing with the right of illegitimate children to receive their father's Social Security benefits, the Court stated:

"[I]rrationality in some classifications [relating to illegitimacy] does not in itself demonstrate that other, possibly rational, distinctions made in part on the basis of legitimacy are inherently untenable. Moreover, while the law has long placed the illegitimate child in an inferior position relative to the legitimate in certain circumstances, perhaps in part because the roots of discrimination rest in the conduct of the parents rather than the child, and perhaps in part because illegitimacy does not carry an obvious badge, as race and sex do, this discrimination against illegitimates has never approached the severity or pervasiveness of the historic legal and political discrimination against women and Negroes.

"We therefore adhere to our earlier view that discrimination between individuals on the basis of their legitimacy does not 'command extraordinary protection from the majoritarian political process.' "

It would be fair to say that the Court seesawed on this subject, but that classifications based on legitimacy now would undoubtedly be considered quasi-suspect. As we shall see, however, most States no longer discriminate on the basis of illegitimacy.

Alienage. As with classifications based on legitimacy, classifications based on alienage seemed to be suspect, but the Court was not totally clear on this point. *Plyler v. Doe*, *supra*, made clear, however, that classifications based on illegal alienage were not suspect. The Court stated:

"We reject the claim that 'illegal aliens' are a 'suspect class.' No case in which we have attempted to define a suspect class, has addressed the status of persons unlawfully in our country. Unlike most of the classifications that we have recognized as suspect, entry into this class, by virtue of entry into this country, is the product of voluntary action. Indeed, entry into the class is itself a crime. In addition, it could hardly be suggested that undocumented status is a 'constitutional irrelevancy.' With respect to the actions of the Federal Government, alienage classifications may be intimately related to the conduct of foreign policy, to the federal prerogative to control access to the United States, and to the plenary federal power to determine who has sufficiently manifested his allegiance to become a citizen of the Nation."

The children of illegal aliens, however, were held to fall into a quasi-suspect class. The Court stated:

"Persuasive arguments support the view that a State may withhold its beneficence from those whose very presence within the United States is the product of their own unlawful conduct. These arguments do not apply with the same force to classifications imposing disabilities on the minor children of such illegal entrants. At the least, those who elect to enter our territory by stealth and in violation of our law should be prepared to bear the consequences, including, but not limited to, deportation. But the children of those illegal entrants are not comparably situated. Their 'parents have the ability to conform their conduct to societal norms,' and presumably the ability to remove themselves from the State's jurisdiction; but the children who are plaintiffs in these cases 'can affect neither their parents' conduct nor their own status.' Even if the State found it expedient to control the conduct of adults by acting against their children, legislation directing the onus of a parent's misconduct against his children does not comport with fundamental conceptions of justice. '[V]isiting . . . condemnation on the head of an infant is illogical and unjust. Moreover, imposing disabilities on the . . . child is contrary to the basic concept of our system that legal burdens should bear some relationship to individual responsibility or wrongdoing. Obviously, no child is responsible for his birth and penalizing the . . . child is an ineffectual—as well as unjust—way of deterring the parent.' ''

Wealth. The case of *San Antonio Independent School District v. Rodriguez, supra,* 411 U.S. 1, seemed to indicate that classifications based on wealth are not inherently suspect. However, the Court described the class discriminated against by the Texas system of school finance, not as a class of poor parents, but as a:

"large, diverse, and amorphous class, unified only by the common factor of residence in districts that happen to have less taxable wealth than other districts. [This class has] none of the traditional indicia of suspectness: the class is not saddled with such disabilities, or subjected to such a history of purposeful unequal treatment, or relegated to such a position of political powerlessness as to command extraordinary protection from the majoritarian political process.''

A classification based solely on wealth may thus be suspect, but it is probably not inherently suspect.

Mental retardation. In *City of Cleburne, Tex. v. Cleburne Living Center,* 473 U.S. 432 (1985), which involved a zoning ordinance that had been interpreted to prevent a group home for the mentally retarded from locating in a residential neighborhood, the Court ruled that classifications based on mental disability are neither suspect nor quasi-suspect. The Court stated:

"The lesson of [our cases] is that where individuals in the group affected by a law have distinguishing characteristics relevant to interests the state has the authority to implement, the courts have been very reluctant, as they should be in our federal system and with our respect for the separation of powers, to closely scrutinize legislative choices as to whether, how and to what extent those interests should be pursued. In such cases, the Equal Protection Clause requires only a rational means to serve a legitimate end. Against this background, **we conclude for several reasons that . . . mental retardation [is not] a quasi-suspect classification calling for a more exacting standard of judicial review than is normally accorded economic and social legislation.**

"First, it is undeniable . . . that those who are mentally retarded have a reduced ability to cope with and function in the everyday world. Nor are they all cut from the same pattern: as the testimony in this record indicates, they range from those whose disability is not immediately evident to those who must be constantly cared for. They are thus different, immutably so, in relevant respects, and the states' interest in dealing with and providing for them is plainly a legitimate one.

"Second, the distinctive legislative response, both national and state, to the plight of those who are mentally retarded demonstrates not only that they have unique problems, but also that the lawmakers have been addressing their difficulties in a manner that belies a continuing antipathy or prejudice and a corresponding need for more intrusive oversight by the judiciary. Thus, the federal government has not only outlawed discrimination against the mentally retarded in federally funded programs, but it has also provided the retarded with the right to receive 'appropriate treatment, services, and habilitation' in a setting that is 'least restrictive of [their] personal liberty.' In addition, the government has conditioned federal education funds on a State's assurance that retarded children will enjoy an education that, 'to the maximum extent appropriate,' is integrated with that of non-mentally retarded children. The government has also facilitated the hiring of the mentally retarded into the federal civil service by exempting them from the requirement of competitive examination. Such legislation thus singling out the retarded for special treatment reflects the real and undeniable differences between the retarded and others. That a civilized and decent society expects and approves such legislation indicates that governmental consideration of those differences in the vast majority of situations is not only legitimate but desirable.

"Third, the legislative response, which could hardly have occurred and survived without public support, negates any claim that the mentally retarded are politically powerless in the sense that they have no ability to attract the attention of the law-makers. Any minority can be said to be powerless to assert direct control over the legislature, but if that were a criterion for higher level scrutiny by the courts, much economic and social legislation would now be suspect.

"Fourth, if the large and amorphous class of the mentally retarded were deemed quasi-suspect . . . it would be difficult to find a principled way to distinguish a variety of other groups who have perhaps immutable disabilities setting them off from others, who cannot themselves mandate the desired legislative responses, and who can claim some degree of prejudice from at least part of the public at large. One need mention in this respect only the aging, the disabled, the mentally ill, and the infirm. We are reluctant to set out on that course, and we decline to do so."

But, in holding that the zoning ordinance was unconstitutional as applied, the Court seemed to use a somewhat heightened scrutiny and seemed less willing than it was in cases like *Dandridge v. Williams, supra*, 397 U.S. 471, to accept any rational basis as a justification for a discrimination affecting important individual interests.

Protected rights

In a footnote in *Plyler v. Doe, supra*, the Court stated:

"In determining whether a class-based denial of a particular right is deserving of strict scrutiny under the Equal Protection Clause, [that is, whether the right denied is fundamental], we look to the Constitution to see if the right infringed has its source, explicitly or implicitly, therein."

Thus, to be considered a fundamental right, a right must be found in the Constitution. It need not be explicitly set forth in the Constitution, but may be implied from it, like the right to marital privacy discussed in *Griswold v. Connecticut, supra,* 381 U.S. 479. To give a further example, in *Shapiro v. Thompson,* 394 U.S. 618 (1969), several States' one year residency requirements before one could receive AFDC were subjected to strict scrutiny under the Equal Protection Clause because the requirements, in creating ''two classes of needy resident families indistinguishable from each other except that one is composed of residents who have a resided a year or more, and the second of residents who have resided less than a year, in the jurisdiction,'' impinged on the right to travel. The Court stated:

''This Court long ago recognized that the nature of our Federal Union and our constitutional concepts of personal liberty unite to require that all citizens be free to travel throughout the length and breadth of our land uninhibited by statutes, rules, or regulations which unreasonably burden or restrict this movement. We have no occasion to ascribe the source of this right to a particular constitutional provision.''

If rights are not explicitly or implicitly found in the Constitution, they will not be considered fundamental rights—no matter how important they are—and classifications which impinge on the exercise of these rights will not, for this reason, be subject to strict scrutiny. Thus, many government actions and laws impinging on important, but not fundamental rights and interests, such as the interest in the means to support one's children, the right to employment, the interest in living where one chooses, and the right to a public education, may be sustained merely if they are rationally related to a legitimate government purpose. Some

rights and interests are so important, however, that laws or government actions that impinge on them may be subjected to heightened scrutiny. Thus, in *Plyler v. Doe, supra,* the Court subjected a law that impinged on the right to a public education to intermediate scrutiny. The Court stated:

''Public education is not a 'right' granted to individuals by the Constitution. But neither is it merely some governmental 'benefit' indistinguishable from other forms of social welfare legislation. Both the importance of education in maintaining our basic institutions, and the lasting impact of its deprivation on the life of the child, mark the distinction. The 'American people have always regarded education and [the] acquisition of knowledge as matters of supreme importance.' We have recognized 'the public schools as a most vital civic institution for the preservation of a democratic system of government,' and as the primary vehicle for transmitting 'the values on which our society rests.' '[A]s . . . pointed out early in our history, . . . some degree of education is necessary to prepare citizens to participate effectively and intelligently in our open political system if we are to preserve freedom and independence.' And these historic 'perceptions of the public schools as inculcating fundamental values necessary to the maintenance of a democratic political system have been confirmed by the observations of social scientists.' In addition, education provides the basic tools by which individuals might lead economically productive lives to the benefit of us all. In sum, education has a fundamental role in maintaining the fabric of our society. We cannot ignore the significant social costs borne by our Nation when select groups are denied the means to absorb the values and skills upon which our social order rests.''

REMEDIES FOR VIOLATIONS OF CONSTITUTIONAL RIGHTS

Federal remedies

In the 1960's, significant numbers of the poor, minorities and members of oppressed groups (such as prisoners and mental patients) began using the courts to assert their constitutional rights and to challenge laws that discriminated against or otherwise injured them. Most of the cases were brought in federal courts because it was generally believed that federal courts were more receptive to the needs of the disadvantaged and to their constitutional arguments than State courts. The cases were also brought in federal courts because most of them were against State officials or sought to invalidate State laws and it was believed that federal judges were more likely to rule against State officials or invalidate State laws than were State judges.

The primary vehicle used to assert constitutional claims against State officials and to challenge State laws in federal courts was a cluster of civil rights laws known as the **"Civil Rights Acts"**. These Acts, which are now found at 42 U.S.C. sections 1981-1988, were passed in the Reconstruction Era after the Civil War pursuant to the authority granted to Congress by the 14th Amendment, but had virtually lain dormant until civil rights advocates and social reformers of the 1960's recognized their usefulness, and particularly the usefulness of section 1983. **Section 1983** allows an individual to sue whenever he or she is deprived of "rights, privileges or immunities secured by the Constitution and laws of the United States" by a person acting "under color of any statute, ordinance, regulation, custom or usage of any State."

The language in section 1983 sweeps broadly; its only significant limitation is the requirement that the defendant was acting under color of law when depriving the plaintiff of his or her rights. The color of law requirement is usually interpreted as the equivalent of the state action requirement, but in some cases it is interpreted as requiring no more than that the defendant acted with the knowledge of and pursuant to State law.

Although section 1983 reaches only state action, Congress, in enforcing the 14th Amendment with its guarantee of due process and equal protection, may legislate against private action. Thus, all federal civil rights laws do not require state action. No state action is required under other sections of the Civil Rights Acts, like section 1981, which deals with discrimination in housing and other property interests, and section 1982, which deals with discrimination in contracts. These sections, however, are not as important as section 1983 in that their scope is limited to specific claims of discrimination while section 1983 goes to any violation of any federal civil right—whether constitutional or statutory.

The list of rights which are within the purview of section 1983 is a lengthy one. Every right protected, explicitly or implicitly, by the Constitution can be the subject of a suit under section 1983 as can unconstitutional discrimination. Further, the statutory language in section 1983 allows suits for violations of the Constitution "and laws" of the United States. One may, thus, rely on a federal statute as the source of an asserted right in addition to the Constitution. The sweep of section 1983 is so great that nearly every constitutional case or Supreme Court case excerpted in this book was brought under it, whether or not that is stated in the excerpts. Indeed, its sweep is so great it has been used repeatedly to bring what are essentially malpractice actions against social workers who work for public agencies.

Under the Civil Rights Acts, and several other federal civil rights laws, a successful litigant may usually obtain an injunction, a declaratory judgment or monetary damages. Cases may be brought as class actions. The members of the class in some civil rights suits, like those challenging the operation of statutory benefit provisions, can number in the millions. Having hundreds or even thousands of class members would not be unusual. Many of the cases excerpted in this book are class actions, again whether that is stated in the excerpts or not.

The extensive use of the Civil Rights Acts, particularly section 1983, to assert constitutional and statutory rights, which began in the 1960's, greatly expanded in the 1970's. In the late 1970's, the expansion was fueled, in part, by the Civil Rights Attorney's Fees Act of 1976, 42 U.S.C. § 1988, which provides that the losing party may be required to pay the winning party's attorney's fees in actions brought under sections 1981-1985.[5] In the 1980's, however, the Supreme Court has issued several rulings which restrict access to the federal courts and which sharply curtail federal judicial remedies, including the use of section 1983. Additionally, the Supreme

Court has somewhat curtailed the class action device. As a result, many feel that the federal civil rights litigation boom of the 1960's and 1970's has ended.

In addition to the Civil Rights Acts, there are other routes to raise denials of constitutional and federal rights in federal courts, the most important being the civil rights laws of the 1960's, the Administrative Procedure Act, and the creation of private rights of action by implication.

The civil rights laws of the 1960's (codified in scattered sections of Titles 18, 20, 25, 28 and 42 of the United States Code) are directed primarily at discrimination in such matters as voting, education, employment, housing and public accommodations. Title VII of the Civil Rights Act of 1964, 42 U.S.C. § 2000e, the law dealing with discrimination in employment which has already been discussed, is perhaps the most important and most used of these laws.

Title VII, like most of the federal civil rights laws of the 1960's, deals with discrimination on the basis of race, religion, national origin or sex. Newer civil rights laws deal with discrimination on other grounds. See, e.g., § 504 of the Rehabilitation Act, 29 U.S.C. § 794, prohibiting discrimination by recipients of federal funds on the basis of handicap, and 29 U.S.C. § 621, prohibiting discrimination in employment on the basis of age.

Title VII, also like many of the other federal civil rights laws of the 1960's, creates an administrative agency to consider claims of discrimination and requires exhaustion of administrative remedies before one may sue.

Title VII, again like many of the other federal civil rights laws of the 1960's, is specifically directed at private discrimination. That is, no state action is required. Small private employers or businesses, with no connection to interstate commerce, however, may not be covered. Several other of the newer civil rights laws, are, by way of contrast, directed

---

5. In the United States, in contrast to most Western countries, the losing party to litigation is not required to pay the winning party's attorney's fees. Some federal and State statutes, however, provide for the shifting of attorney's fees from the loser to the winner in public interest cases. Many of these statutes, like the Civil Rights Attorney's Fees Act, provide for this fee shifting only to the plaintiffs. It is widely believed that such fee shifting provisions operate as an incentive to bring cases which vindicate important rights but which are not financially rewarding to the plaintiffs. If the plaintiff's attorney's fees are paid by the losing defendant, the plaintiff will not be out of pocket for bringing the case.

only at government entities and at recipients of federal funds. *See, e.g.*, § 504 of the Rehabilitation Act and 29 U.S.C. § 6101 *et seq.*, prohibiting discrimination on the basis of age by federally assisted programs.

The Administrative Procedure Act, 5 U.S.C. §§ 551 *et seq.*, which allows the federal courts to review actions taken by a federal agency, may be used by those dissatisfied with most federal administrative agency actions. The Act applies to every agency unless expressly excepted.[6] Review under the Act is limited to determining whether the offending agency action was "arbitrary, capricious or an abuse of discretion."

Another source of relief for the poor and other disadvantaged individuals is the willingness of the federal courts to **imply a remedy** from general statutes which do not specifically authorize private actions or from the Constitution itself. For example, in *Bivens v. Six Unknown Named Agents of the Federal Bureau of Narcotics*, 403 U.S. 388 (1971), federal agents had allegedly violated the 4th Amendment prohibition on unreasonable searches and seizures. The Supreme Court concluded that the 4th Amendment expresses policies so basic that a private remedy for damages is implied.

The **implication of remedies** is a matter of great importance to the disadvantaged. They are the intended beneficiaries of federal social welfare programs in such areas as public assistance, housing and education, yet frequently these benefits are denied because of inaction, or even misconduct, by administrators and officials. To allow enforcement of the underlying public policy to depend solely upon those same administrators and officials would frustrate congressional in-

tent, public policy and the legitimate expectations of the intended beneficiaries. Recognizing this, the courts have allowed private actions under several federal statutes in several significant areas, such as relocation benefits, public housing and food stamps. Remedies have not been implied under all federal statutes, however.

Where there is no adequate judicial remedy for the violation of a constitutional right or where a right is not clearly based on the Constitution or found in any federal statute, the poor, minorities and other disadvantaged groups must seek relief, not from the courts, but from the Congress and administrative agencies. Many civil rights laws and other laws which create specific rights or which protect specific groups, like the Education for All Handicapped Children Act, 20 U.S.C. § 1400 *et seq.*, are in large part the result of active lobbying by the disadvantaged and their allies.

State remedies

The poor, minorities and members of oppressed groups have also asserted their rights in State courts. Many States have civil rights laws which authorize suits in State court when State constitutional rights have been violated. In addition, because State courts can hear cases brought under 42 U.S.C. § 1983, many civil rights cases are heard in State courts. Further, many States have laws like the federal Administrative Procedure Act, which allow one to sue a State agency which has violated one's rights, and many State courts imply private remedies from State laws creating State social welfare programs. Finally, many States have special laws according individuals special rights and privileges or giving them special opportunities for lawsuits. For example, Rhode Island has a law forbidding discrimination against

---

6. The Supreme Court has said that the Social Security Administration is excepted insofar as a claimant of benefits seeks review of a decision on benefits. There is, however, a review possible pursuant to the Social Security Act in such cases.

the handicapped which gives handicapped persons who are the victims of prohibited discrimination the ability to go to State court to obtain "equitable relief, compensatory and/or punitive damages, or such other relief as the court deems appropriate." R.I. Gen. Laws, § 42-87-4.

As the federal courts have become more conservative in the 1980's, there has been more focus on State courts to protect the rights of the disadvantaged. Moreover, because, as has been stated, lobbying is often easier and more fruitful at the State level than at the federal level, there has been greater focus on State laws to protect the constitutional rights of minorities and the disadvantaged. As a result, many States have civil rights commissions or agencies with far-reaching power to investigate complaints and take action in behalf of individuals suffering discrimination. Going to court may, thus, not be necessary to protect one's civil rights.

6

Basic Principles of Criminal Law

Social workers may play a variety of roles in the criminal justice system and be involved in many stages of the criminal justice process. They may work with clients referred by a criminal justice agency or they may be employed by a criminal justice agency; they may perform evaluative functions or provide service to clients for the agency. They may work behind the scenes or they may be witnesses in criminal hearings, particularly those involving mentally ill defendants. Whatever a social worker's role, the social worker often makes recommendations which are a major factor in determining if an offender is to continue through the process or how the offender will continue through it.

Social workers who are not otherwise connected with the criminal justice system may intervene in the criminal justice process to prevent further processing of clients or to help clients achieve favorable outcomes. Moreover, social workers may counsel clients who are going through the process, may work with victims of crimes by helping them go through the process and cope with the trauma, and may counsel the families of those who are going through or have gone through the system. The families of criminal defendants and those serving time in jail or prison are often forgotten by the other participants in the criminal justice process.

Despite the potential range of the social worker's involvement in the criminal justice system, few of you will probably be active participants in the process. Nevertheless, you should understand the criminal law and the criminal justice process for at least two reasons.

First, criminal prosecution imposes severe psychological and financial stress on the person being prosecuted as well as on the person's family. As has been noted, many of you, while not working in the criminal justice system, will work with individuals and families affected by criminal prosecution. By understanding the process, you can better appreci-

ate your clients' situations and offer appropriate services.

Second, the criminal justice system is often used as a model when courts are attempting to determine the rights of an individual in another sort of proceeding in which you might be involved. When a juvenile delinquent, a person who is being involuntarily committed to a mental hospital, a parent whose child is being taken away or many others come before the courts, the courts may decide that they are entitled to some or all of the rights accorded to the criminal defendant. You should, thus, be familiar with these rights.

This chapter will review the basic principles of substantive and procedural criminal law and then will describe the criminal justice process, looking closely at the roles of social workers and the rights of the accused at each stage in that process.

AN OVERVIEW OF CRIMINAL LAW

Criminal laws may be found at the federal, State, and local levels. There is a federal criminal justice system which enforces federal criminal laws; each State has a criminal justice system which enforces the criminal laws of the State; and many States have local criminal justice systems which enforce local criminal laws.

Federal substantive criminal laws, that is, the federal laws which define criminal conduct, deal mainly with activities on federal property (e.g., post offices), with behavior that affects the national interest (e.g., treason), or with interstate or international actions (e.g., taking a kidnap victim across state lines; bringing narcotics into the country). In other words, federal substantive criminal laws deal with uniquely federal problems. Because such problems are limited in number, there are not many federal substantive criminal laws. The substantive criminal laws enacted by counties, cities, towns and other local governments generally deal with uniquely local problems (e.g., leash laws, noise limits). Again, because such problems are limited in number, there are not many local criminal laws. Thus, most substantive criminal laws are found at the State level.

There may be an overlap among federal, State, and local substantive criminal laws. The possession or sale of narcotics, for example, may violate the criminal law of all three levels of government. When there is such an overlap, law enforcement agencies may disagree as to which criminal justice system will handle the case. The federal criminal justice system is not considered to be "superior" to the State systems and will not automatically handle the case. Instead, the federal and State criminal justice systems are considered to be parallel systems and decisions will be made as to which system will handle a given case based on principles of **comity**, that is, cooperation and courtesy. In some States, local criminal justice systems have the same relationship to the State system as the State system has to the federal system, that is, they are parallel systems, but, in most States, the local criminal justice systems are inferior to the State system.

Federal criminal law, except for the criminal law found in the Constitution, is also not considered superior to State criminal law. But the Constitution contains a number of provisions that have direct bearing on the criminal law. Indeed, the Bill of Rights establishes the basic procedural protections found in the criminal law. Thus, the federal Constitution is extremely important in criminal law. State constitutions may also contain the basic procedural protections found in the Bill of Rights and other protections. Thus, they too are extremely important in criminal law.

Most substantive criminal law is found in legislation enacted by Congress, State legislatures, and local legislative bodies. This is because it is believed that legislation provides the best notice to the populace of what behavior is criminal and that elected representatives best express the majority's will on this important subject. Most procedural criminal law is also found in legislation.

Because most criminal law is State law, most criminal law is found in State statutes. These statutes may be contained in a special criminal code, but statutes creating crimes may usually also be found in other codes and laws. For example, a juvenile code may contain a statute making child abuse a crime.

Criminal law may also be found in regulations promulgated by federal, State and local administrative agencies. Violating a regulation may be a crime which may be processed through the appropriate criminal justice system or by the administrative agency itself. For example, a violation of a federal environmental regulation dealing with toxic waste disposal may be dealt with by the federal environmental agency or may be prosecuted in a federal court.

Finally, criminal law may also be found in court decisions. Most of the common law establishing which behavior is criminal has been replaced by statutes, however, and, indeed, courts may not create common law crimes in many States. Precedent may, however, interpret statutes and regulations creating crimes, and procedural criminal law may, in large part, be common law.

BASIC PRINCIPLES AND CONCEPTS OF SUBSTANTIVE CRIMINAL LAW

What is a crime?

You, like most people, probably have an idea what behavior constitutes a "crime."

Legally, however, only conduct which is in violation of a law and for which one can be prosecuted and punished by the government is a crime. Without a law forbidding or commanding a certain act, it is not a crime to commit or omit the act—no matter how offensive you may consider the commission or omission. And unless a law authorizes prosecution by the government and prescribes punishment for certain conduct, the prescribed conduct is not criminal—even if it is a violation of the law. Conduct may have severe consequences for the perpetrator, but these consequences will not include an accusation of criminal behavior and a criminal conviction—unless there is a law against the conduct and that law authorizes prosecution and punishment by a government.

To illustrate, suppose you are injured by a man who was driving while under the influence of prescription drugs. You may be able to sue him for damages, but he can only be charged with a crime if it is against the law to drive while under the influence of prescription drugs and if the law provides that one may be prosecuted and punished by the government for driving while under the influence of prescription drugs. A law providing only that it is against the law to drive while under the influence of prescription drugs and authorizing civil suits for damages for violating the law is not enough to make driving while under the influence of prescription drugs criminal. And even a law authorizing the government to take action against those who drive while under the influence of prescription drugs by, for example, suspending their driver's licenses, may not be enough to make a violation of the law a crime. Suspension of a driver's license may be sought in a civil suit and may not be considered punishment.

Sometimes certain behavior can give rise to both civil and criminal suits. Even if driving while under the influence of prescription drugs is a crime and even if the government is criminally prosecuting a man who injured you while driving under the influence of prescription drugs, you would not be precluded from suing him. One government agency would not be precluded from bringing a civil suit to suspend his driver's license just because another government agency is criminally prosecuting him. It would not be considered double punishment if he was sent to jail and was forced to pay you damages or had his license suspended because neither paying compensatory damages nor losing one's license may be considered "punishment."

Societies differ in how they determine what behavior should be made criminal. In America, by and large, as we have said, only elected representatives (or those to whom they have specifically delegated the authority) determine what behavior should or should not be made criminal. When these elected representatives believe that certain behavior is wrong, that private efforts to control it are insufficient, and that the full authority of the government should be put behind the control effort, they will make the behavior criminal. But to be made criminal, behavior should not just be a private wrong. It should be considered a public wrong, that is, it should be viewed as harmful, not just to those who may be injured by it, but to the social order or to society as a whole. Indeed, certain behavior which may actually not injure anyone—except, perhaps, those who engage in the behavior—like prostitution, not wearing a seat belt, or gambling, may be made criminal because legislators consider the behavior as harming society as a whole.

There is substantial debate as to whether some or all crimes without victims, called **"victimless crimes,"** should exist and whether the government should, in effect, legislate morality. Attacks on such crimes as denials of substantive due process and invasions of the right to privacy, however, have generally been unsuccessful. For example, in *Bowers v. Hardwick*, 478 U.S. 186 (1987), the Supreme Court upheld a law making sodomy, even between consenting adults, a crime stating that the due process clause only protects those liberties "deeply rooted in this Nation's history and tradition," and noting that:

> "The law . . . is constantly based on notions of morality, and if all laws representing essentially moral choices are to be invalidated under the Due Process Clause, the courts will be very busy indeed."

The elements of a crime

All statutory definitions of crime, at a minimum, must set forth the conduct which is illegal, the state of mind one must have at the time of the conduct, and the circumstances which make the conduct illegal. These are known as the "elements of a crime."

Criminal conduct. There must be a specific act or a failure to act when action is required in order for there to be a crime.[1] Bad thoughts or being a bad person is not enough. In a case involving this principle, *Robinson v. California*, 370 U.S. 660 (1962), the Supreme Court declared a California law making it a crime for a person "to be addicted to the use of narcotics" unconstitutional. The Court so held since the California law did not forbid specific antisocial conduct, but rather made a status, being addicted, illegal.

---

1.   Henceforth, although certain failures to act may be criminal (e.g., it may be a crime for a social worker to fail to report suspected child abuse), for simplicity, criminal conduct shall be discussed as if it consisted only of acts, not of omissions.

A criminal state of mind. To convict someone of a crime, it must be shown not only that he or she committed the illegal act charged but also that he or she did so in a state of mind appropriate for the imputation of responsibility. This state of mind is known as the "*mens rea*."

The *mens rea* of most crimes used to be a criminal or guilty intent. One had to intend to commit a crime or have an actual consciousness of guilt in order to be found guilty of most crimes. This requirement has now been abandoned for most crimes. One may now be found guilty of committing most crimes even if one did not intend to commit the crime or any other crime; it is enough if one intended to commit the act which is a crime. For a few crimes, it may even be enough if one did not intend to commit the act but committed it recklessly or negligently.

Although the *mens rea* requirement may range from intent to commit the crime to negligent commission of the act, it is always necessary that the illegal act be voluntary and intentional. The intentional and voluntary quality of the illegal behavior is what makes it punishable. Even in those few cases where negligence or recklessness is a sufficient *mens rea*, one must still voluntarily intend to do what was done (e.g., drive recklessly or carelessly).

How the *mens rea* requirement can differ for different crimes is illustrated by statutes involving **homicide**, that is, the killing of another. If one deliberately intended to kill another, a homicide may be considered a first degree murder; if there was an intent to kill, but no deliberation, a homicide may be considered a second degree murder; if there was no intent to kill but an intent to harm another, a homocide may be considered voluntary manslaughter; if a homicide was the result of an act performed recklessly, with no intent to kill or harm another, it may be considered involuntary manslaughter; and if a homicide was solely the result of negligence, there may be no crime. The different categories of homicide created by the different *mens rea* requirements may have different penalties. For example, murder may carry a sentence of death or a long minimum term in prison; voluntary manslaughter may carry a maximum sentence in prison less than the minimum sentence for murder; involuntary manslaughter may carry an even shorter maximum sentence; and reckless homicide may carry a still shorter maximum.

The attendant circumstances. Although there may have been criminal conduct and a criminal state of mind, there may not have been a crime unless certain circumstances accompanied the intent and the conduct. For example, although a woman may have intended to assault a man and did, in fact, assault him, she would not have committed the crime of "assault with a deadly weapon" unless she used something considered a deadly weapon. The circumstances may also affect the degree of and punishment for a crime. For example, theft of something worth more than $500 could be grand theft, usually punishable by imprisonment of more than a year, while theft of something worth less than $500 could only be petty theft, usually punishable by imprisonment for a maximum of six months.

Classification of crimes

Crimes are generally classified as either **felonies** or **misdemeanors**. A felony is a more serious offense. Most States distinguish between felonies and misdemeanors in terms of length or place of punishment. Usually a felony may be punished by incarceration for a year or more in a prison while misdemeanors may only be punished by incarceration for less than a year in a place other than a prison.

Some States also have **petty offenses**, which are minor crimes, like traffic offenses or violations of local laws, such as curfews. The prosecution process may be different and there may be fewer procedural protections for petty offenses than for more serious crimes.

Defenses to criminal charges

A person who engages in criminal conduct with a required *mens rea* may not be guilty of a crime if he or she has a defense to the crime. Some defenses which may be important to social workers are explained below.

Self-defense. A person who is in immediate danger of being harmed by another person's unlawful use of force is generally allowed to use force to ward off the attack. The law will specify when and how force may be used to defend oneself or when, in other words, one may claim self-defense. The law in most States will also specify when a person may use force to defend others from attack, to protect property, or to prevent the commission of a crime, or when, in other words, one may claim a defense related to self-defense. Generally one may use only the minimum level of force which is reasonably necessary to prevent harm. Reasonableness may be assessed subjectively, that is, the trier of fact puts itself in the position of the accused, or objectively, that is, the trier of fact considers what a reasonable person would do in the circumstances. Distinctions are often made between deadly and non-deadly force. A person generally has the right to use deadly force, but only to defend oneself and only if this amount of force is necessary to prevent his or her own death or severe bodily harm. Some States require those who can do so to retreat rather than to use deadly force.

Often the defense of self-defense, and the related defenses like defense of property or defense of others, are confused with the defenses of necessity or duress. These rarely used—and even more rarely successful defenses—excuse criminal conduct when one's conduct is compelled by the circumstances or by a threat of harm.

Intoxication. The law generally does not relieve an individual of responsibility for crimes committed while voluntarily intoxicated, but involuntary intoxication, such as when a person has been tricked into consuming a substance, not knowing that it might result in intoxication, is generally a defense. Voluntary intoxication may operate as a defense, however, if the intoxication is such that it negates a required *mens rea.* For example, voluntary intoxication may be a defense to a charge of theft if the crime of theft requires a specific intent to steal, as it usually does, and if a woman's intoxication was such that she could not form this intent. Further, in some circumstances, voluntary intoxication may be considered to reduce the seriousness of a charge or the punishment upon conviction.

Insanity. There has been considerable debate on the defense of insanity. There has been no consensus on who should be entitled to claim a defense of insanity, how insanity should be defined, and even whether insanity should be a defense at all. Different jurisdictions have come to different conclusions on these questions. Basically all have allowed the insanity defense, but they have used different variations of one of four basic tests of legal insanity or have adopted a combination of two or more of the tests.

The first test, known as the "**M'Naghten Rule,**" is derived from an 1843 English case in which the House of Lords ruled that a criminal defendant is legally insane and not criminally responsible if:

"at the time of the committing of the act, the party accused was laboring under such a defect of reason, from disease of the mind, as not to know the nature and quality of the act he was doing, or if he did know it that he did not know he was doing what was wrong."

The M'Naghten Rule, often referred to as the "right-from-wrong test," has been used in some form by most States, but it has been criticized as not conforming with modern psychiatric concepts and for failing to recognize different degrees of insanity. It has also been argued that individuals who may be able to distinguish right from wrong may be unable to control their behavior because of their insanity. These individuals, it is argued, should be excused from criminal responsibility, but the M'Naghten Rule does not excuse them.

Some States have dealt with the last of these arguments by supplementing the M'Naghten Rule with the **Irresistible Impulse Test.** This test excuses one from responsibility where one is powerless to control one's behavior or where, in other words, an uncontrollable impulse compels one to commit the crime—even when one knows it is wrong to do so.

A few States have used the **Durham Rule,** so-called because it was adopted in the District of Columbia in the case of *Durham v. United States,* 214 F.2d. 863 (D.C. Cir. 1954). In *Durham,* the court stated that an accused is not criminally responsible "if an unlawful act is the product of mental disease or mental defect."

The Durham Rule was seen as too broad, however, and, in 1972, even the District of Columbia abandoned it in favor of a modified version of a test from the Model Penal Code, a criminal code drafted by law professors and other experts which was proposed for adoption by the States. This test, known as the **Substantial Capacity Test,** is now used in some form in most States. It provides that a person is not responsible for criminal conduct:

"if at the time of such conduct as a result of mental disease or defect he lacks substantial capacity either to appreciate the criminality of his conduct or to conform his conduct to the requirements of law."

The Substantial Capacity Test is essentially a combination, modification, and broadening of the M'Naghten Rule and the Irresistible Impulse Test. Of great importance, the test does not require that a defendant be completely unable to distinguish right from wrong or completely unable to control his or her behavior; the defendant need only lack "substantial capacity" to do so.

Whatever the test, legal insanity is generally established through the testimony of expert witnesses, usually psychiatrists, who testify on the defendant's mental state at the time of the crime. Although the jury, or the judge if the case is tried without a jury, must ultimately decide if the defendant met the jurisdiction's test for legal insanity, the decision usually depends on the credence given to the psychiatric testimony. This testimony is necessarily based, at least to some extent, on guess-work since the psychiatric experts may first see the defendant a long time after the crime and since they have to reconstruct the events surrounding the crime. Moreover, psychiatry is hardly an exact science and psychiatrists can and do differ in diagnoses. Thus, in cases where the insanity defense is asserted, there is often a battle of the experts.

If the insanity defense is successfully asserted, defendants are found "not guilty by reason of insanity." This means they are cleared of all criminal charges, but, as we will see in Chapter 14, they may be committed to an institution or required to undergo treatment under the civil law.

Although there is much public discussion of notorious defendants found not guilty by reason of insanity, such as John Hinckley, there are, in fact, few successful assertions of the insanity defense. Nevertheless, some believe that this defense should be abolished, arguing, erroneously, that it is used to free dangerous people. Others emphasize that most criminals are somewhat unbalanced or that psychiatry is too far from an exact science to be relied on in making important decisions like guilt or innocence. Still others argue that the wealthy are able to pay for the testimony of psychiatrists in support of their defense while the poor cannot.

Because of the arguments against the insanity defense, some States have replaced or augmented the "not guilty by reason of insanity" verdict with the "guilty but mentally ill" verdict. This verdict means that one can be punished as if one were not insane but will be sent to a special prison hospital or mental facility for treatment during the term of punishment.

The "not guilty by reason of insanity" verdict must be distinguished from the determination that an accused is **incompetent** or **unfit to stand trial.** Such a determination does not mean that a defendant is freed of criminal responsibility; it means only that a trial to determine criminal responsibility cannot be held because the defendant cannot understand the nature of the proceedings or participate in his or her own defense. The insanity verdict resolves the criminal action; the unfitness determination only postpones it until such time as the defendant is competent to stand trial.[2] With the insanity defense, courts are concerned with a defendant's mental state at the time of commission of the crime;

---

2. State law may provide that if the defendant does not regain competency within a certain period of time or is determined to be unable to ever regain competency, charges must be dismissed.

with the competency determination, courts are concerned with the defendant's mental state at the time of trial. Decisions on insanity are made at the conclusion of a trial; decisions on competency are made before trial after a hearing on a pretrial motion. Psychiatric experts, through their testimony, assist courts in making either determination, but usually only judges may decide competency while juries may decide sanity. In contrast to the insanity defense, the incompetency determination is frequently made and often successful.

Like those found not guilty by reason of insanity, those found unfit to stand trial may be released under the criminal law but may be held under the civil law if they pose a danger to themselves or others.

BASIC PRINCIPLES AND CONCEPTS OF PROCEDURAL CRIMINAL LAW

Adversarial, accusatorial and fair

The American legal system, as we have said, is an adversary system which uses an accusatorial process. This is true in all areas of the law, but it is in the area of criminal law that one often sees the adversary system and the accusatorial process in its purest form. In a criminal case, the opposing parties are the **prosecution**, the State, federal, or local government entity which initiates and pursues criminal cases, and one or more persons, known as the "**defendant(s)**," who are accused of committing a crime by the prosecution.

As we have also said, the adversary system is only fair if each party has the capacity to present its case and if the parties' capacities

are roughly equal. In many criminal cases, however, the defendants may not have the capacity to present their cases because of poverty or another reason. And even when the defendants have the capacity, the prosecution may have so many resources it can simply overpower them. Thus, the criminal justice system has long been subject to various safeguards designed to insure that the prosecution will not win a case simply because it has more money, more lawyers, and the investigative power of the government at its disposal and to insure that defendants will not lose simply because they have no money, no lawyer, or no ability to investigate. The most important safeguards are the requirements that the prosecution carry the burden of proof and that it establish proof beyond a reasonable doubt.

The accusation is viewed as no more than a statement of the belief of the accuser. It may not be assumed that the allegations are true simply because the government is prosecuting the case. Indeed, the accused is presumed to be innocent, a presumption that can only be rebutted by proof of guilt beyond a reasonable doubt.

Although the prosecution has the burden of proof, it is not required to prove the absence of all defenses. Some defenses are considered **affirmative defenses** which must be raised by defendants. Defendants need not always prove affirmative defenses, however. It is enough if they raise a reasonable doubt as to their guilt with their defenses. For example, insanity is generally considered an affirmative defense. Thus, the prosecution does not have to prove that defendants were sane at the time of the crime. But, to prevail with this defense, defendants do not have to prove they were insane. Rather, they merely must present enough evidence to raise a reasonable doubt as to their sanity.

Besides the presumption of innocence and the requirement of proof beyond a reasonable doubt, there are many other protections built into the criminal justice system to remedy the imbalance between the parties to a criminal case and to insure that the innocent are not convicted. Some of these safeguards are specifically required by the Constitution while others have been derived from the due process clause. For example, in *Ake v. Oklahoma*, 470 U.S. 68 (1985), the due process clause was held to require that a State provide some indigent defendants with the assistance of psychiatrists if their sanity is likely to be an issue in their trials. *Ake* is reviewed below because, in addition to demonstrating the use of the due process clause to insure fairness in the criminal justice process, it may help you understand incompetency, the insanity defense, and the role of psychiatric expert witnesses in a criminal trial.

Ake was charged with murdering a couple and wounding their two children. His behavior in jail and in court was so bizarre that the court ordered a psychiatric examination to assess whether Ake was competent to stand trial. The psychiatrist diagnosed Ake as a probable paranoid schizophrenic and recommended a further, prolonged psychiatric evaluation. The court committed Ake to a mental hospital for this further examination.

After Ake had been at the hospital a few weeks, a hospital psychiatrist reported to the court that Ake was not competent to stand trial. The court then held a competency hearing. It found Ake to be incompetent to stand trial, and ordered him committed to a mental hospital. Six weeks later, the same psychiatrist informed the court that Ake, who was heavily medicated, had become competent to stand trial. The criminal proceedings against him were then renewed.

Ake's attorney immediately informed the court that Ake wanted to raise an insanity defense and moved the court to appoint a psychiatrist to examine Ake as to his insanity at the time of the crime. Although Ake had been

committed soon after the murders with which he was charged and had spent three months at the hospital, no inquiry had ever been made into his sanity at the time of the offense. As an indigent, Ake could not afford to pay for a psychiatrist. The court denied the motion.

Ake was tried for two counts of murder. His sole defense was insanity. Nevertheless,

> **"there was no expert testimony for either side on Ake's sanity at the time of the offense**. The jurors were [told] that . . . Ake was to be presumed sane at the time of the crime unless **he** presented evidence sufficient to raise a reasonable doubt about his sanity at that time. If he raised such a doubt in their minds, the jurors were informed, the burden of proof shifted to the State to prove sanity beyond a reasonable doubt.''

The jury rejected Ake's insanity defense and found Ake guilty on all counts. It then sentenced Ake to death. The Supreme Court reversed Ake's conviction. It stated:

> "This Court has long recognized that when a State brings its judicial power to bear on an indigent defendant in a criminal proceeding, it must take steps to assure that the defendant has a fair opportunity to present his defense. This elementary principle, grounded in significant part on the Fourteenth Amendment's due process guarantee of fundamental fairness, derives from the belief that justice cannot be equal where, simply as a result of his poverty, a defendant is denied the opportunity to participate meaningfully in a judicial proceeding in which his liberty is at stake. Meaningful access to justice has been the consistent theme of [our] cases. We recognized long ago that mere access to the courthouse doors does not by itself assure a proper functioning of the adversary process, and that a criminal trial is fundamentally unfair if the State proceeds against an indigent defendant without mak-

ing certain that he has access to the raw materials integral to the building of an effective defense. Thus, while the Court has not held that a State must purchase for the indigent defendant all the assistance that his wealthier counterpart might buy, it has often reaffirmed that fundamental fairness entitles indigent defendants to 'an adequate opportunity to present their claims fairly within the adversary system.'

"In this case we must decide whether, and under what conditions, the participation of a psychiatrist is important enough to preparation of a defense to require the State to provide an indigent defendant with access to competent psychiatric assistance in preparing the defense. Three factors [derived from *Mathews v. Eldridge*, 424 U.S. 319 (1976)] are relevant to this determination. The first is the private interest that will be affected by the action of the State. The second is the governmental interest that will be affected if the safeguard is to be provided. The third is the probable value of the additional or substitute procedural safeguards that are sought, and the risk of an erroneous deprivation of the affected interest if those safeguards are not provided."

After considering the defendant's "obvious" and "uniquely compelling" interest in the accuracy of a criminal proceeding in which life and liberty are at stake and the State's insubstantial interest in denying a defendant the ability to establish a defense to a criminal charge, the Court considered the value of psychiatric evidence to an accurate verdict in a criminal case.

"We begin by considering the pivotal role that psychiatry has come to play in criminal proceedings. [T]he assistance of a psychiatrist may well be crucial to the defendant's ability to marshal his defense. [P]sychiatrists gather facts, both through professional examination, interviews, and elsewhere, that they will share with the judge or jury;

they analyze the information gathered and from it draw plausible conclusions about the defendant's mental condition, and about the effects of any disorder on behavior; and they offer opinions about how the defendant's mental condition might have affected his behavior at the time in question. They know the probative questions to ask of the opposing party's psychiatrists and how to interpret their answers. Unlike lay witnesses, who can merely describe symptoms they believe might be relevant to the defendant's mental state, psychiatrists can identify the 'elusive and often deceptive' symptoms of insanity, and tell the jury why their observations are relevant. Further, where permitted by evidentiary rules, psychiatrists can translate a medical diagnosis into language that will assist the trier of fact, and therefore offer evidence in a form that has meaning for the task at hand. Through this process of investigation, interpretation and testimony, psychiatrists ideally assist lay jurors, who generally have no training in psychiatric matters, to make a sensible and educated determination about the mental condition of the defendant at the time of the offense.

"Psychiatry is not, however, an exact science, and psychiatrists disagree widely and frequently on what constitutes mental illness, on the appropriate diagnosis to be attached to given behavior and symptoms, on cure and treatment, and on likelihood of future dangerousness. Perhaps because there often is no single, accurate psychiatric conclusion on legal insanity in a given case, juries remain the primary factfinders on this issue, and they must resolve differences in opinion within the psychiatric profession on the basis of the evidence offered by each party. When jurors make this determination about issues that inevitably are complex and foreign, the testimony of psychiatrists can be crucial and 'a virtual necessity if an insanity plea is to have any chance of success.' By organizing a defendant's mental history, examination results and behavior, and other information, interpreting it in light of their expertise, and then laying out their investigative and analytic process to the jury, the psychiatrists for each party enable the jury to make its most accurate determination of the truth on the issue before them.

"The foregoing leads inexorably to the conclusion that, without the assistance of a psychiatrist to conduct a professional examination on issues relevant to the defense, to help determine whether the insanity defense is viable, to present testimony, and to assist in preparing the cross-examination of a State's psychiatric witnesses, the risk of an inaccurate resolution of sanity issues is extremely high. With such assistance, the defendant is fairly able to present at least enough information to the jury, in a meaningful manner, as to permit it to make a sensible determination.

"We therefore hold that when a defendant demonstrates to the trial judge that his sanity at the time of the offense is to be a significant factor at trial, the State must, at a minimum, assure the defendant access to a competent psychiatrist who will conduct an appropriate examination and assist in evaluation, preparation, and presentation of the defense.

"This is not to say, of course, that the indigent defendant has a constitutional right to choose a psychiatrist of his personal liking or to receive funds to hire his own. Our concern is that the indigent defendant have access to a competent psychiatrist for the purpose we have discussed, and . . . we leave to the State the decision on how to implement this right."

Screening

In addition to other constitutional safeguards, screening devices are often included in the criminal justice process. At various stages in the process, a judge or some other neutral factfinder may review each case and the prosecution may have to meet progressively higher burdens of proof to justify moving the case to the next stage until, ultimately, the prosecutor will have to prove guilt beyond a reasonable doubt. Screening devices are included in the process because of the recognition that enduring a criminal prosecution, even if one is ultimately found innocent, is a great hardship.

In *Gerstein v. Pugh*, 420 U.S. 103 (1975), the Supreme Court mandated such a screening device as a constitutional requirement. It held that, when a person is held in custody solely on the basis of a prosecutor's charge, the Constitution "requires a judicial determination of **probable cause** [that is, some likelihood the accused is guilty] as a prerequisite to extended restraint of liberty following arrest." The method of making this judicial determination was left up to the States, but the Court specifically stated that an informal, non-adversary hearing would be constitutionally sufficient. It stated:

"The use of an informal [non-adversary] procedure is justified not only by the lesser consequences of a probable cause determination but also by the nature of the determination itself. It does not require the fine resolution of conflicting evidence that a reasonable-doubt or even a preponderance standard demands, and credibility determinations are seldom crucial in deciding whether the evidence supports a reasonable belief in guilt. This is not to say that confrontation and cross-examination might not enhance the reliability of probable cause determinations in some cases. In most cases, however, their value would be too slight to justify holding, as a matter of constitutional principle, that these formalities and safeguards designed for trial must also be employed in making the . . . determination of probable cause."

Diversion

Screening devices, such as those mandated in *Pugh*, remove some of those who are accused of crimes from the criminal justice process. Others are removed from the process, not because the prosecution has insufficient evidence to proceed, but because a decision is made to **divert** them from the process.

Currently there is a trend toward diverting persons out of the criminal justice system. This diversion can take place at a number of points in the process and can be formal, as part of a specific diversion law or program, or informal, as part of an official's exercise of discretion. Informal diversion occurs whenever an official, for whatever reason, decides not to pursue a case. Formal diversion may occur in two different ways: (1) no arrest or formal charge may be made for a crime in exchange for the accused participating in some sort of formal diversion program; or (2) a trial on a formal charge is delayed on certain conditions. In the latter case, if the defendant satisfies the conditions, the charges will be dropped.

To illustrate how formal and informal diversion may operate, consider a police officer who sees a highly intoxicated man walking down a street late at night. She may decide not to arrest him even though public intoxication is a crime in her State. This is informal diversion. Alternatively, she may be required by a State statute to take him to a detoxification center rather than arresting him. This is a kind of formal diversion by statute. Alternatively, she may arrest him, but the prosecutor may informally divert him by choosing not to file any charges against him. Alternatively, the prosecutor may bring formal charges against him, but before trial, the judge may send the man to a alcohol abuse program, telling him the trial will be stayed and the charges will be dropped if the man partici-

pates in the program and is not arrested again for a year. The judge's actions may be purely discretionary, in which case this would be informal diversion and would require the prosecutor's agreement, or the actions may be required by law for this kind of case or this kind of defendant, in which case this would be considered formal diversion.

There are many reasons for the recent growth of formal diversion, a growth to which social workers have contributed. These reasons include congestion and delay in the courts, overcrowding and inhumane conditions in jails where defendants may be held pending their trials, the hardship of undergoing full criminal trials, and a desire to rehabilitate rather than punish those accused of crimes, particularly victimless crimes. Some people question whether this growth has been wholly salutary, however. Formal diversion is criticized as providing officials with an easy way to avoid exercising their discretion and as increasing, rather than reducing, involvement in the criminal justice system and the number of people considered to be criminal or treated like criminals. For example, in situations where police officers previously would have made no arrests in the exercise of their discretion, such as when people were intoxicated in public, they are now sending people to diversion programs, such as detoxification centers, where the people are labeled as some sort of deviates or problems. Others assert that coerced participation in diversion programs may make the programs mere extensions of the justice system with little potential for rehabilitation or that to force someone to participate in a diversion program under the threat of arrest, prosecution, or trial has most of the elements of the formal criminal justice system save due process. And some point to innocent defendants accepting diversion rather than going through the burdensome process of proving their innocence and risking conviction.

THE CRIMINAL JUSTICE PROCESS

The stages of the criminal process described below and pictured in Diagram 6.1 are only an approximation of the stages you may encounter. From the initial arrest to the final sentencing, a criminal case passes through numerous stages and numerous rights come into play. These stages and rights may vary from jurisdiction to jurisdiction and even within jurisdictions, each court may have its own procedures. To complicate matters further, the stages and rights may vary within a jurisdiction or a court according to the severity of the offense. For example, a jury trial might not be allowed and the appointment of counsel might not be mandated for certain petty offenses. Moreover, within a jurisdiction or a court, the stages do not necessarily occur in a set order in each case. For example, a defendant may be formally charged with an offense before she is arrested or she may be arrested and then formally charged. Finally, the criminal justice process is not a straight and narrow route with offenders steadily moving along until they have been convicted and served their sentences. The process is filled with numerous detours, roadblocks and escape hatches. At each stage, officials must decide whether to advance a case to the next stage, reroute it, or terminate it. Moreover, as we have noted, various screening and diversion methods operate to remove some from the process. Not all defendants that begin the process complete it.

Nevertheless, there are similarities in the process everywhere and certain procedures and rights are constitutionally mandated in all jurisdictions. We shall focus on these similarities and mandates in our discussion of the stages of the process. As we review the stages of the process, it might be helpful for you to refer to Diagram 6.1.

Investigating the crime

Many of the procedural protections in the Constitution address the methods that the police and other law enforcement officials[3] may use to investigate and solve crimes. The 4th Amendment provides several of the procedural protections that arise during the investigative stage of the criminal justice process. It establishes a right to be free of "unreasonable searches and seizures" and requires that "**warrants**," that is, documents issued by judicial officers which authorize searches, arrests, or other law enforcement activities, be issued only with "**probable cause**."

The importance of the 4th Amendment, which protects the right to privacy, is unquestioned, but its application into the daily operations of the criminal justice system has caused a number of problems. For example, warrants require "probable cause" but what does this mean? Further, searches and seizures without a warrant are not prohibited; only those that are "unreasonable" are prohibited, but what should be considered unreasonable? Also, when the police search illegally, what should be done as a sanction? In particular, what should be done with evidence that is illegally obtained? Should offenders be let free because a vital piece of evidence was seized unreasonably without a warrant?

There is no clear definition of the term "probable cause" in the 4th Amendment, but a working definition has emerged from the many cases on the subject. Probable cause to search is defined in terms of facts and circum-

---

3. For simplicity, the term "police" will be used to refer to all law enforcement officers.

Diagram 6.1

THE CRIMINAL JUSTICE PROCESS

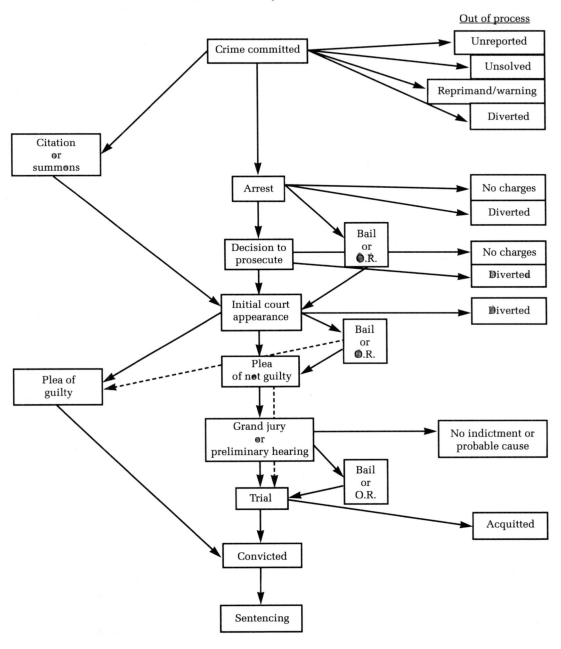

stances which would lead a reasonable person to conclude that crucial evidence would be uncovered.

The Supreme Court has tried on numerous occasions to define what is meant by "reasonable" in the context of the search-and-seizure provisions of the 4th Amendment. No clear definition has emerged but, in deciding each case, the Court has attempted to balance the needs of law enforcement with the right to privacy. The Court has required the police to obtain a search warrant before conducting a search whenever it is reasonably possible to do so. In other words, a search without a warrant may be considered unreasonable. A search of a person without a warrant is generally considered reasonable, however, if it is done at the time of, in other words, incident to, an arrest. Searches without a warrant but with probable cause of suitcases and cars for evidence which can easily be moved are also generally considered reasonable.

Since 1914, federal courts have been required to exclude illegally seized evidence from criminal trials. Since 1961, the Supreme Court has required that such evidence also be excluded from criminal trials in State courts. This requirement, known as the "**exclusionary rule**," is based on the argument that the government must not profit from illegally seized evidence and that without the rule the police would not be deterred from searching in violation of the 4th Amendment. Many are opposed to the exclusionary rule, however, arguing that it has not been effective in deterring police misconduct and that it exacts a high price from society, that is, the release of the guilty. In recent years, the Supreme Court has expressed dissatisfaction with the rule and, accordingly, has been narrowing its scope and giving greater freedom to the police.

It is clear that the 4th Amendment, as other constitutional provisions, does not apply to searches by private individuals, but it is not clear if it applies to searches by government agents other than the police undertaken for purposes other than criminal investigations. In particular, it is not clear if warrants are required for searches conducted by government agents for purposes unrelated to enforcement of the criminal law and if evidence uncovered as part of a warrantless search for such purposes should be excluded from a criminal trial that may occur.

The applicability of the search warrant requirement to so-called "**administrative searches**," that is, searches conducted by government agents for purposes unrelated to enforcement of the criminal law, is important to social workers employed by public agencies. Before undertaking a proposed administrative search, such as a search to investigate a child's care, a social worker should determine if a warrant is required. If a warrant was required and none was obtained, the search may be unlawful and any evidence obtained in the search may be inadmissible should a criminal case, such as for criminal child abuse, occur.

The courts have determined whether warrants are required for administrative searches on a case by case basis. For example, in *Wyman v. James*, 400 U.S. 309 (1971), the Supreme Court, distinguishing other cases on administrative searches, held that a warrant was not required prior to a home visit to determine eligibility for AFDC. The Court stated:

"When a case involves a home and some type of official intrusion into that home, as this case appears to do, an immediate and natural reaction is one of concern about Fourth Amendment rights and the protection which that Amendment is intended to afford. Its emphasis indeed is upon one of the most precious aspects of personal security in the home: 'The right of the people to be secure in their persons, houses, papers, and effects . . .' This Court has characterized that right as 'basic to a free society.' And over the years the Court consistently has been most protective of the privacy of the dwelling.

"This natural and quite proper protective attitude, however, is not a factor in this case, for the seemingly obvious and simple reason that we are not concerned here with any search by the . . . social service agency in the Fourth Amendment meaning of that term. It is true that the governing statute and regulations appear to make mandatory the initial home visit and the subsequent periodic 'contacts' (which may include home visits) for the inception and continuance of aid. It is also true that the caseworker's posture in the home visit is perhaps, in a sense, both rehabilitative and investigative. But this latter aspect, we think, is given too broad a character and far more emphasis than it deserves if it is equated with a search in the traditional criminal law context. We note, too, that the visitation in itself is not forced or compelled . . . If consent to the visitation is withheld, no visitation takes place. The aid then never begins or merely ceases, as the case may be. There is no entry of the home and no search. [And even if the home visit is characterized as a search,] the visit does not fall within the Fourth Amendment's proscription. This is because it does not descend to the level of unreasonableness. **It is unreasonableness which is the Fourth Amendment's standard.**"

The *Wyman* Court made clear, however, that all administrative searches conducted without a warrant would not necessarily be similarly constitutional. It intimated that even some searches conducted to determine welfare eligibility, such as "midnight raids" to find men in AFDC recipients' homes, might not be constitutional. The Court repeated what it said in a prior case:

"the specific content and incidents of [the 4th Amendment right to privacy] must be shaped by the context in which it is asserted."

Thus, an administrative search to determine, for example, whether child abuse has occurred may or may not require a warrant, depending on the circumstances. Of course, if someone refuses to permit a social worker to conduct a search, it may be necessary to obtain a warrant. And, of course, all searches, administrative or criminal, with or without a warrant, are valid if consent is given for the search, even if the consent is somewhat less than voluntary, as in *Wyman*.

The 5th Amendment provides that: "No person shall be compelled in a criminal case to be a witness against himself." Because of this guarantee, known as the guarantee against "**self-incrimination**," criminal defendants may not be compelled to testify and witnesses in any type of proceedings may refuse to answer questions that would incriminate themselves (*i.e.*, they can "take the Fifth"). This guarantee is also important at the investigative stage of the criminal justice process in relation to interrogations and confessions.

Historically, the admissibility of confessions into evidence has hinged on their being voluntary rather than coerced. In the cases of *Escobedo v. Illinois*, 364 U.S. 478 (1964), and *Miranda v. Arizona*, 384 U.S. 436 (1966), the Supreme Court added that confessions obtained without notifying suspects of their right against self-incrimination could not be admitted into evidence.

Miranda gave rise to the now familiar ***Miranda* warnings.** ("You have a right to remain silent. Anything you say can be held against you in a court of law. You have a right to have a lawyer present. If you cannot afford a lawyer, one will be appointed to represent you.") These warnings are routinely given to suspects by the police before they are questioned. If the *Miranda* warnings are not given or if suspects assert their rights after being given the warnings and the assertions of rights are ignored by the police, anything said by the suspects is subject to the exclusionary rule.

The *Miranda* warnings include a notification of the right to have a lawyer present during the interrogation process and the right to have a lawyer appointed if the accused cannot afford one. In cases after *Miranda*, the Supreme Court has emphasized this aspect of *Miranda* and stated that *Miranda* is based, not only on the 5th Amendment right against self-incrimination, but also on the 6th Amendment right to counsel.

As with searches conducted in violation of the 4th Amendment, the present Supreme Court has expressed dissatisfaction with the use of the exclusionary rule in the context of confessions taken in violation of the 5th or 6th Amendment and has been limiting its scope. In particular, the Court has ruled that *Miranda* warnings may not be required if someone is not "in custody." Because of the custody requirement, *Miranda* warnings may not apply if a government official other than a police officer questions someone, even if the questioning is about criminal activities. Thus, in *Minnesota v. Murphy*, 465 U.S. 420 (1984), a probation officer, without *Miranda* warnings, questioned a probationee about a rape and murder he had admitted to his drug counselor. The Court refused to exclude his confession to the probation officer, stating:

"To dissipate 'the overbearing compulsion . . . caused by isolation of a suspect in police custody,' the *Miranda* Court required the exclusion of incriminating statements obtained during custodial interrogation unless the suspect fails to claim the Fifth Amendment privilege after being suitably warned of his right to remain silent and of the consequences of his failure to assert it. We have consistently held, however, that this ex-

traordinary safeguard 'does not apply outside the context of the inherently coercive custodial interrogations for which it was designed.'"

Despite *Murphy* and like cases, social workers employed by public agencies must consider whether they should give clients some kind of warnings, if not the *Miranda* warnings, before they question them about activity that might lead to criminal prosecution, such as possession of illegal drugs, illegal homosexual activity, or criminal child abuse. If they fail to do so, confessions given to them may not be admissible in a criminal trial.

The arrest

The criminal justice process typically begins with the arrest of a suspect by the police. The fact that a suspect to a crime is identified as a result of police criminal investigative techniques does not necessarily mean an arrest, however. The police, instead, may cite suspects and release them upon their promises to appear in court (*i.e.*, give them "**tickets**," "**citations**" or "**summons**"). Or, they may formally or informally divert the suspect from the criminal justice process. This diversion can take several forms.

The police may simply release suspects, perhaps after issuing warning or reprimands, or may release them on the condition that they do something in return, such as participate in a treatment program or engage in a certain activity. The police may also choose or be required to take certain suspects to designated diversion centers, such as detoxification centers, instead of arresting them. Or the police may make referrals to specific social agencies. Finally the police may choose or be required to take certain suspects for screening by formal diversion programs.

The range of programs or activities to which the police may divert offenders is extensive, as is the range of offenders who may be diverted. Social workers may be involved with all the different kinds of programs, activities, and offenders. In addition, many large police departments have special units, often employing social workers or using them as consultants, which work on certain kinds of cases, like domestic disputes or child abuse, or with certain kinds of people, like the emotionally disturbed or the intoxicated. An arresting officer may refer a diversion decision to these units.[4]

In some cases, the police make arrests based on a warrant which authorizes the police to take a person into custody as a suspect or to respond to a formal charge, but generally arrests are made in the field without a warrant or a formal charge. Where there is a warrant, a police officer may have no discretion to divert.

Because arrests are considered "seizures," 4th Amendment objections may be made to warrantless arrests or even to arrests with warrants that were allegedly improperly issued. As with searches and search warrants, the Court has struggled to make clear when an arrest warrant may be issued and when the police may arrest someone without a warrant

consistently with the 4th Amendment. Basically, arrest warrants, like search warrants, require probable cause and the police may arrest without a warrant when they have probable cause to believe a crime has been committed. Some States, by statute, under their common law, or pursuant to their constitutions, require more than probable cause to arrest for misdemeanors as opposed to felonies. They may require that misdemeanors be committed in an officer's presence for a warrantless arrest to be legal. Such a requirement may be relaxed in cases of domestic violence. Citizen's arrests may also be authorized. If the police are not involved in citizen's arrests, the 4th Amendment would not apply.

There is no clear remedy when an arrest violates the 4th Amendment. Confessions taken after unlawful arrests and evidence seized incident to such arrests may be excluded from evidence, but suspects may not be released from custody and freed of all charges simply because of the unlawfulness of their arrests.

A person who is arrested is taken to a police station for processing. Before going to the police station or before processing, a person may generally be searched. The processing generally consists of taking personal data and, where required, photographing and fingerprinting. The word "**booking**" is often used to describe what is done to arrested persons although the "booking" is actually an entry in an arrest record and a minor part of the processing.

After processing, a person is either kept in custody, released on bail, or released on a promise to appear. The nature of the alleged offense determines whether and how one is released. In many jurisdictions, the police must release a suspect who posts bail in an amount set in a schedule of bail amounts for different offenses. In most jurisdictions, the police can make a discretionary decision to release less serious offenders without bail but

---

4. These special units may perform other roles for the police. Much of the police role has nothing to do with crime fighting. Much police time is spent performing social service and order maintenance functions, such as aiding the elderly with health problems, dealing with potential suicides or resolving domestic disputes. Social workers in special police units can assist in the police service role.

Social workers can also assist the police outside of special units, as staff social workers or on a referral basis. Social workers can train the police in crisis intervention techniques or other social work skills. They can also make the police aware of community resources for assisting with behavior and social problems. Without this awareness, the police may respond in ways that are familiar to them. Since they are familiar with the arrest, they may use that tool even when other responses may be more appropriate.

with a promise to appear. Social workers may help the police make decisions about releasing suspects.

After an arrest and processing, it is unlikely that discretionary police diversion will occur, but police departments with special units may have cases screened for diversion by the units after processing or referrals may be made to formal diversion programs at this point.

The charge

If there was no arrest warrant or formal charge before an arrest, the police cannot continue detaining a suspect indefinitely after processing has been completed. There must be a formal charge or warrant to justify continued detention. An arrest and a booking for a particular offense is not the equivalent of such a charge.

Some jurisdictions provide that a suspect cannot be held for more than a set amount of time, like 72 hours, without a formal charge but others trust police discretion. No specific constitutional limitations on the amount of time a suspect can be held without a formal charge have ever been set.

In some jurisdictions, the police may make the formal charges themselves. Usually they may only do so if the crime is a minor one. Often the police make formal charges for minor crimes, like traffic offenses, without making an arrest, as when a traffic ticket is issued and a suspect is released. In most jurisdictions, if a crime is a serious one, the police are required to get a formal charge from the prosecuting attorney to continue holding the suspect.

Prosecutors have wide discretion in deciding whether and what criminal charges should be filed. A major consideration in making this decision is the strength of the evidence, but other factors may also play a role.

The appropriateness of diversion for treatment, for example, may be considered. If there is a formal diversion law or program in a jurisdiction, the prosecutor's discretion to divert may be somewhat limited. Even where there are formal diversion programs, however, the prosecutor may usually decide which cases will be referred to the program.

Among the persons who may assist prosecutors in the exercise of their discretion at this stage of the criminal justice process are social workers who may be asked to evaluate the rehabilitation potential of a suspect or to recommend in favor of or against diversion. Social workers may also work in the formal diversion programs that screen the accused at this stage.

In some jurisdictions and in the federal system, the prosecutor cannot make the formal charges in felony cases. Rather, a **grand jury**, that is, a group of citizens selected to investigate crimes and make criminal charges, must make the charges.[5] In other jurisdictions, prosecutors can make charges themselves or can elect to have a grand jury make them. This is because the 5th Amendment requirement of a grand jury for capital offenses or ''infamous crimes'' has not been incorporated into the due process clause of the 14th Amendment and thus has not been applied to the States.

The grand jury may first get a case after an arrest or before a suspect is even identified. If it first gets a case after an arrest, it is supposed to act as a screening device, protecting defendants from overzealous or unscrupulous prosecutors. In practice, however, the grand jury usually does not function as an independent check on the prosecutor. By and large, grand juries are dominated by the prosecutor. The prosecutor determines which cases will be referred to the grand jury and which wit-

---

5. A trial jury is sometimes distinguished from a grand jury by calling it a ''**petit jury**.''

nesses will be summoned. The prosecutor is the legal advisor to the grand jury and makes recommendations to it. Usually defendants are not present and may not cross-examine witnesses or argue their cases; if they are present, they may not be entitled to counsel. Thus, the grand jury generally charges whom the prosecutor wants charged. In rare cases, however, grand juries exhibit independence. When they do so, they wield a large amount of power.

If a grand jury makes a charge, it is generally called an "**indictment**." A prosecutor's charge may also be called an "indictment," but more commonly it is called a "**complaint**." Other terms, like "**information**" are also used for prosecutors' or police charges.

In some jurisdictions, the victim or complaining witness must sign, join in, or otherwise agree to a complaint. Sometimes social workers counsel victims who are reluctant to sign complaints, such as in domestic violence cases.

The initial appearance

A person who has been arrested and detained must be brought before a judge without unnecessary delay for an initial appearance. Even with formal charges, suspects may not be detained for an indefinite period of time without bringing them before a court. However, the length of time that suspects can be held without appearing before a court has never been definitely established. As with detention before a formal charge, State statutes may set forth the length of time one may be held before being brought before a judge, but no specific time has ever been required constitutionally.

The initial appearance may have different names depending on the charge and the jurisdiction. It is commonly called an "**arraignment**." Whether or not a defendant has been detained, the initial appearance is a defend-

ant's first encounter with the courts for an alleged offense. Defendants who were cited in the field rather than arrested or who were released on bail or a promise to appear after an arrest, are cited to or promise to appear at the initial appearance.

At the initial appearance, defendants are given formal notice of the charges, advised of their rights, and asked to enter a plea to the charges. Most judges make little effort to determine whether defendants understand what is being explained. The advisement of rights may even be given to all defendants in the court at once.

A formal felony charge may not be made until after the initial appearance. Instead, a preliminary charge may be made pending action by a grand jury or a probable cause hearing. Thus, felony defendants often cannot enter a plea at the initial appearance and the initial appearance is a mere formality for them. Defendants who are charged with less serious offenses, however, may enter a plea at the initial appearance. Roughly three out of four misdemeanor defendants do plead guilty at the initial appearance and are sentenced immediately.[6] Thus, the initial appearance may be their only courtroom encounter.

Bail

The 8th Amendment prohibits "excessive" bail. While it would seem that this means that bail must be granted to all defendants, the 8th Amendment has been interpreted not to give a right to bail but only to prohibit excessive bail if bail is granted. Many States do not allow bail for serious charges, such as murder, or for charges carry-

6. David Neubauer, *America's Courts and the Criminal Justice System* (Monterey, CA., Brooks/Cole Publishing, 1984), p. 27.

ing long sentences. Moreover, the amount that is considered excessive has never been defined so that bail can be set in such a high amount that it realistically cannot be paid.

The purpose of bail is to insure that those who have been released from custody while they are awaiting trial will appear at their trials. Nevertheless, many courts use bail to prevent further crimes by an accused. That is, they set bail at a very high amount to keep the defendants in custody and thus prevent them from committing other crimes. This practice, known as "**preventive detention**," has been questioned as going against the presumption of innocence, but in *United States v. Salerno*, 481 U.S. 739, (1987), the Supreme Court upheld a statute authorizing no bail when a defendant is considered dangerous. In other words, it upheld the concept of preventive detention.

Bail is frequently set at the initial appearance. Although, as has been noted, in some jurisdictions there are bail schedules which permit the police to set and take bail before any appearance in court, usually bail schedules cannot be used for more serious crimes and often the bail amounts on the schedules are quite high. Moreover, bail schedules are not binding on judges. Thus, even in jurisdictions with bail schedules, defendants who are arrested and detained seek to have bail set at the initial appearance.

The most common form of bail is a cash bond. For felony defendants, bail may be set at an amount that ranges from $1,000 to over $500,000. Because most defendants do not have that much money, they hire a bail bondsman who, in return for a 10% to 15% non-refundable fee, will post bond. Some States and the federal courts permit the defendant to post the bondsman's usual percentage with the court. This eliminates the unfairness of a non-refundable fee. Whether posting actual bail or paying a bondsman's fee, payments generally must be in cash.

Sometimes courts will accept some other form of security, like a deed on a house.

An alternative to the cash bail system is release **on recognizance**. Certain defendants who are viewed as unlikely to flee are released simply on their promise to return to court; no monetary bail or bond is required.

Defendants who cannot pay the bail or the bond fees or who do not qualify for release on recognizance must await trial in jail. Many defendants are detained for long periods in overcrowded jails awaiting trial. To address this problem, several jurisdictions have established recognizance or bail projects, sometimes employing social workers, to help courts obtain information which can enable them to release more defendants on recognizance or to make better bail decisions. Even without a formal project, court service workers, who may be trained social workers, often help courts in the recognizance or bail decision.

Employing a defense attorney

The 6th Amendment guarantees criminal defendants the right to assistance of counsel. In *Gideon v. Wainwright*, 372 U.S. 335 (1963), the Court interpreted this Amendment to mean that felony defendants not only are entitled to have an attorney present at their trials but also are entitled to have one appointed to represent them if they cannot afford to pay a lawyer. Since *Gideon*, the Supreme Court has extended the right to appointment of counsel for felony defendants to all so-called critical stages of the criminal justice process in addition to the actual trial. One may have an attorney appointed while being questioned by police, while being forced to take part in a line-up, or at an adversary probable cause hearing, for example. Moreover, pursuant to *Argersinger v. Hamlin*, 407 U.S. 25 (1972), and *Scott v. Illi-*

nois, 440 U.S. 367 (1979), those convicted of misdemeanors with a penalty of incarceration are also entitled to appointment of counsel. State statutes in many States provide for further rights to appointment of counsel.

Most criminal defendants (approximately 60 percent and up to 80 percent in some large cities) cannot afford to hire a lawyer.[7] These defendants are represented in one of two ways: **assigned counsel** or **public defender**.[8] Under an assigned counsel system, a judge appoints a member of the local bar, sometimes without pay, to represent the defendant. But, increasingly, indigent defendants are represented by public defenders who are paid government attorneys responsible for representing all indigent defendants in a given jurisdiction. In small communities, the public defender may be a part-time private lawyer, but in larger communities, there may be an office employing a dozen or even several hundred attorneys.

The social worker can perform many functions as part of the defense team, particularly in a public defender's office. The social worker can help with investigation and interviewing; can help justify release on recognizance or reduced bail, can prepare witnesses and defendants for the ordeal of trial, can assist with plea bargaining by arranging for sentencing alternatives to be presented to the prosecution, and can help with the sentencing, also by arranging sentencing alternatives and by assisting the attorneys to understand and critique sentencing reports.

Because of these many possible roles, social workers have been employed in public defender offices for over 60 years and their employment in such offices has been recommended by several commissions.[9]

The preliminary hearing

The **preliminary hearing**, termed a "**preliminary examination**" or "**probable cause hearing**" in some States, is a screening device designed to protect certain defendants against unwarranted prosecutions. At the preliminary hearing, a judge will evaluate the strength of the evidence against the accused and determine if there is probable cause to believe that the defendant committed the crime. The judge may sometimes reduce the charges after a preliminary hearing or propose diversion.

As you saw in *Gerstein v. Pugh*, *supra*, the Supreme Court required some form of preliminary hearing to determine probable cause where there is only a prosecutor's charge and the defendant remains in custody, but a full adversary hearing was not required. Some States do require such adversary hearings for all felony cases by statute, even when the defendant is not in custody.

Sometimes the grand jury is used as a substitute for a preliminary hearing, but, because an accused does not have an opportunity to be heard before a grand jury, a preliminary hearing may be required even where there is a grand jury indictment.

---

7. Neubauer, *op. cit.*, p. 28.

8. In New York City and some other cities, public defenders work out of a legal aid office and are referred to as "**legal aid attorneys**."

9. *See, e.g., The Challenge of Crime in a Free Society*, Project on Standards for Criminal Justice (Chicago: American Bar Association, 1971) p. 151. To the extent that public defender offices also represent juveniles, parents charged in civil proceedings with child abuse or neglect, or people subject to involuntary commitments in mental hospitals, social workers may be of further assistance to the offices.

The plea

After any preliminary hearing or grand jury indictment, a defendant may be brought before a judge to enter a plea again or for the first time in the case of felony defendants in many States. This appearance before a judge to enter a plea is generally called an **"arraignment,"** as is the initial appearance in many jurisdictions.

At the second arraignment, defendants are given copies of the formal accusatory instrument, advised of their rights, usually more extensively than at the initial appearance, and called upon to enter a plea. As at the initial appearance, the plea may be "guilty," "not guilty," "not guilty by reason of insanity," or **"nolo contendere."** This latter plea means the defendant will not contest the charge but does not admit it. A plea of guilty or nolo contendere waives the defendant's right to a trial.

Whatever the initial plea, most criminal defendants ultimately plead guilty. Roughly 80% to 90% of felony defendants (and an even higher percentage of misdemeanor defendants) plead guilty.[10] Not all of these pleas are the result of a bargain with the prosecutor, but many are. And even when a case has gone to trial, it is likely that plea bargaining occurred—albeit unsuccessfully.

Plea bargaining is pervasive, but it is conducted differently in different jurisdictions and the participants may vary. Some judges are active participants; others may refuse to take part. The nature of the bargain also varies widely. In some instances, the defendant pleads guilty to a less serious charge than the one initially charged (*e.g.*, simple robbery rather than armed robbery) or to one or more of the counts in return for a dismissal of others, but there is no agreement as to a sentence.

In another type of plea bargain, the defendant admits guilt to the crime as charged in return for a specified sentence.

As noted, social workers can assist defense attorneys with plea bargaining by arranging for alternative sentences for defendants, such as treatment in a residential drug abuse center. Also where no agreement is made on the defendant's sentence as part of a plea bargain, the judge may ask a social worker for a recommendation before sentencing the defendant.

Pretrial motions

As had been stated, **motions** are oral or written requests for a judge to make a legal ruling in a case. Before (and during and after) trial, lawyers in a criminal case may make various types of motions. A prosecutor may file a motion to require the defendant to produce documents or to give a handwriting sample, to give two examples, but most pretrial motions are filed by the defense. The most common ones are motions to suppress evidence which the police allegedly obtained illegally (that is, motions to invoke the exclusionary rule), motions to suppress confessions which were allegedly coerced or taken in violation of *Miranda* (also motions to invoke the exclusionary rule) and motions to determine the competency of a defendant to stand trial. Even in cases where a jury is demanded, motions will be decided by judges.

The trial

The 6th Amendment guarantees criminal defendants a "speedy" and "public" trial. The word "speedy," however, has never been defined. Moreover, the Supreme Court has recognized that the defendant's interest in a speedy trial may be in conflict with other

---

10. Neubauer, *op.cit.*, p. 29.

interests of society as well as with other interests of the defendant. It has, thus, not established rigid time requirements for trials but rather has adopted a balancing test designed to give judges guidance in determining when the right to a speedy trial has been violated. State statutes may, however, set the maximum time period between arrest and trial for all crimes, for certain types of crimes, or when the defendant is in custody.

The right to a public trial is based on the assumption that if justice is done in the open, courts will act according to the law. As with the matter of speed, however, the Supreme Court has recognized that there may be circumstances when the need for a public trial has to be balanced against other interests. For example, in trials for sex crimes, particularly when the victim is a minor, courts have temporarily barred the public to spare embarrassment to the parties involved and to make witnesses more comfortable.

The 6th Amendment also guarantees a right to an "impartial jury" in all criminal cases. Nevertheless, in some criminal cases, there is no right to a jury. As with the 8th Amendment prohibition on excessive bail, the 6th Amendment right to an impartial jury does not guarantee a defendant a jury—only an impartial jury if there is a jury. The Supreme Court did, however, rule in *Duncan v. Louisiana*, 391 U.S. 155 (1968), that defendants who are charged with serious offenses have a right to a jury. In *Baldwin v. New York*, 379 U.S. 66 (1970), the Court defined this as offenses with a possible sentence of more than six months. In other rulings, the Supreme Court has said that the size of the jury is left up to the State (*see Williams v. Florida*, 379 U.S. 78 (1970), allowing a six person jury) and that unanimous verdicts are not required in any criminal trial. State laws generally specify when a criminal defendant has a right to be tried by a jury, the size of the jury, and whether a jury

verdict must be unanimous within constitutional guidelines.

To insure impartial juries, the Supreme Court has forbidden the systematic exclusion of certain types of jurors, such as Blacks or women, from jury panels. Also, although prosecutors and defendants in criminal cases, as in civil cases, may be able to *voir dire* jurors, and usually have a certain number of **peremptory challenges**, that is, challenges without a stated reason and without a requirement of good cause, the Court ruled in *Batson v. Kentucky*, 476 U.S. 79 (1986), that the prosecution may not exercise its peremptory challenges to systematically exclude Blacks from a criminal jury. The Court stated:

> "Exclusion of black citizens from service as jurors constitutes a primary example of the evil the Fourteenth Amendment was designed to cure."

The rules of evidence and of procedure of a jurisdiction control the conduct of a trial. The rules of evidence may be stricter in criminal trials to protect the rights of the accused. For example, hearsay may be more restricted in criminal trials than in civil trials because of the constitutional right to confront one's accusers.

If there has been a jury trial, at the conclusion of the presentation of evidence and any argument, the judge will instruct the jurors on the applicable law and the jurors will retire to deliberate in secret. As in a civil case, the jury's decision is known as a "**verdict**." If its verdict is "guilty" or the judge decides the defendant is guilty in a bench trial, the judge enters a judgment of **conviction**.[11] If the jury's or judge's verdict is "not guilty," there will be a judgment of **acquittal**.

---

11. There will also be a judgment of conviction entered where there has been a plea of guilty or nolo contendere.

The **double jeopardy** guarantee in the 5th Amendment means that a person charged with a criminal act can be subjected to only one trial for that act in the same jurisdiction. Thus, if a criminal defendant is acquitted rather than convicted, the prosecution may not retry the defendant. But the prohibition against double jeopardy may not always rule out successive prosecutions for an illegal act which violates the law in two jurisdictions (see, e.g., Bartkus v. Illinois, 411 U.S. 423 (1973), where a single act violated State and federal law) or where a single act constitutes two distinct offenses. The double jeopardy guarantee further does not rule out a civil and a criminal trial for the same act.

The double jeopardy guarantee may attach at an earlier point in the criminal justice process than the verdict, although what point is not clear. Generally, if a case is dismissed for some reason before the jury is seated, there may be a subsequent prosecution for the same offense, but between this point and the verdict is a large grey area. If a jury cannot agree, that is, there is a so-called "hung jury," or something extremely prejudicial has occurred, like a witness becoming hysterical under questioning, the judge may declare a **mistrial** and the defendant can be retried without violating the double jeopardy guarantee.

Sentencing

If a defendant is found guilty or has pleaded guilty with no agreement as to the sentence, the question of the appropriate sentence arises. The only constitutional stricture at this point is the 8th Amendment prohibition of "cruel and unusual punishment."

In a few States, primarily in the South, the jury may decide on the sentence, but, usually, except for the imposition of the death penalty, sentencing is left up to the judge.

Judges generally have wide discretion in imposing sentences. The law may only specify a maximum sentence, leaving the judge free to choose one or a combination of the following as the sentence:

1. **Probation**: the sentence is for a period of supervised time in the community, perhaps combined with a requirement of counseling or treatment;

2. A **suspended sentence**: the sentence is for a specific time in custody but the imposition of the sentence is suspended if the defendant fulfills certain conditions (e.g., drug treatment) or, more commonly, does not have further problems with the law;

3. A **fine**: the defendant must pay a certain amount of money to the court or into a special fund;

4. **Community service**: the defendant is sentenced to perform a certain number of hours of work for the benefit of the community;

5. **Restitution**: the defendant must pay compensatory damages to the victim of the crime;

6. A **split sentence**: a short jail sentence is combined with probation, usually for a long period;

7. **Work release** or **periodic imprisonment**: the defendant is sentenced to jail but only for weekends or only at night so that he or she may work or look for work;

8. **Imprisonment**: the defendant is sentenced to serve a term in jail or prison;

9. **Death**: also known as **"capital punishment,"** usually reserved for murder; possibly for other extremely serious crimes.

Many courts are experimenting with alternative sentences beyond these traditional sentencing options, such as chemical castration for sex offenders or bumper stickers or apologies in newspapers for drunk drivers, and several social agencies have developed pilot programs to propose alternative sentences to judges. For example, the National Center on Institutions and Alternatives has "client specific planning" projects in three test sites to propose structured alternative sentences for judges.[12] Some alternative sentences, however, may be argued to violate the 8th Amendment prohibition on cruel and unusual punishment.

It should be noted that **jails** and **prisons** are differentiated in criminal justice terminology. Jails are local institutions used to detain all those who are awaiting their initial court appearance, trial, or sentencing. Jails are also used to incarcerate those who have been convicted of misdemeanors and occasionally felonies. Prisons, on the other hand, are State or federal institutions used only to incarcerate those who have been convicted of felonies. Usually jail sentences cannot exceed one year while prison sentences are for at least one year. Because of the short time generally spent in jails and because of the combination of serious offenders awaiting trial and minor offenders serving short sentences, jails, unlike prisons, rarely have organized rehabilitation or training programs.

It should also be noted that probation is different from **parole**. In some jurisdictions, prison or jail authorities have discretion to release inmates after they have served a certain minimum term or a certain portion of the term to which they have been sentenced. This early release is known as "parole." Usually those who are paroled must have a period of supervision in the community much like probation except it occurs after being incarcer-

ated. The period of supervision is usually for the remainder of the term.

If there is no parole in a jurisdiction, there usually is a system of **good-time**. With a good-time system, inmates get credit for time served without problems or disciplinary actions. When a one day good-time credit is given for each day served without problems, the usual formula, inmates with clean records will be released after serving one half their sentences.

In some jurisdictions, **mandatory** sentencing laws require judges to give defendants convicted of certain crimes specific sentences prescribed by law. For example, those convicted of drunk driving may have to serve a jail sentence while prison may be mandatory for certain serious crimes or if certain circumstances exist (e.g., the defendant used a gun when committing the crime or the defendant committed a third felony). Under **determinate sentencing** laws, also called "mandatory" sentencing laws in some jurisdictions, a judge may have discretion to decide whether to imprison defendants, but if the judge decides to imprison them, the judge has little discretion and must sentence the defendant to a term set by the legislature or within a narrow range set by the legislature. If there are aggravating or mitigating circumstances, the judge may raise or lower the sentence, but only according to a fixed formula. By way of contrast, with **indeterminate** sentencing laws, a judge has considerable discretion in setting a sentence. If a judge imprisons a defendant, the judge may have discretion to set any length for the prison term within a broad range established by the legislature or up to a maximum set by the legislature.[13] Whether sentencing to prison is

---

12. *See* Gary Burchfield, "Alternative Sentencing: Does it Work?" *Barrister*, Vol. 11, No. 1, Winter 1984, p. 17, for a discussion of this project and other alternative sentencing approaches.

13. It should be noted that in some jurisdictions there may be both mandatory and indeterminate sentencing for particular crimes. That is, prison may be mandatory for the crimes but the judge has discretion in setting the prison term. It should also be noted that in some jurisdic-

mandatory, determinate or indeterminate, prison or parole authorities may have discretion to parole sentenced defendants.

Usually sentencing for misdemeanors is indeterminate. A mandatory jail term may be specified for certain misdemeanors (e.g., drunk driving), but the judge usually has discretion to sentence the defendant to a far longer term.

There has been substantial debate over which is the best type of sentencing law, determinate or indeterminate, mandatory or discretionary, for felonies. The trend, however, is toward mandatory and determinate sentencing, at least for the most serious crimes, if not all felonies.

There has also been considerable debate on the death penalty. Those who oppose it have used the 8th Amendment's prohibition against cruel and unusual punishment as a vehicle to challenge it. In *Furman v. Georgia*, 408 U.S. 238 (1972), the Supreme Court ruled that the death penalty, because it was so "capriciously" administered, was cruel and unusual "in the same way that being struck by lightning is cruel and unusual."

After *Furman*, many States passed laws designed to maintain the death penalty by removing the arbitrary aspects of the proceedings. Some of these new laws were invalidated, but others have been upheld. Since the first one was upheld, the death row population has rapidly risen and many have been executed, primarily in the South. The Court continues to face death penalty questions. One recurring question has been whether the death penalty reflects racial discrimination. More than one half of those executed since the first post-*Furman* execution have been Black and most of the victims of

those executed were White, but a challenge to the death penalty on this ground as a violation of equal protection was rebuffed by the Supreme Court in *McClesky v. Kemp*, 481 U.S. 279 (1987). Another recurring question has been whether the execution of youths or those who are mentally ill or mentally retarded violates the 8th Amendment.

When the judge has discretion in sentencing, a judge may ask for a **presentence report** prepared by a probation officer or court service worker, either of whom may be a trained social worker. Many jurisdictions require presentence reports before sentencing for most or many major crimes, even where the judge has no or little discretion in sentencing. The judge knows relatively little about defendants except for what was revealed in any hearings. Judges may not have defendants' official criminal records or may have records which are inaccurate or incomplete. The presentence report provides the necessary information to make a good sentencing decision. At a minimum, the presentence report will contain the defendant's criminal record, a brief social history and a description of the defendant's present employment and living situation, but the contents of the presentence report and the weight given to it by a judge varies from jurisdiction to jurisdiction and from court to court. The educational qualifications of those who prepare presentence reports similarly varies, but often they are prepared by trained social workers.

The collection, interpretation, and presentation of information about the defendant in the presentence report is a major social service role in the criminal justice process, but the role of the social worker in corrections is also important. Social workers may work in prisons, jails, in alternative sentencing settings, or in treatment programs for convicted offenders. Social workers may provide counseling or treatment in these settings or may perform evaluative functions, such as deter-

---

tions, sentencing is called "determinate," whether or not judges have discretion in setting sentences, if sentences are for a fixed term (e.g., 7 years) and "indeterminate," again whether or not judges have discretion, if sentences are for a range (e.g., 3 to 15 years).

mining whether offenders who are sentenced to prison should be sent to maximum or minimum security institutions or when they should be paroled. Social workers are also employed to do planning for inmates after their release and may work as probation or parole officers, supervising convicted criminals.

Since the Supreme Court cases of *Morrissey v. Brewer*, 408 U.S. 471 (1972), and *Gagnon v. Scarpelli*, 411 U.S. 778 (1973), due process hearings must be held where probation or parole officers recommend incarceration for parole or probation violations. This puts the parole or probation officer in a difficult position. As stated in a text on criminal justice:

> "The Parole Officer generally must fulfill two separate and distinct roles: that of social caseworker and that of rule enforcer. In the first instance, he assumes the traditional role of the social caseworker, 'the helping person,' and is supportive, understanding, and forgiving. He aids his charges in their readjustment problems and offers them a wide range of social services from counseling to employment referrals to treatment for drug addiction. At the same time, however, in his role of rule enforcer he enforces the rules of parole and the rules of society generally. He can and often, indeed, must exercise severe sanctions against parolees who substantially violate their proscribed limits.

> "That there is a role conflict here is obvious and that this creates problems for the practitioner is equally obvious. . . . Moreover, the . . . Parole Officer must deal with parolees who have a more heightened awareness of their rights and make increasing demands upon the practitioner based on these rights. The system itself has become more formal, legalistic and technical than heretofore, and, with increasing frequency, attorneys have become involved in the parole process.

> "Parole violation hearings have clearly become highly technical adversarial proceedings which have placed the parole officer in a unique, if unenviable position. Where, in the past, he has been in the virtually unassailable position of the social caseworker cloaked in 'righteous virtue,' he now, in a quasi-judicial arena, finds his actions and, indeed, even his motives under scrutiny and attack."[14]

Appeals

Criminal defendants have a right to appeal from their convictions, and, in several cases, the Supreme Court has insured that the right is meaningful by, for example, holding that indigent criminal defendants must be provided with free transcripts of their trials and, in certain instances, with appointed counsel. In many jurisdictions with two levels of trial courts, however, appeals of convictions for less serious offenses tried in the lower level courts may only be taken, as of right, to the higher level trial court. Any further appeals would be discretionary.

Sometimes convicted defendants attempt to challenge their convictions by seeking **writs of habeas corpus**. A writ of habeas corpus alleges that one is being illegally confined or restrained in some way. If the petitioner asserts that the illegality is a federal constitutional violation, the writ may be sought in federal court wherever the case was tried. Writs of habeas corpus may also be sought to challenge allegedly illegal pretrial confinement, for example, when bail is denied, and conditions of confinement at any time. We will look at the rights of prisoners to humane conditions of confinement in Chapter 17.

---

14. Howard Abadinsky, *Social Service in Criminal Justice* (New Jersey: Prentice-Hall 1979) pp. 117-118.

Because of the prohibition against being put twice in jeopardy, the prosecution may not appeal acquittals. If a defendant appeals a conviction and the conviction is reversed, however, the prosecution may retry the defendant. The defendant, in effect, waives the protection against double jeopardy by appealing.

Criminal records

A person who has been convicted of a crime, particularly of a felony, may lose various civil rights, like the right to vote or hold public office. Also a conviction, or even an arrest, may affect a person's ability to get employment, to get credit, or to get other benefits or privileges you may take for granted. For these reasons, those who have been convicted of crimes, and often those who have been arrested but not convicted, may seek to have their records cleared. A **pardon** will clear the record but pardons, which generally are purely discretionary acts by the chief executive officer of the jurisdiction where the crime was committed, are difficult to obtain. There may be no procedures established to get pardons. There may be clear procedures established to obtain an **expungement**, that is, an erasure, of a criminal record, but one may only obtain expungement if one meets the criteria set forth in an expungement law. These criteria may severely limit the opportunity for expungement. Records may be **sealed**, that is, closed to the public, but if one's record is sealed rather than expunged, one must admit convictions and arrests when asked in most circumstances and convictions may be brought up in subsequent cases. Further, the criteria for sealing records may also be stringent.

One should have no record of a conviction if one has been diverted but the record of the arrest may remain. If diversion occurs formally pursuant to a statute, often the record of the arrest is expunged or sealed.

SECTION II

JUVENILE LAW

INTRODUCTION TO JUVENILE LAW

In this section, we turn to the law related to youth. We will look first at the areas of juvenile delinquency, child protection and adoption—fields of practice chosen by many social workers and fields where social work practice cannot be separated from the law.

As we shall see, the family is protected from government intervention by the Constitution and parents have a constitutional right to raise their children as they wish, but, in instances of juvenile delinquency or where there is a need to protect children, the state may intervene in the family. It generally does so under the authority of statutes which have established either special courts to hear cases involving children or special procedures in regular courts for such cases. These statutes, which are exclusively State statutes, define the circumstances under which the State can intervene in the family, outline the procedures for intervening, and specify the responsibilities of the State once it has intervened.[1]

The names of these statutes authorizing intervention into the family to protect society against criminal acts of children or to protect children differ from State to State, but many are simply called "juvenile court acts." This text will use that term. The specific names and the structure of the special courts established by these statutes or the special procedures created by the statutes which regular courts employ for cases involving children also vary from State to State. For example, in New York family courts are juvenile courts, the higher level trial courts in California sit as juvenile courts, departments of the general trial courts in Illinois employ special procedures for cases under the Illinois juvenile court act, and in Michigan, there is a juvenile division of the probate court. This text will refer to all special courts for youth or all regular courts employing special procedures for cases involving youth as "juvenile courts."

The details of juvenile court acts differ from State to State, but all are essentially similar, and, despite the differences in name and structure of juvenile courts, all operate in much the same way. The juvenile court acts authorize the state to intervene in the family in four basic instances: (1) when a child has committed a crime; (2) when a child's behavior is thought to be injurious to his or her own welfare; (3) when a child has been neglected or abused; and (4) when a child has no parent able to care for him or her. The juvenile courts

---

1. The federal government has some laws on the procedures to follow in federal courts when a youth has violated a federal criminal statute, see U.S.C. § 5031 et seq., but treatment in State courts under State laws is preferred—even when a federal crime is committed. Moreover, the federal government does not have laws which authorize intervention in the family to protect a child although there are some federal programs to assist the States when they intervene in the family to protect children or to address delinquent behavior. These federal programs attach some conditions to the State laws authorizing intervention in the family and, thus, federal law has some impact on these areas.

have jurisdiction over cases in which it is asserted that a youth falls into one of these categories. States differ in the labels they assign to the categories, the precise definitions of the categories, and the age limits for children within each category. However, the purposes of the statutes in all States are the same: to protect children whose behavior is illegal or troublesome or whose parents cannot or will not care adequately for them. These purposes are to be served without jeopardizing the rights of parents and children who appear before the juvenile courts.

The first law creating a juvenile court was enacted in Illinois in 1899, in part as a result of the efforts of Jane Addams and other social workers. The juvenile court in Illinois and the juvenile courts that were eventually created in all the other States following the Illinois model were considered to be a product of the state's **parens patriae** authority, not its **police power**. Under the *parens patriae* authority, the state, literally as a parent, has the obligation to protect individuals who are unable to care for themselves, such as children and adults with severe mental or physical disabilities. The doctrine of *parens patriae* gives the government the authority to intervene in the family to protect children. By way of contrast, the police power gives the state the power to intervene in the family to protect society against public wrongs, to preserve law and order, and to foster morality. The criminal law is based on the police power.

Because the juvenile courts were based on the *parens patriae* authority, not the police power, they were intended to be civil, not criminal, courts. To best serve children's interests, proceedings were to be flexible, informal, and non-adversarial. The legislation in Illinois allowed "any reputable person" to file a petition asking the juvenile court to intervene in behalf of a child. It directed the court simply to "hear and dispose of the case

in a summary manner" after summons to the child's parents had been issued.

Juvenile law and juvenile courts have changed significantly since 1899. The changes reflect continuing attempts to balance society's interest in protecting children with the family's interest in privacy. The changes also reflect continuing attempts to balance the right to due process of law against the State's *parens patriae* authority to protect children and its police power to protect society. Both the family and the child should be free from government interference unless the interference comports with due process— that is, unless the interference is fundamentally just and unless the process by which the decision to interfere is made and the way in which the state interferes are fundamentally fair.

In the first two chapters of this section, we will look at juvenile court acts and juvenile courts. We will outline juvenile court jurisdiction and procedure, identify the rights of persons who come before the juvenile courts, consider other laws which permit the state to intervene in the family to protect children, and discuss the issues related to the state's intervention into family life.

Sometimes the juvenile courts determine that it would be in the best interest of children who have come before the court to permanently terminate their relationship with their parents. Sometimes parents voluntarily terminate their relationships with their children without coming before the juvenile courts. Sometimes parents die or abandon their children. Whenever children are without parents, for whatever reason, the courts may establish new parent-child relationships for them through the process of adoption. In some States in some cases, this process occurs in the juvenile courts under juvenile court acts. In most States, and in most cases, the adoption process occurs under separate laws in regular trial courts. Wherever and however it occurs, social workers play an important role in the adoption process. We will, thus, look closely at this process in the third chapter in this section.

No discussion of law related to youth would be complete without a discussion of the law related to education. Thus, the final chapter of this Section will look at legal issues related to education, reviewing those areas of greatest importance to social workers: school attendance; discipline in the schools; and special education services for handi-capped children. These areas are important to social workers because they frequently work with children who are truants or otherwise present troublesome behavior or who are handicapped. And, because social workers have a particular concern about persons who have historically suffered discrimination under the law, this Chapter will also review legal prohibitions against discrimination in public primary and secondary education.

7

Juvenile Delinquency

WHO IS DELINQUENT?

The juvenile court acts in the various States typically define a delinquent as a minor who has violated or attempted to violate any federal, State, or local criminal law. The acts in all the States further specify that those who are alleged to be delinquents fall under the exclusive jurisdiction of the juvenile court. There are, however, two exceptions to this exclusive jurisdiction.

First, many States establish a maximum age for juvenile court jurisdiction on the basis of delinquency that is less than 18, the age of legal majority. For example, the maximum age in Michigan is 17 while it is 16 in New York. Thus, 17-year-old minors who commit crimes in New York or Michigan will be tried as adults.

Second, the juvenile court acts may provide that certain minors who are under the maximum age for juvenile court jurisdiction either may or must be prosecuted as adults. For example, the juvenile court act in Illinois provides that: (1) any minor alleged to have violated a traffic law may be prosecuted under the authority of that law rather than under the provisions of the juvenile court act; (2) any minor who is charged with certain serious crimes, including murder, armed robbery and the sale of drugs, and who was at least 15 years old at the time the alleged crime was committed must be prosecuted as adult; and (3) any minor 13 years of age or older who is alleged to have violated a State criminal statute may be tried as an adult if a court determines "it is not in the best interests of the minor or of the public to proceed under this Act." Ill. Rev. Stat. ch. 37, par. 805-4(3).

Most States provide in their juvenile court acts, as does Illinois, that the juvenile court may transfer a delinquency case to adult court, or, in other words, waive its exclusive juris-

diction over the case, where it would not be in the best interests of the juvenile or society to remain in juvenile court, where serious crimes are alleged, or where the juvenile is not amenable to treatment in the juvenile court. This situation must be distinguished from the situation where minors under the maximum age for delinquency in a jurisdiction are automatically prosecuted as adults for certain serious crimes, as is also done in Illinois. In the case of waiver, the juvenile court has jurisdiction but makes a decision that the case is not appropriate for juvenile court action and releases or waives its authority. In the case of automatic prosecution as an adult, because of the statutory definition of delinquency, the juvenile court never has jurisdiction.

The Supreme Court recognized the serious consequences of waiver to adult court and set forth the due process requirements before a delinquency case may be waived in *Kent v. United States*, 383 U.S. 541 (1966), a case arising in the District of Columbia. *Kent* concerned a 16 year old, charged with housebreaking, robbery and rape, who, under the authority of the District of Columbia Juvenile Court Act, had been waived to adult court by the juvenile court judge. Kent contended that waiver was invalid because, among other things, no hearing was held, no findings were made by the judge, the judge stated no reasons for the waiver, and his counsel was denied access to certain records. The Court agreed that the waiver was invalid, stating:

"The provision of the Juvenile Court Act governing waiver . . . reads as follows: 'If a child sixteen years of age or older is charged with an offense which would amount to a felony in the case of an adult, or any child charged with an offense which if committed by an adult is punishable by death or life imprisonment, the judge may, after full investigation, waive jurisdiction and order such child held for trial under the regular procedure of the court which would have jurisdiction of such offense if committed by an adult.' [T]he statute contemplates that the Juvenile Court should have considerable latitude within which to determine whether it should retain jurisdiction over a child or—subject to the statutory delimitation—should waive jurisdiction. But this latitude is not complete. At the outset, it assumes procedural regularity sufficient in the particular circumstances to satisfy the basic requirements of due process and fairness, as well as compliance with the statutory requirement of a 'full investigation.' The statute gives the Juvenile Court a substantial degree of discretion as to the factual considerations to be evaluated, the weight to be given them and the conclusion to be reached. It does not confer upon the Juvenile Court a license for arbitrary procedure. The statute does not permit the Juvenile Court to determine in isolation and without the participation or any representation of the child the 'critically important' question whether a child will be deprived of the special protections and provisions of the Juvenile Court Act. It does not authorize the Juvenile Court, in total disregard of a motion for hearing filed by counsel, and without any hearing or statement or reasons, to decide—as in this case—that the child will be taken from [a juvenile facility] and transferred to jail along with adults, and that he will be exposed to the possibility of a death sentence instead of treatment for a maximum, in Kent's case, of five years, until he is 21.

"The theory of the District's Juvenile Court Act, like that of other jurisdictions, is rooted in social welfare philosophy rather than in the *corpus juris.*[1] Its proceedings are designated as civil rather than criminal. The Juvenile Court is theoretically engaged in determining the needs of the child and of society rather than adjudicating criminal conduct. The objectives are to provide measures of guidance and rehabilitation for the child and protection for society, not to fix criminal re-

sponsibility, guilt and punishment. The State is *parens patriae* rather than prosecuting attorney and judge. But the admonition to function in a 'parental' relationship is not an invitation to procedural arbitrariness.

"It is clear beyond dispute that the waiver of jurisdiction is a 'critically important' action determining vitally important statutory rights of the juvenile. The statutory scheme makes this plain. The Juvenile Court is vested with 'original and exclusive jurisdiction' of the child. This jurisdiction confers special rights and immunities. He is, as specified by the statute, shielded from publicity. He may be confined, but with rare exceptions he may not be jailed along with adults. He may be detained, but only until he is 21 years of age. The court is admonished by the statute to give preference to retaining the child in the custody of his parents 'unless his welfare and the safety and protection of the public can not be adequately safeguarded without . . . removal.' The child is protected against consequences of adult conviction such as the loss of civil rights, the use of adjudication against him in subsequent proceedings, and disqualification for public employment.

"The net, therefore, is that petitioner—then a boy of 16—was by statute entitled to certain procedures and benefits as a consequence of his statutory right to the 'exclusive' jurisdiction of the Juvenile Court. In these circumstances, considering particularly that decision as to waiver of jurisdiction and transfer of the matter to the [adult] Court was potentially as important to petitioner as the difference between five years' confinement and a death sentence, **we conclude that, as a condition to a valid waiver order, petitioner was entitled to a hearing, including access by his counsel to the social records and probation or similar reports which presumably are considered by the court, and to a statement of reasons for the Juvenile Court's decision.** We believe that this result is required by the statute read in the context of constitutional principles relating to due process and the assistance of counsel.

---

1.   Literally, the body of the law.

As a further protection for juveniles whose waiver is sought, the Supreme Court ruled in *Breed v. Jones*, 421 U.S. 519 (1975), that transferring a juvenile to adult court for prosecution after an adjudication of delinquency violates the 5th Amendment protection against double jeopardy.

Despite these constitutional barriers to waiver and the preference for juvenile court treatment, as expressed in *Kent*, recently more juveniles are being tried in adult court. This is due not only to more waivers but also to revisions in the juvenile court acts of many States lowering the age at which the juvenile court has jurisdiction over minors and providing for automatic prosecution as adults for certain minors committing certain serious crimes. Both actions are in response to the fact that juveniles can and do commit very serious crimes and to the view that the juvenile court, as a court under the *parens patriae* authority, not the police power, is not an appropriate place to deal with such crimes.

It should be noted that provisions for automatic prosecution of certain minors as adults, without any hearing, do not violate the due process guarantees set forth in *Kent*. As stated by the Illinois Supreme Court in *People v. J.S.*, 103 Ill. 2d. 395, 469 N.E.2d 1090 (1984), *Kent* imposed due process protections to limit the discretion of the judge, but the Illinois' automatic prosecution law does:

> "not leave room for disparity in treatment between individuals within its proscription. All 15- and 16-year-olds who have committed the enumerated offenses . . . are to be prosecuted in the adult criminal court system. There is no discretionary decision to be made by the juvenile court, and therefore we do not believe that . . . *Kent* is dispositive . . ."

If a minor's case is waived to adult court or if prosecution as an adult is automatic, the minor, if convicted, will have a criminal record and will be sentenced as if he or she were an adult—with one possible exception. Despite the statement in *Kent* that the minor could be subjected to the death penalty if he were tried in adult court, as we shall see, a major question today is whether imposition of the death penalty on minors is constitutional.

The discussion of waiver up to this point is based on the premise that the minor does not wish to be prosecuted as an adult. It should be noted that the statutes in some States allow the minor to request waiver, and if a request is made, the court must grant it.

Why would a minor ask to be tried as an adult? First, a minor who is tried as an adult has the right to trial by jury. As we will see, a minor who is tried in the juvenile court might not have this right. Second, it is possible that a sentence imposed after conviction as an adult might be less severe than a disposition following adjudication as a delinquent. For example, a 14-year-old girl convicted of vandalism as an adult is likely to be placed on probation and ordered to clean up and repair the damage or to make restitution. Any sentence would be served quickly, and the girl would then be free of the court's jurisdiction. However, if she were found to be delinquent on the basis of the vandalism, as we will also see, she might be removed from the custody of her parents and committed to a correctional institution for several years. She could remain under the jurisdiction of the court until she was 18 years old, or even older in some States.

JUVENILE COURT PROCEDURE FOR DELINQUENCY

The juvenile court process in cases of delinquency is outlined in Diagram 7.1 on the following page. You should refer to this diagram as you read the following section. You

Diagram 7.1

The Juvenile Justice Process

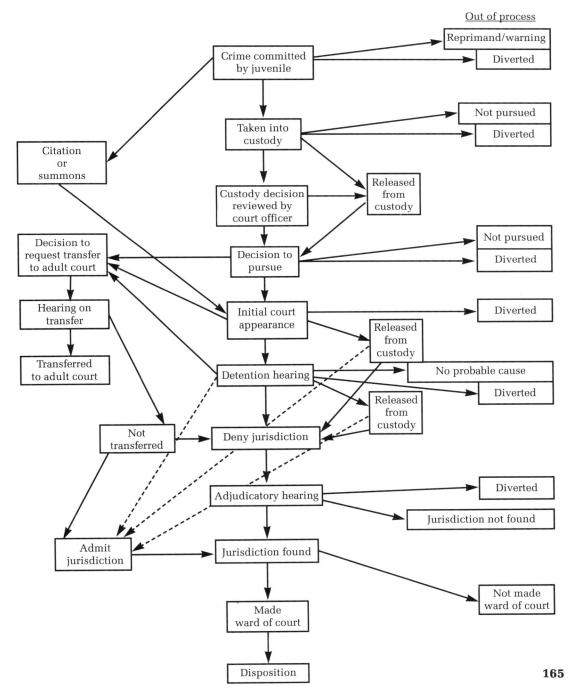

should also refer to Diagram 6.1, setting forth the criminal justice process, and compare the two processes.

Taking a juvenile into custody

If a minor commits a criminal act that is discovered, his or her first encounter with the juvenile justice system will probably be with a police or other law enforcement officer. In many States, the officer who first encounters the juvenile in the field may not be authorized to make a decision concerning the minor but must refer the minor to a special juvenile officer or a probation officer. An officer in the field in these States may be able to release a minor without making a referral to such special officers, but, unless a minor is released immediately without any further action taken, a referral to a special officer must be made.

Whoever makes the decision to take a juvenile into custody, it is important to note that juveniles are not arrested. Because juvenile court proceedings are considered to be civil and because, at least in theory, society does not wish to stigmatize juvenile offenders, the police merely take juveniles into custody. This use of special terminology is important to the juvenile offender, who, as an adult, can honestly assert ''I have no arrest record.''

There are essentially three options available to officers who make the decisions to take minors believed to have committed crimes into custody. The officers may release the minors to their parents without referring the case to the juvenile court; the officers may release the minors to their parents and refer the case to the juvenile court; or the officers may detain the minors. If minors are detained, their cases must be referred to the juvenile court.

Juveniles who are taken into custody are not ''booked.'' Rather, **intake** or the equiva-

lent is done. As suggested above, the intake decision and the decision to detain may be made by a special youth police officer. In addition or alternatively, a probation officer, who may be a trained social worker, may or must make these decisions. For example, in Illinois, a specially designated youth officer must first see a juvenile who has been taken into custody, and if the juvenile is not to be immediately released, a probation officer must screen the case. Ill. Rev. Stat. ch. 37, pars. 805-6 (1); 805-8. In many jurisdictions, the whole intake process occurs, not at a police station (except perhaps for the initial stages) or a jail, but at a juvenile hall or special youth detention center.

Juveniles who are taken into custody are entitled to full *Miranda* rights. However, in *Fare v. Michael C.*, 442 U.S. 707 (1979), the Supreme Court refused to consider a minor's request to talk to his probation officer during a police interrogation as an assertion of *Miranda* rights which would stop an interrogation as would a request for a lawyer. The dissenting opinion in *Fare* points out the serious problems with this decision.

''In *Miranda*, this Court sought to ensure that the inherently coercive pressures of custodial interrogation would not vitiate a suspect's privilege against self-incrimination. Noting that these pressures can operate very quickly to overbear the will of one merely made aware of his privilege, the Court held:

'If [a suspect in custody] indicates in any manner, at any time prior to or during questioning, that he wishes to remain silent, the interrogation must cease. At this point he has shown that he intends to exercise his Fifth Amendment privilege; any statement taken after the person invokes his privilege cannot be other than the product of compulsion, subtle or otherwise. If the individual states that he wants an attorney, the interrogation must cease until an attorney is present.'

"As this Court has consistently recognized, the coerciveness of the custodial setting is of heightened concern where, as here, a juvenile is under investigation. In [a 1948 case], the plurality reasoned that because a 15 1/2 year old minor was particularly susceptible to overbearing interrogation tactics, the voluntariness of his confession could not 'be judged by the more exacting standards of maturity.' The Court reiterated this point [in a 1962 case], observing that a 14-year-old suspect could not 'be compared with an adult in full possession of his senses and knowledgeable of the consequences of his admissions.' And, in *In re Gault*, 387 U.S. 1 (1967), [excerpted later in this chapter] the Court admonished that 'the greatest care must be taken to assure that [a minor's] admission was voluntary.'

"It is therefore critical in the present context that we construe *Miranda*'s prophylactic requirements broadly to accomplish their intended purpose—'dispel[ling] the compulsion inherent in custodial surroundings.' To effectuate this purpose, the Court must ensure that the 'protective device' of legal counsel be readily available, and that any intimation of a desire to preclude questioning be scrupulously honored. Thus, I believe *Miranda* requires that interrogation cease whenever a juvenile requests an adult who is obligated to represent his interests. Such a request, in my judgment, constitutes both an attempt to obtain advice and a general invocation of the right to silence. For, 'it is fatuous to assume that a minor in custody will be in a position to call an attorney for assistance,' or that he will trust the police to obtain a lawyer for him. A juvenile in these circumstances will likely turn to his parents, or another adult responsible for his welfare, as the only means of securing legal counsel. Moreover, a request for such adult assistance is surely inconsistent with a present desire to speak freely. Requiring a strict verbal formula to invoke the protections of *Miranda* would 'protect the knowledgeable accused from stationhouse coercion while abandon-

ing the young person who knows no more than to ask for the . . . person he trusts.'

"On my reading of *Miranda*, a California juvenile's request for his probation officer should be treated as a *per se* assertion of Fifth Amendment rights. Because the Court's contrary determination withdraws the safeguard of *Miranda* from those most in need of protection, I respectfully dissent."

The decision to detain

In *Schall v. Martin*, 467 U.S. 253 (1984), a class action arising from New York, the Supreme Court upheld a statute allowing minors to be detained prior to an adjudicatory hearing on the basis of the likelihood that they would commit further delinquent acts. In effect, the Court said that alleged delinquents may be held in preventive detention. The Court's analysis of the constitutionality of preventive detention of juveniles is excerpted below.

> "**There is no doubt that the Due Process Clause is applicable in juvenile proceedings. 'The problem,' we have stressed, 'is to ascertain the precise impact of the due process requirement upon such proceedings.'** We have held that certain basic constitutional protections enjoyed by adults accused of crimes also apply to juveniles. But the Constitution does not mandate elimination of all differences in the treatment of juveniles. The State has 'a *parens patriae* interest in preserving and promoting the welfare of the child,' which makes a juvenile proceeding fundamentally different from an adult criminal trial. **We have tried, therefore, to strike a balance—to respect the 'informality' and 'flexibility' that characterize juvenile proceedings, and yet to ensure that such proceedings comport with the 'fundamental fairness' demanded by the Due Process Clause.**

"The statutory provision at issue in this case, permits a brief pretrial detention based on a finding of a 'serious risk' that an arrested juvenile may commit a crime before his [trial]. [This] [p]reventive detention . . . is purportedly designed to protect the child and society from the potential consequences of his criminal acts. When making any detention decision, the . . . judge is specifically directed to consider the needs and best interests of the juvenile as well as the need for the protection of the community. As an initial matter, therefore, we must decide whether, in the context of the juvenile system, the combined interest in protecting both the community and the juvenile himself from the consequences of future criminal conduct is sufficient to justify such detention.

"**The 'legitimate and compelling state interest' in protecting the community from crime cannot be doubted.** We have stressed before that crime prevention is 'a weighty social objective,' and this interest persists undiluted in the juvenile context. The harm suffered by the victim of a crime is not dependent upon the age of the perpetrator. And the harm to society generally may even be greater in this context given the high rate of recidivism among juveniles.

"**The juvenile's countervailing interest in freedom from institutional restraints, even for the brief time involved here, is undoubtedly substantial as well.** But that interest must be qualified by the recognition that juveniles, unlike adults, are always in some form of custody. Children, by definition, are not assumed to have the capacity to take care of themselves. They are assumed to be subject to the control of their parents, and if parental control falters, the State must play its part as *parens patriae*. In this respect, **the juvenile's liberty interest may, in appropriate circumstances, be subordinated to the State's '*parens patriae* interest in preserving and promoting the welfare of the child.'**

"[I]n upholding the statute at issue here, [the court below] stressed at some length 'the desirability of protecting the juvenile

from his own folly.' Society has a legitimate interest in protecting a juvenile from the consequences of his criminal activity—both from potential physical injury which may be suffered when a victim fights back or a policeman attempts to make an arrest and from the downward spiral of criminal activity into which peer pressure may lead the child.

"The substantiality and legitimacy of the state interests underlying this statute are confirmed by the wide-spread use and judicial acceptance of preventive detention for juveniles. Every State . . . permits preventive detention of juveniles accused of crime. A number of model juvenile justice acts also contain provisions permitting preventive detention. And the courts of eight States, including the [highest New York appellate court,] have upheld their statutes with specific reference to protecting the juvenile and the community from harmful pretrial conduct, including pretrial crime.

"The fact that a practice is followed by a large number of states is not conclusive in a decision as to whether that practice accords with due process, but it is plainly worth considering in determining whether the practice 'offends some principle of justice so rooted in the traditions and conscience of our people as to be ranked as fundamental.' **In light of the uniform legislative judgment that pretrial detention of juveniles properly promotes the interests both of society and the juvenile, we conclude that the practice serves a legitimate regulatory purpose compatible with the 'fundamental fairness' demanded by the Due Process Clause in juvenile proceedings.**"

It should be noted that under the statute in question in *Schall*, if juveniles were detained at their initial appearances and denied the charges against them, they were entitled to a judicial hearing within three days. At this hearing, to justify continued detention, a judge had to determine both that there was probable cause to believe the juvenile committed the crime alleged and that there was a continued need to detain the juvenile. Moreover, detained juveniles were entitled to a final hearing within a very short time—17 days from the initial appearance for serious offenses and 6 days for less serious offenses. The Court stated:

> "These time-frames seem suited to the limited purpose of providing the youth with a controlled environment and separating him from improper influences pending the speedy disposition of his case."

It is unlikely that the Court in *Schall* would have found detention for a more extended period and without a judicial hearing constitutional. Although it found the New York statute authorizing preventive detention valid with these procedural protections, it also stated that "in some circumstances detention of a juvenile would not pass constitutional muster."

Many States have more stringent time limits than those approved in *Schall* and require immediate judicial hearings to determine probable cause and the need for continued detention. Although the Court did not say so in *Schall*, such judicial hearings, generally known as "**detention hearings**," are probably constitutionally required.

Generally, the decision to detain, whether made by a police or probation officer or by a judge after a detention hearing, is based not so much on the offense charged but on other considerations, such as the willingness and ability of the parents to supervise the minor and the minor's attitude and history. Many States' juvenile court acts list factors to consider in deciding whether to release a minor. The acts may provide that preference should be given to releasing a minor.

Juveniles have no constitutional right to release on bail (unless they are being tried as adults), but a few States do give them a right to release on bail, for all cimes or for certain crimes.

Where to detain juveniles has posed a problem for many years. It is alien to the philosophy and special nature of the juvenile courts to detain juveniles in jails with adults, many of whom are awaiting trial for crimes like murder and rape, but many jurisdictions do precisely that. Many jurisdictions have no special facilities for juveniles. To remedy this, the federal Juvenile Justice and Delinquency Prevention Act, 42 U.S.C. § 5601 *et seq.*, mandated as early as 1974, that in order to receive federal funds for delinquency prevention, a State must:

> "provide that juveniles alleged to be or found to be delinquent . . . shall not be detained or confined in any institution in which they have regular contact with adult persons incarcerated because they have been convicted of a crime or are awaiting trial on criminal charges." § 5633 (13).

A State must further:

> "provide that . . . no juvenile shall be detained or confined in any jail or lock up for adults." § 5633 (14).

Exceptions were and continue to be allowed to the latter mandate in areas with a low population density and for juveniles accused of serious crimes against persons when no existing alternative placement is available. Moreover, many States are out of compliance with the federal law, and there is nothing under federal law to prohibit detention of alleged delinquents in the same facility in which adjudicated delinquents are held. Further, there is nothing requiring that a facility for delinquents be homelike. Indeed, the dissent in *Schall* pointed out the prison-like nature of the detention center in New York where the named plaintiffs in the case were held.

The decision to pursue a case

Juvenile court action is initiated through the filing of a petition. The petition presents information about a minor, alleges that a minor falls under the jurisdiction of the court, and specifies reasons for the petitioner's belief that the minor falls under the jurisdiction of the court. The petition will typically be entitled "In re (the child's name)" or "In the Matter of (the child's name)."

The decision to proceed with a delinquency petition is typically made by a probation officer, but it may be made by the police or, in serious cases, by a prosecuting attorney. The petition usually is prepared and filed by a prosecuting attorney if serious crimes are alleged or if the juvenile is being detained and therefore must have a detention hearing.

Often a decision is made to divert a minor from the juvenile court system instead of filing a petition. Many juvenile court acts urge diversion as an alternative to pursuing a case in juvenile court. Also, often a decision is made to seek a transfer of a case to adult court instead of pursuing the case in juvenile court. In some States, like Colorado, when certain crimes are alleged to have been committed, a prosecutor has discretion to decide whether to prosecute the case in adult court or pursue it in juvenile court, but in most States, a prosecutor must move a juvenile court to waive its exclusive jurisdiction of the juvenile.

The jurisdictional or adjudicatory hearing

The petition alleges that the juvenile court has jurisdiction over a minor and why, because juvenile courts technically do not decide whether a youth is guilty or innocent of committing a crime. Rather, they determine whether they have jurisdiction over minors because they committed crimes or adjudicate minors to be a delinquent because of their commission of a crime. This occurs at a hearing called the "**jurisdictional**" or "**adjudicatory**" hearing or, because the purpose of the hearing is to determine whether the allegation in the petition that a crime was committed by the juvenile is supported by the evidence, the "**fact-finding**" hearing. If the judge finds that the minor committed the crime, the judge will enter a finding of delinquency and assume jurisdiction. The judge may then determine the appropriate intervention in behalf of the minor, but, generally, this determination will be made at a later hearing, usually known as a "**dispositional hearing**."

The judge typically has several options at the jurisdictional hearing. The judge may, as just stated, find the minor to be delinquent. The judge also may find, after hearing all evidence, that the minor is not delinquent. If this is the case, the judge will dismiss the petition. The judge may also be able to arrange some form of diversion. For example, the judge may be able to delay a finding of delinquency and ultimately dismiss the petition if the minor abides by certain conditions that the judge imposes, such as that the minor commit no more illegal acts, attend school regularly, and participate in counseling. If the judge learns that the minor has violated these conditions, the judge can resume the hearing.

In *In re Gault*, 387 U.S. 1 (1967), the Supreme Court set forth many of the elements of due process essential to a fair jurisdictional hearing of a minor. In *Gault*, Gerald Gault, a 15 year old from Arizona, had been taken into custody after he allegedly made lewd remarks to a neighbor in a telephone call. He was on probation at the time. Gerald's parents were not notified that their son had, in effect, been arrested. They were not served with a copy of the petition alleging delinquency. The petition did not include specific notice of the charges. Gerald had several appearances before the juvenile court judge, but no formal hearing was ever held, the complaining witness was not present at any appearance, no transcript or recording of the appearances was ever made, and Gerald was not represented by counsel. Gerald nevertheless was found to be delinquent and was committed to the State Industrial School until he reached the age of majority. Gerald sought release through a writ of *habeas corpus* since no appeal of his adjudication and commitment was allowed under Arizona law. He challenged the proceedings that led to his commitment as a violation of due process. The Arizona Supreme Court upheld his commitment, but the Supreme Court reversed it. It stated:

"From the inception of the juvenile court system, wide differences have been tolerated—indeed insisted upon—between the procedural rights accorded to adults and those of juveniles. In practically all jurisdictions, there are rights granted to adults which are withheld from juveniles. In addition to the specific problems involved in the present case, for example, it has been held that the juvenile is not entitled to bail, to indictment by grand jury, to a public trial or to trial by jury. It is frequent practice that rules governing the arrest and interrogation of adults by the police are not observed in the case of juveniles.

"The history and theory underlying this development are well-known . . . The Juvenile Court movement began in this country at the end of the last century. From the juvenile court statute adopted in Illinois in 1899, the system has spread to every State in the Union, the District of Columbia, and Puerto Rico. The early reformers were appalled by adult procedures and penalties, and by the fact that children could be given long prison sentences and mixed in jails with hardened criminals. They were profoundly convinced that society's duty to the child could not be confined by the concept of justice alone.

They believed that society's role was not to ascertain whether the child was 'guilty' or 'innocent,' but 'What is he, how has he become what he is, and what had best be done in his interest and in the interest of the state to save him from a downward career.' The child—essentially good, as they saw it—was to be made 'to feel that he is the object of [the state's] care and solicitude,' not that he was under arrest or on trial. The rules of criminal procedure were therefore altogether inapplicable. The apparent rigidities, technicalities, and harshness which they observed in both substantive and procedural criminal law were therefore to be discarded. The idea of crime and punishment was to be abandoned. The child was to be 'treated' and 'rehabilitated' and the procedures, from apprehension through institutionalization, were to be 'clinical' rather than punitive.

"These results were to be achieved, without coming to conceptual and constitutional grief, by insisting that the proceedings were not adversary, but that the state was proceeding as *parens patriae*. The Latin phrase proved to be a great help to those who sought to rationalize the exclusion of juveniles from the constitutional scheme; but its meaning is murky and its historic credentials are of dubious relevance. [T]here is no trace of the doctrine in the history of criminal jurisprudence. At common law, children under seven were considered incapable of possessing criminal intent. Beyond that age, they were subjected to arrest, trial, and in theory to punishment like adult offenders. In these old days, the state was not deemed to have authority to accord them fewer procedural rights than adults.

"The right of the state, as *parens patriae*, to deny to the child procedural rights available to his elders was elaborated by the assertion that a child, unlike an adult, has a right 'not to liberty but to custody.' He can be made to attorn to his parents, to go to school, etc. If his parents default in effectively performing their custodial functions—that is, if the child is 'delinquent'—the state may intervene. In doing so, it does not deprive the child of any rights, because he has none. It merely provides the 'custody' to which the child is entitled. On this basis, proceedings involving juveniles were described as 'civil' not 'criminal' and therefore not subject to the requirements which restrict the state when it seeks to deprive a person of his liberty.

"Accordingly, the highest motives and most enlightened impulses led to a peculiar system for juveniles, unknown to our law in any comparable context. The constitutional and theoretical basis for this peculiar system is—to say the least—debatable. And in practice, . . . the results have not been entirely satisfactory. Juvenile Court history has again demonstrated that unbridled discretion, however benevolently motivated, is frequently a poor substitute for principle and procedure. In 1937, [the Dean of Harvard Law School] wrote: 'The powers of the Star Chamber were a trifle in comparison with those of our juvenile courts . . .' The absence of substantive standards has not necessarily meant that children receive careful, compassionate, individualized treatment. The absence of procedural rules based upon constitutional principle has not always produced fair, efficient, and effective procedures. Departures from established principles of due process have frequently resulted not in enlightened procedure, but in arbitrariness. [It has recently been] observed: 'Unfortunately, loose procedures, high-handed methods and crowded court calendars, either singly or in combination, all too often, have resulted in depriving some juveniles of fundamental rights * * * '

"Due process of law is the primary and indispensable foundation of individual freedom. It is the basic and essential term in the social compact which defines the rights of the individual and delimits the powers which the state may exercise. As Mr. Justice Frankfurter has said: 'The history of American freedom is, in no small measure, the history of procedure.' But, in addition, the pro-

cedural rules which have been fashioned from the generality of due process are our best instruments for the distillation and evaluation of essential facts from the conflicting welter of data that life and our adversary methods present. It is these instruments of due process which enhance the possibility that truth will emerge from the confrontation of opposing versions and conflicting data. 'Procedure is to law what "scientific method" is to science.'

"It is claimed that juveniles obtain benefits from the special procedures applicable to them which more than offset the disadvantages of denial of the substance of normal due process. As we shall discuss, the observance of due process standards, intelligently and not ruthlessly administered, will not compel the States to abandon or displace any of the substantive benefits of the juvenile process. But it is important, we think, that the claimed benefits of the juvenile process should be candidly appraised. Neither sentiment nor folklore should cause us to shut our eyes, for example, to such startling findings as that reported in an exceptionally reliable study . . . [that found, among other things, that 66% of the 16- and 17-year-old juveniles referred to the juvenile court had been before the court previously and that 56% of those held in a detention center were repeaters.]

"Certainly, these figures and the high crime rates among juveniles . . ., could not lead us to conclude that the absence of constitutional protections reduces crime, or that the juvenile system, functioning free of constitutional inhibitions as it has largely done, is effective to reduce crime or rehabilitate offenders. We do not mean by this to denigrate the juvenile court process or to suggest that there are not aspects of the juvenile system relating to offenders which are valuable. But the features of the juvenile system which its proponents have asserted are of unique benefit will not be impaired by constitutional domestication. For example, the commendable principles relating to the processing and treatment of juveniles separately from adults are in no way involved or affected by the procedural issues under discussion. Further, we are told that one of the important benefits of the special juvenile court procedures is that they avoid classifying the juvenile as a 'criminal.' The juvenile offender is now classed as a 'delinquent.' There is, of course, no reason why this should not continue. It is disconcerting, however, that this term has come to involve only slightly less stigma than the term 'criminal' applied to adults. It is also emphasized that in practically all jurisdictions, statutes provide that an adjudication of the child as a delinquent shall not operate as a civil disability or disqualify him for civil service appointment. There is no reason why the application of due process requirements should interfere with such provisions.

''Beyond this, it is frequently said that juveniles are protected by the process from disclosure of their deviational behavior. [T]he summary procedures of Juvenile Courts are sometimes defended by a statement that it is the law's policy 'to hide youthful errors from the full gaze of the public and bury them in the graveyard of the forgotten past.' This claim of secrecy, however, is more rhetoric than reality. [And] . . . there is no reason why, consistently with due process, a State cannot continue if it deems it appropriate, to provide and to improve provision for the confidentiality of records of police contacts and court action relating to juveniles.

''Further, it is urged that the juvenile benefits from informal proceedings in the court. The early conception of the Juvenile Court proceeding was one in which a fatherly judge touched the heart and conscience of the erring youth by talking over his problems, by paternal advice and admonition, and in which, in extreme situations, benevolent and wise institutions of the State provided guidance and help 'to save him from a downward career.' Then, as now, goodwill and compassion were admirably prevalent. But recent studies have, with surprising unanimity, entered sharp dissent as to the validity of this gentle conception. They suggest that the appearance as well as the actuality of fairness, impartiality and orderliness—in short, the essentials of due process—may be a more impressive and more therapeutic attitude so far as the juvenile is concerned. For example, in a recent study, . . . [it is observed] that when the procedural laxness of the 'parens patriae' attitude is followed by stern disciplining, the contrast may have an adverse effect upon the child, who feels that he has been deceived or enticed. [The study] conclude[s] as follows: 'Unless appropriate due process of law is followed, even the juvenile who has violated the law may not feel that he is being fairly treated and may therefore resist the rehabilitative efforts of court personnel.' Of course, it is not suggested that juvenile court judges should fail appropriately to take account, in their demeanor and conduct, of the emotional and psychological attitude of the juveniles with whom they are confronted. While due process requirements will, in some instances, introduce a degree of order and regularity to Juvenile Court proceedings to determine delinquency, and in contested cases will introduce some elements of the adversary system, nothing will require that the conception of the kindly juvenile judge be replaced by its opposite.

''Ultimately, however, we confront the reality of that portion of the Juvenile Court process with which we deal in this case. A boy is charged with misconduct. The boy is committed to an institution where he may be restrained of liberty for years. It is of no constitutional consequence—and of limited practical meaning—that the institution to which he is committed is called an Industrial School. The fact of the matter is that, however euphemistic the title, . . . an 'industrial school' for juveniles is an institution of confinement in which the child is incarcerated for a greater or lesser time. His world becomes 'a building with whitewashed walls, regimented routine and institutional hours . . . .' Instead of mother and father and sisters and brothers and friends and class-mates, his world is peopled by guards, cus-todians, state employees, and 'delinquents' confined with him for anything from way-wardness to rape and homicide.

"In view of this, **it would be extraordinary if our Constitution did not require the proce-dural regularity and the exercise of care im-plied in the phrase 'due process.' Under our Constitution, the condition of being a boy does not justify a kangaroo court**. The tradi-tional ideas of Juvenile Court procedure, in-deed, contemplated that time would be available and care would be used to establish precisely what the juvenile did and why he did it—was it a prank of adolescence or a brutal act threatening serious consequences to himself or society unless corrected? Un-der traditional notions, one would assume that in a case like that of Gerald Gault, where the juvenile appears to have a home, a work-ing mother and father, and an older brother, the Juvenile Judge would have made a care-ful inquiry and judgment as to the possibil-ity that the boy could be disciplined and dealt with at home, despite his previous transgressions. [But, in this case,] . . . the points to which the judge directed his atten-tion were little different from those that would be involved in determining any charge of violation of a penal statute. **The es-sential difference between Gerald's case and a normal criminal case is that safe-guards available to adults were discarded in Gerald's case. The summary procedure as well as the long commitment was possi-ble because Gerald was 15 years of age in-stead of over 18.** So wide a gulf between the State's treatment of the adult and of the child requires a bridge sturdier than mere verbi-age, and reasons more persuasive than cli-che can provide. As . . . [has been observed by two sociologists:] 'The rhetoric of the ju-venile court movement has developed with-out any necessarily close correspondence to the realities of court and institutional rou-tines.'"

The Court went on to conclude that in juve-nile court proceedings to adjudicate delin-quency, due process requires at a minimum:

(1) "notice which would be deemed con-stitutionally adequate in a civil or crimi-nal proceeding . . . [Due Process] does not allow a hearing to be held in which a youth's freedom and his parents' right to his custody are at stake without giving them timely notice, in advance of the hear-ing, of the specific issues that they must meet."

(2) that "the child and his parents must be notified of the child's **right to be repre-sented by counsel** retained by them, **or if they are unable to afford counsel, that counsel will be appointed** to represent the child."

(3) that "**the constitutional privilege against self-incrimination** is applicable in the case of juveniles as it is with respect to adults," and

(4) that "absent a valid confession, a deter-mination of delinquency and an order of commitment to a state institution cannot be sustained in the absence of sworn testi-mony subjected to the opportunity for cross-examination in accordance with our law and constitutional requirements."

In a later decision, *In re Winship*, 397 U.S. 358 (1970), the Supreme Court added proof beyond a reasonable doubt to these essential elements of due process established by *Gault*. The Court stated:

"The constitutional safeguard of proof be-yond a reasonable doubt is as much required during the adjudicatory stage of a delin-quency proceeding as are those constitu-tional safeguards applied in *Gault*—notice of charges, right to counsel, the rights of confrontation and examination, and the privilege against self-incrimination.

[W]here a 12-year-old child is charged with an act of stealing which renders him liable to confinement for as long as six years, then, as a matter of due process . . . the case against him must be proved beyond a reasonable doubt.''

Taken together *Gault* and *Winship* gave minors accused of committing a crime all the basic rights at trial accorded to adults accused of committing a crime except one—trial by jury. The Supreme Court later held in *McKeiver v. Pennsylvania*, 403 U.S. 441 (1971), that trial by jury was not a ''constitutional requirement'' for juveniles. The Court offered a number of reasons for its conclusion, among them that trial by jury was disallowed by either statute or court opinion in the majority of the States and a number of model juvenile court acts had not provided for trial by jury. But as the following excerpts from *McKeiver* illustrate, the Court perhaps was simply unwilling to abandon the belief in the wisdom of less formal proceedings that underlies the juvenile court philosophy.

''There is a possibility, at least, that the jury trial, if required as a matter of constitutional precept, will remake the juvenile proceeding into a fully adversary process and will put an effective end to what has been the idealistic prospect of an intimate, informal protective proceeding.

''The juvenile concept held high promise. We are reluctant to say that, despite disappointments of grave dimensions, it still does not hold promise, and we are particularly reluctant to say . . . that the system cannot accomplish its rehabilitative goals. So much depends on the availability of resources, on the interest and commitment of the public, on willingness to learn, and on understanding as to cause and effect and cure. In this field, as in so many others, one perhaps learns best by doing. We are reluctant to disallow the States to experiment further and to

seek in new and different ways the elusive answers to the problems of the young, and we feel that we would be impeding that experimentation by imposing the jury trial. The States, indeed, must go forward. If, in its wisdom, any State feels the jury trial is desirable in all cases, or in certain cases, there appears to be no impediment to its installing a system embracing that feature. That, however, is the State's privilege and not its obligation.

''Finally, the arguments advanced by the juveniles here . . . equate the juvenile proceeding—or at least the adjudicative phase of it—with the criminal trial. [In seeking to equate the two types of proceedings, they] . . . ignore, it seems to us, every aspect of fairness, of concern, of sympathy, and of paternal attention that the juvenile court system contemplates. If the formalities of the criminal adjudicative process are to be superimposed upon the juvenile court system, there is little need for its separate existence. Perhaps that ultimate disillusionment will come one day, but for the moment we are disinclined to give impetus to it.''

The dispositional decision

The dispositional alternatives available to the court following an adjudication of delinquency are generally defined by State statutes. The commonly available dispositions are court supervision, probation, commitment to a child welfare agency and commitment to a correctional agency. The choice of disposition reflects both the offense and the minor's characteristics and is usually not made until an investigation of the minor and the minor's potential for rehabilitation has been completed, generally by a probation officer or other court officer.

Court supervision, probation, and commitment to a child welfare agency may occur with or without an order removing the child from his or her home. Court supervision and probation are similar in that in both cases, the minor must comply with certain orders of the court. For example, the minor may be ordered to go to school, work part-time, attend counseling sessions, be home by 9:00 p.m. every night and so on. The difference is that under probation, the minor must report regularly to a probation officer while under court supervision, the minor is not required to report to a probation officer. If the minor is ordered removed from the home and committed to a child welfare agency or to a correctional agency, usually the agency will assess the minor and determine the proper placement for the minor, consistent with any orders made or restrictions imposed by the court. Some courts make placement decisions themselves.

A minor who has been adjudicated delinquent may or may not be made a **ward of the court**, a term used in most States to describe the continuing authority of the court over the minor. If the minor is made a ward of the court, certain rights and responsibilities may be removed from the minor's parents and vested with the court. The court will, in turn, typically delegate these rights and responsibilities to the probation office, a child welfare agency or a correctional agency as part of its disposition. The court will often give the agency **custody** of the minor—that is, the responsibility for the minor's daily care—and **guardianship** over the minor—that is, the right and responsibility to make legal decisions for the minor.

It is important to note that even if custody and guardianship of a minor are given to an agency, the minor may remain at home with his or her parents. It is also important to note that while foster care is usually associated with neglected or abused minors, delinquents may also be placed with foster parents.

Whatever the disposition of a juvenile adjudicated delinquent, if he or she is made a ward of the court, the court will retain jurisdiction over him or her and may modify its disposition at any time. Often it will retain jurisdiction until the minor reaches majority or possibly older. During the period it retains jurisdiction, the agency to which the court delegated authority will report periodically to the court.

The retention of jurisdiction and the ability to modify a disposition are major ways in which the juvenile court differs from the adult criminal court. When adults are sentenced, the sentencing court loses jurisdiction of the case and has no continuing authority to modify orders. Even if a defendant is sentenced to probation or if the sentence is suspended, the court may only intervene if the defendant violates specific conditions of probation or of the suspension of the sentence. If this occurs, the court may only revoke probation or impose the suspended sentence.

THE DEATH PENALTY FOR JUVENILES

Many States permit the execution of persons who are convicted of committing a capital crime when still a minor, and at least three such persons have been executed since 1985. Nevertheless, whether the imposition of the death penalty for crimes committed while a minor is constitutional remains a major question.

In *Eddings v. Oklahoma*, 455 U.S. 104 (1982), the Supreme Court held that the death penalty as it was imposed on a person who was 16 years old at the time he committed a murder was unconstitutional in that the sentencing judge did not consider mitigating circumstances as required by an earlier Supreme Court decision. It further held that courts were required to consider age as a mitigating factor. The Court specifically stated, however: "we do not reach the question of whether—in light of contemporary standards—the 8th Amendment forbids the execution of a defendant who was 16 at the time of the offense."

Six years later, in *Thompson v. Oklahoma*, 108 S.Ct. 2687 (1988), the Court answered this question by holding that the 8th and 14th Amendments prohibit the execution of those who are under 16 years of age at the time of their offenses. The constitutional question concerning persons less than 16 has, thus, been answered, but the Court has not addressed the question concerning minors who are 16 or 17 years old at the time of the offense. How the Court might rule is uncertain; the decision in *Thompson* was a plurality decision, with four justices joining in the opinion, one justice concurring only in the judgment, and three justices dissenting. Excerpts from the plurality opinion in *Thompson* that review the 1988 status of the death penalty for juvenile offenders and the arguments about it follow.

"The authors of the Eighth Amendment drafted a categorical prohibition against the infliction of cruel and unusual punishment, but they made no attempt to define the contours of that category. They delegated that task to future generations of judges who have been guided by the 'evolving standards of decency that mark the progress of a maturing society.' In performing that task [in the present case] the Court has reviewed the work product of state legislatures and sentencing juries, and has carefully considered the reasons why a civilized society may accept or reject the death penalty in certain types of cases.

"The line between childhood and adulthood is drawn in different ways by various States. There is, however, complete or near unanimity among all 50 States and the District of Columbia in treating a person under 16 as a minor for several different purposes. [Those noted by the Court are voting; serving on a jury; purchasing pornographic materials; and driving, marrying, and gambling without parental consent.] Most relevant, however, is the fact that all States have enacted legislation designating the maximum age for juvenile court jurisdiction at no less than 16. All of this legislation is consistent with the experience of mankind, as well as the long history of our law, that the normal 15-year-old is not prepared to assume the full responsibilities of an adult.

"Most state legislatures have not expressly confronted the question of establishing a minimum age for imposition of the death penalty. In 14 States [Alaska, District of Columbia, Hawaii, Iowa, Kansas, Maine, Massachusetts, Michigan, Minnesota, New York, North Dakota, Rhode Island, West Virginia, and Wisconsin], capital punishment is not authorized at all, and in 19 others [Alabama, Arizona, Arkansas, Delaware, Florida, Idaho, Louisiana, Mississippi, Missouri, Montana, Oklahoma, Pennsylvania, South Carolina, South Dakota, Utah, Vermont, Virginia, Washington, and Wyoming] capital punishment is authorized but no minimum age is expressly stated in the death penalty statute. [All of the] 18 States that have expressly established a minimum age in their death penalty statutes [California, Colorado, Connecticut, Georgia, Illinois, Indiana, Kentucky, Maryland, Nebraska, Nevada, New Hampshire, New Jersey, New Mexico, North Carolina, Ohio, Oregon, Tennessee, and Texas] . . . require that the defendant have attained the age of at least 16 at the time of the capital offense. The conclusion [of all the States that have addressed the issue] that it would offend civilized standards of decency to execute a person who was less than 16 years old at the time of his or her offense is consistent with the views that have been expressed by respected professional organizations, by other nations that share our Anglo-American heritage, and by the leading members of the Western European community.

"[Looking to the behavior of juries in] the past four decades—in which thousands of juries have tried murder cases—leads to the unambiguous conclusion that the imposition of the death penalty on a 15-year-old offender is now generally abhorrent to the conscience of the community.

"Although the judgments of legislatures [and] juries . . . weigh heavily in the balance, it is for us ultimately to judge whether the Eighth Amendment permits imposition of the death penalty 'on one such petitioner who committed a heinous murder when he was only 15 years old. In making that judgment, we first ask whether the juvenile's culpability should be measured by the same standard as that of an adult, and then consider whether the application of the death penalty to this class of offenders 'measurably' contributes to the social purposes that are served by the death penalty.

"The Court has already endorsed the proposition that less culpability should attach to a crime committed by a juvenile than to a comparable crime committed by an adult. The basis for this conclusion is too obvious to require extended explanation. Inexperience, less education, and less intelligence make the teenager less able to evaluate the consequences of his or her conduct while at the same time he or she is much more apt to be motivated by mere emotion or peer pressure than is an adult. The reasons why juveniles are not trusted with the privileges and responsibilities of an adult also explain why their irresponsible conduct is not as morally reprehensible as that of an adult.

"[In *Gregg v. Georgia*, 428 U.S. 153 (1976), we said:] 'The death penalty is said to serve two principal social purposes: retribution and deterrence of capital crimes by prospective offenders.' [W]e concluded that as 'an expression of society's moral outrage at particularly offensive conduct,' retribution was not 'inconsistent with our respect for the dignity of men.' Given the lesser culpability of the juvenile offender, the teenager's capacity for growth, and society's fiduciary obligations to its children, this conclusion is simply inapplicable to the execution of a 15-year-old offender.

"For such a young offender, the deterrence rationale is equally unacceptable. With respect to those under 16 years of age, it is obvious that the potential deterrent value of the death sentence is insignificant for two reasons. The likelihood that the teenage offender has made the kind of cost-benefit analysis that attaches any weight to the possibility of execution is so remote as to be virtually nonexistent. And, even if one posits such a cold-blooded calculation by a 15-year-old, it is fanciful to believe that he would be deterred by the knowledge that a small number of persons his age have been executed in the 20th century. In short, we are not persuaded that the imposition of the death penalty for offenses committed by persons under 16 years of age has made, or can be expected to make, any measurable contribution to the goals that capital punishment is intended to achieve."

Protection of Children

Through a series of decisions beginning in 1923, the Supreme Court has affirmed that parents have a broad authority over their children which they may generally assert without interference from the government. These decisions established the supremacy of parents and the concomitant legal disability of children. They further established the right to family privacy and the concomitant freedom of the family from government intervention. The following excerpt from *Parham v. J.R.*, 442 U.S. 584 (1979), which affirmed the right of parents to admit their children to mental institutions against the children's wishes, illustrates how firmly rooted these traditions are.

> "Our jurisprudence historically has reflected Western civilization concepts of the family as a unit with broad parental authority over minor children. Our cases have consistently followed that course; our constitutional system long ago rejected any notion that a child is 'the mere creature of the State' and, on the contrary, asserted that parents generally 'have the right, coupled with the high duty, to recognize and prepare [their children] for additional obligations.' The law's concept of the family rests on a presumption that parents possess what a child lacks in maturity, experience, and capacity for judgment required for making life's difficult decisions. More important, historically it has recognized that natural bonds of affection lead parents to act in the best interests of their children."

Although the family has long been protected from government intervention, it has long been recognized that the state, under the doctrine of *parens patriae*, can intervene in the family to protect the children from abuse and neglect that threaten their well-being. As the Court went on to say in *Parham*:

> "We have recognized that a state is not without constitutional control over parental discretion in dealing with children when their physical or mental health is jeopardized."

Moreover, there are times when children have no parents able to care for them, that is, they are **dependent** minors, and there are children whose behavior is not criminal, but may be injurious to their own welfare or the welfare of society. The government also has the authority to act in these situations under its *parens patriae* authority and its police power.

This chapter will review, first, the laws allowing the state to intervene in the family to protect children who are abused, neglected or dependent, and, then, the laws related to children whose behavior is injurious.

LAWS RELATED TO ABUSE, NEGLECT AND DEPENDENCY

In addition to juvenile court acts, three sets of civil laws specifically address the problems of child abuse, neglect and dependency in all States: reporting acts; acts creating public social services; and adoption acts. Moreover, as we shall see in the next Section of the book, some States have civil laws related to domestic violence which are primarily designed to help women who are abused by their husbands or lovers, but which can be invoked in behalf of children who have been abused. Further, the criminal law may also be invoked to protect children by prosecuting and punishing those who injure them. Intervention in any given case may occur under the authority of one or more of these laws as well as under the authority of juvenile court acts.

Reporting acts

Reporting acts have three primary purposes: to encourage identification of children at risk; to designate an agency to receive and investigate reports of suspected abuse and neglect of children; and to offer, where appropriate, services to children and their families. Reporting acts require a variety of individuals and professionals who regularly come into contact with children, typically doctors, teachers and social workers, to report suspected abuse or neglect to a designated agency. The acts generally allow or encourage others to report. They also typically specify procedures to be followed in filing and investigating reports and in recording the results of the investigation. In some States, reporting acts also allow certain professionals—typically physicians, police officers and designated social workers—to take immediate protective custody of children in emergencies, that is, to temporarily remove children from the custody of their parents without a court order when necessary to protect the children from serious harm.

Reporting acts encourage reporting in several ways. First, they offer anonymity to reporters. Second, they grant persons reporting in good faith immunity from civil and criminal liability and reinforce the immunity by creating a presumption of good faith. Third, in most States reporting is made an exception to confidentiality laws. Finally, in almost all the States, the reporting acts provide that mandated reporters who willfully fail to report may be found guilty of committing a misdemeanor and may be subject to license suspension or revocation.

Acts creating public child welfare services

These acts assign responsibility for providing services to children who have been abused or neglected or who are dependent to one or more social agencies and authorize public monies to support the services. The statutes typically define what services will be provided and by whom, specify who is eligible to receive services, grant the agencies the authority to promulgate regulations as neces-

sary in order to carry out their duties, and allow the agencies to provide services directly as well as to purchase services from private agencies.

Adoption acts

In some cases of abuse, neglect or dependency, it becomes clear that the parents will never be able to adequately care for the child. In addition, in some cases, parents wish to surrender their rights to their child. In either of these instances, the best alternative is usually for the child to be adopted by other parents. Adoption acts allow for the termination of the legal relationship between a child and his or her parents and for the creation of a new legal parent-child relationship.

Adoption law will be discussed in the next chapter.

Domestic violence legislation

This legislation, which will be discussed in detail in Chapter 13, allows courts to enter orders in cases when one member of a household has abused or threatened to abuse another member of the household. The laws also create mechanisms to enforce the orders. Under the authority of domestic violence laws, the court may order the abuser to leave the home, refrain from contacting the victim, pay support to family members remaining at home, and participate in counseling. Such measures allow a child who has been abused to remain at home and require the abuser to leave. They may be a desirable alternative to juvenile court action—which typically results in the child being removed from the home—when there is a responsible caregiver in the home.

Criminal laws

Criminal laws may authorize the state to prosecute and punish those who abuse or neglect children. Child abuse or neglect may or may not be a distinct crime but may be prosecuted and punished as assault, battery, a sexual offense or even manslaughter or murder. Typically, the criminal law is only invoked in the most serious cases and does not address the question of what happens to the children who are the victims.

Juvenile court acts

Juvenile court acts generally give the juvenile court jurisdiction over children who are abused, neglected or dependent. Indeed, child welfare agencies and adoption services may only be able to intervene if given authority to do so by a juvenile court.

All of these laws attempt to balance society's responsibility to protect vulnerable children with the family's right to privacy. They also attempt to balance the parents' and children's rights to due process with the need for rapid and decisive action when a child is at risk.

It is important to reiterate that more than one of these laws may be invoked in a particular case. That is, intervention may occur in behalf of a single child under the authority of some, or even all, of these laws simultaneously. We shall, however, focus on juvenile court acts.

DEFINITIONS OF ABUSE, NEGLECT, AND DEPENDENCY

States differ in how they define child abuse, neglect and dependency and, in some jurisdictions, the terms used. Definitions of abuse and neglect or equivalent terms may be found in all the laws discussed above while definitions of dependency or equivalent terms are generally found only in juvenile court acts or adoption acts. Definitions within a jurisdiction may also differ from law to law, but this discussion will look only at definitions in juvenile court and reporting acts.

Abuse

Child abuse refers generally to action by a parent, caretaker, or guardian which harms or injures a child. Definitions of abuse usually include nonaccidental physical injury, sexual abuse and excessive corporal punishment, as illustrated in the statutory definition from Illinois set forth below. They may also include emotional harm. Note that the Illinois definition, like the definitions in many States, incorporates not only a person who has injured a child but also a person who allows a child to be injured. This means that, as often occurs, a mother who knows her boyfriend is beating her child and takes no steps to protect the child is by definition just as abusive as the boyfriend who actually beat the child. Note also that in Illinois, like in many other States, anyone who lives with a child, not just a parent, caretaker or guardian, can commit abuse.

"Those who are abused include any minor under 18 years of age:

"(a) whose parent or immediate family member, or any person responsible for the minor's welfare, or any individual residing in the same home as the minor, or a paramour of the minor's parent:

(i) inflicts, causes to be inflicted, or allows to be inflicted upon such child physical injury, by other than accidental means, which causes death, disfigurement, impairment of physical or emotional health, or loss or impairment of bodily function;

(ii) creates a substantial risk of physical injury to such child by other than accidental means which would be likely to cause death, disfigurement, impairment of physical or emotional health, or loss or impairment of any bodily function;

(iii) commits or allows to be committed any sex offense against such minor, as such sex offenses are defined in the Criminal Code . . . ;

(iv) commits or allows to be committed an act or acts of torture upon such minor;

(v) inflicts excessive corporal punishment; or

"(b) whose environment is injurious to his or her welfare." Ill. Rev. Stat. ch. 37, par. 802-3(2).

Neglect

Neglect occurs when parents, guardians or caretakers, by an act of omission, cause injury to a child. This is illustrated in the definition of neglect in the Illinois statutes below.

"Those who are neglected include any minor under 18 years of age whose parent or other person responsible for the minor's welfare does not provide the proper or necessary support, education as required by law, or medical or other remedial care recognized under State law as necessary for a minor's well-being, including adequate food, clothing and shelter, or who is abandoned by his or her parents or other person responsible for the minor's welfare." Ill. Rev. Stat. ch. 37, par. 802-3(1).

Perhaps the most controversial aspects of neglect relate to the provision of medical care to children. Parents have the right and the responsibility to make decisions regarding the medical care of their children, and under the common law, physicians generally cannot treat a minor without the consent of a parent. Thus, some question whether it should be considered neglect when a parent refuses to consent to life-saving surgery for a child born with severe and multiple birth defects, either on or against the advice of physicians. Similarly, it is asked whether it is neglect when a parent chooses to treat a child with a nontraditional, not generally acceptable treatment, such as laetrile treatment for cancer, when the child's physicians recommend a different, more generally acceptable course of treatment, like chemotherapy or radiation. And, it is asked whether it is neglect when a parent refuses to consent to surgery or another course of treatment because the treatment is not consistent with the parent's religious beliefs.

These are profound legal and ethical questions which have not been fully answered by the courts. The Supreme Court has heard few cases related to these questions, which, by and large, do not raise federal questions. Decisions of lower courts are generally specific to individual cases and may provide little guidance in decision-making. Statutes or regulations may provide some answers, however. For example, an Illinois statute provides:

"A child shall not be considered neglected or abused for the sole reason that such child's parent or other person responsible for his or her welfare depends upon spiritual means through prayer alone for the treatment or cure of disease or remedial care." Ill. Rev. Stat. ch. 23, par. 2053.

The federal government has, in recent years, been particularly concerned about the medical care of critically ill infants. In 1983, the federal government took the position that "failure to feed and care for handicapped infants" in hospitals receiving federal funds was a violation of federal law, specifically section 504 of the Rehabilitation Act of 1973, which forbids discrimination against the handicapped by a recipient of federal funds. *See* 48 Fed. Reg. 9630. Hospitals which were not in compliance with this law, as so interpreted, risked loss of federal funds. The regulations implementing this interpretation were, however, struck down by the Supreme Court in *Bowen v. American Hospital Association*, 476 U.S. 610 (1986). The Court held that a hospital's withholding of medical treatment when the parents did not consent to the treatment could not be defined as discrimination under the Rehabilitation Act. Further, it held that the Department of Health and Human Services exceeded the authority given to it by Congress in issuing the regulations.

Congress responded to *Bowen* by enacting the Child Abuse Amendments of 1984, P.L. 98-457. This legislation directs the States, as a condition of receipt of federal funds under the Child Abuse Prevention and Treatment Act, 42 U.S.C. § 5101 *et seq.*, to include "medical neglect," defined as the "withholding of medically indicated treatment" to critically ill newborns, in their reporting acts. The regulations implementing these amendments, 45 C.F.R. § 1340, specify three, and only three, situations in which physicians are justified in withholding medical treatment: (1) when the infant is chronically and irreversibly comatose; (2) when treatment would merely delay an inevitable and imminent death; or (3) when treatment is so extreme and so likely to be futile that it becomes inhumane to administer it.

The federal law, however, does not answer all questions. Determinations of when an infant is chronically and irreversibly comatose and of what treatment is inhumane to administer are not easy to make. Hospitals, with the encouragement of the federal government and the medical profession, have responded by creating ethics committees to review cases in which critical and complex life-saving decisions must be made. Social workers are often among the members of such committees.

In compliance with the federal law, States have amended their reporting laws and juvenile court acts to include medical neglect as defined in federal law. Thus, Illinois has added the following language to its definition of neglect in its reporting act. Interestingly, it has not added this language to its juvenile court act.

> " 'Neglected child' means any child whose parent or other person responsible for the child's welfare withholds or denies nourishment or medically indicated treatment including food or care denied solely on the basis of the present or anticipated mental or physical impairment as determined by a physician acting alone or in consultation with other physicians . . ." Ill. Rev. Stat. ch. 23, par. 2053.

Dependency

A dependent child is usually defined as a child who has been deprived of parental support or care without fault on the part of the parent. Children are dependent when their parents are deceased, hospitalized, or incarcerated for a reason not related to their care of their children. Children may also be defined as dependent when their parents cannot care for them because of mental illness, developmental disability, or drug or alcohol addiction or when their parents no longer wish to care for them. This is illustrated in the Illinois definition.

"Those who are dependent include any minor under the age of 18 years:

(a) who is without a parent, guardian or legal custodian;

(b) who is without proper care because of the physical or mental disability of his parent, guardian or custodian; or

(c) who is without proper medical or other remedial care recognized under State law or other care necessary for his or her well being through no fault, neglect or lack of concern by his parents, guardian or custodian . . . ; or

(d) who has a parent, guardian or legal custodian who, with good cause, wishes to be relieved of . . . parental rights and responsibilities . . . " Ill. Rev. Stat. ch. 37, par. 802-4.

Questions concerning the definitions

Statutory definitions of abuse, neglect, and dependency have been challenged as being at best an invitation to impose middle class standards on families who are not middle class, and at worst a violation of the due process clause and other constitutional protections. It has been argued that the definitions are unconstitutionally vague and overbroad, permitting undue intervention into the family and failing to provide fair notice of what is expected of parents. Moreover, it has been argued that the vague definitions give state officials unbridled discretion, which is "especially grave in the highly subjective context of determining an approved mode of child-rearing." *Alsager v. Iowa*, 406 F.Supp. 10 (S.D. Iowa 1975).

Despite the undoubted vagueness and overbreadth of many definitions of abuse, neglect and dependency, and despite the courts' "solicitude for the family enclave" and the constitutional right to "family integrity" recognized in a "plethora of opinions by the United States Supreme Court," *id.*, courts have rarely, if ever, declared the definitions unconstitutional. This is because the courts recognize both the need to protect children from mistreatment and the difficulty in defining abuse, neglect and dependency with precision.

Over the years, a number of proposals have been offered to address concerns regarding vagueness of abuse, neglect and dependency definitions and the consequent broad power of the state to intervene in the family. One such proposal was offered by a joint project of the Institute of Judicial Administration and the American Bar Association.[1] The project proposed the following six grounds for state intervention into the family in order to protect children and further recommended that a court must find, not only that the child met one of the conditions, but also that state intervention was necessary to protect the child before intervention would be allowed.

"(1) when a child has suffered, or there is a substantial risk that a child will imminently suffer, a physical harm, inflicted nonaccidentally upon him/her by his/her parents, which causes, or creates a substantial risk of causing disfigurement, impairment of bodily functioning, or other serious physical injury;

"(2) when a child has suffered, or there is a substantial risk that the child will imminently suffer physical harm causing disfigurement, impairment to bodily functioning or other serious physical injury as a result of conditions created by his/her parents or by

---

1. Institute of Judicial Administration/American Bar Association, Juvenile Justice Standards Project, "Standards relating to Abuse and Neglect, Standard 2.1" (1977).

the failure of the parents to adequately supervise or protect him/her;

"(3) when a child is suffering serious emotional damage, evidenced by severe anxiety, depression, withdrawal, or untoward aggressive behavior toward self or others, and the child's parents are not willing to provide treatment for him/her;

"(4) when a child has been sexually abused by his/her parent or a member of his/her household (alternative: a child has been sexually abused by his/her parent or a member of his/her household, and is seriously harmed physically or emotionally, thereby);

"(5) when a child is in need of medical treatment to cure, alleviate, or prevent him/her from suffering serious physical harm which may result in death, disfigurement, or substantial impairment of bodily functions, and his/her parents are unwilling to provide or consent to the medical treatment;

"(6) when a child is committing delinquent acts as a result of parental encouragement, guidance or approval."

Despite such proposals, definitions of abuse, neglect, and dependency remain vague, and there has been continuing concerns with these definitions. For example, in 1987, a large group of child protection professionals convened under the auspices of numerous agencies, such as the American Bar Association's National Legal Resource Center for Child Advocacy and Protection, the American Public Welfare Association, and the National Center on Child Abuse and Neglect, to address the vague definitions. The consensus that emerged was for intervention only if "the parent has seriously harmed the child or engaged in behavior capable of seriously harming the child, whether or not actual harm resulted"; or "the parent is suffer-

ing from a mental disability that *demonstrably* prevents the parent from adequately caring for the child."[2]

The federal government has taken a different approach in the Indian Child Welfare Act, 25 U.S.C. § 1901 *et seq*. This legislation, designed to prevent unnecessary removal of Native American children from their families and their tribes, does not address the definitions directly. Rather it requires a showing by clear and convincing evidence—a higher standard than that demanded in most States—that active efforts to protect the child at home have failed before a child can be removed temporarily from parental care. It states:

"Any party seeking to effect a foster care placement of . . . an Indian child under State law shall satisfy the court that active efforts have been made to provide remedial services and rehabilitative programs designed to prevent breakup of the Indian family and that these efforts have proved unsuccessful.

* * *

"No foster care placement may be ordered . . . in the absence of a determination, supported by clear and convincing evidence, including testimony of qualified expert witnesses, that the continued custody of the child by the parent or Indian custodian is likely to result in serious emotional or physical damage to the child." 25 U.S.C. § 1912.

The impact of the requirements is uncertain. However, they clearly attest to the belief that Native American children should be removed from their parents' care only as a last resort. They reflect the findings of Congress "that an alarmingly high percentage of Indian families are broken up by the removal, often unwarranted, of their children from

---

2. Douglas J. Besharov, *Protecting Children from Abuse and Neglect* (Springfield, IL: Charles C. Thomas, 1988), p.343.

them by nontribal public and private agencies'' and ''that the States . . . have often failed to recognize the essential tribal relations of Indian people and the cultural and social standards prevailing in Indian communities and families.'' 25 U.S.C. § 1901. These statements reflect the primary concern about vague and broad definitions of abuse and neglect: acting under the authority of such definitions, social workers who are predominantly white and middle class are free to impose their standards on parents who are poor and who are disproportionately of minority race or ethnicity. The result is the breakup of families in the absence of clear and present danger to children.

JUVENILE COURT PROCEDURE IN ABUSE, NEGLECT, AND DEPENDENCY

Minors who are alleged to be abused, neglected, or dependent generally will proceed through the same set of hearings through which the alleged delinquent will proceed. In other words, Diagram 7.1, without the provisions for transfer to adult court, could be a diagram for the process in abuse, neglect, or dependency. However, there are differences in terminology and there are significant differences in the way in which neglected, abused, or dependent children come to the attention of the court and in their rights attendant to court action. Moreover, parents have an interest in these proceedings that they do not necessarily have in delinquency proceedings.

Cases are usually brought to the attention of the court not by the police, but by a child welfare agency. In most cases, the child will have been the subject of an abuse or neglect report, and, in many cases, the child will be in temporary protective custody at the time a court action is initiated. If the child is in custody, the court will be asked to allow a child welfare agency to retain custody pending an adjudication. In some cases, the child has remained at home while the agency worked with the parents in an effort to improve the child's care—an effort consistent with the intent expressed in most juvenile court and reporting acts to keep children in their own homes whenever possible. Court action is only sought when the efforts to protect the child at home are unsuccessful. When court action is initiated, the agency may be asking for authority to take custody of the child or the agency might be asking the court to order certain actions on the part of the parents with the intent of allowing the child to remain in the home.

Whether or not a child is in custody, as with a delinquency case, an action is initiated through the filing of a petition. The petition will provide identifying information about the child and the parents. It will also state the basis for the juvenile court to assume jurisdiction (abuse, neglect or dependency as defined by statute) and the facts justifying an assumption of jurisdiction. Just as with a delinquency petition, the petition will be in the name of the child. The petition may be prepared and filed by a child welfare worker, an attorney working for a child welfare agency, or a prosecuting attorney.

If the child is in protective custody or if the agency believes the child should be taken into custody immediately, there will be an immediate judicial hearing, generally called a **''shelter care''** or **''temporary custody''** hearing, to address the question of the need for custody. This hearing is the equivalent of a detention hearing for delinquents. Essentially the court decides if there is probable cause to believe the child is abused, neglected, or dependent, as alleged in the petition, and if the child should remain in custody or be taken into custody.

As is true of detention hearings for delinquents, shelter care hearings are often quite perfunctory. Decisions will often be made simply on the basis of testimony of caseworkers involved in placing the child. At this stage, the government's interest in protecting the child clearly outweighs the interests of parents.

An adjudicatory or jurisdictional hearing will be held soon after the shelter care hearing or, if there is no shelter care hearing, soon after the filing of the petition. As with delinquents, the court will determine if it has jurisdiction over the minor by determining if the child is abused, neglected, or dependent as alleged in the petition. If the court does determine it has such jurisdiction, it will later hold a dispositional hearing to decide what should be done for and to the child.

At the dispositional hearing, if a court desires to retain its jurisdiction over the minor for a long period, it typically makes the minor a ward of the court, as it makes a delinquent a ward of the court. Usually, the same dispositional alternatives available to the court in cases of delinquency are available in cases of abuse, neglect, or dependency—except placement in a correctional institution.

The most common disposition for minors adjudicated as abused, neglected or dependent is to make them wards of the court and to award custody and guardianship to a child welfare agency or a designated person in the agency. An agency, even if it has legal custody and guardianship, may leave children in the physical custody of their parents. In some States, only the court can make the decision to remove children from their parents even if they are placed in the custody and/or guardianship of an agency. If children are removed from their homes, the agency or the court may place them with relatives, in foster care, or in an institution. Whichever placement is chosen, attempts will generally be made to improve parental functioning so that the chil-

dren can return to their homes. In most cases, children will ultimately return home, but, in extreme cases, a court may permanently sever parental ties with the child, at the disposition stage or after efforts to reunify the family have failed.

As in the case of delinquents, court involvement will not end after the court has assumed jurisdiction on the basis of abuse, neglect, or dependency. If an abused, neglected or dependent minor is made a ward of the court, the court will retain jurisdiction until the child reaches legal majority (unless the court decides to release jurisdiction at some earlier point) or beyond majority in some States. The court can be involved at several times during the retention of jurisdiction.

First, if the child remains out of the home for an extended period, the court will periodically review the case plan and the status of the child. States are required, as a condition of receipt of federal child welfare funds, to provide for administrative or court review of the status of each child in placement every 6 months and to provide for a court hearing no later than 18 months after the original placement and periodically thereafter as long as the child remains in placement. 42 U.S.C. §§ 670, 675. Second, in many States, before a child who has been removed from a home because of abuse can be returned home, the court must approve of the plan. Third, typically after a child has returned home and the child's parents have demonstrated their ability to care for the child, the agency will petition the court for release of custody and guardianship or for release from whatever responsibilities the court has imposed in the case. Fourth, the agency can petition to be relieved of its responsibilities at any time if it believes it can no longer serve the child. This might occur when the child has been placed with relatives or it might occur when an older adolescent is unwilling to use agency services. Fifth, the parents may petition the court to terminate wardship and to regain the custody and guardianship of their child. Last, if it becomes apparent that the parents are unwilling or unable to ever safely resume caring for their child, the agency can petition the court for a permanent termination of parental rights and to free a child for adoption.

The rights of children and parents in the process

The process of investigating reports of abuse and neglect and the juvenile court process in abuse and neglect cases raise many constitutional questions related to the rights of parents and children, but there are few dispositive court opinions in this area. The apparent reluctance of the Supreme Court to become involved in these areas of law is suggested in its opinion in *Moore v. Sims*, 442 U.S. 415 (1978), a case challenging the constitutionality of various provisions of the Texas law related to the investigation of abuse and neglect reports, documentation of the results of the investigation, release of information to the subjects of reports, and temporary custody of the children—provisions that were and are similar to those in many other States. The Court stated the law:

> "defines the contours of the parent-child relationship and the permissible areas and modes of state intervention. This suit presents the first broad constitutional challenge to interrelated parts of that statutory scheme. It raises novel constitutional questions of the correlative rights and duties of parents, children, and the State in suits affecting the parent-child relationship."

That said, the Court, in a 5-4 decision, reversed and remanded the decision of the federal district court on essentially procedural grounds without ruling on the constitutional claims.

Under the authority of the reporting acts, social workers and other officials designated in reporting acts have broad authority to investigate reports of alleged abuse and neglect. The authority includes questioning third parties such as teachers, neighbors and physicians regarding reports; making unannounced visits to the homes of subjects of reports; and asking children to disrobe in order to check for signs of abuse. All these actions may be taken regardless of the source of a report, without a parent's consent, and without a warrant. Such actions have been challenged as violative of the rights to privacy, due process, and freedom from unreasonable search—rights protected by the 4th, 9th and 14th Amendments to the Constitution—but the challenges have largely been unsuccessful. The courts have consistently held that at the investigation stage of the process, States should have broad authority to intervene in order to protect children. The opinions have echoed the Supreme Court opinion in *Wyman v. James*, 400 U.S. 309 (1971), which, as you saw in Chapter 6, considered a State requirement that AFDC recipients and applicants allow home visits by caseworkers. The Court examined the purpose of the home visit, found it to be the welfare of the dependent child, and held that it did not offend the 4th Amendment, explaining:

> "There is no more worthy object of the public's concern [than a child]. The dependent child's needs are paramount, and only with hesitancy would we relegate those needs, in the scale of comparative values, to a position secondary to what the mother claims as her rights."

Questions have also been raised concerning the *Miranda* rights of parents being investigated for abuse or neglect. No court has authoritatively determined whether parents should be advised of their right against self-incrimination or to an attorney before being questioned, but given that parents generally are not "in custody" while being questioned, *Miranda* probably does not apply. It would apply, of course, if parents were arrested for criminal abuse or neglect.

The emergency removal of a child from a home raises serious due process questions. It has been asserted that children should not be removed from the home without providing parents notice and an opportunity to be heard. However, the potential harm to the child in abuse and neglect situations has led courts to sustain placement of children in protective custody without a prior hearing or even without prior notice as long as there will be notice and a prompt opportunity to be heard after the removal and there are clear standards to guide official discretion in making the removals.

The rights of the child and parent at shelter care hearings, adjudicatory hearings, and dispositional hearings have been the subject of much debate. The parent is undoubtedly entitled to notice and an opportunity to be heard, but the content of the notice and the nature of the opportunity are unresolved. Most States offer the parent a right to appointed counsel by statute or case law, but the Supreme Court ruled in *Lassiter v. Dept. of Social Services*, 452 U.S. 18 (1981), that, while it may be wise to provide counsel in proceedings to permanently terminate parental rights, there is no constitutional right to appointed counsel in such proceedings. This ruling undoubtedly means there is no constitutional right to appointed counsel in hearings on abuse, neglect, and dependency. Most States also offer counsel or a guardian *ad litem* for the child. The latter is a requirement for receiving federal funds under the Child Abuse Prevention and Treatment Act. 51 U.S.C. § 5101 *et seq.*

Juvenile court hearings on abuse, neglect, and dependency have tended to be informal. This informality, as in the delinquency proceedings considered in *Gault*, may result in unconstitutional denials of due process. Thus, many States now require more formality, especially in adjudicatory hearings. They permit cross-examination and confrontation of witness and require that the rules of evidence be followed. However, most States do not allow witnesses to claim testimonial privileges or assert confidentiality, and the parents may not have a right against self-incrimination, except to the extent that they may be criminally prosecuted for their statements.

The standard of proof in adjudicatory hearings may not be clearly allocated or defined. Many States allow a finding of abuse, neglect, or dependency on the basis of preponderance of the evidence, a way of allowing broad authority to intervene in order to protect children. In contrast, as stated earlier, a court order for the removal of an Indian child from Indian caretakers must be supported by clear and convincing evidence. 25 U.S.C. § 1912. Moreover, if the State provides a "higher standard of protection," the State standard must be applied by the court. 25 U.S.C. § 1921.

The role of social workers in the process

Social workers are an integral and essential part of the juvenile court process for abused, neglected, and dependent children. Social workers investigate complaints involving such children, take such children into custody, file petitions requesting juvenile court action, assist attorneys in gathering evidence, recommend dispositional alternatives for children found to be within the jurisdiction of the courts, develop case plans and reports for the court on the status of children, and provide treatment and services for children and their parents under the direction of the court. In much of their work with children who come before the juvenile court, social workers are, in fact, agents of the court.

When social workers intervene in the family to protect abused, neglected, and dependent children, they have a tremendous amount of discretion. The broad and vague definitions in the statutes in most States and the lack of procedural protections for children and parents all require the exercise of sound professional judgment on the part of the social worker. The courts have tended to trust that social workers will use such judgment. Most, if not all, of the orders made by juvenile court judges reflect, in significant part, the recommendations of social workers. Moreover, the reluctance of the Supreme Court and other appellate courts to require clearer definitions in statutes on abuse, neglect, and dependency and to mandate procedural protections for children and parents indicates, in part, a deference to professional judgment.

Legislators, however, have sometimes questioned social workers' exercise of discretion and the services social workers have provided, particularly to children who are in foster care. For example, the federal requirement of periodic court reviews of children in out-of-home placements, found in 42 U.S.C. sections 670 and 675, reflects a distrust of social worker discretion. The same legislation establishes priorities for placement of children, with the highest priority the reunification of families, and mandates **permanency planning**. Permanency planning is an attempt to avoid so-called "foster care limbo," where children who have been made wards of the court and have been removed from their parents' custody go from foster home to foster home, never returning home or being placed for adoption. While there is consensus that long term foster care with its risk of frequent and disruptive moves is damaging to children and costly to society, that reunification is a commendable goal, and that permanency planning, although it may conflict with the goal of reunification, is necessary, these federal requirements are largely a Congressional statement that social workers will not act forcefully to return children home or to place them for adoption if not required to do so.

LEGAL QUESTIONS CONCERNING THE RIGHTS OF FOSTER PARENTS

The majority of children who are removed from their homes because of abuse, neglect or dependency are placed with foster parents by agencies. The relationship between the agency and the foster parent is contractual: foster parents provide child care under the direction of the agency and are reimbursed by the agency for the costs of the care they provide. Foster care, in theory, offers temporary, time-limited care to children until they can either return home or be placed for adoption. However, despite the theory of foster care and the mandate of permanency planning, many children spend many years in foster care, often with the same foster parents. And the longer the child remains in the foster home, the stronger the psychological tie between the child and the foster parent becomes.

Given the ties that develop, there is a question as to what rights foster parents should have regarding children in their care. Moreover, how can the rights of foster parents, if any, be balanced against the rights of a child's biological parents and of the child? These questions were addressed by the Supreme Court in *Smith v. Organization of Foster Families For Equality and Reform*, 431 U.S. 782 (1977), a class action arising in New

York. Each foster parent named as a plaintiff in the case had been a foster parent to a child for a substantial length of time, in some cases, beginning when the child was an infant. In each case, an agency proposed to remove the child from the foster home, either to return the child to his or her parents or to place the child in a different home or an institution. The foster parents objected to the removal of their foster children and claimed that, like natural parents, they were entitled to a due process hearing before a foster child could be taken from them. The Court held that foster parents were not entitled to the same rights as natural parents and that New York's procedures governing the removal of foster children from foster homes, which provided foster parents notice, an opportunity for conferences, and in some cases, administrative hearings or even judicial review of proposals to remove children, were constitutionally sufficient. The Court's reasoning provides insight into the realities of foster care as well as some of the legal questions that arise when children are in care.

"Foster [family] care has been defined as '[a] child welfare service which provides substitute family care for a planned period for a child when his own family cannot care for him for a temporary or extended period, and when adoption is neither desirable nor possible.' [T]he distinctive features of foster care are, first, 'that it is care in a family, it is noninstitutional substitute care,' and, second, 'that it is for a planned period either temporary or extended. This is unlike adoptive placement, which implies a permanent substitution of one home for another.'

"Under the New York scheme children may be placed in foster care either by voluntary placement or by court order. Most foster care placements are voluntary. They occur when physical or mental illness, economic problems, or other family crises make it impossible for natural parents, particularly single parents, to provide a stable home life for their children for some limited period. Resort to such placements is almost compelled when it is not possible in such circumstance to place the child with a relative or friend, or to pay for the services of a homemaker or boarding school.

"[When a voluntary placement is made,] [t]he New York system divides parental functions among agency, foster parents, and natural parents, and the definitions of the respective roles are often complex and often unclear. The law transfers 'care and custody' to the agency, but day-to-day supervision of the child and his activities, and most of the functions ordinarily associated with legal custody, are the responsibility of the foster parent. Nevertheless, agency supervision of the performance of the foster parents takes forms indicating that the foster parent does not have the full authority of a legal custodian. Moreover, the natural parent's placement of the child with the agency does not surrender legal guardianship; the parent retains authority to act with respect to the child in certain circumstances. The natural parent has not only the right but the obligation to visit the foster child and plan for his future; failure of a parent with capacity to fulfill the obligation for more than a year can result in a court order terminating the parent's rights on the ground of neglect.

"The consequences of foster-care placement by court order [after a court has found a child to be abused, neglected, delinquent or in need of supervision] do not differ substantially from those for children voluntarily placed, except that the parent is not entitled to return of the child on demand; termination of foster care must then be consented to by the court.

"Foster care of children is a sensitive and emotion-laden subject, and foster-care programs consequently stir strong controversy. From the standpoint of natural parents, . . . foster care has been condemned as a class-based intrusion into the family life of the poor. It is certainly true that the poor resort to foster care more often than other citizens. For example, over 50% of all children in foster care in New York City are from female-headed families receiving Aid to Families with Dependent Children. Minority families are also more likely to turn to foster care; 52.3% of the children in foster care in New York City are black and 25.5% are Puerto Rican. This disproportionate resort to foster care by the poor and victims of discrimination doubtless reflects in part the greater likelihood of disruption of poverty-stricken families. Commentators have also noted, however, that middle- and upper-income families who need temporary care services for their children have the resources to purchase private care. The poor have little choice but to submit to state-supervised child care when family crises strike.

"The extent to which supposedly 'voluntary' placements are in fact voluntary has been questioned on other grounds as well. For example, it has been said that many 'voluntary' placements are in fact coerced by threat of neglect proceedings and are not in fact voluntary in the sense of the product of an informed consent. Studies also suggest that social workers of middle-class backgrounds, perhaps unconsciously, incline to favor continued placement in foster care with a generally higher-status family rather than return the child to his natural family, thus reflecting a bias that treats the natural parents' poverty and lifestyle as prejudicial to the best interests of the child. This accounts, it has been said, for the hostility of agencies to the efforts of natural parents to obtain the return of their children.

"[The foster parents] note that children often stay in 'temporary' foster care for much longer than contemplated by the theory of the system. The [trial court in this case] found as a fact that the median time spent in foster care in New York was over four years. Indeed, many children apparently remain in this 'limbo' indefinitely. [The trial court] also found that the longer a child remains in foster care, the more likely it is that he will

never leave. It is not surprising then that many children, particularly those that enter foster care at a very early age and have little or no contact with their natural parents during extended stays in foster care, often develop deep emotional ties with their foster parents.*

"Yet such ties do not seem to be regarded as obstacles to transfer of the child from one foster placement to another. The record in this case indicates that nearly 60% of the children in foster care in New York City have experienced more than one placement, and about 28% have experienced three or more. The intended stability of the foster-home management is further damaged by the rapid turnover among social work professionals who supervise the foster-care arrangements on behalf of the State. Moreover, even when it is clear that a foster child will not be returned to his natural parents, it is rare that he achieves a stable home life through final termination of parental ties and adoption into a new permanent family.

"[Given this summary of the "complex and controversial system with which this lawsuit is concerned," we turn to the issue presented by this law suit:] "[I]s the relation of foster parent to foster child sufficiently akin

---

* "The development of such ties points up an intrinsic ambiguity of foster care that is central to this case. The warmer and more homelike environment of foster care is intended to be its main advantage over institutional child care, yet because in theory foster care is intended to be only temporary, foster parents are urged not to become too attached to the children in their care. Indeed, the New York courts have upheld removal from a foster home for the very reason that the foster parents had become too emotionally involved with the child.

"On the other hand, too warm a relation between foster parent and foster child is not the only possible problem in foster care. Qualified foster parents are hard to find, and very little training is provided to equip them to handle the often complicated demands of their role; it is thus sometimes possible that foster homes may provide inadequate care. Indeed, situations in which foster children were mistreated or abused have been reported. And the social work services that are supposed to be delivered to both the natural and foster families are often limited, due to the heavy caseloads of the agencies."

to the concept of 'family' recognized in our precedents to merit similar [substantive and procedural] protection? Although considerable difficulty has attended the task of defining 'family' for purposes of the Due Process Clause. . . we are not without guides to some of the elements that define the concept of 'family' and contribute to its place in our society.

"First, the usual understanding of 'family' implies biological relationships, and most decisions treating the relation between parent and child have stressed this element. A biological relationship is not present in the case of the usual foster family. But biological relationships are not exclusive determination of the existence of a family. The basic foundation of the family in our society, the marriage relationship, is of course not a matter of blood relation. Thus the importance of the familial relationship, to the individuals involved and to the society, stems from the emotional attachments that derive from the intimacy of daily association, and from the role it plays in 'promot[ing] a way of life' through the instruction of children, as well as from the fact of blood relationship. No one would seriously dispute that a deeply loving and interdependent relationship between an adult and a child in his or her care may exist even in the absence of blood relationship. At least where a child has been placed in foster care as an infant, has never known his natural parents, and has remained continuously for several years in the care of the same foster parents, it is natural that the foster family should hold the same place in the emotional life of the foster child, and fulfill the same socializing functions, as a natural family. For this reason, we cannot dismiss the foster family as a mere collection of unrelated individuals.

"But there are also important distinctions between the foster family and the natural family. First, unlike the earlier cases recognizing a right to family privacy, the State here seeks to interfere, not with a relationship having its origins entirely apart from

the power of the State, but rather with a foster family which has its source in state law and contractual arrangements. [W]hatever emotional ties may develop between foster parent and foster child have their origins in an arrangement in which the State has been a partner from the outset. While the Court has recognized that liberty interests may . . . arise [in such cases,] . . . in such a case, and particularly where, as here, the claimed interest derives from a knowingly assumed contractual relation with the State, it is appropriate to ascertain from state law the expectations and entitlements of the parties. In this case, the limited recognition accorded to the foster family by the New York statutes and the contracts executed by the foster parents argue against any but the most limited constitutional 'liberty' in the foster family.

"A second consideration related to this is that ordinarily procedural protection may be afforded to a liberty interest of one person without derogating from the substantive liberty of another. Here, however, such a tension is virtually unavoidable. Under New York law, the natural parent of a foster child in voluntary placement has an absolute right to the return of his child in the absence of a court order obtainable only upon compliance with rigorous substantive and procedural standards, which reflect the constitutional protection accorded the natural family. Moreover, the natural parent initially gave up his child to the State only on the express understanding that the child would be returned in those circumstances. These rights are difficult to reconcile with the [claimed] liberty interest in the foster family relationship . . . It is one thing to say that individuals may acquire a liberty interest against arbitrary governmental interference in the family-like associations into which they have freely entered, even in the absence of biological connection or state-law recognition of the relationship. It is quite another to say that one may acquire such an interest in the face of another's constitutionally recognized liberty interest that derives from blood relationship, state-law sanction, and basic human right [which] the foster parent has recognized by contract from the outset. Whatever liberty interest might otherwise exist in the foster family as an institution, that interest must be substantially attenuated where the proposed removal from the foster family is to return the child to his natural parents.

"We deal here with issues of unusual delicacy, in an area where professional judgments regarding desirable procedures are constantly and rapidly changing. In such a context, restraint is appropriate on the part of courts called upon to adjudicate whether a particular procedural scheme is adequate under the Constitution. [W]e hold that the procedures provided [in New York] . . . are adequate to protect whatever liberty interest [foster parents] may have . . . ''

MINORS WHOSE BEHAVIOR IS INJURIOUS TO THEIR OWN WELFARE

Minors whose behavior is injurious to their own welfare are frequently termed "**status offenders**," suggesting that they have not committed crimes but have a certain status, such as incorrigibility, or that they have committed offenses that are crimes only by virtue of the status of being a minor, such as truancy or curfew violations. Despite the fact that the term "status offender" is commonly used, it is not a label that accurately describes either the behavior or the way in which the juvenile court intervenes. Nor is it a term that is found in definitions in most juvenile court acts. Minors who have been termed "status offenders" are better thought of as youth who are troubled and who present troublesome behavior in the eyes of their parents and other adults in authority.

Statutory definitions

States differ in the statutory labels assigned to minors whose behavior is injurious to their own welfare. Common terms are "minors," "children" or "persons" "in need of supervision" (MINS, CHINS or PINS), and "children in need of protection and services" (CHIPS). Some States recognize that troubled and troublesome behavior in children reflects dysfunction in the family and provide for a "family in need of supervision" (FINS).

States also differ in what behavior is included within their statutory definitions. Most States include minors who repeatedly run away or who are otherwise beyond the control of their parents, who are chronically truant, or who are drug or alcohol dependent within their definitions. Many States include such vague bases for intervention as "incorrigibility," "dissolute behavior," and "promiscuity."

Given the broad and vague definitions, traditionally, juvenile courts have been able to assume jurisdiction over minors in numerous situations. Recently, however, some States have placed restrictions on the assumption of juvenile court jurisdiction over minors whose behavior is not criminal. These restrictions reflect a modern preference for use of community-based services, a desire to avoid stigmatizing children and excessive out-of-home placements, and a recognition that traditional correctional or child welfare services have not, and perhaps cannot, serve such children well. For example, in 1983, Illinois amended its juvenile court act to restrict intervention over minors whose behavior is injurious to themselves to "addicted minors" and to "minors requiring authoritative intervention" (MRAI). An MRAI was defined as

"any minor under 18 years of age (1) who is (a) absent from home without consent of parent, guardian or custodian, or (b) beyond the control of his or her parent, guardian or custodian, in circumstances which constitute a substantial or immediate danger to the minor's physical safety; and who after 21 days from the date the minor is taken into limited custody, . . . and having been offered crisis intervention services, where available, refuses to return home after the minor and his or her parent, guardian or custodian cannot agree to an arrangement for an alternative voluntary residential placement . . . " P.A. 83-180.

The Illinois provisions differed from those in the majority of States in several important ways. First, they specifically excluded truancy as a basis for juvenile court intervention. Second, they limited the statutory definition to three specific situations and eliminated the vague definitions found in other statutes. Third, they allowed juvenile court intervention over MRAI's only if the minors were offered services, were out of their homes for at least three weeks, refused to return home, and could not agree with their parents on a voluntary placement outside the home.

Because of difficulties with this law and objections from law enforcement and school officials, Illinois has repeatedly amended these provisions and has, once again, included truancy as a basis for juvenile court intervention in its law, with the proviso that there can be no jurisdiction over a minor alleged to be a truant unless crisis intervention services have been offered. Ill. Rev. Stat. ch. 37, par. 803-33.

Juvenile court procedure

States also differ in the process for minors whose behavior is injurious to themselves. The process may be identical or substantially similar to that for delinquents or to that for children who are abused, neglected, or de-

pendent, or may be substantially different from either in all instances or in certain instances. For example, under the 1983 version of the Illinois law, addicted minors were treated as delinquents, with some differences in places of detention and dispositional alternatives, while MRAI's had their own special procedures and services with strict limitations on custody and emphasis on voluntary agreement. The juvenile court would be involved with MRAI's, only if crisis intervention failed and voluntary agreement could not be reached. If the juvenile court was involved, the process for MRAI's would be the same as for abused, neglected, or dependent minors but some dispositional alternatives available for delinquents could be used. Moreover, because a failure to provide education or shelter to a child was defined as neglect in the Illinois juvenile court act, as a matter of practice, truants and runaways were sometimes brought to court as neglected minors.

If the process for minors whose behavior is injurious to themselves is similar to that for delinquents, cases would proceed as in Diagram 7.1, but there would be a greater emphasis throughout the proceedings on arranging in-home, community-based services for the minors and their parents. However, because the constitutional protections provided by *Gault* and *Winship* apply only to alleged delinquents, not to other minors who come before the juvenile court, and because the Supreme Court has not addressed the question of the rights of minors whose behavior is alleged to be injurious to themselves, but who are not alleged to have committed crimes and, thus, are not alleged to be delinquent, the rights of such minors are dependent on State statutes and court decisions and possibly federal court decisions addressing a particular State's law. These rights therefore vary from State to State.

The dispositional alternatives that are

available to the courts for minors whose behavior is injurious to themselves are generally similar to those available either for abused, neglected, and dependent minors or for delinquents. One dispositional alternative that may be available to the courts for such minors is **emancipation**.

Emancipation is a legal process through which children are freed from the custody, care and control of their parents before they reach the age of legal maturity. Emancipated minors can live independently and make most decisions for themselves; they are no longer entitled to support from their parents. The process may be a matter of common law, but many States[3] have statutes providing for emancipation if certain requirements are met and certain procedures are followed. The statutes usually look to such issues as minors' age, their ability to manage their own financial affairs and support themselves, whether they live apart from their parents, whether they are married or have children of their own, and whether their parents agree to their emancipation. Some juvenile court acts specifically provide for emancipation as an alternative disposition for minors who are beyond the control of their parents or who are habitual runaways or for all minors, including delinquent, abused, neglected, or dependent minors.

Federal law has some impact on the process for minors whose behavior is injurious to themselves, at least in States receiving federal funds for delinquency prevention and treatment. Federal law prohibits such States from holding minors who are not delinquent in detention, 42 U.S.C. § 5633. Therefore, such minors will generally be held in custody as abused, neglected, or dependent children

pursuant to a temporary custody order, not a detention order. Further, minors who are not adjudicated delinquent cannot be committed to a correctional facility.

The question of appropriate policy

Current approaches to intervention with difficult minors largely reflect the lead of the federal government through the Juvenile Justice and Delinquency Prevention Act. 42 U.S.C. § 5601 *et seq.* This Act favors deinstitutionalization of such minors. According to a report published in 1986 by the Attorney General's Advisory Board on Missing Children, all but five States receive funds through the Act and therefore have enacted laws that deinstitutionalize minors whose behavior is injurious to themselves. It is therefore significant to note that the Advisory Board is now recommending changes in the Act that would allow courts to assume jurisdiction over children who have run away and to order them held in secure detention. While the original Act was a response to the belief that minors were essentially treated as criminals—often in violation of constitutional rights—simply because they presented problems for parents and other adults in authority, the Advisory Board takes quite a different position. It stated in its report to the President and to the Congress:

"The Juvenile Justice and Delinquency Prevention Act of 1974 influenced States to create a child's right of freedom from both parental and appropriate government control. A law that was intended to benefit America's children, in fact, handcuffs those most able to help them and contributes to the very hazards it seeks to eliminate. As children are set free to a life on the street—one that often includes drugs, street crime, sexual exploitation, prostitution, and grave physical danger—frustrated parents, police, and ju-

---

3.   These States include Alabama, Alaska, California, Connecticut, Indiana, Illinois, Kansas, Louisiana, Maine, Michigan, Mississippi, New Mexico, North Carolina, Oklahoma, Oregon, Tennessee, Texas, and West Virginia.

venile judges are denied authority to exercise effective control over them. Restrictions on detaining children who have not been charged or convicted of delinquent conduct have made it virtually impossible to hold a runaway for more than a few hours, or at most, a few days. The result is that these children are simply ignored—permitted to walk out of police stations or runaway shelters and resume their flight before parents or authorities have time to make arrangements to return them home safely or provide a caring environment.''

The report goes on to recommend that ''juvenile courts should be given authority to detain such children pending appropriate placement when they are at risk.'' Many, however, would disagree, arguing that ''appropriate'' placements simply do not exist, and that therefore the States should not intervene in essentially punitive ways—or should not intervene at all.

As we saw, Illinois adopted an approach of limited intervention and provision of voluntary social services, but has somewhat retreated from this position. Other States have experimented with other approaches. As did Illinois, some States may take different approaches to different categories of minors whose behavior is injurious to themselves, choosing, for example, one approach for truants and another for runaways. There is no clear consensus on the best approach to minors whose behavior is not criminal, but is troublesome. Among the available approaches are: (1) intervention as for delinquents; (2) intervention as for delinquents but with an emphasis on deinstitutionalization and in-home services; (3) intervention as for abused, neglected, or dependent minors; (4) juvenile court intervention under special procedures; or (5) no coercive intervention by juvenile or other courts, but provision of services on a voluntary basis.

9

Adoption

Adoption is a legal process through which a new legal parent-child relationship is created. While both children and adults may be adopted, adoption of adults rarely occurs, and when it does, it rarely involves social workers. Thus, this chapter will only address the law and legal issues concerning adoption of children.

Adoption of children involves two legal processes, both of which are governed entirely by State law except in the case of Native American children. One process, which may not occur in all cases, dissolves any existing legal relationship between a living parent and his or her child. The other process creates a new legal parent-child relationship. The dissolution of an existing legal parent-child relationship may or may not involve court action although, to be effective, the dissolution must be recognized by a court. The creation of a new legal parent-child relationship always involves court action.

FORMS OF ADOPTION

Adoption may be arranged in several ways, some of which may involve social workers and some of which may not. The form of adoption that is perhaps most familiar is what might be termed "traditional agency adoption." In such an adoption, prospective adoptive parents apply to an agency to adopt a child and are evaluated by agency staff. If the applicants are approved for adoption and if a suitable child becomes available for adoption through the agency, the agency places the child with them. A court later approves of the arrangement the agency has made.

Closely related to traditional agency adoption is adoption by foster parents, a form of adoption that is occurring more and more frequently. Adoption by foster parents is similar to traditional adoption in that an adoption is arranged and approved by an agency, and a court simply approves the arrangement.

There are two forms of foster parent adoption. In the first form, the parents did not apply to the agency for adoption of any suitable child and a child was not originally placed with them for the purpose of adoption. Instead the parents applied to provide foster care and a child was placed with them for temporary care. The child later became eligible for adoption, the child's foster parents wished to adopt the child, and adoption by the foster parents was determined to be the best plan for the child.

In the other form of foster parent adoption, sometimes termed "legal risk" adoption, the foster parents from the outset agree to accept a child for foster care who the agency believes will ultimately be free for adoption, with the understanding the if the child becomes free, they will adopt the child, subject to court approval.

Another form of adoption is termed "private adoption." A private adoption is arranged between a child's birth parents and the adoptive parents, typically with the assistance of an intermediary. The intermediary is generally a physician or an attorney. Social workers may be asked by a court to evaluate the suitability of the adoptive parents, but social workers will not have been involved in arranging the adoption, at least not as employees of an agency.

All States forbid paying a parent for a child, so-called "black market adoption," but the States may allow adoptive parents to reimburse a mother's expenses in bearing a child. This is often referred to as "grey market adoption" because the reimbursement may be tantamount to payment. Because grey market adoptions are frowned upon, some States forbid or very carefully regulate private adoptions.

Yet another form of adoption is adoption by

relatives. In this form of adoption, the child is adopted by a relative, often a step-parent. Social workers usually are not involved in step-parent adoptions in any way unless State statute or local practice requires some sort of investigation of the adoptive applicant. Depending on State law, social workers may be involved when another relative, such as a grandparent, seeks to adopt the child. Such situations often occur when a child has been found by a court to be abused, neglected, or dependent and is in the custody of an agency.

DISSOLUTION OF AN EXISTING LEGAL PARENT-CHILD RELATIONSHIP

In this country, a child can have only two parents at a time, one mother and one father. Therefore, before a new parent-child relationship can be created, any existing relationship must be dissolved. This is true for agency, private, and relative adoptions.

An existing relationship can be dissolved in one of three ways: consent; surrender; or termination of parental rights. Because consent and surrender are similar and raise similar issues, they will be discussed together.

Consent and surrender

A parent may consent to the adoption of his or her child by another person. Consents are typically used when the adoptive parent or parents are known to the birth parent or have been identified. In most private adoptions, the child's birth parents consent to their child's adoption by the prospective adoptive parents. In many adoptions by a step-father, the child's birth father consents to the adoption of the child by the step-father.

A surrender is similar to a consent in that a parent voluntarily agrees to the adoption of his or her child. It is different in that a consent is typically used when specific adoptive parents are identified and presumably approved by the birth parents, while a surrender is typically used to grant an agency the authority to choose adoptive parents and to approve of the child's adoption by the adoptive parents. Essentially the parents give their authority to consent to the child's adoption to an agency. Unless agency policy states differently, the birth parent who surrenders a child to an agency has no right to select the adoptive parent or to approve or disapprove of the adoption.

State statutes generally require that both consents and surrenders be in writing and prescribe the forms to be used or the content of the consent or surrender. Social workers frequently are involved in taking consents and surrenders, meaning that the parent signs the required forms in the presence of the social worker. Attorneys and judges also often take consents and surrenders.

Once parents have signed a consent or a surrender, they have no further legal rights regarding their child. State statutes typically provide that consents and surrenders are final and irrevocable immediately after they are given or after a brief period of time unless they are given under duress or fraud, and that even if they are given under duress or fraud, no action can be taken to revoke them after a certain period of time. Thus, while parents might decide that they made a mistake soon after executing a consent or surrender, they cannot reclaim their parental rights unless they can show that they gave up their rights under duress or fraud. And even if they can show duress or fraud, they may not necessarily be able to reclaim their child.

The irrevocability of consents and surrenders is much more than a legal technicality. It is important because if a consent or surrender is revoked, a child's adoption must also be re-voked.

California and several other States, in a desire to protect birth parents' rights, have liberalized the provisions for revocation of consents and surrenders or made them revocable for a long time after they are executed, often as long as six months. Either approach causes serious problems for adopted children and adoptive parents. A better approach may be to insure that consents and surrenders are given knowingly and voluntarily.

The statutes in most States include provisions designed to assure that consents and surrenders are given knowingly and voluntarily. For example, the statutes may provide that a mother cannot surrender her child or consent to her child's adoption before or within a specified period after the child is born. The statutes may require the parent to indicate in writing or in open court that the consent or surrender was given knowingly and voluntarily. Moreover, special provisions may be made for parents who are minors or who are mentally disabled. For example, a guardian *ad litem* may be appointed for them.

The enormity of the decision to give up a child for adoption and the possible consequences for children if proper practices are not followed in taking consents or surrenders dictate extreme caution on the part of social workers who are involved in taking consents and surrenders. Social workers are obligated to explore fully the emotional, social, and legal consequences of the decision with a parent who is considering giving up a child for adoption. In addition, although it may not be required by statute, it is good practice not to allow parents to execute consents or surrenders immediately after they have decided to give up a child. Moreover, it is good practice to encourage, and perhaps insist, that the parents discuss the decision with an attorney or a trusted professional who is not involved in

the decision and to have the parent sign the consent or surrender before a judge who has, at least for the record, fully informed the parent of the legal consequences of the action and obtained assurances that it is being done voluntarily.

Termination of parental rights

A legal parent-child relationship can be dissolved involuntarily through a court action, commonly called a "**termination of parental rights**." Courts may terminate parental rights when: 1) a parent is unwilling or unable to consent to his or her child's adoption or to surrender the child for adoption; 2) there is sufficient evidence that the parent is an unfit parent as defined by State law; and 3) termination is in the best interests of the child. Occasionally courts will also terminate parental rights after a child's parents have either surrendered or consented to their child's adoption, thus reinforcing the validity of the surrenders or consents and protecting the subsequent adoption from later attack.

The terminology concerning termination varies from State to State. Statutes in some States speak specifically of termination of parental rights. Statutes in other States allow courts to waive the requirement that a parent consent to the adoption of his or her child if the conditions specified above are met—that is, if there is sufficient evidence of parental unfitness and adoption is in the best interests of the child. Whatever the terminology, a termination means a total and final end to all parental rights and responsibilities. In other words, it causes a complete severance of the legal parent-child relationship.

Substantive law. There must be a showing that there is a legal basis or grounds for termination of parental rights. These grounds, all of which relate to the unfitness of the parent, will be specified in State statutes. Typical grounds are: character flaws in the parent, as depravity or immorality; mental disability; abandonment; extreme or repeated abuse or neglect; failure to make reasonable efforts to correct the conditions that were the basis for removing a child from the parent's custody; failure to make reasonable progress toward the return of a child who has been removed from the parent's custody; and failure to visit, meaningfully communicate with, or plan for the future of a child who is in foster care.

While a finding of unfitness is usually required before parental rights can be terminated, in a few cases, it has been argued that a termination should occur solely because it is in the best interest of a child. Usually, in these cases, a parent has had no or limited contact with a child, through no fault of the parent's or for reasons unrelated to the parent's relationship with the child, and the child has formed strong emotional bonds with a non-parent who wishes to adopt the child. Although the parent is not unfit, it is argued that the parent's rights should be terminated and the non-parent allowed to adopt the child. In a few such cases around the country, courts have terminated parental rights, but their rulings have been questioned. The Supreme Court agreed to review such a case, *In re Baby Girl M.*, 191 Cal. App. 3d 786, 236 Cal. Rptr. 660 (1987), *cert. granted* 1988, *sub nom. McNamara v. San Diego Dept. of Soc. Serv.*, to decide whether a termination solely on the grounds of a child's best interest is constitutional but later decided that certiorari was improvidently granted and dismissed by the case. Thus, the constitutional issue remains undecided.

The different grounds for termination related to unfitness raise somewhat different legal and practical questions. In considering these questions, it is important to remember that termination of parental rights actions typically are taken in behalf of children who have been adjudicated abused, neglected, or dependent, and who have been removed from the custody of their parents. The actions are often initiated by the social workers who have been providing services to the children and their parents with the goal of returning the child home. The actions are initiated only when it becomes apparent that reunification is impossible.

Many of the grounds, particularly the grounds that relate to a parent's character, may be unconstitutionally vague and overbroad. Because, unlike a mere finding of abuse or neglect in a proceeding under a juvenile court act, a termination means a final and complete deprivation of parental rights, courts may be more willing to find grounds for termination unconstitutionally vague and overbroad than definitions of neglect and abuse in juvenile court acts. For example, in *Alsager v. Iowa*, 406 F.Supp. 10 (S.D. Iowa 1975), among other claims, the Alsagers argued that an Iowa statute on the basis of which their parental rights to five of their six children were terminated was unconstitutionally vague. The statute allowed termination, among other grounds, when parents:

". . . have substantially and continuously or repeatedly refused to give the child necessary parental care and protection.

". . . although financially able, . . . have substantially and continuously neglected to provide the child with necessary subsistence, education, or other care necessary for physical or mental health or morals of the child . . . .

". . . are unfit by reason of debauchery, intoxication, habitual use of narcotic drugs, repeated lewd and lascivious behavior, or other conduct found by the court likely to be detrimental to the physical or mental health or morals of the child."

The court agreed with the Alsagers that the statutory grounds for termination were unconstitutionally vague, stating:

"Vague statutes . . . carry three dangers: the absence of fair warning, the impermissible delegation of discretion, and the undue inhibition of the legitimate exercise of a constitutional right. An analysis of these dangers in the context of the challenged standards of the Iowa parental termination statute leads the Court to conclude that the portions of the Iowa parental termination statute invoked against the Alsagers are unconstitutionally vague.

"The initial danger present in a vague statute is the absence of fair warning. Citizens should be able to guide their conduct by the literal meaning of phrases expressed on the face of statutes. When the standard embodied in a statute is susceptible to multifarious meanings, a person may believe that his actions comply with the law, only to have the law used against him. The standards of 'necessary parental care and protection,' and of '[parental] conduct . . . detrimental to the physical or mental health or morals of the child,' are susceptible to multifarious interpretations which prevent the ordinary person from knowing what is and is not prohibited. An examination of these phrases will not inform an ordinary person as to what conduct is required or must be avoided in order to prevent parental termination. For instance, a parent might follow a rigid scheme of 'discipline-instilling' corporal punishment believing himself in full compliance with the law, only to learn of his folly at a termination proceeding. The standards challenged here simply fail to give 'the person of ordinary intelligence a reasonable opportunity to know what is prohibited.'

"The second danger present in a vague statute is the impermissible delegation of discretion from the state legislature to the state law enforcement body. The Iowa parental termination standards of 'necessary parental care and protection,' and of '[parental] conduct . . . detrimental to the physical or mental health or morals of the child,' afford state officials with so much discretion in their interpretation and application that arbitrary and discriminatory parental terminations are inevitable. Indeed, the Supreme Court has recently noted that 'perhaps the most meaningful aspect of the vagueness doctrine is . . . the requirement that a legislature establish minimal guidelines to govern law enforcement.' Under Iowa's current scheme, state officials may subjectively determine, on an *ad hoc* basis, what parental conduct is 'necessary' and what parental conduct is 'detrimental.' The termination of the parent-child relationship in any given case may thus turn upon which state officials are involved in the case, rather than upon explicit standards reflecting legislative intent. This danger is especially grave in the highly subjective context of determining an approved mode of child-rearing. The Court finds these standards unconstitutionally vague in that they are permeated with the 'dangers of arbitrary and discriminatory application.'

"The third danger present in a vague statute is the risk that the exercise of constitutional rights will be inhibited. The Iowa parental termination standards of 'necessary parental care and protection,' and of '[parental] conduct . . . detrimental to the physical or mental health or morals of the child,' serve to inhibit parents in the exercise of their fundamental right to family integrity. Wary of what conduct is required and what conduct must be avoided to prevent termination, parents might fail to exercise their rights freely and fully. The risk that parents will be forced to steer far wider of 'the unlawful zone' than is constitutionally necessary is not justified when the state is capable of enacting less ambiguous termination standards. The Court finds the aforementioned standards unconstitutionally vague in that they deter parents from conduct which is constitutionally protected.

"This Court is not indifferent to the difficulties confronting the State of Iowa when attempting to regulate parental conduct vis-a-vis the child. Nevertheless, Due Process requires the state to clearly identify and define the evil from which the child needs protection and to specify what parental conduct so contributes to that evil that the state is justified in terminating the parent-child relationship.''

Even if grounds for termination are not unconstitutionally vague, grounds related to the character of parents can be so vague that they are difficult to prove. This point is illustrated by *In re Abdullah*, 85 Ill.2d 300, 423 N.E.2d 915 (1981), involving an order terminating the parental rights of a father over his son on the basis of ''depravity'' after the father was sentenced to a 60-year prison term for the murder of his ex-wife, his son's mother. The Illinois Supreme Court held that the ''mere fact of conviction'' of murder did not constitute depravity, but it did find evidence of depravity in the case because of the nature of the murder.

It may also be difficult to prove that a parent's criminal or alleged immoral conduct is harmful to a child, and absent this showing, many courts will not terminate parental rights.

Courts have also historically been reluctant to terminate parental rights on the basis of abandonment, holding that as long as the parent shows ''a flicker of interest'' in the child, the child is not abandoned. Therefore, parents who occasionally visited their children in foster care or who sent birthday gifts but had little meaningful contact with their children have been found not to have abandoned them.

Extreme or repeated abuse or neglect as a basis for termination presents a different set of problems. Once a child has been removed from a parent's care, there is or should be little opportunity for the parent to continue to abuse or neglect the child; at this point the child is under the protection of a child welfare agency. Children in foster care usually will visit their parents, and parents can and do abuse or neglect children during visits. However, if the caseworker suspects abuse or neglect during visits, the visits will be restricted and supervised, thus preventing extreme or repeated abuse or neglect and eliminating the possibility of using this as a basis for termination.

Because of the problems inherent in using grounds related to character, abandonment, or extreme or repeated abuse or neglect, States have shifted to an emphasis on parental behavior while children are in foster care. Termination statutes have been amended to allow termination when parents fail to maintain contact with or plan for their children who are in foster care, or when parents do not make reasonable efforts to correct the conditions which were the basis for the child originally being removed from their custody. The statutes, where they provide for such grounds, also typically require the agency having custody or guardianship of the child to make diligent efforts to encourage contact between parents and children and to help the parents correct the conditions that resulted in the child being removed.

It should be remembered that most children who are removed from the custody of their parents will be returned to the custody of their parents. While the child is in foster care, the agency will, or at least should, given federal and State statutory provisions, work with the parent to correct the conditions that necessitated removal. This work, as well as efforts to terminate parental rights if reunification is impossible, will be facilitated by written case plans specifying the responsibilities of parents and caseworkers. The case plans can direct intervention. The case plans can also implicitly define ''reasonable efforts'' and ''reasonable contact,'' common phrases in the statutes setting forth grounds for termination of parental rights. Documentation that parents failed to make reasonable efforts or maintain reasonable contact as operationally defined in case plans can be introduced as evidence in termination proceedings.

Procedural law. The procedures that must be followed in terminating parental rights are specified in State statutes. These statutes may be part of a State's juvenile court act and/or part of a separate law dealing specifically with adoption. Wherever located, the statutes in all States provide for notice and for a full evidentiary hearing before parental rights are terminated.

In most States, children who are the subject of termination proceedings will have guardians *ad litem* appointed for them, and indigent parents will have appointed counsel. But appointment of counsel is not constitutionally required. The Supreme Court held in *Lassiter v. Department of Social Services of Furham County, North Carolina*, 452 U.S. 18 (1981), that a State provision permitting a court to decide whether counsel should be appointed to represent an indigent parent in a termination proceeding met the 14th Amendment requirement of due process. However, the Court noted:

> "a wise public policy . . . may require that higher standards be adopted than those minimally tolerable under the Constitution. Informed opinion has clearly come to hold that an indigent parent is entitled to the assistance of appointed counsel not only in parental termination proceedings, but also in dependency and neglect proceedings as well. Most significantly, 33 States and the District of Columbia provide statutorily for the appointment of counsel in termination cases. The Court's opinion today in no way implies that the standards increasingly urged by informed public opinion and now widely followed by the States are other than enlightened and wise."

Less than a year after *Lassiter*, the Supreme Court addressed the standard of proof in termination proceedings in *Santosky v. Kramer*, 455 U.S. 745 (1982). As in *Lassiter*, the Court in *Santosky* evaluated the constitutionality of the challenged termination proceedings in light of the three factors set forth in *Mathews v. Eldridge*, 424 U.S. 319 (1976), but unlike in *Lassiter*, the Court concluded that due process required a specific procedural protection in termination proceedings: proof by at least clear and convincing evidence. The decision, as in *Lassiter*, was 5-4. Justice Blackmun, who sharply dissented from the majority in *Lassiter*, wrote the opinion for the Court in *Santosky*, a portion of which is excerpted below.

> "The fundamental liberty interest of natural parents in the care, custody, and management of their child does not evaporate simply because they have not been model parents or have lost temporary custody of their child to the State. Even when blood relationships are strained, parents retain a vital interest in preventing the irretrievable destruction of their family life. If anything, persons faced with forced dissolution of their parental rights have a more critical need for procedural protections than do those resisting state intervention into ongoing family affairs. When the State moves to destroy weakened familial bonds, it must provide the parents with fundamentally fair procedures.

> "In *Lassiter*, the Court and three dissenters agreed that the nature of the process due in parental rights termination proceedings turns on a balancing of the 'three distinct factors' specified in *Mathews v. Eldridge*: the private interests affected by the proceeding; the risk of error created by the State's chosen procedure; and the counter-

vailing governmental interest supporting use of the challenged procedure. While the respective *Lassiter* opinions disputed whether those factors should be weighed against a presumption disfavoring appointed counsel for one not threatened with loss of physical liberty, . . . that concern is irrelevant here. Unlike the Court's right-to-counsel rulings, its decisions concerning constitutional burdens of proof have not turned on any presumption favoring any particular standard.

''In *Lassiter*, to be sure, the Court held that fundamental fairness may be maintained in parental rights termination proceedings even when some procedures are mandated only on a case-by-case basis, rather than through rules of general application. But this Court never has approved case-by-case determination of the proper standard of proof for a given proceeding. Standards of proof, like other '[p]rocedural due process rules[,] are shaped by the risk of error inherent in the truth-finding process as applied to the generality of cases, not the rare exceptions.' Since the litigants and the fact-finder must know at the outset of a given proceeding how the risk of error will be allocated, the standard of proof necessarily must be calibrated in advance. Retrospective case-by-case review cannot preserve fundamental fairness when a class of proceedings is governed by a constitutionally defective evidentiary standard.

''In parental rights termination proceedings, the private interest affected is commanding; the risk of error from using a preponderance standard is substantial; and the countervailing governmental interest favoring that standard is comparatively slight. Evaluation of the three *Eldridge* factors compels the conclusion that use of a 'fair preponderance of the evidence' standard in such proceedings is inconsistent with due process.''

The question of best interests

As has been stated, State statutes generally provide that parental rights can be terminated only when a court finds that a parent is unfit and that a termination is in the child's best interests. But when is termination in a child's best interests? Given that many parents are encouraged by social workers to surrender their children, often under the threat of court action to terminate their rights, the same question might be posed regarding surrenders: when is it in a child's best interests to encourage a parent to surrender a child?

In answering these questions, one needs to consider the consequences of a surrender or a termination. Both a surrender and a termination leave a child without a legal parent. While the child and the parent may maintain an emotional attachment and may even continue to see each other, they have no legal relationship and no enforceable rights to contact. Moreover, a surrender or a termination ends the legal relationship between a child and his or her siblings and other relatives to whom there may be strong attachments. The agency may desire or plan for continued contact between the child and siblings or other relatives, but once again, there is no legal relationship and no right to continued contact.

Termination is often justified on the basis that it will ultimately provide a child with a stable life in a caring family and that this stability outweighs any losses the child might suffer. But some children may not be easily adopted. These include children of minority race, children with handicaps, older children, and children who are to be adopted with siblings. And, as demonstrated in the following excerpts from *Alsager v. Iowa, supra*, stability may by no means be assured after a termination. After noting that the Alsagers were ''affectionate parents, of below average but by no means inadequate intelligence, who lost their children through application of the loose standards, if any, contained within'' the Iowa law, and that it was never established that the children faced ''actual or imminent harm'' if they remained with their parents, the court stated:

> If anything has been made clear throughout these proceedings, it is that the area of predicting what will be in the best future interests of the child is a delicate one. Through the benefit of the hindsight, this Court can today see no apparent benefit to the 1970 termination. [D]uring the interim from 1969 to 1974, [four] Alsager children . . . between them experienced some 15 separate foster home placements, and eight juvenile home placements. The uncertainty of post-termination life is further depicted by the fact that when the case was first argued . . . , [the] experts recommended that even if the termination proceedings were ruled unconstitutional, two of the children should be permanently placed in their present foster homes. Some months later, [at another hearing] the situation had changed in that the two 'well-adjusted' boys had apparently rejected their foster homes and were being considered for probationary placements with their parents.

> ''Termination has thus failed to provide the Alsager children with either stable or improved lives. Based on their parents' capabilities, the Court cannot say that separation has benefited the children in any discernible way. In the eyes of [some] experts, they have been harmed. One lesson emerges clearly from this sad testament. **Termination is a drastic, final step which, when improvidently employed, can be fraught with danger.**''

The fact that a termination or surrender can leave a child with no parent and can end other significant relationships suggests the need for the social workers who are involved, and who are often in the position of arguing for termination, to exercise extreme caution. They must be sure they have something to offer the child through adoption before they move to terminate. They also must do whatever they can to assure that termination does not end contact with people who are important to the child.

CREATION OF A NEW PARENT-CHILD RELATIONSHIP

Adoption proceedings, like juvenile court proceedings, are initiated by the filing of a petition. The petition generally is filed by the prospective adoptive parent or parents. It typically presents information about the prospective adoptive parents, the child to be adopted, the relationship between the child and the prospective adoptive parents, and the child's legal status. If the adoption is an agency adoption, the petition will also include information about the agency. If the child's birth parents have not consented to the adoption, surrendered the child to an agency, or had their parental rights terminated, the petition will also present information about them and seek to terminate their rights.

If the adoption is not of a related child, soon after the petition is filed, the court will appoint an agency or an individual to investigate the prospective adoptive parents. In some jurisdictions, an investigation will also be ordered for an adoption of a related child. If the child is being placed through an agency, the investigation will be completed by staff in that agency; usually it will have been completed before the petition was filed. Whenever it is done, the social worker completing the investigation will file a report of the investigation with the court.

In most cases there will be two court hearings related to the adoption. The first is usually called an "**interim hearing**," and it will occur soon after the petition is filed. The primary purpose of the hearing is to assure that the consents, surrenders, or termination orders are valid.[1] This hearing is particularly important in private adoptions of unrelated children because in these instances, there is less assurance of the validity of consents or surrenders than there is when an agency has been involved with the parent or when the adoption is by a relative. If parental rights have not been terminated, the court may terminate rights at this point. The court may also appoint a guardian *ad litem* to represent the child. All these steps are necessary to protect the adoptive parent-child relationship from later attack. The custody of a child pending the adoption may also be considered at an interim hearing.

At some later point, after the report of the investigation is filed with the court, another hearing will be held. The judge will hear evidence regarding the prospective adoptive parents and their relationship with the child. If the judge has not done so at an interim hearing, the judge will rule on the validity of the consents, surrenders or termination orders. If satisfied that the child is legally free to be adopted and that the proposed adoption is in the best interests of the child, the judge will enter an order of adoption. This order generally is final—another protection against disruption of the adoptive parent-child relationship. It is, however, subject to appeal.

The order of adoption creates a legal relationship between the adoptive parent and child identical to the legal relationship between a child and a birth parent. The adoptive parent has all of the rights and responsibilities of a birth parent. The adoptive legal relationship, like the relationship between a child and birth parents, can be ended only through consent, surrender or termination of parental rights; the State has no authority to intervene in the relationship except as it can with birth parents.

Following the adoption, a new birth certificate will be issued for the child. The new certificate will list the child's new name if different from the name given by his or her birth parents, and it will list the adoptive parents' names as parents and the age they were at the time the child was born. The original birth certificate will be sealed. While provisions vary from State to State, the statutes in most States also allow the judge to seal all court records related to an adoption.

WHO MAY ADOPT?

The question of who may adopt a child arises in two contexts. It arises, first, when prospective adoptive parents apply to an agency for adoption and are rejected. Agencies can and do reject applicants for a variety of reasons, such as they are overweight, diabetic, or too old, they have been divorced, or they have no religious affiliation or profess to be atheists. While rejections for the reasons cited above may be questionable, they have seldom been challenged and, when challenged, have been upheld by the courts. Agencies have no obligation to place a child for adoption with someone who has no existing legal claim to a child.

The question of who may adopt also arises with respect to foster parents who wish to adopt a child in their care. Foster parents may also be rejected as adoptive parents for a variety

---

1.   It should be noted that when the term "consent" is used in this chapter, it refers to a consent to adopt a child by the child's parent or by an agency acting under the authority of a surrender or a termination order. The consent of the child to be adopted may also be required. The statutes in most States specify an age beyond which a child's consent to the adoption is required.

of reasons, but many have challenged rejections on racial grounds, specifically, rejections of white foster parents who wish to adopt black children. The National Association of Black Social Workers has argued forcefully that adoption of black or mixed race children by white parents is not in the best interests of the child. The position of the Association has been widely accepted, and, either by policy or in practice, transracial adoption is discouraged. Similarly, representatives of tribes have argued that placing Native American children with non-Native American adoptive parents was not in the best interests of either the child or the child's tribe. The Indian Child Welfare Act, discussed in Chapter 8, includes procedures to prevent placement of Indian children with non-Indian parents.

An important case related to transracial adoption is *Drummond v. Fulton County Department of Family and Children's Services*, 563 F.2d 1200 (5th Cir. 1977); *cert. den'd*. 437 U.S. 910 (1978). The case was brought by the Drummonds after their application for the adoption of a mixed race child in their care was denied by the placing agency. The Drummonds were white, and their application was denied in part because of their race and their racial attitudes. The Court of Appeals held that since the denial was not totally or automatically based on race, it did not violate equal protection, noting the following factors:

"First, consideration of race in the child placement process suggests no racial slur or stigma in connection with any race. It is a natural thing for children to be raised by parents of their same ethnic background.

"Second, no case has been cited to the Court suggesting that it is impermissible to consider race in adoption placement. The only cases which have addressed this problem indicate that, while the automatic use of race is barred, the use of race as one of the factors in making the ultimate decision is legitimate.

"Third, the professional literature on the subject of transracial child placement stresses the importance of considering the racial attitudes of potential parents. The constitutional strictures against racial discrimination are not mandates to ignore the accumulated experience of unbiased professionals. A couple has no right to adopt a child it is not equipped to rear, and according to the professional literature race bears directly on that inquiry. From the child's perspective, the consideration of race is simply another facet of finding him the best possible home. Rather than eliminating certain categories of homes from consideration it avoids the potentially tragic possibility of placing a child in a home with parents who will not be able to cope with the child's problems.

"Fourth, in the analogous inquiry over the permissibility of considering the religion of would-be adoptive parents, numerous courts have found no constitutional infirmity. Those cases make the same distinction as this Court makes in the racial context. So long as religion is not an automatic factor, its consideration as one of a number of factors is unobjectionable.

"Finally, adoption agencies quite frequently try to place a child where he can most easily become a normal family member. The duplication of his natural biological environment is part of that program. This Court does not have the professional expertise to assess the wisdom of [this practice], but it is our province to conclude, as we do today, that the use of race [in duplicating the biological environment] is not unconstitutional."

LEGAL MECHANISMS TO FACILITATE ADOPTION OF CHILDREN WITH SPECIAL NEEDS

The popular image of agency adoption is of a woman who has desperately wanted to be a mother cradling a smiling infant while her husband looks down adoringly. The infant has been surrendered by his or her young, unmarried mother who loved the child but recognized other parents could offer her child more than she could. To be sure, this image fits reality in some cases. However, as stated earlier, agency adoptions increasingly involve children who have entered foster care because they were abused or neglected and who cannot return home. The children may be older and handicapped. Many are of minority race or ethnicity. Many are members of sibling groups who wish to be adopted together.

There are several provisions in the statutes of most States that encourage adoption of children who are termed as having special needs—children who are older, handicapped, of minority race or ethnicity, or members of sibling groups. These provisions also indicate awareness that close relationships often develop between children and their foster parents. Specifically, the statutes may give foster parents preference in adoption if a child has remained in their care for a given period of time, usually twelve months. Moreover, the statutes may provide for subsidies to parents—most of whom are foster parents—who adopt children with special needs. These subsidies may be somewhat equivalent to the payments received by foster parents. The types of subsidies, the basis for computing the amount to be paid, and the duration of subsidies vary from State to State. The subsidies may assist the parents in meeting the routine costs of caring for a child, may reimburse the parents for the legal costs entailed in adoption or they may cover the costs of a child's medical care.

UNMARRIED FATHERS' RIGHTS

A large proportion of children who are adopted have birth fathers who are not married to their birth mothers and who have not been providing physical care or financial support to them. What rights do such fathers have and what rights should they have? These questions have caused substantial debate among lawyers and social workers.

The question of unmarried fathers' rights often arises when unmarried mothers have surrendered their children or consented to their adoption by a stepfather and courts have entered orders allowing for the adoption without notifying and/or obtaining the consent or surrender of the fathers. The Supreme Court has wrestled with this question in a series of cases. In *Lehr v. Robertson*, 463 U.S. 248 (1983), excerpts of which follow, the Court addressed this question and also reviewed its earlier significant cases regarding the rights of unmarried fathers.

In *Lehr*, the child in question, Jessica, was born out of wedlock. Jessica's mother, Lorraine, and Lehr had lived together for several years before Jessica's birth, and Lorraine always acknowledged Lehr was the father of her unborn child. Lehr visited Jessica and Lorraine every day in the hospital after Jessica was born, but when they were discharged from the hospital, Lorraine hid herself and Jessica from Lehr. Eight months after Jessica was born, Lorraine married Robertson, and when Jessica was two, Robertson sought to adopt her. Although the trial court was aware that Lehr had been seeking Jessica and had filed a court action to establish his rights to Jessica, the court approved Robertson's petition to adopt Jessica without providing Lehr notice of the adoption and an opportunity to be heard. The Supreme Court upheld the court's action, which was in accordance with the New York statutory scheme. It stated:

"The State of New York maintains a 'putative father registry.' A man who files with that registry demonstrates his intent to claim paternity of a child born out of wedlock and is therefore entitled to receive notice of any proceeding to adopt that child. Before entering Jessica's adoption order, the . . . Family Court had the putative father registry examined. Although [Lehr] claims to be Jessica's natural father, he had not entered his name in the registry.

"In addition to the persons whose names are listed on the putative father registry, New York law requires that notice of an adoption proceeding be given to several other classes of possible fathers of children born out of wedlock—those who have been adjudicated to be the father, those who have been identified as the father on the child's birth certificate, those who live openly with the child and the child's mother and who hold themselves out to be the father, those who have been identified as the father by the mother in a sworn written statement, and those who were married to the child's mother before the child was six months old. [Lehr] admittedly was not a member of any of those classes.

"[Lehr] . . . offers two alternative grounds for holding the New York statutory scheme unconstitutional. First, he contends that a putative father's actual or potential relationship with a child born out of wedlock is an interest in liberty which may not be destroyed without due process of law; he argues therefore that he had a constitutional right to prior notice and an opportunity to be heard before he was deprived of that interest. Second, he contends that the gender-based classification in the statute, which both denied him the right to consent to Jessica's adoption and accorded him fewer procedural rights than her mother, violated the Equal Protection Clause.

"The intangible fibers that connect parent and child have infinite variety. They are woven throughout the fabric of our society, providing it with strength, beauty, and flexibility. It is self-evident that they are sufficiently vital to merit constitutional protection in appropriate cases. This Court has examined the extent to which a natural father's biological relationship with his illegitimate child receives protection under the Due Process Clause in precisely three cases: *Stanley v. Illinois*, 405 U.S. 645 (1972), *Quilloin v. Walcott*, 434 U.S. 246 (1978), and *Caban v. Mohammed*, 441 U.S. 380 (1979).

"*Stanley* involved the constitutionality of an Illinois statute that conclusively presumed every father of a child born out of wedlock to be an unfit person to have custody of his children. The father in that case had lived with his children all their lives and had lived with their mother for eighteen years. There was nothing in the record to indicate that Stanley had been a neglectful father who had not cared for his children. Under the statute, however, the nature of the actual relationship between parent and child was completely irrelevant. Once the mother died, the children were automatically made wards of the state. [T]he Court held that the Due Process Clause was violated by the automatic destruction of the custodial relationship without giving the father any opportunity to present evidence regarding his fitness as a parent.

"*Quilloin* involved the constitutionality of a Georgia statute that authorized the adoption of a child born out of wedlock over the objection of the natural father. The father in that case had never legitimated the child. It was only after the mother had remarried and her new husband had filed an adoption petition that the natural father sought visitation rights and filed a petition for legitimation. The trial court found adoption by the new husband to be in the child's best interests, and we unanimously held that action to be consistent with the Due Process Clause.

"*Caban* involved the conflicting claims of two natural parents who had maintained joint custody of their children from the time of their birth until they were respectively two and four years old. The father challenged the validity of an order authorizing the mother's new husband to adopt the children; he relied on both the Equal Protection Clause and the Due Process Clause. Because this Court upheld his equal protection claim, the majority did not address his due process challenge. The comments on the latter claim by the four dissenting Justices are nevertheless instructive, because they identify the clear distinction between a mere biological relationship and an actual relationship of parental responsibility. Justice Stewart correctly observed:

> 'Even if it be assumed that each married parent after divorce has some substantive due process right to maintain his or her parental relationship, . . . it by no means follows that each unwed parent has any such right. **Parental rights do not spring full-blown from the biological connection between parent and child. They require relationships more enduring.**' (emphasis added [by the Court]).

"In a similar vein, the other three dissenters in *Caban* were prepared to 'assume that, **if and when one develops**, the relationship between a father and his natural child is entitled to protection against arbitrary state action as a matter of due process.' (emphasis added [by the Court]).

"The difference between the developed parent-child relationship that was implicated in *Stanley* and *Caban*, and the potential relationship involved in *Quilloin* and this case, is both clear and significant. **When an unwed father demonstrates a full commitment to the responsibilities of parenthood by 'com[ing] forward to participate in the rearing of his child,' his interest in personal contact with his child acquires substantial protection under the due process clause. At that point it may be said that he 'act[s] as a father toward his children.' But the mere existence of a biological link does not merit equivalent constitutional protection.** The significance of the biological connection is that it offers the natural father an opportunity that no other male possesses to develop a relationship with his offspring. If he grasps that opportunity and accepts some

measure of responsibility for the child's future, he may enjoy the blessings of the parent-child relationship and make uniquely valuable contributions to the child's development. If he fails to do so, the Federal Constitution will not automatically compel a state to listen to his opinion of where the child's best interests lie.

"[Turning to the equal protection claim,] [t]he legislation at issue in this case, is intended to establish procedures for adoptions. Those procedures are designed to promote the best interests of the child, protect the rights of interested third parties, and ensure promptness and finality. To serve those ends, the legislation guarantees to certain people the right to veto an adoption and the right to prior notice of any adoption proceeding. The mother of an illegitimate child is always within that favored class, but only certain putative fathers are included. [Lehr] contends that the gender-based distinction is invidious.

"As we noted above, the existence or non-existence of a substantial relationship between parent and child is a relevant criterion in evaluating both the rights of the parent and the best interests of the child. In *Quilloin*, we noted that the putative father, like appellant, 'ha[d] never shouldered any significant responsibility with respect to the daily supervision, education, protection, or care of the child. Appellant does not complain of his exemption from these responsibilities . . . ' We therefore found that a Georgia statute that always required a mother's consent to the adoption of a child born out of wedlock, but required the father's consent only if he had legitimated the child, did not violate the Equal Protection Clause. Because, like the father in *Quilloin*, [Lehr] has never established a substantial relationship with his daughter, the New York statutes at issue in this case did not operate to deny [him] equal protection.

"We have held that these statutes may not constitutionally be applied in that class of cases where the mother and father are in fact similarly situated with regard to their relationship with the child. In *Caban*, the Court held that it violated the Equal Protection Clause to grant the mother a veto over the adoption of a four-year-old girl and a six-year-old boy, but not to grant a veto to their father, who had admitted paternity and had participated in the rearing of the children. The Court made it clear, however, that if the father had not 'come forward to participate in the rearing of his child, nothing in the Equal Protection Clause [would] preclude[] the State from withholding from him the privilege of vetoing the adoption of that child.'

"Jessica's parents are not like the parents involved in *Caban*. Whereas [Lorraine] had a continuous custodial responsibility for Jessica, [Lehr] never established any custodial, personal, or financial relationship with her. **If one parent has an established custodial relationship with the child and the other parent has either abandoned or never established a relationship, the Equal Protection Clause does not prevent a state from according the two parents different legal rights.**"

Frequently, the location of an unmarried father may be unknown or the mother may be unwilling to provide information on him. In such cases, notice to the father may be by publication in a newspaper or by other means such as those mentioned in *Lehr*. Such notice may be constitutionally sufficient, as implied in *Lehr*. State statutes will specify which fathers must be notified and how.

Despite *Lehr* and the provisions of any applicable State statutes, it is good practice to attempt to locate and involve fathers, not only when termination is being considered, but also early on in the process of intervention. The father and his family may be viable placement resources.

ACCESS TO ADOPTION AND BIRTH RECORDS

As has been stated, a child's birth certificate is typically amended following an adoption and, under the authority of State statutes, the original birth certificate and the court records related to the adoption are typically sealed. Once sealed, the original birth certificate and the records generally can be opened only by court order upon a showing of "good cause" for opening them.

Because records are sealed and may be opened only upon a showing of good cause, adoptees who want information about their birth family often cannot get it. Two cases, one from Illinois and one from New York, illustrate the response of courts to constitutional challenges to statutes allowing or requiring the sealing of records and to claims of "good cause." The Supreme Court denied *certiorari* in the two cases, *In re Roger B.*, 84 Ill.2d 323, 418 N.E.2d 751 (1981), and *Linda F. M. v. Department of Health of the City of New York*, 52 N.Y. 2d 236, 418 N.E.2d 1302 (1981), at the same time. *Cert. den'd.* 454 U.S. 806 (1981).

In *Roger B.*, the adoptee contended that the Illinois statute providing for sealing of adoption records, among other claims, deprived him of a fundamental right "to know his own identity." The Illinois Supreme Court disagreed, stating:

"We have found no case holding that the right of an adoptee to determine his genealogical origin is explicitly or implicitly guaranteed by the Constitution. Although information regarding one's background, heritage, and heredity is important to one's identity, it does not fall within any heretofore delineated zone of privacy implicitly protected within the Bill of Rights. We believe the adoptee does not have a fundamental right to examine his adoption records.

"Inasmuch as a fundamental right is not involved, the statute will be upheld if it is not arbitrary and bears a rational relationship to a legitimate State objective. [The challenged statute] represent[s] a considered legislative judgment that confidentiality promotes the integrity of the adoption process. Confidentiality is needed to protect the right to privacy of the natural parent. The natural parents, having determined it is in the best interest of themselves and the child, have placed the child for adoption. This process is done not merely with the expectation of anonymity, but also with the statutory assurance that his or her identity as the child's parent will be shielded from public disclosure. Quite conceivably, the natural parents have established a new family unit with the expectation of confidentiality concerning the adoption that occurred several years earlier.

"Confidentiality also must be promoted to protect the right of the adopting parents. The adopting parents have taken into their home a child whom they will regard as their own and whom they will love, support, and raise as an integral part of the family unit. They should be given the opportunity to create a stable family relationship free from unnecessary intrusion. The [statute] creates a situation in which the emotional attachments are directed toward the relationship with the new parents. The adoptive parents need and deserve the child's loyalty as they grow older, and particularly in their later years.

"The State certainly must protect the interest of the adoptee, as well as the rights of the natural and adopting parents. When the adoptee is a minor, there is no dispute that the sealed-record provisions serve this end. The child, in his new family environment, is insulated from intrusion from the natural parents. The child is protected from any stigma resulting from illegitimacy, neglect, or abuse. The preclusion of outside interfer-

ence allows the adopted child to develop a relationship of love and cohesiveness with the new family unit. Prior to adulthood, the adoptee's interest is consistent with that of the adopting and natural parents.

"Upon reaching majority, the adoptee often develops a countervailing interest that is in direct conflict with the other parties, particularly the natural parents. The adoptee wishes to determine his natural identity, while the privacy interest of the natural parents remains, perhaps stronger than ever. The [statute] recognizes that the right of privacy is not absolute. It allows the court to evaluate the needs of the adoptee as well as the nature of the relationships and choices made by all parties concerned. The statute, by providing for release of adoption records only upon issuance of a court order, does no more than allow the court to balance the interests of all the parties and make a determination based on the facts and circumstances of each individual case.

"**We find the statute to be rationally related to the legitimate legislative purpose of protecting the adoption process. Consequently, [it] does not unconstitutionally infringe upon an adoptee's right to discover his own identity.**"

Linda F. M. also focused on the reasons for confidentiality in denying an adoptee's claim of "good cause" to discover her identity. The court stated:

"[C]onfidentiality serves several purposes. It shields the adopted child from possibly disturbing facts surrounding his or her birth and parentage, it permits the adoptive parents to develop a close relationship with the child free from interference or distraction, and it provides the natural parents with an anonymity that they may consider vital. A natural parent understandably can feel deep effects when the records of an adoption are opened years after the child was surrendered for adoption. Although the sudden reappearance of the child may often be a source of great pleasure to the natural parent, in other cases it may be a destructive intrusion into the life that the parent has built in the years since the adoption. It may be the source of much discomfort. In some cases, it may even open the way for the child or others to blackmail the natural parents by threatening to disclose embarrassing circumstances surrounding the birth.

"Petitioner . . . summarized her reasons for wanting access to her records as a desire '[t]o know who I am. I feel cut off from the rest of humanity. I was given birth to the same way as everyone else, but everyone else can send away $3 and get a copy of their birth certificate. I want to know who I am. The only person in the world who looks like me is my son. I have no ancestry. Nothing.' A desire to learn about one's ancestry should not be belittled. When balanced against the interests of other parties to the adoption process, however, it cannot alone constitute good cause [to breach confidentiality.] This is not to say that concrete psychological problems, if found by the court to be specifically connected to the lack of knowledge about ancestry, would never constitute good cause. By its very nature, good cause admits of no universal, black-letter definition. Whether it exists, and the extent of disclosure that is appropriate, must remain for the courts to decide on the facts of each case. Nevertheless, mere desire to learn the identity of one's natural parents cannot alone constitute good cause, or the requirement of [confidentiality] would become a nullity."

In contrast to the courts, legislatures in many States have allowed adoptees access to records. Access is granted in several ways. Idaho and South Dakota allow access to court adoption records on the adoptee's demand and Alabama, Alaska, and Kansas release an adoptee's birth certificate on demand. Other States, including Florida and Ohio, allow release of either identifying or non-identifying information about birth parents to the adoptee or the adoptive parents, in some States with the consent of the birth parents and in others without any requirement of such consent. In addition, some States, including Illinois, have created registries and intermediary systems designed to help adult adoptees locate birth parents, with the birth parents' consent, and to facilitate exchange of information.

Moreover, statutes mandating confidentiality generally apply to birth and court records, not to agency records. Many agencies do seal records, making them unavailable to adoptees, but there is usually nothing in the law to prevent agencies from sharing information, and many agencies, in recognition of the value of sharing information, have developed various forms of what is termed "open adoption." Open adoption may involve birth and adoptive parents meeting each other prior to the adoption and continuing to have contact after the adoption, either directly or by exchanging information through the agency. Many private adoptions, moreover, are open adoptions and, indeed, a birth parent may choose a private adoption in order to be able to have an open adoption and to maintain contact with the adopted child.

SURROGATE MOTHERING

Couples in which a wife is infertile or unable to bear a child have increasingly turned to surrogate mothering rather than traditional adoption as a means of having a child. Surrogate mothering, as it has generally been practiced to this point, involves a contract between a woman and a couple. The woman agrees to bear a child for the couple. She is then artificially inseminated with the sperm of the man desiring to have a child. Surrogate parenting involves adoption because, under the terms of the contract, the surrogate agrees to consent to the child's adoption by either the man's wife or by both the husband and wife. The husband and wife, in turn, agree to pay the surrogate for the expenses of the pregnancy, or perhaps a fee for bearing the child.

The practice is extremely controversial and raises several legal and policy questions which have not been definitively answered. For example: does the practice violate provisions prohibiting compensation for placing a child for adoption? Who are the child's legal parents? Most important, is the contract enforceable? That is, can and should a court enforce the contract if either the surrogate or the adoptive couple refuses to comply with its terms?

Some of these questions were addressed by the Supreme Court of New Jersey in the well-known Baby M case, *Matter of Baby M.*, 109 N.J. 396, 537 A.2d 1227 (1988). In *Baby M.*, the court held that surrogate contracts conflicted with State statutes: 1) prohibiting compensation for adoptions; 2) requiring proof of parental unfitness or abandonment before a termination of parental rights is ordered or an adoption is granted; and 3) making surrenders of custody and consents to adoption revocable in private adoptions. The court also held that the contract conflicted with public policy. The court then reversed the earlier order of the trial court that declared the contract valid and enforceable. This opinion is in contrast to an earlier decision of the Kentucky Supreme Court which held that there are fundamental differences between surrogate arrangements and baby selling. *Surrogate Parenting Assocs. v. Commonwealth ex. rel. Armstrong*, 704 S.W.2d 209 (Ky. 1986).

Many State legislatures have tried to address surrogacy. In an attempt to provide guidance to the States in developing law in this controversial and emotional area, in 1988, a Model Surrogacy Act was drafted by the American Bar Association's Section of Family Law. The model act allowed surrogacy, provided for a reasonable fee to be paid the surrogate mother, and specified a simplified procedure through which the intended parents would be certified as the child's legal parents, thus avoiding the adoption process and provisions under adoption law concerning some forms of compensation.[2] In a "heated" session, however, the Section's model act was rejected by the full Association in favor of a model act which gave two options to lawmakers: either to declare surrogacy contracts void for public policy reasons or to allow the contracts but only with certain rights guaranteed to the children born of such contracts."[3]

Michigan, the State where the Baby M. surrogacy contract was arranged, was the first State to make arranging a surrogate contract a crime. The law was immediately challenged, but the suit was settled when the law was interpreted to only apply to contracts where a surrogate agreed to give up her maternal rights.[4]

At this time, in most States, the legality and enforceability of surrogate contracts is an open question which may be resolved by the courts or by legislatures. Should surrogacy be determined to be legal, other questions will remain such as whether psychological and medical screening of surrogate mothers and fathers should be required, whether standards should be imposed on surrogacy centers and lawyers who act as intermediaries, and whether the process should involve adoption or a new process for determinining parentage should be developed.

---

2. 22 Fam. L.Q. 125 (Summer, 1988).
3. A.B.A.J. (April 1, 1989), p.128.
4. New York Times, September 22, 1988, p. 12.

Public Primary and Secondary Education

As was noted in the introduction to this Section, this chapter will review the legal issues in public primary and secondary education of particular importance to social workers, that is, the law related to school attendance, discipline in the schools, special education services for handicapped children, and discrimination in the schools.

Before considering these topics, it should be noted that education is the only area of the law we consider in this text where local law is significant, if not predominant. In all the States but Hawaii, public primary and secondary schools are created, financed, and operated by local school districts, which typically are coextensive with towns or cities in populated areas and which may include several small towns and unincorporated areas or an entire county in rural areas. State governments may provide some funds to local school districts, and State laws may regulate some aspects of the operation of the schools, but local financing is generally primary, and the local laws enacted by the elected school boards that typically govern school districts generally controls the day-to-day operation of the schools. The federal government also provides some funds to local school districts and conditions receipt of the funds on compliance with certain federal laws, but the schools are primarily financed by their local districts and governed by their local school boards.

DISCRIMINATION

Throughout our history, certain groups of children have been denied educational opportunities. Handicapped children were excluded from the schools. Separate school systems for white children and black children existed under the authority of the law. Children were prevented from taking certain classes simply because they were boys or they were girls, and there were few opportunities for women to participate in athletics. While such discrimination is now prohibited by statute and through court interpretations of the equal protection clause of the 14th Amendment, vestiges of discrimination remain and continue to affect children. Moreover, debate continues over exactly what violates equal protection in the context of education.

Race

The Supreme Court held in *Brown v. Board of Education*, 347 U.S. 483 (1954), a case consolidating four cases arising from Delaware, Kansas, South Carolina, and Virginia, that laws either requiring or permitting segregation by race in public schools violate the equal protection guarantee of the 14th Amendment. In so holding, the Court overruled the "separate but equal" doctrine it had established in *Plessy v. Ferguson*, 163 U.S. 537 (1899), stating: "In the field of public education the doctrine of 'separate but equal' has no place. Separate educational facilities are inherently unequal." The Court reasoned:

"In these days, it is doubtful that any child may reasonably be expected to succeed in life if he is denied the opportunity of an education. Such an opportunity, where the State has undertaken to provide it, is a right which must be made available to all on equal terms.

"We come then to the question presented: Does segregation of children in public schools solely on the basis of race, even though the physical facilities and other 'tangible' factors may be equal, deprive the children of the minority group of equal educational opportunities? We believe it does.

"To separate [blacks] from others of similar age and qualifications solely because of their race generates a feeling of inferiority as to their status in the community that may affect their hearts and minds in a way unlikely ever to be undone."

The Court concluded its opinion by inviting further argument on the appropriate relief from the parties, the Attorney General of the United States, and the Attorneys General of all States requiring or permitting racial segregation in public schools. It essentially asked what should be done to implement its decision in the four consolidated cases. After considering the arguments, the Court rendered a second *Brown* decision, 349 U.S. 294 (1955), in which it stated:

"Full implementation of [desegregation] may require solution of varied local school problems. School authorities have the primary responsibility for elucidating, assessing, and solving these problems; courts will have to consider whether the action of the school authorities constitutes good faith implementation of the governing constitutional principles.

"In fashioning and effectuating the decrees, the courts will be guided by equitable principles. Traditionally, equity [special courts which operate under equitable principles and give special kinds of remedies or regular courts which so operate] has been characterized by a practical flexibility in shaping its remedies and by a facility for adjusting and reconciling public and private needs.

"While giving weight to [various] public and private considerations, the courts will require that the defendants [in the four cases] make a prompt and a reasonable start toward full compliance with our [earlier] ruling. Once such a start has been made, the courts may find that additional time is necessary to carry out the ruling in an effective manner. The burden rests upon the defendants to establish that such time is necessary in the public interest and is consistent with good faith compliance at the earliest practicable date."

This decision was followed by a long line of federal court decisions ruling that schools were segregated in violation of *Brown* and that officials were not making sufficient efforts to desegregate. The decisions at first merely ordered compliance with *Brown* and later, when compliance did not occur, imposed desegregation plans. The federal government's commitment to desegregation, and then integration of the public schools, was later articulated in the Civil Rights Act of 1964, 42 U.S.C. § 2000 *et seq*. This Act includes provisions prohibiting federal assistance to schools that discriminate on the basis of race and providing funds to support the costs of integrating the schools and remedying the effects of past discrimination.

Despite these court decisions and the provisions in the Civil Rights Act of 1964, segregation in the public schools has not been eliminated and integration has not been achieved. There are several factors that account for this.

First, there has been resistance by school boards to integration, manifested, not only in outright refusals to comply with court orders, but also in the development of unacceptable plans for integration such as so-called "free transfer plans" or "freedom of choice" plans. Such plans, which require voluntary action that may not be forthcoming, have lead to extended court battles. Further, white parents have demonstrated their resistance to integration by enrolling their children in white private schools or by moving from integrated communities to communities that are entirely or almost entirely white, leaving the public schools in some areas almost entirely black.

Second, as the previous paragraph suggests, it may be difficult to achieve integration as long as America has a system of community schools and as long as communities remain racially segregated. In other words, integration is difficult to achieve when there is **de facto** **segregation**—that is, segregation resulting from housing patterns, not laws forbidding integration—rather than **de jure** **segregation**—that is, segregation resulting from the law, not economic and geographic factors. Bussing has been the only solution devised to deal with de facto segregation, but bussing is controversial to say the least. Moreover, where entire school districts are predominantly composed of children of one race, integration can only be achieved if children are bussed across district lines. Plans that order such interdistrict bussing have been imposed by lower courts but have been struck down by the Supreme Court. Therefore, such plans must be voluntary—an unlikely event given the structure and financing of public education in this country.

Third, racial segregation may result from "**tracking**," the placing of students in separate classes or schools according to "ability." Research has consistently shown that students of minority race and ethnicity are disproportionately placed in classes for persons of lower ability, leading to charges that placement is made on the basis of tests and judgments that are racially and culturally biased.

Wealth and alienage

As we have seen, in *San Antonio Independent School District v. Rodriguez*, 411 U.S. 1 (1973), the Supreme Court refused to rule that dependence on local property taxes to finance the schools, a dependence which results in an inferior education for poor children in poor school districts, was an unconstitutional denial of equal protection. Some States and the federal government, however, have sought to remedy discrimination on the basis of wealth by easing local school districts' dependence on local property taxes. But, as long as public education is financed primarily through local property taxes, there will be differences between districts in the financing, and therefore the quality, of education. And because black children are disproportionately poor and tend to live in poor districts, many will continue to receive an education inferior to that of white children. Further, just as ability groupings tend to segregate on the basis of race, they tend to segregate on the basis of wealth. This results from the relationship between race and income. It may further be a function of differences in the ability of parents to purchase services or to access resources for their children.

While discrimination on the basis of wealth may be constitutional, as we have also seen, the Supreme Court ruled in *Plyler v. Doe*, 457 U.S. 202 (1982), that to exclude alien children, including illegal alien children, from the schools violated the 14th Amendment.

Sex

Discrimination on the basis of sex has occurred through restrictions on enrollment in certain classes and unequal access to participation in athletic programs. Title IX of the Education Amendments of 1972, 20 U.S.C. § 1681, as amended by the Civil Rights Restoration Act of 1987, P.L. 100-259, forbids such discrimination by any school which receives federal funds, which means virtually all public elementary and secondary schools. In addition, many State constitutions and statutes prohibit discrimination on the basis of sex in public education.

A subcategory of sex discrimination is discrimination on the basis of pregnancy. In the past, pregnant girls often were not allowed to attend school or were exempt from compulsory education laws. Presently, because of sex discrimination claims, pregnant girls generally may continue their education in school unless continuing is contraindicated by health. Moreover, if a pregnant student cannot attend school because of health, the school must generally provide a home education equivalent to that in the classroom.

Disability

In 1971 and 1972, two lower federal courts ruled that disabled children could not be excluded from the schools, essentially extending to disabled children the equal opportunity rights of *Brown*. These cases, *Pennsylvania Association for Retarded Children v. Pennsylvania*, 334 F.Supp. 1257 (E.D.Pa. 1971), and *Mills v. D.C. Board of Education*, 348 F.Supp. 866 (D.D.C. 1972), led to the 1975 enactment of the Education for All Handicapped Children Act (EAHCA), P.L. 94-142, 20 U.S.C. § 1401 *et seq.* The EAHCA, together with Section 504 of the Rehabilitation Act of 1973, 29 U.S.C. § 794, which forbids discrimination against the handicapped by federally assisted entities, enforces the goal of providing full educational opportunity for handicapped children. Because of EAHCA, which will be discussed later in the chapter, it is no longer permissible for local school districts to deny children an education on the basis of mental or physical disability. Whether children with AIDS may be denied an education solely because of the possibility of contagion, however, is not fully resolved.

As long as children with AIDS do not have symptoms which could interfere with their ability to be educated, they may not be covered by the EAHCA, but they should be covered by Section 504 of the Rehabilitation Act

under *School Bd. of Nassau County, Fla. v. Arline*, 480 U.S. 273 (1987). In *Arline*, which dealt with discrimination against a teacher, not a student, on the basis of tuberculosis, not AIDS, the Court stated that when Congress amended Section 504 to prohibit discrimination not only against those who were impaired but also against those "regarded as impaired":

"Congress acknowledged that Society's accumulated myths and fears about disability and disease are as handicapping as are the physical limitations that flow from actual impairment. Few aspects of handicap give rise to the same level of public fear and misapprehension as contagiousness. [People fear contagion even from those who have diseases which are not infectious, such as cancer.] The Act is carefully structured to replace such reflexive reactions to actual or perceived handicaps with actions based on reasoned and medically sound judgments . . ."

ATTENDANCE

In addition to ruling that discrimination in education on the basis of wealth may not be a violation of the 14th Amendment, the Supreme Court ruled in *San Antonio Independent School District v. Rodriguez*, that education was not a fundamental right either explicitly or implicitly protected by the Constitution. However, either the constitution or statutes in all the States but Mississippi guarantee a free public education to all children through the 12th grade. These constitutional and statutory provisions guaranteeing a free education are supported by statutes in all the States requiring children within certain ages to attend school and imposing civil and criminal penalties on parents who fail to educate their children in compliance with the law. The provisions in Texas are illustrative of the constitutional and statutory scheme creating public education and requiring attendance. The Texas Constitution states:

> "A general diffusion of knowledge being essential to the preservation of the liberties and rights of the people, it shall be the duty of the Legislature of this State to establish and make suitable provision for the support and maintenance of an efficient system of public free schools." Tex. Const. art. VII, § 1.

The Texas statutes provide that, with limited exceptions related to illness, weather or other factors, every child from 7 to 16 years old "shall be required to attend the public schools in the district of his residence [or a private or parochial school] . . . a minimum of 170 days of the regular school term." Tex. Educ. Code Ann. §§ 21.032,.033,.035.

The statutes in Texas further: 1) include within the definition of a minor in need of supervision (MINS) under the juvenile law a child who is absent from school for extended periods, Tex. Fam. Code Ann. § 51.03(b)(2); 2) require child abuse and neglect reports when a child has "violated the compulsory school attendance laws on three or more occasions," *Id.* at § 34.02(a); 3) provide that the parent-child relationship may be terminated when a parent has been the cause of the child's failure to be enrolled in school, *Id.* at § 15.02(1)(J)(i); and 4) make it a criminal offense for a parent to fail to require a child to attend school as required by law, Tex. Educ. Code § 4.25(a).

The ability of the State to require school attendance is not absolute. For example, in *Pierce v. Society of Sisters*, 268 U.S. 510 (1925), the Supreme Court held that a State could not compel attendance in public schools, thereby allowing parents to send

their children to private schools. The Court later held in *Wisconsin v. Yoder*, 400 U.S. 205 (1972), that a State could not require Amish children to attend school until the age of 16 when doing so conflicted with their parents' religious beliefs and when the parents provided continuing informal vocational instruction consistent with their beliefs. Lower courts have upheld a parent's right to teach a child at home as long as the parent complies with State requirements concerning instructional hours and curriculum.

Where school attendance is required, the statutes in some States recognize that truancy may reflect social and educational problems. Thus, the statutes may require schools to offer services in an effort to correct truant behavior before the case is referred to court or may address truancy under special provisions in the State's juvenile court act.

DISCIPLINE

School authorities have an obligation to maintain discipline on school grounds and are typically given broad discretion in the administration of discipline. But two forms of discipline that are frequently used, corporal punishment and exclusion from school, raise numerous legal questions.

Corporal punishment

Corporal punishment is any physical striking or paddling of a child. In *Ingraham v. Wright*, 430 U.S. 662 (1977), a 5-4 decision with a vigorous dissent, the Court considered and rejected a challenge to corporal punishment. The Court ruled that corporal punishment did not violate the 8th Amendment's prohibition on cruel and unusual punishment, holding that the 8th Amendment was designed to protect only convicted criminals. The Court did rule that the use of corporal punishment is governed by the 14th Amendment. It stated:

> "Among the historic liberties [protected by the Due Process Clause] was a right to be free from and to obtain judicial relief, for unjustified intrusion on personal security. While the contours of this historic liberty interest . . . have not been defined precisely, they always have been thought to encompass freedom from bodily restraint and punishment. It is fundamental that the state cannot hold and physically punish an individual except in accordance with due process of law.

> "[W]here school authorities, acting under color of state law, deliberately decide to punish a child for misconduct by restraining the child and inflicting appreciable pain, we hold that Fourteenth Amendment liberty interests are implicated."

However, the Court was not willing to hold that the imposition of corporal punishment necessarily violates substantive due process guarantees in the 14th Amendment. It noted that corporal punishment has long been used in this country and has been widely accepted by the courts.

> "The use of corporal punishment in this country as a means of disciplining school children dates back to the colonial period. [T]he practice continues to play a role in the public education of school children in most parts of the country. Professional and public opinion is sharply divided on the practice, and has been for more than a century. Yet we can discern no trend toward its elimination.

> "Although the early cases viewed the authority of the [schools to impose corporal punishment] as deriving from the parents, the concept of parental delegation has been replaced by the view—more consonant with

compulsory education laws—that the State itself may impose such corporal punishment as is reasonably necessary for the maintenance of group discipline."

As of 1988, fourteen States had statutes which specifically authorized the use of corporal punishment in the schools. For example, a South Dakota law gives school personnel the authority

> "to administer such physical punishment on an insubordinate or disobedient student that is reasonable and necessary for supervisory control over the student." S.D. Codified Laws Ann. § 13-32-2.

Some States prohibit use of corporal punishment. For example, a statute in California provides:

> "No person employed by or engaged in a public school shall inflict, or cause to be inflicted corporal punishment upon a pupil. Every resolution, bylaw, rule, ordinance, or other act or authority permitting or authorizing the infliction of corporal punishment upon a pupil attending a public school is void and unenforceable." Cal. Educ. Code § 49001.

This law was enacted because:

> "The Legislature finds and declares that the protection against corporal punishment, which extends to other citizens in other walks of life, should include children while they are under the control of the public schools. Children of school age are at the most vulnerable and impressionable period of their lives and it is wholly reasonable that the safeguards to the integrity and sanctity of their bodies should be, at this tender age, at least equal to that afforded to other citizens." *Id.* at § 49000.

Other States have no statutes forbidding or authorizing the use of corporal punishment, but the courts have held that corporal punishment is allowed. For example, while the Indiana statutes on school discipline list specific grounds for suspension and expulsion and set forth other punishments that may be imposed on students, such as restriction of extracurricular activities, corporal punishment is nowhere mentioned. Ind. Code §§ 20-8.1-5-4, 20-8.1-5-7. Nevertheless, it has been held that school officials in Indiana have the power to use corporal punishment. *Cole ex rel. Cole v. Greenfield-Central Community Schools*, 657 F.Supp. 56 (S.D. Ind. 1986). As the Supreme Court stated in *Ingraham*:

> "Where the legislatures have not acted, the . . . courts have uniformly preserved the common-law rule permitting teachers to use **reasonable** force in disciplining children . . ."

The use of unreasonable or excessive force, however, may give rise to due process claims, as the Court made clear in *Ingraham*. Thus, the courts have allowed students who were badly hurt or had corporal punishment imposed for minor infractions to bring civil rights actions against their teachers or schools for damages. *See, e.g., Garcia v. Miera*, 817 F.2d 650 (10th Cir. 1987) *cert den'd*. 108 S. Ct. 1220, where a 9-year-old girl was beaten so hard she was permanently scarred; *Metzger by and through Metzger v. Osbeck*, 841 F.2d 518 (3d Cir. 1988); *Hall v. Tawney*, 621 F.2d 607 (4th Cir. 1980).

Moreover, while reasonable corporal punishment may be constitutional, there may be limitations on its use, under local or State law, and certain procedural protections may be required before it may be imposed. In *Baker v. Owen*, 423 U.S. 907 (1975), the Supreme Court, without opinion, affirmed a lower court decision allowing schools to paddle students, even over parental objection, but requiring minimal notice and an opportunity for the student to be heard before the punishment could be administered. Later in *Ingraham*, however, the Court held that the 14th Amendment procedural due process requirements were met even if no notice or hearing preceded the administration of corporal punishment because a child could sue school officials if the punishment were excessive. The Court stated:

> "In view of the low incidence of abuse [of corporal punishment], the openness of our schools, and the common law safe-guards that already exist, the risk of error that may result in violation of a schoolchild's substantive rights can only be regarded as minimal. Imposing additional administrative safeguards as a constitutional requirement might reduce that risk marginally, but would also entail a significant intrusion into an area of primary educational responsibility. We conclude that the Due Process Clause does not require a notice and a hearing prior to the imposition of corporal punishment in the public schools."

Ingraham leaves school authorities with great freedom in use of corporal punishment, but there is nothing in the opinion to prevent States and local school boards from requiring procedural protections. Thus, certain protections, such as review by an administrator before a teacher can paddle a student, may be required by local or State law.

Exclusion from school

Students can be excluded from school through suspension or expulsion. If a child is suspended, he or she is not allowed to attend school for a short period of time, typically 3 to 10 days. If a child is expelled, he or she is typically not allowed to attend school for the remainder of the school year or is permanently excluded from school. The student is not given credit for any work due during the period of suspension or expulsion. Some schools use in-school suspension in which children are required to continue attending school and receive credit for work done but do not attend their regular classes and may receive counseling or special supervision.

As we saw, the Supreme Court held in *Goss v. Lopez*, 419 U.S. 565 (1975), that if a State offers free public education to all children and requires all children within certain ages to attend school, it creates a property right protected by the 14th Amendment. Having created a protected right, a State cannot deprive a child of the right, even for a short period of time, without due process. A child, therefore, cannot be suspended or expelled unless certain protection is offered.

Goss gave students facing up to a 10-day suspension only a right to notice and a minimum right to be heard. Such students were not accorded a right to an evidentiary hearing with the right of confrontation, a right to counsel, or any of the rights we have come to expect when one is deprived of a significant interest. With a longer suspension or with an expulsion, given the traditional due process balancing test, however, one should expect more procedural protection. This protection is generally set forth in State statutes and regulations and in local school district laws. These State and local laws may also provide more procedural protections attendant to short suspensions than those required as a minimum by *Goss*.

Grounds for punishment in the schools

Given that corporal punishment and exclusion from school are governed by the 14th Amendment, in addition to the question of what procedural protections must surround the administration of punishment by exclusion from school or corporal punishment, the question arises as to what constitutes reasonable grounds for such punishment.

The Supreme Court stated in *Tinker v. Des Moines School District*, 393 U.S. 503 (1968), that:

> "In our system, state-operated schools may not be enclaves of totalitarianism. School officials do not possess absolute authority over their students. Students in school as well as out of school are 'persons' under our Constitution. They are possessed of fundamental rights which the State must respect, just as they themselves must respect their obligations to the State."

Tinker concerned high school students who were suspended for wearing black arm bands in protest of American involvement in Vietnam. The Court held that the students' conduct was protected by the 1st and the 14th Amendments because it constituted political speech, it was not disruptive and it did not impinge on the rights of others. Suspension for such conduct, therefore, was not justified. In *Bethel School District No. 403 v. Fraser*, 478 U.S. 675 (1986), however, the Supreme Court distinguished wearing an arm band from making a speech which was considered lewd and obscene by school officials. Although the speech was only lewd by innuendo and was given at a rally in support of a candidate for student office, and was thus clearly political, the Court held that it was not protected by the 1st Amendment and therefore was a legitimate ground for disciplinary action.

As stated in *Tinker*, school officials have the authority "to prescribe and control conduct in the schools." Although, as *Tinker* also made clear, this authority must be balanced against the rights of individual students, school officials have the right and responsibility to maintain order and protect all students.

Because of the need to maintain order in the schools, school authorities may have wider powers than law enforcement officials to question and search students for evidence of misbehavior. In *New Jersey v. T.L.O.*, 469 U.S. 325 (1985), the Court ruled that a search of a student's purse after she was caught smoking in the lavatory did not violate the 4th Amendment. The Court stated that, while the 4th Amendment applies to searches in schools,

> "[i]t is evident that the school setting requires some easing of the restrictions to which searches by public authorities are ordinarily subject. The warrant requirement, in particular, is unsuited to the school environment: requiring a teacher to obtain a warrant before searching a child suspected of an infraction of school rules (or of the criminal law) would unduly interfere with the maintenance of the swift and informal disciplinary procedures needed in the schools. [Further,] the accommodation of the privacy interests of schoolchildren with the substantial need of teachers and administrators to maintain order in the schools does not require strict adherence to the requirement that searches be based on probable cause to believe that the subject of the search has violated or is violating the law. Rather, the legality of a search of a student should depend simply on the reasonableness, under all the circumstances, of the search."

The opinions in *T. L. O.*, *Bethel*, and *Tinker*, read together, indicate that while students have certain constitutionally protected rights, they may exercise these rights only to the extent that they do not disrupt the educational process. Moreover, they indicate that the Constitution gives school officials broad authority to maintain order and that the grounds for discipline may be broad and left largely to their discretion.

What conduct, then, justifies punishment? The statutes in some States are not specific, providing only that the school authorities must maintain discipline and establish a policy on discipline. For example, an Illinois statute provides:

> "Teachers and other certified educational employees shall maintain discipline in the schools . . . In all matters relating to the discipline in and conduct of the schools . . . , they stand in the relation of parents and guardians to the pupils. [E]ach board must establish a policy on discipline, and the policy so established must provide that a teacher may remove a student from the classroom for disruptive behavior and must include provisions which provide due process to students." Ill. Rev. Stat. ch 122, par. 24-24.

The local policies established under this Illinois statute or similar statutes in other States, may be specific or may similarly give broad discretion to teachers and administrators.

The statutes in some States list specific grounds for punishment. For example, as has been noted, an Indiana statute lists specific grounds for suspension or expulsion, including certain drug offenses, serious violent behavior, possession of a weapon, or failing to obey school authorities. Ind. Code § 20-8.1-5-4.

EDUCATION OF HANDICAPPED CHILDREN

As has been noted, after two courts ruled that physically and mentally disabled children had a right to an education as long as a free public education was provided for non-handicapped children, Congress enacted the Education for All Handicapped Children Act (EAHCA), 20 U.S.C. § 1401 et seq.[1]

The EAHCA essentially provides that, in order to receive any federal funds, a school district must provide handicapped children with a free, appropriate education and related services, preferably in public schools with non-handicapped children, but definitely in the least restrictive appropriate environment and in an environment tailored to each handicapped child's needs. The EAHCA further establishes the procedures that school districts must follow in providing an education for handicapped children and establishes procedural protection for parents. Basically, when a child is identified as handicapped, an individualized education program (IEP) must be prepared by appropriate professionals with parental input. The child must be provided with an education and related services in accordance with this IEP, at no cost to the parents. If the parents object to the IEP or to the school's refusal to recognize a child as requiring an IEP, that is, as educationally handicapped, they are entitled to have an informal conference, a formal administrative hearing, and a judicial hearing.

Because the EAHCA requires that qualified professionals prepare IEP's and states that handicapped children are entitled to "related services," including social work and psychological counseling, most school districts now employ social workers. Because a major function of school social workers is working with handicapped children and because many other social workers work with handicapped children or their parents, all social workers must understand the EAHCA.

---

1. The Act is commonly referred to as such, and will be so referred to in this text, but because the Act amended the Education of the Handicapped Act, it is sometimes referred to simply as the "Education of the Handicapped Act."

The provisions of the EAHCA and the history of its enactment were reviewed by the Supreme Court in its opinion in *Board of Education of the Hendrick Hudson Central School District v. Rowley*, 458 U.S. 176 (1982). This case is excerpted as Appendix 10-1 to this chapter. You should read it carefully, not only because of the issues it resolved, but also because of its thorough summary and analysis of the EAHCA.

The EAHCA has raised and still raises many questions of interpretation. The Supreme Court has answered some of these questions in *Rowley* and other cases, but many questions remain, and the Supreme Court opinions have raised further questions. Some of these questions are discussed below.

The definition of "handicap"

The first question posed by the EAHCA is who is "handicapped." The Act defines handicapped children to include children who are mentally retarded, hard of hearing, deaf, speech impaired, visually handicapped, seriously emotionally disturbed, orthopedically impaired, health impaired or with specific learning disabilities. § 1401(1). This definition has been interpreted, however, to include only handicaps which interfere with learning or social development and does not include handicaps which may be solely due to social or cultural background (but may include such handicaps when the student, because of social or cultural background, has a definable "educational maladjustment.") In other words, to be considered handicapped under the EAHCA, a child must be "educationally" handicapped, not just handicapped. Thus, as has been noted, a child with AIDS who has no symptoms of the disease which interfere with learning may not be considered handicapped under the EAHCA.

The definition of "appropriate"

Perhaps the most serious question posed by EAHCA is what is the "appropriate" education that must be provided. The Supreme Court said in *Board of Education of Hendrick Hudson Central School District v. Rowley,* excerpted in Appendix 10-1, that this does not mean an education to maximize a student's potential, an education which would put a handicapped child in exactly the same position as a child without the handicap, or an equal educational opportunity. It means only enough education to permit a student to benefit from the education. This education must be individualized according to an IEP, but as long as the education provided to the student pursuant to the IEP provides some educational benefit, the education provided will be considered sufficient. If "related services" are required to achieve this benefit, they must be provided in addition to pure educational services, but if related services are only necessary to maximize educational potential, they do not have to be provided.

It should be noted that it is "free" appropriate education which must be provided. The EAHCA makes clear that if the most appropriate education is in a private school, the school district must pay the tuition at the private school regardless of the parents' wealth. After all, public education is provided free regardless of wealth. Moreover, the Supreme Court held in *Burlington School Committee v. Department of Education,* 471 U.S. 359 (1985), that when parents pay for private special education they believe is necessary for their child in opposition to an IEP, while they are in the process of protesting the IEP, if a court ultimately determines that the IEP was wrong and the school district should have provided for the private special education for the child, the court may order the school dis-

trict to reimburse the parents for their expenditures. The Court stated:

"In a case where a court determines that a private placement desired by the parents was proper under the EAHCA and that an IEP calling for placement in a public school was inappropriate, it seems clear beyond cavil that [the provision in the EAHCA, allowing a court to order] 'appropriate' relief would include a prospective injunction directing the school officials to develop and implement at public expense an IEP placing the child in a private school. If the administrative and judicial review under the Act could be completed in a matter of weeks, rather than years, it would be difficult to imagine a case in which such prospective injunctive relief would not be sufficient. As this case so vividly demonstrates, however, the review process is ponderous. [The Supreme Court decision was rendered six years after the child in question was placed in a private school by his parents. The six-year review process included numerous administrative hearings, numerous trial court hearings, including a four-day trial, and two Court of Appeals decisions.] A final judicial decision on the merits of an IEP will in most instances come a year or more after the school term covered by that IEP has passed. In the meantime, the parents who disagree with the proposed IEP are faced with a choice: go along with the IEP to the detriment of their child if it turns out to be inappropriate or pay for what they consider to be the appropriate placement. If they choose the latter course, which conscientious parents who have adequate means and who are reasonably confident of their assessment normally would, it would be an empty victory to have a court tell them several years later that they were right but that these expenditures could not in a proper case be reimbursed by the school officials. If that were the case, the child's right to a free appropriate public education, the parents' right to participate fully in developing a proper IEP, and all of the procedural safeguards [in the

EAHCA] would be less than complete. Because Congress undoubtedly did not intend this result, we are confident that by empowering the court to grant 'appropriate' relief Congress meant to include retroactive reimbursement to parents as an available remedy in a proper case.''

The definition of ''related services''

What are the ''related services'' that must be provided as part of a free, appropriate education for handicapped children? The EAHCA defines related services as:

> ''transportation, and such developmental, corrective and other supportive services (including speech pathology and audiology, psychological services, physical and occupational therapy, recreation and medical and counseling services, except that such medical services shall be for diagnostic and evaluation purposes only) as may be required to assist a handicapped child to benefit from special education. . . .'' 20 U.S.C. § 1401(a).

There is no question that social work services are related services, but questions often arise as to what are impermissible medical services. In *Irving v. Tatro*, 468 U.S. 883 (1984), the Supreme Court, ruled that clear intermittent catheterization (CIC) was a related service which must be provided to an 8-year-old girl with spinal bifada, Amber, by her school. The Court noted that CIC could easily be done by anyone with a minimal amount of training, but that Amber could not do it for herself at this point, and that without CIC, she could not remain in school. The Court then reasoned:

> ''A 'free appropriate public education' is explicitly defined [in the EAHCA] as 'special

education and related services.' § 1401(18). The issue in this case is whether CIC is a 'related service' that [the school district] is obliged to provide to Amber. We must answer two questions: first, whether CIC is a 'supportive servic[e] . . . required to assist a handicapped child to benefit from special education'; and second, whether CIC is excluded from this definition as a 'medical servic[e]' serving purposes other than diagnosis or evaluation.

''. . . CIC is a 'supportive servic[e] . . . required to assist a handicapped child to benefit from special education.' It is clear on this record that, without having CIC services available during the school day, Amber cannot attend school and thereby 'benefit from special education.' CIC services therefore fall squarely within the definition of a 'supportive service.'

''A service that enables a handicapped child to remain at school during the day is an important means of providing the child with the meaningful access to education that Congress envisioned. The [EAHCA] makes specific provision for services, like transportation, for example, that do no more than enable a child to be physically present in class, *see* 20 U.S.C. § 1401(17); and the [EAHCA] specifically authorizes grants for schools to alter buildings and equipment to make them accessible to the handicapped, § 1406. Services like CIC that permit a child to remain at school during the day are no less related to the effort to educate than are services that enable the child to reach, enter, or exit the school.

''[P]rovision of CIC is not a [medical service], which a school is required to provide only for purposes of diagnosis or evaluation. [T]he regulations of the Department of Education, which are entitled to deference . . . [,] define 'related services' for handicapped children to include 'school health services,' which are defined in turn as 'services provided by a qualified school nurse or other qualified person.' 'Medical services' are defined as 'services provided by a licensed physician.' This definition of 'medical services' is a reasonable interpretation of congressional intent.

"Congress plainly required schools to hire various specially trained personnel to help handicapped children, such as 'trained occupational therapists, speech therapists, psychologists, social workers and other appropriately trained personnel.' School nurses have long been a part of the educational system, and the Secretary could therefore reasonably conclude that school nursing services are not the sort of burden that Congress intended to exclude as a 'medical service.' By limiting the 'medical services' exclusion to the services of a physician or hospital, both far more expensive, the Secretary has given a permissible construction to the provision.

"In [the school district's] view, CIC is a 'medical service,' even though it may be provided by a nurse or trained layperson [because it may only be used] in accordance with a physician's prescription and under a physician's ultimate supervision. Aside from conflicting with the Secretary's reasonable interpretation of congressional intent, however, such a rule would be anomalous. Nurses in [Amber's] school district are authorized to dispense oral medications and administer emergency injections in accordance with a physician's prescription. This kind of service for nonhandicapped children is difficult to distinguish from the provision of CIC to the handicapped. It would be strange indeed if Congress, in attempting to extend special services to handicapped children, were unwilling to guarantee them services of a kind that are routinely provided to the nonhandicapped."

It is still not clear whether psychiatric services performed by a physician rather than a psychologist or non-medically trained psychotherapist should be considered excludable medical services. Further, it is not clear

whether residential psychiatric treatment is similarly excludable. In *Gary B. v. Cronin,* 542 F.Supp. 102 (N.D.Ill. 1980), the court ruled that psychotherapy provided in a residential setting may be a related service which must be provided at no cost to the parent, but in *Darlene L. v. Illinois State Board of Education,* 568 F. Supp. 1340 (N.D.Ill. 1983), the same court ruled that psychiatric hospitalization was a medical service which need not be provided by a school.

It should be pointed out that just as a private education must be provided at no cost to parents if an IEP indicates the private education is necessary, any required related services must be provided at no cost. Thus, for example, a school would have to pay the full cost of a sign language interpreter if such an interpreter was required for a deaf child to benefit from an education.

The setting for special education

Many questions relate to the setting for special education. The EAHCA favors "mainstreaming," that is, educating handicapped children with the non-handicapped whenever possible, in these words:

"to the maximum extent appropriate, handicapped children, including children in public or private institutions or other care facilities, are [to be] educated with children who are not handicapped and . . . special classes, separate schooling, or other removal of handicapped children from the regular educational environment [should] occur only when the nature or severity of the handicap is such that education in regular classes with the use of supplementary aids and services cannot be achieved satisfactorily." § 1412(5).

Many wonder whether mainstreaming is really a good idea and whether mainstreaming helps or harms handicapped children. On the one hand, handicapped children and non-handicapped children can benefit from being with each other. On the other hand, handicapped children may not be able to perform as well as non-handicapped children and may be ridiculed as well as being always at the bottom of the class in performance. But, whatever one's view, for now, the law mandates mainstreaming.

Where mainstreaming or even public education is not appropriate, questions arise as to the cost of private education, a cost that, as has been noted, must be borne by a school district regardless of a parent's wealth. For example, if the only appropriate school identified in an IEP is excessively expensive, may a school district refuse to pay?

In addition to questions of cost, problems arise when the most appropriate education for a child is far from the child's home or even out-of-state. The EAHCA provides that a placement is supposed to be as close as possible to a child's home, but distant placements are often necessary. If a parent refuses a distant placement suggested in a proper IEP, should a school be relieved of all responsibility to provide a free appropriate education? If a distant placement is far cheaper than an equally appropriate local placement, which must be chosen? These and other questions remain unanswered.

Procedural protections

A fifth series of problems and questions relates to the procedures which must be followed by school districts and the procedures available to parents to challenge school district actions. These procedures are set forth in some detail in *Rowley*. Basically, local, state, and federal legislation and regulations all set forth procedures for developing an IEP and for making placements pursuant to it. All procedures established in regulations must be consistent with any authorizing statutes and with any regulations on a higher level. All procedures established in statutes must be consistent with any statutes and regulations at a higher level. All these procedures must be followed by school districts. As can be expected, construing all this legislation and these regulations and following all these procedures cause many problems for school districts. Nevertheless, *Rowley* stressed the importance of following the proper procedures.

In *Burlington School Committee v. Dept. of Educ., supra,* the Court stated that Congress recognized that school officials and parents would not always achieve consensus and that "in any disputes the school officials would have a natural advantage" and thus it "incorporated an elaborate set of what is labeled 'procedural safeguards' to insure the full participation of the parents and proper resolution of substantive disagreements." These procedural safeguards insure that parents have a right: to notice; to participate in developing an IEP; to an administrative hearing to protest an IEP or the school's refusal to do an IEP; and to judicial review. Parents, however, do not have a right to appointed counsel (although they may retain counsel[2]), to any special burden of proof, or to juries.

Questions have also arisen as to the function of the courts in special education cases. *Rowley* made clear, however, that courts are not supposed to second-guess local and State school officials or to consider questions of methodology or educational approaches. Rather, courts are merely supposed to insure

---

2. In *Irving v. Tatro, supra,* the Court held that because the parents prevailed under the EAHCA, they were not also entitled to relief under section 504 of the Rehabilitation Act. This holding is significant because, under section 504, the prevailing party is entitled to a reimbursement of attorney's fees but is not similarly entitled under the EAHCA.

that all procedures are followed, that individualized attention is given to a child's needs, and that a child is given all that is required to realize an educational benefit.

Exclusion

Finally, it has been questioned whether handicapped students can be suspended or expelled because of troublesome behavior, and if so, under what circumstances.

The Supreme Court addressed these questions in *Honig v. Doe*, 484 U.S. 305 (1988). The two students in *Honig*, who were receiving special education services because they were considered emotionally disturbed, were suspended from school indefinitely by the their school district for violent and disruptive conduct related to their disabilities. The Court held that such indefinite suspensions were "changes of placement" under the EAHCA and that if parents objected to the changes, the children could not be moved while the parents challenged the change. It so ruled because of the so-called "stay-put" provision in section 1415(e)(3) of the EAHCA, which provides:

"During the pendency of any proceedings . . . [challenging a school district decision], unless the State or local educational agency and the parents or guardian otherwise agree, the child shall remain in the then current educational placement of such child. . . ."

The Court stated, however: "Our conclusion that § 1415 (e)(3) means what it says does not leave educators hamstrung." It noted that: 1) a school could suspend a child for up to ten days without the suspension being considered a change of placement; 2) a school was not precluded from using other "normal procedures for children who are endangering themselves or others," such as "the use of study carrels, timeouts, detentions, or the restriction of privileges;" and, 3) when a child was considered a danger, school officials could seek immediate injunctive relief in court without exhausting administrative remedies. Nevertheless, *Honig* does not free schools from their obligation to educate children who pose a danger because of their disruptive or violent conduct. The Court stated:

"We think it clear . . . that [in adopting the stay-put provision without an exception for dangerousness] Congress very much meant to strip schools of the **unilateral** authority they had traditionally employed to exclude disabled students, particularly emotionally disturbed children, from school. In so doing, Congress did not leave school administrators powerless to deal with dangerous students; it did, however, deny school officials their former right to 'self-help,' and directed that in the future the removal of disabled students could be accomplished only with the permission of parents or, as a last resort, the courts."

APPENDIX 10-1
BOARD OF EDUCATION OF THE HENDRICK HUDSON CENTRAL SCHOOL DISTRICT v. ROWLEY

"The Education of the Handicapped Act (Act) provides federal money to assist state and local agencies in educating handicapped children, and conditions such funding upon a State's compliance with extensive goals and procedures. The Act represents an ambitious federal effort to promote the education of handicapped children, and was passed in response to Congress' perception that a majority of handicapped children in the United States 'were either totally excluded from schools or [were] sitting idly in regular classrooms awaiting the time when they were old enough to "drop out." ' The Act's evolution and major provisions shed light on the question of statutory interpretation which is at the heart of this case.

"Congress first addressed the problem of educating the handicapped in 1966 when it amended the Elementary and Secondary Education Act of 1965 to establish a grant program 'for the purpose of assisting the States in the initiation, expansion, and improvement of programs and projects . . . for the education of handicapped children.' That program was repealed in 1970 by the Education of the Handicapped Act, which established a grant program similar in purpose to the repealed legislation. Neither the 1966 nor the 1970 legislation contained specific guidelines for state use of the grant money; both were aimed primarily at stimulating the States to develop educational resources and to train personnel for educating the handicapped.

"Dissatisfied with the progress being made under these earlier enactments, and spurred by two District Court decisions holding that handicapped children should be given access to a public education, Congress in 1974 greatly increased federal funding for education of the handicapped and for the first time required recipient States to adopt 'a goal of providing full educational opportunities to all handicapped children.' The 1974 statute was recognized as an interim measure only, adopted 'in order to give the Congress an additional year in which to study what if any additional Federal assistance [was] required to enable the States to meet the needs of handicapped children.' The ensuing year of study produced the Education for All Handicapped Children Act of 1975.

"In order to qualify for federal financial assistance under the Act, a State must demonstrate that it 'has in effect a policy that assures all handicapped children the right to a free appropriate public education.' 20 U.S.C. § 1412(1). That policy must be reflected in a state plan submitted to and approved by the Secretary of Education, § 1413, which describes in detail the goals, programs, and timetables under which the State intends to educate handicapped children within its borders. §§ 1412, 1413. States receiving money under the Act must provide education to the handicapped by priority, first 'to handicapped children who are not receiving an education' and second 'to handicapped children . . . with the most severe handicaps who are receiving an inadequate education,' § 1412(3) . . .

"The 'free appropriate public education' required by the Act is tailored to the unique needs of the handicapped child by means of an 'individualized educational program' (IEP). § 1401(18). The IEP, which is prepared at a meeting between a qualified representative of the local educational agency, the child's teacher, the child's parents or guardian, and, where appropriate, the child, consists of a written document containing '(A) a statement of the present levels of educational performance of such child, (B) a statement of annual goals, including short-term instructional objectives, (C) a statement of the specific educational services to be provided to such child, and the extent to which such child will be able to participate in regular educational programs, (D) the projected date for initiation and anticipated duration of such services, and (E) appropriate objective criteria and evaluation procedures and schedules for determining, on at least an annual basis, whether instructional objectives are being achieved.' § 1401(19). Local or regional educational agencies must review, and where appropriate revise, each child's IEP at least annually. § 1414(a)(5).

"In addition to the state plan and the IEP already described, the Act imposes extensive procedural requirements upon States receiving federal funds under its provisions. Parents or guardians of handicapped children must be notified of any proposed change in 'the identification, evaluation, or educational placement of the child or the provision of a free appropriate public education to such child,' and must be permitted to bring a complaint about 'any matter relating to' such evaluation and education. §§ 1415(b)(1)(D) and (E).* Complaints brought by parents or guardians must be resolved at 'an impartial due process hearing,' and appeal to the state educational agency must be provided if the initial hearing is held at the local or regional level. §§ 1415(b) (2) and (c). Thereafter, '[a]ny party aggrieved by the findings and decision' . . . has 'the right to bring a civil action with respect to the complaint . . . in any State court of competent jurisdiction or in a district court of the United States * * * ' § 1415(e)(2).

"Thus, although the Act leaves to the States the primary responsibility for developing and executing educational programs for handicapped children, it imposes significant requirements to be followed in the discharge of that responsibility. Compliance is assured by provisions permitting the withholding of federal funds upon determination that a participating state or local agency has failed to satisfy the requirements of the Act, §§ 1414(b)(2)(A), 1416, and by the provision for judicial review. . . .

"This case arose in connection with the education of Amy Rowley, a deaf student. . . . Amy has minimal residual hearing and is an excellent lipreader. As required by the Act, an IEP was prepared for Amy during the fall of her first-grade year. The IEP provided that Amy should be educated in a regular classroom at [the school where she went to kindergarten], should continue to use the FM hearing aid [she was provided in kindergarten], and should receive instruction from a tutor for the deaf for one hour each day and from a speech therapist for three hours each week. The Rowleys agreed with parts of the IEP, but insisted that Amy also be provided a qualified sign-language interpreter in all her academic classes in lieu of the assistance proposed in other parts of the IEP. The school administrators [had] . . . concluded that Amy did not need such an interpreter. . . . They reached this conclusion after [an interpreter who had been placed in Amy's kindergarten class for a 2-week experimental period reported that Amy did not need his services at that time, and after] consulting the school district's Committee on the Handicapped, which had received expert evidence from Amy's parents on the importance of a sign-language interpreter, received testimony from Amy's teacher and other persons familiar with her academic and social progress, and visited a class for the deaf.

"When their request for an interpreter was denied, the Rowleys demanded and received a hearing before an independent examiner. After receiving evidence from both sides, the examiner agreed with the administrators' determination that an interpreter was not necessary because 'Amy was achieving educationally, academically, and socially' without such assistance. The examiner's decision was affirmed on appeal by the [State education agency] on the basis of substantial evidence in the record. Pursuant to the Act's provision for judicial review, the Rowleys then brought an

---

*"[These]requirements . . . represent only two examples of Congress' effort to maximize parental involvement in the education of each handicapped child. In addition, the Act requires that parents be permitted [to examine all relevant records and applications for funds and be consulted in the development of state policies and plans and local educational programs.]''

action in the [appropriate federal District Court], claiming that the administrators' denial of the sign-language interpreter constituted a denial of the 'free appropriate public education' guaranteed by the Act.

"The District Court found that Amy 'is a remarkably well-adjusted child' who interacts and communicates well with her classmates and has 'developed an extraordinary rapport' with her teachers. It also found that 'she performs better than the average child in her class and is advancing easily from grade to grade,' but 'that she understands considerably less of what goes on in class than she could if she were not deaf' and thus 'is not learning as much, or performing as well academically, as she would without her handicap,' This disparity between Amy's achievement and her potential led the court to decide that she was not receiving a 'free appropriate public education,' which the court defined as 'an opportunity to achieve [her] full potential commensurate with the opportunity provided to other children.' [The Court of Appeals affirmed.] We granted certiorari to review the lower courts' interpretation of the Act. Such review requires us to consider two questions: What is meant by the Act's requirement of a 'free appropriate public education'? And what is the role of state and federal courts in exercising the review granted by 20 U.S.C. § 1415?

"According to the definitions contained in the Act, a 'free appropriate public education' consists of educational instruction specially designed to meet the unique needs of the handicapped child, supported by such services as are necessary to permit the child 'to benefit' from the instruction. Almost as a checklist for adequacy under the Act, the definition also requires that such instruction and services be provided at public expense and under public supervision, meet the State's educational standards, approximate the grade levels used

in the State's regular education, and comport with the child's IEP. Thus, if personalized instruction is being provided with sufficient supportive services to permit the child to benefit from the instruction, and the other items on the definitional checklist are satisfied, the child is receiving a 'free appropriate public education' as defined by the Act.

"Other portions of the statute also shed light upon congressional intent. Congress found that of the roughly eight million handicapped children in the United States at the time of enactment, one million were 'excluded entirely from the public school system' and more than half were receiving an inappropriate education. [T]he Act requires States to extend educational services first to those children who are receiving no education and second to those children who are receiving an 'inadequate education.' § 1412(3). When these express statutory findings and priorities are read together with the Act's extensive procedural requirements and its definition of 'free appropriate public education,' the face of the statute evinces a congressional intent to bring previously excluded handicapped children into the public education systems of the States and to require the States to adopt procedures which would result in individualized consideration of and instruction for each child.

"Noticeably absent from the language of the statute is any substantive standard prescribing the level of education to be accorded handicapped children. [T]he language of the statute contains no requirement . . . that States maximize the potential of handicapped children 'commensurate with the opportunity provided to other children.'

"[The Rowleys] contend that 'the goal of the Act is to provide each handicapped child with an equal educational opportunity.' We think, however, that the requirement that a State provide specialized educational services to handicapped children generates no additional requirement that the services so provided be sufficient to maximize each child's potential 'commensurate with the opportunity provided other children.' [The Rowleys] . . . correctly note that [the legislative history of the Act reveals that] Congress sought 'to provide assistance to the States in carrying out their responsibilities under . . . the Constitution of the United States to provide equal protection of the laws.' But we do not think that such statements imply a congressional intent to achieve strict equality of opportunity or services.

"The educational opportunities provided by our public school systems undoubtedly differ from student to student, depending upon a myriad of factors that might affect a particular student's ability to assimilate information presented in the classroom. The requirement that States provide 'equal' educational opportunities would thus seem to present an entirely unworkable standard requiring impossible measurements and comparisons. Similarly, furnishing handicapped children with only such services as are available to nonhandicapped children would in all probability fall short of the statutory requirement of 'free appropriate public education'; to require, on the other hand, the furnishing of every special service necessary to maximize each handicapped child's potential is, we think, further than Congress intended to go. Thus to speak in terms of 'equal' services in one instance gives less than what is required by the Act and in another instance more. The theme of the Act is 'free appropriate public education,' a phrase which is too complex to be captured by the word 'equal' whether one is speaking of opportunities or services.

"Assuming that the Act was designed [as its legislative history indicates] to provide a 'basic floor of opportunity' consistent with equal protection [,] . . . neither the Act nor its history persuasively demonstrates that Congress thought that equal protection required anything more than equal access. Therefore, Congress' desire to provide specialized educational services, even in furtherance of 'equality,' cannot be read as imposing any particular substantive educational standard upon the States.

"**The District Court and the Court of Appeals thus erred when they held that the Act requires [school authorities] to maximize the potential of each handicapped child commensurate with the opportunity provided nonhandicapped children. Desirable though that goal might be, it is not the standard that Congress imposed upon States which receive funding under the Act. Rather, Congress sought primarily to identify and evaluate handicapped children, and to provide them with access to a free public education.**

"Implicit in the congressional purpose of providing access to a 'free appropriate public education' is the requirement that the education to which access is provided be sufficient to confer some educational benefit upon the handicapped child. It would do little good for Congress to spend millions of dollars in providing access to a public education only to have the handicapped child receive no benefit from that education. The statutory definition of 'free appropriate public education,' in addition to requiring that States provide each child with 'specially designed instruction,' expressly requires the provision of 'such . . . supportive services . . . as may be required to assist a handicapped child to **benefit** from special education.' § 1401(17). **We therefore conclude that the 'basic floor of opportunity' provided by the Act consists of access to specialized instruction and related services which are individually designed to provide educational benefit to the handicapped child.**

"When the language of the Act and its legislative history are considered together, the requirements imposed by Congress become tolerably clear. **Insofar as a State is required to provide a handicapped child with a 'free appropriate public education,' we hold that it satisfies this requirement by providing personalized instruction with sufficient support services to permit the child to benefit educationally from that instruction. Such instruction and services must be provided at public expense, must meet the State's educational standards, must approximate the grade levels used in the State's regular education, and must comport with the child's IEP. In addition, the IEP, and therefore the personalized instruction, should be formulated in accordance with the requirements of the Act and, if the child is being educated in the regular classrooms of the public education system, should be reasonably calculated to enable the child to achieve passing marks and advance from grade to grade.**

"As mentioned . . . , the Act permits '[a]ny party aggrieved by the findings and decision' of the state administrative hearings 'to bring a civil action' in . . . [a State or federal trial court.] § 1415(e)(2). The complaint, and therefore the civil action, may concern 'any matter relating to the identification, evaluation, or educational placement of the child, or the provision of a free appropriate public education to such child.' § 1415(b)(1)(E). In reviewing the complaint, the Act provides that a court 'shall receive the record of the [state] administrative proceedings, shall hear additional evidence at the request of a party, and, basing its decision on the preponderance of the evidence, shall grant such relief as the court determines is appropriate.' § 1415(e)(2).

"The parties disagree sharply over the meaning of these provisions . . . [In determining what authority they give the courts to review school officals' actions,] . . . we think the fact that [the grant of authority] is found in sec-

tion 1415, which is entitled 'Procedural safeguards,' is not without significance. When the elaborate and highly specific procedural safeguards embodied in section 1415 are contrasted with the general and somewhat imprecise substantive admonitions contained in the Act, we think that the importance Congress attached to these procedural safeguards cannot be gainsaid. It seems to us no exaggeration to say that Congress placed every bit as much emphasis upon compliance with procedures giving parents and guardians a large measure of participation at every stage of the administrative process, see, e.g., §§ 1415(a)-(d), as it did upon the measurement of the resulting IEP against a substantive standard. We think that the congressional emphasis upon full participation of concerned parties throughout the development of the IEP, as well as the requirements that state and local plans [for development of IEPs] be submitted to the [federal government] for approval, demonstrates the legislative conviction that adequate compliance with the procedures prescribed would in most cases assure much if not all of what Congress wished in the way of substantive content in an IEP.

"Thus the provision that a reviewing court base its decision on the 'preponderance of the evidence' is by no means an invitation to the courts to substitute their own notions of sound educational policy for those of the school authorities which they review. The very importance which Congress has attached to compliance with certain procedures in the preparation of an IEP would be frustrated if a court were permitted simply to set state decisions at nought. The fact that section 1415(e) requires that the reviewing court 'receive the records of the [state] administrative proceedings' carries with it the implied requirement that due weight shall be given to these proceedings. And we find nothing in the Act to suggest that merely because Congress was rather sketchy in establishing substantive requirements, as opposed to procedural requirements for the preparation of an IEP, it intended that reviewing courts should have a free hand to impose substantive standards of review which cannot be derived from the Act itself.

"**Therefore, a court's inquiry in suits brought under section 1415(e)(2) is twofold. First, has the State complied with the procedures set forth in the Act? And second, is the individualized educational program developed through the Act's procedures reasonably calculated to enable the child to receive educational benefits? If these requirements are met, the State has complied with the obligations imposed by Congress and the courts can require no more.**

"In assuring that the requirements of the Act have been met, courts must be careful to avoid imposing their view of preferable educational methods upon the States. The primary responsibility for formulating the education to be accorded a handicapped child, and for choosing the educational method most suitable to the child's needs, was left by the Act to state and local educational agencies in cooperation with the parents or guardian of the child. The Act expressly charges States with the responsibility of 'acquiring and disseminating to teachers and administrators of programs for handicapped children significant information derived from educational research, demonstration, and similar projects, and [of] adopting, where appropriate, promising educational practices and materials.' § 1413(a)(3). In the face of such a clear statutory directive, it seems highly unlikely that Congress intended courts to overturn a State's choice of appropriate educational theories. . . .

"[In *San Antonio Independent School Dist. v. Rodriguez*, we] . . . cautioned that courts lack the 'specialized knowledge and experience' necessary to resolve 'persistent and difficult

questions of educational policy.' We think that Congress shared that view when it passed the Act. . . . Congress' intention was not that the Act displace the primacy of States in the field of education, but that States receive funds to assist them in extending their educational systems to the handicapped. **Therefore, once a court determines that the requirements of the Act have been met, questions of methodology are for resolution by the States.**

"Entrusting a child's education to state and local agencies does not leave the child without protection. Congress sought to protect individual children by providing for parental involvement in the development of state plans and policies . . . and in the formulation of the child's individual educational program. . . . As this very case demonstrates, parents and guardians will not lack ardor in seeking to ensure that handicapped children receive all of the benefits to which they are entitled by the Act.

"Applying these principles to the facts of this case, we conclude that . . . [Amy's school was not required to provide her with a sign-language interpreter.] Neither the District Court nor the Court of Appeals found that [the school officials] had failed to comply with the procedures of the Act, and the findings of neither court would support a conclusion that Amy's educational program failed to comply with the substantive requirements of the Act. On the contrary, the District Court found that the 'evidence firmly establishes that Amy is receiving an "adequate" education, since she performs better than the average child in her class and is advancing easily from grade to grade.' In light of this finding, and of the fact that Amy was receiving personalized instruction and related services calculated . . . to meet her educational needs, the lower courts should not have concluded that the Act requires the provision of a sign-language interpreter."

SECTION III

LAW AND THE FAMILY

INTRODUCTION TO LAW AND THE FAMILY

The legal system has always had a special relationship with the family. On the one hand, as we have seen, the family is recognized as an institution which is protected from interference by the State. As the Court stated in *Smith v. OFFER*, 431 U.S. 816 (1977):

> "[The] 'freedom of personal choice in matters of . . . family life is one of the liberties protected by the Due Process Clause of the Fourteenth Amendment.' There does exist a 'private realm of family life which the state cannot enter,' and that has been afforded both substantive and procedural protection."

But, on the other hand, as was stated in *Prince v. Commonwealth of Massachusetts*, 321 U.S. 158 (1944), the family "is not beyond regulation in the public interest." You learned in the chapters on juvenile law that, as was also stated in *Prince*, "the state has a wide range of power for limiting parental freedom and authority in things affecting the child's welfare." In the chapters in this Section, you will learn other ways that the state may intervene in or regulate the family. You will learn that while the state must recognize the integrity of the family and not infringe "the liberty interest in family privacy [which] has its source . . . in intrinsic human rights, as they have been understood in 'this Nation's history and tradition,' " *Smith v.*

OFFER, the state will act to preserve the family and to protect the interests of family members and of society. Moreover, the state may itself define the family. As was further stated in *Smith*:

> "the usual understanding of 'family' implies biological relationships . . . [b]ut biological relationships are not the exclusive determination of the existence of a family. The basic foundation of the family in our society, the marriage relationship, is, of course, not a matter of blood relation."

It is, instead, a relationship which is legally defined and recognized. Similarly, as you saw in Chapter 9, adoption is a legal action which is the legal equivalent of biological parenthood.

In this Section of the book, we will look at the ways the law and the legal system define, regulate, and protect the family. In Chapter 11, we will look at how the law defines marriage, regulates the marriage relationship, and protects, or fails to protect, the parties to a marriage. We will also look to the law on the termination of marriage and to the rights and obligations of the parties that survive the end of a marriage.

While social workers should be familiar with the laws on marriage and termination of marriage and while some social workers may play active roles in the legal process followed to terminate a marriage, social workers generally only have an indirect counseling role in relation to marriage and termination of marriage—except where children are involved. If there are children in a family, the issues of child custody and support may arise and social workers have several direct and crucial roles to play in the legal system. Among other roles, social workers may be actively involved in negotiations and mediation related to child custody and support, may prepare reports or make recommendations for the courts in disputed custody cases, may appear as witnesses in custody cases, may act as guardians *ad litem* for children involved in custody disputes, or may work in offices which impose and enforce child support obligations. Thus, in Chapter 12, we will carefully examine the issues of child custody and support and look closely at the role of the social worker in relation to these issues.

A family law issue of particular importance to social workers is the problem of **domestic violence**, that is, one member of a family or household assaulting or abusing another member. Social workers are frequently employed by shelters for victims of domestic violence or may work with victims of domestic violence in other settings. Social workers may assist the victims of domestic violence obtain the protection of laws designed to aid them or may work with perpetrators of domestic violence who have been ordered to obtain counseling by courts. They may also work with perpetrators of domestic violence who voluntarily seek help. It is, thus, important that social workers be familiar with the laws designed to prevent domestic violence and to protect victims of such violence. These laws are reviewed in Chapter 13.

The laws we shall discuss in this Section related to families are almost exclusively State laws. There is no local law related to marriage, the termination of marriage, or child custody and support, and federal law plays no role in the creation, regulation, or termination of the marriage relationship or in domestic violence—except that State laws related to marriage or domestic violence, as all laws, must be consistent with the Constitution. Federal courts may only entertain cases dealing with the marriage relationship or domestic violence when a State law or practice related to the marriage relationship or domestic violence is challenged as a violation of the Constitution or when a case concerns entitlement to federal benefits through a spouse. There are some federal laws, which we shall discuss, related to child support and child custody, but federal courts do not entertain cases related to these subjects—again, except where the Constitution is implicated.

11

Marriage

In legal terms, marriage is a contractual relationship. The parties to the contract, the husband and wife, agree to certain obligations towards one another, for example, to support one another. The marriage contract is a special kind of contract in that entering into the contract creates a new legal status for the parties. After marrying, one is something new in the eyes of the law and the eyes of others—a married person. Having the status of a married person means having certain rights, privileges and obligations not afforded to non-married persons, such as the right to have sexual intercourse with one's spouse legally, the privilege of receiving Social Security benefits on one's spouse's account, and the obligation to support one's spouse.

Marriage may also affect the legal status of a couple's children. Children conceived or born while their birth parents were married to one another are considered **legitimate** while children whose birth parents were not married at the time of their conception or birth may be considered **illegitimate**.[1] The legitimacy of a child was once highly significant because there was pervasive and invidious discrimination against illegitimate children in the law and in social conduct. There are still vestiges of such discrimination in the law today, but legitimacy is far less important today than it was formerly. Indeed, several States have totally eliminated the distinction between legitimate and illegitimate children or recognize some children who were conceived or born when their natural parents were not married as legitimate. We shall look closer at legitimacy in Chapter 12.

---

1.   This term, which replaced the stigmatizing term "bastard," has been replaced in much legal writing by the less stigmatizing term "**children born out of wedlock**."

GETTING MARRIED

There are certain legal prerequisites to entering into the marriage contract. These prerequisites, which are both substantive and procedural, vary in certain respects from State to State but are essentially the same. All have similar purposes. They were established primarily to protect the public health, to assure that the parties have the legal capacity to understand and assume the obligations of marriage, and to provide an official record that a marriage has, in fact, occurred.

Substantive prerequisites

The parties must have capacity.   Generally, in order to marry, the parties must have the legal capacity to enter into a marriage contract or be legally competent to do so. That is, they must be of a certain age and have the requisite mental capacity to form a contract.

The age at which persons can marry without parental consent is 18 years old in almost all of the States. The statutes in many States allow marriage at an earlier age, generally age 16 for both parties or for the woman: 1) if the woman is pregnant or has given birth; 2) if the couple's parents or guardians consent; or 3) if a court approves.

Some States have specific restrictions limiting marriage by persons who are mentally ill or mentally disabled in addition to the general requirement that one must have the mental capacity to enter into a contract.

The parties must be unrelated.   All States prohibit certain blood relatives from marrying one another, but the specific relatives who are forbidden to intermarry differ from

State to State. Relatives by adoption or marriage are also often forbidden to intermarry, but this prohibition has been declared invalid in at least one State. *See, Israel v. Allen*, 185 Colo. 263, 577 P.2d 762 (1978), allowing an adopted brother and sister to marry.

The parties must be of different sexes.   No State recognizes marriages between two people of the same sex. In *Singer v. Hara*, 11 Wash. App. 247, 522 P.2d 1187 (1974), the Washington Supreme Court explained this refusal to recognize a marriage between two gay men, appellants in the case, on several grounds. First, it stated that although the Washington statutes did not explicitly say so, "it is apparent from a plain reading of our marriage statutes that the legislature has not authorized same-sex marriages."

Second, the court stated that, despite Washington's enactment of the Equal Rights Amendment (ERA), which provides, in relevant part: "Equality of rights and responsibility under the law shall not be denied or abridged on account of sex," and which, in the words of the appellants, made "sex an impermissible legal classification," a prohibition of marriage between persons of the same sex is not barred. This prohibition, the court reasoned, is unlike the prohibition on interracial marriages held unconstitutional in *Loving v. Virginia*, 388 U.S. 1, (1967). The Washington court stated:

"The operative distinction lies in the relationship which is described by the term 'marriage' itself, and that relationship is the legal union of one man and one woman. Washington statutes, specifically those relating to marriage and marital property are clearly founded upon the presumption that marriage, as a legal relationship, may exist only between one man and one woman who are otherwise qualified to enter that relationship. Similarly, although it appears that the appellate courts of this state until now have

not been required to define specifically what constitutes a marriage, it is apparent from a review of cases dealing with legal questions arising out of the marital relationship that the definition of marriage as the legal union of one man and one woman who are otherwise qualified to enter into the relationship not only is clearly implied from such cases, but also was deemed by the court in each case to be so obvious as not to require recitation."

"Given the definition of marriage which we have enunciated, the distinction between the case presented by appellants and . . . *Loving* is apparent. In *Loving* . . . , the parties were barred from entering into the marriage relationship because of an impermissible racial classification. There is no analogous sexual classification involved in the instant case because appellants are not being denied entry into the marriage relationship because of their sex; rather, they are being denied entry into the marriage relationship because of the recognized definition of that relationship as one which may be entered into only by two persons who are members of the opposite sex."

"The ERA does not create any new rights or responsibilities, such as the conceivable right of persons of the same sex to marry one another; rather, it merely insures that existing rights and responsibilities, or such rights and responsibilities as may be created in the future, which previously might have been wholly or partially denied to one sex or to the other, will be equally available to members of either sex. [I]t is apparent that the state's refusal to [allow two men] to marry one another is not based upon [their] status as males, but rather it is based upon the state's recognition that our society as a whole views marriage as the appropriate and desirable forum for procreation and the rearing of children. This is true even though married couples are not required to become parents and even though some couples are incapable of becoming parents and even though not all couples who produce children are married. These, however, are exceptional situations. The fact remains that marriage exists as a protected legal institution primarily because of societal values associated with the propagation of the human race. Further, it is apparent that no same-sex couple offers the possibility of the birth of children by their union. Thus the refusal of the state to authorize same-sex marriage results from such impossibility of reproduction rather than from an invidious discrimination 'on account of sex.' "

Finally, the court held that the State's refusal to let two men marry does not deny gays equal protection, rejecting the appellants' argument that gays constitute a suspect class.

"[Appellants] argue homosexuals constitute 'a politically voiceless and invisible minority;' that being homosexual, generally speaking, is an immutable characteristic; and that homosexuals are a group with a long history of discrimination subject to myths and stereotypes. We are not unmindful of the fact that public attitude toward homosexuals is undergoing substantial, albeit gradual, change. Notwithstanding these considerations, we express no opinion upon the desirability of revising our marriage laws to accommodate homosexuals and include same-sex relationships within the definition of marriage. That is a question for the people to answer through the legislative process. [S]uch a legislative change is not constitutionally required."

"[T]o define marriage to exclude homosexual or any other same-sex relationships is not to create an inherently suspect legislative classification requiring strict judicial scrutiny to determine a compelling state interest . . . [Thus,] the exclusion of same-sex relationships from our marriage statutes may be upheld under the traditional 'reasonable basis' or 'rational relationship' test . . . There can be no doubt that there exists a rational basis for the state to limit the defini-

tion of marriage to exclude same-sex relationships. Although, as appellants contend, other cultures may have fostered differing definitions of marriage, marriage in this state, as elsewhere in the nation, has been deemed a private relationship of a man and a woman (husband and wife) which involves 'interests of basic importance in our society.' [M]arriage is so clearly related to the public interest in affording a favorable environment for the growth of children that we are unable to say that there is not a rational basis upon which the state may limit the protection of its marriage laws to the legal union of one man and one woman."

The parties must not already be married. All States require that both parties to a marriage be unmarried and make **bigamy**, that is, marriage to more than one person at a time, a crime. This requirement and the crime of bigamy have been challenged as violating freedom of religion in that certain religions allow or even advocate polygamy. Over 100 years ago, in the case of *Reynolds v. United States*, 98 U.S. 145 (1878), the Court rejected such a challenge by a Mormon, stating that:

"it is within the legitimate scope of the power of every civil government to determine whether polygamy or monogamy shall be the law of social life under its dominion."

The parties must be free of certain diseases or disabilities. Early statutes forbade marriage by "insane" persons, "alcoholics", or "mentally deficient" persons. Most modern statutes have eliminated these prohibitions except to the extent that they relate to capacity to contract. Early statutes also forbade marriage by persons with certain venereal disease. Testing for some venereal diseases is still required in almost all States, but the prohibition on marriage by those with certain venereal diseases has been eased in many States. Some States allow marriage by persons with certain venereal diseases if the party who is free of the diseases consents, if the parties are beyond child bearing age, if the woman is pregnant, or if the parties have children.

Limits on substantive prerequisites

The States' authority to establish substantive prerequisites to marriage is not unlimited. Because there is a fundamental right to marry, if the substantive prerequisites unreasonably interfere with the right or disproportionately burden certain classes of people, the prerequisites may violate the due process or equal protection clauses. This is illustrated by *Zablocki v. Redhail*, 434 U.S. 374 (1978), in which the Court struck down a Wisconsin statute that made it difficult or impossible for certain poor people to marry as violative of equal protection. The statute provided that no one who was obligated to support any children could marry unless he or she submitted proof that the children "are not then and are not likely thereafter to become public charges."

Procedural prerequisites

Blood tests. As has been noted, almost all States require blood tests for certain venereal diseases as a condition of obtaining a marriage license, and in some States, positive results may bar marriage in all or some circumstances. Some States also require tests for sickle cell anemia or for rubella immunity, but positive results do not bar marriage. Rather, those with positive results are warned of the dangers involved.

Licenses. All States require the parties to obtain a marriage license. Licenses are required to give States control over who marries and to maintain statistics. Obtaining a marriage license does not mean that the parties are married; the license merely give the parties the authority to marry.

Most States require a couple to wait a period of time after applying for or obtaining a marriage license before they can be married. This waiting period is intended as a "cooling off" period or a time to "think it over." It is also designed to prevent marriage under the influence of alcohol or drugs.

Solemnization. All the States require some kind of formal ceremony in order for a marriage to be valid. The ceremony solemnizes the event and impresses its seriousness on the participants. It also serves as proof that the marriage occurred.

Depending on State law, the marriage ceremony may be performed by members of the clergy, judges, or certain public officials, like city clerks or mayors. The formal requirements of the ceremony depend on State law.

COMMON LAW AND INVALID MARRIAGE

If there has been no marriage license issued and no solemnization, in most States there is no marriage. Fourteen States, however, recognize so-called "**common law marriage**," that is, a marriage where the parties live together and hold themselves out as husband and wife but have never had a ceremony.[2] If a

---

2. These States are Alabama, Colorado, Georgia, Idaho, Iowa, Kansas, Montana, Ohio, Oklahoma, Pennsylvania, Rhode Island, South Carolina, Texas and the District of Columbia. New Hampshire and Tennessee have limited recognition of common law marriages.

State recognizes common law marriage, a couple who live together and hold themselves out as married, are considered married for all intents and purposes. In other words, they must divorce if they wish to terminate their relationship, they are entitled to all the rights, privileges, and benefits of married persons, and they owe to each other all the rights and obligations of married persons. The children of their union would be considered legitimate.

If a State does not recognize common law marriage, it still may impose some or all of the rights and obligations of marriage on the partners to a common law union. In the famous case of *Marvin v. Marvin*, 18 Cal.3d 660, 557 P.2d 106 (1977), involving the actor Lee Marvin, the California Supreme Court did not recognize common law marriage but held that an alleged oral agreement between Lee Marvin and the woman with whom he lived for many years, Michelle Marvin, to treat his property as marital property and to impose an obligation of support on him, like a husband's obligation of support, in consideration of Michelle ceasing to work outside the home and performing wifelike duties could be recognized and enforced. The court reasoned that:

"Although the past decisions hover over the issue in the somewhat wispy form of the figures of a Chagall painting, we can abstract from those decisions a clear and simple rule. The fact that a man and woman live together without marriage, and engage in a sexual relationship, does not in itself invalidate agreements between them relating to their earnings, property, or expenses. Neither is such an agreement invalid merely because the parties may have contemplated the creation or continuation of a nonmarital relationship when they entered into it. Agreements between nonmarital partners fail only to the extent that they rest upon a consideration of meretricious sexual services.

"[W]e base our opinion on the principle that adults who voluntarily live together and engage in sexual relations are nonetheless as competent as any other persons to contract respecting their earnings and property rights. Of course, they cannot lawfully contract to pay for the performance of sexual services, for such a contract is, in essence, an agreement for prostitution and unlawful for that reason. But they may agree to pool their earnings and to hold all property acquired during the relationship in accord with the law governing community property; conversely they may agree that each partner's earnings and the property acquired from those earnings remains the separate property of the earning partner. So long as the agreement does not rest upon illicit meretricious consideration, the parties may order their economic affairs as they choose, and no policy precludes the courts from enforcing such agreements."

The court also held that Michelle Marvin could be entitled to a share of defendant's property under a theory of **implied contract**. Under this theory, even if there is no express contract, if the conduct of the parties is such as to give rise to an implied agreement, the courts will enforce the agreement as if it were an express contract.

The Court rejected all arguments that recognizing explicit or implied agreements to divide property made in non-marital relationships would undermine marriage or foster immorality. It stated:

"Although we recognize the well-established public policy to foster and promote the institution of marriage, perpetuation of judicial rules which result in an inequitable distribution of property accumulated during a nonmarital relationship is neither a just nor an effective way of carrying out that policy. [T]he prevalence of nonmarital relationships in modern society and the social acceptance of them, marks this as a time when our courts should by no means apply the doctrine of the unlawfulness of the so-called meretricious relationship to the [division of property.] As we have explained, the nonenforceability of agreements expressly providing for meretricious conduct rested upon the fact that such conduct, as the word suggests, pertained to and encompassed prostitution. To equate the nonmarital relationship of today to such a subject matter is to do violence to an accepted and wholly different practice.

"We are aware that many young couples live together without the solemnization of marriage, in order to make sure that they can successfully later undertake marriage. This trial period, preliminary to marriage, serves as some assurance that the marriage will not subsequently end in dissolution to the harm of both parties. We are aware, as we have stated, of the pervasiveness of nonmarital relationships in other situations. The mores of the society have indeed changed so radically in regard to cohabitation that we cannot impose a standard based on alleged moral considerations that have apparently been so widely abandoned by so many."

The court made clear, however, that in removing the judicial barriers to division of the property of partners in a non-marital relationship:

"[w]e do not seek to resurrect the doctrine of common law marriage, which was abolished in California by statute in 1895. Thus we do not hold that plaintiff and defendant were 'married,' nor do we extend to plaintiff the rights which the [law] grants . . . spouses; we hold only that she has the same rights to enforce contracts and to assert her equitable interest in property acquired through her effort as does any other unmarried person."[3]

Several courts in other States have followed *Marvin* and have granted property rights to non-marital partners using the *Marvin* express or implied contract theory or other theories.[4] Minnesota has recognized non-marital property rights by statute. Interestingly the Minnesota statutes provide that a contract between "co-habitants" establishing rights to property will be enforced by a court only if it is in writing; if there is no written contract between the parties:

"the courts of this state are without jurisdiction to hear and shall dismiss as contrary to public policy any claim by an individual if the claim is based on the fact that the individuals lived together in contemplation of sexual relations and out of wedlock within or without this state." Minn. Stat. §§ 513.075; 513.076.

In *Hewitt v. Hewitt*, 77 Ill.2d 49, 394 N.E. 2d 1204 (1979), the Illinois Supreme Court was not willing to recognize a contract between the parties to a non-marital relationship and said no marital rights and obligations should arise from such a relationship on any theory. This was so even though, unlike in *Marvin*, the partners had a long-time relationship from their college days on, had three children, and everyone believed they were married. The court stated:

"[W]e believe . . . [t]he issue of unmarried cohabitants' mutual property rights . . . cannot appropriately be characterized solely in terms of contract law, nor is it limited to con-

---

3.   It should be noted that the court in *Marvin* only held that implied or explicit contracts could be recognized and enforced. On remand of the case, no implied or explicit contract for Lee Marvin to support Michelle Marvin after they ceased living together was found to exist.

4.   *See, e.g., Pickens v. Pickens*, 490 So. 2d 872 (Miss. 1986), using a trust theory; *Kenkenon v. Hue*, 207 Neb. 698, 301 N.W. 2d 77 (1981) *Kozlowski v. Kozlowski*, 80 N.J. 378, 403 A.2d 902 (1979), and *Morone v. Morone*, N.Y. 2d 481, 407 N.E. 2d 438 (1980), recognizing claims of express contracts; and *Beal v. Beal*, 282 Or. 115, 577 P.2d 507 (1978), *Caroll v. Lee*, 148 Ariz. 10, 712 P.2d 923 (1979), and *Watts v. Watts*, 137 Wis. 2d 506, 405 N.W.2d 303 (1987), recognizing implied contracts or other equitable remedies.

siderations of equity or fairness as between the parties to such relationships. There are major public policy questions involved in determining whether, under what circumstances, and to what extent it is desirable to accord some type of legal status to claims arising from such relationships. Of substantially greater importance than the rights of the immediate parties is the impact of such recognition upon our society and the institution of marriage. Will the fact that legal rights closely resembling those arising from conventional marriages can be acquired by those who deliberately choose to enter into what have heretofore been commonly referred to as 'illicit' or 'meretricious' relationships encourage formation of such relationships and weaken marriage as the foundation of our family-based society? And . . . what of the children born of such relationships? What are their support and inheritance rights and by what standards are custody questions resolved? What of the sociological and psychological effects upon them of that type of environment? Does not the recognition of legally enforceable property and custody rights emanating from nonmarital cohabitation in practical effect equate with the legalization of common law marriage at least in the circumstances of this case? And, in summary, have the increasing numbers of unmarried cohabitants and changing mores of our society reached the point at which the general welfare of the citizens of this State is best served by a return to something resembling the judicially created common law marriage our legislature outlawed in 1905?''

The court felt that these questions had been answered long ago when the legislature outlawed common law marriage and the courts ruled that ''an agreement in consideration of future illicit cohabitation . . . is void.'' The court was unwilling to abandon this rule despite the ''changes in societal norms and attitudes.'' The Court stated:

''It is urged that social mores have changed radically in recent years, rendering this principle of law archaic. It is said that because there are so many unmarried cohabitants today the courts must confer a legal status on such relationships. If this is to be the result, however, it would seem more candid to acknowledge the return of varying forms of common law marriage than to continue displaying the naivete we believe involved in the assertion that there are involved in these relationships contracts separate and independent from the sexual activity, and the assumption that those contracts would have been entered into or would continue without that activity.

''[Moreover, e]ven if we were to assume some modification of the rule of illegality is appropriate, we return to the fundamental question earlier alluded to: If resolution of this issue rests ultimately on grounds of public policy, by what body should that policy be determined? *Marvin*, viewing the issue as governed solely by contract law, found judicial policy-making appropriate. In our view, however, the situation alleged here was not the kind of arm's length bargain envisioned by traditional contract principles, but an intimate arrangement of a fundamentally different kind. The issue, realistically, is whether it is appropriate for this court to grant a legal status to a private arrangement substituting for the institution of marriage sanctioned by the State. The question whether change is needed in the law governing the rights of parties in this delicate area of marriage-like relationships involves evaluations of sociological data and alternatives we believe best suited to the superior investigative and fact-finding facilities of the legislative branch in the exercise of its traditional authority to declare public policy in the domestic relations field. That belief is reinforced by the fact that judicial recognition of mutual property rights between unmarried cohabitants would, in our opinion, clearly violate the policy of our . . . [new marriage act, which was enacted soon after]

Marvin was decided and received wide publicity. [This act, which nowhere mentions non-marital contracts, but which continues to outlaw common law marriage] constitute[s] a recent and unmistakable legislative judgment disfavoring the grant of mutual property rights to knowingly unmarried cohabitants. Even if we disagreed with the wisdom of that judgment, it is not for us to overturn or erode it.''

The court also noted that, in its view, the practical effect of recognizing non-marital contracts would be the reinstatement of common law marriage, something which the court could not and should not do.

The recognition of agreements made by those who live in non-marital sexual relationships to share property and to assume some of the rights and obligations of marriage is of some moment to gays and lesbians, who, as we have seen, are not allowed to marry their same-sex lovers. Because their agreements may not be recognized, some gays and lesbians have chosen, instead, to adopt their partners. Adoption could also provide legal recognition for a longstanding relationship. In *Matter of Adoption of Robert Paul P.*, 63 N.Y. 2d, 471 N.E.2d 424 (1984), however, a man was not permitted to adopt his male lover. The court stated:

"Adoption is not a means of obtaining a legal status for a non-marital sexual relationship—whether homosexual or heterosexual. Such would be a 'cynical distortion of the function of adoption.' Nor is it a procedure by which to legitimize an emotional attachment, however sincere, but wholly devoid of the filial relationship that is fundamental to the concept of adoption.''

The situation where there is an unrecognized common law union or cohabitation without a marriage license or solemnization must be contrasted with the situation where there has been a marriage license issued and a solemnization of the marriage and one or both of the parties have a good faith belief that the marriage is valid, but the marriage is, in fact, invalid. In the latter situation, the States may recognize marital rights and obligations of the parties. It may make a difference if the marriage is **void**, that is, prohibited or impossible for some reason, or **voidable**, that is, merely technically invalid, but a party with a good faith belief in the validity of a solemnized marriage is generally recognized as a **putative spouse**, entitled to all the rights and privileges of a married person as long as the invalidity of the marriage is not due to his or her fault. Thus, a man who marries a woman believing in good faith that her prior marriage has been terminated by divorce would generally be considered a putative spouse entitled to all the rights of a spouse even if the woman's divorce was not final at the time of the marriage, but the woman might not be recognized as a putative spouse even if she believed in good faith that her divorce was final.

Putative spouses are generally entitled to all the rights of a "real" or legal spouse, but they would not be given these rights if to do so would adversely affect a legal spouse. Thus, for example, if a man were a bigamist, both his putative spouse and his legal, that is, his first, spouse should be entitled to widow's Social Security benefits upon his death, but the putative spouse would not be entitled to full inheritance rights of two-thirds of her husband's property because granting her full inheritance rights would deny the first spouse her full inheritance rights. Both wives cannot have two-thirds of the husband's property.

INTERSTATE RECOGNITION OF MARRIAGES

Article IV, section 1 of the Constitution provides ''Full Faith and Credit shall be given in each State to the Public Acts, Records and judicial Proceedings of every other State." Pursuant to this clause, known as the **"Full Faith and Credit Clause,"** a marriage that is valid in the State in which it was entered into, even a common law marriage, must be recognized as valid in all other States. However, a State need not recognize as valid a marriage entered into in one State (State A) by residents of another State (State B) who married in State A solely to evade the requirements of State B. For example, if State A allows marriages between first cousins while State B forbids such marriages and John and Mary are first cousins who live in State B and intend to continue to reside in State B, State B need not recognize John and Mary's marriage which was entered into in State A solely to avoid State B's requirements.

PROPERTY RELATIONSHIPS DURING MARRIAGE

There are two very different systems for determining the property rights between a husband and wife during the marriage: the common law, also known as the "separate property" system, and the community property system.

Forty-one States plus the District of Columbia use the common law system. Under this system, property acquired during marriage may be held jointly, but unless a couple decides to hold property jointly, property acquired during marriage by one spouse remains that spouse's separate property; the other spouse has no right to or interest in that property during the marriage. Eight States (Arizona, California, Idaho, Louisiana, Nevada, New Mexico, Texas, and Washington) use the community property system. Under this system, each spouse is deemed to have a

one half interest in all property acquired during marriage except property inherited or received by one spouse as a gift.

There are variations in the community property systems from State to State. For example, who controls the community property differs from State to State as does the status of income earned during marriage from property acquired before marriage. There are also variations in the separate property systems from State to State. For example, whether one spouse must pay the other's debts and which debts differs from State to State. Whatever the variations, the community property system is seen as fairer to the wife, who generally earns less than the husband or who may earn nothing at all. Under the separate property system, the wife may own little or no property. Even her clothes may not belong to her if they were paid for out of her husband's earnings and are not considered a gift to her. Further, under a separate property system, a wife with no earnings has traditionally not been able to obtain credit in her own name; she has no right to her husband's earnings and a creditor cannot necessarily collect her debts from her husband. Under the community property system, by way of contrast, the wife may obtain credit in her own name whether or not she earns any money. Because she has a right to one-half of her husband's earnings and a creditor can collect from this one-half share, there is no problem giving her credit despite her lack of earnings.

The Equal Credit Opportunity Act, 15 U.S.C. § 1691, has somewhat eased the problem of a woman obtaining credit in separate property States. The Act prohibits discrimination by creditors on the basis of sex or marital status. It also permits a woman to use as a credit reference jointly used credit cards. However, under the Act, creditors can inquire into marital status. Further, while the Act explicitly preempts all State laws which prohibit separate extension of credit to married persons, the Act provides that if a spouse receives credit separately, the other spouse is not responsible for the debt. 15 U.S.C. § 1691d.

Because the community property system is seen as fairer to the wife, some separate property States are considering adopting variations of the community property system. Wisconsin has adopted such a system, but it is called a "marital property" system, not a "community property" system, probably because of negative associations with the latter term. See Wisc. Stat. § 766.001 et seq.

Whether a State uses a community or separate property system to allocate property during marriage, one spouse may have a right to a division of the property acquired during marriage after the marriage ends. Thus, one spouse may inherit a set share, like one-third or one-half, of the other spouse's property following his or her death whether or not there is a will and even if a will does not provide for inheritance of this share. And one spouse may have a right to division of the property acquired during marriage following a divorce. How much may be inherited regardless of a will or when there is no will varies from State to State and, as we shall see, how the property will be divided and how much each spouse will receive after a divorce also differ from State to State.

Further, whichever property system is used by a State to divide property during marriage, the States generally require spouses to support one another. Nevertheless, courts may not be willing to intervene into the marriage relationship to enforce the duty of support. Thus, in the case of *McGuire v. McGuire*, 157 Neb. 226, 59 N.W.2d 336 (1953), it was held that a 66-year-old woman who was in failing health was not entitled to court ordered support payments from her husband although he had substantial assets and income and although he had given her no money for three or four years with the result

that she was living in a state of considerable deprivation. She was provided with food but was not provided with any new clothing during this time except a coat. The furnishings and furnace in the home were very old, the newest appliance in the kitchen was a wood burning stove, the house had no bathroom or inside toilet, and water came from a well. The couple had one very old car. The court stated:

> "The living standards of a family are a matter of concern to the household, and not for the courts to determine, even though the husband's attitude toward his wife, according to his wealth and circumstances, leaves little to be said in his behalf. As long as the home is maintained and the parties are living as husband and wife it may be said that the husband is legally supporting his wife and the purpose of the marriage relation is being carried out."

AGREEMENTS CONCERNING PROPERTY RELATIONSHIPS

The parties to a marriage may enter into agreements to create their own property relationships during their marriage or after it ends. Such agreements, which are called "**pre-nuptial**" or "**ante-nuptial**" **contracts** when they are entered into before marriage and "**post-nuptial**" **contracts** when they are entered into during marriage, are generally recognized, although State law differs on requirements for valid nuptial contracts, and although post-nuptial contracts are less commonly recognized than pre-nuptial ones. Typically, to be recognized, the contracts must be in writing and be entered into knowingly and voluntarily with full knowledge of the other party's assets and income. Generally, the contracts may not alter certain obligations, such as the obligation to support one another. Also, contracts which set forth what may happen if the couple divorces may not be recognized on the theory that before they even marry, couples should not be contemplating divorce.

Nuptial contracts may address aspects of the marital relationship in addition to property relationships, such as the responsibility for housework and the religion of any children of the marriage. The courts may not be willing to enforce such provisions, however, believing that courts should not intervene in certain sensitive areas despite a contract. This does not mean that a contract in such sensitive areas is not a good idea. While some may object that entering into a formal contract undermines the trust necessary to marriage, others believe that setting forth expectations and obligations in writing may avoid later misunderstanding and conflict.

People who are living together without marriage might be well-advised to write contracts related to property rights and other aspects of their relationships. Written contracts are far more likely to be recognized and enforced by the courts than tacit agreements. Written contracts may not, however, resolve inheritance rights. If people who are living together, particularly gays and lesbians whose relationship may not be acknowledged or accepted by relatives, wish their partners to inherit their property, it is necessary that they execute a proper will. Moreover, written contracts establishing a marital-like distribution of property or relationship cannot confer the status of marriage upon the partners. As long as the parties to the contract are not married, without the benefit of a law recognizing their relationship for a particular purpose, they may not be allowed, for example, to be included in their partner's insurance coverage as dependents, to file a joint income tax return, to file a law suit for the wrongful death of their partner, to collect a pension or Social Security benefits on their partner's account, or to claim a partner's rent controlled apartment upon a partner's death.

TERMINATION OF MARRIAGE

All States have laws specifically prescribing how one may terminate a marriage. All such laws are premised on the principle that the State should uphold the stability of marriage and should protect all the parties involved in a marriage. Thus, until fairly recently, in most States, one could get a divorce only if there were specific legal grounds for divorce such as desertion, adultery, or conviction of a felony. Now all the States have some kind of so-called "no-fault divorce" which permits the parties to obtain a divorce if the marriage has "irretrievably broken down," if the parties "mutually agree" to divorce, or if the parties have "irreconcilable differences."[5] This does not mean, however, that a divorce is available simply at the will of one party or that it is simple to terminate a marriage. In all States, a divorce may only be granted at the conclusion of a court proceeding and if the parties have met certain procedural and substantive requirements.

A divorce, called a "**dissolution of marriage**" in many States, is the legal termination of a valid marriage. A judgment of divorce not only terminates a marriage. It also may resolve the rights and obligations of the parties that are incident to the marriage. Specifically, it may divide the property acquired during the marriage, order spousal and child support payments, and determine child cus-

---

5. The previous "fault" standards may still be able to be asserted as the basis for a divorce. Whether or not they are specifically asserted, they may affect the resolution of matters related to a divorce, such as distribution of property or child custody.

tody and visitation. These rights and obligations resolved in a divorce judgment are sometimes referred to as "ancillary matters."

While a divorce is the termination of a valid marriage, an **annulment** is the termination of an invalid one. A statute usually sets forth a few specific grounds for an annulment, all of which go to the validity of the marriage. An annulment cannot be obtained unless one or more of these grounds exist. Typical annulment statutes provide that a marriage may be terminated by an annulment if, and only if: 1) the marriage was not valid at the time of solemnization (e.g., the wife's previous marriage was not yet finally terminated; the husband was under age); 2) the marriage is prohibited (e.g., the husband and wife are uncle and niece; the wife had a venereal disease); 3) the marriage has not been consummated (i.e., the parties have not had sexual relations); or 4) consent to the marriage was obtained through fraud. The last ground has generally been interpreted to require fraud about an essential element of the marriage or that was essential to obtaining consent; mere boasting or a false inducement to obtaining consent may not be considered fraud. Thus, lying about one's income may not be the kind of fraud which constitutes a ground for annulment, but lying about one's sexual impotence may be.

It should be noted that the legal grounds for an annulment may differ from the grounds recognized for an annulment by a religion. Moreover, an annulment granted by a court may not be recognized by a religion and an annulment granted by a religious body would generally have no legal effect.

The consequences of a legal annulment differ from State to State. Generally, the children of an annulled marriage will be considered legitimate. The rights and entitlement of parties to annulled marriages may be equal to that of divorced spouses, may be equal to that of divorced spouses only where they are putative spouses, or may depend on the entitlement in question. For example, a woman whose marriage was annulled may be entitled to alimony if, and only if, she were a putative spouse, but she may not be entitled to her husband's retirement benefits even if she were a putative spouse. The consequences of an annulment and the rights and entitlements of the parties may also depend on the grounds for the annulment and whether a marriage was void or voidable. Whether a spouse in an annulled marriage is entitled to the social welfare benefits of a divorced spouse, including federal social welfare benefits like Social Security or Veteran's benefits, usually depends on the spouse's State law status.

Sometimes the parties to a marriage may not be eligible for an annulment and may not want to divorce for religious or other reasons, but may want to live apart and cease all marital relations. If they separate without any judicial action, there may be no legal consequences to their separation. All rights, obligations, entitlements, and incidents of marriage will probably be unaffected by the separation except that, if the parties have physically separated, the courts generally feel free to intervene in the marriage to enforce the support obligation. If, however, the parties go to court for a **judicial decree of separation**, that is, a **legal separation**, depending on State law, all or some of the rights, obligations, entitlements, and incidents of marriage will probably be affected. In most States, the parties will be treated exactly like divorced people with one essential difference—they are not free to marry again. The tax consequences, including the federal tax consequences, of a separation depend on State law.

THE DIVORCE PROCESS AND
THE SOCIAL WORKER'S ROLE IN
THE PROCESS

We shall discuss only the divorce process, but the process may be very similar for an annulment except that one has to allege and prove that legal grounds exist for an annulment. The process may also be similar for a judicial decree of separation.

A party to a marriage who wants a divorce must file a petition for a divorce in a State court. Several States, including New York, have special courts, called "Family Courts" or "Domestic Relations Courts," which hear all divorce cases and other matters related to families, that is, **domestic relations** matters. Most States simply hear divorces in their trial courts of general jurisdiction or in special departments of these courts. If there are two levels of trial courts in a State, usually only the higher level court is a court of general jurisdiction which can grant a divorce.

The party who is seeking the divorce must generally have been a resident of the State where the divorce is filed for a certain period of time, such as six months. In *Sosna v. Iowa*, 419 U.S. 393 (1975), the Court upheld a one year residency requirement to file for a divorce. Usually a court in a State in which only one party resides has jurisdiction to grant a divorce. However, a court in a State where only one party resides may not have jurisdiction to make certain ancillary orders related to property in the divorce judgment. If it proceeds to make such orders without jurisdiction, its orders are void and need not be recognized in another State despite the command of the Full Faith and Credit Clause of the Constitution. Thus, if one spouse deserts and moves to another State, unless the deserted spouse can seek an order in the deserting spouse's State, the deserted spouse

may never get certain orders on ancillary matters.

In *Boddie v. Connecticut*, 401 U.S. 371 (1971), the Court ruled that Connecticut's fee to file a petition for a divorce that indigents could not afford to pay was an impermissible barrier to divorce in violation of due process. Thus, any filing fee for a petition for divorce must be waived if a petitioner is indigent.

The petition may be a very simple form which the party who seeks a divorce can complete without the assistance of an attorney. Generally, however, people seeking divorces need attorneys to assist them, particularly if there is substantial property or the ancillary matters are complex or hotly contested.

A person's inability to afford a lawyer to assist in filing the necessary papers and obtaining a divorce may appear to be a substantial barrier to divorce like the high filing fee found to violate due process in *Boddie v. Connecticut*, but no court has ever held that there is a right to the appointment of a lawyer in a divorce case, either for the petitioner or the respondent, and several courts have held that there is no such right.[6] State law generally provides, however, that one party to a divorce may be required to pay the other party's attorney's fees at the conclusion of a divorce. Thus, an attorney may be willing to accept a divorce case for a party who has no funds on the contingency that the other party will be ordered to pay all fees.

A divorce petition, like other petitions,

---

6. *See, e.g., In re Smiley*, 36 N.Y.2d 433, 330 N.E. 2d 53 (1975); *Kiddie v. Kiddie*, 563 P.2d 139 (Okla. 1977); *Parsley v. Knuckles*, 346 S.W.2d 1 (Ky. 1961); *Wilson v. Wilson*, 218 Pa.Super. 344, 280 A.2d 665 (1961). Some courts have held that while there is no right to appointment of an attorney, a court has discretion to appoint counsel for an indigent party to a divorce in certain situations. *See, e.g., Barkowski v. Barkowski*, 90 Misc.2d 957, 396 N.Y.S.2d 962 (1977), appointing a counsel for the child custody aspects of a divorce only, and *Flores v. Flores*, 598 P.2d 893 (Alaska 1979), stating counsel may be appointed when a public agency represents one party).

must be served on the respondent. Where the respondent is out of State or his or her whereabouts are unknown, publication of a notice in a newspaper may be sufficient service.

Because publication is often the method of service, because respondents may not be able to afford a lawyer, and because divorces are often not contested, respondents may not answer divorce petitions, that is, they may **default**. They are then not entitled to further notice or an opportunity to contest the contents of the petition.

In an effort to prevent divorce, most States require the parties to a divorce to wait a period of time, often several months, from the time a divorce petition is filed until a judgment can be granted. Such waiting periods are designed to prevent hasty divorces. Also in an effort to prevent divorce, some States require divorcing couples to have counseling, often called ''**divorce conciliation**,'' aimed at reconciling them. Some States only require such counseling in certain circumstances, as when the couple has children or when the marriage has been of long duration. Other States have laws giving a judge discretion to order conciliation in an appropriate case.

Divorce conciliation, whether it is mandatory or ordered by a court in its discretion, may be done by special court employees, who may be social workers, or by private social workers who work under contract with the court. Couples may also go to counselors of their choice or be referred to independent counselors by the court. The counseling may be free of charge, may be paid for by the court, or may be paid for by the parties.

In contrast to divorce conciliation, **divorce mediation** assumes that a couple's divorce will occur, and rather than trying to help them reconcile, it helps them reach a fair agreement, through the use of a neutral mediator, on the ancillary matters related to their divorce. As of 1987, thirty-three jurisdictions had adopted laws making mediation manda-

tory in some divorce cases, such as those involving young children. Other States have adopted laws specifically giving a judge discretion to order mediation. In other States, judges may be able to order mediation in their discretion without benefit of such a law.

Social workers can and often do act as divorce mediators, sometimes acting in tandem with a lawyer. Indeed, the California mediation law, the first mandatory mediation law in the country, specifically provides that social workers may be appointed as mediators. Calif. Civ. Code § 4607(b); Code of Civ. Proc. § 1745.

While all ancillary matters associated with divorce may be mediated and while social workers may mediate on any subject, they generally do not have the professional expertise to address property distribution and other financial arrangements, especially when the couple has substantial assets and income. Thus, social workers most often mediate child custody and visitation agreements and related child (and possibly spousal) support arrangements.

Whether or not there has been a formal effort to arrange a settlement of ancillary matters through divorce mediation, divorcing couples, like other litigants, often settle certain ancillary matters without a trial. In divorce cases, as in most other types of litigation, settlement is the norm. Unlike in most other types of litigation, however, in divorce cases, judges may not always honor the parties' settlement. If judges believe that a settlement or mediated agreement is not in the best interests of a party or does not protect the party's interests, they may refuse to recognize it.

Social workers can assist in negotiating divorce settlements. Persons involved in divorces often act irrationally and have unrealistic expectations; lawyers are often ill-equipped to address the psychological dimensions of divorce and the negotiating process. Social workers can play an important role in the negotiating process by helping the parties reduce their ambivalence towards divorce, guiding the parties away from destructive and stressful ways of interacting, and assisting the parties to formulate realistic and reasonable settlements.

Even when there has been a settlement agreement or a divorce is uncontested, most States require a hearing before a divorce judgment can be granted. The hearing is designed to insure that the divorce is fair to all parties. In some States the parties must speak to an officer of the court, who may be a social worker, before the final hearing. This officer of the court provides a recommendation on certain ancillary matters, particularly those related to children, to the court. In other States any final hearing is before a special magistrate or referee who is not officially a judge. This referee or magistrate makes a recommendation to the judge who ultimately decides the case.

After a contested or uncontested final hearing, the court generally grants a divorce and resolves all ancillary matters in one judgment. This judgment is final insofar as it grants a divorce, but some ancillary matters resolved in the judgment may be modified if the circumstances of the parties change. In some States, in some cases, because there may be substantial delays in resolving the ancillary matters, as a matter of court practice or pursuant to statute, courts may grant a judgment of divorce and then consider the ancillary matters. This process is known as "**bifurcating a divorce.**"

Either party may have obtained a temporary order for property division, child custody and support before judgment. Such temporary orders, which may be referred to as orders "***pendente lite***," can be sought at any time before judgment, including at the time of filing a petition. Orders *pendente lite* generally remain in effect until the final judgment, but may be modifiable if circumstances change.

Social workers may help those involved in the divorce process throughout the process and after the process has been completed. People contemplating a divorce frequently need counseling to help them make a wise decision. Peo-

ple who have decided on a divorce frequently need counseling to help them cope with the process. As has been noted, they also frequently need the help of social workers to negotiate settlements of the ancillary matters. Social workers may be particularly helpful when it comes to arranging workable child custody and visitation agreements. After a divorce, people need help adjusting to their new status, coping with the guilt and ambivalent feelings they may have, and living with any child custody and visitation orders, among other things. Throughout and after the process, social workers may help the children involved in a divorce adjust to the divorce and to any child custody arrangements.

PROPERTY RELATIONSHIPS AFTER TERMINATION OF MARRIAGE

Alimony

At the termination of marriage, one spouse may be required to pay an amount, known as "**maintenance**," "**support**," or "**alimony**," to the other spouse: 1) for a set period; 2) until a certain event occurs, such as the remarriage of the spouse receiving alimony or the retirement of the spouse paying alimony; or 3) indefinitely. Alimony may be paid monthly, yearly, or in a lump sum. Until the Supreme Court ruled in *Orr v. Orr*, 440 U.S. 268 (1979), that the practice was an unconstitutional denial of equal protection, in some States, men were required to pay alimony to women, but there was no reciprocal obligation on women to pay alimony to men. Despite the gender-neutral alimony laws compelled by *Orr*, however, it is the rare case where a woman is ordered to pay alimony to a man. Thus, and for convenience, the discussion of alimony in this chapter will ignore the possibility that an ex-wife could be ordered to pay alimony to her ex-husband. Of course, everything that is said about the award of alimony to a woman would apply with equal force to the award of alimony to a man.

Many argue that the greater equality between men and women which we have today and the ever increasing opportunities for women's employment mean that alimony should never be granted to the wife. While there undoubtedly are cases where an award of alimony would be unnecessary and unjust, it cannot be doubted that alimony is necessary in some cases. As was said in *In re Marriage of Brantner*, 67 Cal.App. 3d 416, 136 Cal.Rptr. 635 (1977):

> "A marriage license is not a ticket to a perpetual pension and, as women approach equality in the job market, the burden on the husband will be lessened . . . . However, in those cases in which it is the decision of the parties that the woman becomes the homemaker, the marriage is of substantial duration and at separation the wife is to all intents and purposes unemployable, the husband simply has to face up to the fact that his support responsibilities are going to be of extended duration—perhaps for life. This has nothing to do with feminism, sexism, male chauvinism or any other trendy social ideology. It is ordinary common sense, basic decency and simple justice."

A belief in the equality of women and of their opportunity for employment, however, has lead to a decrease in awards of alimony and a decrease in the amount awarded. Not only is alimony no longer routinely awarded, in fact, it is rarely granted. Where it is awarded, it is often in a low amount, representing a small percentage of the husband's income. Even this low amount often is not paid.

Whether alimony should be awarded as a matter of course, in certain circumstances, or never is a question that may trouble courts and legislatures for years to come. And even if it is finally decided that alimony should be awarded in certain kinds of cases, troubling questions will remain. How much alimony should be awarded? Should alimony be awarded based on the husband's income or the wife's needs? Should the wife's income or the husband's income be decisive? Should alimony be in an amount calculated to keep the wife's standard of living equivalent to that during marriage or only in an amount calculated to meet basic needs? Should it make a difference whether there are children and who has custody of them? Should the amount of alimony be determined in conjunction with the property division and the award of child support or independently? Does the duration of the marriage make a difference? Does fault make any difference? (E.g., if the wife committed adultery, should she be denied alimony despite her needs?) Should alimony be designed to "rehabilitate" the unemployable wife by providing her with an amount she can use to acquire training for as long as is necessary to complete the training?

An alimony order is generally modifiable or terminable. A judgment may provide when alimony is to be terminated or modified (e.g., when the wife remarries; if the husband retires; in seven years), but it will usually be modifiable or terminable, after a motion and hearing, even if nothing is said about modification or termination in the decree. The modifiability and terminability of alimony payments also raise many questions, such as: Should alimony be lowered if the husband assumes new responsibilities by remarrying or fathering more children? May the husband quit his job without regard for his ex-wife's needs? What should happen if the wife begins living with a man but does not marry him to avoid losing her alimony?

The answers to these and the many other questions posed by alimony may be resolved by legislatures as a matter of social policy or by courts on a case-by-case basis.

Property division

A decree terminating a marriage generally divides the property acquired by the couple during the marriage. In all the separate property jurisdictions and in half the community property States, the courts, in accordance with case law or with statutory mandates, will distribute the property "equitably." This means the property will be distributed as fairly as possible in light of such considerations as who acquired the property, the contribution of the party who did not actually acquire the property to the acquisition of the property and to the household, and the needs of the parties.

Equitable distribution is not the equivalent of equal distribution, the system used in Wisconsin and four of the community property States. Indeed, only a few of the equitable distribution jurisdictions presume that an equitable distribution is an equal distribution; and most specifically do not equate equity with equality. Thus, the usual distribution of property, rather than being equal, is two-thirds to the husband and one-third to the wife.[7]

Some excerpts from the majority and concurring opinions in *LaRue v. LaRue*, 304 S.E. 2d 312 (W.Va. 1983), may help you to understand the concept of equitable distribution of property and some of the issues that arise when equitable, or equal, distribution is attempted. In *LaRue*, an appeal from a divorce judgment, the West Virginia Supreme Court reversed the trial court's refusal to equitably distribute the property acquired during the LaRue's thirty-year marriage. The LaRue marriage was "a traditional one in the sense that Mr. LaRue exclusively handled the family's financial affairs and Mrs. LaRue was mainly a homemaker." Mrs. LaRue only worked in the first years of their marriage. "Mr. LaRue encouraged his spouse to be a housewife and homemaker, and accordingly she raised two children, cared for the house and the comfort of her family, and entertained her husband's business associates." In the judgment, Mrs. LaRue was awarded alimony and an allowance for health insurance, but, except for some items of personal property, she was awarded none of the property acquired during the marriage, all of which was in Mr. LaRue's name only.

MAJORITY OPINION

"The concept of equitable distribution of marital property has achieved an almost universal acceptance in the divorce laws of the various states. It originated when courts applied their equitable powers to secure equitable rights for one spouse in property titled or held by the other spouse based on the claim that a resulting or constructive trust should be impressed on the property. The basis for such a claim was that the spouse seeking an interest in the property had made a substantial economic contribution toward the acquisition of the property. Consequently, under the principles of unjust enrichment, it would be unfair to permit the spouse with title or possession to keep the entire interest. [The general rule is:]

'Where a wife has made a material contribution to the husband's acquisition of property during coverture [marriage], she acquires a special equity in the property so accumulated which equity entitles her, on divorce, to an award in satisfaction thereof; and it is not a necessary prerequisite that the wife show that she has contributed by funds or efforts to the acquiring of the specific property awarded to

---

7. Lenore Weitzman, *The Divorce Revolution* (Free Press: New York 1985) at p. 47. It should be noted that if the wife has been awarded custody of any children of the marriage, which is true in 90% of the cases studied by Weitzman, *id.*, at p. 49, even an equal distribution of property between the wife and husband would not be an equal distribution among all the parties involved. Moreover, it should be noted that most States will consider alimony along with property distribution and that courts in seven States have specifically held that alimony is precluded where the property is divided equitably.

her, but division may be had even though the wife has not contributed funds or efforts to the acquisition of the specific property awarded to her.'

"Judicial decisions involving these equitable principles have more recently been supplemented and enhanced by various forms of legislative enactments. A . . . common statute which a majority of [the separate property] states have enacted, permits the court upon the dissolution of a marriage to make an equitable distribution of the marital property based upon a detailed list of factors. [Another] category of statutes, used in a few states, is more general and provides that an equitable distribution of property may be made by the court without specifying any guidelines. Finally, in those few jurisdictions that have no specific statute on equitable distribution, the courts have continued to evolve their concepts of equitable distribution with a broad interpretation of traditional equity principles. We are in this category.

'Thus, it would appear that in virtually every state either by way of express statute or through court interpretation, some mechanism exists to permit a court in granting a final divorce to provide the wife with some distribution for her homemaker and economic contributions.'

"In determining an appropriate amount for equitable distribution where there have been economic contributions made (other than homemaker services), it is necessary to consider the respective economic contributions made by both parties during the marriage as weighed against the net assets that are available at the time of the divorce. The term 'net assets' does not include assets acquired by a party prior to the marriage, or obtained during the marriage by way of inheritance or gifts from third parties. In computing the value of any net asset, the indebtedness owed against such asset should ordinarily be deducted from its fair market value. In an appropriate case, the court in calculating the amount of equitable distribution arising from economic contributions may take into account the value of gifts made to the spouse seeking equitable contribution by the other spouse.

"Homemaker services . . . present a more complex problem than economic contributions. In the traditional view of marriage, the husband's obligation was to support his wife and she in turn rendered domestic or homemaker services. The theory of alimony is based upon the husband's legal obligation to support his wife, and thus upon the dissolution of a marriage where she was not at fault, the wife is entitled to alimony. Thus, to some extent, it may be argued that homemaker services were the consideration for the husband's traditional obligation to support his wife. There is, however, an increasing recognition that homemaker services cannot be viewed as a mere adjunct to the husband's duty of support. [They may, instead, be viewed as a contribution to the marriage which can be recognized in the distribution of property.]

"[As a contribution to the marriage,] . . . homemaker services is not to be measured by some mechanical formula, but instead rests on a showing that the homemaker has contributed to the economic well-being of the family unit through the performance of the myriad of household and child-rearing tasks which make up the term 'homemaker services.' In valuing this service, the length of the marriage is an important factor and consideration should be given to the quality of the services. Some consideration should also be given to the age, health, and skills of the homemaker as well as the amount of independent assets possessed. [Further], we believe that fault is a factor to consider when valuing homemaker services even though it is not a factor where economic contributions have been made. The reason for considering fault is that, historically, homemaker services were the wife's marital contribution upon which rested the husband's countervailing support obligation and his duty to pay alimony if the marriage was dissolved without fault on the wife's part. We do not suggest that fault on the wife's part is an absolute bar to her receiving some equitable distribution for homemaker services. [W]e do not foreclose the trial court from giving some equitable distribution for homemaker services even where traditional fault grounds exist, where an otherwise compelling case for equitable distribution for homemaker services can be shown.

"Just as in the economic contribution area, a court may consider the value of any gifts given to the homemaker spouse during the marriage by the other spouse. The value of homemaker services must also be considered in relation to the net assets available at the time of the divorce and in light of the alimony award.

"Applying these principles of equitable distribution to the facts of the present case, . . . Mrs. LaRue was entitled to some equitable distribution on both theories. First, during the early years of her marriage, she had contributed her earnings . . . . This economic contribution must be considered, but its value will have to be determined based on a comparison of the contributions made by Mr. LaRue as weighed against the net assets at the time of the divorce. Second, Mrs. LaRue's homemaker services, which were contributed over a considerable period of time, also entitle her to some equitable consideration. Again, her contributions must be calculated against the net marital assets."

CONCURRING OPINION

"A marriage is, as the majority has stated, to some degree an economic partnership. Both partners contribute services that have a recognizable value to the household. In most marriages a surplus is generated by the parties' forbearance from immediate consumption of the marital income. This marital surplus is commonly invested in a dwelling, and in insurance and other investments to assure the protection of the partners from penury should sudden and unforeseen events, or the quiet onslaught of age, diminish the family earnings. It does no violence to [West Virginia law], I believe, to recognize that contributions of a party to his or her marriage give rise to a property right to a proportionate share of that marital surplus.

"My enthusiasm for today's holding arises largely from my understanding of the economic plight of women in America. Simply put, women are poorer than men. The mean wage for women who work full time is 59 percent of the equivalent mean wage for men. Among single men and women who are not living with relatives, the poverty rate for men is 18.1 percent; the rate for women is 27.7 percent. Once a man and woman are married, if both are working full time, the woman's wage on average amounts to only 34.7 percent of the family earnings. When a marriage has ended, the situation becomes bleaker; 10.3 percent of male single parents fall below the poverty line (a total of 205,000); 34.6 percent of single women with children, or a total of 3.4 million such women, fall below the poverty line. In fact, divorced women with children now make up a new class of the poverty-stricken. By contrast, the poverty rate for families headed by a married couple is only 6.8 percent.

"Among the factors leading to [these statistics] two are prominent. The first is that court-ordered awards. . . are frequently not paid. The second [is] that divorced women often do not have access to that part of the marital surplus invested in pensions or insurance. . . .

"Among divorced or currently separated women, 14.3 percent were entitled to alimony or maintenance as of the spring of 1979. The alimony or maintenance award amounted to over 25 percent of the mean income of those women who actually received it. However, of those women entitled to receive alimony or maintenance payments in 1978, 28.4 percent did not receive the full amount due them, and 30.5 percent received nothing at all.

"Our growing experience with the financial

position of divorced women leads me to the conclusion, confirmed by this statistical data, that West Virginia's current scheme for allocating marital property acquired through joint efforts is inadequate to protect women . . . from unfair results. Since the statute [on distribution of property] does not by its terms foreclose us from developing equitable doctrines that will provide greater financial security upon divorce, it is incumbent upon us to do so.

"This Court's holding today opens a wide field of opportunity to the [trial] courts, whose options previously were by and large limited to alimony and child support. It is my hope that the courts . . . will creatively avail themselves of the opportunities that equitable distribution presents. Unfortunately, there are many problems which are beyond the capacity of courts to solve. Courts can only distribute wealth, they cannot create any. The economies of scale that prevail in joint households are irretrievably lost when a married couple separates. Pensions adequate to support two retired people living together may not be adequate to support the two retired people living separately. Similarly, when an active head of a household becomes disabled, he may still be able to support a joint household with insurance proceeds, but may no longer be able to meet his alimony . . . obligations.

"However, there is a second problem which courts may successfully address, which comes to mind because of some of the peculiar forms the marital surplus is likely to assume. The 'savings' of the average American family no longer take the form of cash on hand in a savings account in the local bank. Rather, the 'savings' are invested in the family home, plowed back into ongoing business ventures, or used to buy institutional insurance and pension programs. These forms of 'savings' are often tied to the family wage-earner personally, or held in the name of the partner who is responsible for taking care of the financial affairs of the family. The advent of societal institutions selling finan-

cial protection in a pension/insurance package has transformed the nature of America's wealth from present capital to future interest. To the extent that these various forms of savings represent investments rather than assets—and some are investments under very strict terms—they present a new challenge to courts attempting to effect among divorcing parties a fair financial reconciliation. With a little effort and imagination courts can see that divorcing parties, who own an apple orchard for instance, leave the courthouse with apples for life rather than a truckload each of applewood kindling.

"We must be aware, for instance, of the importance of the family home in terms both of its emotional and financial value. I am concerned that the dominant financial value of the family home will cause inequities, and even forced sale, as a result of our adoption of equitable distribution. My concern is particularly aroused when I contemplate minor children, who are the innocent victims of their parents' inability to maintain the marriage. Our courts should bend over backward to maintain minor children with a custodial parent in the family home when appropriate. This can be accomplished under traditional child support and alimony doctrines.

"Pension rights and insurance plans present a particularly challenging opportunity for . . . creative solution. Investment in pensions and insurance is probably the largest slice of the investment pie. In addition to social security are myriad company, union, and public employee pensions. These programs are generally tied to the wage-earner in a family, and would therefore seem to be an asset ripe for redistribution under a court's equitable powers. However, pension rights present one of the most complex problems in equitable distribution cases [as do problems with] . . . private insurance. Many middle income people have whole life insurance policies but their cash surrender values are negligible until people have reached comfortable middle age. A husband whose insurance policy is paid for with marital assets may on termination of the marriage eliminate the former wife's beneficiary status. . . . Where alimony is not a charge on a former husband's estate the wife may then be left with nothing upon his death. Although the present cash surrender value of the policy may be negligible, its value as insurance (particularly if the husband is in poor health) may be substantial."

As can be seen from *LaRue*, the distribution of property after a divorce, whether it be an equitable or an equal distribution, poses many questions. Some of the questions are similar to the questions posed by alimony, such as: Should fault matter? Does it make any difference who was awarded custody of the children? Does the amount of the wife's or husband's separate income and property make any difference? Other questions are unique to property distribution. Two of these unique questions warrant further discussion.

First, what should happen to the wife's and children's health insurance coverage if, as is often the case, the wife and children have been included in a group plan through the husband's job? Can they remain on the plan as long as the husband remains on the plan? Should it make any difference if the husband or the employer pays for dependents' insurance coverage? Should it make a difference if the husband remarries and acquires new dependents? If the wife is required to obtain new health insurance because she and the children cannot be included on her husband's policy, what happens if she or the children have pre-existing conditions which the new insurance company will not cover? Many States have adopted laws which address some of these questions. Some of these laws require insurance companies to continue divorced spouses and children in group plans upon payment of the group rate premium. Other States routinely make orders

that the husband continue providing insurance coverage for the wife and children as part of alimony or child support orders instead of as part of property distribution.

Second, what should be done with pensions? Should the wife get a share of a husband's pension which will be paid upon his retirement many years in the future? Does it make any difference if the pension is the major asset of the husband and that the family sacrificed in the present because of the future pension, as is often the case with military families? In *McCarty v. McCarty*, 435 U.S 210 (1981), the Court ruled that a federal military pension could not be divided by a State divorce court based on its view of federal versus State authority, but Congress has now provided that a State divorce court may make certain orders related to a military pension and the military can pay a portion of a pension directly to an ex-wife. See 10 U.S.C § 1408.

Pensions provided by private employers are probably the most common type of pension. Most such pensions are regulated by a federal law, the Employee's Retirement Income Security Act, 29 U.S.C. § 1001 *et seq.*, known as "ERISA." The Supreme Court also held that a State court could not make an order dividing a pension regulated by ERISA, again because of the relation between federal and State law, and again Congress reversed the Supreme Court. *See*, 26 U.S.C. § 414(p).

Despite Congress' actions, other problems arise with respect to pensions. Courts may be unwilling or unable to divide pensions that will be paid in the future. They may be willing or able to order the payment of future dependents' benefits to former spouses, but the wage earner may be able to opt for pension plans which pay the wage earner a higher amount in return for eliminating dependents' benefits. Some statutes prevent married persons from so electing without notice to or the consent of a spouse or a former spouse. However, special pension benefits for dependents may be in a small amount on the assumption that they supplement the wage earner's pension, an assumption which is not valid when the spouses are living apart.

One other problem in the area of property distribution must be discussed. Typically divorcing American couples have little property; it is their income (or their earning capacity) which determines their standard of living. When couples divorce young, the husband's future earning capacity may not yet be realized. He may have just obtained a professional degree or just begun a professional practice or a business. Should a wife get an equitable share of her husband's professional degree or license if she supported him while he obtained it? Can a wife somehow put a lien on future earnings if she contributed to the foundation of such earnings? The States are split on this. At least four have ruled that a professional degree is property that can be distributed on divorce. At least ten have held it is not property that can be distributed, but some of these States and some other States say that future earning capacity should be taken into account when distributing property.

As with the questions that arise in the area of alimony, some of the questions that arise in the area of distribution of property may be answered by legislatures as a matter of policy or by courts on a case-by-case basis.

12

Custody and Support of Children

CHILD CUSTODY AND VISITATION

Whenever a marriage is terminated or a husband and wife legally separate, the courts must determine which parent will be awarded custody of any children of the marriage. Child custody disputes may also arise when the parents never married and when a non-parent seeks custody of a child. The discussion in this chapter will, however, focus on the most common kind of custody dispute—between divorcing parents.

Standards used in awarding custody

Until well into the nineteenth century, the father was routinely awarded custody of his children. The children were considered his ''property''; he had a right to their ''services.'' Moreover, women's limited civil rights meant men were the logical choice as legal guardians of children.

As society became more urban, it was recognized that fathers generally worked away from the home and were not responsible for child care and child rearing and that mothers were the parents who were home with the children and who had primary responsibility for their care. Moreover, the fact that the mother was generally the more nurturing and caring parent, particularly for young children, began to be considered important. The courts adopted the **tender years presumption** under which they presumed that the mother was the ''natural'' parent of a child of ''tender'' years and awarded her custody unless she was shown to be unfit.

In the 1920's, the idea took hold that child custody decisions should be based, not on the father's interests in his ''property'' or on the alleged ''natural'' relationship between mother and child, but rather on the best inter-

ests of the child. Nevertheless, mothers still were routinely awarded custody. The courts continued to use the tender years presumption, presuming that, absent a showing of unfitness, it was in the best interest of a child, particularly a young child, to be raised by his or her mother.

The idea that custody awards should be based on the best interests of the child is now part of the law in every State. The continued use of the tender years presumption, however, has been called into question by the increased equality of men and women and the increased use of the equal protection clause to challenge laws fostering or perpetuating sexual inequality. Most States have officially abandoned the presumption. Nevertheless, it is still likely that child custody will be awarded to the mother for several reasons. First, judges may still assume, even though the assumption is unstated, that child rearing is a woman's role and that, absent a showing of unfitness, it is in the best interests of young children that they be placed in the custody of their mothers. Second, many jurisdictions follow the ''**primary caretaker rule**,'' which requires that, other things being equal, a child's primary caretaker in the past should be given his or her custody in the future. Because mothers are generally children's primary caretakers, mothers are generally given custody under this rule. Further, few fathers seek custody and many mothers agree to settlements giving up alimony or giving them a disadvantageous property division if they are given custody.

Despite the likelihood that the mother will be awarded custody of her children, as has been stated, all courts are required to make custody determinations on the basis of the best interests of the child. Typically, a statute mandates the use of the best interests standard. Sometimes the statute sets forth the factors which should be considered by a judge in deciding what is in a child's best interests, as does the Uniform Marriage and Divorce Act, which has been adopted in some form by Arizona, Colorado, Illinois, Kentucky, Minnesota, Missouri, Montana and Washington. For example, the Arizona version of the Uniform Act provides:

"The court shall determine custody in accordance with the best interest of the child. The court shall consider all relevant factors including:

(1) The wishes of the child's parent or parents as to his custody;

(2) The wishes of the child as to his custodian;

(3) The interaction and interrelationship of the child with his parent or parents, his siblings, and any other person who may significantly affect the child's best interest;

(4) The child's adjustment to his home, school, and community;

(5) The mental and physical health of all individuals involved; and

(6) Which parent is more likely to allow the child frequent and continuing contact with the non-custodial parent." Ariz. Rev. Stat. Ann. § 25-332A.

The Arizona law further provides that "evidence of spouse abuse" shall be considered "as being contrary to the best interest of the child," and that the court shall not prefer a parent as custodian because of that parent's sex. § 25-332B, C.

Sometimes a statute sets forth no factors and it is solely up to the judge to decide what factors to consider. Usually even if there is a list of relevant factors in a statute, as in Arizona, a judge may still consider other factors. As in Arizona, sometimes factors that may not be considered, like the sex of a custodian, are listed in a statute. A provision of the

Uniform Marriage and Divorce Act that Arizona did not adopt provides that: "The court shall not consider conduct of a proposed custodian that does not affect his relationship to the child."

Many factors could conceivably come into play in making child custody determinations. Sometimes courts make these determinations based on factors that are neither included in statutes nor relevant to the best interests of the child, such as a parent's wealth or religion. Basing child custody determinations on such factors would be contrary to law. Sometimes the factors that a judge considers may be relevant to a child's best interests but consideration of the factors is nevertheless erroneous as a violation of equal protection guarantees or as otherwise contrary to law. For example, as we shall see, basing a custody determination on one parent's interracial marriage has been held to violate equal protection.

Child custody orders are usually accompanied by orders granting visitation to non-custodial parents, but visitation may be denied if a court believes visitation would not be in a child's best interests. Factors that lead to a denial of custody may equally lead to a denial of visitation. Further, the more acrimonious a divorce, the more difficult and potentially disruptive visitation may be. Nevertheless, a complete denial of all visitation would be extreme and unusual. Far more commonly, visitation may be curtailed, conditions may be imposed on any visitation (for example, all visits must occur in a certain location), or visitation may be supervised, often by a social worker.

The best interest standard and the factors related to it are used not only in making initial custody and visitation determinations but also when a parent seeks to change an initial custody or visitation determination. Child custody orders and accompanying visitation orders, like other ancillary matters related to divorce, are generally modifiable for changed circumstances. But, the modifiability of child custody orders is usually limited because of the belief that a child needs the stability of one parent and because it is believed that uprooting a child from a parent with whom he or she has lived for many years, even if the parent may no longer be the ''best'' parent for the child, can cause lasting harm to a child. Statutes and court decisions in most States provide that a child custody order may not be changed unless the circumstances have changed substantially since the initial custody order and unless the changed circumstances will have a substantial, identifiable adverse effect on the child.

The use of experts

Making an initial determination of custody and visitation or deciding when custody or visitation should be changed is not easy. It is particularly difficult for a judge whose training and experience have probably not provided any expertise in the area. Moreover, judges must make custody determinations in adversary hearings where mud-slinging and recriminations rather than dispassionate truth seeking are the norm. Thus, many judges ask social workers and other mental health professionals to provide them with assistance in child custody matters.

Referring a child custody dispute to a social worker or another mental health professional may be authorized by a statute, such as the Colorado statute discussed in Chapter 4 and set forth in Appendix 4-1, or may be a discretionary act of a judge, done without benefit of a statute. Whichever is the case, it is often done. And because social workers are generally recognized as experts in child custody, the parties themselves may hire social workers to appear as their expert witnesses.

Even with a complete social work report or several expert witnesses, determining child custody and visitation may still not be an easy matter for a judge. There may be conflicting recommendations made by the experts on each side, and reports of court social workers or the testimony of experts may not be persuasive or credible. As stated in *Pact v. Pact*, 70 Misc.2d 100, 332 N.Y.S.2d 940 (1972), a case where several psychiatric and social worker expert witnesses expressed conflicting views on a mother's request to terminate the father's visitation of their two girls and a father's request to transfer custody of both girls to him:

> ''Starting with King Solomon's famous decision in the first recorded custody case and down through the ages, experienced jurists will unreservedly agree that child custody proceedings are the most trying, vexatious and complex of all legal proceedings.

A lengthy excerpt from *Pact* is set forth below because it reveals some of the factors considered by judges in making child custody determinations. It should be noted that this is a trial, not an appellate, court decision. New York is one of the few States that publishes such decisions.

> ''Custody is perhaps the most critical phase in the growing pains of a child's life and should not provide an arena where parents will engage in an unenviable contest of undermining the child's love for the other parent. It is precisely to that point that Judge Cardozo [a famous and well-respected judge] addressed himself in the celebrated case . . . when he enunciated his 'best interests' rule [stating that the judge in custody cases] '* * * acts as *parens patriae* to do what is best for the interest of the child. . . . He is not adjudicating a controversy between adversary parties, to compose their private differences. He is not determining rights ''as between a parent and a child,'' or as between

one parent and another . . . [The court's concern is not with the disputants.] Its concern is for the child.'

"The cardinal rule of custody law is now well established that the court must be governed above all by a concern for the best interests or welfare of the child. In all cases there shall be no *prima facie* right to the custody of the child in either parent, and [custody shall be awarded] as justice requires, having regard to the circumstances of the case and of the respective parties and to the best interests of the child. Questions of custody are generally for the court in its discretion, but that discretion is not an absolute or uncontrolled one. Discretion should encompass a full and incisive review of the facts adduced including the social, spiritual, psychological and economic conditions prevailing at the alternative environments. **To guide the Court in cases of this kind psychiatrists, psychologists and trained social workers should be consulted and their findings given serious consideration.**

"To avoid the pitfall of balancing the rights of either parent in total disregard of the best interests and welfare of the children the Court [in this case] did reach out for guidance of the psychiatric, psychological and social work professions and seriously considered their reports and conclusions yet always mindful that the ultimate decision must be made by the Court.

"In transferring custody from one parent to another, the Court must be aware of the child's need for stability in the home in the early years of his developing personality and through his formative years. Psychiatrists maintain that stability is practically the principal element in raising children. A child can handle almost everything better than he can handle instability. Shuttling children between parents is therefore not to be looked upon with favor if stability is an important ingredient in the development of a child. The overriding consideration of the child's welfare dictates that a continual shifting back and forth of custody should be avoided

whenever possible. Yet we cannot deny that time does bring about changes in a person's lifetime and more so during his infancy and formative years. A child's needs are in a constant state of dynamic alteration. They change with age and in response to daily experiences. Plans for children must keep these changes in mind. If a child's needs change as time goes along then courts of law must be ever alert to the fact that orders of custody must likewise be flexible and courts should not hesitate to modify custody where the exigencies of the case so demand.

"While an award of custody is always subject to modification or change if conditions or the requirements of the children so warrant, the change of circumstances or requirements must be material and should be used sparingly and under extraordinary circumstances.

"If the balancing of equities between parents was the determinative factor in deciding child custody cases [Mr. Pact's] application for change of custody would be denied since Mrs. Pact is doing her utmost to adequately care for the children even in the face of opposition from the children and their father. But . . . a custody hearing should not be relegated to a contest between parents bent on victory for each other at the expense of the welfare and future happiness of their children. [Mr. Pact] readily admits to encouraging the children to rebel against their mother but he attributes his action solely to his sympathy for their strong and unwavering desire to live with him. He joins them in pleading for their custody.

"In the absence of any grave disability such as the unfitness of a parent a child's preference will be given paramount consideration if it further appears that her best interests, welfare and development will be improved by awarding custody to the preferred parent. The Court . . . interrogate[d] the children as to their experience in the mother's home and elicit[ed] their wishes as to the place in which they would prefer to live. The expressed wishes of a child, provided it is of sufficient age and understanding, as to the parent in whose custody it desires to be placed is a factor taken into consideration by the court in determining the child's custody as between contesting parents. However, the weight to be given the preference is within the discretion of the trial court and may be disregarded altogether. It is not, in the final analysis, controlling and will not bar the court from making a contrary determination in the best interest of the child. . . . 'Any other policy would be practically to abandon the jurisdiction of the Court and make the child the sole judge of his own best interests and welfare.' [W]here the stated preference is deemed to have been inspired by pressure or 'brain washing', it will not be given any weight.

"After carefully reviewing all of the evidence adduced including the findings of the psychiatrists and the social workers, the Court is now firmly convinced of Debra's strong and unyielding desire to reside with her father even absent the incidents of his encouragement and inducement. The desire to live with her father has increased rather than diminished during the past year as evidenced by her constant refusal to accommodate her mother and the two attempts of absconding from her home. She does not appear to be motivated toward making any type of adjustment in regard to her mother psychotherapy notwithstanding. The prevailing opinion of the psychiatrists and social workers who examined the parties and the children is that the older child would not be affected psychologically if she was permitted to reside with her father. Even . . . [the] psychiatric social worker who was most critical in his evaluation of [the father] indicated that the child is extremely dependent on her father. The Law Guardian, [a guardian *ad litem*] who represented the children during the hearing, indicated that she too believes that the sisters should be separated although she looked askance at the thought of Debra being awarded to [the father.]

"Under all the circumstances the Court finds that as to Debra there exists a clear showing of a substantial change of circumstances to justify modification of the existing order of custody. There does not seem any justification . . . [however, for changing the custody of her sister Allison and] disrupting her home stability at this time. Division of the siblings between the parties seems to furnish the only sensible answer to their continued welfare. If at all possible, it is assumed that children should be reared together, rather than partitioned off, unless there is a clear necessity that separate custody be awarded due to the circumstances of the parties. From all of the evidence adduced the Court believes that Allison's best interest would be served if she remained with her mother and free from the manipulative acts of both her sister and her father."

Unlike the court in *Pact*, sometimes courts pay no attention to social work experts and erroneously decide custody cases based on their own biases and prejudices. For example, in *Pikula v. Pikula*, 349 N.W.2d 322 (Minn. App. 1984), an appellate court reversed a divorce judgment awarding custody of the couple's two children, aged 4 and 3, to the father, because the trial court ignored the experts and the statutory factors, and decided custody based on irrelevant factors. The appellate court stated:

"A court ordered custody evaluation, involving at least three social workers, recommended that custody of both daughters remain with the mother and that she undergo counselling, not to overcome 'any deficit in her ability to parent, but rather as recognition that the role of the single parent is extremely demanding.' Witnesses testifying at trial disputed the abilities of each parent. Both parties claimed the best interests of the two children lay with their having legal custody with visitation to the other.

"Little reference was made by the trial court

to the factors found in [the custody statute.] Instead, the court emphasized the desirability of the father's extended family. The custody evaluation, virtually ignored by the court, noted that appellant-mother, as the primary care giver and person most able to provide a loving environment, was the most functional parent. The custody study contained a clear statement of preference for appellant as custodian. **The court dismissed the expert opinions of three social workers on the ground that only the court had the benefit of all the evidence.**

"The court chose not to examine the mental and physical health of the parents, . . . gave no weight to testimony that respondent-father is chemically dependent, habitually untruthful, is extremely dependent upon his parents, has poor control of his temper and is unable to give the children's welfare priority over his own desires. The court noted that respondent's environment is improving, but ignored all evidence of appellant's growing maturity and gains made in counselling. The court apparently placed great importance on the continuation of religious training for the children. Despite appellant's plans to continue raising her daughters in the Catholic faith, the court concluded that [the custody statute] required contact with the 'respondent and significant other persons' to raise the children 'in their religion, creed and culture.' No reference was made to the ability of either party to give the children love and affection.

"Both parties are imperfect parents. However, the trial court noted only the father's good points and the mother's problems. The trial court, for all practical purposes, disregarded the custody evaluation. The court indicated it was better qualified than the social workers to evaluate the complete facts.

"A trial court ruling on child custody has broad discretion. However, because this record . . . fails to support the findings, this court is obligated to apply the [custody] statute and grant custody to the mother."

Sometimes courts do pay attention to social work reports when they should not. For example, in *Goodman v. Goodman*, 180 Neb. 83, 141 N.W.2d 445 (1966), the Nebraska Supreme Court criticized a trial court for deciding a custody case based on its own prejudice and an inadequate and biased social worker's report. The mother in the case, who had raised the children as Catholic, had been found unfit three years earlier, and custody had been awarded to the father. The mother now sought to have custody returned to her, primarily because the father was raising the children as Jewish. A social worker made a report for the judge recommending that the children be returned to the mother and stating, among other things, that the children would be emotionally damaged by having two religions. Primarily on the basis of this report, the court changed custody back to the mother. The Nebraska Supreme Court reversed, stating:

"[I]t is quite obvious that a social worker, largely on information submitted by the children and the [mother] in one interview, expressed fear of emotional damage to the children. The testimony of public school teachers, of . . . the children, the Rabbi, and virtually every other witness was to the contrary, and the social worker herself found the children to be 'relatively well adjusted for their age.' The social worker's opinion was that the absence of a 'mother figure' in the home of the [father] made it unstable. No reference is made to the absence of a 'father figure' if custody be changed. She termed the [father's] housekeeper a 'servant figure,' but did not even meet the [maternal grandmother] who was going to care for the children while the mother worked, nor did she visit her home where the [mother] intended to leave them for such care.

"Hearsay, opinion, gossip, bias, prejudice, and the hopes and fears of social workers should not be the basis for a change of custody. Findings of fact must rest on a prepon-

derance of evidence, the verity of which has been carefully and legally tested. The relationship of parent and child should not be severed or disturbed unless the facts justify it.''

Perhaps, the case of *Fritschler v. Fritschler*, 60 Wis.2d 283, 208 N.W.2d 336 (1973), best sums up the role of social work experts in custody cases. The divorce decree in the case granted custody of the two children, then aged 3 and 4, to their mother. When their mother moved from Wisconsin to Colorado, however, custody was awarded to the father and the mother appealed.

''The main issue on appeal is whether the lower court abused its discretion in not allowing Mrs. Fritschler to have custody of the children except in Wisconsin. It is claimed the trial court disregarded the recommendations of three family specialists [from Colorado] who had recommended in effect that Mrs. Fritschler should have custody of the children in Colorado. The trial court considered [the letters and reports that were submitted into evidence] and commented thereon to the effect that it was not very helpful to a determination of the issue presented.

''This court has held social workers' reports are not binding upon a trial court which may determine the weight to be given to the reports of social workers. It has recommended the use of social workers as a helpful tool in determining the best interests of the child. But neither the use of such witnesses nor the acceptance of their recommendations is mandatory. If it were, the social workers would be performing the function of a judge on the bench rather than that of a witness. [W]e can find no abuse of discretion in its failure to accept or give more weight to the social workers' reports . . . ''

The appointment of a guardian *ad litem*

Because a child's preference may be considered in child custody proceedings, as many cases and statutes provide, and because custody proceedings are focused on the child, many courts provide an opportunity for a child to be heard, in their discretion or pursuant to a statute. Courts may interview a child in chambers or appoint a counsel or a guardian *ad litem* for a child. The guardian *ad litem* may be a social worker, but he or she usually is a lawyer.

In *Provencal v. Provencal*, 122 N.H. 793, 451 A. 2d 374 (1982), the court stated the role of the guardian *ad litem* in these words:

''[A] guardian ad litem represents the interests of the child and is treated as a full party to all proceedings. The guardian ad litem serves primarily as an advocate for the best interests of the child. Nevertheless, the guardian ad litem should also assist the court and the parties in reaching a prompt and fair determination, while minimizing the acrimony during this process.''

One issue raised in *Provencal* was the confidentiality of the guardian *ad litem*'s report. The court stated:

''Although we recognize that confidentiality brings anonymity to individuals who might otherwise be reluctant to provide information to a guardian ad litem, we find that the parental interest in disclosure outweighs the need for anonymity. However, because the guardian ad litem serves [in some respects] as an attorney for his ward, the attorney-client evidentiary privilege will apply to all communications between the guardian and the child. References in the report to these communications should remain confidential, and . . . [t]he court should determine the circumstances under which [they] will be made available to the parties.''

Permissible and impermissible factors to consider

Some of the factors which a court may or may not be permitted to consider in deciding a child custody case are reviewed below.

Who is the child's primary caretaker? As was stated earlier, in the absence of a showing of unfitness, many courts will award custody to a child's primary caretaker. Some courts have elevated the inclination to award custody to a child's primary caretaker to a presumption. In *Garska v. McCoy*, 278 S.E.2d 357 (W.Va. 1981), the rationale for so doing was the fear that otherwise the child could suffer economically. The court stated:

> "The loss of children is a terrifying specter to concerned and loving parents; however, it is particularly terrifying to the primary caretaker parent who, by virtue of the caretaking function, was closest to the child before the divorce or other proceedings were initiated. Since the parent who is not the primary caretaker is usually in the superior financial position, the subsequent welfare of the child depends to a substantial degree upon the level of support payments which are awarded in the course of a divorce. Our experience instructs us that uncertainty about the outcome of custody disputes leads to the irresistible temptation to trade the custody of the child in return for lower alimony and child support payments. Since trial court judges generally approve consensual agreements on child support, underlying economic data which bear upon the equity of settlements are seldom investigated at the time an order is entered. [T]he one enormously important function of legal rules is to inspire rational and equitable settlements in cases which never reach adversary status in court."

The court then concluded that a rule creat-

ing a presumption in favor of primary caretakers would tend to make primary caretakers less likely to fear loss of custody and thus less likely to give up property and support in return for custody.

Other courts have not adopted a presumption in favor of the primary caretaker. They may, however, recognize that a court should consider who the child's primary caretaker is in awarding custody and should give preference to that parent. For example, in *In re Maxwell*, 8 Ohio App.3d 302, 456 N.E.2d 1218 (1982), the court stated that the Ohio custody statute precluded it from adopting the presumption, but also stated that who a child's primary caretaker is

> "is a factor which must be given strong consideration as it bears on the child's interaction and interrelationship with his parents, as well as the child's adjustment to his home. Not to do so ignores the benefits likely to flow to the child from maintaining day to day contact with the parent on whom the child has depended for satisfying his basic physical and psychological needs."

Morality of a parent. The States are split on whether the morality or sexual misconduct of a parent is relevant to a custody determination. Some courts consider the sexual misconduct of a parent and his or her immoral activities as directly bearing on the best interests of a child. Others like the court in *Dunlap v. Dunlap*, 475 N.E.2d 723 (Ind.App. 1985), assert:

> "In order to deprive a parent of the custody of a child because of sexual misconduct, the misconduct must be shown to have an adverse effect upon the welfare of the child. Although it is a factor to be considered, evidence of sexual misconduct alone is insufficient to deny a parent the custody of a

child. Without some evidence that the [misconduct] is in some way detrimental to the welfare of . . . [the child, a custody award] based solely upon [misconduct] is improper.''

In some States, a consideration of morality is mandated by statute. For example, a Utah statute provides:

"In determining custody, the court shall consider the best interests of the child and the past conduct and demonstrated moral standards of each of the parties.'' Utah Code Ann. § 30-3-10

By way of contrast, in other States, as in the Uniform Marriage and Divorce Act, consideration of ''conduct of a present or proposed custodian that does not affect his relationship to the child'' is precluded.

Wealth. The relative wealth of the parents may or may not be considered in awarding custody. If, however, courts gave great weight to the financial resources of the parties in awarding custody and did not favor the primary caretaker, fathers would receive most custody awards and mothers who had only been homemakers would never receive custody. Thus, many argue that financial considerations should never come into play or that they cannot be allowed to outweigh the primary caretaker rule.

The dissenting opinion in *Fritschler v. Fritschler, supra,* in which custody of children was changed from the mother to the father because the mother wished to move with them from Wisconsin to Colorado, points out, in vivid language, what can happen when wealth is a factor in child custody decisions.

"[O]nly proper and relevant factors are to be considered in determining what custody

placement order would best serve the welfare and well-being of the children involved. The financial income, the professional status and the community standing of the two ex-spouses are not such proper factors. Here the trial court obviously gave heavy weight to such income, such status and such standing. In its memorandum opinion, the trial court stated:

'. . . children should be able to enjoy and bask in the delights of their father's reputation as a competent and leading attorney of the City of Madison and the State of Wisconsin. . . . Fortunately in this matter, Mr. Fritschler has a good reputation and there is no reason that the Court sees, why that reputation should not continue, and the Court is of the opinion that there is no reason why those two (2) children should not become a part of that reputation.'

"Earlier in the same opinion, the trial court added to status and standing as an attorney, the matter of the substantial income earned in his profession by the father, stating:

'The Defendant is a very successful attorney—is well respected in the community as evidenced by his substantial income over a long period of time. . . .'

"Wherever the father is a successful attorney and the mother is a full-time homemaker, giving weight to these considerations puts a butcher's thumb on the scales. Of course, the barrister father will have a greater income, professional status and standing in the community than the mother who stayed home to raise the children. By such scales, so weighted, an F. Lee Bailey or Melvin Belli would be assured custody of children should lawyer-husband and homemaker-wife go separate ways. The best interests of a child are not to be determined by a comparison of income tax returns or resort to a Martindale directory [a directory of attorneys]. Success, status or standing in any one of what in Italy are termed the *le grande professions* does not make one a preferred custodian of minor children. One's law school diploma and license to practice law, or the financial success or community prestige one attains in this profession are not relevant or proper foundation stones for a change of custody order.''

In a further twist on the consideration of wealth, in *Buchard v. Garay*, 42 Cal. 3d 531, 724 P.2d 486 (1986), the trial court awarded custody of a 2½-year-old child, who was born out of wedlock and who had lived exclusively with his mother since birth, to the father because of the father's better economic circumstances and because the mother worked and had to place the child in day care. The California Supreme Court reversed, stating:

"The trial court's decision referred to [the father's] better economic position, and to matters such as homeownership or ability to provide a more 'wholesome environment' which reflect economic advantage. But comparative income is not a basis for a custody award. '[T]here is no basis for assuming a correlation between wealth and good parenting or wealth and happiness.' If in fact the custodial parent's income is insufficient to provide . . . proper care for the child, the remedy is to award child support, not to take away custody.

"The court also referred to the fact that [the mother] worked and had to place the child in day care while the father's new wife could care for the child in their home. But in an era when over 50 percent of mothers and almost 80 percent of divorced mothers work, the courts must not presume that a working mother is a less satisfactory parent or less fully committed to the care of her child. A custody determination must be based upon a true assessment of the emotional bonds between parent and child . . . [and reflect] a factual determination of how best to provide continuity of attention, nurturing, and care. It cannot be based on an assumption, unsupported by scientific evidence, that a working

mother cannot provide such care—an assumption particularly unfair when, as here, the mother has in fact been the primary caregiver.''

Sexual preference of a parent. The States are also split on the question of the impact of the sexual preference of a parent. Some courts consider homosexuality immoral and would deny custody to a gay or lesbian parent on that ground. Others would consider it as having an adverse impact on children. Thus, in *Jacobson v. Jacobson*, 314 N.W.2d 78 (N.D. 1981), a lesbian mother was denied custody. The court stated:

"It is not inconceivable that one day our society will accept homosexuality as 'normal.' Certainly it is more accepted today than it was only a few years ago. We are not prepared to conclude, however, that it is not a significant factor to be considered in determining custody of children, at least in the context of the facts of this particular case. Because the trial court has determined that both parents are 'fit, willing and able' to assume custody of the children we believe the homosexuality of [the mother] is the overriding factor. [D]espite the fact that the trial court determined the relationship [between the mother and her lover] . . . to be a 'positive one,' it is a relationship which, under the existing state of the law, never can be a legal relationship. Furthermore, we cannot lightly dismiss the fact that living in the same house with their mother and her lover may well cause the children to 'suffer from the slings and arrows of a disapproving society' to a much greater extent than would an arrangement wherein the children were placed in the custody of their father with visitation rights in the mother.

"We . . . cannot determine whether or not the fact the custodial parent is homosexual or bisexual will result in an increased likelihood that the children will become homosexual or bisexual. However, that issue does not control our conclusion. Rather, we believe that because of the mores of today's society, because [the mother] is engaged in a homosexual relationship in the home in which she resides with the children, and because of the lack of legal recognition of the status of a homosexual relationship, the best interests of the children will be better served by placing custody of the children with [the father.]''

By way of contrast, based on near unanimous psychiatric testimony that a lesbian lifestyle, in and of itself, would not have adverse affect on a child, the court in *Doe v. Doe*, 16 Mass.App. 499, 452 N.E.2d 293 (1983), permitted a lesbian mother, who was living with her lover, to share joint custody of her ten-year-old son. This ruling was made despite a Massachusetts statute which provided:

"In making an order or judgment relating to the custody of children . . . the rights of the parents shall, in the absence of misconduct, be held to be equal, and the happiness and welfare of the children shall determine their custody or possession. When considering the happiness and welfare of the children, the court may consider whether or not the child's present or past living conditions adversely affect his physical, mental, moral or emotional health . . . '' Mass. G.L. c. 208, § 31, as amended through St. 1982, c. 252.

The question of the relevance of the sexual preference of a parent has been complicated by the AIDS crisis. Cases have arisen where custody or visitation has been denied because of a parent's AIDS or the mere fear that a parent could have AIDS. In *Stewart v. Stewart*, 521 N.E.2d 956 (Ind. App. 1987), however, the court held that it was improper to deny a father visitation solely because he had AIDS.

Handicap of a parent. Despite laws forbidding discrimination against the handicapped, the handicap of a parent may be considered in making a custody award. In *Carney v. Carney*, 24 Cal.3d 725, 598 P.2d 36 (1979), however, a change of custody based solely on the custodial parent's handicap was reversed. In *Carney*, when a couple separated after four years of marriage, the father took custody of their two young boys, moving with them from New York to California, where he began living with a woman by whom he later had a daughter. Four years later, he was injured in an accident and rendered a quadriplegic. He spent a year in a hospital, but his children, who remained in the care of the woman with whom he had been living, visited him several times a week and he came home most weekends. After his release from the hospital, when he finally sought a divorce in order to marry the woman with whom he had been living, the mother of the boys sought custody. She was awarded custody by the trial court, although it was undisputed that from the date of separation until a few days before the hearing on custody, a period of almost five years, she never visited the children or contributed to their support and her sole contact with them consisted of some telephone calls and a few letters and packages. The California Supreme Court reversed the custody award. It stated:

"In this case . . . we are called upon to resolve an apparent conflict between two strong public policies: the requirement that a custody award serve the best interests of the child, and the moral and legal obligation of society to respect the civil rights of its physically handicapped members, including their right not to be deprived of their children because of their disability. As will appear, we hold that upon a realistic appraisal of the present day capabilities of the physically handicapped, these policies can both be accommodated. The trial court herein failed to make such an appraisal, and instead premised its ruling on outdated stereotypes of both the parental role and the ability of the handicapped to fill that role. Such stereotypes have no place in our law.

"[It is plain that the trial court's] judgment was affected by serious misconceptions as to the importance of the involvement of parents in the purely physical aspects of their children's lives. We do not mean, of course, that the health or physical condition of the parents may not be taken into account in determining whose custody would best serve the child's interests. In relation to the issues at stake, however, this factor is ordinarily of minor importance; and whenever it is raised . . . it is essential that the court weigh the matter with an informed and open mind. In particular, if a person has a physical handicap it is impermissible for the court simply to rely on that condition as *prima facie* evidence of the person's unfitness as a parent or of probable detriment to the child; rather, in all cases the court must view the handicapped person as an individual and the family as a whole. To achieve this, the court should inquire into the person's actual and potential physical capabilities, learn how he or she has adapted to the disability and manages its problems, consider how the other members of the household have adjusted thereto, and take into account the special contributions the person may make to the family despite or even because of the handicap. Weighing these and all other relevant factors together, the court should then carefully determine whether the parent's condition will in fact have a substantial and lasting adverse effect on the best interests of the child.

"The record shows the contrary occurred in the case at bar. To begin with, the court's belief that there could be no 'normal relationship between father and boys' unless William engaged in vigorous sporting activities with his sons is a further example of the conventional sex-stereotypical thinking that we [have] condemned in [the context of employ-ment discrimination.] Even more damaging is the fact that the court's preconception herein, wholly apart from its outdated presumption of proper gender roles, also stereotypes William as a person deemed forever unable to be a good parent simply because he is physically handicapped. Like most stereotypes, this is both false and demeaning. [I]t mistakenly assumes that the parent's handicap inevitably handicaps the child. But children are more adaptable than the court gives them credit for; if one path to their enjoyment of physical activities is closed, they will soon find another. In addition, it is erroneous to presume that a parent in a wheelchair cannot share to a meaningful degree in the physical activities of his child, should both desire it. Although William cannot actually play on his children's baseball team, he may nevertheless be able to take them to the game, participate as a fan, a coach, or even an umpire and treat them to ice cream on the way home. Nor is this companionship limited to athletic events: such a parent is no less capable of accompanying his children to theaters or libraries, shops or restaurants, schools or churches, afternoon picnics or long vacation trips. Thus it is not true that, as the court herein assumed, William will be unable 'to actively go places with [his children], take them places, . . .'

"On a deeper level, . . . the stereotype [that handicapped parents cannot be effective parents] is false because it fails to reach the heart of the parent-child relationship. Contemporary psychology confirms what wise families have perhaps always known that the essence of parenting is not to be found in the harried rounds of daily carpooling endemic to modern suburban life, or even in the doggedly dutiful acts of 'togetherness' committed every weekend by well-meaning fathers and mothers across America. Rather, its essence lies in the ethical, emotional, and intellectual guidance the parent gives to the child throughout his formative years, and often beyond. The source of this guidance is the adult's own experience of life; its motive power is parental love and concern for the child's well-being; and its teachings deal with such fundamental matters as the child's feelings about himself, his relationships with others, his system of values, his standards of conduct, and his goals and priorities in life. Even if it were true, as the court herein asserted, that William cannot do 'anything' for his sons except 'talk to them and teach them, be a tutor,' that would not only be 'enough,' contrary to the court's conclusion, it would be the most valuable service a parent can render. Yet his capacity to do so is entirely unrelated to his physical prowess: however limited his bodily strength may be, a handicapped parent is a whole person to the child who needs his affection, sympathy, and wisdom to deal with the problems of growing up. Indeed, in such matters his handicap may well be an asset: few can pass through the crucible of a severe physical disability without learning enduring lessons in patience and tolerance.

"Both the state and federal governments now pursue the commendable goal of total integration of handicapped persons into the mainstream of society: the Legislature declares that 'It is the policy of this state to encourage and enable disabled persons to participate fully in the social and economic life of the state . . . .' Thus far these efforts have focused primarily on such critical areas as employment, housing, education, transportation, and public access. No less important to this policy is the integration of the handicapped into the responsibilities and satisfactions of family life, cornerstone of our social system. Yet as more and more physically disabled persons marry and bear or adopt children or, as in the case at bar, previously nonhandicapped parents become disabled through accident or illness, custody disputes similar to that now before us may well recur. In discharging their admittedly difficult duty in such proceedings, the trial courts must avoid impairing or defeating the foregoing public policy. [W]e are confident of their ability to do so."

Race. In *Palmore v. Sidoti*, 466 U.S. 429 (1984), the Supreme Court held that race was an invalid consideration in a custody case. In that case, when the parents divorced, the mother was awarded custody of their three year old daughter. The mother, father and daughter were White. Approximately 1 1/2 years later, the father sought custody of the daughter on the ground that the mother married a Black. Although the Florida trial court found both parents fit, it awarded custody to the father stating that "despite the strides that have been made in bettering relations between the races in this country, it is inevitable that [the child] will, if allowed to remain in her present situation . . . suffer from the social stigmatization that is sure to come." The Supreme Court reversed, stating:

"A core purpose of the Fourteenth Amendment was to do away with all governmentally-imposed discrimination based on race. Classifying persons according to their race is more likely to reflect racial prejudice than legitimate public concerns; the race, not the person, dictates the category. Such classifications are subject to the most exacting scrutiny; to pass constitutional muster, they must be justified by a compelling governmental interest and must be 'necessary . . . to the accomplishment' of its legitimate purpose. The State, of course, has a duty of the highest order to protect the interests of minor children, particularly those of tender years. In common with most states, Florida law mandates that custody determinations be made in the best interests of the children involved. The goal of granting custody based on the best interests of the child is indisputably a substantial governmental interest for purposes of the Equal Protection Clause.

"It would ignore reality to suggest that racial and ethnic prejudices do not exist or that all manifestations of those prejudices have been eliminated. There is a risk that a child living with a step-parent of a different race may be subject to a variety of pressures and stresses not present if the child were living with parents of the same racial or ethnic origin. The question, however, is whether the reality of private biases and the possible injury they might inflict are permissible considerations for removal of an infant child from the custody of its natural mother. We have little difficulty concluding that they are not. The Constitution cannot control such prejudices but neither can it tolerate them. Private biases may be outside the reach of the law, but the law cannot, directly or indirectly, give them effect. 'Public officials sworn to uphold the Constitution may not avoid a constitutional duty by bowing to the hypothetical effects of private racial prejudice that they assume to be both widely and deeply held.'

"This is by no means the first time that acknowledged racial prejudice has been invoked to justify racial classifications. In [a 1917 case], for example, this Court invalidated a Kentucky law forbidding Negroes from buying homes in white neighborhoods. Whatever problems racially-mixed households may pose for children in 1984 can no more support a denial of constitutional rights than could the stresses that residential integration was thought to entail in 1917. The effects of racial prejudice, however real, cannot justify a racial classification removing an infant child from the custody of its natural mother found to be an appropriate person to have such custody."

Religion.   The religion, or lack of religion, of a parent is often considered in making custody determinations. Because of the freedom of religion established in the 1st Amendment to the Constitution, however, courts should not decide that one parent's religion is preferable to the other's religion and should not deny a parent custody solely because of his or her religion or lack of religion. As the Ne-

braska Supreme Court stated in *Goodman v. Goodman, supra,* where a Catholic mother was favored over a Jewish father by the trial court:

"The courts preserve an attitude of impartiality between religions and will not disqualify a parent because of his or her religious beliefs. Particularly is this true where there is no showing that the religious beliefs . . . seriously threaten the health or well-being of the child."

Joint custody

Because an award of custody to one parent may not be wholly satisfactory and because contested child custody cases may be difficult for all concerned, many people favor **joint custody**, also called "shared responsibility" or "divided custody." As stated in *Beck v. Beck,* 86 N.J. 480, 432 A.2d 63 (1981):

"In recent years the concept of joint custody has become topical, due largely to the perceived inadequacies of sole custody awards and in recognition of the modern trend toward shared parenting in marriage. Sole custody tends both to isolate children from the noncustodial parent and to place heavy financial and emotional burdens on the sole caretaker, usually the mother, although awards of custody to the father, especially in households where both parents are employed outside the home, are more common now than in years past. Moreover, because of the absolute nature of sole custody determinations, in which one parent 'wins' and the other 'loses,' the children are likely to become the subject of bitter custody contests and post-decree tension. The upshot is that the best interests of the child are disserved by many aspects of sole custody.

"Joint custody attempts to solve some of the problems of sole custody by providing the child with access to both parents and granting parents equal rights and responsibilities regarding their children. At the root of the joint custody arrangement is the assumption that children in a unified family setting develop attachments to both parents and the severance of either of these attachments is contrary to the child's best interest.

"Properly analyzed, joint custody is comprised of two elements, **legal custody** and **physical custody**. Under a joint custody arrangement, legal custody, the legal authority and responsibility for making 'major' decisions regarding the child's welfare, is shared at all times by both parents. Physical custody, the logistical arrangement whereby the parents share the companionship of the child and are responsible for 'minor' day-to-day decisions, may be alternated in accordance with the needs of the parties and the children. Through its legal custody component joint custody seeks to maintain these attachments by permitting both parents to remain decision-makers in the lives of their children. Alternating physical custody enables the children to share with both parents the intimate day-to-day contact necessary to strengthen a true parent-child relationship."

In recent years, most States have adopted statutes providing that there is a preference for or presumption in favor of joint custody or that authorize courts to award joint custody in their discretion. A few States have no statutes on the subject, but the courts nevertheless make joint custody awards in their discretion. These courts may establish a presumption or preference for joint custody, or, as in *Beck*, a decision from New Jersey which, at the time, had no statute on joint custody, may only "endorse its use as an alternative to sole custody" in "the proper case." The courts or statutes may also establish a preference or presumption against joint custody. For example, a Minnesota statute

provides that joint custody may be ordered only after consideration of the ability of the parents to cooperate and a determination that they have methods to resolve disputes and only if it would be detrimental to the child if one parent were to have sole custody. Minn. Stat. §518.17, subd. 2. Finally, there may be a preference for or presumption in favor of joint custody, but the presumption may not apply in certain circumstances, such as if there has been spouse abuse. The Florida shared responsibility statute, for example, provides:

"The court shall order that the parental responsibility for a minor child be shared by both parents unless it finds that shared responsibility would be detrimental to the child. The court shall consider evidence of spouse abuse as evidence of detriment to the child. If the court . . . finds that spouse abuse has occurred between the parties, it may award sole parental responsibility to the abused spouse and make such arrangements for visitation as will best protect the child and abused spouse from further harm." Laws of Florida, § 61.13(2)(b)2.

As you saw from *Beck v. Beck, supra,* joint custody is of two types. Generally a parent with sole custody is able to make all major decisions concerning a child, such as the religion of the child, the type of education and the need for medical care. With joint legal custody, however, decision making would be shared. Less common is joint physical custody where the children actually live with both parents, moving back and forth on a daily, weekly or monthly basis. Because of the disruption of frequent moves, joint physical custody orders are rare or may resemble sole custody orders with liberal visitation. Also, statutes or court opinions favoring joint custody may actually only favor joint legal custody. For example, in *Beck v. Beck, supra,* which expressed a preference for joint custody, the court stated:

"The physical custody element of a joint custody award requires examination of practical considerations such as the financial status of the parents, the proximity of their respective homes, the demands of parental employment, and the age and number of the children. Joint physical custody necessarily places an additional financial burden on the family. Although exact duplication of facilities and furnishings is not necessary, the trial court should insure that the children can be adequately cared for in two homes. The geographical proximity of the two homes is an important factor to the extent that it impinges on school arrangements, the children's access to relatives and friends (including visitation by the noncustodial parent), and the ease of travel between the two homes. If joint custody is feasible except for one or more of these practical considerations, the court should consider awarding legal custody to both parents with physical custody to only one and liberal visitation rights to the other. Such an award will preserve the decision-making role of both parents and should approximate, to the extent practicable, the shared companionship of the child and non-custodial parent that is provided in joint physical custody."

Florida's shared responsibility law is really a law providing for joint legal custody, but it permits the parties to share decisions on the physical residence of a child. The law provides:

" 'Shared parental responsibility' means that both parents retain full parental rights with respect to their child and requires both parents to confer so that major decisions will be determined jointly. In ordering shared parental responsibility, the court may consider the expressed desires of the parents and may grant to one party the ultimate responsibility over specific aspects of

the child's welfare or may divide those aspects between the parties based on the best interests of the child. When it appears to the court to be in the best interests of the child, the court may order or the parties may agree how any such responsibility will be divided. Such areas of responsibility may include **primary physical residence**, education, medical and dental care, and any other responsibilities which the court finds unique to a particular family and/or in the best interests of the child." Laws of Florida, § 61.13(2)(b)2a.

Many people are opposed to joint custody. As stated in *Beck v. Beck, supra:*

"Joint custody . . . is not without its critics. The objections most frequently voiced include contentions that such an arrangement creates instability for children, causes loyalty conflicts, makes maintaining parental authority difficult, and aggravates the already stressful divorce situation by requiring interaction between hostile ex-spouses. Although these same problems are already present in sole custody situations, some courts have used these objections either to reject or strictly limit the use of joint custody."

A serious problem with joint custody is the restrictions it imposes on a parent's ability to relocate. If a parent who shares joint custody of a child moves out of State or even to a distant place in the same State, joint custody would probably be impossible.

This problem also arises in relation to visitation. A distant move with a child may deprive the other parent of visitation. Yet, the movement of a custodial parent should not be unduly restricted. Sometimes there are good reasons for relocating. Thus, some States provide by statute that a parent with sole custody of a child may move out of State or out of the area, but only with court permission, and many custody orders, even where there is no such statute, provide that a parent with sole custody may only move with court approval. And even if there is no such provision in an order or a statute, a non-custodial parent with visitation rights may always go to court to oppose a move by the custodial parent. Courts do not lightly approve of a custodial's parents desire to move. As stated in *Fritschler v. Fritschler, supra,* in which a custodial mother wished to move from Wisconsin to Colorado:

> "[O]ne having custody of a child is not free to move about the country disregarding state lines, as that person would be if she did not have custody. The parent's responsibility to the child and its interests and the rights of the other parent qualify and limit the right and liberty to move about freely—that is one of the burdens of having custody of minor children.

> "In the present case, the trial court thought the children's best interests would be harmed by their removal from Wisconsin and the resulting separation from frequent contacts and a closer relationship with their father. There was apparently no question in the trial court's mind that Mr. Fritschler could afford to exercise his visitation rights by going to Colorado; nor was the court unaware of the possibility that the father could have custody of the children for several months during the summer if Mrs. Fritschler were permitted to exercise custody outside the state. Such alternatives were believed not to be in the children's best interests. Living in Colorado is not as conducive to a normal relationship between a father and his children, from the children's standpoint as living in the same city. While a divorce terminates a marriage, it does not terminate parenthood and should not in effect do so."

Restrictions on a custodial parent's ability to move have been challenged as unconstitu-

tionally infringing the right to travel, but such arguments have generally been dismissed by courts. For example, in *Rowsey v. Rowsey,* 329 S.E.2d 57 (Va. 1985), the court stated:

> "This Court has recognized a right to travel, under the Federal Constitution. The paramountcy of child welfare may, however, supersede the right to travel."

Interstate custody issues

As has been stated, a court in a state where only one spouse resides may have jurisdiction to grant a divorce but not to resolve certain ancillary matters related to the divorce. A court in a State where a child resides with one parent may, however, have jurisdiction to award custody of the child in a divorce decree even if the child's other parent lives in another State. This is because a court has jurisdiction over a resident child—even if it does not have jurisdiction over both the child's parents.

The ability of a court to make a child custody order when only the child and one parent are residents of the State can cause problems when a parent takes a child from one State to another State to evade an order awarding custody of the child to the other parent. A court in the State where a child has been brought (State 2) does not have to recognize the child custody order of the State from which the child has been taken (State 1) pursuant to the Full Faith and Credit Clause of the Constitution because child custody orders are generally modifiable, and only nonmodifiable orders need be recognized under the Full Faith and Credit Clause. Alternatively, a court in State 2 could recognize State 1's custody order but could exercise its authority to modify it. Either way, a court in

State 2 is likely to rule in favor of the parent who is before it and is unlikely to return a child to an out-of-state parent—despite the resident parent's action in bringing the child into State 2 in violation of State 1's custody order.

Further problems could arise when a parent takes a child from one State to another to avoid a valid child custody order. The court in the State from which the child has been taken may still have jurisdiction to enforce its child custody order, but how is a parent who lives in one State going to enforce an order in another State? What should happen if parents do not have the financial ability to take their cases to the State where their children now reside? And what should happen if two States make conflicting orders on child custody and both orders were within the courts' jurisdiction.

To resolve some of these problems, all the States have adopted the Uniform Child Custody Jurisdiction Act. The Uniform Act enables a parent in one State to initiate a child custody action and enforce a child custody award when the child lives in another State without going to the State where the child lives. The Uniform Act also limits a court's jurisdiction to make a child custody order or modify another State's custody order. The Act does not, however, resolve the problem of a court's natural bias for the parties before it, a bias which encourages interstate child-snatching. To resolve this problem, in 1980 the federal government enacted the Parental Kidnapping Prevention Act, 28 U.S.C. § 1738A. The Act further limits court's jurisdiction to make a child custody order and provides that a court in one State must recognize a child custody order of another State if the court which made the order had jurisdiction to do so. It also provides that a court in one State cannot modify a properly made child custody order of another State unless it has jurisdiction to do so and the other State

no longer has jurisdiction or has declined jurisdiction. Finally, as part of the Act, Congress declared that

> "28 U.S.C. § 1073, the law making interstate flight to avoid prosecution or giving testimony a federal crime, should be interpreted to apply to cases involving parental kidnapping." P.L. 96-611, § 10.

Unfortunately, the natural bias of state courts for their own residents has not been eliminated by this law, and the Supreme Court has ruled that this law does not give federal courts jurisdiction to consider interstate custody disputes. *Thompson v. Thompson*, _____ U.S. _____, 108 S.Ct. 513 (1988).

Non-parents' rights to custody and visitation

In the last few years, there has been increased agitation for grandparents' rights to visit their grandchildren after a divorce or the death of a parent. Forty-eight States now afford grandparents some visitation rights by statute. A problem arises if grandparents have been given visitation rights and a child is subsequently adopted by a step-parent. As we have seen, adoption is intended to sever biological relationships and replace them with new familial relationships. Thus, if a stepfather adopts a child, severing her relationship with her natural father, her paternal grandparents should no longer have visitation rights. Some States, however, will continue natural grandparents' visitation rights after an adoption provided that visitation is not contrary to the child's best interests.

Very recently, there has been agitation for and concern for step-parents' rights. The trend is still small, but step-parents are beginning to get visitation in negotiated settlements and in divorce decrees, and a few States have laws spelling out step-parents' rights to visitation.

In a few cases around the country, step-parents, grandparents, and other relatives, and even non-relatives, have been awarded custody over birth or adoptive parents despite many State laws expressing a strong preference for a parent over a non-parent in custody disputes. When a child has been living with a non-parent for a substantial period, courts may be unwilling to remove the child from the non-parent's home and return the child to the parent—even where there is no evidence that the parent is unfit.

CHILD SUPPORT

Children are entitled to financial support from their parents unless and until the parents' rights are terminated. An order denying a parent custody of a child does not relieve the parent of the obligation to support the child. Indeed, sole custody awards often impose a child support obligation on the noncustodial parent.

In *Gomez v. Perez*, 409 U.S. 535 (1973), the Court held that children born out of wedlock are entitled to the same support from their parents as children born in wedlock. With children born out of wedlock, however, it may not be clear on whom the child support obligation can be imposed. There is usually no dispute as to who a child's mother is, and thus there is usually no problem imposing a support obligation on the mother, but there may be a dispute as to who is the father of a child born out of wedlock. A support obligation cannot be imposed on a man merely because the mother says he is the father of a child born out of wedlock. It must be legally

established that he is the father. In other words, **paternity** must be established.

By way of contrast, if a child is born during wedlock, the mother's husband is presumed to be the father of the child. In the past, the husband could not rebut this presumption. It now may be rebutted in most States, but, in the absence of satisfactory rebuttal evidence presented by the father in a legal action, the support obligation can be imposed on the husband.

Children born out of wedlock may be **legitimated**, that is, have their legal status changed from illegitimate to legitimate. Legitimation procedures may be set forth in a statute or may be a matter of common law. Usually children are automatically legitimated if their natural parents marry after their birth. Sometimes a further step in addition to marriage, such as an acknowledgement of paternity by the father, is required. Because the father usually has to take certain steps to legitimate a child (and, in fact, usually only the father can legitimate a child), paternity is established when a child born out of wedlock is legitimated.

Legitimating a child is different than **acknowledging a child.** Acknowledging a child does not affect the child's status; the child remains illegitimate, but the child's father, or possibly mother, has admitted being the child's parent. There may be certain legal requirements for an acknowledgement to be legally binding, but once a father has acknowledged a child in accordance with these requirements, paternity is established.

The legal action to establish that a certain man is the natural father of a child is known as a ''**paternity action.**'' Because, in the absence of legitimation or an acknowledgement of paternity, it is necessary to establish legally that a man is the father of a child born out of wedlock before a support obligation can be imposed on him, we will review paternity actions before discussing child support.

The establishment of paternity

Paternity actions, like all other domestic relations actions, are authorized and controlled by State law. The laws differ from State to State, but there are basic similarities in all the laws. Moreover, as of 1989, seventeen States had adopted the Uniform Parentage Act (UPA) which, among other things, establishes a procedure for determining paternity,[1] and several more States had not adopted the UPA in its entirety, but had adopted portions of it or had modeled their paternity procedures on it.

Under the UPA and the law in many States, paternity petitions may be filed by the mother in the name of the child, by the mother in her own name, or by the child in his or her own name. The UPA and some States also permit the father to bring a paternity action to establish his rights to a child or to establish nonpaternity. A **maternity action** in which it is established that a woman is or is not the mother of a child is also theoretically possible.

A major legal issue related to paternity actions is how long after the child's birth can they be brought or, in other words, what is the **statute of limitations** for paternity actions? A statute of limitations establishes how long after an event a suit concerning the event may be brought. Generally, statutes of limitations may be **tolled**. This means time will not run during a certain period. Tolling may occur for a variety of reasons, such as in-

ability to bring a suit because one is in prison or is abroad in the military. Minority, a legal disability which prevents one from suing, generally tolls a statute of limitations.

In *Mills v. Habluetzel*, 465 U.S. 91 (1982), and in *Pickett v. Brown*, 462 U.S.1 (1983), the Supreme Court struck down, respectively, a one-year and a two-year statute of limitations for paternity actions, with no tolling allowed for minority, on the grounds that the statutes unconstitutionally discriminated against illegitimate children and "did not provide illegitimate children with an adequate opportunity to obtain paternal support." The Court strongly suggested in *Pickett* that longer statutes of limitations for paternity actions also may not pass constitutional muster, but the Court has not determined the permissible outer limits on statutes of limitations. It has, without an opinion, vacated and remanded a case upholding a six year statute of limitations "for further consideration in light of *Pickett v. Brown.*" *Daniel v. Collier*, 113 Mich. App. 74, 317 N.W.2d 293 (1983), *vacated and remanded*, 464 U.S. 805 (1983).

The UPA has no statute of limitations if a child has a presumed father. In some situations, such as when a child is born in wedlock or a man lives with and supports a child, a man is presumed to be the natural father of the child. If there is no presumed father, a paternity action must be brought within three years of the child's birth or, if it is brought by or on behalf of the child, within three years of the time the child attains majority.

Because a paternity action may result in the imposition of a long and substantial burden of support and may have other serious repercussions for both father and child, many procedural protections for the father have been included in the UPA and in other State statutes. The courts have also mandated procedural protections for the father as a matter of due process. The necessary state action exists because many paternity actions are brought

---

1. The UPA also eliminates any distinction between legitimate and illegitimate children. It provides in section 2: "The parent and child relationship extends equally to every child and to every parent, regardless of the marital status of the parents."

The seventeen states which have adopted the UPA are: Alabama, California, Colorado, Delaware, Hawaii, Illinois, Kansas, Minnesota, Missouri, Montana, Nevada, New Jersey, North Dakota, Ohio, Rhode Island, Washington, and Wyoming.

by welfare authorities on behalf of children receiving welfare. They are brought by welfare authorities because no support obligation can be imposed on a father unless paternity is established and because it is believed that children should be supported by their parents rather than the State.

The Supreme Court has not considered whether the father is entitled to the appointment of an attorney if he cannot afford to retain one, but courts in several States have held that the appointment of a counsel for the father is constitutionally required in all cases or if the action is brought by a welfare department. Courts in several States have held otherwise, but many State statutes and the UPA require appointment of counsel for the father in all cases.

In *Little v. Streater*, 452 U.S. 1 (1981), the Supreme Court held that a defendant in a paternity action brought by the State for a mother on welfare who cannot afford to pay for blood tests has a constitutional right to have the blood tests paid for by the State. Because blood tests are so reliable and probative, the Court concluded that a defendant in a paternity action is denied due process if he is denied the means to obtain a blood test.

In *Rivera v. Minnich*, 483 U.S. 574, (1987), the Court held that the preponderance of evidence standard is constitutionally sufficient in a paternity case, but many States require clear and convincing evidence for a judgment of paternity. No Supreme Court case has addressed the issue of a right to a jury trial, but, again, many States give the alleged father a right to a jury trial by statute. The UPA does not allow a jury trial, and because the standard of proof is not specified, it is a mere preponderance of the evidence.

The UPA permits a court to impose a specific support obligation on a man found to be the father at the conclusion of the paternity action. Most State statutes similarly provide.

The federal government requires States receiving federal AFDC funds to develop programs to establish paternity and obtain child support for children on welfare. The federal law mandating such State programs is known as the "**IV-D Program**" because it is found in Part D of Title IV of the Social Security Act, 42 U.S.C. § 651 *et seq.* Pursuant to the IV-D program, mothers of children on AFDC are required to cooperate with authorities in ascertaining the paternity of their children and in obtaining child support from the fathers. States receive financial incentives from the federal government for vigorous pursuit of delinquent fathers and reimbursement of enforcement costs. Further, State law on paternity ascertainment and child support collection must follow certain federal guidelines, and the States must institute certain mechanisms to collect child support. These guidelines apply to all paternity and child support actions, not just those brought by welfare departments, and the enforcement mechanisms may be used by all children, not just those on AFDC. For example, Title IV-D authorizes the withholding of federal income tax refunds for past due child support, whether the child support was ordered paid for a welfare or a non-welfare family, and requires States to establish programs to garnish wages for past due support, again for all families, not just welfare families.

As part of the 1988 reform of welfare, Congress strengthened many of the child support provisions found in Title IV-D and added to them. Under the 1988 revisions, child support can be ordered withheld from wages at the time of an initial support order instead of only after an arrearage has accumulated; child support awards must be reviewed every three years if a family is on welfare or requests review; States will have to increase the numbers of cases in which they determine paternity; and to aid in determining paternity, States must attempt to include the social security numbers of both parents on birth certificates.

The collection of child support

Unlike alimony, child support is generally ordered in all cases where a non-custodial parent is before the court, but as with alimony, there is no unanimity as to how child support should be set. Many of the same questions that arise with alimony arise with child support. For example, should child support be based on the non-custodial parent's income or the child's needs? Other questions that are unique to child support also arise. For example, should the child support obligation of a non-custodial parent be reduced if a child is living with a wealthy step-parent even if the step-parent has no legal obligation to support the step-child?

However these questions are answered, every study on the subject has concluded that child support is generally set at an amount which lowers children's standard of living after a divorce and which keeps many children born out of wedlock in poverty. Judges have generally had considerable discretion in setting child support awards and have felt that child support should not take a large percentage of a non-custodial parent's income. Moreover, as was stated in *Garska v. McCoy, supra*, 278 S.E.2d 357, divorcing mothers may bargain away child support in return for custody, and courts may approve their settlements without inquiry. Thus, non-custodial parents generally pay only a small amount of child support.

In an attempt to address this problem, many States established formulas or schedules for child support based on the parents' income. In 1984, the federal government, as part of the IV-D program, mandated that all States adopt such guidelines for child support awards. Because many judges ignored

discretionary guidelines, however, in 1988, Congress said such guidelines must be mandatory and can be ignored only if a specific finding is made that the formula would impose an unfair burden in a particular case.

Even with mandatory minimum guidelines or formulas for setting child support, questions will remain. For example, how long should child support continue? Should child support continue after a child reaches majority while a child is continuing his or her education, in college or beyond? Should it be continued indefinitely for a disabled child?

Like alimony awards, child support awards are modifiable. The modifiability of child support awards raises other questions. For example, how and when can child support be modified? Should a non-custodial parent be able to quit a job and thus reduce his or her ability to pay child support obligations? Should a non-custodial parent's child support obligation be reduced if he or she assumes new responsibilities by remarrying and having more children?

These and other questions may be answered by legislatures as a matter of policy or by courts on a case-by-case basis. However these questions are answered and whatever the amount of child support ordered, it is clear that many fathers[2] have failed and will fail to make court ordered child support payments.[3] Increasing attention has been paid to

---

2. Because most non-custodial parents are fathers and because non-custodial mothers are rarely ordered to pay child support, for convenience, we will hereinafter discuss only fathers, but what is said about fathers could apply equally to mothers.

3. Of the approximately 5 million women who lived with children with absent fathers in 1982, only 71.6 percent received the child support due to them in 1981. And although the average amount ordered paid was $2,460 per year, the average amount received was $1,510. U.S. Bureau of the Census, *Child Support and Alimony: 1981 (Advance Report)*, Series P-23, No 124 (May 1983). *See also* David Chambers, *Making Fathers Pay: The Enforcement of Child Support* (University of Chicago Press, 1979).

the failure of fathers to pay court ordered child support. This attention has led to new mechanisms, many of which were created or required by the IV-D program, to enforce child support obligations. These mechanisms include: mandatory **wage garnishments**, that is, judicial orders which require an employer to withhold a certain percentage of an employee's wages or salary from his or her paycheck and to pay the withheld amount to the court; withholding of income tax refunds; reporting of child support arrearages to consumer credit agencies; reporting the names of delinquent fathers in newspapers; and placement of liens on delinquent fathers' property. This attention has also led to renewed interest in old enforcement mechanisms, like arrest and imprisonment of delinquent fathers for contempt of child support orders or for non-support, a crime in most jurisdictions.

Interstate support problems

As has been stated, child support is generally ordered when a non-custodial parent comes before a court, but many of the women living with children with an absent father are not awarded child support for their children.[4]

---

4. As of Spring 1982, of the 8.4 million women who were living with a child whose father was not in the household, only 59 percent were awarded child support from the absent father. *Id*.

One reason for this is that many mothers do not know where the father of their children is or have not been able to establish paternity. Another reason is that a court may not have jurisdiction to award child support if the non-custodial parent lives out of state and does not voluntarily appear before the court. A court also may not have jurisdiction to entertain a paternity action involving an out-of-state father.

In an attempt to collect child support from out-of-state absent fathers, all of the States have adopted the Uniform Reciprocal Enforcement of Support Act. This Act allows a parent with custody of a child to seek and enforce child support orders from a parent in another State without great difficulty or expense. Through this Act, a custodial parent may file an action for support in the State where he or she lives. The action will be transferred to the State where the non-custodial parent lives and will be pursued by a public attorney in that State.

The Uniform Act greatly assists with interstate collection and enforcement of child support, but it is still difficult to pursue a case from a distance. A poor mother may not be able to go to a distant State to testify in a case. A public official from one State may give low priority to a case from another State. Moreover, the Act, as the Uniform Child Custody Jurisdiction Act, does not resolve the problem of a court's natural bias for its residents. Resident fathers may, thus, be favored over non-resident children.

13

Domestic Violence

It has been estimated that almost 2 million women in America suffer from domestic violence each year. The problem arises within marriage and outside of marriage. Women are assaulted and abused by their husbands or ex-husbands, their lovers or ex-lovers, or by other members of their families or households. Men are also assaulted by family or household members, but the problem is far more acute for women. Thus, we shall focus on domestic violence against women in the first sections of this chapter.

There are persons of both sexes who are particularly vulnerable to domestic violence, including children, the elderly, and persons who are mentally or physically disabled. As we have seen, children are protected from domestic violence through juvenile court acts, child abuse and neglect reporting legislation, and through other laws discussed in Chapter 8, including domestic violence legislation. We shall not further discuss the protection of children from domestic violence in this chapter, but you should note when they might be protected by the laws designed to protect adult women. In the last section of this chapter, we will discuss the laws designed to protect the elderly and disabled who are living alone or with family members in the community. Protection of such persons who are institutionalized is addressed in Chapter 17.

WOMEN'S NEED FOR PROTECTION AGAINST DOMESTIC VIOLENCE

The problem of the domestic violence suffered by women was largely ignored until fairly recent times. By and large, domestic violence was a well-kept secret. Its extent and severity were unknown. And even if it was known that some men beat their wives, generally their behavior was excused. Husbands were believed to have a right to beat their wives just as parents are believed to have a right to physically discipline their children. Indeed, the expression "rule of thumb" was derived from an English rule, adopted widely in America, that a husband could discipline his wife with any reasonable instrument, including a rod no thicker than his thumb.

A few legal methods existed to combat domestic violence, but most were inadequate or totally ineffective. We will review the remedies against domestic violence available in the past and consider their inadequacies in order to put the present situation into perspective. Also many of the remedies, despite their inadequacies, are still used today.

In the past, criminal prosecutions could have been initiated against men who beat their wives or lovers. Domestic violence, in and of itself, may not have been a crime, but where a beating was not excused as proper disciplining of a wife, it could have constituted the crime of assault or battery. Victims of crimes, however, generally cannot initiate criminal prosecutions themselves. Thus, a woman could not herself initiate a criminal action against a man who beat her. Only the police could arrest the man who beat her, and only the prosecutor could bring criminal charges against him. But police officers were reluctant to arrest men who beat their wives or lovers, and prosecuting attorneys were reluctant to prosecute them. Thus, criminal prosecutions for domestic violence were few and far between. Only the most severe and egregious instances of domestic violence were prosecuted.

In some instances, the police or prosecutors were willing to pursue criminal actions against batterers, but the victims of the battering were reluctant to cooperate with them. There could have been several reasons for this reluctance.

First, a criminal prosecution could have left a woman quite vulnerable. A woman would not be protected against further violence if a man who beat her were released on bail while a prosecution was pending. Even if he were convicted, a woman would not be protected against further violence at his hands. Violence could occur when he was released after serving his sentence or if he did not serve time at all. Indeed, more serious violence could occur after a criminal prosecution as retaliation for the victim initiating the prosecution.

Second, a woman could have been prevented from taking action against a man who assaulted her by psychological forces and by social pressure. Pursuing a criminal action is often difficult; victims are sometimes made to feel guilt or responsibility for their situation. Both were particularly true for battered women in the male dominated courts. Moreover, social pressure, psychological forces, and the persuasiveness of husbands and lovers could operate to prevent a woman from taking action against a man who beat her, in addition to a quite natural fear of the criminal process.

Finally, homemakers with no possibility of employment might have reasonably refused to prosecute a man upon whom they were financially dependent, knowing they would be unable to support themselves and their children if the men who supported them were jailed.

Even if the police, the prosecutors, and the victims of domestic violence were willing to pursue a criminal prosecution, most States had laws which prevented many arrests and prosecutions. As has been noted, it was believed that a man had a right to beat his wife; a beating which would be considered a battery if the victim were a stranger might have been considered perfectly acceptable if the victim were one's wife. Moreover, no State considered forced sexual intercourse with one's wife a crime until quite recently. Further, even if an incident of domestic violence was

considered to be a crime, it was likely to be considered a misdemeanor, and the police might not have been able to arrest the man. Laws in many States provided that misdemeanor arrests could not be made without warrants unless they occurred in the arresting officer's presence; getting a warrant was often cumbersome and difficult and could cause dangerous delays.

Thus, criminal prosecution was an inadequate answer to the problem of domestic violence. Another possible answer, a civil suit for assault or battery, was perhaps even more inadequate.

A person who has been beaten or assaulted may bring a civil action for damages against the person who did the beating or committed the assault. But until recently many States prohibited law suits between spouses under a doctrine known as "**interspousal immunity**." If there was no interspousal immunity, a woman still might not have been able to bring suit against her husband. In many States, married women did not have the right to bring suit in their own name without the consent of their husbands.

Although some women were not barred from bringing suits for assault and battery against the men who beat them, such suits would probably have been impossible to bring without a lawyer, would have been difficult and expensive, and could have taken years before they came to trial or were resolved. Moreover, women bringing such suits would have been provided with absolutely no protection from the men who beat them. All a woman could receive if she successfully pursued such a suit would be monetary damages for her past injuries.

Some States permitted women to obtain a **peace bill**, **peace bond**, **restraining order**, or an **injunction** against their husbands to prevent further violence. Again, a lawyer would probably be required to bring suit and the suit would be difficult, expensive, and slow.

Moreover, the effectiveness of the orders was questionable; many considered them as worth little more than the paper on which they were written since the police would not assist in enforcing them and the only method of enforcement, a civil contempt action for violating a court order, was also difficult, slow, and expensive.

Wives could generally seek orders protecting them against further violence in conjunction with a divorce, but the procedure to obtain such orders was usually cumbersome, and the orders, like peace bills and other such civil orders, were often ineffective. Seeking a divorce was often impossible without a lawyer, and until the advent of no-fault divorce, specific grounds were required for a divorce. A husband's hitting a wife might not have been one of these grounds. Moreover, residency requirements for divorce actions and religious beliefs prevented some women from bringing divorce actions. Perhaps most important, many women wanted the violence to stop but did not want a divorce.

A woman could always leave her home to get away from the violence, but then she left herself vulnerable to a charge of desertion in a divorce action. If found to be a deserting spouse, she could be denied alimony and a share in her husband's property as the party considered "at fault" in the divorce. And if she left her home without her children, she could be denied their custody at the conclusion of any divorce action because of her so-called "abandonment."

PROVISIONS OF MODERN DOMESTIC VIOLENCE LEGISLATION

In the 1960's and 1970's, the woman's movement changed the public's view of the acceptability of wife beating. Moreover, it made the public aware that domestic violence was a serious and pervasive problem in this country, affecting women at all levels in society, and that the existing remedies to deal with domestic violence were inadequate. It became clear that these remedies had to be improved and that new remedies had to be fashioned—that there was a need for simple, fast procedures which were accessible to all women; for mechanisms, not only to protect women against violence, but also to provide them with necessary financial support while they took action against their batterers; and for ways to help women overcome the barriers to taking action against their batterers. In addition, there was recognition of the need to develop mechanisms to provide services to batterers, services that many of them were unwilling or reluctant to seek.

Beginning in the 1970's, every State enacted laws to address the problem of domestic violence. These laws differ from State to State. Some States just improved and expanded existing remedies, but slightly more than half of the States enacted laws which provided a new legal remedy for victims of domestic violence—a quick and easy procedure for them to obtain meaningful protection against violence. These laws also differ, but they all permit a court to issue an order, generally called a "**protective order**," a "**restraining order**," or an "**order of protection**," enjoining a person from assaulting, harming, or even seeing a family or household member. All of the laws establish special procedures for obtaining an order and all of the laws permit issuance of an emergency order without notice to the batterer. Many of the laws also recognize, create, and/or fund special temporary shelters for victims of domestic violence.

Procedures for obtaining a protective order

The procedure employed to obtain a protective order differs from State to State, but it is usually fairly uncomplicated. Generally a petition is filed in the trial court that hears domestic relations matters. The petition may be

hearsay, could be barred by confidentiality rules, and would probably not be helpful.

The law may set forth the factors that may and may not be considered by a judge in determining whether to issue a protective order. In Illinois, among other things, a judge must consider:

"the nature, frequency, severity, pattern and consequences of the respondent's past abuse of the petitioner or any family or household member . . .; any unauthorized physical violence by respondent; . . . the likelihood of danger of future abuse to petitioner or any member of petitioner's or respondent's family or household [and] . . . the danger that any minor child will be abused or neglected or improperly removed from the jurisdiction, improperly concealed within the State or improperly separated from the child's primary caretaker." Ill. Rev. Stat. ch. 40, par. 2312-14(c)(1)(i), (ii).

A judge may not consider, among other things, evidence that:

"Respondent has cause for any physical abuse, unless that cause satisfies the standards for justifiable use of force [in the Illinois Criminal Code];

"Respondent was voluntarily intoxicated;

"Petitioner acted [or did not act] in self-defense or defense of another . . .; [and]

"Petitioner left [or did not leave] the residence or household to avoid further abuse by respondent" Ill. Rev. Stat. ch. 40, par. 2312-14(e).

If a protective order is issued, it can be of long duration, typically one year. The relief that can be included in the protective order varies from State to State. All States allow issuance of a protective order forbidding a respondent from assaulting, molesting, harassing, or harming a respondent in any way. In most States, the respondent can also be required to move from the residence he shares with the petitioner and to stay away from the petitioner's place of work or other locations where he might encounter the petitioner. The protective order can include an order placing any children in the custody of the petitioner and requiring the respondent to pay support to the petitioner and the children. It may include an order requiring the respondent to compensate the petitioner for expenses incurred filing and pursuing the petition and related to any injuries. It may require the respondent to have counseling.

Special provisions may be made for service of the order on the respondent and execution of the order. In Minnesota,

"upon request of the petitioner, the court shall order the sheriff or constable to accompany the petitioner and assist in placing the petitioner in possession of the dwelling or residence, or otherwise assist in execution or service of the order of protection." Minn. Stat. § 518.01, subd. 9.

Some States require the court to send a copy of the protective order to State law enforcement agencies or establish a procedure whereby the petitioner can file a copy with law enforcement agencies. Whether or not the order is provided to law enforcement, generally law enforcement officers are required to arrest those who violate an order. The arrest may be without a warrant with probable cause only.

In most States, a man who violates the order can be prosecuted criminally for assault or for criminal contempt. Contempt of a protective order may be established as a distinct crime or may be included in the general crime of contempt of a court order. A petitioner can also seek civil contempt against a respondent who violates a protective order. Civil contempt may result in jail in many States.

Problems with the procedures

Domestic violence legislation establishing special procedures for obtaining a protective order has definitely been helpful, but the legislation has not solved all the problems of domestic violence. And, there are problems with many States' laws.

First, the laws may only be available to certain victims of domestic violence. A victim of domestic violence may not be able to get a protective order against someone who is not a relative by blood or marriage or who does not live in the same household. Thus, many women are unprotected against their lovers, particularly if they do not live with them, or against their ex-husbands. The Washington law protects anyone from violence by "family or household members" which is defined to include:

> "spouses, former spouses, parents, adult persons related by blood or marriage, persons who are presently residing together, or who have resided together in the past, and persons who have a child in common regardless of whether they have married or have lived together at any time." Wash. Rev. Code § 26.50.010(2).

Even this law, although it is more comprehensive than many, will not protect a woman from violence by a lover with whom she has never lived or had a child.

Second, the definition of "domestic violence" in many of the laws may be too restrictive. Acts of harassment and non-physical abuse may not be included in the laws. Further, forced sexual intercourse with a wife may not be considered "domestic violence."

Third, many victims of domestic violence who are unquestionably covered by their State's law may be unaware of the law and of the availability of protective orders. To address this problem, some laws provide that the police must inform the victims of domestic violence about the law or tell them about shelters where they can learn about the law whenever they respond to a domestic violence call. Further outreach may be necessary, however, particularly in areas where there are no or few shelters.

Fourth, even if the victims of domestic violence are aware of the laws, there may be psychological and social barriers to using the laws. To address this problem, some laws provide that the police should not only tell women about shelters but also should transport them to shelters or refer them to other social service agencies where they may be counseled.

Fifth, some victims of domestic violence may be aware of the laws and have no psychological or other opposition to the laws, but may believe it is difficult to obtain a protective order and that the assistance of an attorney and the expenditure of substantial sums are necessary. Others may be intimidated by the mere thought of going to court. Thus, many women will not use the laws available to them, especially if they do not have help in doing so.

Sixth, while the domestic violence laws are generally intended to establish simple procedures that all victims of domestic violence can follow without the assistance of an attorney, in fact, this may not be the case. The laws are often far more complex than legislators realize and use words which non-lawyers may not understand. Victims of domestic violence who are uneducated may have great difficulties understanding and using the laws. It may be impossible for those victims who are illiterate to use the law. And despite provisions in some laws that court personnel are to assist the victims to complete the necessary papers, court personnel may not be helpful. Court staff may be too busy or too impatient to help the victims of domestic violence. Some are frankly hostile towards victims of domestic violence or towards anyone who tries to go to court without a lawyer to lead the way. The situation is usually worse in States where the law does not impose a duty on court personnel to help the victims. The combination of the intimidating nature of courts and the impatience or hostility of court personnel can keep many victims from pursuing their cases.

Seventh, judges may also be impatient with unrepresented litigants who do not do things "right." They may, indeed, be hostile towards victims of domestic violence. For example, in a Massachusetts case, a judge told a woman who came before him for a protective order that "she was wasting the court's time, that her fears of [her husband] were unfounded and that she should act more like an adult." He gave her a protective order but refused her request for police protection. A few months later, she was murdered by her husband.[1] A 1985 statewide study of the Massachusetts domestic violence legislation in response to this case and other complaints about judges concluded that the legal system's response to the domestic violence law was "non-compliance," and that "judges misapply or refuse to apply the law."[2]

Finally, if an order can be obtained, it may be difficult to enforce it or to pursue a violator for contempt. A proceeding for civil contempt may be far more complex than a proceeding for a protective order. The police may not be willing to arrest violators of protective orders and prosecutors may not be willing to pursue criminal charges if the police do make arrests. Interestingly, Minnesota law specifically provides that a peace officer "shall arrest and take into custody a person whom the peace officer has probable cause to believe has violated an order," but also provides that "[a] peace officer is not liable . . . for a failure to perform [this] duty." Minn. Stat. § 518.01, subd. 14.

All of these problems with the legislation creating special procedures to obtain a protective order underscore the importance of social services to battered women. Given the social isolation and fears of many women who are abused, obtaining the protection accorded by the law may be impossible in the absence of services.

Other protective legislation and remedies

Because of problems with the laws permitting women to use special procedures to obtain protective orders and because not all States have such laws, many battered women have to rely on the criminal justice system for relief. Most States have amended their criminal laws to provide that domestic violence is a crime or have made clear that domestic violence is included within the definition of other crimes, such as assault. Most States still do not consider forced sexual intercourse with a spouse a crime, however.[3] Moreover, in all States, in practice, it is difficult, if not impossible, to establish a rape by someone with whom a woman previously had voluntary sexual intercourse, by someone whom a woman was dating, or even by someone with whom a woman is acquainted. So-called "date rapes" or "acquaint-

<hr>

1. "Judges in Massachusetts Criticized in Harassment," New York Times, November 30, 1986.
2. *Id.*

3. As of 1983, 34 States did not permit prosecutions for spousal rape. The remaining States consider spousal rape a crime, but often the crime of spousal rape is limited to spouses who are separated or in the process of divorce or to situations where extreme force is employed.

ance rapes'' are rarely prosecuted and, when prosecuted, are rarely successful.

Where it is clear that a crime has been committed, the police may, nevertheless, be unwilling to make arrests for domestic violence—even in States where special domestic violence laws impose duties on law enforcement officers to arrest batterers or ease warrant requirements in cases of domestic violence. The Massachusetts study of domestic violence enforcement, referred to earlier, concluded that: ''Police do not treat domestic violence as a crime.''

To address this problem, the Illinois domestic violence law provides that law enforcement officers must investigate and make a written report on every ''*bona fide* allegation'' of domestic violence, which ''shall include the abuse victim's statements as to the frequency and severity of prior incidents of abuse by the same family or household member and the number of prior calls for police assistance to prevent such further abuse.'' Ill. Rev. Stat. ch. 40, par. 2313-3. The Illinois law further provides that if an officer does not make an arrest, he or she must ''inform the victim of abuse of the victim's right to request that a criminal proceeding be initiated, including specific times and places for meeting with [a prosecutor or other official] in accordance with local procedure.'' Ill. Rev. Stat. ch. 40, par. 2313-4(b).

Despite this strong law, the supervisor of the Domestic Violence Court Advocacy Project in Chicago has stated:

> ''The Illinois Domestic Violence Act is very good. . . . Unfortunately, the act is not enforced. Police almost never arrest the batterer. Women call '911' when they are being assaulted and they are told it's not a police matter. Or they may ask the woman, 'What are you doing to make him hit you?' Or they may threaten her and say, 'If you keep calling, we'll arrest you.''[4]

And, although Minnesota has had a law requiring police to arrest batterers on probable cause since 1978, police have not been making arrests unless they witnessed the assault, according to the director of the Minnesota Program for Battered Women.[5]

If the police do make arrests, prosecutors may not pursue cases and judges may respond with leniency. This may serve to make police less willing to arrest batterers.

In some cases, women have successfully sued the police for their non-compliance with the law. *See, e.g., Thurman v. City of Torrington*, 595 F.Supp. 1521 (D.Conn. 1984), where a woman won $1.9 million after the police refused to arrest her husband for severe abuse, and *Bartalone v. County of Berrien*, 643 F.Supp. 574 (W.D. Mich. 1986), where the court stated that a police officer's failure to arrest a batterer may have violated a wife's right to equal protection if he failed to act ''because she was a spouse seeking protection from an abusive husband.'' Similar suits have been brought against prosecutors who refuse to criminally prosecute those who engage in domestic violence or who violate protective orders, but less successfully. Suits may not be brought against judges because of their immunity from civil suits.

Despite some successful suits, enforcement has been and remains the major problem with the criminal laws protecting battered women. Moreover, the very laws designed to protect victims of domestic violence, the laws enabling them to obtain protective orders, have been used to deny them access to the criminal justice system. The attitude of some police and prosecutors is that women have a civil remedy and thus do not need a criminal remedy.

Even if enforcement problems are solved, some women will not want to use the crimi-

---

4. Nancy Blodgett, ''Violence in the Home,'' 73 A.B.A.J. 66, 68-69 (May 1, 1987)

5. *Id.* at 68.

nal justice system. As in the past, a criminal prosecution, particularly when no protective order is issued, can leave a women quite vulnerable, psychological forces and social pressures can prevent a woman from seeking to prosecute her batterer; and a women who relies on her batterer for support for herself or her children may not wish to see him jailed.

Of course, wives who are abused can still seek protection against their husbands in divorce actions. No-fault laws have made getting a divorce easier, but other barriers to di-

... ...en, the ...ce for a ..., a husvent his

vil suits n in the ch suits, d a marher own milarly, d enforc-gh some modern

legal ult besocial ttered gnore, e the ttered l rem-

THE BATTERED WOMAN SYNDROME

Some women have taken matters into their own hands and killed their batterers. If these women are able to establish that they acted in self-defense, they are generally not charged with or convicted of murder. But, traditionally, the claim of self-defense is only available in a homicide case if the killer was in imminent danger of physical injury or death, and often women kill their batterers at a time when they are in no immediate danger of serious injury, such as when their batterers are asleep. Thus, the traditional claim of self-defense is not available to them.

In recent years, battered women for whom the traditional claim of self-defense is not available have been asserting a special kind of self-defense based on what is known as the **"battered woman syndrome."** It is argued that some victims of repeated domestic violence develop this syndrome, which blankets them in "psychological numbness," and engulfs them "in a whirlpool of pain and violence" in which only two alternatives emerge: submit to abuse and risk death or "strike back."[7] It is further argued that if these women do chose to strike back and kill their batterers, their actions are really done in self-defense—even if they are not done at the time of a battering episode. They are done in self-defense, it is asserted, because they stem from the battered woman's constant fear of violence.

State v. Leidholm, 334 N.W.2d 811 (N.D. 1983),is a case accepting the battered woman syndrome as a form of self-defense. In *Leidholm*, the court stated.

"[A] correct statement of the law of self-

---

6. "Poor Women and Family Law," *supra*, 14 Clearinghouse Review at 1070.

7. Buda and Butler, "The Battered Wife Syndrome: A Backdoor Assault on Domestic Violence," 23 Fam. L. J. 359, 369 (1985).

defense [in an instruction to the jury] is one in which the court directs the jury to assume the physical and psychological properties peculiar to the accused, viz., to place itself as best it can in the shoes of the accused, and then decide whether or not the particular circumstances surrounding the accused at the time he used force were sufficient to create in his mind a sincere and reasonable belief that the use of force was necessary to protect himself from imminent and unlawful harm.

"[The] battered woman syndrome is not of itself a defense. . . . 'The existence of the syndrome in a marriage does not of itself establish the legal right of the wife to kill the husband, the evidence must still be considered in the context of self-defense.' [But a jury may be instructed to consider the] battered woman syndrome and the psychological effects it produces in the battered spouse when deciding the issue of the existence and reasonableness of the accused's belief that force was necessary to protect herself from imminent harm."

Other courts have not accepted the battered woman syndrome as a form of self-defense or have refused to allow expert witnesses to testify on the battered woman syndrome. Without expert testimony, establishing self-defense may be impossible.

As was stated in Chapter 3, in order for expert testimony to be admissible, the testimony must be on a subject beyond the knowledge of an ordinary person, be based on reliable and scientific data, and be helpful to the trier of fact. Some courts have been unwilling to accept expert testimony on the battered woman syndrome as meeting any or all of these criteria. Thus, in *Buhrle v. State*, 627 P.2d 1374 (Wyo. 1981), the trial court refused to allow Dr. Lenore Walker, the author of *The Battered Woman* (Harper & Row: New York, 1979), and a recognised expert on the syndrome, to testify in the murder case before it. The court refused to allow Dr. Walker's testi-

mony although, as the court recognized, she had testified as an expert witness on the battered woman syndrome in numerous cases, including *Leidholm*. The court's reasons were that:

"1) *Voir dire* did not adequately demonstrate that the state of the art permitted a reasonable opinion.

"2) The reasons for [Dr. Walker's] opinions were not adequately explained, were difficult to understand; and therefore, would not aid the jury.

"3) [The battered woman's] state of mind at the time of the shooting [in this case] was not adequately explained; and therefore, this testimony would not aid the jury in its determination."

The Supreme Court of Wyoming, also recognizing that Dr. Walker had testified as an expert witness in numerous cases, upheld the trial court, stating:

"The record indicates that research in the 'battered woman syndrome' is in its infancy; that objectives are difficult to identify; that statistical analysis was in the preparation stage; and that acceptance or recognition of the phenomenon is largely limited to the people who are actively engaged in the research and the people making research grants. This is not to deny a battered woman syndrome and all its ramifications. Suffice it to say defendant failed to demonstrate to the trial court that the state of the art would permit a reasonable expert opinion, nor would the proposed opinions . . . aid the jury.

"The quotation from Dr. Walker's book, *The Battered Woman*, and . . . her *voir dire* suggests that Dr. Walker may make certain conclusions and state certain theories, then engage in research to attempt to substantiate those theories and conclusions. The trial judge may have concluded that she did this with Mrs. Buhrle. Dr. Walker was vague in her explanation of Mrs. Buhrle's behavior if such behavior did not fit into the pattern of battered women.

"The trial judge expressed some difficulty in understanding Dr. Walker's explanations. . . . This court experienced the same difficulty. It might reasonably be assumed, therefore, that if the trial court and the appellate court had difficulty understanding the expert's explanations, so would the jury. The 'aura of special reliability and trustworthiness' surrounding scientific or expert testimony, particularly calls for trial court discretion.

"In our holding here we are not saying that this type of expert testimony is not admissible; we are merely holding that the state of the art was not adequately demonstrated to the court, and because of inadequate foundation the proposed opinions would not aid the jury."

PROTECTION OF THE ELDERLY OR DISABLED

Protection through domestic violence statutes

Violence against an elderly or disabled member of a household would be covered by a State's domestic violence statute if the victim and the abuser are spouses. Further, depending on the definitions of domestic violence in a State's law, it may be covered when the victim and the abuser are not spouses but are living in the same household, as in the case of an elderly woman living with her daughter or a mentally retarded adult living with his parents. When violence against the elderly or the disabled is covered by domestic violence statutes, the victim can obtain orders of protection just as an abused woman can obtain an order of protection—with all, or more, of the attendant difficulties. If it is difficult, practically and psychologically, for an adult woman to obtain a protective order, consider the practical and psychological difficulties for a person who is elderly and frail or mentally retarded.

Protection through criminal laws

Violence or threat of violence against anyone is a crime in every State. Many States, moreover, either define violence against a person who is elderly or disabled as a more serious offense than violence against someone who is younger or able-bodied, or create separate criminal offenses for abuse of an elderly or disabled person. An example of the first approach is seen in Colorado where the statutes, after specifying sanctions for different types of assault against elderly or disabled persons, state:

"Elderly persons and handicapped persons are seldom as physically or emotionally equipped to protect themselves or aid in their own security as are their younger or more physically able counterparts in society. At the same time, they are far more susceptible than other groups to the adverse long-term effects of assault. The general assembly therefore finds that the penalty for the crime of assault on an elderly or handicapped person should be more severe than the penalty for assault on other members of society." § 18-3-209 C.R.S.

An example of the second approach is found in California which permits imprisonment for up to four years of any caretaker of an

mits the person's health to be injured or places the person in a situation that endangers the person's health. Calif. Penal Code § 368.

Protection through adult protective services legislation

Just as in the case of child abuse and neglect, the States have come to recognize that criminal prosecution is usually an ineffective way to address the problem of abuse of elderly and disabled persons. Abuse of the elderly and disabled by caregivers typically evolves from the physical, emotional, and often financial stress of caring for a person who is dependent. As in the case of child abuse, the maltreatment occurs within a relationship that is conflicted but caring in many ways. To criminally prosecute the abuser in such situations will harm the family and put the victim at risk of institutionalization, outcomes that may ultimately be more detrimental to the victim than the abuse itself. In recognition of these facts, the majority of States have enacted adult protective services legislation designed to protect the elderly and persons who are mentally or physically disabled.

The definition of adult protective services varies widely from State to State. To illustrate, protective services in California are defined primarily in terms of the conditions that necessitate the need for societal intervention:

" 'Adult protective services' means those preventive and remedial activities performed on behalf of elders and dependent adults who are unable to protect their own interests; harmed or threatened with harm; caused physical or mental injury due to the action or inaction of another person or their own action due to ignorance, illiteracy, incompetence, mental limitation or poor health; lacking in adequate food, shelter, or clothing; exploited of their income and resources; or deprived of entitlement due them." Calif. Welf. and Inst. Code § 15610.

In contrast, Florida defines protective services primarily in terms of social and other services that might be offered.

" 'Protective services' means those services, the objective of which is to protect an aged or disabled adult from abuse, neglect, or exploitation. Such protective services include, but are not limited to: evaluation of the need for protective services; casework for the purpose of planning and providing needed services; obtaining financial benefits to which the aged person or disabled adult is entitled; securing medical and legal services; maintenance of the aged person or disabled adult in his own home through the provision of protective services; assistance in obtaining out-of-home services, including respite care, emergency housing, and placement settings, as necessary; and seeking protective placement, as necessary." Fla. Stat. Ann. § 415.102(14)

Similarly, the specific provisions of protective services legislation vary widely from State to State, but all the statutes have similar elements. The statutes define who is elderly or disabled for the purposes of providing services; define what constitutes abuse, neglect, or exploitation; require or encourage the reporting of suspected abuse, neglect, or exploitation to designated authorities; provide immunity from civil or criminal liability to those who report in good faith; outline procedures for investigating reports; and state the conditions under which services can be provided with and without the consent of a person found to be in need of services. As you can see, the provisions are much like those of the child abuse and neglect reporting statutes. As you can also see, the provisions typically offer broader protection than do domestic violence statutes and the criminal code in that they include neglect and exploitation.

In most States, the protective services legislation covers persons living at home or with relatives or friends as well as persons who live in nursing homes or other institutions.

Protection of vulnerable adults who are living in the community is complex, both legally and practically, and the statutes represent an attempt to balance the difficult problems involved in offering this protection. The legal issues revolve around privacy and liberty. While children are assumed to be incompetent and thus in need of the *parens patriae* protection of the State, adults are assumed to be competent and thus capable of making decisions on their own behalf. This is often not an issue in instances where a frail elderly person has been physically abused by a caregiver, but it is clearly an issue when a frail elderly person is living, apparently by his or her own choice, in a home that is unsanitary and unsafe. Such is the case with many elderly persons who want at all costs to continue living in their own homes. Should the State intervene against the individual's wishes in such cases, especially when the intervention might result in the individual being placed in a nursing home because no community services are available? This ques-

tion relates to competency and guardianship, topics that will be discussed later in the text.

The practical problems in protection are perhaps more complex than the legal problems. Because abuse, neglect, and exploitation of the elderly or the disabled are criminal offenses, to report such instances, even under the authority of protective services statutes, is to risk criminal prosecution of the abuser and, as stated before, displacement of the victim. This is especially the case when the report, as is true in many States, can be made to law enforcement agencies rather than social service agencies. In addition, there is an unwillingness on the part of society and on the part of victims to identify neglect or abuse and therefore to report mistreatment. And even if mistreatment is reported and identified, there may be no services available to be offered.

Overriding all these concerns is recognition that the elderly and the disabled are vulnerable and with limited resources and that they therefore will find it difficult or impossible to access any protective services that are available. This recognition underscores the importance of advocacy on the part of persons with whom the elderly and disabled have regular contact.

SECTION IV

LEGAL ASPECTS OF
HEALTH AND
MENTAL HEALTH CARE

14

Mental Health Commitment

DEFINITION OF COMMITMENT

Commitment is any state-imposed, compulsory treatment, hospitalization, confinement, or other restriction of liberty premised on mental illness or a mental condition. A commitment can occur with or without court involvement depending on the State and the circumstances in the individual case. The conditions under which an individual may be committed and the process for making decisions regarding commitment are defined by State law.

Many people assume commitment always involves court action and involuntary hospitalization. Neither assumption is true. Individuals may be involuntarily hospitalized under the authority of State statutes without a court hearing and may remain hospitalized for extended periods of time without court review; the commitment is authorized by a mental health professional, not ordered by a judge. Individuals who are committed through court action might not be hospitalized. Instead they might be ordered by the court to participate in an out-patient treatment program, or they might be placed by the court in the custody of relatives or other persons.

The definition of commitment used in this text and the discussion that follows excludes voluntary psychiatric hospitalization or receipt of mental health services. It is, of course, possible for individuals in need of psychiatric care to obtain the care voluntarily, and it is desirable for them to do so. But voluntary receipt of services raises few legal questions and results, at least in theory, in no unwanted restrictions of an individual's rights. It should be noted, however, that some hospitalizations which are called "voluntary" are, in fact, only agreed to under threat of commitment. Moreover, sometimes voluntary hospitalizations turn into commitments when a voluntary patient seeks to be released. Some States have statutes which are designed to minimize these problems.

LEGAL AUTHORITY FOR COMMITMENT

The authority for commitment derives both from the doctrine of *parens patriae* and from the police power of the state. According to the doctrine of *parens patriae*, the state has the responsibility to care for persons who cannot care for themselves. It therefore can require persons who might harm themselves or who are in need of psychiatric treatment to submit to treatment. The state also has the responsibility to protect the public. It does so by confining under the authority of its police power a person who, because of a mental condition, has harmed or is likely to harm another person.

STANDARDS FOR COMMITMENT

The standards used to determine who is subject to commitment are found in State statutes. The language differs considerably from State to State. Generally, however, a person may be committed only if he or she is mentally ill and a danger to others, a danger to self, or in need of psychiatric treatment. Two conditions must be met: mental illness and a consequence of the mental illness. It is not sufficient to be mentally ill nor is it sufficient to be dangerous or in need of treatment.

The definitions of the terms typically found in the statutes, like "mental illness," "dangerous," or "in need of treatment," are usually not included in the statutes or are very general. In practice, therefore, the definitions are provided by mental health professionals. Given the vague definitions, it may be possible to commit persons who are not mentally ill as the term is commonly understood but who are mentally retarded or developmentally disabled. Commitment statutes, however, are generally not used in such cases. Instead, such individuals may be found incompetent and have a guardian appointed for them. The guardians may, in turn, "voluntarily" admit them to facilities either for the mentally ill or for the mentally retarded, with or without specific court authority. This procedure will be discussed further in Chapter 15. Alternatively, mentally retarded or developmentally disabled adults may have been placed in institutions by their parents when they were minors. They may remain in the institutions when they become adults without court review or with only minimal review.

Some States do specifically define conditions such as mental retardation or developmental disability in their commitment statutes. Usually these States have special commitment procedures for those who are mentally disabled but not mentally ill which differ from those for the mentally ill in several respects. Primarily, emergency commitment procedures may not be used, and commitment orders may be for extended periods or permanent. Further, hearings may be provided only upon request rather than automatically and there may be no automatic reviews of commitment orders.

In the landmark case of *O'Connor v. Donaldson*, 422 U.S. 563 (1975), the Supreme Court considered a substantive due process challenge to the fifteen-year involuntary hospitalization of a man, Kenneth Donaldson, who was committed for "care, maintenance, and treatment" after having been found by a court on a petition of his father to be suffering from "paranoid schizophrenia." Despite Donaldson's many re-

quests to be released over the years, the hospital staff refused to release him although it had the power to do so. He was finally released after filing suit. Because he sought damages for his alleged unconstitutional confinement, Donaldson continued with his suit and a four-day jury trial was held. As the Court stated:

> "The testimony at the trial demonstrated, without contradiction, that Donaldson had posed no danger to others during his long confinement, or indeed at any point in his life. There was no evidence that Donaldson had ever been suicidal or been thought likely to inflict injury upon himself. . . . Donaldson could have earned his own living outside the hospital. He had done so for some 14 years before his commitment, and immediately upon his release he secured a responsible job . . . Furthermore, Donaldson's frequent requests for release had been supported by responsible persons willing to provide him any care he might need on release.

> "The evidence showed that Donaldson's confinement was a simple regime of enforced custodial care, not a program designed to alleviate or cure his supposed illness. O'Connor [the hospital superintendent] described Donaldson's treatment as 'milieu therapy.' But witnesses from the hospital staff conceded that 'milieu therapy' . . . was a euphemism for confinement in the 'milieu' of a mental hospital. For substantial periods, Donaldson was simply kept in a large room that housed 60 patients, many of whom were under criminal commitment."

At the conclusion of the trial, the jury "found that Donaldson was neither dangerous to himself nor dangerous to others, and also found that, if mentally ill, Donaldson had not received treatment," and awarded him damages for the denial of his constitutional right to freedom. The Supreme Court agreed that Donaldson had been unconstitutionally confined. It stated:

"A finding of 'mental illness' alone cannot justify a State's locking a person up against his will and keeping him indefinitely in simple custodial confinement. Assuming that that term can be given a reasonably precise content and that the 'mentally ill' can be identified with reasonable accuracy, there is still no constitutional basis for confining such persons involuntarily if they are dangerous to no one and can live safely in freedom.

"May the State confine the mentally ill merely to ensure them a living standard superior to that they enjoy in the private community? That the State has a proper interest in providing care and assistance to the unfortunate goes without saying. But the mere presence of mental illness does not disqualify a person from preferring his home to the comforts of an institution. Moreover, while the State may arguably confine a person to save him from harm, incarceration is rarely if ever a necessary condition for raising the living standards of those capable of surviving safely in freedom, on their own or with the help of family or friends.

"May the State fence in the harmless mentally ill solely to save its citizens from exposure to those whose ways are different? One might as well ask if the State, to avoid public unease, could incarcerate all who are physically unattractive or socially eccentric. Mere public intolerance or animosity cannot constitutionally justify the deprivation of a person's physical liberty.

"In short, a State cannot constitutionally confine without more a nondangerous individual who is capable of surviving safely in freedom by himself or with the help of willing and responsible family members or friends."

The phrase "without more" has been difficult to interpret, and the Court's statement that, since the jury found that Donaldson received no treatment, "there is no reason now to decide whether . . . the State may compulsorily confine a non-dangerous mentally ill individual for the purpose of treatment" specifically left open the constitutionality of committing a person for treatment. Nevertheless, *O'Connor* has led to the view that commitment is allowed only when there is clear evidence that an individual is a danger to self or others. This, in turn, has led to questions concerning the ability of mental health practitioners to predict dangerousness.

Questions also have arisen as to the vagueness of the terms in many commitment statutes. Because *O'Connor* made clear that commitments implicate 14th Amendment liberties, standards in commitment statutes should be narrowly drawn and not leave a great deal to officials' (or mental health professionals') discretion.

There are some who believe that the States have gone too far in following *O'Connor* and restricting the standards for commitment, pointing to the number of people who are mentally ill and homeless. However, others point out that homelessness among persons who are mentally ill is more a reflection of the failure of States to develop comprehensive community based service systems than an indication that grounds for commitment have become too narrow. To attribute homelessness to the inability to commit under existing standards, they assert, simply obscures the fact that services in the community do not exist.

THE COMMITMENT PROCESS FOR MENTALLY ILL ADULTS

Most States provide for at least two types of involuntary commitments: (1) emergency commitments and (2) commitments by court order. With an emergency commitment, an individual is involuntarily hospitalized pending a court hearing. Anyone may initiate the commitment but usually a psychiatrist, another sort of mental health professional or a physician must certify the need for an emergency commitment. The commitment is authorized on the basis of a professional judgment that hospitalization is required immediately.

The emergency commitment usually must be followed immediately or in a specified brief period of time by the filing of a petition and other documentation concerning the need for commitment with a court. After the filing of the petition, the court will hold a hearing within a time period specified by law to determine whether a commitment by court order is justified. In other words, the emergency commitment is followed by a commitment by court order or by a discharge.

Because, with an emergency commitment, a person may be deprived of freedom merely on the basis of someone's judgment that the person should be committed, due process would seem to mandate an immediate judicial screening of the commitment or some sort of preliminary hearing. Many courts have so held, and many States by statute require such hearings within 24 to 72 hours of an emergency commitment. Other States have no requirement of a preliminary hearing, but require a full examination by a psychiatrist, who did not prepare the certification of the need for emergency hospitalization, within 24 to 72 hours of admission, and the concurrence of this psychiatrist on the need for an emergency commitment to justify continued hospitalization. Typically, such States also require a full hearing within a short time of the initial commitment, ranging from 5 to 14 days.

While the statutes generally provide for commitments by court order which are not preceded by emergency commitments and hospitalization, such commitments seldom occur. Given the requirement in most States

that in order to be committed there must be imminent danger of serious harm if one is not committed, almost all court ordered commitments follow emergency hospitalization. Court ordered commitments without prior hospitalization, may, however, be used for the mentally disabled or for *parens patriae* commitments for treatment.

Whether or not there is an emergency commitment, court action is initiated by the filing of a petition. The petition typically contains a statement of facts about the person alleged to be in need of commitment, that is, the respondent, justifying the need for commitment. The specific contents of the petition are governed by statute. In many States, the petition is a court form which is simply completed in handwriting. Such form petitions are often completed by non-lawyers, including social workers.

The petition typically must be accompanied by reports of psychiatric examinations of the respondent. If a petition is not accompanied by the required reports, the judge may order that the respondent be examined before further court action is taken or may dismiss a case. The reports accompanying a petition or submitted after a petition is filed are typically called "**certifications**" or "**affidavits**." Their contents are often prescribed by statute. Generally they must include a detailed description of the respondent's behavior which suggests that commitment is required. Sometimes they are made on a court form. While they usually must be completed by a psychiatrist or a medical doctor, social workers are often involved in gathering the information that is reported and in some States may be authorized to make certifications themselves.

Commitment hearings

The sections that follow may suggest to you that there are always formal and lengthy hearings for court commitments. If you expect this, you will be surprised. In most cases, the respondent is already hospitalized through an emergency commitment, and mental health professionals and the respondent's family members all agree that the respondent is in need of commitment. No witnesses may appear for the respondent and he or she may be so disabled as to be unable to testify or to play any role in the hearing. Thus, the hearing is often perfunctory and merely a means to assure that the respondent receives continued care. In addition, many State statutes authorize holding hearings at the mental health facility where the respondent is being held. Even if there is a courtroom in the facility, this courtroom is probably a far less formal setting than a normal courtroom. Moreover, in many cases there will not even be a hearing. Even though many respondents object to being committed, they may not formally contest petitions. That is, like criminal defendants who plead guilty, and waive their rights to trials, respondents in commitments may waive their right to a hearing.

A private party usually may prepare and file a petition for a commitment and may have a private lawyer to represent his or her interests at the hearing, but typically a public attorney, such as the prosecutor, will prepare and file a commitment petition, perhaps with the signature of an initiating relative or other private party, and will present the case as the representative of the State.

Any testimony that is heard in court focuses on information contained in the petition and the reports of psychiatric examinations. While the testimony is usually that of professionals, the friends, relatives, co-workers, and neighbors of the respondent—indeed, anyone who knows the respondent or has witnessed incidents involving the respondent, including law enforcement officers—may be called to testify about the respondent's behavior or particular incidents involving the respondent. Those who are called to testify are subject to both direct and cross examination and must expect to justify and document any statements made in written documents they have filed with the court. Usually, unless the respondent waives his or her right to a hearing, the respondent cannot be committed merely on the basis of written reports; at least one mental health professional who has examined the respondent must testify.

Possible outcomes of hearings

The judge or the jury, if there is one, after evaluating the evidence presented at the hearing, determines whether the respondent meets the standards for commitment. If the respondent meets the standards, the judge will determine the proper disposition of the matter. The judge, as has been noted, may not necessarily commit the respondent to an institution just because he or she has been found to meet the standards for commitment. In some States, the commitment decision is made by special agencies to whom the judge commits the respondent. In some States, the judge might, instead of committing the respondent to an institution, order another disposition, like requiring the respondent to participate in out-patient treatment or placing the respondent in the custody of a responsible relative. When judges make the commitment decision, they typically rely on information provided by qualified professionals, including social workers, concerning appropriate settings and treatment alternatives.

Several federal district courts and State courts have accepted the application of the least restrictive alternative doctrine to mental health commitments. This doctrine requires that courts consider less restrictive alternatives to institutionalization and order institutionalization only when no other alternatives are available or appropriate. The rationale for the application of this doctrine and the requirement that alternatives to involuntary hospitalization be considered were articulated well in *Lessard v. Schmidt*, 349 F. Supp. 1078 (E.D. Wisc. 1972), in which the court stated:

"Even if [government intervention is justified] a court should order full-time involuntary hospitalization only as a last resort. A basic concept of American justice is the principle [as stated by the Supreme Court] that 'even though the governmental purpose be legitimate and substantial, that purpose cannot be pursued by means that broadly stifle fundamental personal liberties when the end can be more narrowly achieved. The breadth of legislative abridgement must be viewed in the light of less drastic means for achieving the same basic purpose' Perhaps the most basic and fundamental right is the right to be free from unwanted restraint. It seems clear, then, that persons suffering from the condition of being mentally ill, but who are not alleged to have committed any crime, cannot be totally deprived of their liberty if there are less drastic means for achieving the same basic goal. We believe that the person recommending full-time hospitalization must bear the burden of proving: (1) what alternatives are available; (2) what alternatives were investigated; and (3) why the investigated alternatives were not deemed suitable. These alternatives include . . . out-patient treatment, day treatment in a hospital, night treatment in a hospital, placement in the custody of a friend or relative, placement in a nursing home, referral to a community mental health clinic, and home health aide services."[1]

---

1. It should be noted that although *Lessard* was vacated on technical grounds by the Supreme Court and, as a district court opinion, is of little value as precedent, it has been widely cited and followed.

Of greater significance than court application of the least restrictive alternative doctrine to commitment is that many States statutorily require that less restrictive alternatives to institutionalization be explored and considered. Commitment to an institution is only authorized if there is no feasible alternative. For example, Michigan requires by statute that if a person is found to meet the standards for commitment, the judge must consider a report, usually prepared by a social worker at the community mental health center, on alternative treatment plans and may only order commitment to an institution if there is no alternative treatment plan available. Mich. Comp. Laws § 330.1425.

Procedural safeguards

Whether a commitment involves institutionalization or a less restrictive alternative, a person who is committed loses liberty. He or she may also lose the rights to privacy and of freedom of speech and association. Thus, respondents are entitled to due process in commitment proceedings. The extent of the procedural protection due is not clear, however. Because the Supreme Court has not considered the impact of the due process clause on civil commitment procedures except regarding the standard of proof, the protection that is provided is dependent on State statute and lower court decisions. Further, because there is no complete constitutional answer to the question of the extent of the protection, the protection afforded varies from State to State.

Several essential elements of procedural due process which have been mandated by the courts or are set forth in statutes are considered below.

Notice. Although notice is considered a fundamental element of due process, some

State commitment statutes either do not require notice or require the provision of only minimal amounts of information to the respondent. This policy is based on the belief that the commitment procedure is designed to help a person who is mentally ill and that the service of legal papers might only confuse and distress the person. In accordance with this policy, the statutes in some States allow notice to be waived if there is a showing that it would distress the person. In most States, however, notice is required at several points in the commitment process, including at the time of an emergency involuntary hospitalization and in advance of any court hearings. This notice must be given sufficiently in advance to allow the respondent time to seek assistance and prepare any response.

The elements of notice differ from State to State. They typically include a statement of the date, time and place of any hearing, the alleged facts supporting commitment, the respondent's rights before and at the hearing, including any right to counsel, the names of examining physicians and all other persons who might testify in favor of commitment, and a summary of their proposed testimony. Much of this information may be provided by giving the respondent a copy of the petition and any accompanying certificates.

Any notice typically must be given personally to respondents and may additionally have to be provided to respondents' attorneys, guardians, or guardian *ad litems*, any responsible relatives they might have, and, if they are currently in mental health facilities, the directors of the facilities. Specific requirements differ from State to State.

Simply providing a written copy of information concerning a hearing or orally informing a person upon admission to a facility of his or her rights to a hearing may not be effective notice. Notice is effective only if it is given in language understandable to the recipient and if it is given when the recipient is not overly agitated, confused, or medicated. Social workers, because of their interaction with patients following admission, are in a position to assure that not only the respondent but also others who might assist the respondent receive effective notice.

Presence at the hearing. The respondent generally has the right to be present at the hearing. However, the statutes in some States allow the court to excuse the respondent's presence if it might be detrimental to the respondent's health.

A question which has not been resolved is whether the right to be present includes the right to be present without being medicated. California handles this in the case of hearings to review the need for continuing commitment by requiring that the hearing officer be informed if the patient has taken psychotropic drugs within 24 hours and told of their possible effects. Michigan only allows the person to be medicated within 24 hours of the hearing if he or she consents in writing to such medication. The court ruled in *Lessard v. Schmidt, supra,* that persons subject to commitment must be informed of their right to refuse medication which renders them unable to adequately prepare a defense.

Appointed counsel. Most States provide a right to counsel for respondents in commitment proceedings. Some States additionally or alternatively provide a guardian *ad litem.* Counsel is typically provided either by the office which represents indigent criminal defendants or by an independent State agency. It is important to note, however, that no Supreme Court opinion has established a constitutional right to counsel in commitment hearings.

Trial by jury. The Supreme Court has not held that a respondent in a commitment hearing is entitled to a jury trial, but many States accord a jury trial to a respondent on demand. The jury may have less than twelve members, and its verdict need not be unanimous, however. Moreover, in practice, requests for a jury trial are extremely rare.

Clear and convincing evidence. The Supreme Court established clear and convincing evidence as the minimum standard of proof in civil commitment proceedings in *Addington v. Texas*, 441 U.S. 418 (1979). As can be seen in the following excerpt from *Addington*, in requiring more than the mere preponderance of the evidence standard then used in Texas, the Court balanced the individual's interest in not being involuntarily confined against the state's interest in confining the individual.

> "In considering what standard should govern in a civil commitment proceeding, we must assess both the extent of the individual's interest in not being involuntarily confined indefinitely and the state's interest in committing the emotionally disturbed under a particular standard of proof. Moreover, we must be mindful that the function of legal process is to minimize the risk of erroneous decisions.

> "This Court repeatedly has recognized that civil commitment for any purpose constitutes a significant deprivation of liberty that requires due process protection. Moreover, it is indisputable that involuntary commitment to a mental hospital after a finding of probable dangerousness to self or others can engender adverse social consequences to the individual. Whether we label this phenomena 'stigma' or choose to call it something else is less important than that we recognize that it can occur and that it can have a very significant impact on the individual.

> "The state has a legitimate interest under its *parens patriae* powers in providing care to its citizens who are unable because of emotional disorders to care for themselves; the state also has authority under its police power to protect the community from the dangerous tendencies of some who are mentally ill. Under the Texas Mental Health Code, however, the State has no interest in confining individuals involuntarily if they are not mentally ill or if they do not pose some danger to themselves or others. Since the preponderance standard creates the risk of increasing the number of individuals erroneously committed, it is at least unclear to what extent, if any, the state's interests are furthered by using a preponderance standard in such commitment proceedings.

> "At one time or another every person exhibits some abnormal behavior which might be perceived by some as symptomatic of a mental or emotional disorder, but which is in fact within a range of conduct that is generally acceptable. Obviously, such behavior is no basis for compelled treatment and surely none for confinement. However, there is the possible risk that a factfinder might decide to commit an individual based solely on a few isolated instances of unusual conduct. **Loss of liberty calls for a showing that the individual suffers from something more serious than is demonstrated by idiosyncratic behavior. Increasing the burden of proof is one way to impress the factfinder with the importance of the decision and thereby perhaps to reduce the chances that inappropriate commitments will be ordered.**

> "The individual should not be asked to share equally with society the risk of error when the possible injury to the individual is significantly greater than any possible harm to the state. **We conclude that the individual's interest in the outcome of a civil commitment proceeding is of such weight and gravity that due process requires the state to justify confinement by proof more substantial than a mere preponderance of the evidence.**"

The Court was not willing to mandate the

"beyond a reasonable doubt" standard of proof used in criminal cases. It stated:

"There are significant reasons why different standards of proof are called for in civil commitment proceedings as opposed to criminal prosecutions. In a civil commitment state power is not exercised in a punitive sense. In addition, the 'beyond a reasonable doubt' standard historically has been reserved for criminal cases. This unique standard of proof, not prescribed or defined in the Constitution, is regarded as a critical part of the 'moral force of the criminal law,' and we should hesitate to apply it too broadly or casually in noncriminal cases.

"The heavy standard applied in criminal cases manifests our concern that the risk of error to the individual must be minimized even at the risk that some who are guilty might go free. The full force of that idea does not apply to a civil commitment. It may be true that an erroneous commitment is sometimes as undesirable as an erroneous conviction. However, even though an erroneous confinement should be avoided in the first instance, the layers of professional review and observation of the patient's condition, and the concern of family and friends generally will provide continuous opportunities for an erroneous commitment to be corrected. Moreover, it is not true that the release of a genuinely mentally ill person is no worse for the individual than the failure to convict the guilty. One who is suffering from a debilitating mental illness and in need of treatment is neither wholly at liberty nor free of stigma. It cannot be said, therefore, that it is much better for a mentally ill person to 'go free' than for a mentally normal person to be committed.

"Finally, the initial inquiry in a civil commitment proceeding is very different from the central issue in either a delinquency proceeding or a criminal prosecution. In the latter cases the basic issue is a straightforward factual question—did the accused commit the act alleged? There may be factual issues to resolve in a commitment proceeding, but the factual aspects represent only the beginning of the inquiry. Whether the individual is mentally ill and dangerous to either himself or others and is in need of confined therapy turns on the meaning of the facts which must be interpreted by expert psychiatrists and psychologists. Given the lack of certainty and the fallibility of psychiatric diagnosis, there is a serious question as to whether a state could ever prove beyond a reasonable doubt that an individual is both mentally ill and likely to be dangerous.

"The subtleties and nuances of psychiatric diagnosis render certainties virtually beyond reach in most situations. The reasonable doubt standard of criminal law functions in its realm because there the standard is addressed to specific, knowable facts. Psychiatric diagnosis, in contrast, is to a large extent based on medical 'impressions' drawn from subjective analysis and filtered through the experience of the diagnostician. This process often makes it very difficult for the expert physician to offer definite conclusions about any particular patient. Within the medical discipline, the traditional standard for 'factfinding' is a 'reasonable medical certainty.' If a trained psychiatrist has difficulty with the categorical 'beyond a reasonable doubt' standard, the untrained lay juror—or indeed even a trained judge—who is required to rely upon expert opinion could be forced by the criminal law standard of proof to reject commitment for many patients desperately in need of institutionalized psychiatric care. Such 'freedom' for a mentally ill person would be purchased at a high price.

"That some states have chosen—either legislatively or judicially—to adopt the criminal law standard gives no assurance that the more stringent standard of proof is needed or is even adaptable to the needs of all states. The essence of federalism is that states must be free to develop a variety of solutions to problems and not be forced into a common, uniform mold. As the substantive standards for civil commitment may vary from state to state, procedures must be allowed to vary so long as they meet the constitutional minimum. We conclude that it is unnecessary to require states to apply the strict, criminal standard."

The Court, thus, turned to "a middle level of burden of proof that strikes a fair balance between the rights of the individual and the legitimate concerns of the state," noting that 25 states used this standard of proof, usually defined as "clear and convincing evidence. However, as you can see from the opinion in *Addington*, there is nothing there that prevents States from adopting a higher standard than clear and convincing evidence, and many States have done so.

Review of the need for commitment

The statutes typically provide that the need for continuing commitment be periodically reviewed by the court. This occurs by statutorily limiting the length of time for which a person can be committed or by requiring review of commitment orders after a specified period of time. Moreover, persons who have been committed can generally request court reviews of their commitments at any point. Whether the court must consider each request for review and when a hearing must be given on the committed person's request depends on State law.

THE COMMITMENT PROCESS FOR MINORS

As we saw in the section of the text on juvenile law, minors often may not make crucial legal decisions for themselves. Their parents and legally appointed guardians usually make such decisions for them, including the decision to be admitted to a psychiatric facility. Thus, a child's admission to a mental hospital by his or her parents or guardians, even over the child's vigorous objection, may be considered a "voluntary" admission, not a commitment.

In *Parham v. J. R.*, 442 U.S. 534 (1979), the Supreme Court held that parents may commit their children for psychiatric care with only minimal procedural protection. In *Parham*, J. R. was one of two minors who brought a class action suit against various officials in the Georgia mental health system. The minors alleged that the statutes establishing commitment procedures for children under age 18 violated due process. Like the statutes in most States, the Georgia statutes permitted a parent or guardian to apply for hospitalization for his or her child. The child could then be admitted by the hospital superintendent for observation. If the superintendent found evidence of mental illness and found that the child was suitable for treatment, the child could be admitted indefinitely, subject to the parent's or guardian's right to request discharge and the superintendent's duty to release a child who had recovered or no longer required hospitalization.

The trial court, after considering extensive evidence and viewing several hospitals, held that the statutes were unconstitutional, enjoined commitments under them, and ordered Georgia to appropriate funds to establish non-hospital facilities so that members of the class could be treated in less restrictive environments. On appeal, in testing the validity of the statutes, the Supreme Court used the test established in *Mathews v. Eldridge*, 424 U. S. 319 (1976). That is, having found a protectible interest, the Court balanced this interest, the risk of error and the value of additional or different procedural safeguards, and the state's interest, including the fiscal and administrative burden that the additional or different procedures would entail. The Court's analysis, which lead it to conclude that the Georgia statutes were constitutional, follows.

"For purposes of this decision, we assume that a child has a protectible interest not only in being free of unnecessary bodily restraints but also in not being labeled erroneously by some persons because of an improper decision by the state hospital superintendent. [It is argued] that the constitutional rights of the child are of such magnitude and the likelihood of parental abuse is so great that the parents' traditional interests in and responsibility for the upbringing of their child must be subordinated at least to the extent of providing a formal adversary hearing prior to a voluntary commitment.

"Our jurisprudence historically has reflected Western civilization concepts of the family as a unit with broad parental authority over minor children. Our cases have consistently followed that course; our constitutional system long ago rejected any notion that a child is 'the mere creature of the State' and, on the contrary, asserted that parents generally 'have the right, coupled with the high duty, to recognize and prepare [their children] for additional obligations.' Surely, this includes a 'high duty' to recognize symptoms of illness and to seek and follow medical advice. The law's concept of the family rests on a presumption that parents possess what a child lacks in maturity, experience, and capacity for judgment required for making life's difficult decisions. More important, historically it has recognized that natural bonds of affection lead parents to act in the best interests of their children.

"As with so many other legal presumptions, experience and reality may rebut what the law accepts as a starting point; the incidence of child neglect and abuse cases attests to this. That some parents 'may at times be acting against the interests of their children' creates a basis for caution, but is hardly a rea-

son to discard wholesale those pages of human experience that teach that parents generally do act in the child's best interests. The statist notion that governmental power should supersede parental authority in all cases because some parents abuse and neglect children is repugnant to American tradition.

"In defining the respective rights and prerogatives of the child and parent in the voluntary commitment setting, we conclude that our precedents permit the parents to retain a substantial, if not the dominant, role in the decision, absent a finding of neglect or abuse, and that the traditional presumption that the parents act in the best interests of their child should apply. We also conclude, however, that the child's rights and the nature of the commitment decision are such that parents cannot always have absolute and unreviewable discretion to decide whether to have a child institutionalized. They, of course, retain plenary authority to seek such care for their children, subject to a physician's independent examination and medical judgment.

"The State obviously has a significant interest in confining the use of its costly mental health facilities to cases of genuine need. The Georgia program seeks first to determine whether the patient seeking admission has an illness that calls for inpatient treatment. To accomplish this purpose, the State has charged the superintendents of each regional hospital with the responsibility for determining, before authorizing an admission, whether a prospective patient is mentally ill and whether the patient will likely benefit from hospital care. In addition, the State has imposed a continuing duty on hospital superintendents to release any patient who has recovered to the point where hospitalization is no longer needed.

"The State in performing its voluntarily assumed mission also has a significant interest in not imposing unnecessary procedural obstacles that may discourage the mentally ill or their families from seeking needed psychiatric assistance. The *parens patriae* interest in helping parents care for the mental health of their children cannot be fulfilled if the parents are unwilling to take advantage of the opportunities because the admission process is too onerous, too embarrassing, or too contentious. It is surely not idle to speculate as to how many parents who believe they are acting in good faith would forgo state-provided hospital care if such care is contingent on participation in an adversary proceeding designed to probe their motives and other private family matters in seeking the voluntary admission.

"The State also has a genuine interest in allocating priority to the diagnosis and treatment of patients . . . rather than to time-consuming procedur[es]. One factor that must be considered is the utilization of the time of psychiatrists, psychologists, and other behavioral specialists in preparing for and participating in hearings rather than performing the task for which their special training has fitted them. One consequence of increasing the procedures the state must provide prior to a child's voluntary admission will be that mental health professionals will be diverted even more from the treatment of patients in order to travel to and participate in—and wait for—what could be hundreds—or even thousands—of hearings each year. Obviously the cost of these procedures would come from the public moneys the legislature intended for mental health care.

"We now turn to consideration of what process protects adequately the child's constitutional rights by reducing risks of error without unduly trenching on traditional parental authority and without undercutting 'efforts to further the legitimate interests of both the state and the patient that are served by' voluntary commitments. We conclude that the risk of error inherent in the parental decision to have a child institutionalized for mental health care is sufficiently great that some kind of inquiry should be made by a 'neutral factfinder' to determine whether the statutory requirements for admission are satisfied.

"That inquiry must carefully probe the child's background using all available sources, including, but not limited to, parents, schools, and other social agencies. Of course, the review must also include an interview with the child. It is necessary that the decisionmaker have the authority to refuse to admit any child who does not satisfy the medical standards for admission. Finally, it is necessary that the child's continuing need for commitment be reviewed periodically by a similarly independent procedure.

"We are satisfied that such procedures will protect the child from an erroneous admission decision in a way that neither unduly burdens the states nor inhibits parental decisions to seek state help.

"Due process has never been thought to require that the neutral and detached trier of fact be law trained or a judicial or administrative officer. Surely, this is the case as to medical decisions, for 'neither judges nor administrative hearing officers are better qualified than psychiatrists to render psychiatric judgments.' Thus, a staff physician will suffice, so long as he or she is free to evaluate independently the child's mental and emotional condition and need for treatment.

"It is not necessary that the deciding physician conduct a formal or quasi-formal hearing. A state is free to require such a hearing, but due process is not violated by use of informal traditional medical investigative techniques. Since well-established medical procedures already exist, we do not undertake to outline with specificity precisely what this investigation must involve. The mode and procedure of medical diagnostic procedures is not the business of judges. What is best for a child is an individual medical decision that must be left to the judgment of physicians in each case. We do no more than emphasize that the decision should represent an independent judgment of what the child requires and that all sources of information that are traditionally relied on by physicians and behavioral specialists should be consulted.

"Although we acknowledge the fallibility of medical and psychiatric diagnosis, . . . we do not accept the notion that the shortcomings of specialists can always be avoided by shifting the decision from a trained specialist using the traditional tools of medical science to an untrained judge or administrative hearing officer after a judicial-type hearing. Even after a hearing, the nonspecialist decisionmaker must make a medical-psychiatric decision. Common human experience and scholarly opinions suggest that the supposed protections of an adversary proceeding to determine the appropriateness of medical decisions for the commitment and treatment of mental and emotional illness may well be more illusory than real.

"By expressing some confidence in the medical decisionmaking process, we are by no means suggesting it is error free. [But] that there may be risks of error in the process affords no rational predicate for holding unconstitutional an entire statutory and administrative scheme that is generally followed in more than 30 states. **In general, we are satisfied that an independent medical decisionmaking process, which includes the thorough psychiatric investigation described earlier, followed by additional periodic review of a child's condition, will protect children who should not be admitted; we do not believe the risks of error in that process would be significantly reduced by a more formal, judicial-type hearing.**"

The Court went on to conclude that different procedures are not required when an agency requests admission for one of its minor wards, such as the other named plaintiff in the case. The Court concluded that Georgia's procedures were "reasonable and consistent with constitutional guarantees" when a guardian commits a ward as much as when a parent commits a child.

It should be noted that the fact that in *Parham* the Supreme Court approved a procedure offering few procedural protections for minors does not mean that a State may not offer greater procedural protections. As with the standard of proof in *Addington*, the Supreme Court in *Parham* only set forth the minimum required. Thus, in Washington, for example, minors are entitled to a full judicial hearing before they can be admitted to mental hospitals over their objections. Wash. Rev. Code § 71.05.240.

It should also be noted that *Parham* applies to children whose parents or guardians seek to admit them to state hospitals, not private psychiatric facilities. While the decision might be interpreted to apply to all psychiatric admissions, the Court paid particular attention to the use of public facilities. Thus, protection of minors admitted to private facilities may be left entirely to State law with no constitutional restrictions.

THE INTERFACE OF CRIMINAL PROSECUTION AND COMMITMENT

A problem that has long concerned the courts is what should happen to persons who are accused of committing a crime and who are either determined to be unfit to stand trial or who are found not guilty by reason of insanity. Holding those who are only accused of committing a crime and who, under the law, are presumed to be innocent in secure mental institutions for an indefinite or extended period of time because they are incompetent to stand trial seems clearly contrary to our system of justice. Holding those who have been found not guilty by reason of insanity in secure mental institutions for an indefinite period of time that may extend beyond the length of the sentence that would have been imposed following conviction also seems contrary to fundamental constitutional principles. Both types of detention, moreover, seem to violate the mentally ill criminal's right to equal protection. Because they are mentally ill, they may be detained longer than persons who committed the same crimes but who are not mentally ill.

These questions were addressed by the Supreme Court in several cases of which two, *Jackson v. Indiana*, 406 U.S. 715 (1972), and *Jones v. United States*, 463 U.S. 364 (1983), are of particular significance. The Court held in *Jackson* that indefinite commitment of a criminal defendant solely on account of his unfitness to stand trial violates due process. The Court further held that such persons cannot be held more than a reasonable period of time necessary to determine whether they will regain competence in the foreseeable future. If it is determined that they will not attain competency, the State must institute civil commitment proceedings or release them. Moreover, the Court held that to impose more lenient standards for commitment of those found unfit to stand trial than those generally applicable and more strict standards for release of such persons violated equal protection. Somewhat in contrast, the Court ruled in *Jones* that to confine a person found not guilty by reason of insanity for a longer period than he or she would have been incarcerated if convicted did not violate due process or equal protection guarantees, and that employing procedures for commitment of persons found not guilty by reason of insanity that were different from and had less procedural protections than those used for other civil commitments was constitutional.

It should be emphasized that even if the commitment procedures and standards for those found not guilty by reason of insanity or unfit to stand trial differ from those used in ordinary civil commitments, the commitments are civil, not criminal, proceedings. If a criminal defendant is found not guilty by reason of insanity, he or she is no longer subject to the jurisdiction of the criminal court for the crime charged and cannot be "sentenced" for this crime; the defendant may only be held if he or she is civilly committed. If a criminal defendant is found unfit to stand trial, the criminal court may retain jurisdiction over him or her for the crime charged, but criminal proceedings must be suspended, and the defendant may be held longer than the reasonable period necessary to determine when and if he or she will regain competency only if he or she is civilly committed.

INVOLVEMENT OF SOCIAL WORKERS IN COMMITMENT

Social workers are often involved in commitment proceedings as petitioners or as advocates for those who are subject to commitment. As a petitioner, the social worker is asking the court to commit a person. As an advocate, the social worker is questioning the validity of committing a person.

Social workers are also often involved in providing information to the court. The information might be related to the need for commitment or to the services that should be provided if the person is committed. The statutes in many States require the court to consider not only psychiatric diagnoses but also measures of adaptive behavior in making commitments. Social workers may make these assessments and provide reports of their evaluation to the courts. Social workers also routinely present treatment plans to courts which must decide the appropriate treatment for those found subject to commitment or which must determine the least restrictive alternative for the respondent. Further, social workers may prepare the reports on the treatment provided to those who have been committed for courts which are conducting reviews of the commitments.

Social workers occasionally serve as administrative hearing officers or as qualified examiners in some jurisdictions. Hearing officers administratively review the validity of continuing commitment, and qualified examiners complete psychiatric examinations of persons alleged to be in need of commitment.

The most important role played by social workers in commitment, however, may be that of interpreter. Commitment is a complicated proceeding, but all too often the professionals that are involved incorrectly assume that it is understood by the patient and by his or her family. Social workers can help by explaining the proceeding, the possible outcomes of the proceeding, and the alternatives to the proceeding. In doing so, the social worker can make the proceeding less threatening and perhaps can help the patient and the family find another way to obtain needed services. The social worker can also interpret the desires of the person who may be subject to commitment proceedings to his or her family or friends. Often the social worker can develop a mutually agreeable plan which will make commitment proceedings unnecessary.

15

Competency and Guardianship of Disabled Adults

There are times when adults are unable to make sound decisions or exercise basic rights because of mental or physical disabilities. The law may define them as legally **incompetent**. When they are so defined, a court appoints someone to make certain or all decisions for them. The name given to the person who is appointed varies. The most common name is "**guardian**," which is the term that will be used in this text. Regardless of the terminology, the state intervenes in such instances under the *parens patriae* authority. That is, it intervenes in order to protect the disabled person. The procedures and specific bases for intervention are governed by State statutes and vary from State to State.

In order to put the discussion that follows in context, it is useful to keep in mind the reality of guardianship. You are probably familiar with reports in the press of individuals who believe a member of their family is squandering a large estate and ask a court to find the family member incompetent. While such cases are noteworthy and perhaps illustrate the abuse of guardianship, they are not common. In the vast majority of cases, the person who is alleged to be incompetent is either developmentally disabled or seriously mentally ill, has an incapacitating condition, such as Alzheimer's disease or brain damage resulting from an accident, or is extremely elderly. The person who petitions for guardianship is typically a family member, but the family member is not trying to protect a large estate. Instead, the family member is doing what is necessary to protect and provide for the care of the disabled person.

Although guardianship proceedings, in theory and, in most cases, in fact, are initiated to protect the disabled person, it is important to recognize that a finding of incompetence and the appointment of a guardian deprive the disabled person of basic rights and freedoms. In addition, guardianship can impose a heavy responsibility on the guardian who stands in relation to the disabled person as a parent stands to his or her child. Therefore, guardianship is not an action that should be undertaken lightly. A number of alternatives should be considered before a petition is filed requesting appointment of a guardian.

Guardianship involves two procedures: 1) finding a disabled person incompetent as defined in the law; and 2) appointing a guardian. Every State has a statutory process by which a person may be declared incompetent and a guardian appointed. The terminology used in the guardianship statutes; the standards used to determine when someone is incompetent and a guardian may or must be appointed; the procedures used to determine incompetency and appoint a guardian; the procedural protections and rights afforded to the alleged incompetent; the authority, powers, and responsibilities of the guardian; and the rights lost by the incompetent differ from State to State.

The difference between jurisdictions is more marked in this area of the law than in many of the other areas of law we have considered because there are very few constitutional cases in this area and no authoritative Supreme Court decisions establishing basic substantive or procedural rights of those alleged to be or determined to be incompetent. Unlike in commitment law, where the Supreme Court has established some standards for commitment (*i.e.*, danger to self or others) and some minimum procedural safeguards (e.g., right to proof by clear and convincing evidence), the Supreme Court has established no minimum standards or safeguards in guardianship law. Moreover, most of the scattered lower court decisions have been resolved against the incompetent. Despite the loss of rights an incompetent may endure, the courts have generally not seen the determination of incompetence and the imposition of a guardian as a deprivation warranting due process protection.

Legislatures have, however, begun to change guardianship laws to protect the rights of incompetents and to provide needed assistance to them without depriving them unnecessarily of the right of self-determination and of individual autonomy. Moreover, legislatures, courts, and social agencies have developed several alternatives to guardianship which protect individuals without the loss of freedom entailed in guardianship. We shall examine these alternatives in this chapter, but before examining them, it is necessary to understand both the concept of competence and the process of guardianship.

COMPETENCY

In the United States, as we have seen, minors are presumed to be legally incompetent and are not generally entitled to make legal decisions for themselves. Ordinarily, a minor's parent or parents will act as his or her guardian and will make all or most decisions for the minor. If a minor has no living parent or no parent capable of making sound decisions for him or her, a court will appoint an adult to serve as the minor's guardian.

By way of contrast, adults in the United States are presumed to be legally competent and are entitled to make all decisions for themselves. Only if they are determined to be incompetent by a court can they be deprived of the right to make their own decisions and can a guardian be appointed to make decisions for them. The determination of incompetence can only be made if the presumption of competence is overcome. In other words, an adult must be proven to be incompetent. An adult need not establish his or her own competence; it is assumed.

A definition of incompetence is found in the statutes in all the States. The definition varies somewhat, but the following definition from Florida is typical.

> "An 'incompetent' is a person who, because of minority, mental illness, mental retardation, senility, excessive use of drugs or alcohol, or other physical or mental incapacity, is incapable of either managing his property or caring for himself, or both." Fla. Stat. § 744.102.

This definition, like many others, includes both a status and a functional component: a person must have a disability and, because of that disability, be unable to manage property or care for himself or herself. With such a definition, some evidence of impaired social skills and adaptive behavior must be presented in addition to evidence of mental or physical impairment in order to establish incompetency. Such a definition recognizes that one may be mentally ill but competent to make decisions concerning one's life, that one may be developmentally disabled but capable of caring for oneself, or that one may be an alcoholic, but capable of managing one's money.

Because the right of self-determination and the right to control one's own life are considered to be basic in this country, the presumption of competency should not be lightly overcome. It should only be overcome if a person is incapable of making certain or all decisions and it is necessary to have another make the decisions to protect the incapable person. The presumption should not be overcome merely because a person might make unwise decisions or decisions that could cause harm to himself or herself. Adults have a right to be wrong. The state may intervene to protect a person incapable of making a rational decision on a certain matter or any rational decisions under the doctrine of *parens patriae*, but "[t]his is not to say that any personal decision that causes harm or risk, or that is otherwise ill-advised, demonstrates a lack of legal competency warranting state intervention. The law permits us to smoke, to drink, and to overeat; it allows us to make foolish purchases and imprudent investments. . . . In short, the law does not require that one make wise decisions. It requires only that one's ability to make decisions not be so impaired as to substantially threaten one's safety or welfare."[1]

However, the breadth and vagueness of the definition of incompetence in many statutes, as well as the lack of procedural protections in guardianship proceedings, may result in findings of incompetence that are not justified.

Limitations on findings of incompetency

Traditionally people were assumed to be incompetent simply because they had been involuntarily committed for psychiatric care. Many States now recognize that a person may be a danger to oneself or others and thus subject to commitment, but may be quite capable of making sound and mature decisions on a variety of matters. Thus, they have clearly separated commitment and incompetence. For example, a Texas statute provides:

"Court-ordered mental health services or emergency detention . . . or receipt of voluntary mental health services shall not constitute a determination or adjudication of mental incompetency and shall not abridge the person's rights as a citizen or the person's property rights or legal capacity. Mental competency is presumed in the absence of a contrary judicial determination under [the

guardianship law.]" Tex. Mental Health Code, Art. 5547-83.

However, some States continue to, in effect, merge the two decisions. For example, an Indiana statute provides:

"Commitment to a hospital for the insane pursuant to a statute shall be equivalent to a prior adjudication of incompetency." Ind. Code. § 29-1-18-20.

While historically incompetence was an all or none proposition—either a person was competent for all purposes or a person was incompetent for all purposes—many States now require that the decision on competence be related to specific circumstances. Under this approach, for example, a different standard of competency may be used to determine whether an individual can decide where to live than may be used to determine whether an individual can refuse life saving treatment. To give a further example, a person may be determined incompetent to manage a family business but determined to be quite competent to decide where and how to live. This approach recognizes the relativity of competence and the fact that no single test for competency for all purposes can be developed. It requires a court to consider the purposes for which competency is being tested (e.g., money management, consent to medical care, or need for assistance in daily living) and the particular facts and circumstances of each case. Using this approach, a court can, for example, find a person incompetent to manage financial affairs but competent to make decisions about medical care or daily living. It can then appoint a guardian only to manage the disabled person's estate or income. This guardian will not have the authority or responsibility to determine where the disabled person will live. However, it must

---

1. Herr, Arons, & Wallace, *Legal Rights and Mental Health Care* (Lexington, MA: D. C. Heath, 1983), p. 25.

be recognized that the disabled person's decisions regarding living arrangements and life style may be dictated by the financial resources over which he or she has lost control.

Consequences of an incompetency determination

State laws differ on the rights retained or lost by a person found to be incompetent. Generally the person is, like a child, unable to make significant personal decisions. Some rights that the person loses may be transferred to a guardian, like the right to decide where to live or the right to consent to medical or psychiatric treatment, but other rights are simply lost, like the right to vote.

In determining the rights that a person found to be incompetent loses, the constitutional principle of least restrictive alternative (LRA) should come into play. The person should only lose those rights which he or she cannot properly exercise. But few courts have recognized the applicability of LRA in this context. Many legislatures, however, have adopted laws which recognize LRA. Instead of a court making a general determination of incompetency whenever a person is incompetent to make some decisions, thus depriving the person of all rights, and appointing a guardian with full powers over the person, the guardianship laws may provide that a court can or should determine that a person is incompetent only for specific purposes, that it can or should only deprive the person of specific rights, and that it can or should only give the guardian specific powers. In other words, a **limited guardianship** is recognized. For example, Texas law provides for limited guardianship and further provides that:

> "Limited guardianship for incapacitated persons shall be utilized only as necessary to promote and protect the well-being of the in-

dividual, shall be designed to encourage the development of his maximum self-reliance and independence in the individual, and shall be ordered only to the extent necessitated by the individual's actual mental or physical limitations." Texas Probate Code § 130A.

The statute further provides that a person for whom a limited guardian is appointed is not presumed to be incompetent, and "shall retain all legal and civil rights and powers" except those which the court designates "as legal disabilities by virtue of having been specifically granted to the limited guardian."

GUARDIANSHIP

Guardianship can best be understood as the method by which a court protects a person who has been found to be legally incompetent. After a court has found a person to be incompetent for any or all purposes, it must appoint a guardian to act in those areas where the person has been found to be incompetent. If a guardian were not appointed, there would be no one to make legally effective decisions for the incompetent person. Once a guardian is appointed, he or she acts under the authority of the court and must report to the court.

Terminology

There is a distinction between a **guardian of the estate**, who is responsible for decisions relating to property, such as money, income, investments and assets, and a **guardian of the person**, who is responsible for life decisions, such as where an incompetent lives, how he or she lives, or what medical treatment he or she will receive. The guardian of the estate and the guardian of the person may be different people or entities.

Some States use the term "**conservator**" for the guardian of the estate and others use it for the guardian of the person. Some use the term as a substitute for "guardian." Some States use the terms "guardian" and "conservator" interchangeably, but suggest the use of the term "conservator" to avoid the stigma often associated with the term "guardian." Other States use entirely different terms as "**committee**," "**curator**" or "**fiduciary**."

The person over whom a guardianship is imposed is usually called a "**ward**." A person over whom a conservatorship is imposed is sometimes called a "**conservatee**." Sometimes the person is simply called "the incompetent."

The term "**plenary guardian**" is sometimes used to refer to a guardian who is both guardian of the estate and the person. Sometimes it is used to describe a guardian who has full powers over a ward in contrast to a "**limited guardian**" who may only make certain decisions for or exercise limited authority over a ward.

Often when a person is appointed a guardian, he or she is said to have been given "**letters of guardianship**." If a guardianship is terminated, the letters are withdrawn.

The guardian's authority and responsibility

A guardian generally has the same power to make decisions for his or her ward as a parent has to make decisions for his or her child. Like a parent with a child, the guardian must take good care of a ward and act in the ward's best interest, but unlike a parent of a minor child, a guardian of an adult has no responsi-

bility to support a ward. Indeed, a guardian may be paid for his or her services by taking money from the ward's estate.

Consistent with the modern approach towards incompetence discussed earlier, courts may specifically limit the authority of a guardian in the order appointing a guardian. States which recognize the concept of limited guardianship may provide that a guardian only has the powers specifically set forth in the order of appointment. Such States, and some States which do not recognize the concept of limited guardianship, may also have laws which limit the authority of a guardian to do certain things without a court order or express authorization, such as to commit a ward to a mental hospital or to consent to psychosurgery for a ward. These laws may be found in guardianship laws or elsewhere. For example, the Illinois guardianship law provides that no guardian "shall have the power unless specified by court order, to place his ward in a residential facility," while the Illinois law related to mental health commitments provides that a guardian of a person who has been committed may consent to "electro-convulsive therapy, or to any unusual, hazardous or experimental services or psychosurgery" for the ward— but "only with the approval of the court." Ill. Rev. Stat. ch. 110 1/2, par. 11a-14.1; ch. 91 1/2, par. 2-110.

Some courts have held that certain rights are so important that they cannot be lost without specific authority. Thus, because of the importance of the right to procreate and raise a family, a guardian may not be able to consent to the sterilization of a ward or the relinquishment of a ward's parental rights.

Whether a guardian is a plenary or a limited guardian, a guardian of the estate or of the person, guardians must account to the court. That is, guardians must make a report, often called an "**accounting**," to the court annually or at more frequent intervals setting forth what they have done for their wards. Usually the law is more concerned with the ward's estate than the ward's person and detailed financial records, but no reports on personal decisions, are required. Whatever reports are required by courts, however, studies have shown that guardians often fail to make reports and that courts rarely sanction guardians who neglect to make reports or pay much attention to the reports that are received, at least where only small estates are involved.

Who may be appointed as a guardian?

In most States, any legally competent adult may be appointed a guardian of an incompetent. Additionally certain public agencies, private non-profit corporations, private social agencies, or even private profit-making institutions, like banks, may be appointed as a guardian under State law. A conflict of interest may arise if an agency providing residential care for an incompetent is appointed an incompetent's guardian. Thus, some States forbid such an appointment, but others specifically authorize it.

The wishes of the ward are typically considered in making an appointment. A relative or a friend is generally chosen as guardian if at all possible. If no relative or friend is available, a private or public agency may be appointed. While some States simply specify who courts may or should consider, others set forth a hierarchy of potential guardians. For example, Arizona law provides that "any competent person" may be appointed as a guardian and that persons "who are not disqualified have priority for appointment as guardian in the following order:" the incapacitated person's spouse; one of his or her adult children; his or her parent, "including

a person nominated by will or other writing signed by a deceased parent;" any relative "with whom [the incapacitated person] has resided for more than six months prior to the filing of the petition;" or "the nominee of a person who is caring for the incapacitated person or paying benefits to him." Ariz. Rev. Stat. § 14-5311. Such a priority list may serve to prevent disputes between potential guardians.

Some States have special public officials, often called "**public guardians**," whose sole or chief function is to serve as guardians of the person of an indigent or when no friend or family member is willing to serve as guardian. Public guardians are often necessary for indigents because guardians are usually paid for their services by taking money from the ward's estate. People who are indigent by definition have no estates from which payments can be made.

As noted earlier, the guardian of the person and the guardian of the estate may be two different people or entities. It is common, for example, for a family member to be appointed guardian of the person and a trust department of a bank or an attorney to be appointed guardian of the estate when an estate is large. Similarly, it is not unusual for a person of limited mental capacity to not require a guardian of the person but to require a guardian of the estate. In either of these cases, conflict can arise because the guardian of the estate, who may wish to conserve the ward's assets for a variety of reasons, may refuse to pay for residential care and other services desired by the guardian of the person or by the ward. If such disputes cannot be resolved informally, the case can be brought to the court appointing the guardian or guardians. Such action may require advocacy on the part of an interested third party, such as a social worker, because without assets, access to the courts is difficult.

PROCEDURES AND PROCEDURAL PROTECTIONS

As has been stated, guardianship actions are typically regulated by State statutes. These statutes are often found in a State's **probate code**, the code that governs trusts and wills and the administration of estates after a person's death.

A guardianship action is typically initiated by a relative of a person alleged to be incompetent. Where there is no relative, a public agency may initiate the action. In most States, the relative or another "interested person," the definition of which varies from State to State, files the petition with the court. In some States, the petition is filed by a public attorney.

The statutes generally provide that the person alleged to be incompetent, that is, the respondent to the petition, be given full notice of the petition. The statutes also typically provide that notice be given to any person having the care and custody of the respondent and to close family members. However, many States laws waive the requirement of notice if the petition requests appointment of a temporary guardian that is, a guardian who is appointed on an emergency basis, or a **successor guardian**, that is, a guardian who merely succeeds another guardian. These are questionable practices given that a temporary appointment can often extend for 60 to 90 days and that appointment of a successor guardian can extend indefinitely.

In most States, petitions must be accompanied by certificates of qualified professionals attesting to the respondent's incapacity. A court may also order an examination of the respondent after the filing of a petition to determine if the respondent is, in fact, incapacitated. States differ on who is authorized to perform such examinations and how the examinations must be conducted. Social workers often are authorized to examine and report on mentally disabled adults, or the elderly.

If the appointment of a temporary guardian is sought on an emergency basis pending the final determination on competency, an abbreviated, probably *ex parte*, hearing may be held.

All States require some kind of formal hearing to determine competency, usually within a short time of the filing of a petition, but few specify the exact number of days. The hearings, as illustrated by the Florida law, are often "conducted in as informal a manner as may be consistent with orderly procedure and in a physical setting not likely to have a harmful effect on the mental health of the alleged incompetent." Fla. Stat. § 744.331.

Generally very few procedural safeguards are afforded to the respondent at the hearing. Although the respondent faces significant losses of basic rights, such as the right to marry, the right to vote, or the right to determine where and how he or she may live, no court opinion has declared that the respondent in a guardianship proceeding has a constitutional right to appointed counsel if he or she cannot afford one, and only a small minority of the States give the respondent a statutory right to appointed counsel. About half of the States do authorize the appointment of a guardian *ad litem*, but a guardian *ad litem* may be no substitute for an attorney who must advocate for his or her client. In some States, however, a guardian *ad litem*, who may be a social worker, must perform several specified tasks which may be of value to the respondent. For example, Washington law provides that a court shall appoint a guardian *ad litem* "to represent the best interests of the alleged incompetent or disabled person." This guardian *ad litem* must be "free of influence" from anyone involved with the case and have "the requisite knowledge, training, or expertise to perform the duties required by this section." These duties include: (1) explaining "in language which [the respondent] can reasonably be expected to understand" the nature of the proceedings and the respondent's rights; (2) providing the court with a written report setting forth a "description of the degree of incompetence or disability;" an "evaluation of the appropriateness" of the proposed guardian; the "appropriate duration" of any limited guardianship which may be ordered and "the limits and disabilities to be placed on the disabled person;" "any expression of approval or disapproval made by the [respondent]" on the proposed guardian or guardianship; and a "recommendation as to whether or not counsel should be appointed to represent the [respondent] and the reasons for such recommendation;" (3) to arrange for a written medical report on the respondent's "degree of incompetency or disability including the medical history . . . , the effects of any current medication on appearance or the ability to participate fully in the proceedings, and a medical prognosis specifying the estimated length and severity of any current disability;" and (4) if a prospective guardian is not named in the petition, "to investigate the availability of a possible guardian." Wash. Rev. Code § 11.88.090.

Many State statutes specifically permit the hearing to be conducted *ex parte*, that is, without notice to or the presence of the respondent "for good cause." Washington, alternatively, allows the court "to remove itself to the place of residence of the alleged incompetent or disabled person." Wash. Rev. Code § 11.88.040(3). About half the States permit a jury trial, but no court opinions have established a constitutional right to a jury in guardianship proceedings. A few States specifically grant the respondent a right of confrontation (*i.e.*, to cross-examine witnesses), but many

deny the right against self-incrimination (*i.e.*, to refuse to testify). Few States authorize an independent examination at no cost to the respondent if the respondent cannot afford an examination and, even more important, most States permit a determination of incompetency to be made by a mere preponderance of the evidence, the lowest standard of proof. Combining this low standard of proof with the vague statutory standards readily permits a finding of incompetence.

If there is a finding of general or limited incompetence and a guardian is appointed, it would seem that the ward should be afforded periodic reviews to determine the continuing necessity of guardianship. Only a handful of States, however, provide for a full hearing to review a guardianship appointment on an annual basis. Other States provide for very limited reviews, and still other States provide for no automatic reviews. All the States but Virginia permit a ward to petition for termination or modification of guardianship, but a court may be permitted to deny such petitions without a hearing, and a ward may be required to bear the burden of proving his or her competence, a difficult burden in most cases and particularly difficult where a ward, because of the guardianship, has been unable to make many important decisions on his or her own and to otherwise demonstrate competence. Once again, the advocacy of interested third parties, such as social workers, may be required in order to gain access to the courts and to assist in demonstrating competence.

GUARDIANSHIP OF VETERANS

Seventeen States have adopted the Uniform Veterans Guardianship Act which provides that the Administrator of the Veterans Administration be a party to all guardianship proceedings involving a respondent who is receiving money from the Veterans' Administration (V.A.) or who has assets purchased with V.A. funds. In addition, the Act provides that a certificate of incompetency from the V.A. is enough to establish a *prima facie* case of incompetency and puts some limits on who may be a guardian and how much the guardian may take from the ward's estate as fees. Other States have not adopted the entire Act but have incorporated some of its provisions into their laws. For example, Illinois makes a V.A. certificate of incompetency *prima facie* evidence of incompetence, Ill. Rev. Stat. ch. 110 1/2, par. 11a-11g, but Illinois has not adopted the Act.

ALTERNATIVES TO GUARDIANSHIP

As we have seen, a finding of incompetence and the appointment of a guardian may result in severe restrictions on a person's rights and basic freedom of action, and most guardianship laws offer minimal procedural protections to the person alleged to be incompetent. In addition, a person who is made a guardian assumes a significant burden, often at some personal cost. Therefore it is not surprising that social workers and others have sought acceptable alternatives to guardianship which would protect those who cannot fully protect themselves without depriving them of rights and which may avoid the costs and obligation of guardianship. These alternatives are discussed in this section.

Self-imposed guardianship

While not truly an alternative to guardianship, in some States one may avoid the restrictions of guardianship by petitioning for a guardianship for oneself. Such an action allows the person in need of guardianship to exercise more control over the process and may avoid involuntary action later. Further, in those States which recognize the concept of limited guardianship, such an action may preclude an action for a plenary guardian. Moreover, because of the individual planning that precedes such an action, the guardian is more likely to have been identified in advance and to have agreed to serve, providing greater assurance that the guardian will, in fact, act in accord with the ward's wishes. Thus, this is an alternative that might be appropriate in certain cases, especially those where an individual is diagnosed as having a degenerative disease or where a person is physically frail but mentally alert.

Some States simply specify that a person in need of guardianship may file the petition. The fact that the petition is filed by the person in need of guardianship has no effect on subsequent procedures. Other States provide that if a petition is filed by the person subject to guardianship, the guardian can be appointed without a finding of incompetence, thus protecting the dignity of a person who is physically frail but mentally competent. This is illustrated in the Florida statutes, which provide:

> "Without adjudication of incompetency, the court shall appoint a guardian of the estate of a . . . person who, though mentally competent, is incapable of the care, custody, and management of his estate by reason of age or physical infirmity and who has voluntarily petitioned for the appointment." Fla. Stat. § 744.341.

Less satisfactory but still helpful, one may execute a document while one is still of sound mind and while one still has full physical capacities asking that, should it ever be necessary to appoint a guardian, a designated person be selected. A court is not bound by the previous self-designation but generally will give it great weight in deciding who to appoint. This may be specified by statute. *See, e.g.*, Ill. Rev. Stat. ch. 110 1/2, par. 11a-6, which requires a court to appoint a previously self-designated guardian if the court finds he or she "will secure the best interests and welfare of the ward."

Representatives for receipt of benefits

Another person may be appointed to receive the checks of someone who is receiving public benefits, like AFDC or Old Age, Survivor's or Disability Insurance (Social Security), and to spend the money on behalf of the actual recipient. The person who is appointed is called a "**legal representative**" under the AFDC program or a "**representative payee**" under the Social Security program. The representative is not appointed by a court but by the agency that administers the benefit program; there is usually no need for a court determination of legal incompetence or even an agency determination—just a finding that such an appointment is necessary. There may be no specific procedures to follow in making the finding or the appointment.

Where an allegedly incompetent person's chief source of income is a public benefit program, the appointment of a representative payee or legal representative may sufficiently protect the person and may avoid appointment of a guardian with the resultant loss of rights. For example, a representative payee can insure that rent is paid, that money is not wasted and that there is enough money for food and other necessities. No further protection may be necessary.

The appointment of a representative may not always be a good alternative to guardianship, however. Appointing a representative

deprives a person of freedom of choice, yet there are few, if any, procedural safeguards in most agencies' appointment process. Moreover, agencies may not take care to select responsible representatives and may not oversee them adequately. Representatives may not act to protect beneficiaries, but rather may steal from them or otherwise take advantage of them. A 1983 study of representative payees by the Social Security Administration found problems in 20% of the cases reviewed and recommended the replacement of 5% of the representatives.[2]

Agency agreements or powers of attorney

When a person is of sound mind, he or she may generally authorize another person to act for him or her in certain matters. The one who authorizes the action is called the "**principal**," and the one who is authorized to act is the "**agent**." Often this authorization takes the form of a **power of attorney** which gives the agent the authority to make certain legal decisions or even execute certain legal documents, like deeds, for the principal. An agency or a power of attorney agreement may be as broad or as narrow as the principal wishes, authorizing the agent to manage all the principal's income and property or make all important decisions or authorizing the agent to sell a specific piece of property or make a particular decision.

In order to prevent guardianship proceedings, one may execute a broad agency agreement with a person of one's choice. The agreement may specify what the agent is to do and how he or she is to do it. However, an agency agreement, including a power of attorney, must be executed while one is of sound mind,

---

2. "U.S. Trying to Halt Abuses of Incompetent Pensioners," *New York Times*, March 22, 1989.

and, in most States, the agreement becomes invalid if the principal becomes incompetent, even if there is no legal determination of incompetency. To avoid this problem, most States have adopted **durable power of attorney** laws. These laws still require that the principal be of sound mind when executing the power of attorney but allow the agreement to continue even if the principal becomes incapacitated. Indeed, durable power of attorney laws may specify that powers of attorneys executed under the law are only effective when the principal becomes incapacitated.

Durable power of attorney laws create a workable and less restrictive alternative to guardianship which permits one to shape the restrictions one would wish should one become incapacitated. The durable power of attorney is also relatively inexpensive to execute and avoids the formality and public disclosures of court action.

There are problems with powers of attorney, however. Some people may not recognize the power of attorney and permit the agent to, for example, withdraw money from a bank account or sell an investment. Because the power of attorney has historically been used to facilitate action on financial matters, not to support decisions related to personal care, medical and other service providers may be unfamiliar with powers of attorney and unsure of their effect. Further, it may not be accepted that the principal was of "sound mind," however this may be defined, when a power was executed. Finally, there are no safeguards to assure the honesty of the agent and to assure that the agent acts in the principal's best interests.

Living wills

Often a guardianship action is initiated after a medical crisis, and a guardian is needed to consent to or withhold consent for medical care. Such may be the case when an individual becomes comatose following an accident or in the course of an illness. Living wills provide a mechanism by which persons, while still of sound mind, can express their desires about medical treatment should they become incompetent to express them, thus avoiding guardianship action and any doubts a guardian might have as to a ward's wishes. Living wills will be discussed in the next chapter.

Trusts

Trusts operate like agency agreements. Trusts allow one person, known as the "**trustee**," to control the property of another, known as the "**beneficiary**" or "**legal owner**," which is placed in a trust or which is the subject of a trust agreement. The powers of the trustee over the trust property may be limited by the trust agreement, but generally the trustee may do anything that will further the purpose of the trust. This purpose may be stated as generally as "to serve the best interest of the trust beneficiary." Usually, after property is placed in a trust, the beneficiary no longer has any power over it or only has such power as is reserved in the trust agreement.

One may put all or part of one's property in a trust at any time when one is of sound mind or one may execute a so-called "**living trust**" which will put all or a part of one's property in a trust when a "triggering" event, such as one's incapacity, occurs. Such trusts are generally revocable at any time while a person is still competent.

The problems with trust agreements are that they only relate to property, there are often complex laws and rules which must be followed to create or administer a trust, and it is easy to make an ineffectual living trust. Still where one has substantial property, a trust may prevent a guardianship. Moreover, one may put money or property in trust for another. Thus, a parent may specify by will that all an incompetent child will inherit from the parent be put into a trust. It may then not be necessary for the child to have a guardian appointed to manage the estate and it can be managed according to the specific instructions of the parent.

Case management and protective services

Many State and local mental health departments offer case management services through which a client is given assistance managing his or her daily affairs. In other States, special protective services offices have been opened to assist mental health clients or elderly clients in managing their affairs. Federal funds have been provided for such offices which may assist persons in "achieving or maintaining self-sufficiency" or in preventing "inappropriate institutional care." 42 U.S.C. § 1397(2)(and 4). These funds may be used to provide "services related to the management and maintenance of the home, day care services for adults, transportation services, . . . training and related services, employment services, information, referral and counselling services, the preparation and delivery of meals," in other words, services that would be provided by a guardian or that make appointment of a guardian unnecessary. 42 U.S.C. § 1397a(a)(2).

While case management services may be most helpful, like most other alternatives to guardianship discussed here, they are purely voluntary. If an incapacitated person is unwilling to use the services or did not chose to use one of the alternatives, coercive measures may have to be considered.

Health Care

Earlier chapters of this text have discussed several topics related to health care which are of relevance to social workers, including medical neglect of minors, discrimination on the basis of handicap, commitment of the mentally ill, and guardianship. This chapter discusses three additional topics: access to medical care; consent to treatment, including the right to withhold consent; and human reproduction. This chapter also discusses aspects of medical treatment of minors other than those discussed previously.

THE RIGHT TO RECEIVE MEDICAL CARE

The American health care system, unlike the system in many other countries, is predominantly private. America has predominantly private hospitals and predominantly private doctors whose services are paid for by predominantly private insurance companies and private funds. There is some direct provision of health care by governments at the federal, State, and local level; a substantial amount of money is expended on health care by all three levels of governments; and there is government regulation of the health care system, primarily at the federal and State levels of government. But, the American health care system remains a private system.

The Supreme Court has never said there is a constitutional or fundamental right to medical care in America. Although there are some public hospitals and clinics in America, although some health care in America is provided to members of the public free of charge, and although the government pays for some private medical care through such programs as Medicaid and Medicare, there is no right to medical care at public expense in America. No State constitution includes a right to med-

ical care. No statutes create a system of free universal health care in America. Most Americans are not entitled by law to the services of any or a particular health care provider—at public or private expense. Indeed, in America, a private hospital or doctor, and in many instances a public hospital or a publicly employed doctor, may generally refuse to treat anyone.

There are several important exceptions to the broad statement that health care providers can refuse to treat anyone. There are, for example: requirements that a person be given emergency treatment if a failure to provide such treatment would cause serious injury or death; requirements to provide certain services imposed by funding sources; and civil rights requirements that no person be refused treatment for reasons like race or sex. But, in general, even if the cost of a patient's medical care will be subsidized by the government through Medicare or Medicaid, a doctor or hospital cannot be forced to treat a patient.

Although there is no right to receive medical treatment in America, there is a common law and constitutional right to refuse treatment. Americans are considered to have a constitutional right to privacy and a common law right of bodily integrity which preclude involuntary medical treatment. With a few limited qualifications and exceptions, no medical treatment can proceed in America unless the patient, or one who is authorized to act for the patient, such as a guardian or a parent, voluntarily consents to the treatment with knowledge of the risks and alternatives to treatment—that is, unless there is **informed consent** to the treatment. If a patient is treated without informed consent, depending on the jurisdiction, the health care provider may be civilly liable for assault, battery, malpractice or negligence or may even be criminally liable.

Because the right to refuse treatment and

the concept of informed consent are important to social workers, both will be discussed in some depth below, first in relation to adults, and then, in the section on health care of children, in relation to children.

INFORMED CONSENT OF
ADULTS FOR HEALTH CARE

Informed consent generally need not be in writing, but most health care providers obtain written consent as documentation. The written consent should be specific. A general consent may not be considered sufficient to establish informed consent for a specific treatment.

Informed consent has three elements: competence; voluntariness; and knowledge.

Adults must be of sound mind to be competent to give informed consent to medical treatment for themselves. As a general matter, unless they have been declared legally incompetent, adults should be considered competent to make treatment decisions for themselves. However, some adults may be temporarily incompetent to consent to necessary treatment. They may be under the influence of prescribed (or non-prescribed) drugs or alcohol, in shock, unconscious or suffering from a medical condition which has affected their otherwise sound minds. In an emergency, when treatment must proceed and there is no time to get a court to appoint someone to consent to the treatment, a health care provider will usually ask the closest available relative of a temporarily incompetent patient to consent to the treatment of the patient, but, in most jurisdictions, this consent is invalid—unless the relative is a legally appointed guardian with power to consent to treatment. Only the patient or a legally appointed guardian is competent to consent to a patient's treatment. And, it should be noted, even a guardian may be legally incompetent to consent to any or to certain medical treatment for a ward as specified by law or by an order of appointment.

Consent to treatment must also be voluntary. That is, consent must be given freely and willingly to be valid. It also may be withdrawn at any moment. There may be questions of fraud and coercion in some cases, but generally, except for the involuntarily institutionalized, where the situation is itself coercive, there are few problems with the voluntariness of informed consent when consent is given by adults for their own treatment. There may be voluntariness problems, however, when guardians consent to treatment for their wards against the ward's wishes.

Consent cannot be informed unless one has knowledge of what one is consenting to. You would think that doctors would have to tell a patient about the nature of a proposed treatment and all the risks of, alternatives to and consequences of the treatment in order to obtain a patient's informed consent, but in many jurisdictions a doctor is only required to tell a patient what a "reasonable" or the "average" doctor would tell a patient in the circumstances. This is considered an "objective" test. In other jurisdictions, doctors only have to tell their patients what they need to know to make intelligent choices; in other words, the focus is on the patient, not the doctor and the test used to determine how much a doctor must tell a patient is subjective rather than objective. But, using either test, patients need not be told everything for consent to be informed; they only must be told that which is reasonable to tell a patient in the patient's particular circumstances. Patients may even be told nothing about a proposed treatment if disclosure would be unreasonable; the informed consent requirement would not be violated if telling the patient nothing about the treatment was reasonable in the circumstances.

In certain situations, statutes, regulations or the common law may require specific disclosures by doctors. For example, as of 1987, 17 States had statutes requiring doctors to inform women about the alternative forms of treatment for breast cancer and the risks and consequences of each form of treatment. In most of these States, women have to be provided with specific written material containing the information and must sign a form indicating they have received the material.

Social workers may help health care providers inform patients about proposed treatment, primarily by translating and interpreting medical information for patients and by providing information about services. Moreover, social workers may assist health care providers determine the voluntariness and competence of a patient's consent. And when patients do not make their own decisions about their medical care, that is, when their informed consent is not required, social workers can help them understand why treatment proceeded without their informed consent. But the social workers' primary role when it comes to informed consent is assisting patients and their families decide when they should give informed consent to medical treatment. Social workers are not dispensing medical advice or interfering with a doctor's care of a patient if they help patients understand the psychological or social dimensions of their medical decisions, help them reach decisions with which they will be comfortable, and make sure that their doctors understand the decisions they have reached.

There are three main exceptions to the requirement of informed consent.

First, in an emergency, health care providers may and must dispense with informed consent. They need not wait for court orders appointing guardians to consent to treatment before providing life-saving treatment to those who cannot consent to treatment because they are, for example, unconscious after an accident.

Second, in some circumstances, treatment may be forced on people under the state's *parens patriae* authority or the police power. For example, people who are mentally ill may be required to submit to treatment for their own good or to prevent them from injuring others, and people who have been exposed to or who have a communicable disease may be treated against their will for their own good or to prevent the spread of the disease. Similarly, people may be compelled to submit to vaccinations over their objections.

Third, we may not always allow people to refuse life-saving treatment. People may sometimes be treated against their will if treatment will save their lives. That is, they may be denied what has been referred to as the "right to die," the "right to death with dignity" or the "right to die a natural death."

Although social workers are usually not directly involved in the legal battles related to this last exception to the informed consent rule, they may be indirectly involved. For example, they may counsel patients who are making decisions to accept or reject treatment or they may take part in hospital committees which make decisions to provide or withhold treatment. Moreover, medical social workers' ability to find appropriate and affordable care for patients may play a significant part in the patients' decision to refuse treatment, and all social workers may be helping patients and their families and friends cope with guilt and doubt after making a decision to refuse treatment. Thus, it is necessary for social workers to understand this exception.

ADULTS' RIGHT TO REFUSE
LIFE-SAVING TREATMENT

The right to refuse life-saving treatment has become more and more important as technological advances permit many people who formerly would have died to live, albeit in hospitals connected to machines, and as more and more dying people go to hospitals or nursing homes instead of remaining at home. As this right has become increasingly important, the law on it has been changing and becoming more complex. This changing and complex law may be best understood if the right is examined in three contexts in which it may arise: 1) when competent adults refuse treatment; 2) when adults who are rendered incompetent by their medical condition never expressed their desires when competent; and 3) when adults who are rendered incompetent by their medical condition expressed their desires when they were competent.

Competent adults

As a corollary to the requirement of informed consent, competent adults have a right to refuse to consent to medical treatment. But, if a refusal of treatment means death and acceptance of treatment means life, the assertion by a patient of the right to refuse may conflict with beliefs in the sanctity of life, a moral and legal abhorrence of suicide, the medical profession's obligation and desire to save life, the *parens patriae* notion that the state may protect people from themselves, and the state's desire to protect innocent third parties. Thus, competent adults right to refuse treatment may be disputed by their relatives, friends, or doctors or by the government. Sometimes these disputes will end up in a court. Patients may go to court to prevent or stop treatment provided against their will. Their relatives, friends, or doctors may go to court to force treatment the patients have refused or to have guardians appointed to consent to the treatment. Such disputes may also reach courts after patients have been treated against their will or have died without treatment.

When such disputes end up in court, the modern trend is to uphold a competent adult's right to refuse to treatment. It is, however, difficult to predict how a court will rule in a given case. Each case and court is different. But, the factors which will influence a court's decision can usually be predicted. On the one hand, a competent adult's right to refuse treatment may be denied: 1) if the patient has minor children or other dependents; 2) if the treatment is of minor intrusiveness or constitutes a minor invasion of bodily integrity; 3) if the proposed treatment is a generally accepted mode of treatment; 4) if the quality of life will not be adversely affected by the treatment or if the patient will not live a limited or painful life after treatment; or 5) if the treatment does not merely prolong the patient's life for a short time but actually will save the patient's life. On the other hand, a competent adult's right to refuse treatment may be upheld: 1) if the patient has no dependents and his or her friends and family agree with the decision to refuse treatment; 2) if the treatment is highly intrusive and/or exceptionally painful; 3) if the treatment is risky, experimental and/or has a small chance of success; 4) if the quality of the patient's life will be seriously affected by the treatment or by the medical condition even with the treatment; 5) if the treatment will only postpone imminent death; or 6) if the patient has a deeply held religious belief opposing the treatment. It may also make a difference whether there is or was a request to withdraw treatment (e.g., to disconnect a respirator) or a refusal to submit to treatment (e.g., a patient asks that she not be given a respirator). In other words, it may matter whether the health care provider is playing an active or passive role in causing a patient's death. It further may matter whether the underlying medical condition or the provider's action or inaction causes a death. An action or inaction by a health care provider which is perceived as causing a patient's death, such as disconnecting an intravenous feeding tube of a paralyzed patient, thereby starving the patient, may be considered a violation of medical ethics—or even murder. Although such an action may be called "euthanasia" or "mercy killing" if the patient was dying or in great pain, it may still be murder under the law.

Passive conduct by a health care provider which is usually acceptable is failure to resuscitate a patient who is in a permanent state of great pain or who has a terminal condition. Such a failure to resuscitate may be a spontaneous decision, but more commonly it is the result of a previous, probably written, do not resuscitate" order, known as a "**DNR**" order, or "**no code**."

Incompetent adults

Sometimes adult patients are unable to make decisions to accept or reject medical treatment for themselves. Decisions about whether treatment should be initiated or discontinued often must be made for patients who had been competent adults but whose medical conditions have rendered them unconscious, comatose, or otherwise incompetent to make decisions for themselves. Social workers play a role in medical decision-making with such patients by assisting the patients' families make and live with decisions for the patients.

Many argue that incompetent adults should have the same right to refuse treatment as competent adults. In other words, they should not be prevented from exercising their right to die merely because they are incompetent. But how do incompetent patients exercise this right? How do health care providers determine what comatose or unconscious patients want? And how do providers protect themselves from civil or criminal liability if available treatment is withheld and incompetent patients die?

As we have learned, when adults are unable to make decisions for themselves or to exercise their legal rights, guardians may be appointed for them. These guardians stand in their wards' shoes, making decisions and exercising their rights for them. But is it consistent with the nature and purpose of guardianship for a guardian to make a decision which, not only does not protect a ward, but also may cause the ward's death? How does a guardian decide whether or not to refuse treatment for a ward? Should a guardian's exercise of a ward's right to die override the desires and ethics of the ward's health care providers? And is the informed consent of a guardian sufficient to protect a health care provider from liability if a ward dies without available treatment?

Courts may get involved in questions related to treatment of incompetent persons in several ways. First, someone may seek to be appointed the guardian of an incompetent patient and to be given authority to exercise the patient's right to refuse treatment. Second, a health care provider may seek to have a guardian appointed for an incompetent patient to authorize treatment for the patient or may otherwise seek judicial authority to provide treatment to the patient. Third, relatives or friends of an incompetent patient may sue a health care provider to stop or prevent treatment of the patient. Fourth, relatives of an incompetent patient may sue a health care provider civilly for providing treatment without the informed consent of the patient or his or her guardian or for causing injury or death to the patient by withholding treatment. Occasionally, a provider may also be criminally prosecuted for assault or battery for providing treatment without informed consent or for murder for withholding treatment from a patient who died. Finally, because of the potential for civil and criminal liability—no matter which course health care providers may wish to take—they may go to court to determine whether treatment may be provided to or withheld from an incompetent patient without incurring civil or criminal liability. That is, they may seek a declaratory judgment setting forth their rights and obligations.

When a court is asked to decide a case involving an incompetent person's right to die, it may use either a subjective or an objective test to determine whether the patient would assert the right. If it uses a subjective test, also known as a "**substituted judgment test**," it will attempt to determine what the patient would want; if it uses an objective test, it will attempt to determine what a reasonable person in the position of the patient would want. Whichever test the court uses, if it determines the right to refuse treatment would be asserted, it would uphold or deny the right based on the factors mentioned in the discussion of a competent patient's right to die above.

Matter of Quinlan, 70 N.J. 10, 355 A.2d 647 (1976), is the highly publicized case involving Karen Quinlan, a young woman who was in an irreversible coma. Her father asked the court to be appointed her guardian and to be given the power to consent to the removal of her respirator. The trial court denied his request, and he appealed. In reversing the denial, the New Jersey Supreme Court noted that:

"No form of treatment which can cure or improve [Karen's] condition is known or avail-

able. As nearly as may be determined, considering the guarded area of remote uncertainties characteristic of most medical science predictions, she can **never** be restored to cognitive or sapient life. She is debilitated and moribund and although fairly stable . . . no physician risked the opinion that she could live more than a year and indeed she may die much earlier. Her life . . . is sustained by the respirator and tubal feeding, and removal from the respirator would cause her death soon, although the time cannot be stated with more precision.''

Karen, however, still had some brain function and, thus, was not considered "brain dead." Moreover, her doctors "asserted that no physician would have failed to provide respirator support at the outset, and none would interrupt its life-saving course thereafter . . ." The court respected the doctors' position, but also concluded that Karen had a constitutional right of privacy which was violated by the forced treatment. It stated:

"We have no hesitancy in deciding . . . that no external compelling interest of the State could compel Karen to endure the unendurable, only to vegetate a few measurable months with no realistic possibility of returning to any semblance of cognitive or sapient life. We perceive no thread of logic distinguishing between such a choice on Karen's part and a similar choice which, under the evidence in this case, could be made by a competent patient terminally ill, riddled by cancer and suffering great pain; such a patient would not be resuscitated or put on a respirator and . . . would not be kept **against his will on a respirator**.

"The claimed interests of the State in this case are essentially the preservation and sanctity of human life and defense of the right of the physician to administer medical treatment according to his best judgment. In this case the doctors say that removing Karen from the respirator will conflict with their professional judgment. [Karen's father] answers that Karen's present treatment serves only a maintenance function; that the respirator cannot cure or improve her condition but at best can only prolong her inevitable slow deterioration and death; and that the interests of the patient, as seen by her surrogate, the guardian, must be evaluated by the court as predominant, even in the face of an opinion *contra* by the present attending physicians.

"[Karen's father's] distinction is significant. The nature of Karen's care and the realistic chances of her recovery are quite unlike those of the patients . . . in many of the cases where treatments were ordered. In many of those cases the medical procedure required (usually a transfusion) constituted a minimal bodily invasion and the chances of recovery and return to functioning life were very good. We think that the State's interest *contra* weakens and the individual's right to privacy grows as the degree of bodily invasion increases and the prognosis dims. **Ultimately there comes a point at which the individual's rights overcome the State interest.** It is for that reason that we believe Karen's choice, if she were competent to make it, would be vindicated by the law. Her prognosis is extremely poor,—she will never resume cognitive life. And the bodily invasion is very great,—she requires 24 hour intensive nursing care, antibiotics, the assistance of a respirator, a catheter and feeding tube.

"Our affirmation of Karen's independent right of choice, however, would ordinarily be based upon her competency to assert it. The sad truth, however, is that she is grossly incompetent and we cannot discern her supposed choice based on the testimony of her previous conversations with friends . . . **Nevertheless we have concluded that Karen's right of privacy may be asserted on her behalf by her guardian under the peculiar circumstances here present.**"

"If a putative decision by Karen to permit this non-cognitive, vegetative existence to terminate by natural forces is regarded as a valuable incident of her right of privacy, as we believe it to be, then it should not be discarded solely on the basis that her condition prevents her conscious exercise of the choice. The only practical way to prevent destruction of the right is to permit the guardian and family of Karen to render their best judgment, subject to the qualifications hereinafter stated, as to whether she would exercise it in these circumstances. If their conclusion is in the affirmative this decision should be accepted by a society the overwhelming majority of whose members would, we think, in similar circumstances, exercise such a choice in the same way for themselves or for those closest to them."

The court's conclusion that Karen's father could be appointed her guardian and could assert her right to refuse treatment did not resolve the case. The court noted that many questions remained, such as whether Karen's doctors could be forced to withdraw treatment, whether, in this or like cases, the institution or withdrawal of life-sustaining procedures was the subject of medical discretion, and whether doctors in cases like Karen's risked civil or criminal liability if they terminated treatment. The court stated that, in the past, courts have placed full responsibility "in the hands of the physician." But this placement of responsibility needs to reexamined in light of "underlying human values and rights."

"Determinations as to [the distribution of responsibility in cases like Karen's] must, in the ultimate, be responsive not only to the concepts of medicine but also to the common moral judgment of the community at large. In the latter respect the Court has a nondelegable judicial responsibility. Put in another way, the law, equity and justice must not themselves quail and be helpless in the face of modern technological marvels presenting questions hitherto unthought of. Where a Karen Quinlan, or a parent, or a doctor, or a hospital, or a State seeks the process and response of a court, it must answer with its most informed conception of justice in the previously unexplored circumstances presented to it. That is its obligation and we are here fulfilling it, for the actors and those having an interest in the matter should not go without remedy.''

But courts, ''having no inherent medical expertise, . . . [should not necessarily] overrule a professional decision made according to prevailing medical practice and standards.'' Although the ''modern proliferation of substantial malpractice litigation and the less frequent but even more unnerving possibility of criminal sanctions would seem, for it is beyond human nature to suppose otherwise, to have bearing on the practice and standards as they exist,'' courts should attempt to discern the prevailing practice and standards. In this case, the practice and standards seemed clear to the court.

> ''We glean from the record here that physicians distinguish between curing the ill and comforting and easing the dying; that they refuse to treat the curable as if they were dying or ought to die, and that they have sometimes refused to treat the hopeless and dying as if they were curable. [M]any of them have refused to inflict an undesired prolongation of the process of dying on a patient in irreversible condition when it is clear that such 'therapy' offers neither human nor humane benefit. We think these attitudes represent a balanced implementation of a profoundly realistic perspective on the meaning of life and death and that they respect the whole Judeo-Christian tradition of regard for human life. No less would they seem consistent with the moral matrix of medicine, 'to heal,' very much in the sense of the endless mission of the law, 'to do justice.'
>
> ''Yet this balance, we feel, is particularly difficult to perceive and apply in the context

of the development by advanced technology of sophisticated and artificial life-sustaining devices. For those possibly curable, such devices are of great value, and, as ordinary medical procedures, are essential. Consequently, . . . they are necessary because of the ethic of medical practice. But in light of the situation in the present case (while the record here is somewhat hazy in distinguishing between 'ordinary' and 'extraordinary' measures), one would have to think that the use of the same respirator or like support could be considered 'ordinary' in the context of the possibly curable patient but 'extraordinary' in the context of the forced sustaining by cardio-respiratory processes of an irreversibly doomed patient. And this dilemma is sharpened in the face of the malpractice and criminal action threat which we have mentioned.''

The court ''hesitate[d], in this imperfect world,'' to give doctors absolute immunity from malpractice and criminal liability, but it did give Karen's and other doctors a qualified immunity which could ''free physicians, in the pursuit of their healing vocation, from possible contamination by self-interest or self-protection concerns which would inhibit their independent medical judgments for the well-being of their dying patients.'' Moreover, the court urged the institution and use of a Hospital Ethics Committee as a ''technique aimed at the underlying difficulty.'' It described such a committee, quoting from a law review article, as ''a regular forum'' to provide ''input and dialogue in individual situations and to allow the responsibility of [physicians' ethical] judgments to be shared,'' and further quoted from the article:

> ''Many hospitals have established an Ethics Committee composed of physicians, social workers, attorneys, and theologians, . . . which serves to review the individual circumstances of ethical dilemma and which has provided much in the way of assistance

and safeguards for patients and their medical caretakers. Generally, the authority of these committees is primarily restricted to the hospital setting and their official status is more that of an advisory body than of an enforcing body.''

The court stated:

''The most appealing factor in [this] technique seems to us to be the diffusion of professional responsibility for decision, comparable in a way to the value of multi-judge courts in finally resolving on appeal difficult questions of law. Moreover, such a system would be protective to the hospital as well as the doctor in screening out, so to speak, a case which might be contaminated by less than worthy motivations of family or physician. In the real world and in relationship to the momentous decision contemplated, the value of additional views and diverse knowledge is apparent.''

Whether or not a hospital ethics committee is constituted, the court stated doctors should make decisions on the treatment of incompetent patients without courts.

''We consider that a practice of applying to a court to confirm such decisions would generally be inappropriate, not only because that would be a gratuitous encroachment upon the medical profession's field of competence, but because it would be impossibly cumbersome. This is not to say that in the case of an otherwise justiciable controversy access to the courts would be foreclosed; we speak rather of a general practice and procedure.

''And although the deliberations and decisions which we describe would be professional in nature they should obviously include at some stage the feelings of the family of an incompetent relative. Decision-making within health care if it is considered as an expression of a primary obligation of the physi-

cian, . . . should be controlled primarily within the patient-doctor-family relationship . . .

''If there could be created not necessarily this particular system but some reasonable counterpart, we would have no doubt that such decisions, thus determined to be in accordance with medical practice and prevailing standards, would be accepted by society and by the courts, at least in cases comparable to that of Karen Quinlan.''

The court concluded its opinion by ordering the following declaratory relief.

''Upon the concurrence of the guardian [Karen's father] and family of Karen, should the responsible attending physicians conclude that there is no reasonable possibility of Karen's ever emerging from her present comatose condition to a cognitive, sapient state and that the life-support apparatus now being administered to Karen should be discontinued, they shall consult with the hospital 'Ethics Committee' or like body of the institution in which Karen is then hospitalized. If that consultative body agrees that there is no reasonable possibility of Karen's ever emerging from her present comatose condition to a cognitive, sapient state, the present life-support system may be withdrawn and said action shall be without any civil or criminal liability therefor on the part of any participant, whether guardian, physician, hospital or others.''

Quinlan has been most influential. It has been interpreted to stand for the proposition, which has been widely accepted, that ''extraordinary measures'' may be withheld from an incompetent patient if there is ''no hope of recovery'' or if the patient is ''irrevocably doomed.'' This is an objective test, but it is not an easy test to apply. It raises many questions.

First, what is an "extraordinary" measure? Is a respirator, an intravenous feeding system, chemotherapy, or resuscitation an "extraordinary" measure? You probably believe that putting an artificial or a baboon heart into a human is an extraordinary measure, but would you say that a human heart transplant is extraordinary?

Second, what is "recovery?" Is life with great suffering or life in a permanent vegetative state recovery? In *Quinlan*, and in a later case involving an 84 year old woman who was "incompetent with severe and permanent mental and physical impairments and a life expectancy of approximately one year or less," *Matter of Conroy*, 98 N.J. 321, 486 A.2d 1209 (1985), the New Jersey Supreme Court stated that it did not want to consider the value of life or the quality of life or make decisions "based on assessments of the personal worth or the social utility of another's life," but it seemed to do precisely that. The Court said in *Conroy* that if the patient is suffering and the "burdens" of life outweigh the "benefits," life support measures, extraordinary or not, may be withdrawn.

Third, are doctors competent to decide if a patient is "irreversibly doomed?" In Karen Quinlan's case, the doctors were wrong when they all stated, as reported in the opinion, that she would die immediately if her respirator was removed and would die in a short time even with the respirator. In fact, her respirator was removed soon after the opinion was rendered, and she lived another nine years.

No matter what test is used to decide if treatment may be withheld from an incompetent adult, other questions may arise. Three of the most important of these questions are posed below.

First, what should or can be done if a health care provider refuses to go along with a request of a legally appointed guardian for an incompetent adult to withhold or withdraw treatment? Can a doctor, who cannot be forced to treat someone, be forced not to treat someone? *Quinlan* said "no," but three New Jersey cases after *Quinlan* said "yes."

Second, at what point should someone be considered legally "dead" so that treatment can be terminated without any legal questions? In the past, people were considered dead if they stopped breathing or their hearts stopped, but people can now be kept alive for years on life-support machines after they have stopped breathing on their own and people can now be resuscitated after their hearts have stopped. Should people who display no signs of brain activity but whose hearts and lungs are working with the aid of machines be considered "alive?" As of 1985, forty-three States decided "no." These States all recognize, in their statutes or common law, the concept of **brain death**. The definitions of brain death in the different States differ but in all these States, one can be considered dead even if one is breathing and one's heart is beating with the aid of machines. Many now urge a broadening of the States' definitions of brain death to include those, like Karen Quinlan, who are in a permanent vegetative state but who have some brain function, while others urge a tightening of the definitions, arguing that present definitions are contrary to religious and moral precepts and permit euthanasia.[1]

Last, who should make a decision for an incompetent adult? Are courts competent to decide these matters? Are these matters best decided in adversary hearings? Should doctors

---

1. The definition of brain death is also important in relation to organ transplants. Before an organ can be removed from a person for transplant, the person must be legally dead, but often healthy organs deteriorate while a terminal patient is comatose but not brain dead. Thus, to facilitate transplants, some urge the broadening of the definition of brain dead. Social workers, who may counsel family members who are asked to authorize organ transplants of terminally ill or injured relatives, need to be able to explain the concept of brain death to them.

be allowed to make certain decisions for incompetent adults on their own or does this give doctors too much power and ignore the right to privacy? Should guardians be allowed to make the necessary decisions or does this give guardians too much power? Should hospital ethics committees or other bodies specially constituted to make such decisions be entrusted with life and death decisions for incompetent patients as *Quinlan* urged? Should the decision ultimately be one for a patient's family? What if a patient's family disagrees among themselves?

There is one possible answer to the questions related to who should make the decision for an incompetent patient: incompetent patients may decide for themselves through a prior expression of their desires.

Incompetent adults who assert the right to die in advance

Courts have recognized an incompetent patient's prior expression of desires related to treatment even when such desires were not documented in writing and, in fact, were evidenced only by abstract or philosophical discussions. *See, e.g., Eichner v. Dillon*, 73 A.D. 2d 431, 426 N.Y.S.2d 517 (1980). But no one can trust that his or her desires will be taken into account unless they are expressed in a written document recognized under the law. The court in *Quinlan*, for example, declined to give probative weight to Karen Quinlan's discussions with friends on being kept alive connected to machines.

Documents prepared by competent adults which state what lifesaving or life-prolonging treatment they would like to be provided or withheld should they become ill and incompetent are sometimes referred to as "**living wills.**" Living will, or so-called "natural death" acts authorize competent adults to prepare such documents. As of 1987, 39

States had such acts. The acts may specify the contents and form of such documents, but living wills may be recognized by courts, guardians, and doctors even if they do not conform to the requirements of an applicable act and even if there is no living will act in the jurisdiction. Any sort of living will would be helpful to courts using subjective tests to determine if treatment may be withheld from incompetent adults. Of course, a living will is most likely to be effective if it is prepared in conformity with the law.

Living will acts differ. As noted, some acts require that the wills be in a particular form; they may further require witnesses or other formalities. Other acts permit any type of document and require no formalities. Some acts only authorize terminating certain types of life support measures. Thirteen of the acts, for example, do not authorize the withdrawal of artificial feeding. Some acts apply only when death is imminent; other acts have a wider scope. None of the acts compel a doctor to honor a living will, but all give doctors some kind of qualified immunity, as in *Quinlan*, for honoring one.

Where a jurisdiction has no living will act or has an act that is narrow in scope and the courts are hesitant to recognize a non-statutory living will, an alternative may be for competent adults to designate in advance guardians who are authorized to make medical decisions for them should they become incompetent and who are aware of and willing to follow their future ward's wishes. Similarly, a durable power of attorney can be given to another person for the purpose of having that person make medical decisions for oneself. Several States have passed laws to supplement their living will acts or instead of living will acts which recognize durable powers of attorney specifically for medical care.

The proliferation of living will and related acts and the increased use of living wills pose a danger that guardians, courts and health care providers may be hesitant to recognize incompetent adults' right to die if they have not executed living wills or otherwise expressed their desires in writing. In other words, they may presume that the failure to execute a living will indicates a desire to forego the right to die. Some living will acts address this problem. *See, e.g.,* Iowa Code § 144A.11(4) which provides: "This Chapter creates no presumption concerning the intention of an individual who has not executed [a living will]." Eliminating the presumption as a matter of law, however, does not eliminate it as a matter of human psychology.

Even the most comprehensive living will act can only provide a partial solution to the problem of an incompetent adult's right to die. For one thing, most people will not execute living wills, and living wills do not solve the problem posed by those who are incompetent because of infancy or retardation. For another thing, even the best drafted law may still raise serious questions such as what type of treatment may be withheld or terminated and when the provisions of a living will should be put into effect.

Social workers can help patients with terminal diseases who are facing incompetence, such as those with Alzheimer's disease or AIDS, and their families achieve peace of mind by advising them of the availability of living wills and other means to express their desires before they become incompetent, and by referring them to lawyers who can draft effective documents for them which accurately express their desires.

MEDICAL CARE OF CHILDREN

In general, minors are not considered competent to consent to their own medical treatment. The necessary informed consent for their treatment must come from a parent or a legal guardian.[2] There are, however, several exceptions to the rule that only a parent can provide informed consent for a minor child's medical care. Some of these exceptions come from the common law, some are constitutionally based and some are statutory. The four most important exceptions are reviewed below.

First, in an emergency, minors can consent to treatment for themselves or health care providers can treat minors without parental consent. Determining what is an "emergency" for the purpose of this exception may pose a problem. Some States, have statutes defining "emergency" or have statutes permitting health care providers to proceed with treatment of a child without the consent of a parent whenever a failure to provide immediate treatment could have adverse effects. For example, New York law allows treatment of a minor without parental consent when

> "in the physician's judgment an emergency exists and the person is in immediate need of medical attention and an attempt to secure consent would result in delay of treatment which could increase the risk of the person's life or health." N.Y. Public Health Law, § 2504(4).

Second, health care providers may provide minor treatment of children without parental consent. As with deciding what is an "emergency," deciding what is "minor" may not be simple. Treatment like the cleaning and bandaging of a child's small cut by a school nurse would unquestionably be considered minor, however.

Third, emancipated or mature minors may be permitted to consent to their own medical

---

2. For convenience, the term "parent" will be used to refer to both parents and legal guardians unless the context otherwise requires.

treatment. As has been noted, **emancipation** is generally a statutory or common law status with specific substantive or procedural prerequisites, but maturity is rarely legally recognized or defined. Nevertheless, courts have allowed "mature" minors to make treatment decisions under some circumstances.

Fourth, minors may be allowed to get certain types of treatment without parental consent, or even notification. It is thought that minors would not seek certain kinds of treatment which they should be encouraged to get, such as treatment for substance abuse, assistance with birth control, or treatment for venereal disease, if they had to discuss the treatment with their parents or if they had to get their parents' consent. This exception may be found in statutes or regulations or may arise from constitutional interpretation.

The requirement that a parent provide the informed consent for treatment of a child poses a problem when the child opposes the treatment or when the treatment does not benefit the child. While a parent's desires will generally override those of a child, a parent may be deprived of the right to consent to treatment of a child which does not benefit the child. For example, a parent may not be permitted to consent to an organ transplant from one child to an ailing sibling. Older, mature children may be asked their wishes in such cases.

Courts may be asked to determine when a parent can withhold informed consent for treatment of a child or, in other words, when a parent has the right to refuse medical treatment for a child. As in *Quinlan*, they may be asked to give declaratory relief by parents or health care providers. For example, in *In re L.H.R.*, 253 Ga. 439, 321 S.E.2d 716 (1984), a critically ill newborn's doctor, parents, and the hospital's Infant Care Review Committee, consisting of two doctors, a nurse, a social worker, a hospital administrator and the parent of a handicapped child, all wished to remove life support from the infant. The hospital filed a motion for declaratory relief. The case was treated as if it involved an incompetent adult, except that the parent was considered to have the right to speak for the child, and *Quinlan* was followed. The court concluded:

> "[T]he right to refuse treatment or indeed terminate treatment may be exercised by the parents or legal guardian of [an] infant after diagnosis that the infant is terminally ill with no hope of recovery and that the infant exists in a chronic vegetative state with no reasonable possibility of attaining cognitive function."

As we have seen, courts may also get involved in such cases through a child neglect action in a juvenile court. Most child neglect statutes include the failure to provide medical care within their definitions of neglect, but even if they do not, failing to provide such care would normally be considered a failure to provide "proper" or "appropriate" care within the purview of a neglect statute. Further, courts may get involved when criminal neglect, or even homicide, cases are brought against parents who fail to provide medical care for their children.

Many people view parental refusals to consent to treatment for severely handicapped children or critically ill newborns not as child neglect but as examples of discrimination against the disabled. They believe that rather than bringing such cases in juvenile courts under juvenile law or in criminal courts under criminal law, they should be brought as civil rights cases in the appropriate courts for such cases. Others reject the use of civil rights laws where parents refuse treatment for severely handicapped children or critically ill newborns, but would still assert that neither the juvenile court nor the criminal court is the appropriate forum for most such cases, which raise different issues than the usual juvenile or criminal court child neglect action.

Whatever the route to a court, a court which is determining when a parent has the right to refuse medical treatment for a child must weigh parental autonomy against the *parens patriae* authority of the state. Generally a court will not allow a parental refusal to consent to stand if a child's life is at stake. However, if a proposed treatment involves some risk, if it may be painful, if it has little chance of success, if it is not a generally accepted mode of treatment, if the quality of life after treatment is questionable, if there is a strong religious basis for the refusal, or if an older or mature child concurs with the parental refusal, a court may tip the scale in favor of the parents' right to refuse.

As counselors to bereaved families of critically ill newborns, as counselors to families with severely handicapped children and as child welfare workers, social workers are often involved in cases involving a parent's right to refuse treatment for their children.

LEGAL ISSUES RELATED TO HUMAN REPRODUCTION

Many legal issues related to human reproduction are of concern to social workers who will work with clients, particularly teenagers, making medical decisions related to reproduction. The most significant of these issues are reviewed below.

Birth control

In *Griswold v. Connecticut*, 381 U.S. 479 (1965), the Supreme Court held that a State

violated the constitutional right to privacy when it forbade a married couple's use of birth control. In subsequent cases, the Court has struck down State laws restricting unmarried persons' and even minors' use of or access to birth control because of this right.

As with any other medical treatment, prescription birth control devices and drugs can only be provided after informed consent is given. Various State statutes, however, allow all minors or all minors of a certain age to obtain birth control without the informed consent of a parent or guardian. The Supreme Court has held that a State may not forbid "mature" minors from receiving birth control without parental consent. *Carey v. Population Services International*, 431 U.S. 678 (1977). The law is in flux on requirements of parental notification but generally mature minors may also receive birth control without parental notification.

Sterilization

Sterilization as a method of birth control raises several legal issues. Voluntary sterilization raises issues related to access and consent. Access to voluntary sterilizations may be limited in some States by so-called "conscience laws," allowing doctors to refuse to perform sterilization, by laws requiring long waiting periods after consent to sterilization is given, by lack of public or health insurance funding for voluntary sterilizations, and by consent requirements. A spouse's consent generally cannot be required, but parental consent may be required.

Other issues arise for involuntary sterilizations. In the past, the mentally ill and the developmentally disabled were sometimes involuntarily sterilized. Less frequently, criminals or the poor were sterilized against their will. Such sterilizations were done because of a belief in eugenics, a theory that the human "stock" would be improved if people with "bad genes" were kept from reproducing. In an early case, the Supreme Court, permitted such a sterilization under the police power with the statement that "three generations of imbeciles are enough." *Buck v. Bell*, 274 U.S. 200 (1927). In a later case, *Skinner v. Oklahoma*, 317 U.S. 535 (1942), the Court struck down a statute authorizing sterilization of certain criminals, but the statute was invalidated only on the ground that it impermissibly distinguished among classes of criminals in violation of the equal protection clause. The Court recognized a right to procreate which could be violated by involuntary sterilization, but it also upheld the practice where there was a substantial state interest in the sterilization.

Only a few States currently have statutes authorizing involuntary sterilizations. These statutes have been attacked but because *Buck* and *Skinner* upheld the practice of involuntary sterilization, the legal arguments against the statutes have focused on procedural rather than substantive due process rights. That is, they have focused on the standards defining who may be involuntarily sterilized and the procedural protections for those facing sterilization.

An important issue related to involuntary sterilizations is whether a parent or guardian can consent to the sterilization of a child or ward. Some States require a specific court order before a parent's or guardian's consent to a sterilization of a child or ward is effective or consider all such consents ineffective.

Abortion

As you must know, a woman's right to obtain an abortion is a hotly contested and highly controversial issue. In *Roe v. Wade*, 410 U.S. 113 (1973), the Supreme Court upheld a woman's right to obtain an abortion, based on the right to privacy theory of *Griswold v. Connecticut*, but allowed certain restrictions on abortions. Many cases after *Roe* addressed questions related to these and other restrictions on abortion. For example, cases considered whether abortions should be allowed in the second or third trimesters of pregnancy; whether abortions should be performed in hospitals or whether they could be performed in clinics, doctors' offices, or anywhere; whether doctors should perform abortions or whether they could be performed by nurses or others; whether doctors could be required to tell a woman about the viability of the fetus, the likelihood of the fetus living after abortion, or anything in particular before a woman's informed consent to an abortion was valid; and whether consent from a woman's husband or the man who impregnated her could be required.

Most cases have struck down restrictions on abortions, except those restrictions related to funding, insurance coverage, or access to an abortion. The courts have consistently ruled that public hospitals can refuse to perform abortions, that public funds, such as Medicaid funds, can be denied for abortions, that private insurance plans need not provide coverage for abortions merely because they provide coverage for birth control or childbirth, and that doctors can refuse to perform abortions under conscience laws. Court decisions upholding such restrictions have effectively limited access to abortions; a woman may obtain an abortion—but only if she can afford it and can find a doctor to perform it.

In 1989, the Supreme Court, in effect, overruled *Roe v. Wade* when it held in *Webster v. Reproductive Health Services*, _____ U.S. _____, 109 S.Ct. 3040, that States may limit the right to an abortion. After 1989, abortions may be even less accessible or even illegal.

Whether a minor has a right to an abortion without parental consent or notification has not been fully resolved. In *Planned Parent-*

hood v. Danforth, 428 U.S. 52 (1976), the Court held that during the first trimester of pregnancy, a State lacked the authority to require parental consent for a minor's abortion. The State's interest in the "safeguarding of the family unit and parental authority" were held insufficient to intrude on a minor's right to privacy, but the Court made clear that not "every minor, regardless of age or maturity, may give effective consent for termination of her pregnancy." Similarly, in *Bellotti v. Baird,* 428 U.S. 132 (1976), the Court suggested that a State can prohibit abortions by minors without parental consent—but only if the minors do not possess sufficient maturity and competency to make independent decisions on their own. On the issue of notification, in *H.L. v. Matheson,* 450 U.S. 398 (1981), the Court upheld a statute providing for parental notification, but only in the case of an unemancipated 15 year old. Later cases have further defined the circumstances when a minor may obtain an abortion without parental consent and without parental notification, but the law remains unclear and is constantly changing.

New reproductive technologies

New reproductive technologies like artificial insemination, *in vitro* fertilization, and embryo transfer raise many legal issues.

With artificial insemination by donor, there are questions related to the child's legitimacy. Most States now provide that a child who is born during a marriage after the artificial insemination of the wife by an anonymous donor with the consent of the husband is the legitimate child of husband, but the question of legitimacy may still arise when the donor is not anonymous. Further, there may be questions as to a known donors' responsibilities for and rights in relation to the child. With any donor, anonymous or known, there may be a question as to whether the child has a right to learn the identity of his or her natural father. Finally, questions arise as to the kind of genetic counseling that should be required before an artificial insemination may occur.

In vitro fertilization and embryo transfer may cause similar problems of parentage if an egg or sperm of a "non-parent" are used. Further, as we saw in Chapter 9, many legal problems can arise when a surrogate mother is used in conjunction with these techniques. In addition, some States have laws which define destroying a fertilized egg as child abuse. Because many fertilized eggs must be destroyed in the process of *in vitro* fertilization or embryo transfer, such laws may inhibit these techniques. They may be further inhibited by State statutes which forbid fetal research. *In vitro* fertilization and embryo transfer may be encompassed by such laws.

The Rights of Institutionalized Adults

Whatever their field of practice, social workers may work with adults who are institutionalized because of their physical or mental health, as punishment for a crime, or for other reasons. Social workers may be employed by the institutions where adults are voluntarily or involuntarily admitted or may be employed outside of such institutions but be instrumental in placing individuals in the institutions, or work with persons in institutions or with their relatives.

It is important that social workers understand the rights of institutionalized adults. Many times, it is social workers who must inform those who have been institutionalized or who face institutionalization of their rights or interpret their rights for them. Many times, only social workers are available to act as advocates for those who are institutionalized, insuring that their rights are recognized and respected. Further, social workers should not recommend placement in an institution without knowing the rights lost and retained by those in the institution, and cannot work successfully with the institutionalized without knowing their rights.

This chapter will review the basic rights of adults in three types of institutions with which social workers are likely to be involved: institutions for the mentally ill or disabled; nursing homes; and correctional facilities. Many of the rights of those in other health-related institutions which we will not review, such as veterans' hospitals or residential facilities for substance abusers, are derived from or analogous to the rights of those in these three types of institutions.[1]

A word of caution is necessary. As you read the sections concerning rights of mental patients and nursing home residents, you may get the impression that these people are well protected. In a sense they are—statutes, regulations, and court opinions have conferred many rights. But mental patients and nursing home residents are vulnerable and dependent on their caregivers. In practice, they will have the rights that are granted to them by law only if these rights are respected by the institution's staff or if they have strong and effective advocates.

THE RIGHTS OF MENTAL HEALTH PATIENTS

The right to treatment

The involuntarily admitted mentally ill. No Supreme Court case has decided whether involuntarily committed mentally ill adults have a right to treatment. Although many people expected the Supreme Court decision in *O'Connor v. Donaldson*, 422 U.S. 563 (1975), to establish the right of involuntarily committed mentally ill adults to treatment, the Court did not consider the right to treatment argument presented to it because, as we saw, it resolved the case on the ground that Donaldson's commitment was not justified, whatever treatment may have been provided

---

1. We will not review the rights of institutionalized children in these chapters. As we have seen, children have limited rights in American society—in and out of institutions. They are in the custody and control of their parents or legal guardians at all times and are not free to make decisions for themselves. Their parents can decide to place them in institutions, such as boarding schools or mental hospitals, and the State has only a limited interest in intervening or power to intervene in such decisions, as you saw in *Parnham v. J.R.*, 442 U.S. 534 (1979). Thus, when children are placed in institutions by their parents, generally the only rights they have are those on which their parents insist. This is particularly so if they are placed in private institutions. The rights of children who are removed from the care and custody of their parents and are placed in institutions under the authority of juvenile court acts may be specified in those or other acts or may be insisted upon by child welfare agencies.

to him. Some lower courts have, however, considered and accepted the argument that those who have been civilly committed have a right to treatment. *See, e.g., Wyatt v. Stickney*, 325 F. Supp. 781 (M.D. Ala. 1971). These courts have reasoned that if one has been involuntarily committed under the *parens patriae* authority, treatment is an essential corollary of the state's action while if one has been involuntarily committed under the police power, treatment is necessary to avoid lifetime detention.

Two problems arise with a judicially recognized right to treatment: the courts' limited expertise and their limited ability to implement their decisions. Courts may not be able to develop and prescribe the treatment to be afforded to those involuntarily committed; the type of treatment to be provided and the manner of its provision must be left to mental health professionals. Courts may be powerless if their orders are ignored; they cannot run mental hospitals and provide treatment themselves.

Both of these problems are illustrated by the case of *Wyatt v. Stickney*, where the court, in its first decision, recognized the class of involuntarily institutionalized plaintiffs' right to treatment but refused to determine the standards "to be used in effectuating that right," merely ordering the institutions involved in the case to develop plans for providing treatment to the class. When no adequate plans were developed six months after the decision, the court refused to appoint special masters to run the institutions, as requested by the plaintiffs. Instead, the court scheduled a hearing to allow the parties and interested experts to propose "minimum constitutional standards for adequate treatment of the mentally ill." 334 F. Supp. 1341 (1972) The court found none of the proposed standards acceptable, however, and thus developed its own standards, issuing a detailed order mandating such matters

as patients' clothing allotments and telephone privileges, hospital staff qualifications, number of staff required (*e.g.*, 10 housekeepers, 15 food service workers, 1 messenger), the content of individualized treatment plans, the interval between reviews of plans, the number of tubs and showers per patient and the content of patients' records. *Wyatt v. Stickney II*, 344 F. Supp. 373 (M.D. Ala. 1972). "Even this detailed system of supervision, however, produced no magical solutions, and the *Wyatt* litigation required many more decisions by the court."[2]

The Mental Health Patients' Bill of Rights expresses the "sense of Congress that each State should review and revise, if necessary, its laws to ensure that mental patients receive the protection and services they require" and are afforded certain rights, including "the right to appropriate treatment." 42 U.S.C. § 9501(1)(A), reaffirmed in 1984, 42 U.S.C. § 10841. In response to this law, or on their own initiative, several States, by statute, require that treatment be provided to involuntarily committed mentally ill adults. *See, e.g.*, N.Y. Mental Hygiene Law, § 33.03, requiring that each patient receive "care and treatment that is suited to his needs and skillfully, safely and humanely administered with full respect for his dignity and personal integrity."

The problems with judicial imposition of the right to treatment may also arise where the right is created by statute. The courts may still have to act to define and enforce statutory mandates. *See, e.g., Rouse v. Cameron*, 373 F.2d 451 (D.C. Cir. 1966), determining the scope of the District of Columbia's mandate of treatment.

Private hospital accreditation agencies,

---

2. Eisenberg and Yeazell, *The Ordinary and Extraordinary in Institutional Litigation*, 93 Harv. L. Rev. 465, 470 (1980).

such as the Joint Commission on Hospital Accreditation, and public hospital accreditation and licensing agencies, such as State health departments, may also require treatment of involuntarily admitted mentally ill adults. The courts will normally not be involved in interpreting and enforcing private requirements of treatment, but they will interpret public regulatory requirements.

Because there is no definitive case establishing a constitutional right to treatment for the involuntarily committed mentally ill, there may be no right to treatment in the absence of a statutory or regulatory mandate of treatment. Thus, a statute such as Indiana Code section 16-14-1.6-2, which provides that the involuntarily committed are entitled to "mental health services . . . in accordance with standards of professional practice" but which also provides that "there may be certain conditions for which there is no known effective treatment" and that, in such cases, a "service provider is not required to afford mental health services" may be valid.

Where there is a right to treatment, advocates for the mentally ill have sought and obtained statutory, regulatory, and judicial refinements of the right such as requirements that: (1) treatment be on the basis of individualized treatment plans with short-term, intermediate and long-range treatment goals and projected timetables, *see Davis v. Watkins*, 384 F. Supp. 1196 (N.D. Ohio 1974); (2) there be periodic review and revision of treatment plans, *see Wyatt v. Stickney II, supra*; 42 U.S.C. § 9501(1)(B); 42 C.F.R. § 441.102; (3) there be patient participation in the development of these plans, *see* 42 U.S.C. § 9501(1)(C); and, of particular interest to social workers, (4) there be provision of appropriate social services, *see* 42 C.F.R. § 441.102(b)(5).

The voluntarily admitted mentally ill. Because, as we saw in Chapter 16, there is no

constitutional right to medical care in America, there is no constitutional right to be voluntarily admitted to mental hospitals and those who are voluntarily admitted have no constitutional right to treatment. They may, however, have a statutory right to treatment or a right to treatment stemming from private accreditation or public licensing of mental health facilities.

The developmentally disabled. In *Youngberg v. Romeo*, 457 U.S. 307 (1982), the Supreme Court established a minimal right to habilitation for the mentally retarded. Romeo was a profoundly retarded adult with the "mental capacity of an 18-month-old child, with an I.Q. between 8 and 10," who could not talk and lacked "the most basic self-care skills." He was committed to a State institution by his mother when he was age 26. In the institution, he "was injured on numerous occasions, both by his own violence and by the reactions of other residents to him." After his mother complained, he "was physically restrained during portions of each day." His mother sued on Romeo's behalf, seeking damages for his injuries, his prolonged restraint, and for the institution's "failure to provide him with appropriate 'treatment or programs for his mental retardation.'" On appeal, the Court reasoned:

"[Romeo's] first two claims involve liberty interests recognized by prior decisions of this Court, interests that involuntary commitment proceedings do not extinguish. The first is a claim to safe conditions. In the past, this Court has noted that the right to personal security constitutes a 'historic liberty interest' protected substantively by the Due Process Clause. And that right is not extinguished by lawful confinement, even for penal purposes. If it is cruel and unusual punishment to hold convicted criminals in unsafe conditions, it must be unconstitutional to confine the involuntarily committed—who may not be punished at all—in unsafe conditions.

"Next, [Romeo] claims a right to freedom from bodily restraint. In other contexts, the existence of such an interest is clear in the prior decisions of this Court. Indeed, '[l]iberty from bodily restraint always has been recognized as the core of the liberty protected by the Due Process Clause from arbitrary governmental action.' This interest survives criminal conviction and incarceration. Similarly, it must also survive involuntary commitment.

"[Romeo's] remaining claim is more troubling. In his words, he asserts a 'constitutional right to minimally adequate habilitation.' The term 'habilitation,' used in psychiatry, is not defined precisely or consistently . . . [but it] refers to 'training and development of needed skills.'

"As a general matter, a State is under no constitutional duty to provide substantive services for those within its border. When a person is institutionalized—and wholly dependent on the State—. . . a duty to provide certain services and care does exist, although even then a State necessarily has considerable discretion in determining the nature and scope of its responsibilities. Nor must a State 'choose between attacking every aspect of a problem or not attacking the problem at all.' [However,] [a]s we have recognized that there is a constitutionally protected liberty interest in safety and freedom from restraint, . . . training may be necessary to avoid unconstitutional infringement of those rights. [W]e . . . conclude that **[Romeo's] liberty interests require the State to provide minimally adequate or reasonable training to ensure safety and freedom from undue restraint.**"

The Court then addressed the issue of the standards to employ in determining what was "undue" restraint and what training was required to prevent it. The Court stated:

". . . Romeo retains liberty interests in safety and freedom from bodily restraint. Yet these interests are not absolute; indeed to some extent they are in conflict. In operating an institution [for the mentally retarded,] there are occasions in which it is necessary for the State to restrain the movement of residents—for example, to protect them as well as others from violence. Similar restraints may also be appropriate in a training program. And an institution cannot protect its residents from all danger of violence if it is to permit them to have any freedom of movement. The question then is not simply whether a liberty interest has been infringed but whether the extent or nature of the restraint or lack of absolute safety is such as to violate due process.

"[T]he standard [which may be used to determine if there has been a violation of due process and which] . . . reflects the proper balance between the legitimate interests of the State and the rights of the involuntarily committed to reasonable conditions of safety and freedom from unreasonable restraints[,] . . . [may be stated as follows:] 'the Constitution only requires that the courts make certain that professional judgment in fact was exercised. It is not appropriate for the courts to specify which of several professionally acceptable choices should have been made.' [A stricter standard] . . . would place an undue burden on the administration of institutions such as [Romeo's] and also would restrict unnecessarily the exercise of professional judgment as to the needs of residents.

"In determining what [training] is 'reasonable'—in this and in any case presenting a claim for training by a State—we emphasize that courts must show deference to the judgment exercised by a qualified professional. By so limiting judicial review of challenges to conditions in state institutions, interference by the federal judiciary with the internal operations of these institutions should be minimized. Moreover, there certainly is no reason to think judges or juries are better qualified than appropriate professionals in making such decisions. **For these reasons, the decision, if made by a professional, is presumptively valid; liability may be imposed only when the decision by the professional is such a substantial departure from accepted professional judgment, practice, or standards as to demonstrate that the person responsible actually did not base the decision on such a judgment.** In an action for damages against a professional in his individual capacity, however, the professional will not be liable if he was unable to satisfy his normal professional standards because of budgetary constraints . . .

"In this case, therefore, the State is under a duty to provide [Romeo] with such training as an appropriate professional would consider reasonable to ensure his safety and to facilitate his ability to function free from bodily restraints. It may well be unreasonable not to provide training when training could significantly reduce the need for restraints or the likelihood of violence."

This minimal right to habilitation has been augmented by numerous statutes, regulations, and lower court cases. Of great importance, in the Developmentally Disabled Assistance and Bill of Rights Act, 42 U.S.C. § 6000 *et seq.*, Congress has provided financial assistance to State programs for the developmentally disabled, and made clear that: "Persons with developmental disabilities have a right to appropriate treatment, services, and habilitation for such disabilities." § 6009(1). Congress has further required that, in order to receive federal funds for a program for the developmentally disabled, a State must assure the federal government that it is providing habilitation to "each developmentally disabled person who receives services from or under the program" pursuant to an annually reviewed written habilitation plan which shall:

". . . be developed jointly by (A) . . . representatives of the program primarily responsible for delivering or coordinating the delivery of services to the person for whom the plan is established, (B) such person, and (C) where appropriate, such person's parents or guardian or other representative.

". . . contain a statement of the long-term habilitation goals for the person and the intermediate habilitation objectives relating to the attainments of such goals. Such goals should include the increase or support of independence, productivity, and integration into the community for the person. . . . The plan shall (A) describe how the objectives will be achieved and the barriers that might interfere with the attainment of them, [and] (B) state an objective criteria and an evaluation procedure and schedule for determining whether such objectives and goals are being achieved . . .

". . . contain a statement (in readily understandable form) of specific habilitation services to be provided, . . . identify each agency which will deliver such services, . . . describe the personnel (and their qualifications) necessary for the provision of such services, and . . . specify the date of the initiation of each service to be provided and the anticipated duration of each such service. [and]

". . . specify the role and objectives of all parties to the implementation of the plan." § 6023(a).

In *Pennhurst State Sch. & Hospital v. Halderman*, 451 U.S. 1 (1981), however, the Supreme Court stated that this law did not create substantive rights in favor of residents of institutions. It stated:

"Congress in recent years has enacted several laws designed to improve the way in which this Nation treats the mentally retarded. The Developmentally Disabled Assistance and Bill of Rights Act is one such law. It establishes a national policy to provide better care and treatment to the retarded and creates funding incentives to induce the States to do so. But the Act does no more than that. We would be attributing far too much to Congress if we held that it required the States, at their own expense, to provide certain kinds of treatment.''

Nevertheless, in order to obtain Medicaid reimbursement, a public institution for ''the mentally retarded or persons with related conditions'' must provide health or rehabilitation services pursuant to an individualized treatment plan. 42 U.S.C. § 1396d(d)(1) & (2); see, generally, 42 C.F.R. Part 442, Subpart G, spelling out specific treatment requirements.

The right to refuse treatment

As we have seen, medical treatment generally cannot proceed without the informed consent of the person being treated. As we also saw, informed consent must be voluntary, competent, and given with knowledge of the risks of and alternatives to treatment. These last two elements of informed consent may be problematical in the context of the mentally ill or disabled. Further, the very nature of involuntary commitment may preclude voluntary consent. As was stated in *Kaimowitz v. Department of Mental Health, State of Michigan*, Wayne County Circuit Court, 1973 C.A. No. 73-19434-AW, reprinted in Ralph Reisner, *Law and the Mental Health System* (St. Paul, MN: West, 1985), in which the court held that a patient involuntarily committed to a State mental hospital could not give informed consent for experimental psychosurgery:

''It is obvious that the most important thing to a large number of involuntarily detained mental patients incarcerated for an unknown length of time, is freedom. [To be vol-

untary, consent should be free of] any element of force, fraud, deceit, duress, overreaching, or other **ulterior form of constraint or coercion**. It is impossible for an involuntarily detained mental patient to be free of ulterior forms of restraint or coercion when his very release from the institution may depend upon his cooperating with the institutional authorities and giving consent to [treatment. Further,] [t]he privileges of an involuntarily detained patient and the rights he exercises in the institution are within the control of institutional authorities. Nearly every important aspect of his life [is] decided without an opportunity to participate in the decision-making process. Involuntarily confined mental patients live in an inherently coercive institutional environment. Indirect and subtle psychological coercion has profound effect upon the patient population. Involuntarily confined patients cannot reason as equals with the doctors and administrators over whether they should undergo [treatment.] They are not able to voluntarily give informed consent because of the inherent inequality in their position.''

Despite their inability to give informed consent, involuntarily committed mental patients may be treated. Moreover, they may be denied the right to withhold their informed consent for treatment, that is, the right to refuse treatment. Indeed, involuntary commitment is itself a form of involuntary treatment.

The courts have wrestled with the problems associated with the right of mentally ill or disabled adults to refuse treatment for many years. The Supreme Court, rather than deciding the issue in a case before it dealing with a refusal to take psychotropic drugs, remanded the case to be resolved as a matter of State law. *Mills v. Rogers*, 457 U.S. 291 (1982). The Court did indicate in its opinion remanding the case, however, that the right to refuse may be constitutionally protected.

The ultimate State decision in *Mills, Rogers v. Commissioner*, 390 Mass. 489, 458 N.E.2d 308 (1983), and numerous other State and lower federal court decisions, have recognized institutionalized mentally ill and disabled individuals' constitutional right to refuse treatment, even when they have been involuntarily committed. As was stated in *Rennie v. Klein*, 653 F.2d 836 (3d Cir.1981):

> "Just as the power to confine is accepted, but its nature limited, so may involuntary administration of [treatment] be justified only when accompanied by appropriate restrictions. The involuntarily committed patient retains a 'residuum of liberty,' and he correspondingly retains the right to be free from 'unjustified intrusions on [his] personal security.' Even though a person may be mentally ill, and has been properly committed involuntarily, he nonetheless is considered competent to some extent. His constitutional rights to be free from confinement and personal intrusion are necessarily limited by commitment, but they are not totally extinguished. The Constitution is . . . viable behind the walls of a psychiatric hospital . . ."

There may be qualifications on the judicially recognized right to refuse. *Rennie* stated the Constitution

> "does not prohibit all intrusions. It merely directs attention to and requires avoidance of those which are unnecessary or whose cost benefit ratios, weighed from the patient's standpoint, are unacceptable. There must be a careful balancing of the patient's interest with those to be furthered by administering the [treatment.]"

In general, the more intrusive or experimental the treatment, the more right to refuse and, conversely, the less intrusive or the more generally accepted the treatment, the less right to refuse. In other words, mental pa-

tients may not be able to refuse medication but may be able to refuse electro-shock therapy and should be able to refuse psychosurgery. Where medication is mind-altering, however, a right to refuse may be recognized under 1st Amendment, that is, freedom of speech, theories.

Some courts have not recognized any right of the involuntarily committed to refuse treatment or have recognized only a limited right to refuse, asserting that if the purpose of an involuntary commitment is treatment, treatment should proceed despite a refusal to consent or an incapacity to give informed consent. For example, a Wisconsin statute which provided that judicially committed mental patients do "not have the right to refuse medication and treatment" except, in limited circumstances, for religious reasons, and except for psychosurgery or electroconvulsive treatment was upheld in *Stensvad v. Reivitz*, 601 F. Supp. 128 (W.D. Wisc. 1985). The court stated:

> "[A] person subjected to involuntary commitment has been afforded a hearing concerning whether or not he can be forced to undergo psychiatric treatment. [I]nvoluntary treatment by antipsychotic drugs must be considered to be within the contemplation of the committing court. It seems clear . . . that an involuntary commitment is a finding of incompetency with respect to treatment decisions. Nonconsensual treatment is what involuntary commitment is all about."

Several States have adopted statutes which recognize a right of mental patients to refuse treatment. *See, e.g.,* Cal. Welf. & Inst. Code § § 5325(f),(g) & 5326.2. The federal Mental Health Patients' Bill of Rights recognizes:

> "The right not to receive a mode or course of treatment . . . in the absence of . . . informed,

voluntary, written consent to such mode or course of treatment, except treatment

(i) during an emergency situation if such treatment is pursuant to or documented contemporaneously by the written order of a responsible mental health professional; or

(ii) as permitted under applicable law in the case of a person committed by a court to a treatment program or facility." 42 U.S.C. § 9501(D).

The right to humane treatment in the least restrictive manner

Many court cases and statutes recognize the right of the mentally ill or disabled to humane treatment in the least restrictive manner. See, e.g., 42 U.S.C. § 6009(2), requiring that:

"The treatment, services, and habilitation for a person with developmental disabilities should be designed to maximize the developmental potential of the person and should be provided in the setting that is least restrictive of the person's liberty."

For many mentally ill or disabled adults, recognition of the right to humane treatment in the least restrictive manner has meant de-institutionalization or institutionalization in small community facilities, such as group homes. For those who remain in large institutions, recognition of the right has meant recognition of a variety of rights, some of which are reviewed below. Many of these rights are provided for in State statutes or are mandated by courts.

The right to be free of restraints and seclusion. As you saw, in *Youngberg v. Romeo*,

the Supreme Court held that an involuntarily committed mentally retarded patient has a liberty interest in being free of restraint which implicates the due process clause. However, the Court was not willing to condemn the use of all restraint or even to restrict restraints to cases of compelling or substantial necessity. In response to growing criticism of the use and abuse of restraints and seclusion, a number of States and the federal government have restricted their use. See, e.g., Ind. Code § 16-14-1.6-6; Cal. Welf. & Inst. Code § 5325.1; and 38 C.F.R. § 17.34a(d), restricting their use in Veterans Administration hospitals. But like the cases considering the use of restraints or seclusion, most statutes only restrict certain uses of restraints or seclusion. See, e.g., *New York State Association for Retarded Children v. Rockefeller*, 357 F. Supp. 752 (E.D.N.Y. 1973); Cal. Welf. & Inst. Code § 5325.1, forbidding "unnecessary or excessive physical restraint [or] isolation." Some statutes, alternatively, focus on procedural safeguards before restraints or seclusion may be used. This approach is exemplified by the federal Mental Health Patients' Bill of Rights which provides that patients should have:

"The right to freedom from restraint or seclusion, other than as a mode or course of treatment or restraint or seclusion during an emergency situation if such restraint or seclusion is pursuant to or documented contemporaneously by the written order of a responsible mental health professional." 42 U.S.C. § 9501(F).

Institutional employment. For many years, mental institutions routinely required patients to work: (1) for institutional rewards (e.g., "tokens" good for such things as television privileges); (2) for therapeutic reasons; (3) for minimal monetary rewards; or (4) to maintain the institution with minimal paid staff. A number of cases have forbidden institutional employment for any of these reasons on several grounds.

First, it has been held that mandatory institutional employment constitutes involuntary servitude in violation of the 13th Amendment to the Constitution. The standard employed to determine if work assignments violate the 13th Amendment, however, makes most challenges to institutional employment on this ground unsuccessful. Work must be both involuntary and completely non-therapeutic to violate the 13th Amendment. Thus, in *Estate of Buzelle v. Colorado State Hospital*, 76 Colo. 554, 491 P.2d 1369 (1971), for example, the court considered 6000 hours of work preparing food and cleaning and maintaining the hospital "related to a therapeutic program of rehabilitation" and, therefore, not violative of the 13th Amendment.

Second, it has been held that insofar as institutionalized persons are paid less than the minimum wage for non-therapeutic work, mandatory work assignments violate minimum wage laws. Claims under the minimum wage laws are sustained where a claimant merely demonstrates that the institution derives a substantial economic benefit from the enforced employment.

Third, it has been held that insofar as institutionalized persons must work to secure privileges, work assignments violate the right to treatment in a humane environment. That is, the privileges should be afforded without the work. Claims using this theory are sustained if the claimant demonstrates that the mandatory work is neither voluntary nor therapeutic, is not compensated in accordance with minimum wage laws, and is of a type for which the institution would otherwise have had to pay a regular employee.

Some State statutes and regulations explicitly forbid involuntary or uncompensated work for non-therapeutic reasons, *see, e.g.*,

Ill. Rev. Stat. ch. 91 1/2, par. 2-106, or require "compensation in accord with labor laws." N.Y. Mental Hygiene Law, § 3309.

The right to privacy. Privacy is often considered an essential part of an humane treatment environment. The right to privacy may mean the right to confidentiality of records and the right to privacy in treatment. Often, however, privacy may be sacrificed because of institutional needs. Patients may not be entitled to private rooms or to private bathrooms, but, wherever possible, they should be entitled to privacy.

The right to personal property. As part of a humane treatment environment, advocates have claimed the right to have personal property, including the right to wear one's own clothes. States statutes, federal and State regulations, and court decisions have upheld this right, but the right may be qualified or strictly limited at times. That is, one cannot simply bring all one's furniture to a mental institution or be allowed to wear inappropriate clothing.

First Amendment rights and freedoms. Those who are committed to mental institutions should not be deprived of their essential 1st Amendment freedoms—freedom of speech, religion, and association—merely because they are in institutions. Many States restrict these freedoms, however, particularly by restricting the right to communicate and visit with outsiders and by denying the right to worship in a church of choice. These rights have been restricted because of therapeutic concerns and institutional needs. That is, certain communications and visits may be upsetting or may threaten the security and administration of a facility; a mental health facility cannot provide a means to worship in every possible faith. Such restrictions on 1st Amendment freedoms of institutionalized mental patients are strictly scrutinized by the courts and upheld only if they are justified by compelling state interests.

Under the 1st Amendment, institutionalized mental patients should have the right to petition for redress of grievances. Thus, the federal Mental Health Patients' Bill of Rights provides that a mental patient should have:

"The right to be informed promptly at the time of admission and periodically thereafter, in language and terms appropriate to such person's condition and ability to understand, of [his or her] rights . . .

"The right to assert grievances with respect to infringement of [any] rights . . . , including the right to have such grievances considered in a fair, timely, and impartial grievance procedure provided for or by the program or facility.

". . . the right of access to (including the opportunities and facilities for private communication with) any . . . rights protection service . . . [or] qualified advocate . . . for the purpose of receiving assistance to understand, exercise, and protect [his or her] rights . . ." 42 U.S.C. § 9501.

In order to facilitate mentally ill and developmentally disabled persons' assertion of their 1st Amendment and other rights, the federal government provides funds to States to establish programs for "protection and advocacy" for the mentally ill, 42 U.S.C. § 10801 *et seq.*, and developmentally disabled, 42 U.S.C. § 60401 *et seq.* Many such programs employ social workers.

Transfers

Involuntarily committed persons may be committed to particular institutions by a court or by mental health authorities, but, after a period of time, a need may arise to transfer them to different institutions. Due process protections should come into play when one is transferred to a more secure institution or to an institution far from one's friends and family. Generally, however, only minimal protections are provided to the transferred person. Nevertheless, there should be some justification for a transfer and a person being transferred should be given notice and an opportunity to be heard prior to a transfer—if not a full-blown administrative or judicial hearing. This is particularly so if an individual has been committed to a particular institution by a court.

If involuntarily committed patients are released on out-patient status by an institution, they may also have a right to a hearing before they can be returned to the institution—even if they remain under a court commitment order. *See In re Richardson*, 481 A.2d 473 (D.C. App. 1984).

THE RIGHTS OF NURSING HOME RESIDENTS

Residents of nursing homes should be afforded all of the rights afforded to those in mental health facilities. However, while many mental health facilities are public, many nursing homes are private, and while many of those in mental health facilities have been committed involuntarily pursuant to a court order, most residents of nursing homes have admitted themselves voluntarily or been admitted by their relatives without a court order. In other words, in contrast to the situation with many mental patients, there may be no government involvement with a nursing home patient's confinement. Without government involvement, that is, without "state action," no rights may arise under the 14th Amendment or other sections of the Constitution. *See, e.g. Doyle v. Unicare Health Services, Inc., Aurora Center,* 399 F. Supp. 69 (N.D. Ill. 1975), aff'd. 541 F.2d 283, holding that being subject to extensive federal regulation and receiving federal funds did not make an otherwise private nursing home subject to a suit for deprivation of civil rights under 42 U.S.C. section 1983. Thus, many residents of nursing homes only have rights derived from statutes or regulations or from private contracts, and thus, have less rights than those confined in mental health facilities.

The almost 2 million residents of nursing homes whose care is paid for, wholly or partially, by Medicaid or Medicare do have substantial rights derived from federal law. Nursing homes have to meet certain standards and provide certain rights to residents in order to qualify for Medicaid reimbursement or for the limited reimbursement available for nursing home care under Medicare. The imposition of these standards and the provision of these rights also benefits the residents of the nursing homes whose care is not reimbursed by Medicaid or Medicare, but these residents may bear the brunt of the cost of meeting the standards.

For many years, the federal government, through regulations, required nursing homes to comply with a nursing home patients' bill of rights in order to receive Medicaid or Medicare reimbursement. This bill of rights provided each resident, among other rights, with the right to be "fully informed by a physician of his health and medical condition unless the physician decides that informing the resident is medically contraindicated;" the right "to participate in planning his total care and treatment;" the right to refuse treatment; the right to exercise all rights "as a citizen" and to submit complaints "free from restraint, interference, coercion, discrimination, or reprisal;" the right to privacy; the freedom from restraints except under certain conditions and with certain safeguards; the right to "be treated with consider-

ation, respect, and full recognition of his dignity and individuality;" the freedom from compulsory employment; and the freedom to "communicate, associate, and meet privately with individuals of his own choice," to "send and receive personal mail unopened," and "to participate in social, religious, and community group activities." *See,* 42 C.F.R. § 405.1121(k) (Medicare), § 442.311 (Medicaid) (1987).

In 1987, as part of the Omnibus Budget Reconciliation Act of 1987 (OBRA), P.L. 100-203, Congress enacted a sweeping law to further protect the rights of residents of nursing homes that receive Medicaid or Medicare. Among other things, the law provides that nursing home residents have the right: "to chose a personal attending physician;" to notice of any change of room or roommate; "to be free from physical or mental abuse, corporal punishment, involuntary seclusion and any physical or chemical restraints imposed for purposes of discipline or convenience;" and to have grievances addressed promptly. The law further requires nursing homes to maintain or enhance "the quality of life of each resident" and requires annual comprehensive assessments of each resident's ability to perform such everyday tasks as bathing, dressing, eating, and walking. These assessments will be used to develop written plans of care for each resident, describing how the resident's medical, psychological, and social needs will be met. Moreover, requirements are set forth for staffing, including the requirement that any nursing home with more than 120 beds must employ at least one full-time social worker with a degree in social work or similar qualifications. 42 U.S.C. §§ 1396r,1396r-3,1396s.

In addition to the regulation of private nursing homes that stems from Medicaid and Medicare reimbursement, private nursing homes generally have to be licensed. State licensing laws may mandate certain rights of residents of nursing homes. *See, e.g.* Tex. Civ. Stat. art. 4442c § 7B, requiring licensed nursing homes to honor the "Rights of the Elderly" set forth in Tex. Human Resources Code § 102.003. Many States additionally or alternatively have statutes specifically providing for rights for nursing home residents akin to those afforded mental patients by statute or court decision. *See, e.g.,* Colo. Rev. Stat. § 25-1-120; Mich. Comp. Laws § 333.20201. Further statutory protection of nursing home residents' rights may derive from the laws discussed in Chapter 13 which mandate the reporting of abuse of the elderly or of residents of nursing homes or from laws prohibiting such abuse. *See, e.g.,* Ill. Rev. Stat. ch. 111 1/2, par. 4161 *et seq.*; Tex. Civ. Stat. art. 4442, § 16.

Contracts for private nursing home care may specify residents' rights, but few people are in a position to negotiate for their rights when entering into a contract for nursing home care. Thus, some States now regulate the content of nursing home contracts. *See, e.g.,* Cal. Health & Safety Code § 1599.60 *et seq.* Comprehensive consumer protection laws may also regulate the contents of such contracts.

A particular problem for nursing home residents is involuntary transfers or discharges. Such transfers or discharges may occur for several reasons. A nursing home may want to replace Medicaid recipients with patients using insurance which pays at a higher rate than Medicaid; a nursing home may have been decertified for Medicaid or Medicare reimbursement or lost its license; a nursing home may not want to keep a troublesome or difficult patient. As has been noted:

> "An involuntary transfer can be a traumatic experience for the resident, an experience quaintly called 'transfer trauma.' Some believe involuntary transfer may increase mortality rates as much as 90%."[3]

Accordingly, many patients' advocates have gone to court to prevent involuntary transfers or discharges. In *O'Bannon v. Town Court Nursing Center,* 447 U.S. 773 (1980), the Supreme Court assumed that transfer trauma exists but held that it did not amount to a deprivation of liberty which would entitle nursing home residents to a pre-transfer hearing. Various federal and State statutes and regulations do exist, however, to protect nursing home residents against transfer trauma. OBRA, for example, restricts transfers and discharges and provides procedural protections before residents may be discharged or transferred; a resident patient may challenge the discharge or transfer through an administrative process which must be established by each State.

THE RIGHTS OF PRISONERS[4]

For many years, no rights of prisoners were established. In a series of cases beginning in the 1970's, however, the Supreme Court ruled that conviction of a crime and incarceration should not lead to a forfeiture of all constitutional rights, and that prisoners should keep those rights which were not inconsistent with their status as prisoners or with legitimate correctional objectives. *See, e.g., Bell v. Procunier,* 417 U.S. 817 (1974), *Bell v. Wolfish,* 441 U.S. 520 (1979). Following the Supreme Court's lead, through application of the 8th Amendment prohibition on cruel and unusual punishment, 1st Amendment guarantees of freedom of

---

3. Joan M. Krauskopf, *Advocacy for the Aging* 475 (1983).

4. Hereinafter, for convenience, the term "prison" will be used to refer to prisons, jails, and all other types of correctional facilities and the term "prisoner" will be used to refer to convicted criminals institutionalized in any type of correctional institution. It should be noted that the rights of those accused of crimes who are detained in jails while awaiting their trials, will not be discussed.

speech and religion, and other constitutional protections, the federal courts provided prisoners with a wide variety of substantive and procedural rights like those discussed above which have been accorded to mental patients and nursing home residents. For example, prisoners were given rights to privacy, to communicate with outsiders, and to practice their religion and were given freedom from undue restraint and excessive use of seclusion. Prisons were required to provide inmates with such necessities as medical care, personal security, sanitary facilities, and adequate diets. Prison overcrowding, which threatened personal security and deprived inmates of privacy through such mechanisms as double-celling, was frequently condemned. The federal courts repeatedly found that the totality of conditions in a prison or prison system was such that confinement in the prison or the system constituted cruel and unusual punishment in violation of the 8th Amendment.[5] During the 1970's, the federal courts found more than one hundred correctional institutions to have unconstitutional conditions of confinement and subjected them to sweeping orders related to the conditions of confinement and inmates' rights.

Prisoners' rights were always limited by the need to maintain order in the prisons and by a recognition that prisoners were, after all, convicted criminals who were being subjected to punishment. Nevertheless, through the efforts of the federal courts, the conditions of confinement for prisoners greatly improved in the 1970's. This improvement slowed, and many say was reversed, in the 1980's.

Primarily because of a new "get tough" policy on crime, the population of State and federal prisons more than doubled in the 1980's and almost every State faced a severe shortage of prison space. About 40 State prison systems and many of the largest jails were under federal court orders to reduce overcrowding and improve conditions, but it was prohibitively expensive to comply with these orders without releasing large numbers of prisoners, and such releases caused public outcry. Faced with this situation, the federal courts began to retreat from their active engagement in prison reform. Further, in several cases, the Supreme Court sharply restricted the use of 42 U.S.C. section 1983 to challenge prison conditions. *See, e.g., Parratt v. Taylor*, 451 U.S. 527 (1983); *Hudson v. Palmer*, 468 U.S. 517 (1984); *Daniels v. Williams*, 474 U.S. 327 (1986).

The new attitude of the federal courts towards prisoners' rights is typified by *Hudson v. Palmer*, in which the Court held that prisoners have no right to privacy in their cells and that their cells can be searched and their private property seized without regard to 4th Amendment guarantees. The Court stated:

> "We have repeatedly held that prisons are not beyond the reach of the Constitution. No 'iron curtain' separates one from another. Like others, prisoners have the constitutional right to petition the Government for redress of their grievances, which includes a reasonable right of access to the courts. Prisoners must be provided 'reasonable opportunities' to exercise their religious freedom guaranteed under the First Amendment. Similarly, they retain those First Amendment rights of speech 'not inconsistent' with [their] status as . . . prisoner[s] or with the legitimate penological objectives of the corrections system.' They enjoy the protection of due process. And the Eighth Amendment ensures that they will not be subject to 'cruel and unusual punishments.' The continuing guarantee of these substantial rights to prison inmates is testimony to a belief that the way a society treats those who have transgressed against it is evidence of the essential character of that society.

---

5. Ironically, because the Supreme Courts has held that the 8th Amendment only applies to prisons and other modes of punishing criminals, involuntarily committed mental patients, retarded youths in training institutions and students in public schools, to give three examples, may actually be entitled to less constitutional protections than convicted criminals.

"However, while persons imprisoned for crime enjoy many protections of the Constitution, it is also clear that imprisonment carries with it the circumscription or loss of many significant rights. These constraints on inmates, and in some cases the complete withdrawal of certain rights, are 'justified by the considerations underlying our penal system.' The curtailment of certain rights is necessary, as a practical matter, to accommodate a myriad of 'institutional needs and objectives' of prison facilities, chief among which is internal security. Of course, these restrictions or retractions also serve, incidentally, as reminders, that under our system of justice, deterrence and retribution are factors in addition to correction.

"Prisons, by definition, are places of involuntary confinement of persons who have a demonstrated proclivity for antisocial criminal, and often violent, conduct. Inmates have necessarily shown a lapse in ability to control and conform their behavior to the legitimate standards of society by the normal impulses of self-restraint; they have shown an inability to regulate their conduct in a way that reflects either a respect for law or an appreciation of the rights of others. Within this volatile 'community,' prison administrators are to take all necessary steps to ensure the safety of not only the prison staffs and administrative personnel, but also visitors. . . . [and] the inmates themselves.

"A right of privacy in traditional Fourth Amendment terms is fundamentally incompatible with the close and continual surveillance of inmates and their cells required to ensure institutional security and internal order. We are satisfied that society would insist that the prisoner's expectation of privacy always yield to what must be considered the paramount interest in institutional security. We believe that it is accepted by our society that '[l]oss of freedom of choice and privacy are inherent incidents of confinement.' "

The new attitude of the federal courts towards prisoners' suits is most significant since legislatures, administrators, and State court judges are generally more concerned with controlling crime than with "coddling" criminals by providing them rights.

SECTION V

LEGAL ASPECTS OF
SOCIAL WORK PRACTICE

INTRODUCTION TO LEGAL ASPECTS
OF SOCIAL WORK PRACTICE

As you have learned in reading this book, the law regulates the practice of social work in many ways. For example, the law determines when and how a social worker can involuntarily commit a client to a mental hospital or place a child in a foster home. In a sense, almost every law we have discussed so far indirectly affects or regulates some aspect of social work practice. Now we are going to look at the laws that directly affect or regulate social work practice. We are going to discuss the laws which are not directed at particular activities you may engage in as professional social workers, but towards you as professional social workers—whether you work for a public or private agency or in the private practice of social work.

The practice of the profession of social work is directly regulated in many States by statutes which determine who may call themselves social workers or who may practice the profession of social work or both. We are going to look at these statutes in Chapter 18. In this chapter, we will also look at the regulation of the profession, not by the law, but by the profession itself.

In Chapter 19, we are going to consider the laws which regulate the practice of social work by imposing legal obligations on social workers to maintain client confidences. We will also consider the professional requirements of confidentiality.

Social work practice is also regulated by laws which establish the consequences when social workers do not practice their profession properly. In Chapter 20, we are going to examine these laws, which answer the question: What can happen to social workers when they injure their clients through poor professional practice?

In Chapter 21, we are not going to be looking at the law, but at lawyers. We will discuss how social workers can go about referring their clients who are in need of legal help to lawyers and how social workers can work effectively with lawyers to aid their clients.

This section of the text may be the most important one for the growing numbers of social workers in private practice. Indeed, many of the laws we will be discussing were developed with only such social workers in mind. For example, licensing laws and laws making social workers accountable for their practices were developed in large part because of concern that increasingly social workers were practicing outside of the protective confines of agencies. But this section of the text is also important for social workers in agencies. Once developed, laws regulating the practice of social work may apply to all social workers.

18

Credentialing, Licensing, and Other Direct Regulation of Social Work Practice

CREDENTIALING OF SOCIAL WORKERS

LICENSING OF SOCIAL WORKERS

ADDITIONAL REGULATION OF SOCIAL WORK PRACTICE

REGULATION OF SOCIAL WORK AGENCIES

CREDENTIALING OF SOCIAL WORKERS

Some States may **credential** those who engage in an occupation. Credentialing is of two types: **registration** and **certification**. With registration, the State maintains a list or register of persons who are entitled to give themselves a certain title, like "marriage counselor" or "family therapist" but it does not certify that those in the register are competent to engage in the occupation for which they are registered. With certification, the State again lists those who may give themselves a certain title, but, in contrast to registration, it certifies that the people on the list are qualified to be on it. There may be specified requirements (e.g., certain educational attainment, certain experience or passing an examination) for either certification or registration, but usually the requirements are more stringent for certification than for registration.

The distinction between registration and certification is blurred by some commentators and in some laws. Indeed, in some laws, the term "registration" may be used when there is, in fact, certification and the term "certification" when there is only registration.

Whether it entails registration or certification, credentialing only protects a job title, not a job. If a law credentials an occupation, uncredentialed people can engage in the occupation, doing exactly what a credentialed person does, without violating the law. They run afoul of the law only if they use a credentialed person's title without authority to do so. Thus, if a State credentialed social workers, anyone could practice social work, but only those who were credentialed could call themselves "social workers." It would not be against the law to practice social work without being credentialed, but it would be against the law to use the title "social worker."

By way of contrast, **licensing** protects both the title and the job. No one can use a certain title or engage in a certain occupation without a license. Thus, if social workers were licensed and a man called himself a social worker and practiced social work without a social work license, he would be breaking the law, not only by calling himself a social worker, but also by practicing social work.

As with the distinction between certification and registration, the distinction between credentialing and licensing is blurred by some commentators and in some laws. Some laws which only protect a title are called licensing laws. Unlike the distinction between certification and registration, however, the distinction between credentialing and licensing is quite significant and easy to detect. Whatever a law is called, unless it actually restricts the practice of an occupation to those who have a license, it is not a licensing law.

An occupation which is neither licensed nor credentialed by the State may be privately controlled and regulated. Unions, professional associations and other private organizations may grant recognition to, that is, credential, certain people who engage in an occupation. These organizations then control and regulate the occupation by withholding this recognition from some people.

Private credentialing may have important ramifications. One may not be able to get a certain job or do certain things without a private credential. For example, a court may only order divorce conciliation with a privately certified marriage counselor or an agency may only hire privately credentialed family therapists.

There is extensive private regulation of the profession of social work, primarily through the Council on Social Work Education (CSWE) and the National Association of Social Workers (NASW). For example, only those who have obtained degrees from schools accredited by CSWE may get certain jobs as social workers or, in many States, get licenses to practice social work or publicly granted credentials to call themselves social workers. Only those who have master's degrees in social work from CSWE accredited schools, who have two years of postgraduate social work experience, and who pass a written examination administered by NASW may be admitted to the Academy of Certified Social Workers and may use the initials "**A.C.S.W.**," indicating membership in the academy, after their names.

Unlike regulation under the law, the regulation of social work through CSWE, NASW, and other private organizations, is voluntary. Nevertheless, this voluntary regulation is powerful and respected in the profession. It may have great impact on those who practice or wish to practice social work. For example, membership in the A.C.S.W. may be necessary for certain public and private agency jobs, particularly at supervisory levels, to obtain consulting contracts with or referrals from public and private agencies, to receive insurance reimbursement for services rendered in private social work practice, or to attract clients.

While private credentialing may be quite important to an individual who desires to engage in a privately recognized occupation, and while NASW recognition is undoubtedly important to professional social workers, private credentialing, like NASW's A.C.S.W. certification, is not backed by the government. There is no public enforcement of private recognition. The government will not stop someone from or punish someone for using a privately granted title; engaging in a privately credentialed occupation without the private authority to do so breaks no laws.

If credentialing is established by a law, the credentialing is publicly enforced. The government may take action to stop a non-

credentialed person from using a credentialed person's title or to punish a person for having used it.

Private credentialing may exist in addition to public credentialing, but only the public credentialing will be publicly enforced. For example, Montana credentials social workers and authorizes credentialed social workers to put the letters "LSW," standing for "Licensed Social Worker," after their names. If a woman in Montana who is not entitled to do so puts "LSW" after her name, the State of Montana may take action against her. The State will not take action, however, if a man in Montana who is not entitled to do so puts the private NASW credential, "A.C.S.W.," after his name. NASW or someone who is defrauded by the unauthorized use of the A.C.S.W. title may be able to sue the man who falsely used the A.C.S.W. title, but, although Montana will provide a forum for resolution of the suit, the suit is a private action.

It should be noted that although the title used in Montana is "licensed" social worker, in fact, social workers in Montana are only credentialed, not licensed. The law merely provides:

> "No person may represent himself to be a licensed social worker by adding the letters 'LSW' after his name or by any other means . . ." Mont. Code Ann. § 37-22-305(1).

And it specifically states, as does the credentialing law in many States, that it

> "does not prohibit qualified members of other professions . . . or the general public engaged in social work like activities from doing social work consistent with their training if they do not hold themselves out to the public by a title or description incorporating the words 'licensed social work' or 'licensed social worker.' " Mont. Code Ann. § 37-22-305, (2)(a).

It should also be noted that under the Montana law, uncredentialed social workers in Montana can call themselves "social workers" or say they practice "social work" without any legal sanction. Only the specific title "licensed social worker" cannot be used without a credential. This is similar to the law in many States which credential social workers. Many States do not prohibit using the term "social worker," but only prohibit using a specific term which indicates government credentialing, like "certified social worker," (e.g., New York, N.Y. Educ. Law § 7702) or "registered social worker" (e.g., South Carolina, S.C. Code Ann. § 40-63-10). The North Carolina credentialing law is broader than most, but it also only prohibits the use of a term indicating credentialing. It provides:

> "[I]t is unlawful for any person who is not certified under this Chapter, to represent himself or herself out to the public by any title or description denoting that he or she is certified under this Chapter. . . . Nothing herein shall be construed as prohibiting social workers who are not certified by the N.C. Certification Board for Social Work from practicing social work." N.C.Gen. Stat. § 90B-4.

Sometimes credentialing of social workers recognizes different levels of practice. Thus, for example, Illinois formerly recognized social workers with bachelor's degrees as "social workers" entitled to use the initials "S.W." after their names while master's level social workers were recognized as "certified social workers" entitled to use the initials "C.S.W." Ill. Rev. Stat. ch. 111, par. 6307.[1] Sometimes credentialing is only intended for clinical or independent social

workers; social workers employed by public agencies, or even by certain private agencies, are not credentialed. Thus, for example, Florida only protects the titles "clinical social worker," "licensed social worker," and "psychiatric social workers," Fla. Stat. § 490.012, while New Hampshire only protects the title "certified clinical social worker." N.H. Rev. Stat. § 330-A:21.

Private credentialing may also recognize different levels of practice. For example, NASW maintains a national Register of Clinical Social Workers for master's level social workers with specific post-master's clinical experience. NASW has also cooperated with other private groups interested in clinical social work practice to have the American Board of Examiners grant certfication as a "diplomate" in clinical social work to social workers who have an MSW and five years of acceptable postgraduate experience, have completed specific course work and passed an examination administered by the board, and have the highest level license possible in their State of residence.

Private or public credentialing may, further, be intended only for a certain type of practice, which may include but not be limited to social workers. For example, a few States credential marriage and family counselors, who could have degrees in social work or related fields, such as psychology, and the American Association for Marriage and Family Therapy recognizes as clinical members those who have master's or doctoral degrees in marriage and family therapy or who have completed a specified graduate level course of study, which could be offered by schools of social work, and have two years of supervised experience in marital and family therapy.

Government credentialing of occupations is always done by statute. There can be no common law credentialing and credentialing cannot occur by regulation without statutory authority. Regulations are often used to inter-

---

1. This law was repealed in 1987 and replaced with a licensing law, Ill. Rev. Stat. ch.111, par. 6351.

pret and implement credentialing statutes, but regulations cannot themselves authorize credentialing. The credentialing of occupations is also always at the State level. There is no local or federal public credentialing of occupations.

As of 1986, according to NASW and a study conducted by the United States General Accounting Office, seventeen States, no matter what their social work regulatory acts are called, merely credentialed social workers.[2] Because many States first established an official relationship with social workers in the 1980's, more States may credential social workers now.

LICENSING OF SOCIAL WORKERS

As of 1986, fifteen States had statutes licensing social workers.[3] These licensing laws may only apply to social workers in private, independent practice or engaged in clinical social work or may recognize different levels of social work practice. The Kansas licensing law, for example, recognizes two levels of social work practice. It is, moreover, interesting in that it restricts participation "in the delivery of social work service" without a licensed supervisor. It provides:

"No person may engage in the private, independent practice of social work unless he or she is: . . . licensed under this act as a master social worker . . .

"No person shall engage in the practice of social work for compensation or hold forth as performing the services of a social worker unless such person is licensed in accordance with the provisions of this act, nor may any person participate in the delivery of social work service unless under the supervision of a person who is licensed under this act." Kan. Stat. Ann. § 75-5353(a), 5348(a).

Also as of 1986, another five States had laws credentialing certain types of social workers and licensing other types, again generally those in private, independent practice or engaged in clinical practice.[4] For example, the Colorado law provided for credentialing of two levels of social workers: "licensed social workers," that is, social workers with master's degrees in social work and two years of supervised experience who pass written examinations; and "registered social workers," that is, social workers with bachelor's degrees in social work with two years supervised experience or with master's degrees. There was no practice restriction at these levels; only the use of these titles was restricted. But the law also provided that "no person may engage in the private, independent practice of social work" unless he or she met certain licensing requirements. Specifically, he or she must have a credential as a "licensed social worker," have had five years of supervised experience "in the field of specialization in which [he or she] will practice," and have passed an advanced examination on this field of specialization.

As with credentialing, licensing is always established by a statute at the State level. Un-

---

2.   These States were: Connecticut; Florida; Georgia; Illinois; Iowa; Maryland; Michigan; Montana; New Hampshire; New York; North Carolina; Oregon; Rhode Island; South Carolina; Tennessee; Texas; and the Virgin Islands. NASW, *State Comparison of Laws Regulating Social Work*, reprinted Oct. 1985 with corrections as of Feb. 1986; U.S. GAO, *Clinical Social Work: State Laws Governing Independent Practice and Reimbursement of Services*, Feb. 1986.

3.   According to the NASW and GAO studies, these States were: Alabama; Arkansas; Delaware; Idaho; Kansas; Kentucky; Louisiana; Massachusetts; North Dakota; Oklahoma; South Dakota; Utah; Virginia; the District of Columbia; and Puerto Rico.

4.   These five States were: California; Colorado; Maine; Ohio; and West Virginia.

like with credentialing, there cannot be private licensing. By definition, licensing is government regulation of an occupation. A State may sanction private credentialing and may make private credentialing a requirement for a license, but the State's action in recognizing the private credentialing does not convert the private credentialing into licensing. Thus, a State could require a social worker to obtain A.C.S.W. certification from NASW in order to obtain a license to practice social work, but the private A.C.S.W. credential would not thereby become a license. It is merely a prerequisite to obtaining a license.[5]

Licensing is always publicly enforced. If social workers were licensed by a State and if a woman called herself a social worker and practiced social work without a license, the State generally could bring a civil suit against her to stop her from using the title and from continuing to practice social work without a license and to assess penalties against her for the unlawful use of the title and the unlawful practice. It could probably also bring a criminal action against her for using the title "social worker" and engaging in the practice of social work. One of her clients, who was mislead by her into believing she was licensed, could also sue her, but this private action would be additional to the possible public enforcement.

Because licensing protects not only an occupational title, but also an occupation, a State must be able to define with a reasonable degree of specificity what licensed people in an occupation may do that no one else may do. This may be difficult for social work. No two social workers may agree on a definition of social work let alone a definition that does not include many counselors, psychothera-

pists, community organizers, or others who legislators would not wish to prevent from engaging in social work like activities.

The definitions of social work practice in State laws licensing social work are typically broad and may encompass many people who do not really practice social work. Consider the definitions of social work practice in the Oklahoma and Massachusetts licensing laws.

> " 'Practice of social work' means the professional activity of helping individuals, groups or communities enhance or restore their capacity for physical, social and economic functioning and the professional application of social work values, principles and techniques in areas such as clinical social work, social service administration, social planning, social work consultation and social work research to one or more of the following ends: Helping people obtain tangible services; counseling with individuals, families and groups; helping communities or groups provide or improve social and health services; and participating in relevant social action. The practice of social work requires knowledge of human development and behavior; of social, economic and cultural institutions and forces; and of the interaction of all these relevant factors. Social work practice includes the teaching of relevant subject matter and of conducting research into problems of human behavior and conflict." Okla. Stat., tit. 59, § 1250.1, par. 2

> " 'The practice of social work,' [means] rendering or offering to render professional service for any fee, monetary or otherwise, to individuals, families, or groups of individuals, which services involve the application of social work theory and methods in the prevention, treatment, or resolution of mental and emotional disorders or family or social dysfunctioning caused by physical illness, intrapersonal conflict, interpersonal conflict or environmental stress. Such professional services may include, but shall not be limited to, the formulation of psychoso-

---

5. In fact, West Virginia does recognize A.C.S.W. membership as a substitute for its licensing examination, and Louisiana requires inclusion in the national Register of Clinical Social Workers for a social worker to be entitled to insurance reimbursement.

cial evaluation, counseling, psychotherapy of a nonmedical nature, referral to community resources, and the development and provisions of educational programs.'' Mass. Gen. Laws, ch. 112, § 130.

These definitions could encompass people who do assertiveness training workshops, debt counselors, people who run support groups for cancer patients, low-income tenant organizers, people who run shelters for the homeless, and numerous others not considered social workers, although the requirement in the Massachusetts law that the services offered ''involve the application of social work theory and methods,'' could narrow the definition to exclude such people. Do you think Massachusetts and Oklahoma would take action against such people on the basis of their laws restricting the practice of social work to licensed social workers, and that taking such action is what the legislature intended?

To deal with the problems that can arise because of broad definitions of social work practice in licensing laws, there may be exclusions or exemptions for related professions or reliance on the use of a title to distinguish who is and who is not practicing social work. Thus, a 1986 NASW model licensing act provides:

''No provisions in this Act shall be construed to prevent individuals licensed by this State, whose activities overlap with the practice of social work, from carrying out the functions covered by their respective license provided that such individuals shall not hold themselves out to the public by any title or description of services likely to cause public confusion with the titles or descriptions of services set out in this Act.''

Taking a slightly different approach, the Virginia licensing statute provides:

''The 'practice of social work' means rendering or offering to render to individuals, families, groups organizations, governmental units, or the general public service which is guided by special knowledge of social resources, social systems, human capabilities, and the part conscious and unconscious motivation play in determining behavior. Any person regularly employed by a licensed hospital or nursing home who offers or renders such services in connection with his employment in accordance with patient care policies or plans for social services adopted pursuant to applicable regulations when such services do not include group, marital or family therapy, psychosocial treatment or other measures to modify human behavior including child abuse, newborn intensive care, emotional disorders or similar issues, shall not be deemed to be engaged in the 'practice of social work.' Va. Code § 54-941, par. c.

NASW has been seeking licensing for social workers for many years. It has argued that licensing, and to a lesser extent credentialing, can protect the public against untrained and incompetent practitioners and can enhance the profession of social work.

NASW asserts that clients of social welfare agencies, who generally have no choice in picking their social workers, need licensing to insure they receive competent service. It asserts that without licensing or credentialing, public agencies and other employers have hired ''workers without any professional social work training or education'' and who do not have ''the professional knowledge or skill to know what their clients need or how to help them.'' While the large numbers of persons who voluntarily seek social work services or seek help from private practitioners do have a choice in picking their social workers, NASW asserts they are ''in no position to effectively judge the possible competence'' of their chosen social workers and that "[w]ithout some form of licensing, clients and potential clients of social work services have no basis for understanding the qualifications of those persons presenting themselves as 'social workers.' "[6]

Further NASW "believes that one of the most important reasons for enacting licensure [for social work] is the accountability it provides to the public."[7] NASW can suspend or revoke its credentials for unethical conduct, but not for incompetent conduct, and it cannot prevent social workers, even unethical ones, from continuing to practice. However, public licensing and credentialing agencies can institute mechanisms a client can use to raise charges of malpractice easily and can suspend or revoke the licenses or credentials of incompetent practitioners. Moreover, NASW asserts standards of practice can be more easily imposed and enforced when an occupation is licensed, or to a lesser extent, credentialed. If anyone who wants to can practice an occupation or use an occupational title, it may not be easy to establish standards of practice. Similarly, it may not be possible to impose or enforce confidentiality requirements which further protect the public.

NASW acknowledges that it is interested in licensing because licensing, and to a lesser extent, credentialing, can help develop and protect the profession of social work. If charlatans and untrained and unskilled people are kept from practicing social work or using the title social worker, the professional reputation of social workers is enhanced and protected. Licensing and credentialing can insure that professional and ethical standards are maintained and that practitioners participate in continuing education requirements. Perhaps most important, licensing and credentialing would grant official recognition

that social workers have special skills and require special training and that social work is important enough to require regulation. That is, official recognition may be valued for its own sake. Moreover, official recognition may lead to other benefits. For example, for social workers in private, independent practice, licensing or credentialing may lead to a benefit of great importance: health insurance payment for their services.

As of 1986, fifteen States had so-called "freedom of choice" or "vendorship" laws that required insurance companies to provide coverage for social work services if mental health services were covered or to reimburse insureds if they chose social workers over psychiatrists or psychologists for covered services.[8] Such vendorship provisions usually only are established where social workers are licensed or credentialed and only apply to licensed or credentialed social workers. For example, New York law provides:

> "[A] group policy for delivery in this state which policy provides reimbursement to insureds for psychiatric or psychological services or for the diagnosis and treatment of mental, nervous or emotional disorders and ailments, however defined in such policy, by physicians, psychiatrists or psychologists, must provide the same coverage to insureds for such services when performed by a social worker, within the lawful scope of his or her practice, who is certified . . . and in addition shall have . . . three or more years post degree experience in psychotherapy." New York Insur. Law § 3221(1)(4)(A).

More States would undoubtedly have vendorship provisions if more States licensed or credentialed social workers—or even recog-

---

6. NASW, "Answers to Questions State Legislators Ask About Social Work Licensing," (NASW: Md 1986)
7. Id.

8. According to NASW, these States are: California; Florida; Kansas; Louisiana; Maine; Maryland; Massachusetts; Montana; New Hampshire; New York; Oklahoma; Oregon; Tennessee; Utah; and Virginia.

nized that social work requires special skills and training. Indeed, in 1986 forty States had vendorship provisions for psychologists, who were licensed in every State, as compared to the fifteen States having such provisions for social workers, who were licensed in considerably less than half the States.

The benefits of a particular licensing or credentialing law for the public or an occupation may be assessed by determining if it contains certain elements. Continuing education and periodic renewal requirements indicate a desire to insure competence. Confidentiality requirements, accessible mechanisms for making complaints, and provisions for thorough investigation of complaints and for suspension and revocation of licenses also protect the public. Grandfathering provisions allow people who are practicing at the time a law goes into effect to be licensed or credentialed without meeting the law's requirements. The more people grandfathered, the less protection of the public. Similarly, the more exclusions of like professionals and members of a profession from licensing requirements, the less protection of the public. Recognition of other States' licensing laws provides mobility for professionals, allowing them to move freely from State to State. Often such provisions require reciprocity. In other words, State A will recognize State B's action in licensing an individual if State B would recognize State A's licensing of an individual. Finally, whether the policing and regulating of an occupation is done by members of the profession, the general public, or others may determine whether licensing or credentialing serves primarily to protect the public or enhance the profession.

NASW has identified several essential elements to a social work licensure act, including: (1) recognition of different levels of practice; (2) regulation of independent or private practice; (3) "valid means of objectively assessing the qualifications, knowledge and competencies of applicants for licensure, in addition to requirements for educational attainment;" (4) coverage of all areas of social work practice, "including public and voluntary, profit and non-profit;" (5) periodic renewal and continuing education requirements; (6) confidentiality provisions; and (7) the "authority to hold practitioners accountable for their professional and ethical conduct."[9]

ADDITIONAL REGULATION OF SOCIAL WORK PRACTICE

Statutes or regulations, at the State, federal or local level, may regulate aspects of the practice of social work by requiring certain training, experience or expertise to perform certain tasks. For example, a Colorado statute provides:

"A person shall not be allowed to testify regarding a [child] custody or visitation evaluation which he has performed . . . unless the court finds that he is qualified as competent, by training and experience, in the areas of:

(i) the effects of divorce and remarriage on children, adults and families;

(ii) appropriate parenting techniques;

(iii) child development, including cognitive, personality, emotional, and psychological development;

(iv) child and adult psychopathology;

(v) applicable clinical assessment techniques; and

(vi) applicable legal and ethical requirements of child custody evaluation." § 14-10-127 C.R.S.

---

9. NASW, "Answers to Questions," *supra.*

How a court is to determine competency in these areas is not set forth. One can only assume that it would rely on standards established by credentialing and licensing laws or by private professional associations, such as NASW or the American Association for Marriage and Family Therapy.

Other laws may set forth standards more easily applied by a judge. For example, the California law which sets forth standards for those who may perform divorce conciliation and mediation only permits conciliation by social workers with a master's degree in social work and a set number of years of experience, Calif. Code of Civ. Proc. § 1745; the Illinois law which provides that "clinical social workers" may act as "qualified examiners" in proceedings to involuntarily commit mentally disabled adults requires:

> "a master's or doctoral degree in social work . . . [and] at least 3 years of supervised post-master's clinical social work practice which shall include the provision of mental health services for the evaluation, treatment and prevention of mental and emotional disorders." Ill. Rev. Stat. ch. 91 1/2, par. 1-122.1.

The Illinois law also provides:

> "To the extent that social workers are, by law, regulated . . . a clinical social worker shall also be in compliance with such law." Ill.Rev. Stat. ch. 91 1/2, par. 1-122.

Often statutes or regulations set forth requirements for employment, not as consultants, as in the Colorado, California, and Illinois laws above, but as staff of public agencies. These requirements may be similar to licensing or credentialing requirements or may refer to them. For example, many States set forth specific education requirements for certification as a school social worker and preclude public schools from employing school social workers who are not certified.

REGULATION OF SOCIAL WORK AGENCIES

Many of the agencies or facilities where social workers are employed, such as adoption agencies, day care centers, clinics, nursing homes, hospices or drug rehabilitation centers, are subject to government supervision and regulation. The government may supervise and regulate even those social service agencies and facilities which are purely private and which are affiliated with religious organizations.

Usually public social service agencies need not be licensed. They are closely regulated, but any regulation may be self-regulation established by the same law which established the agency. Alternatively, a public agency established by one type or level of government, such as a town clinic, may be regulated by another type or level of government, such as a State health department.

Most private social service agencies and facilities must be licensed in order to operate. The licensing requirement is generally found in a State statute which typically provides that a designated public agency with expertise in the services provided will license the agency or facility. For example, day care centers are typically licensed by a public child welfare agency, and nursing homes typically are licensed by a health department.

In order to be licensed, a private agency or facility must meet standards set forth in the licensing statute and in any regulations promulgated by the designated licensing agency. The standards typically relate to a facility's physical structure or to a facility's or agency's program and the number and qualifications of its staff.

Private social work agencies are often publicly regulated, not only through licensing, but also through government purchase of service, that is, through contracts with public agencies. For example, a public child welfare agency might purchase counseling services or foster care services for its clients from a private agency. The private agency must meet certain requirements imposed by the public agency if it wishes to enter into a purchase of service agreement. Again these requirements may relate to staff qualifications.

Public funding sources may also regulate private social work agencies insofar as specific requirements are established to receive public funds or grants. For example, there may be specific requirements to receive State funds to operate a drug abuse program or federal funds to operate a job training program. Again these requirements may relate to staff qualifications.

Any requirements related to social work staff qualifications in licensing laws, purchase of service agreements, or funding programs serve to regulate the practice of social work itself. For example, if a hospice must have a staff social worker with certain training and experience in order to be licensed, that training will probably be offered in schools of social work, and social workers interested in working in hospices will have to practice in a way that provides the necessary experience.

Most private social work agencies are organized as **corporations**. Corporations are special kinds of entities recognized by the law. An association, an organization, or an agency which wants to become a corporation must follow the procedures for incorporation and meet the requirements for a corporation, both of which will be established by law, generally in a State statute. There may be different procedures and requirements for profit-making versus non-profit corporations.

Once an organization is granted corporate status, whether as a profit-making or non-profit corporation, it becomes an entity that is equivalent in many ways to a person in the eyes of the law. For example, it can sue and be sued in its own name; it cannot be denied due process; and it can be taxed.

The major reason for incorporating is protection from liability. Once an organization becomes a corporation, its stockholders or members, its board of directors, and its officers cannot generally be held personally liable for actions of the corporation. Only the corporation will be held responsible to the extent of its assets.

Those in the private practice of social work for profit, even those in a solo practice, may incorporate for this reason. Incorporation of a private practice also can have tax advantages.

A major reason for non-profit social work agencies to incorporate also relates to taxes. Organizations incorporated as non-profit corporations are exempt from most taxes while unincorporated organizations may not be exempt from taxes even if they operate as non-profit charitable organizations.

Just because a corporation is exempt from taxes, contributions to the corporation are not necessarily deductible on the contributor's tax return. There are additional requirements imposed on tax exempt corporations to obtain tax deductible status. Neither tax exempt status nor tax deductibility are automatic for non-profit corporations; both must be applied for and will be granted only if certain requirements are met, such as a charitable or educational purpose. Non-profit corporations which engage in substantial lobbying may be tax exempt, but contributions to them are usually not tax deductible.

Most incorporated social work agencies are incorporated as non-profit corporations and are both tax exempt and have tax deductible status.

Social work agencies may also incorporate

because licensing agencies may require incorporation as a way to assure the stability and responsibility of an agency. For the same reason, funding sources may require incorporation. Thus, for example, a shelter for battered women may not be eligible for State domestic violence funds unless it is incorporated.

Corporations are subject to regulation by the State which incorporated them. Their books and records must be made available to appropriate officials. They must periodically apply to maintain their corporate status. Further, corporations are subject to regulation by State and federal taxing authorities. Corporations must file tax returns even if they are exempt from taxation and they must make their books and records available to taxing authorities to justify maintaining their tax exempt or tax deductible status.

19

Confidentiality of Communications and Records

AN OVERVIEW OF THE LAW

In order to understand the law related to confidentiality of communications to social workers and social work records, it is necessary to understand both the terms which are defined below and the law related to confidentiality in professional relationships in general.

Records may be defined as written documentation maintained by a social worker or another professional of interactions with or related to clients; written comments, notes or observations placed in a clients' file; documents, like letters, medical reports or court orders, included in a client's file; or the file itself.

Communications are statements made to a social worker or another professional in the course of practice. Communications may be from a client or from another person, may be oral or written, and may be recorded in clients' records or only remembered.

Confidentiality is the obligation of a social worker or other professional not to reveal records of or communications from or about a client obtained in the course of practice.

Finally, a **privilege**, broadly defined, is the right of a client to keep a social worker or another professional from revealing records and communications from or about the client. Narrowly defined, as it usually is and as it shall be used in this book, a privilege is the right of a client to keep a social worker or another professional from testifying in a court or an administrative tribunal about communications from the client. Sometimes the right to keep a professional from testifying is called a **"testimonial privilege."**

Privileges generally are considered to belong to clients, not to professionals. Professional must assert privileges on their clients' behalf, but they may not assert privileges if their clients waive them. In other words, a professional may not be able to refuse to testify if a client allows his or her testimony—unless another confidentiality rule precludes the testimony.

Confidentiality may be required by law or by professional or ethical standards. Where confidentiality is legally required, legal actions may be taken to prevent a breach of confidentiality. Someone who is injured by a breach of confidentiality may also sue for damages. Even if confidentiality is legally required, however, a client may not be able either to stop a professional from breaching confidentiality by testifying or producing records in court or to collect damages for the breach of confidentiality. Only if there is a privilege not to testify or produce records, in addition to a confidentiality requirement, can testimony or a disclosure of records in court be stopped. A privilege must be legally recognized to be a privilege. Unless there is legally recognized privilege, a professional can be ordered to testify or produce records by a court. A refusal to testify or produce records in the face of such an order can result in being jailed for contempt of court for a set time or until one complies with the order.

Confidentiality laws are generally found in statutes or regulations. Privileges may also be found in statutes, in regulations in rare cases, and quite often in the common law. Confidentiality and privilege laws are often State laws, but federal and local laws may also establish confidentiality requirements or privileges. Many federally assisted activities of importance to social workers, such as education, welfare assistance, health care, and substance abuse treatment, are covered by federal confidentiality laws, and some local activities are covered by local confidentiality laws. Indeed, one activity may be covered by federal, State, and local confidentiality laws. For example, the federal law, known as the "Buckley Amendment,'' 20 U.S.C. § 1232g mandates that schools receiving federal funds keep their records confidential; most States have statutes imposing confidentiality requirements on public schools within the State consistent with the Buckley Amendment; and most school districts have confidentiality rules implementing the federal and State laws. Thus, the records of a social worker employed by a public school receiving federal funds may be covered by federal, State, and local confidentiality laws.

Confidentiality

A legal requirement of confidentiality in a professional practice is usually based on a combination of constitutional and common law notions of privacy, a belief that confidentiality is essential to the particular professional relationship, and a desire to foster this relationship. In other words, confidentiality requirements usually stem from the desire to preserve people's privacy in their relationships with certain professionals and from the belief that if confidentiality is not assured, clients will not seek necessary help from these professionals or will not reveal the information to the professionals that must be revealed for a fruitful relationship. Thus, social workers will not be required to maintain confidentiality unless confidentiality is considered essential to successful social work and social work itself is considered important.

Even where confidentiality is not required for a certain profession, it may be required for certain records maintained by or certain communications made to members of the profession. Indeed, confidentiality may be required for certain records or communications whoever has possession of the records or received the communications, whether professional or not. For example, as we have seen, it is generally required that records of adoptions be kept confidential. Even if there is no requirement that social workers maintain confidentiality in a jurisdiction, social workers in that jurisdiction must keep their records related to adoptions confidential. And the court clerks who prepare and maintain adoption records for the courts must also make sure that the records are kept confidential.

Confidentiality laws that apply to certain records or communications usually have exceptions which authorize the release of records or the disclosure of communications in certain circumstances. Similarly, even where confidentiality is legally required as a general matter for a certain profession, it usually is excused for certain records or certain communications. Indeed, a breach of confidentiality may not only be excused but also required. Child abuse and neglect reporting laws are examples of laws requiring breaches of confidentiality because of the societal view of the importance of preventing child neglect and abuse.

Exceptions to confidentiality laws may be built into the confidentiality laws themselves, may be found in other laws, like a child abuse and neglect reporting law, or may be generally recognized in a jurisdiction's common law although not stated explicitly in any law. The exceptions differ from jurisdiction to jurisdiction, from profession to profession, from record to record, and from communication to communication. Nevertheless, a few common exceptions should be noted.

Despite confidentiality laws, it is often permissible to reveal records for purposes of research, program evaluation, or public statistical gathering. Depending on to whom the records are revealed, client names and identifying information may have to be deleted.

It is usually permissible to disclose records and reveal communications if the client consents. Sometimes this consent must be in writing. Often the written consent must specify a particular record or communication which may be disclosed. In other words, a general consent for release of records or disclosure of information may not be valid. The consent always must be voluntary. It may be difficult to determine the voluntariness of consent in certain situations which may be coercive by nature, such as when someone is required to execute a consent for the release all medical records to obtain welfare benefits, or where a patient is mentally disabled.

It is often not considered a disclosure at all if one professional consults another professional in the same agency about a client, if a professional reviews a file with a supervisor, or if a professional makes a disclosure for the benefit of the client to another professional who is bound by similar or stricter confidentiality rules. However, before making such disclosures, "the clinician would be well advised to seek consent, if not as a personal precaution then as an act of deference to the client. It cannot hurt legally and may help clinically."[1]

Confidentiality may not be allowed or required if it aids in the furtherance of a crime. Similarly, a professional may be required to disclose confidential communications to prevent an injury or if a danger is posed if a communication or record is not disclosed. For example, in *Tarasoff v. Board of Regents*, 17 Cal. 3d 425 (1976), the California Supreme Court held that a psychotherapist, who was bound by statutory confidentiality laws, could be liable to the parents of a woman murdered by one of his patients because he failed to warn the woman of the patient's threat to kill her.

---

1. Herr, Arons, and Wallace, *Legal Rights and Mental Health Care* (Lexington Books, 1984)

Privilege

A law requiring a professional to maintain confidentiality may not accord the professional a testimonial privilege, but certain professionals may have a privilege not to testify, in addition to having legal recognition of confidentiality. Certain records of or communications to professionals may also be privileged whether or not the professional is generally accorded a privilege. Usually, testimonial privileges are granted in accordance with criteria established by a noted law professor, Dean Wigmore. Using Wigmore's criteria, a privilege will be recognized for a professional if:

(1) communications to the professional originate in the expectation that they will not be disclosed and the particular communications for which a privilege is claimed so originated;

(2) confidentiality is essential to a full and satisfactory relation between the professional and his or her clients;

(3) the professional relationship is one which society thinks should be "sedulously fostered;" and,

(4) the injury to the relationship, in general or in a particular case, if a disclosure is made is greater than the benefit gained from the disclosure.

In addition, a privilege is more likely to be accorded if confidentiality has been legally recognized for the type of professional, communication or record. It also may be more likely to be recognized if there are professional, or generally recognized ethical, requirements of confidentiality.

The four Wigmore factors may be considered by a legislature in creating a privilege statute, by a court in developing a common law privilege rule, or by a court in deciding a case before it. If there is a specific statute or an established common law rule granting a privilege, a court may or may not be able or willing to make an exception in a specific case based on these factors. The Wigmore factors may also be considered in deciding whether or not to establish confidentiality requirements.

As with confidentiality laws, most statutes or common law rules creating privileges have built in or generally recognized exceptions. Also, as with confidentiality laws, exceptions to laws creating privileges may be found in other laws. For example, almost all child abuse and neglect reporting laws specifically abrogate all or most privileges.

All or some privileges may not apply in certain types of proceedings such as civil commitments, child abuse cases, or malpractice cases against the professional who is required to maintain confidentiality. Some privileges do not apply in murder cases or in cases involving other serious crimes. Because the privilege belongs to the client, the client may always waive the privilege. Waivers are generally readily found by courts.

LEGAL CONFIDENTIALITY
REQUIREMENTS AND PRIVILEGES

Jurisdictions differ as to which professions are granted testimonial privileges or are bound by confidentiality laws and as to which kinds of records and communications are protected by privileges and confidentiality laws. Almost universally, lawyers are granted privileges not to testify and are bound by strict confidentiality rules which have few and limited exceptions. Doctors generally are privileged not to testify about their patients and are bound by confidentiality rules but less universally than lawyers, and generally there are more and broader ex-

ceptions to the privileges and confidentiality rules than for lawyers. Some States grant privileges to and require confidentiality of all licensed psychotherapists whether or not they are doctors; a few States even grant privileges to and require confidentiality of psychotherapists but not doctors. The confidentiality rules and privileges may be broader for psychotherapists than for doctors. The priest-pentinent privilege is quite common. It encompasses all recognized clergy, not just Catholic priests.

Privileges and legal confidentiality requirements for the profession of social work as a whole are fairly rare. As of 1986, only twenty two of the thirty seven jurisdictions that licensed or credentialed social workers included privileges or confidentiality requirements in their social work licensing or credentialing statutes. Moreover, these privileges and confidentiality requirements were generally limited in scope and full of exceptions. A common law privilege is usually not recognized for social workers as such.

Allred v. State, 554 P.2d. 411 (Alaska 1976), in which the five member Alaska Supreme Court produced four opinions on whether a social worker should be granted a testimonial privilege, illustrates some of the attitudes courts may have towards social workers' assertions of testimonial privileges.

While Allred, a suspect in a murder case, was being questioned at the police station, he asked to see Dr. Wolf, his psychiatrist at a public psychiatric clinic, or Shirley Henderson, a psychiatric social worker at the clinic who was his counselor under the supervision of Dr. Wolf. Henderson was summoned to the police station where she talked with Allred extensively about his involvement in the killing. At Allred's subsequent trial for the murder, she was called to testify, over Allred's objection, on her conversation with him. The judge allowed her testimony, and she testified that Allred told her he committed the murder as part of a suicide pact, but he had been unable to kill himself. Despite this testimony, the jury was unable to reach a verdict and a mistrial was declared. Because a retrial was contemplated, the Alaska Supreme Court granted review to determine whether any privilege would prevent Mrs. Henderson from testifying at the retrial.

A majority of the court recognized a common law psychotherapist-patient privilege, but two justices thought it should not apply to Mrs. Henderson. Two justices thought it should apply, and one justice thought her testimony was privileged by a psychologist's confidentiality statute. Excerpts from the four opinions follow.

MAJORITY OPINION

"Privilege was originally conceived of in England as a judicially recognized point of honor among lawyers and other gentlemen not to reveal confidential communications. This general rule of honor was conclusively repudiated in 1776, although lawyers were able to maintain a privilege for their profession. The common law did not recognize a physician-patient privilege [but Alaska has created a statutory one.] This privilege does not extend to criminal cases, however. Even if it did, the rule would not cover communications to a psychiatric social worker.

"Allred relies on [an Alaska statute] to provide a statutory psychotherapist privilege in criminal cases.[2] The provision nowhere states that it was intended as creating a privilege. It does not refer to courtroom testimony. The general thrust of its language seems to point towards 'anti-gossip' considerations. [Moreover,] [t]he legislature's fail-

---

2. The statute provides: "No psychologist or psychological associate may reveal to another person a communication made to him by a client of his about a matter concerning which the client has employed the psychologist or psychological associate in a professional capacity."

ure to create expressly an evidentiary privilege for psychotherapists while doing so for newspapermen [in the same legislative session as it enacted the psychotherapist's confidentiality law] indicates a legislative intent that psychotherapists were not to be so favored.

"It is only as an 'anti-gossip' measure that [the psychotherapist's confidentiality law] makes sense. The statute provides that only a writing may waive whatever rights a patient acquires under the section. But evidentiary privileges are traditionally much more easily waived, in light of the strong competing policy in favor of compulsory testimony. By enacting [the law] as an 'anti-gossip' measure, the legislature has opened the door to professional licensing sanctions and possibly broadened the scope of common law duty in suits against indiscreet psychotherapists.

"Allred argues that the federal and Alaska constitutions require an evidentiary psychotherapist privilege resulting from the right to privacy [which is specifically included in the Alaska Constitution and which has been recognized as included in the United States Constitution.] Since it is apparent that Mrs. Henderson was not a police agent, we do not perceive any state action that would trigger the constitutional privacy guarantees . . .

"The question remains whether a common law psychotherapist privilege should be recognized and, if so, what its scope ought to be. Because of the strong need for compulsory testimony, the creation of new privileges is generally looked upon with disfavor by the commentators. The courts have created privileges in modern times, however, when they have found sufficient policy justification for doing so. One American trial court has specifically created a psychotherapist-patient privilege as a matter of decisional common law, although the result has been criticized. In the federal area, the United States Congress is apparently of the opinion that the creation of a psychotherapist-patient privilege is properly one of common law development through court decision.[3]

"Professor Wigmore has proposed four canons to be used as basis for determining whether, for any particular relationship, a common law privilege is desirable. In our view the psychotherapeutic relationship satisfies each of these canons.

First, communications to a psychotherapist in the course of therapy are inherently confidential. Patients often make statements in psychotherapy which they would not make to even the closest members of their families. Psychotherapy tends to explore the innermost recesses of the personality, the very portions of the self which the individual seeks to keep secret from the world at large. Revelation of such matters could have an irrevocably harmful effect upon the reputation and well being of the patient.

"Second, inviolability of the confidence is essential to achievement of the psychotherapeutic goal. Without foreknowledge that confidentiality will attach, the patient will be extremely reluctant to reveal to his therapist the details of his past life and his introspective thoughts and feelings. Without the patient's confidence, a psychiatrist's efforts are worthless. In therapy the patient must often lay bare his entire inner life, including his fantasies, his past behavior, and his feelings of guilt or shame.

"Third, the relationship between psychotherapist and patient is unquestionably one which should be fostered. Psychiatry and its techniques of therapy are relatively young as specialized fields, but they have received widespread recognition as a valid sphere of medical science. Indeed, our legislature has recognized the importance of psychotherapy by prohibiting certain revelations by

psychologists and psychogical associates in [the confidentiality law] discussed earlier in this opinion.

"Finally, in balancing injury to the relation, by fear of disclosure, against the benefit to justice by compelling disclosure, the scales weigh heavily in favor of confidentiality. We believe that the goals of therapy may be frustrated if the privilege does not attach. Reason indicates that the absence of a privilege would make it doubtful whether either psychotherapists or their patients could communicate effectively if it were thought that what they said could be disclosed compulsorily in a court of law. We are also aware of the delicate position occupied by the psychotherapist himself. Because of the special nature of a patient's confidences, the psychotherapist is subject to an even more stringent honorable obligation not to disclose, under any circumstances, than are other professionals. We do not wish psychotherapists to be faced with the dilemma of either violating this extraordinary trust or being incarcerated.

"In conclusion, **we recognize a common law privilege, belonging to the patient, which protects communications made to psychotherapists in the course of treatment**.

"We now turn to a consideration of the scope of the privilege. At the outset **it appears to us that the psychotherapist privilege cannot be extended to all manner of counselers, and psychological associates**. The number of persons engaged in such capacities is so great that it is hard to estimate the number of relationships and conversations which would fall within the privilege. **Moreover, it appears to us that there is a substantive difference between the activities comprehended under the term 'psychotherapy' and those covered by the fields of counseling and psychiatric social work**.

"Much psychological counseling has as its direct or indirect goal the improvement of the client or patient in his current adaptation to reality, his relationships with others, and

---

3. Congress so stated when it rejected a proposed rule for federal courts creating a psychotherapist-patient privilege.

his ability to handle his personality problems more adequately. But this does not mean that all forms of psychological counseling should be equated with 'psychotherapy' in the serious sense of that term. Psychotherapy literally means 'treatment of the mind.' It commonly refers to the use of psychological means to modify mental and emotional disorders of a serious, disabling nature. In its technical application the therapist, through interview sessions, verbally explores the patient's conflicts, feelings, memories and fantasies in order to provide insight into the causes of the disorder.

" 'Psychotherapy' implies treatment by medical personnel, or treatment by non-medical professionals (clinical psychologists) who are as well trained as physicians to employ psychological methods of treating emotional and personality disturbances. By contrast 'counseling' most often refers to psychological efforts of a nomedical nature, administered by non-medical personnel. Counseling is aimed not primarily at uncovering deep psychological processes but at enabling the patient to make more effective use of his present resources. Counseling includes vocational, educational, employee, rehabilitation, marriage, and personal guidance within its spheres of operation.

"An additional distinction between psychotherapy and counseling must be drawn according to the type of training which is a prerequisite for practicing each of those fields of endeavor. Counselors may have little or no training in formal psychology and methods of treatment. Psychotherapy should be practiced only by persons who have undergone rigorous intellectual and practical training. Only psychiatrists, who are medically qualified, and a limited number of professional psychologists should be permitted to practice psychotherapy. It is only a few highly qualified psychologists [with a doctorate plus experience] who should practice psychotherapy at all, and even then it should be done in collaboration with licensed medical personnel in all but exceptional instances.

"Moreover, counseling is considerably more superficial and less searching than what we understand to be included within the term 'psychotherapy.' Counseling either does not, or should not, have as its aim a deep penetration into the psychic processes of the patient or client. The need for a privilege to foster the counsel-client relationship is, correspondingly, less readily apparent. It is true that clients of counselors may reveal incriminating or degrading acts about themselves, but this cannot be considered a necessary concomitant of the counseling relationship. Such revelations are more in the nature of an unintended byproduct of the counseling activity. Such utterances are neither essential nor necessary to the successful realization of the counseling goal. There may be instances in which counselors attempt to uncover the intimate, personal secrets of their clients, but we do not view such activity to be essential or proper to the counseling function. In any event, such occurrences would not provide sufficient justification for extending an evidentiary privilege to the field of counseling as a whole.

"We note that the legislature has drawn a similar distinction in the statutes regulating the practice of professional psychology. To be a licensed psychologist in Alaska one must hold a doctoral degree in psychology from an accredited school, must have at least one year's [acceptable] experience . . ., and must have passed an examination . . . To be licensed as a psychological associate in Alaska it is necessary that the applicant hold a master's degree from an accredited or approved educational institution, with at least 24 credit hours of course work directly related to counseling or another specialized area in which licensure is required including a practicum, that he have three years' experience within the past ten years, two of which are in Alaska, including one year of [acceptable] supervised postgraduate experience . . ., and that he have the recommendation of his immediate supervisor, if a licensed psychologist, or two licensed psychologists. He must also pass an examination.

"Statutorily only a psychologist may practice psychology. A psychological associate may practice counseling. A psychologist may employ psychotherapeutic techniques in his practice. A psychological associate may only employ counseling techniques. While the statutory definitions are not too helpful about the distinction between psychotherapeutic techniques and counseling techniques, it is noteworthy that the legislature employed a sharp semantic demarcation between them. The statutes do evidence a policy that psychotherapy be practiced only by licensed psychologists, and that others, such as psychological associates be limited to the practice of counseling. If even psychological associates, whose qualifications are considerable, may not practice psychotherapy, it follows that the legislature did not intend that persons with lesser qualification should practice psychotherapy. We find this legislative distinction helpful, not because it sets the boundaries of the privilege—to us a matter of common law development—but because it evinces the public policy of Alaska and fortifies us in deciding a question of common law.

"We believe that the psychotherapist-patient privilege can be held within proper bounds—while still fulfilling the purposes of the privilege—by using a two-fold test of applicability. The first criterion focuses upon the professional status of the person to whom the communication is made. As we have shown above, **the evidentiary privilege should extend only to communications made to a psychiatrist or a licensed psychologist**. The second criterion focuses upon the type of communication in question. We believe that **the evidentiary privilege should extend to communications made in the course of intensive, deep psychotherapy, of the type which requires confidentiality for its success**. This necessarily includes communications made in the course of diagnostic interviews and examinations which might reasonably lead to psychotherapy, as we have delineated that term. Excluded from the privilege, for example, would be statements made by a patient to a psychiatrist or psychotherapist outside of the therapeutic relationship.

"Measured against this test, it is apparent that Allred's statements to Mrs. Henderson do not qualify as privileged, as she was neither a psychiatrist nor a licensed psychologist, and the statements were not given in the course of psychotherapeutic treatment.

"Allred asserts that a distinction between licensed and unlicensed practitioners is a violation of . . . equal protection . . . He argues that the psychiatric social worker is 'the poor man's psychiatrist,' and that limiting the evidentiary privilege to licensed practitioners results in impermissible practical discrimination based on wealth.

"We find, however, that the line we have drawn is a means closely and substantially related to our ends. The need for an evidentiary privilege decreases with the privacy of the communications involved, and hence with the 'depth' of psychological probing and the seriousness of the case. This gradation can be equated, roughly, to the skill and training of the practitioner. The dividing line chosen provides a workable estimate of this skill and training. As with any drawing of lines, no absolute certainty is possible, but the line is not drawn arbitrarily or as a matter of caprice.

"[In] *San Antonio Ind. School Dist. v. Rodriguez*, 411 U.S. 1, 20-21, (1973) . . . the United States Supreme Court indicated that wealth discriminations would require strict scrutiny only if the facts involved an 'absolute deprivation' of the benefit at issue, because the disadvantaged persons were 'completely unable to pay.' Allred does not offer sufficient data . . . [to establish this deprivation and, from a footnote in the opinion, "[i]n view of the widespread availability of social and health services for economically disadvantaged persons, we will not assume that such persons are absolutely deprived of psychiatric and psychological services by licensed personnel.''']

''In conclusion, a majority of this court agrees that a common-law psychotherapist-patient privilege obtains in Alaska. [But] the author of this opinion and [another justice] are of the view that the privilege does not extend to Allred's communication.''

CONCURRING OPINION

''. . . I believe that the statute establishing a privilege for communications made by a client to a psychologist or psychological associate is here controlling, . . .

''Mrs. Henderson was employed* by Mr. Allred in a professional capacity. She characterized the session during which Allred made his confession as a 'therapeutic session'. Assuming that Mrs. Henderson was acting as a psychological associate, the communication clearly comes under the provision of [the statute.] The scope of the statute in no manner is limited to communications other than in court. In fact, the statute expressly excludes certain communications, specifying: 'This section does not apply to a case conference with other psychologists, psychological associates or with physicians and surgeons, or in the case in which the client in writing authorized the psychologist or psychological associate to reveal a communication.'

''Had the legislature also intended to exclude communications in court, it could easily have added such a provision. Under the well-recognized rule of construction, . . . the exclusion of specified communications from the statute indicates an intent not to exclude additional communications such as those

made in court. [Because there is no] . . . reason for not applying the plain meaning of the statute, [the statute] generally prohibits courtroom testimony in situations such as presented in the instant case. We have [only] for consideration the question of whether Mrs. Henderson is to be regarded as a psychological associate so as to come under the provisions of the statute.

''[The licensing statute] applies to a 'psychologist or psychological associate.' [It] defines a 'psychological associate' as including a 'counselor or psychometrist'. [It] states that a 'psychologist' means a person who practices psychology', and [it] provides that

'to practice psychology' means to apply established principles of learning, motivation, perception, thinking, and emotional relationships to problems of personnel evaluation, group relations and behavior adjustment, including (A) counseling and guidance; (B) using psychotherapeutic techniques with persons or groups of persons who have adjustment problems in the family, at school, or at work; (C) measuring and testing of personality, intelligence, aptitudes, emotions, and attitudes and skills; (D) conducting research on human behavior [.]

''Mrs. Henderson worked directly under the supervision of Dr. Aaron Wolf, a psychiatrist, and was assigned by the . . . Clinic staff as Mr. Allred's counsellor. He often sought her aid in resolving mental and emotional problems, and she worked with Dr. Wolf's staff in attempting to resolve Mr. Allred's mental and emotional problems. She had engaged in some 30-50 extended counseling sessions with him and had been his counsellor for at least a year prior to [his] arrest. It would appear beyond dispute that she constituted a psychologist or psychological associate under the terms of this statute.

I would therefore hold that the psychologist privilege applies in the instant case, and that upon retrial, Mrs. Henderson may be permitted to testify as to the communications made

---

*   ''The fact that the services were provided by the state cannot be regarded as altering the relationship between the client and psychologist. 'Employed' must be construed as meaning 'consulted' or 'utilized.' Otherwise, the statute would violate state and federal 'equal protection' provisions in making the privilege depend on one's ability to pay for the services involved.''

to her by Mr. Allred only in the event that Mr. Allred authorizes her to reveal such communications.''

CONCURRING OPINION

''While I agree that a common law privilege covering communications between patients and psychotherapists should be recognized, on the particular facts of this case, I would hold that the privilege encompasses the relationship between Mrs. Henderson and Allred. [T]he record demonstrates that Mrs. Henderson was intimately familiar with Allred's problems and occupied a central role in Allred's therapy.* Given Professor Wigmore's four canons for determining whether a common law privilege is desirable, and given the conclusion that a psychotherapist-patient privilege should be recognized, then the reason why the privilege ought not extend to the instant case should somehow relate to Wigmore's canons. I fail to see why the rationale which supports a common law privilege is less compelling here than in any case where the psychotherapist-patient privilege is recognized.

''The communication in question which took place between Allred and Mrs. Henderson was viewed by them as a therapeutic session in which Allred discussed his mental problems and looked to Mrs. Henderson for advice and counseling. Allred requested Mrs. Henderson's presence for the purpose of counseling. He talked to her because he needed counseling. His candor with Mrs.

Henderson was based on the belief that he was in therapy with his counselor. Under the circumstances confidentiality was essential to the relationship between them.

''In my opinion Allred's relationship with Mrs. Henderson, initiated to seek mental health, is one which ought to be sedulously fostered by the community. It is not necessarily relationships with psychiatrists or licensed psychologists that ought to be sedulously fostered; rather, what should be fostered is the therapeutic relationship which looks toward improvement of mental health. Whatever trust Allred once had in psychotherapists in general, or Mrs. Henderson in particular, would be significantly undermined if we were to exclude therapists in Mrs. Henderson's position. Were it Dr. Wolf instead of his alter ego who testified in court, the damage to the therapy relationship could be no less in its impact. Thus, I conclude that all of the reasons which support the recognition of a psychotherapist-patient privilege in theory call for the application of that privilege to the circumstances of the case at bar.**

CONCURRING OPINION

''I concur with [the majority opinion] in [its] recognition or creation of a psychotherapist-patient privilege as a matter of decisional common law. But I do not concur

---

* ''Mrs. Henderson was the eyes, ears, and spokeswoman for a therapy group consisting of staff members of various specialties. She would present problems weekly to the group which was led by Dr. Wolf and which consisted of staff members of various specialties. The problems of particular individuals and the resolution of these problems would be discussed among the group. Mrs. Henderson described this therapy as 'community therapy.' In her own words: '. . . it's where the entire staff works together; in other words it's not one person working with one patient. It's one person, with the help of the rest of the staff, working. . . . It's a case of the entire staff relating everything they know about a particular patient.' ''

** ''[The majority opinion] seeks to distinguish the instant situation from the general psychotherapist-patient privilege on the grounds that relationships with psychological associates are less 'intensely personal.' The reasoning which correlates the depth of the patient-therapist relationship with the therapist's fulfillment of state licensing requirements escapes me. The purpose of our licensing requirements is to protect consumers of the service from the charlatan, not to provide the therapist with a license to become 'intensely personal.' Therapists treat mental and emotional problems and do not necessarily delve into the patient's life with a particular degree of personal intensity.

''In view of the community therapy regimen he was undergoing, I cannot conclude that Allred's interview with Mrs. Henderson must have been 'less intensely personal' merely because she was neither a licensed psychologist nor a psychiatrist.

with [the] conclusion that this privilege does not cover the communication made by Allred to Mrs. Henderson. [Moreover, I do not concur with the reasoning of the majority opinion.]

"I do not agree that [in determining whether there is a privilege] the third [Wigmore] canon must be satisfied, *i.e.*, that 'The relation must be one which in the opinion of the community ought to sedulously fostered'. There may be a day when community opinion does not sedulously foster the relation between psychotherapist and patient. If that day should come to pass, my position is that the privilege should still be recognized.

"Professor Wigmore apparently developed his canons to explain privileges then accepted. I feel that the inclusion of a criterion involving community approval is unfortunate if used for any purpose other than in an analysis of how some established privileges arose. I believe that if an antireligious sentiment should sweep the community, the court should still recognize the priest-penitent privilege; and if a substantial majority of the population, because of particular religious tenets, does not believe in medical science, the physician-patient privilege should still apply.

"The need for a privilege should not depend upon community approval of the relationship. Rather, it is the purpose of the relationship and its legitimate value to the participants which should be weighed against the truth-finding function of the courts. Another consideration is the effectiveness of the relationship in terms of the legitimate and valuable goals of that relationship. [I]f community approval for the relationship vanishes, the legitimate interests of the parties to the relationship should still be recognized.

"The psychotherapist-patient privilege is somewhat analogous to both the priest-penitent privilege and the physician-patient privilege. Like the priest-penitent privilege, the relationship between psychotherapist and patient often involves a central part of a person's life. The trust and confidence placed in the psychotherapist is often as deep, if not deeper, than that placed in a priest. Like a physician-patient relationship, the main purpose of the relationship between the psychotherapist and the patient is the well-being of the patient—emotional, mental and frequently physical. Furthermore, often the purpose of the psychotherapist-patient relationship is the prevention and curing of antisocial behavior, such as the therapy in the instant case. If this type of activity is successful, then many potential crimes will not be committed. The prevention of a number of similar defendants being prosecuted in future cases is more than an adequate balance for the hampering of the truth-finding function in an individual case.

"Psychotherapy is a relatively new endeavor, and as with all growing sciences, may not be adequately understood by the community. But it is its effectiveness, *i.e.*, its central value to the participant and legitimate purposes which are to be considered, and not the community's conscious approval. Community approval, although perhaps some evidence of value, is only a secondary indication of what I feel to be the primary considerations.

"I believe that regardless of community opinion, a psychiatrist's efforts to help an emotionally or mentally disturbed person would be fruitless if the patient did not place his entire trust in the psychiatrist and did not have complete confidence that their communications would never be revealed to others. Psychotherapy could never be successful without such trust and confidence.

"Professor Wigmore was an eminent authority on the law of evidence. But his 'authority' does not require this court to unalterably adhere to every rule that he proposes. I would dispense with Wigmore's third condition or canon for recognizing the psychotherapist-patient privilege.

"Finally, I respectfully suggest that [the majority] opinion should not have stated the additional rule of law that the psychotherapist-patient privilege is one 'belonging to the patient'. This clearly implies that the psychiatrist cannot claim the privilege if the patient waives or abandons it. I realize that where the physician-patient privilege is concerned, for example, this is a rule that is generally, if not universally, applied by the courts. And in the few instances where the question has arisen involving the psychotherapist-patient privilege, the same rule has likewise been applied. But I question its validity in the latter instance. A seriously disturbed patient may very well not realize the consequences of his waiver of the privilege. Where there has been intense psycho therapy over an extended period of time, it is more likely than not that to force the psychiatrist to breach the trust the patient has placed in him would destroy the psychiatrist-patient relationship, and could result in incalculable harm to the patient. I believe that circumstances may well exist where the psychiatrist should be permitted to assert the privilege—even in the face of an abandonment or waiver of the privilege by the patient—for the best welfare of the patient."

Another murder case, *State v. Martin*, 274 N.W.2d 893 (S.D. 1979), also illustrates the use of the Wigmore criteria to decide if a privilege exists and the courts' attitude towards social workers' assertion of testimonial privileges, even in the face of a statute specifically requiring social workers to maintain confidentiality.

Lawrence Lawlor, a licensed, certified social worker, received a call at 4:45 a.m. from John Martin, one of his patients. Martin told Lawlor he had just killed someone. With Martin's consent, Lawlor notified the police, telling them where they could find Martin and his victim. Nevertheless, at Martin's trial for the murder, Lawlor and Martin both urged

that the content of the phone conversation was privileged. The trial court disagreed, Lawlor was compelled to testify, and Martin was convicted. On appeal of the conviction, the South Dakota Supreme Court held that a South Dakota statute which provided in pertinent part:

"No licensed certified social worker, social worker, or social work associate or his employee may disclose any information he may have acquired from persons consulting him in his professional capacity that was necessary to enable him to render services in his professional capacity to those persons"

"requires that confidentiality may be inferred only after an examination of the facts and circumstances in each case." The court agreed that this statute created a privilege, but noted that its "specific language" limits the privilege

"to information disclosed to the social worker 'in his professional capacity that was necessary to enable him to render services in his professional capacity to those persons.' This would indicate that the legislative intent in the adoption of the act was to require inquiry into the facts and circumstances in each case."

The court then held that, in the circumstances of the case and using the Wigmore factors, the communication between Martin and Lawlor was not privileged. It stated:

"It appears to be settled law that there are four basic and fundamental conditions which must be present to establish a privilege, whether the privilege is set forth by statute or common law . . . [that is, the four Wigmore factors.]

"There is nothing in the record which would indicate that the conversation was made in confidence or with the expectation of confidentiality. The substance of the conversation would substantiate the lack of confidentiality, or an intent thereof, since Martin advised Lawlor that he understood the need for advising the police before he furnished Lawlor his address. We can only speculate as to Martin's reasons for contacting Lawlor. Martin's family was out of state for the weekend—he had just that evening resigned from his part-time employment which had supplemented his income since he was a college student—he had consulted with Lawlor as a patient for six to eight months and apparently had faith in him. Seemingly he wanted to talk with someone. In any event, the conversations offered in this case did not relate to and did not arise out of their specific relationship.''

Although the courts may not be willing to recognize a privilege for social workers, in general, and although legislatures may not accord privileges to or impose confidentiality requirements on all social workers, many social workers are nevertheless covered by confidentiality laws and have testimonial privileges.

Some States require confidentiality of or grant privileges to social workers in statutes not addressed only or specifically to social workers. For example, Illinois requires confidentiality of and grants privileges to all "therapists" providing "mental health or developmental disabilities services," and specifically includes social workers within its definition of "therapist." Ill. Rev. Stat. ch. 91 1/2, pars. 803, 802 (9). And, as you saw in Allred, one justice of the Alaska Supreme Court interpreted a statute granting privileges to psychotherapists as including psychiatric social workers.

Confidentiality laws and privileges may further apply to the activities of social workers or to their places of employment. Most States have confidentiality laws related to, among other activities of social workers:

adoptions; health care; juvenile court work; public aid or welfare administration; and substance abuse treatment. To encourage openness in certain specific situations which may involve social workers, testimonial privileges may be accorded those who engage in such activities as counseling rape victims, divorce conciliation and mediation, or providing advice on birth control and venereal disease. In most jurisdictions, records of hospitals, clinics, hospices and other health related agencies, community mental health agencies, child welfare agencies, and many other places where social workers are employed must be kept confidential.

In addition, social workers' privileges may be linked to the privileges of others. In many States, social workers who work with doctors, psychotherapists, or others who are covered by professional privileges are considered the agents of the professionals for whom they work and are covered by any privileges applying to the professionals. As you also saw in Allred, however, social workers are not uniformly given a privilege merely because they work with a privileged professional.

The welter of confidentiality and privilege laws applying to social workers and the absence of one simple overriding confidentiality or privilege law applying to social workers in many jurisdictions makes it difficult for social workers to know what must be kept confidential and when they must assert a privilege. The situation is made even more complex and difficult because, as has been stated, each confidentiality law that may apply to social workers may have numerous built in or recognized exceptions which may differ from law to law.

The confidentiality and privilege laws applying to social workers occasionally conflict, causing social workers to face quandaries. For example, each State has a child abuse and neglect reporting law which abrogates all or most other confidentiality laws and testimonial privileges. All of these reporting laws apply to social workers. At the same time, the federal government imposes strict confidentiality requirements on all those who are engaged in substance abuse work if the work is connected in any way, no matter how attenuated the connection, to the federal government. Until 1986, the federal government insisted that its substance abuse confidentiality law contained no exception for child abuse and neglect reporting. Social workers who only did occasional substance abuse work with little connection to the federal government were probably unaware of the federal confidentiality requirements and of the conflict they faced, but many social workers were aware of the conflict and were torn between their obligation to report child abuse and their simultaneous obligation to protect the confidentiality of their substance abuse clients. Fortunately, Congress resolved this conflict in 1986 by amending the substance abuse confidentiality laws to make an exception for child abuse and neglect reporting. 42 U.S.C §§ 290dd-3, 290ee-3.

ETHICAL AND PROFESSIONAL CONFIDENTIALITY REQUIREMENTS

Conflicts may also arise for social workers when they are asked to testify or otherwise reveal information covered by an ethical or professional obligation to maintain confidentiality, but not covered by a privilege or legal protection of confidentiality.

NASW requires its members to "respect the privacy of clients and hold in confidence all information obtained in the course of pro-

fessional service."[4] The NASW Code of Ethics further requires that:

> "The social worker should share with others confidences revealed by clients, without their consent, only for compelling professional reasons;"

> "When providing clients with access to records, the social worker should take due care to protect the confidences of others contained in those records;" and

> "The social worker should obtain informed consent of clients before taping, recording, or permitting third party observation of their activities."[5]

Other professional or personal confidentiality requirements or standards may also preclude a social worker from revealing information about or a communication with a client. If, however, a social worker is somehow required to reveal such information and there is no legal protection of confidentiality or privilege which applies in the particular situation, the social worker must either violate his or her professional or personal standards or face legal or other sanctions, such as being held in contempt of court for refusing to testify or loss of employment. For example, in *Belmont v. California State Personnel Board*, 36 Cal. App.3d 518, 111 Cal.Rptr. 607 (1974), two psychiatric social workers, who were employed by the State welfare department to work with emotionally disturbed welfare recipients, refused to turn over information on the recipients for inclusion in the department's central data bank. Because of their refusal, they were suspended for five days without pay for "willful disobedience." On appeal of the suspension order, they insisted:

---

4. NASW Policy Statements, # 1, "Code of Ethics," adopted 1979.

5. *Id.*

"that a special professional relationship exists between themselves and their 'clients' entitling them to assume an adversary position toward their employer, the State of California, defending 'the rights of their clients.' They speak of a social worker's 'code of ethics' designed to 'protect those clients who come into professional contact with the social worker,' to which they owe a higher duty of obedience than to their employer. And they argue that the Department's order [to turn over the information] tends to 'seriously undercut the relationship between the patient and the psychiatric social worker,' a relationship which they strongly suggest is covered by the psychotherapist-patient privilege against nondisclosure, created by [a California statute.]"

The court of appeals upheld the suspension, stating:

". . . [The social workers] are in no way endowed with the 'privilege to refuse to disclose . . . a confidential communication between patient and psychotherapist.' And . . . assuming, arguendo, a conflict between appellants' allegiance to a code of ethics and their duties as employees of the state, they are legally bound to fulfill the duties of their employment, or suffer disciplinary action."

As has been noted, a professional who breaches confidentiality requirements may be sued. A plaintiff may bring, and win, a law suit alleging a breach of confidentiality, even where there is no legal requirement of confidentiality, if there is a professional requirement of confidentiality. As we shall see, the breach of confidentiality would then constitute malpractice. Moreover, a private credential granted by a professional association, like NASW's A.C.S.W., may be suspended or revoked if a credentialed professional violates the professional confidentiality standards.

RESPONDING TO REQUESTS TO REVEAL INFORMATION OR TO TESTIFY

As has been noted, a professional who breaches confidentiality requirements may be sued for damages. These suits may take the form of suits for malpractice, for breach of contract, for breach of confidentiality, or for invasion of privacy. Further, because many confidentiality and privilege laws provide that their violation is a crime, a professional may be prosecuted for a breach of confidentiality. Finally, a professional's license or credential may be suspended or revoked for breaching confidentiality laws. Thus, it is important that you do not lightly reveal information about client.

As discussed in Chapter 3, when someone is seeking to obtain a social worker's records for a court case, or possibly for an official investigation of some sort, the social worker may be served with a **subpoena** or a **subpoena duces tecum**, which specifically requests records. If you are served with a subpoena, you should consult with your supervisor and, if possible, an agency attorney before responding. You are not required to yield your records just because a subpoena for the records has been issued by a court or other official body. Courts issue subpoenas without any controls; usually a clerk merely hands blank subpoenas to lawyers. Indeed, most lawyers have blank subpoena forms, signed by court clerks, in their offices. One must respond to a subpoena, but one may respond by claiming confidentiality. If the claim is contested, there will be a court hearing, and a judge will decide if the claim is valid or if the records must be turned over.

Even if a court specifically orders a social worker to turn over his or her records, a social worker may refuse to comply with the order. He or she would then probably be held in contempt of court but could test the order in a higher court or in a different court by appealing the contempt order. It would be quite unusual for a professional to be jailed pending an appeal of a contempt order, but a decision to disobey a court order should only be made with the advice of counsel.

Unlike subpoenas, search warrants must be complied with immediately. That is, they cannot be contested at the time they are served and a court contest after a search and seizure would be of little value, except to establish a precedent. Fortunately, it would be rare to have a search warrant issued for social work records and if there were a search warrant for a professional's records, many law enforcement officials would be willing to wait for a court to rule on the validity of the warrant before searching for and seizing the professional's records. Law enforcement officials know that professionals are unlikely to destroy or hide their records while they are contesting a search warrant.

A social worker's records may be sought with a search warrant or a subpoena, but it is far more likely that a social worker's records will be sought informally. Someone, like a probation officer, a potential employer or landlord of a client, a friend or relative of a client, or a welfare worker, will telephone and ask a social worker a question about a client. Without thinking, the social worker may answer the question and thereby disclose information from the client's record. Social workers must be cautious about such casual disclosures of client records. They must respect their clients' right to privacy and be aware of any legal and ethical confidentiality requirements.

If you receive a telephone call seeking information about a client or are otherwise asked to reveal information about a client do not say anything—not even something you believe is favorable or of benefit to the client—without considering whether the in-

formation sought is confidential. Even revealing that the client is, in fact, a client may violate confidentiality laws. When you are in doubt, you should consult with a supervisor, or perhaps a lawyer. You should also consult with your client. Your client may readily agree to your release of information, eliminating any problems for you.

If your testimony is sought at a court or administrative hearing, you will probably also receive a subpoena or summons. The South Dakota murder case, *State v. Martin, supra,* with its description of a social worker's (Lawlor's) efforts to assert a privilege and its dismissal of a claim by Lawlor's client [Martin] that he was forced to waive the privilege, provides several valuable lessons on your proper response should you receive such a subpoena.

> "At the preliminary hearing, over repeated objections by [Martin's] counsel and by Lawlor and his counsel, [the judge] required Lawlor to testify. [Martin] sought an immediate appeal on that issue and this court declined to hear it. At the trial, after additional objections and records were made, Lawlor persistently, if not arrogantly, refused to testify. The trial court specifically advised and admonished the witness at an in camera proceeding. After repeated refusals the trial court quite properly found the witness in contempt. All parties were admonished not to reveal this publicly until after the trial, at which time the court would ascertain the appropriate sanctions. The trial court then indicated, over timely objections, that the witness's testimony from the preliminary hearing would be read to the jury. Upon reconvening, Martin then waived the privilege so that the witness could testify in person. He urges here that the conduct of the trial court in directing that the preliminary transcript be read in essence forced him to waive the privilege.

> "The trial court was confronted with a witness who improperly refused to testify de-

spite being ordered to do so. The witness had previously testified under oath at a proceeding where [Martin] had an opportunity to cross-examine him. When considering the posture of the case and the totality of circumstances before the trial court, we conclude that the court acted properly . . .''

This case should teach you that if you have questions about the propriety of testifying, do not testify at any hearing. You cannot decide your testimony at one hearing will be harmless and thus testify; this testimony may be used at another hearing when it would be quite harmful. Moreover, if you testify at one time, or even reveal information in another manner, such as in a conversation with the police, a court may rule that you or your client have waived any privilege you may have and can force you to testify at a time when you do not wish to do so. Since Lawlor's testimony at the preliminary hearing was over objection, the court could not say there was a waiver in that case, but having testified earlier put Lawlor in a less advantageous position than if he had not testified. If he was determined to refuse to testify, even at the risk of being held in contempt, he should have refused to testify the first time he was asked to do so.

Second, note that Lawlor had his own counsel at the preliminary hearing. While this counsel was not able to prevent Lawlor's testimony, the counsel surely helped Lawlor formulate his position. You cannot rely on your client's counsel to advise you. This counsel has other concerns, which may even be in conflict with your concerns. You must have your own counsel to advise you if there is a privilege and to help you assert any privilege.

Third, Lawlor's refusal to testify at the trial was characterized as ''arrogant'' by the court. This perceived arrogance, whether or not it truly existed, surely hurt Lawlor. An angered judge is not likely to accord a professional privilege and any sanction for a refusal to testify is likely to be worse if a witness is perceived as arrogant.

SPECIAL PROBLEMS RELATED TO SOCIAL WORK RECORDS

One continuing problem that faces social workers is whether clients can have access to their own records. Non-clients' access to records may be limited by confidentiality rules, and a few confidentiality rules, such as the federal Buckley Amendment, which applies to school records, do provide for access to one's own records, but generally clients' access to their own records is not mentioned in confidentiality rules and is otherwise ignored by the law.

As a general matter, however, clients should have access to their own records. These records may be considered their property. Moreover, the NASW Code of Ethics requires that: ''The social worker should afford clients reasonable access to any official social work records concerning them.''[6] Nevertheless, in problematic situations, a social worker should consider carefully and consult with supervisors before providing access. Access may be denied in certain situations, for example, if a social worker believes that a client could become emotionally disturbed if he saw his records. Usually even laws which mandate access to one's own records contain exceptions for such situations. And, NASW only requires ''reasonable'' access.

Before providing access, you should carefully protect the confidences of others which may be contained in the records. For example, if your client's father said something

6. NASW, Code of Ethics, *supra*.

about her, you may take this out of her records before providing her access to them. The NASW Code of Ethics requires you to do this.

A federal law, the Freedom of Information Act, 5 U.S.C. § 552, and similar laws in all States provide for access to records maintained by the government, including public social work agencies. These laws usually allow people to obtain any records maintained by a public agency, whether or not they relate to them, unless access to one's own records would be harmful or access to records which relate to others is precluded by a confidentiality law. There may also be exceptions to access established by freedom of information laws. Most freedom of information laws, for example, except personnel records and records relating to litigation from general access.

A problem that may arise for social workers is whether parents should have access to their children's records. Generally parents are entitled to their children's records if the children would be entitled to the records themselves if they were adults. Records related to birth control, treatment for substance abuse, or treatment for venereal disease are gener-

ally excepted from this rule, however. Parents are specifically granted access to their children's school records by the Buckley Amendment.

Frequently, social workers wonder what records they must keep. The quantity and nature of records which must be maintained by social workers generally depends more on rules of practice than on rules of law. There are some laws that prescribe the keeping of certain records, for example, hospices may have to maintain records on each patient's treatment, and, as we shall see in the next chapter, good records may assist with the defense of a malpractice action. In addition, accrediting and funding agencies may require certain kinds of records. But, by and large, you should decide what records to maintain based on clinical rather than legal considerations, keeping in mind that your records may have to be revealed to clients and third parties.[7]

---

7. Some access laws, such as the Buckley Amendment, specifically except "personal notes" maintained outside of a client's file from access.

Professional Liability

Professionals, including social workers, may be held accountable if they injure someone in the course of their work. They may be found liable for damages in a civil suit; they may be criminally prosecuted; or they may be subjected to the loss of their jobs, professional credentials, or licenses in administrative disciplinary actions. A court action to make a professional liable for injuries stemming from the professional's work can take many forms and can have many legal bases. When you think of professional liability, however, you probably think of **malpractice**. A malpractice action is the usual form of a civil suit against a professional for damages and the most common way to hold professionals accountable for their actions. Thus, we will consider malpractice first.

MALPRACTICE

Malpractice is a type of **tort**, a civil lawsuit brought because of a wrong suffered other than from a breach of contract. In tort actions, the plaintiffs allege that they have been injured by wrongful actions or inactions[1] of the defendants and seek monetary damages from them. Usually, any damages plaintiffs receive are **compensatory**, that is, the damages compensate them for their injuries. In unusual cases, the damages may be **punitive**, that is, the damages are imposed not to compensate plaintiffs, but to punish defendants.

Not all wrongful acts give rise to tort liability. Whether a wrongful action gives rise to tort liability and under what circumstances is

---

1. For convenience, this chapter will use the term "action" for both an action and an inaction. Similarly, the term "act" will be used for both an act and a failure to act and to "do" something may also mean to fail to do something.

often established by court precedent. That is, tort liability often comes from the common law rather than statutory law. Federal tort liability is quite rare. Any federal tort liability that exists is statutory.

To prevail in a tort action, the plaintiff must establish: (1) a duty: the defendant owed a legal duty to the plaintiff to do or to refrain from doing something; (2) a breach of duty: the defendant failed to do what he or she had a legal duty to do or did what he or she had a legal duty to refrain from doing; (3) an injury: the injury may be to the plaintiff's property or person; an injury to the plaintiff's person may be physical or mental; and, (4) a causal relationship between the breach and the injury: the injury must have been foreseeable from the breach and caused by it. The term "**proximate cause**" is sometimes used to refer to this required foreseeability and causal relation.

The tort of malpractice was originally developed as a mechanism to hold physicians accountable for injuries to patients. The above elements of any tort—a duty, a breach of duty, and an injury which was proximately caused by the breach—were adapted to the tort of medical malpractice.

Because physicians were believed to need special skills and training and because it was believed that patients were unable to judge physicians' skill or the adequacy of their training, a legal duty was imposed on doctors to exercise due care in treating their patients. Physicians were held accountable if they breached this duty by failing to perform their jobs with the requisite skill and knowledge or in accordance with professional standards.

The heart of every medical malpractice claim is a failure to perform one's job in a manner consistent with the standard of care of like doctors. For a specialist in Boston, "like doctors" may be similar urban specialists. For a family practitioner in Montana, ''like doctors'' may be other rural generalists. But, whoever is considered a ''like doctor,'' a physician will be held liable for malpractice if he or she caused foreseeable harm to a patient due to a failure to exercise the skill or care ordinarily exercised by such doctors.

The tort of malpractice is now used to impose liability on other professionals, who, like physicians, are considered to need special skills and training which consumers are unable to judge. The courts have tended to use the medical model of malpractice to determine whether and when other professionals should be held liable for malpractice. That is, other professionals have been held liable for malpractice if it is determined that: (1) they owed the plaintiffs a duty to exercise due care; (2) they breached that duty in that professional acts were not performed in a manner consistent with the standard of care of like professionals in the community; and (3) their breaches were the proximate cause of the plaintiffs' injuries.

Given the medical model of malpractice, it may be difficult to impose malpractice liability against social workers for several reasons. Indeed, the tort of malpractice against social workers may not even be recognized. Social work may not be recognized as a profession requiring special skills and training beyond the ability of the client to judge. Thus, it may seem inappropriate to hold social worker's liable for malpractice. Moreover, the profession of social work may not be clearly defined, making it difficult to establish who should be held to a professional standard of care. Social work is particularly unlikely to be recognized as a defined profession in States where social workers are not licensed or credentialed and anyone may use the title ''social worker'' or engage in the practice of social work.

Even where it is recognized that social workers are professionals who need certain skills and training beyond the ability of the client to judge and who, thus, have a duty to exercise due care in the practice of their profession, it may not be easy to determine to whom social workers owe this duty. In medical malpractice cases, doctors are said to owe a duty to their patients and it is easy to determine who is and who is not their patient. But it is not always clear who is a social worker's client and thus, to whom a duty to exercise due care is owed. For example, does a social worker doing family therapy owe a duty to each member of the family individually or to the family unit as a whole? What if the best plan for a family as a whole would be to have one member of the family live apart from the family but this would not be in the best interests of this family member? To whom does the social worker owe a duty in this situation? To give two other examples, does a child welfare worker owe a duty to a child's natural parents to reunite them with their child, to the child to keep him safe from all possible harm, to the child's foster parents, or to the child's prospective adoptive parents? Does a hospital social worker owe a duty to an elderly, unconscious patient or to the patient's family?

Further, if social workers fail to exercise due care in their work, those with whom they have no professional relationship rather than clients may be injured. For example, the abusing husband a social worker is improperly counseling may injure his wife. It is not uniformly accepted, however, that a professional's duty to exercise due care should extend to those with whom the professional has no professional relationship and that those who are injured by a professional with whom they have no professional relationship, may sue the professional for malpractice.

Traditionally, in medical malpractice cases, doctors were considered to have a duty to exercise due care to their patients and to no one else; no one else but patients could sue a doctor for malpractice. Recently, some courts have recognized a duty of due care of professionals, particularly mental health professionals, which extends to those who may be affected by professionals' work even though they have no professional relationship with them. For example, as was discussed in the last chapter, in *Tarasoff v. Board of Regents*, 17 Cal.3d 425, 551 p.2d 334 (1976), the California Supreme Court held that a psychologist had a duty to warn a patient's ex-girlfriend of the patient's murder threats, and psychiatrists who have negligently discharged dangerous patients from mental hospitals have been held to have a duty to those whom the patients injured. *See, e.g., Semler v. Psychiatric Institute of D.C.*, 538 F.2d 121 (D.C. Cir. 1976). Not all courts, however, are willing to so extend professionals' duty to exercise due care and to thus extend their malpractice liability. This unwillingness may shield social workers from malpractice liability. In *Chatman v. Millis*, 257 Ark. 451, 517 S.W.2d 504 (1975), for example, a psychologist, who made a recommendation in a child visitation dispute, as do many social workers, was held to have no duty to exercise due care to the parent who was not his client and was thus relieved of malpractice liability.

In *Chatman*, Mrs. Chatman had been divorced from Chatman, who had visitation privileges with their 2 1/2 year old son, Chris. When Mrs. Chatman, became concerned that Chatman had sexually molested Chris, she went to Dr. Millis, a licensed psychologist, to have him evaluate Chatman's conduct with the idea of seeking an order to terminate Chatman's visitation rights. After talking with Mrs. Chatman and Chris, but without seeing Chatman, Dr. Millis wrote her attorney a letter in which he stated that Chatman was a homosexual and that "I feel that it would not be a good idea to allow Chris to continue to visit

his father . . .'' On the basis of this letter, Chatman sued Dr. Millis for defamation and malpractice. On motion, the trial court dismissed the defamation claim for technical reasons. It also dismissed the malpractice claim, holding that:

> "no action for malpractice exists in this state against a psychologist; that even if such an action were permitted in this jurisdiction, there would have to be a doctor-patient relationship or some similar relationship between the parties, and that . . . Chatman had never been examined by Millis, and in fact, was not even known to the doctor; accordingly, there could be no action for malpractice.''

The Arkansas Supreme Court affirmed, stating it was not necessary to decide whether an action for malpractice was available against a psychologist in Arkansas since, even if it were available, no action would lie in this case because Millis "owed no duty, as a doctor, to [Chatman], and this duty must be in existence before [Chatman] can recover because of negligence, constituting malpractice.'' The court reasoned:

> "We do not flatly state that a cause for malpractice must be predicated upon a contractual agreement between a doctor (psychologist) and patient, but we do say that a doctor-patient relationship must exist, *i.e.*, there must be a duty, as a doctor, owed from the practitioner to the patient. Under the allegations before us, Millis . . . did not even know Chatman, and had never seen him. [Chatman] was not a patient of Millis, and the diagnosis reached was not for the benefit of Chatman. Even if the findings of the psychologist were negligently made, Chatman did not rely upon this diagnosis to his detriment.

> "Of course, all persons owe a duty to refrain from defaming others, but this is simply a

duty that all citizens have toward each other, and has nothing to do with a doctor-patient relationship. After all, Chatman was not damaged by the allegedly negligent diagnosis—he was damaged by the alleged defamation. An example . . . illustrate[s] the point. Let us assume that a physician is engaged in lighthearted pleasure at a large cocktail party. Assume further that this physician openly refers to a non-patient individual, and by name, refers to him as a homosexual. Certainly, under these circumstances, the physician might be found to have slandered that person's character, and, if so found, held to be answerable to that person for damages sustained. However, the fact that the speaker happened to be a physician does not mean that what was said constituted malpractice.''

The dissenting opinion in *Chatman*, with its discussion of the legal definitions of malpractice and the necessary elements of a malpractice claim, is most instructive.

''The allegations relating to negligence (or malpractice) [in the complaint] are as follows:

'Defendant at all times mentioned in the complaint was * * * [a] psychologist duly licensed under the laws of the State of Arkansas, . . .

'* * * defendant diagnosed the plaintiff as a homosexual who had engaged in incestuous activities with his 2½ year old son and such diagnosis was [told to others] . . .

'Defendant was negligent and careless in making such diagnosis by failing to exercise the degree of skill and care, or to possess the degree of knowledge, ordinarily exercised or possessed by other * * * psychologists engaged in this type of practice in . . . similar localities, in that he failed and neglected to ever interview the plaintiff and in fact did not even know him, failed to administer any diagnostic tests

which would reveal any homosexuality tendencies or to use any of the proper methods that psychologists use in exercising ordinary care to protect others from injury or damage * * *

'As a proximate result of [this] negligence and carelessness . . . plaintiff suffered excruciating mental anguish, humiliation, embarrassment and will continue to do so in the future; he suffered financial injury.'

''Malpractice has been defined as 'Any professional misconduct, unreasonable lack of skill or fidelity in professional or fiduciary duties, evil practice, or illegal or immoral conduct.' In Arkansas, malpractice has been recognized as negligence in the practice of various professions, among which are law, medicine, and dentistry. [W]e [have] held that the rules governing duties and liabilities of physicians and surgeons applied to practice of kindred branches of the healing arts. Our statutes make the practice of psychology a profession of the healing arts. They provide for licensing of psychological examiners and psychologists and for suspension and revocation of licenses, for privileged communication between such a licensee and his client, and for a code of ethics governing practice and behavior. It seems so clear such a malpractice action can lie against such a practitioner as to be beyond argument.

''I thoroughly disagree with the view that a doctor-patient relationship—as it is described by the majority—is a necessary prerequisite to a recovery for malpractice by appellant. I submit that the attempt to analogize this case and this issue to cocktail party chatter is illustrative of the majority's approach to the issue and the faulty basis for its result. The dissimilarity of this example to this case should be obvious. It does not involve the professional relationship in any aspect or even remotely approach an involvement of the practice of a profession. I agree with the premise of the majority's result only in the respect that, in order for a presumably skilled professional to be liable, he must have owed a duty to the person who claims to have been injured and he must have violated that duty. Thereafter, I agree only with the conclusion that the physician at the cocktail party might be held answerable for his chatter in defamation, but not in a malpractice action.

"A malpractice action, however it may be necessary to define it in order to give recognition to factors peculiar to the practice of a profession, should be considered nothing more or less than a tort action to recover damages for either willful, ignorant or negligent misconduct of a practitioner in the practice of his profession. [Under an appropriate malpractice standard] . . . any practitioner (including [Millis] and others in his field) would be required to possess and, using his best judgment, apply with reasonable care the degree of skill and learning ordinarily possessed and used by members of his profession in good standing engaged in the same type of practice in the locality in which he practices or in a similar locality; otherwise he is guilty of negligence.

"But . . . there can be no 'negligence in the air.' In other words, there can be no actionable negligence, unless the actor has violated a duty he owed the victim of his act or omission. The question then becomes 'To whom does the practitioner owe a duty?' Actionable negligence must arise from violation of a duty imposed upon the actor by common law, by statute or by contract. [N]egligence [is] a matter of relationship between the parties which must be founded upon the foreseeability of harm to the person in fact injured. 'Duty' is determined by answering the question whether the defendant is under any obligation for the benefit of the other party. '* * * the courts will find a duty where, in general, reasonable men would recognize it and agree that it exists.'

"Arkansas cases hold that a duty to use care arises when it is reasonably foreseeable that injury will probably result to another if care is not used and that it depends upon the foreseeability of injury or damage, not upon [the relationship of the parties or, in legal terms, their **privity**. Other authorities and jurisdictions hold similarly. Thus,] [t]he test of actionable negligence, insofar as 'duty' is concerned, becomes one of foreseeability, *i.e.*, whether the consequences of the alleged wrongful act were reasonably to be foreseen as injurious to the person seeking recovery (either individually or as a member of a class). In making the determination, 'foreseeability is not to be measured by what is more probable than not, but includes whatever is likely enough in the setting of modern life that a reasonably thoughtful man would take account of it in guiding practical conduct.'

"The allegations in this case are that [Chatman] was damaged by Millis'] failure to exercise the requisite degree of skill in making a psychological diagnosis of [Chatman]. Such diagnoses are certainly within the scope of [Millis'] practice. Assuming the allegations of the complaint to be true, as we must, it would border on absurdity to say that [Millis] could not reasonably have foreseen that a misdiagnosis of homosexuality would harm [Chatman]. The fact that the diagnosis was made without [Millis] having known, seen or interviewed appellant or having administered any tests to him would seem, in and of itself, to be malpractice, but whether it is or not is a matter of evidence when the case is tried on its merits. It certainly is a sufficient allegation to state a cause of action. As a matter of fact, the only flaw the majority perceives in the complaint is the fact that Chatman was not a patient of Millis. I submit that reason and logic do not support the majority opinion."

Malpractice actions against social workers may also be difficult because only where a professional standard of care is established can there be a breach of duty which forms the basis of malpractice liability, but there are no such standards in many areas of social work practice. The NASW Code of Ethics and standards for practice in different settings establish clear standards of ethical practice, but there are many different methods of treatment and there may be no generally recognized mode of treatment for given types of problems or clients. For example, there may be no standard or generally recognized method of working with a rape victim, an abusive parent, an alcoholic, or the son of a man in an irreversible coma.

Moreover, to the extent that social workers are not required to be licensed, it may be difficult to determine who are ''like'' professionals whose standards should be compared to a defendant's actions. Are ''like'' professionals all members of NASW, all people doing a certain job, all people with a certain degree or all people who use a certain job title? Should a social worker with an MSW who does marriage and family counseling be compared to someone who does family therapy with no degree or to a psychiatrist who also does family therapy? Should a social worker with 8 years of clinical experience but only a BSW be compared to a newly graduated MSW?

In other words, with social workers, even if one can establish that the social worker owed a duty to a plaintiff in a malpractice action, it may be difficult to establish a breach of that duty.

If plaintiffs in malpractice actions against social workers can establish a duty owed to them by their social workers and can further establish a breach of this duty, the plaintiffs still may not be able to succeed in their malpractice actions. They may be unable to establish an injury which was foreseeable from the breach of duty and which was caused by it.

Generally, the kind of injury that would be caused by social worker malpractice is psychological injury. Judges and jurors may not recognize such injuries. If a doctor amputates the wrong leg, the injury is clear, but if a social worker does not relieve the depression of a depressed client, the injury is far less clear.

Further, social workers have far less control over the physical, emotional, cultural, and environmental stimuli that surround their clients than do doctors. These stimuli, moreover, may have significantly more impact on the success of social workers' work than they would on a doctor's work. Therefore, it is much more difficult with a social worker than a physician to determine who or what is responsible for the outcome of events. For example, if an emotionally disturbed child whom a school social worker is counseling does not succeed in school, is it fair to say that the social worker caused the child's failure to succeed? Further, to the extent that clients of social workers themselves take the actions which cause injuries, can it be said that their social workers caused them to take the injurious actions? For example, if a depressed client commits suicide, can one say the therapist caused the suicide? In other words, it is difficult to establish causation with social workers.

Moreover, when one is dealing with psychological or social problems rather than the physical problems, it is difficult to predict the consequences of treatment. In other words, it is difficult to establish foreseeability with social workers. For example, if a doctor carelessly prescribes the wrong medication for a patient, the consequences may be quite foreseeable, but if a social worker fails to remove a child from neglecting parents or fails to recommend residential treatment for an alcoholic, it is difficult to foresee the consequences for the child or the alcoholic.

Even if a plaintiff could establish that a social worker's breach of duty caused him or her harm, the social worker may have **immunity** from a malpractice suit. Insofar as social workers are public employees or work with public agencies, they may be protected from malpractice liability by the doctrine of **sovereign immunity**. This doctrine protects the government and government employees from law suits. It held sway in America for many years, shielding most government entities and public servants from all liability for their actions. Since the 1950's, however, many government entities have lost all or most of their immunity, and many public servants can be sued for failure to properly perform their jobs. Laws have been developed in most jurisdictions limiting sovereign immunity. In some jurisdictions, these laws make a distinction between those governmental functions which historically have generally been public (like running a jail) and those which historically have generally been private or proprietary (like running a hospital) and have abrogated immunity in the latter instance. In other jurisdictions, a distinction is made between, on the one hand, discretionary acts or acts of a policy-making nature (like setting a salary) and, on the other hand, ministerial acts, in which front line workers are merely following orders (like issuing a salary check). Sovereign immunity may only apply to the former acts.

Drawing the line between public and proprietary functions may be difficult, but drawing the line between discretionary and ministerial acts is even more so. For example, some courts believe that decisions involving the placement of children in foster care are discretionary while some courts believe they are ministerial. Thus, in *Sinhagar v. Parry*, 427 N.Y.S. 2d 216 (App. Div., 1980), the court stated that ''the selection of an appropriate placement for a child . . . is a matter of judgment involving the exercise of executive discretion with due consideration to state policy and the availability of suitable facilities and adequate funds'' and thus held that a social worker was immune from liability for placing three children in a facility where they were

abused, but in *Nat. Bank of South Dakota v. Lehr*, 325 N.W. 2d 845 (S.D. 1982), the court stated that while some discretion was involved when social workers placed foster children, social workers who made such placements do not make policy decisions but rather make placements using established criteria, and thus held that a social worker could be liable for placing two young girls in a home where they were sexually abused.

It is also possible, though not likely, that social workers, insofar as they work for private non-profit agencies dedicated to charitable purposes, like hospitals or adoption agencies, may be protected from malpractice actions by another type of immunity: **charitable immunity**. Charitable immunity used to be widely prevalent in America but few jurisdictions recognize it now.

Specific activities of social workers may also be protected by laws giving anyone who engages in the activity immunity qualified by a requirement of ''good faith.'' For example, many States give qualified immunity to anyone who petitions or assists with a petition to involuntarily commit a mentally ill adult.

For all these reasons, malpractice actions may not lie against social workers or may be very difficult to establish.

The two following cases, which come from the same jurisdiction but reach opposite results on very similar facts, demonstrate the courts' conflicting views on social worker malpractice.

In the first appellate case on social worker malpractice in Illinois, *Martino v. Family Service Agency of Adams Cty.*, 112 Ill. App.3d 593, 445 N.E.2d 6 (1982), Janet Martino sued a family service agency and its social worker director, Jane Balke. The five count complaint alleged that the agency offered family and marriage counseling services to the public; that it contracted with Martino to provide counseling service in an effort to improve the marital relationship between her and her husband; that Balke was Martino's counselor for about 7 months and that during this time Balke "(a) used against [Martino's] interest information [she] obtained from [Martino] during counseling, (b) revealed those confidences to others, (c) fell in love with [Martino's] spouse, pursued him, and engaged in 'intimate relations' with him, and (d) after developing this conflict of interest failed to either inform [Martino] of the conflict or terminate her counseling relationship with [her.]" The first three counts were directed solely against the agency and the other two counts were directed solely against Balke. Count I was based upon the theory that the agency breached a contract with Martino "to furnish counseling services to her that would be performed with skill, care and ethics commonly exercised in the counseling profession in [the community] or similar places." Count II alleged that, as the employer of Balke, the agency was liable for "the tort of malpractice of the profession of social work." Count III maintained that the agency, acting through Balke, violated two Illinois acts, one requiring confidentiality for therapists and one credentialing social workers and requiring confidentiality in social work practice. Counts IV and V charged Balke, as an individual, with social worker malpractice and violations of the two acts.

The trial court, on motion, dismissed the complaint. On appeal, the Court of Appeals affirmed the dismissal of the malpractice claims.[2] The court stated:

"[Martino] has not presented any direct statutory or common law authority of this state as precedent for applying the tort of malpractice to the social work profession. Similarly, we have been unable to discover any such precedent. [Martino] seeks to draw

---

2. As we shall see, it allowed the breach of contract claim and one of the statutory claims.

analogy to the medical profession where a breach of duty has been held to arise from a psychiatrist having intercourse with his patient as part of her prescribed therapy, a psychiatrist beating a patient, and a hospital negligently failing to abide by licensing regulations. [Martino] points out that a Code of Ethics has been adopted by the National Association of Social Workers which would have been violated by the conduct of Balke alleged here. [Martino] also maintains that breach of the social worker's code alleged here would be similar to a breach by a lawyer of codes promulgated by various bar groups such as the American Bar Association.

"[Martino] emphasizes the loyalty and trust that should be at the heart of a relationship between a social worker and a client, likening it to a fiduciary relationship. However, neither of the . . . cases [on such relationships upon which she relies] held a breach of a fiduciary duty to be a tort.

"[Martino] also relies on the following statements [from a legal encyclopedia]:

'The therapist-patient relationship is one of great intimacy and trust, in which the therapist encourages the patient to confide in the therapist, and the therapist has a corresponding fiduciary responsibility to the patient.'

'Psychiatrists, psychologists, and other mental health professions are required to exercise due skill and care in conformity with that ordinarily exercised by qualified professionals in their respective fields.'

"The most authoritative texts give a broad scope to the types of endeavor in which the tort of malpractice may be committed:

'Unless he represents that he has greater or less skill or knowledge, one who undertakes to render services in the practice of a profession or trade is required to exercise the skill and knowledge normally possessed by members of that profession or trade in good standing in similar communities.'

'Beyond this the American courts have extended the tort liability for misfeasance to virtually every type of contract where defective performance may injure the promisee. An attorney or an abstractor examining a title, a physician treating a patient, a surveyor, an agent collecting a note or lending money or settling a claim, or a liability insurer defending a suit, all have been held liable in tort for their negligence. The same is true of contractors employed to build a structure, to transport people or goods, to install a windmill or a lightning rod, or to shoot an oil well, or a beauty shop giving a permanent wave; * * * and of many others.'

"[Martino] also relies on *Nat. Bank of South Dakota v. Lehr,* [discussed *supra* in this text in relation to social worker immunity] and cases cited therein in support of her theory. [T]hose other cases were decided on the issue of whether social workers employed by governmental units had sovereign immunity. However, the implication in *Lehr* and some other cases was that social workers were liable for negligence in their furnishing of services for their clients.

"**Despite the implications of the foregoing cases, the directives of the [texts], and the inference arising from the quoted material that the tort of malpractice is applicable to one engaged in the profession of social work, we are unwilling to recognize such a tort at least when it arises from conduct not intended to harm.** No Illinois court of review has done so in the past. Although the conduct alleged here was clearly improper, determination of the propriety of conduct of social workers and the relationship it might have to injury suffered by clients generally would be most difficult to ascertain. The damages a client might receive from the improper practice of social work are unlikely to be pecuniary in nature and extremely unlikely to be physical in nature.

"The [Illinois Supreme Court has stated:]

'* * * Indiscriminate allowance of actions for mental anguish would encourage neurotic overreactions to trivial hurts, and the law should aim to toughen the psyche of the citizen rather than pamper it. But a line can be drawn between the slight hurts which are the price of a complex society and the severe mental disturbances inflicted by intentional actions wholly lacking in social utility.'

"**In the absence of Illinois precedent we find no compelling policy reason to initiate the recognition of the tort of social worker malpractice for unintended 'hurts' most of which we deem likely to be 'slight hurts which are the price of a complex society.'** We decline to do so. The trial court properly dismissed counts II and IV.''

In the next appellate case on social worker malpractice arising in Illinois, *Horak v. Biris,* 130 Ill.App.3d 140, 474 N.E.2d 13 (1985), the court of appeal for a different district than the court in *Martino,* recognized the tort of social worker malpractice.

As the court stated in *Horak,* the facts were "similar, if not identical" to the facts in *Martino.* Harry J. Horak, Jr., filed a complaint against Dean Biris, a certified social worker, who operated a facility called the "Center for Psychotherapy," alleging Biris had sexual relations with his then wife, Dorothy Horak, during the course of marital counseling sought by the Horaks. Specifically, in counts I to IV, which alleged malpractice based on negligence and intentional conduct, Horak alleged that: (1) Biris "held himself out to the general public as an expert in the field of psychology and mental therapy, and held himself out to professionally counsel individuals, couples, and groups for emotional problems, marriage difficulties, and other conditions which were treatable by the use of psychotherapy, psychiatric techniques, and mental therapy;'' (2) in February of 1978, Biris began ''to provide psychological counseling and psychiatric and mental therapeutic care for Dorothy

Horak;'' (3) during this counseling Biris obtained ''significant information'' from Dorothy Horak ''about the personal profile of [Horak]'' and the Horak's marital relationship; (4) on Biris' request, Horak began ''a course of treatment'' with Biris in October 1978, ''which treatments continued until March 1980;'' and, (5) during this period, Biris had ''a close and confidential relationship with [Horak] and [Horak] therefore communicated numerous confidential facts about his life, personality, and marriage'' to Biris.

In support of his allegations of malpractice, Horak alleged that: (1) Biris owed a duty to Horak ''to perform a course of treatment calculated to lead to the alleviation of [Horak's] condition of ill-being,'' but that he failed to do so; (2) Biris administered ''a course of treatment'' ''ostensibly to cure and aid [Horak's] sense of ill-being, but which was not in accordance with generally accepted standards of psychological, psychiatric and therapeutic care;'' (3) Biris ''appeased [his] own self-interest, in disregard and in violation of professional standards and in detriment to [Horak's] condition;'' (4) Biris caused Horak's condition of ill-being to deteriorate ''without providing any psychological, psychiatric or mental therapeutic treatment;'' and (5) Biris ''began and allowed a course of treatment to continue that was of such a nature as to do great harm to [Horak's] condition of ill-being.'' Further, Horak alleged that Biris: (1) ''failed to inform [Horak] that a conflict of interest existed in counseling both [Horak] and his wife; (2) failed to terminate therapy with [Horak] as soon as he realized that a conflict of interest existed; and (3) failed to understand and guard against the transference phenomenon which occurs between psychotherapists and their patients.'' The original complaint alleged that Biris had sexual relations with Dorothy Horak, but ''[t]he act of sexual involvement . . . was not specifically alleged in the [final] amended complaint but was alluded to in [Horak's] allegation regarding the transference phenomenon.''

Based on *Martino*, the trial court dismissed the first four counts, sounding in malpractice,[3] and Horak appealed, urging the court to reject the reasoning of *Martino*. The court stated:

''We have reviewed the *Martino* decision [but believe] . . . that the tort of social worker malpractice should be recognized under the facts presented here. **Contrary to the reasoning set forth in the *Martino* decision, we believe that the facts alleged and admitted in the instant case are sufficient to establish a cause of action for social worker malpractice.**

'' 'Malpractice' is defined in Black's Law Dictionary [the standard legal dictionary] as '[a]ny professional misconduct, unreasonable lack of skill or fidelity in professional or fiduciary duties, evil practice, or illegal or immoral conduct.' The elements necessary to establish a malpractice action are the same elements required of any negligence case. Thus, plaintiff must plead: (1) that defendant owed him a duty, (2) that defendant failed to perform or breached that duty, (3) that the breach was the proximate cause of plaintiff's injuries, and (4) damages. Whether a duty exists is a question of law to be determined by the court, but whether the duty is properly performed by defendant is a fact question to be decided by the trier of fact. A person's duty to act with reasonable care does not extend to the world at large, but, rather, is defined and limited by various considerations such as the relation between the parties, the gravity and foreseeability of the harm, the utility of the challenged conduct and the burden of guarding against the injury.

''We believe the facts alleged in the instant case, if proved, sufficiently establish a duty

---

3.   Two counts alleging breach of contract were not dismissed and were thus not at issue in the appeal.

owed by defendant Biris to plaintiff Horak
and a subsequent breach of that duty by defendant. It was alleged that plaintiff went to
defendant's office, at defendant's request, to
receive counseling and guidance in his personal and marital relationships, ostensibly
for the purpose of improving those relationships. Defendant held himself out as a social
worker licensed by the State to render such
assistance and insight. His license placed
him in a position of trust, the violation of
which would constitute a breach of the fiduciary relationship. Such a breach has been
held on several occasions to be an actionable
and independent tort [despite what *Martino*
says]. Further, we think that the very nature
of the therapist-patient relationship, which
was alleged and admitted here, gives rise to
a clear duty on the therapist's part to engage
only in activity or conduct which is calculated to improve the patient's mental or emotional well-being, and to refrain from any activity or conduct which carries with it a
foreseeable and unreasonable risk of mental
or emotional harm to the patient.

"Regarding a breach of defendant's duty to
plaintiff, we reiterate that the question
whether the duty is properly performed is a
fact question to be decided by the trier of
fact. We believe plaintiff alleged sufficient
facts which, if proved and believed by the
trier of fact, would establish a breach of defendant's duty to refrain from conduct that is
detrimental to plaintiff's well-being. Defendant operated a facility known as the
'Center for Psychotherapy,' where he performed counseling services defined as 'psychotherapy.' He allegedly held himself out
as possessing a certain expertise in the counseling and treatment of emotional and social
problems. Accordingly, defendant was required to exercise that degree of skill and
knowledge normally possessed by members
of the social work profession practicing in
the same field.

"In recognizing a cause of action for social
worker malpractice under the facts presented
in this case, we note that our legislature [in

the Social Worker Registration Act] has provided for revocation of a social worker's license if he or she is found to be 'unfit or incompetent by reason of gross negligence in
the practice of social work.' Additionally, a
social worker is required to be registered in Illinois pursuant to the Social Workers' Registration Act (the Act), in order to use the title
'social worker.' Defendant in the present case
is a 'certified social worker', and thus must
meet certain educational requirements as prescribed in the Act. Also the legislature was
mindful of the concept of a social worker malpractice cause of action. They provide in section 20 of the Act 'No social worker may disclose any information, . . . except: . . . , (2) in
actions, civil or criminal, against the social
worker for malpractice, ...'

"We believe these provisions, not discussed
in the *Martino* decision, indicate that the
legislature of this State is concerned with the
quality of service rendered by the social
work profession, even to the extent of providing for procedures to eliminate certain
'incompetent' social workers from the practice of social work. Further, these provisions, along with the code of ethics apparently adopted by the National Association of
Social Workers . . . make it clear that certain
minimum standards of professional conduct
do exist for social workers, contrary to the
suggestion in the *Martino* decision that the
propriety of a social worker's conduct would
be difficult to ascertain. While it may be true
that certain fields of social work (*i.e.*, community organization for social welfare, social work research, social welfare administration) may not readily lend themselves to a
malpractice action, we believe that marriage
and family counseling is one area of social
work likely to possess more well-defined
principles of social work practice because of
its close association with the field of psychology. We are also of the opinion that an
adoption by this court of the reasoning set
forth in *Martino* would serve only to shield
mental health professionals from any consequences of their actions to the detriment of

those individuals who turn to them in reliance upon their professional expertise and in a good faith attempt to improve their marital and family relationships. We believe such a result runs contrary to the public policy of this State as gleaned from the statutes heretofore discussed.''

Despite the difficulties in getting some courts to recognize the tort of malpractice against social workers and despite the difficulties in proving a case of malpractice against a social worker,[4] malpractice actions against social workers have been brought throughout the country and have resulted in liability for social workers.[5]

Malpractice actions against social workers in their role as counselors or therapists may be based on incorrect diagnosis, incorrect treatment, bad effects of treatment, poor results, sexual impropriety, failure to consult with or refer to specialists, physical injury from physical contacts during therapy, violation of confidentiality, failure to warn, or abandonment. Malpractice actions against other kinds of social workers may be based on other failures to live up to professional standards. There has been, for example, a steady increase in the number of malpractice cases against child protection workers. These cases include actions alleging failure to report or properly investigate child abuse cases, improper selection of or failure to monitor placements, wrongful removal of children from their homes, wrongful detention of children, failure to locate or arrange for a permanent placement, and failure to treat parents. All social workers may face malpractice actions for breaches of confiden-

tiality, giving poor or unauthorized (e.g., legal) advice, or failing to appropriately refer cases. Further, all social workers may be accused of malpractice if they fail to obtain informed consent for a course of treatment, particularly for an experimental or controversial treatment, such as aversion therapy.

It should also be noted that malpractice actions may be brought not only against the professional who committed the malpractice but also the supervisor who failed to properly supervise the professional who committed the malpractice and against the professional's employer or agency. As you saw, both the agency and the social worker were named as defendants in *Martino*.

It should further be noted that a complaint in malpractice, as the complaints in *Martino* and *Horak*, may allege several different theories of malpractice in different counts or causes of action in the complaint. These theories may be inconsistent or alternative. Moreover, other claims, such as the breach of contract claims in *Martino* and *Horak*, and a claim of breach of a statutory duty in *Martino*, may be joined with malpractice claims.

Malpractice is generally proved by expert testimony. That is, experts are called to establish the standard of care for like professionals. They may testify on: the customary and acceptable practice in the locality or the country as a whole, whether there are any authoritative professional standards, and whether there are any generally accepted treatises and/or scholarly works which establish standards of care.

Besides careful practice, the best defense to a malpractice action may be good records. A social worker's records could show that he or she or exercised care in making decisions and that all actions were thoughtful. Good records could show that a social worker conscientiously followed acceptable professional standards, that there was informed consent to a course of treatment, or that warnings were

---

4.   Note that the plaintiff in *Horak* is a long way from winning his case. He still has to prove a breach of duty and a foreseeable injury caused by the breach. Moreover, he must establish his damages to collect any money.

5.   *See, generally,* Douglas Besharov, *The Vulnerable Social Worker* (NASW: Maryland 1985).

given, either to a patient or client or to a third party. A record could show that a social worker consulted with supervisors, with other experts, or with colleagues. Similarly, a record could show reliance on a specific professional standard, law, or scholarly work. Whenever a social worker feels that he or she is making a controversial decision, making a record showing a thoughtful weighing of options and consideration of alternatives is a wise precaution.

OTHER TORT ACTIONS

Malpractice is a tort which is generally based on negligent conduct. Occasionally the conduct which gives rise to a malpractice action may be intentional, as was alleged in *Horak*. Many torts are only based on intentional conduct. Social workers may be sued for many of the following intentional torts in combination with or instead of a malpractice action.

False imprisonment

False imprisonment cases arise from claims of wrongful commitment, detention or incarceration. A social worker could be sued for false imprisonment, for example, if she allegedly forced a client to enter a residential drug treatment program.

Invasion of privacy or breach of confidentiality

Invasion of privacy or breach of confidentiality cases may arise when social workers improperly release client records or reveal client communications. Social workers have also been sued for invasion of privacy when they conduct allegedly harassing and over-reaching investigations of possible child abuse. *See, e.g., Martin v. County of Weld, 598 P.2d 532 (Colo. 1979).*

Defamation

A **defamation** occurs when someone makes a written or oral derogatory statement about a person which damages the person's reputation. The statement must be untrue. Defamation actions may arise from evaluations or recommendations, as in *Chatman v. Millis, supra,* investigations, or casual comments made to others.

Intentional infliction of mental distress

Intentional infliction of mental distress is a newly recognized tort which may arise if a client alleges trauma as a result of a method of treatment or as a result of certain social worker actions, such as removing children from a parental home. A few jurisdictions also recognize a tort of negligent infliction of mental distress. It should be noted that even if these torts are not recognized, one may recover damages for mental distress in combination with a malpractice or other claim. The court specifically noted in *Horak* that "the plaintiff would be entitled to recover for emotional distress."

Assault or battery

An **assault** or **battery** occurs when one person improperly touches or threatens to touch another. The contact or threat of contact need not be considered offensive generally. Treating persons without their informed consent may be considered an assault or battery, as could having sexual relations with a patient or client, as in *Martino* and *Horak*. Even if a patient or client consents to sexual contact with a professional, the contact may be considered an assault or battery on the theory that the professional exerted undue influence over the patient or client to obtain the consent.

Malicious prosecution or abuse of process

Malicious prosecution or **abuse of process** cases can be brought against social workers for initiating law suits, particularly child protection actions, maliciously and wrongfully. *See, e.g., Doe v. County of Suffolk*, 494 F.Supp. 179 (E.D.N.Y. 1980), in which a social worker allegedly filed an abuse and neglect action "knowing full well that ultimately the said petition must be dismissed."

OTHER CIVIL ACTIONS

Statutory violations

Social workers may be sued for violating statutes applicable to them. In *Martino*, for example, in addition to the counts in the complaint alleging malpractice, two counts alleged the social worker and the agency, through the social worker, violated an Illinois statute requiring social workers to maintain confidentiality. The court allowed these counts.

Sometimes the statutes themselves provide for a civil action against a violator, possibly with statutory penalties or provisions for payment of the plaintiff's attorney's fees. Sometimes the courts imply a remedy for the violation of a statute that does not provide

for a civil action. Sometimes they are not willing to do so. The court in *Martino*, for example, refused to imply a remedy from the Illinois act credentialing social workers and requiring them to maintain confidentiality.

Civil rights actions

Social workers who work with a public agency or in a public capacity (e.g., as a guardian *ad litem*) may also be sued under 42 U.S.C. section 1983, the federal civil rights statute discussed in Chapter 5, for violating a client's or another's civil rights. Child protection workers and employees of public mental health or correctional facilities are particularly vulnerable to such suits, but all social workers employed in a public capacity should be aware of their potential liability for civil rights violations under the statute. Sovereign immunity may serve as a shield against civil rights actions, but there will generally not be immunity where there is particularly egregious conduct or where conduct is intentional.

In *DeShaney v. Winnebago County DSS*, _____ U.S. _____, 109 S.Ct. 998 (1989), the Court limited the use of 42 U.S.C. section 1983 against child protective workers. In *DeShaney*, a 4-year-old child, Joshua, was severely beaten by his father and "suffered from brain damage so severe that he is expected to spend the rest of his life confined to an institution for the profoundly retarded." His non-custodial mother sued the Wisconsin child welfare agency and various agency workers under 42 U.S.C. section 1983 for failing to remove Joshua from his father's custody or to otherwise protect him from injury despite several reports of abuse and several investigations by the agency. The Court stated:

"[N]othing in the language of the Due Process Clause . . . requires the State to protect the life, liberty, and property of its citizens against private actors. The Clause is phrased as a limitation on the State's power to act, not as a guarantee of certain minimal levels of safety and security. It forbids the State itself to deprive individuals of life, liberty, or property without 'due process of law,' but its language cannot fairly be extended to impose an affirmative obligation on the State to ensure that those interests do not come to harm through other means. Its purpose was to protect the people from the State, not to ensure that the State protected them from each other. [O]ur cases have recognized that the Due Process Clauses generally confer no affirmative right to governmental aid, even where such aid may be necessary to secure life, liberty, or property interests of which the government itself may not deprive the individual.

"If the Due Process Clause does not require the State to provide its citizens with particular protective services, it follows that the State cannot be held liable under the Clause for injuries that could have been averted had it chosen to provide them. **As a general matter, then, we conclude that a State's failure to protect an individual against private violence simple does not constitute a violation of the Due Process Clause.**"

Joshua's mother contended, however, that "even if the Due Process Clause imposes no affirmative duty on the State to provide the general public" with protective services, a duty may arise when the State has begun to provide services. She argued that since the agency "knew that Joshua faced a special danger of abuse at his father's hands, and specifically proclaimed, by word and by deed, its intention to protect him against that danger," it "acquired an affirmative 'duty' enforceable through the Due Process Clause to [act] in a reasonably competent fashion." The Court rejected this argument, stating:

"It is true that in certain limited circumstances the Constitution imposes upon the State affirmative duties of care and protection with respect to particular individuals. [W]e [have] recognized that the Eighth Amendment's prohibition against cruel and unusual punishment . . . requires the State to provide adequate medical care to incarcerated prisoners. We reasoned that because the prisoner is unable 'by reason of the deprivation of his liberty [to] care for himself,' it is only 'just' that the State be required to care for him. In *Youngberg v. Romeo*, 457 U.S. 307 (1982), we extended this analysis beyond the Eighth Amendment setting, holding that the substantive component of the Fourteenth Amendment's Due Process Clause requires the State to provide involuntarily committed mental patients with such services as are necessary to ensure their 'reasonable safety' from themselves and others. [In another case, we held that] the Due Process Clause requires the responsible government or governmental agency to provide medical care to suspects in police custody who have been injuried while being apprehended by the police.

"But these cases afford petitioners no help. Taken together, they stand only for the proposition that when the State takes a person into its custody and holds him there against his will, the Constitution imposes upon it a corresponding duty to assume some responsibility for his safety and general well-being. The affirmative duty to protect arises not from the State's knowledge of the individual's predicament or from its expressions of intent to help him, but from the limitation which it has imposed on his freedom to act on his own behalf. [The analysis of these cases] simply has no applicability in the present case. [T]he harms Joshua suffered did not occur while he was in the State's custody, but while he was in the custody of his natural father, who was in no sense a state actor. While the State may have been aware of the dangers that Joshua faced in the free world, it played no part in their creation, nor did it do anything to render him any more vulnerable to them. That the State once took temporary custody of Joshua does not alter the analysis, for when it returned him to his father's custody, it placed him in no worse position than that in which he would have been had it not acted at all; the State does not become the permanent guarantor of an individual's safety by having once offered him shelter. Under these circumstances, **the State had no constitutional duty to protect Joshua.**''

The Court emphasized that its holding that Wisconsin had no duty to protect Joshua under the Due Process Clause, and thus could not be liable under section 1983, did not mean that Joshua and his mother were without a remedy for the State's failure to protect Joshua. It stated:

''It may well be that, by voluntarily undertaking to protect Joshua against a danger it concededly played no part in creating, the State acquired a duty under state tort law to provide him with adequate protection against that danger. A State may, through its courts and legislatures, impose such affirmative duties of care and protection upon its agents as it wishes. But not 'all common-law duties owed by government actors were . . . constitutionalized by the Fourteenth Amendment.' Because . . . the State had no constitutional duty to protect Joshua against his father's violence, its failure to do so—though calamitous in hindsight—simply does not constitute a violation of the Due Process Clause.

''Judges and lawyers, like other human beings, are moved by natural sympathy in a case like this to find a way for Joshua and his mother to receive adequate compensation for the grievous harm inflicted upon them. But before yielding to that impulse, it is well to remember once again that the harm was inflicted not by the State of Wisconsin, but by Joshua's father. The most that can be said of the state functionaries in this case is that they stood by and did nothing when suspicious circumstances dictated a more active role for them. In defense of them it must also be said that had they moved too soon to take custody of the son away from the father, they would likely have been met with charges of improperly intruding into the parent-child relationship, charges based on the same Due Process Clause that forms the basis for the present charge of failure to provide adequate protection.

''The people of Wisconsin may well prefer a system of liability which would place upon the State and its officials the responsibility for failure to act in situations such as the present one. They may create such a system, if they do not have it already, by changing the tort law of the State in accordance with the regular law-making process. But they should not have it thrust upon them by this Court's expansion of the Due Process Clause of the Fourteenth Amendment.''

If section 1983 suits may still be brought after *DeShaney*, they may be brought by those not ordinarily considered ''clients.'' For example, a child welfare worker may face a civil rights suit brought by a child or by a child's natural, foster, or prospective adoptive parents. Whenever there is a conflict of interest between parent and child or between a child's natural, foster, or adoptive parents, a potential for a civil rights suit by a disgruntled party is possible. Note that in *DeShaney*, the plaintiff was a noncustodial mother who, in fact, lived in another State.

It should be noted that civil rights claims under 42 U.S.C. section 1983 may be brought in State courts. Thus, a civil rights claim could be combined with a malpractice or other tort action, most of which must be filed in State courts.

Breach of contract

Social workers may also be sued for breach of contract. Although the court in *Martino* was unwilling to make the social worker liable in malpractice, it was willing to make her agency liable for breach of contract. The court stated:

"We view count I charging breach of contract in a different light [than the counts sounding in malpractice]. It alleged that a contract was entered into between [Martino and the agency] for the furnishing of counseling and that competent counselling was not provided to the damage of [Martino]. It alleged that competent counseling included (1) a duty of loyalty to the client, (2) a withdrawal by a counseling social worker if a conflict of interest developed, and (3) an avoidance of revelation to others or use by the social worker against the interests of the client of confidential information obtained during the counseling. The factual allegations set forth a breach of that promised service.

"We are . . . unaware of case precedent for such a suit in contract. However, no specific precedent is necessary to support the viability of a complaint which alleges a contract from which certain promises are implied, a breach of those implied promises and damages."

The damages that may be allowed in a breach of contract claim may be limited. The court in *Martino* allowed a claim for damages for the revelation and transmittal of "personal and intimate information" which "was used against plaintiff's interests," and for the deprivation "of the opportunity to have relations between [plaintiff] and her husband improved." It would not, however, allow a claim for damages related to plaintiff's giving up her residence and employment or suffer-ing "embarrassment," "emotional distress," and "a loss of confidence in the integrity of counselors" and thus, "an ability to obtain counseling." It stated:

"The giving up of a residence or employment is not a proper element of damages particularly when no monetary loss therefrom is specifically alleged. Embarrassment, emotional distress and loss of confidence in the integrity of counselors are not proper elements of damage for breach of contract."

Other courts would further limit damages for a breach of contract claim to refund of any money paid for professional services.

CRIMINAL LIABILITY

In a few isolated cases, social workers have been subjected to criminal liability for their actions in connection with child protective services. In Colorado, for example, a case worker and her supervisor were criminally prosecuted when a child with whom the case worker was working was killed by her parents. The parents had been reported to the worker as abusive but the worker had chosen to keep the child in the home. The worker and her supervisor were convicted but their convictions were overturned on appeal because of technicalities. *Steinberger v. District Court*, 596 P.2d 755 (Colo. 1979); *People v. Beruman*, 638 P.2d 789 (Colo. 1982).

Many regulatory statutes affecting social workers establish criminal liability for certain actions. For example, in 48 States, it is a crime to for a social worker to fail to report suspected cases of child abuse. While prosecutions under such statutes are rare, if not unheard of, the possibility for prosecution does exist.

DISCIPLINARY ACTIONS

Licensed or certified social workers may be subject to suspension or revocation of their licenses or credentials when they engage in professional misconduct in violation of a licensing or credentialing law. They may also lose their private credentials. For example, the social workers in *Martino* and *Horak* could lose their A.C.S.W. membership, if they had it, for becoming sexually involved with clients in violation of the NASW code of ethics.

Social workers may also be discharged, demoted, or suspended from their employment for misconduct. Such a disciplinary action may occur even if a social worker is in a civil service positions with job security as long as there is good cause for the action.

Sometimes a disgruntled client or patient may make a complaint which initiates a disciplinary action against a social worker. Credentialing and licensing laws should provide mechanisms for processing such complaints.

LIABILITY INSURANCE

Most social workers do not have liability insurance,[6] but liability insurance can provide real protection for social workers—at least from civil law suits. Liability insurance rarely provides assistance with criminal actions or disciplinary actions, but it will provide both legal representation and payment of damages in most civil suits that can be brought against a social worker for professional activities. While malpractice claims against social workers may not be widely recognized and while it may be difficult to succeed in a malpractice

suit against a social worker, 373 claims were made against social workers holding the NASW liability policy between 1965 and 1985[7] and legal representation is necessary to fight such claims. It may cost a great deal to retain a lawyer to defend a lawsuit—even one that has no chance of success.

Social workers who work for public agencies may believe they are immune from suit or that their agencies will represent them in any suit and indemnify them if they must pay damages. But jurisdictions differ on their provisions for representation and indemnification of public employees and, as has been noted, immunity for public employees is no longer the rule. Social workers who work for private agencies may believe that their agencies' liability insurance policies will protect them, but many agencies have no insurance and if they have insurance, it may not cover employees sued as individuals. Thus, individual liability insurance may be necessary for social workers even if they are employed by public or private agencies.

Social worker liability insurance policies differ. Most will not cover intentional wrongdoing; many will not cover claims of sexual impropriety[8] or civil rights violations. Other provisions, including the premium cost, coverage and deductibles, also differ. It is wise to shop around.

LIABILITY OF VOLUNTEERS AND STUDENTS

The liability of volunteers in private and public social work agencies is not clear. Gen-

---

6. Besharov, *supra*, p. 175.

7. *Id.*, at 3. The number of such claims rose rapidly in the last years of this period.

8. The NASW policy stopped covering claims of sexual impropriety in 1985 because the number of such claims became overwhelming. Indeed, they rose from 2 in 1970 to 165 in 1980. *Id.* at 179.

erally, volunteers cannot be held liable for malpractice, not because they are volunteers, but because they may not have special skills and training and, thus, may not be held to have a duty to exercise care. However, if a volunteer represents himself or herself as having special skills and training, he or she may be held liable for malpractice, and, if you do volunteer work as a social worker, you could be held to the standard of care of professional social workers and found liable for malpractice. The fact that you were not paid for your work by the client or the agency for whom you volunteered would be irrelevant. Moreover, an agency which uses volunteers or a paid professional supervisor of volunteers could be liable for the actions of volunteers.

Volunteers could also be liable for intentional torts and for violations of statutes and could be criminally liable. The fact that they were volunteers might not shield them from such liability. However, they would be entitled to the same immunity as paid employees.

Volunteer members of boards of directors of private agencies would be shielded from most liability, as would any members of board of directors, if the agencies are organized as corporations.

The liability of students who are doing supervised work as part of their training is not clear. They may be liable as volunteers or as employees. They would certainly be liable if they misrepresented their status as students, but may be protected from liability if they make clear to clients that they are in training.

CONCLUSION

Social workers, like other professionals, may be liable for damages in civil suits, may be criminally prosecuted, and may be disciplined if they injure someone in the course of their work. While malpractice suits may be rare and criminal prosecutions even rarer, and while many social workers' fears of liability may be overblown, all social workers should be aware of their potential liability. This awareness should not paralyze them in their practices, however. The best defense against professional liability is maintaining a professional practice. A social worker who follows acceptable professional standards; who participates in continuing education and stays abreast of new developments in practice; who is aware of and acts in compliance to the law; who properly supervises those who work for him or her and demands supervision and guidance from those for whom he or she works; and who maintains good records which document his or her sound professional practices is generally not in danger of liability. And liability insurance can provide the cushion against frivolous, unsound and harassing claims.

Referring to and Working with Lawyers

MAKING REFERRALS TO LAWYERS

Referrals for poor clients

In America, despite the right to the "assistance" of counsel in a criminal case guaranteed by the 6th Amendment, to the United States Constitution, there is no general right to free or even affordable legal representation. Indeed, as we have seen, even an indigent criminal defendant does not have a constitutional right to the appointment of counsel at no cost in less serious criminal cases. There are some constitutional and statutory rights to appointment of an attorney at no cost in certain kinds of cases, such as serious criminal cases, cases involving termination of parental rights, paternity actions, or civil commitments, but, in general, if parties to litigation cannot afford attorneys, they are not entitled to the appointment of an attorney at public expense.

Moreover, a party to litigation who has a right to have counsel appointed to represent him or her generally does not have a right to the assistance of an attorney at no cost from the time the legal problem arose. Usually parties who are entitled to the appointment of attorneys are respondents or defendants in certain kinds of cases; they will not have attorneys appointed for them until they appear in court for the first time in the case. Further, attorneys will be appointed for them only if the court is satisfied that they cannot afford to pay for a privately retained attorney. Thus, if you have poor clients with the types of legal problem for which they would be entitled to free representation, your clients may not be entitled to free advice from a lawyer before the problem ripens into litigation, and you may not be able to make referrals for them

since only a court can appoint an attorney for them. The most you may be able to do is advise them that if their problems go to court, they will probably be entitled to appointment of an attorney. You should, additionally, make it clear to them that they must pay attention to all court documents they might receive and must appear in court as they are instructed to do in these documents. If they fail to appear in court, no attorney will come looking for them.

The following example should make your and your clients' position in these kinds of cases clearer to you. Suppose you have a client who has been told he fathered a child out of wedlock and who has been asked by the welfare department to pay child support for the child. Even if defendants in paternity actions in your State are entitled to appointment of an attorney, you may not be able to refer him to an attorney for free advice. You may only be able to advise him that, should he be sued to establish paternity and for child support, he would be entitled to appointment of an attorney at no cost if the court believes he cannot afford an attorney. Further, you should make him understand that it is imperative that he appear in court and ask for an attorney if he is served with a paternity petition. You might also make him aware of the seriousness of his situation, advise him to be cautious about agreeing to or signing anything before he goes to court and gets a lawyer, and assure him that he should not suffer a penalty if he exercises his right to appointment of counsel.

Given that there is generally no right to the appointment of an attorney free of charge in America and given the limited scope of the right to the appointment of an attorney where it exists, where can you refer poor clients who need the assistance of an attorney? What can you do if your client who was asked to pay child support in the above example is being pressured by the welfare department and re-

recovery. Many other kinds of cases are handled on a contingency fee basis. Further, in most worker's compensation, social security, and some other kinds of cases, the attorney's fee is set by a court or hearing officer as a percentage of the amount awarded. And in some kinds of cases, such as civil rights cases brought under 42 U.S.C. section 1983 or employment discrimination cases brought under Title VII, the court may order that all or some of the attorney's fees be paid by the losing party. In domestic relations matter, usually the court will order that fees be paid by the better off party. Thus, even an indigent client may be able to afford a private attorney located through a lawyer referral service.

Before you make a referral to a lawyer referral service, you should know that some lawyer referral services make referrals by lawyers' specialty areas but many simply make referrals to participating attorneys on a strict rotating basis without regard to the nature of the legal problem. You should also know that some lawyer referral services have many participating attorneys and are quite helpful but some have only a few attorneys participating or have only young, inexperienced attorneys, attempting to establish their practices, who may not be able to provide much assistance on an initial consultation. Lawyer referral services usually make no representation of the quality of service provided by the participating attorneys. Finally, you should know that many private lawyers do not charge anything for an initial consultation. A client might be just as well off looking in the yellow pages of the telephone book and calling attorneys to determine if they charge an initial consultation fee, if they take cases like their cases, and if they would take their cases on a contingency fee basis. Many attorneys list their specialties in the yellow pages and provide information on their fees.

A social worker can usually find local lawyer referral services, law school clinics, pro

bono programs, legal services organizations, public defender offices, or other private or publicly funded legal assistance programs in the yellow pages of the phone book under either "Attorneys" or "Lawyers." If there is a local legal services or public defender office, usually it can provide other local referrals. Indeed, some such offices maintain lists of attorneys who are willing to take cases for a reduced fee or on a pro bono basis. Courts may also know of free or reduced fee legal assistance programs.

If a client wants to initiate certain kinds of legal actions, such as an action to obtain a domestic violence protective order, to involuntarily commit or obtain a guardianship over a relative, or to obtain past due child support, the local prosecuting attorney or State attorney general's office may be willing to assist. Indeed, in some jurisdictions, prosecutors are required to initiate such actions in appropriate cases. Prosecutors may always decide, however, that a particular case is not appropriate for action. If they decide to assist, their services would usually be free.

Local prosecutors or State attorney general's offices may also assist clients with consumer complaints. Better Business Bureaus or Chambers of Commerce may also assist with such complaints, but they are unlikely to take legal action on one's behalf.

Referrals for middle-class clients

Referrals may be difficult for poor clients who cannot afford to pay for a lawyer, but referrals are even more difficult for middle class clients. These clients may not be able to pay lawyers' fees, which can be several hundred or even several thousand dollars for a simple case, but may not be eligible for the free legal assistance which is available to the poor. Most law school clinics, pro bono programs, legal services organizations, public defender offices, or other private or publicly funded legal assistance programs have strict financial eligibility requirements. Indeed, the maximum monthly income for a person to be eligible for services from an LSC funded program is less than the monthly welfare grant in some States.[3]

Lawyer referral services usually have no financial eligibility requirements. Thus, this may be the best referral source for middle class clients. Special interest organizations, like the ACLU, also usually have no financial eligibility requirements, but they take only a few selected cases.

There are many private for-profit law offices that provide services on certain kinds of simple cases for relatively low fees. Sometimes these offices are known as "legal clinics." You may find these offices in shopping centers or in other community areas. Many of them are part of nationwide or statewide chains. You should know, however, that the price one pays for reduced fees is assembly line service with limited personal contact. On certain simple cases, like uncontested divorces or stepparent adoptions, this is all one needs, but a client should be aware of the limitations of such offices before contracting for representation by them. Of course, the quality of these offices differs from office to office and from chain to chain.

There are also some self-help offices that help people do their own legal work on certain kinds of cases for a small fee. In some jurisdictions, these self-help offices have been charged with practicing law without a license, but many operate openly and without problems with the law. If you have a client who has a simple legal problem and who can handle legal documents and appearances on

his or her own without the assistance of a lawyer, such self-help clinics may be ideal.

Because of the difficulties involved in making referrals for middle class clients and because trusting a lawyer referral service, the yellow pages, a low-cost law office, or a self-help office, may seem unwise, you might be tempted to make referrals to friends, relatives, or acquaintances who are lawyers. Before making such referrals, however, you should consider the ethics of referring clients, who will be paying fees for the services received, to your friends, relatives, and acquaintances. You should also consider whether you want to be in a position of recommending a particular lawyer to a client. Moreover, if you work for a public agency, or even for some private agencies, making such referrals may be contrary to agency rules.

If you do work for an agency, a far better solution than making referrals to friends, relatives, or acquaintances might be to help the agency prepare a list of private attorneys to whom clients may be referred. The agency can inform local attorney groups that it is preparing such a list, can let any attorney who is interested join the list, and can promise to make referrals on a strict rotating basis. The agency can tell clients and attorneys that it does not certify the quality of service provided by attorneys on the list, but it does certify that these attorneys are willing to take certain kinds of cases for reasonable fees.

Sometimes agencies can make special arrangements with attorneys to provide services to agency clients for a reduced fee or on a *pro bono* basis on special kinds of cases or in return for other kinds of referrals. For example, a local LSC funded program in California had a list of attorneys to whom it referred social security disability cases. If the cases involved initial claims for benefits and if the clients seemed eligible for benefits, the attorneys welcomed the cases because, if the clients were found eligible, the attorneys would

---

3. Welfare recipients may nevertheless be eligible for services. LSC rules permit programs to ignore income derived from public assistance in determining eligibility.

get a fee consisting of a percentage of the retroactive benefits paid.[4] If the cases involved terminations of benefits, however, few of the attorneys were willing to take the cases because, whenever aid was paid pending a hearing, there would be no lump sum payment of retroactive benefits from which the attorney could get a percentage. In order to get representation for clients in termination cases, the LSC program asked the attorneys on the list to agree to take one termination case on a *pro bono* basis for every three referrals of screened initial benefits cases. Most attorneys on the list agreed to this arrangement.

Because of the middle class' problem finding and paying for legal representation, there are more and more legal insurance or prepaid plans being developed. Many unions have included legal insurance or pre-paid plans in their package of benefits. Some auto clubs provide legal representation or assistance on auto related matters as part of their offerings. Some credit card companies provide legal representation in certain situations. Your clients might have such coverage without even knowing it. And, although your clients may not be aware of it, their homeowners or automobile insurance company should provide legal representation for them if anyone seeks compensation from them for injuries related to their homes or autos.

With a legal insurance plan, one may have a choice of attorneys, but with most pre-paid or union plans, one must go to certain attorneys. If representation is provided by an insurance company under a homeowners or automobile insurance policy, the company will provide the lawyer.

---

4. If one is found eligible for social security benefits, benefits are paid from the date of application. If there is a long delay between the application and the determination of eligibility, the retroactive benefits, which are paid in a lump sum, could amount to several thousand dollars.

Making referrals well

As a social worker or a student of social work, you undoubtedly know how you should go about making referrals for clients to other professionals or to community resources. Making referrals to lawyers is no different than making referrals to other professionals.

You may save your clients much time and aggravation if you check first with your referrals to see if and when they will see your clients, what they can do for your clients, and what they will charge for their services.

If you are making a direct referral to a lawyer for a client, you may want to provide the lawyer with your client's history and the history of the problem which the client is bringing to a lawyer. This can save the lawyer's time, and thus the client's expense, and will enable the lawyer to prepare in advance for the first meeting with the client. Of course, you may not breach confidentiality by discussing your client with the lawyer without your client's consent. You must ask your client to consent to the disclosure, but you can assure your client that lawyers are bound by much stricter confidentiality rules than social workers.

Before making referrals to lawyers, without giving the clients the legal advice they will get from the lawyer, you should try to explain something about the legal process to your clients, attempt to ease the stress they may feel at seeing a lawyer, and get them to address the emotional aspects of their legal problems. Lawyers often fail to deal with the emotional dimensions of their clients' legal problems. Whether because they are overworked publicly funded lawyers or because they do not want to charge their clients their high hourly rates for amateur counseling, lawyers usually work exclusively on their clients' legal problems and ignore all other problems facing their clients, including their inability to cope with their legal problems. You can fill in this gap in service, both before and after making a referral.

If you have made a direct referral to a lawyer, it is a good idea to keep in touch with the lawyer—assuming your client has given you permission to do so. If you have continued to counsel the client, you can assure the lawyer that counseling is continuing. You can find out from the lawyer if there is anything you can do to help the client cope with his or her legal problems and with the stress of seeing a lawyer and going to court. Your assistance can make the lawyer's job much easier and the process more satisfactory for the client. Again, be sure in doing this that you are not violating confidentiality. Disclosure should be made only with the client's consent, and although lawyers are bound by strict confidentiality requirements, they do not need to know everything there is to know about a client.

OTHER WORKING ROLES WITH LAWYERS

You may not only be making referrals to lawyers; you may also be getting referrals from them. As has been noted, most lawyers do not have the time, the inclination or the expertise to address clients' psychosocial problems. Yet often resolution of these problems is crucial to the resolution of legal problems. Thus, lawyers may need to make referrals to social workers. For example, a lawyer cannot make a plan for child custody and visitation to present to a court if all the parties have unrealistic or inappropriate expectations. The lawyer might need a social worker's help in getting the client to come up with a reasonable plan. To give another example,

getting a daughter appointed the legal guardian of her elderly mother may not solve the family's problems. The daughter needs assistance finding a place for her mother to live where she can get appropriate care. A social worker can provide this assistance. To give a final example, a lawyer may help a widow deal with her husband's estate after his death, but he may not be able help her deal with her grief at the death. And unless she does come to terms with this grief, she may be incapable of taking the necessary legal actions. She needs a social worker to help her get back on her feet.

Whether you are in private practice or working with an agency, as you get to know the lawyers in your community that work with family problems, you should make it clear to them that you can help them in numerous ways and that you can perform necessary services for their clients. If you do get a referral from a lawyer, you should always keep in touch with the lawyer and should regularly report on the client's progress, assuming your client gives you permission to discuss his or her case with the lawyer. By keeping in touch with the lawyer, you can be assured that the legal service and the social work service are coordinated, to the client's benefit, and you can establish a fruitful professional relationship with the lawyer.

As a private practitioner, you may work with lawyers as professional colleagues, doing divorce mediation with them, helping them arrange private adoptions, finding rehabilitation services for their injured clients, or performing other tasks with or for them and their clients. You can, moreover, assist them directly with their cases. You can help them interview difficult clients; you can do certain kinds of investigations of cases; you can help prepare witnesses, particularly witnesses that are children, rape victims, or emotionally disturbed, for the ordeal of trial; you can assess cases that have psychological or social aspects or that involve other social workers; you can act as expert witnesses for them, and you can evaluate reports of other expert witnesses. For over 60 years, legal aid and public defender offices have employed social workers as staff members to perform such tasks. Remember when you work with attorneys as colleagues, you may be bound by their confidentiality rules.

As a social worker in many public social work agencies, you may also work closely with lawyers as professional colleagues. For example, if you are a child welfare worker, the prosecutor or another public attorney will be bringing cases to court for you. If you are working in a community mental health program, you might also need to have a public attorney initiate civil commitments or guardianships for you. If you work in corrections, prosecuting attorneys might be coming to you for sentencing recommendations.

Whether you are in the private practice of social work or working with an agency, your understanding of the respective roles of social workers and lawyers and your professionalism are the keys to successful working relationships with lawyers. You must perform the role you are trained to perform and not the lawyer's role. You must always act like a professional, doing your work in accordance with your own professional standards. A lawyer will respect you more if you assert your professionalism and your independence rather than bending to the lawyer's wishes. For example, refusing to recommend that a child be placed in the custody of a lawyer's client if you honestly believe such a placement would be contrary to the child's best interests may earn you more respect from the lawyer than making a poor recommendation that is criticized by a judge.

Many times, you may find yourself in an adversarial rather than a cooperative relationship with an attorney. An adversarial relationship does not, however, need to be hostile. Indeed, animosity between the lawyer and the social worker may very well work to everyone's detriment. As when you are acting as a colleague of a lawyer, the keys to the successful performance of your job are your understanding of your respective roles and your professionalism.

THE SOCIAL WORKER AS ADVOCATE

As a social worker, you often must advocate for your clients. While you always want to guide your clients to independence and self-reliance, sometimes you must help them achieve their goals by acting as their advocates. You might talk to the management of a nursing home for a client to assure the client's placement in the home; you might help a client fill out a job application and tell the prospective employer about the client's strengths; you might try to convince a landlord that he should make repairs of his property on behalf of a group of tenants who are your clients.

Sometimes your advocacy for your clients is advocacy within the legal system. Primarily, you may act as the legal representative of a client with an administrative agency or in an administrative hearing. Most administrative agencies permit non-lawyers to act as legal representatives and to perform the advocacy role that one would expect to be performed by a lawyer. In fact, in some types of administrative hearings, Veterans Administration hearings, for example, non-lawyer legal representatives are far more common than lawyer representatives, and some non-lawyer legal representatives do legal representation of clients as their only job.

When social workers are performing as advocates in the legal system, they must do work which they are generally not trained to do. Advocacy is very different than the usual activities of social workers. Advocacy skills are very different than the usual social work skills. This does not mean that a social worker cannot be a good legal advocate or even the best advocate for a particular client. It just means that the social worker must be aware of the special role he or she is performing.

The social worker must also remember that his or her usual role within the legal system is not that of an advocate. Whether the social worker is acting as an expert witness, making a recommendation to a court, filing a petition with a court, working with a lawyer on a case, or performing another of the social worker's usual roles within the legal system, his or her goal should be serving the best interests of all of those involved, not advocating for one of those involved. To the extent the social worker forgets this and becomes an advocate, as has been stated in Chapters 2 and 3, the social worker's own important role is neglected or shirked.

GLOSSARY–INDEX

TABLE OF CASES

All cases are alphabetized under the first proper name (or initial, where an initial is substituted for a proper name) in the case name, as follows: *Beruman, People v.; Bowers v. Hardwick; Gault, In re; Irving v. Tatro; L.H.R., In re; Martin, State v.; Rivera v. Min-* nich; *Robert Paul P., Matter of Adoption of; Roe v. Wade.* Where page references are in **bold type**, the case has been excerpted, not merely referred to or briefly quoted. Only the initial page of any excerpt, quote, or reference is set forth.

INDEX

To locate definitions of legal terms or terms of art, use the Glossary-Index. Court opinions cited in the text are included in the Table of Cases; statutes of importance are listed below.